"I tried hard to find customer questions that I received on managing Exchange 2007 anti-spam that remain unanswered by this book, but this book covers everything. All essential topics in spam filtering for Exchange 2007 are discussed with impressive attention to detail and lab validation. The authors' insistence on engaging Exchange engineers in understanding the inner workings of the messaging hygiene pays back!"

—Mihai Costea,
Senior Program Manager of Exchange Server 2007,
Microsoft Corporation

"There are several great books when it comes to Exchange Server 2007. This one stands out in several ways from the rest, though. The book provides both breadth and depth when it comes to the many components of Exchange, which is a very tough balancing act. I love the writing style and the technical content hits the mark. I will certainly be recommending this book to others."

—Russ Kaufmann
MVP - Windows Clustering
MCT, CTT+, MCSE: Messaging, Security
MCITP: Enterprise Messaging Administrator
ClusterHelp.com, a Microsoft Gold Certified Partner

About the Authors

Richard Luckett is the president of SYSTMS of NY, Inc. (http://systmsny.net), a leading Microsoft Gold Partner providing professional services, managed services, and training solutions. Richard is an MCSE, MCT, MVP, MCITP, and MCTS with specializations in security and messaging and over 15 years of experience as an IT professional. Richard is a Microsoft Certified Trainer with more than nine years Exchange Server instructional experience. He is one of fewer than 120 experts worldwide awarded the Exchange Most Valuable Professional distinction by Microsoft. Richard is an accomplished author and speaker who coauthored *Administering Exchange 2000 Server* by McGraw-Hill and is the course director of seven best-selling Exchange courses for Global Knowledge, Inc. Richard is a contributor to the SearchExchange.com website at TechTarget and is their resident Exchange expert for questions on spam and security.

William Lefkovics, MCSE, A+, BSc, works as the Technical Director for Mojave Media Group, based in Las Vegas, Nevada. He started working with Microsoft products more than 10 years ago and was first certified in Exchange 5.0. He has been a Microsoft Exchange MVP since 2001. While working as a writer, presenter, trainer, and consultant, William contributes articles for Exchange and Outlook Pro VIP online (http://exchangeprovip.com) and Slipstick.com's *Exchange Messaging Outlook (EMO)* newsletter. He was also a coauthor for the book *Configuring Exchange 2000 Server* by Syngress Media. Most recently, William is speaking at Exchange Connections in Orlando in April 2008.

Bharat Suneja is Principal Exchange Architect at Zenprise (www.zenprise.com), maker of automated troubleshooting and monitoring software for Microsoft Exchange and BlackBerry environments. Bharat is an MCSE (+Messaging +Security), MCT, and MVP (Exchange Server), with over 10 years of experience as an IT professional. He actively participates in Microsoft communities as a writer, presenter, and technical contributor. Bharat publishes the Exchangepedia Blog (exchangepedia.com/blog), a popular destination for IT professionals, Exchange administrators, and architects from over 150 countries. He contributes to TechTarget's SearchExchange.com.

About the Contributing Authors

Rev. Dr. Bradford S. Werner, Technical Evangelist, is the president of Werner Training and Consulting, Inc.—a software development, consulting, and training business in Phoenix, Arizona. Brad has over 27 years of experience in systems engineering and software development. He is an expert with embedded systems development and systems integration. Besides embedded systems, Brad has developed operating systems, compilers, and other software for UNIX, Mac, and of course, Windows systems. He's a best-selling author whose software, books, and award-winning course materials have been used worldwide. Windows-related courses include a dozen courses on Windows Server and security topics, and a course on the automation of Windows Server 2008 with Windows PowerShell. Brad holds a B.S. in computer science, completed half of a masters in telecommunications, and holds a doctorate in metaphysics, as well as other certifications.

Nick Cavalancia, MCSE, MCT, MCNE, MCNI, is an accomplished consultant, trainer, author, columnist, and speaker and has been in the IT industry for over 15 years, having designed Exchange environments for some of the most well-known companies today. He has contributed to over a dozen books on topics such as Windows, Active Directory, SQL Server, and Exchange, and is the coauthor of *Exchange 2000 Server Administration: A Beginner's Guide* and *Exchange 2000 Server: The Complete Reference*. Nick currently serves as Vice President of Product Marketing for ScriptLogic Corporation, where he assists in driving innovation and leads the evangelism of ScriptLogic solutions.

Pat Richard is a Messaging Architect for Analysts International, a Microsoft Gold Partner. Pat has been working with messaging environments since the MS Mail days, and spends a majority of his time designing and implementing enterprise messaging solutions based around Microsoft Exchange. Complex migrations and implementations, as well as large scale upgrades, are his specialty. Several years ago, he was given the Microsoft MVP award for his contributions to the Exchange community. Pat continues to be active online, assisting others with Exchange-related issues.

About the Technical Editors

Rodney Fournier has been working in the field for over 22 years. He has been recognized by Microsoft as an MVP in Windows Clustering and is one of six people in the world to receive this distinction. Currently, Rodney is a Principal Computer Scientist working onsite at NASA – Marshall Space Flight Center (MSFC). He works in the NASA Data Center (NDC) Architect and Engineer's group of IT Security. His focus is on Windows Server 2003 Active Directory services, clustering technologies, Exchange 2003, SQL 2000, and infrastructure design.

Rodney also owns and runs Net Working America, Inc. (www.nw-america.com). As the President and Lead Consultant, he does public speaking and technical editing, as well as authors books, publications, and training courses. He has been a Microsoft Certified Trainer for the past 11 years. Rodney has been a source of information in many articles written by other authors and has been quoted in the industry press on many different topics regarding IT. He is also involved in www.ClusterHelp.com, where he teaches, writes the labs, and helps with the courseware.

Steve Music has worked in the IT industry since 1988. He has provided support to a vast range of organizations, including small sole proprietor businesses, international corporations, nonprofit groups, and U.S. Government agencies. His experience as a system administrator for e-mail began in 1998 with Lotus Domino R4 and Exchange 5.5. At the time this book was published, he was the contract Team Lead for messaging at the Bureau of Indian Affairs, where his responsibilities included the planning and deployment of Microsoft Exchange 2007. Steve lives in Virginia with his wife and two children.

Microsoft® Exchange Server 2007: The Complete Reference

Richard Luckett
William Lefkovics
Bharat Suneja

New York   Chicago   San Francisco
Lisbon   London   Madrid   Mexico City
Milan   New Delhi   San Juan
Seoul   Singapore   Sydney   Toronto

The *McGraw·Hill* Companies

Library of Congress Cataloging-in-Publication Data

Luckett, Richard.
  Microsoft Exchange server 2007 : the complete reference / Richard Luckett,
William Lefkovics, Bharat Suneja.
      p. cm.
  ISBN 978-0-07-149084-9 (alk. paper)
  1. Microsoft Exchange server. 2. Client / server computing.
  3. Electronic mail systems. I. Lefkovics, William. II. Suneja, Bharat.
III. Title.
  QA76.9.C55L93 2008
  005.7'1376—dc22

                                                         2008011444

McGraw-Hill books are available at special quantity discounts to use as premiums and sales promotions, or for use in corporate training programs. To contact a special sales representative, please visit the Contact Us page at www.mhprofessional.com.

Microsoft® Exchange Server 2007: The Complete Reference

1234567890 DOC DOC 0198

ISBN   978-0-07-149084-9
MHID   0-07-149084-1

Sponsoring Editor
  Jane K. Brownlow

Editorial Supervisor
  Patty Mon

Project Manager
  Aparna Shukla,
  International Typesetting
  and Composition

Acquisitions Coordinator
  Jennifer Housh

Technical Editors
  Rodney Fournier
  Steve Music

Copy Editor
  Bart Reed

Proofreader
  Carol Shields

Indexer
  Broccoli Information
  Management

Production Supervisor
  Jean Bodeaux

Composition
  International Typesetting
  and Composition

Illustration
  International Typesetting
  and Composition

Art Director, Cover
  Jeff Weeks

Contents

Part I   Exchange Server 2007 Fundamentals

Part II   Designing and Deploying Exchange Server 2007

Foreword

Exchange Server 2007 is a large and complex piece of software—actually many pieces—with many features and capabilities. More than four years in the making, Exchange 2007 (and more recently Exchange 2007 Service Pack 1) represents an entirely new breed of Exchange Server. Exchange 2007 is not simply e-mail. It's many forms of communications: e-mail, voicemail, fax, meeting requests, and more. When combined with the power of rich clients such as Outlook Web Access, Microsoft Outlook, Windows Mobile, and others, it becomes a portal to other forms of collaboration and communication. With many components rewritten from the ground up, and with a new 64-bit architecture, Exchange 2007 will forever change the way you plan for, design, deploy, and manage Exchange Server.

It's hard to believe how far messaging has come since the world's first message was sent back in late 1971. That first message was sent between two computers sitting next to each other. Fast-forward 36 years later to the present day, and we find that the modern business world now runs on e-mail. E-mail has moved beyond mission critical, beyond business critical, and has become a permanent fixture in our lives.

For one-third of those 36 years, Microsoft Exchange Server has been a part of business e-mail around the world. Every day, millions upon millions of messages traverse Exchange servers throughout the globe. At any given second, a message is being processed by an Exchange server somewhere in the world. To make sure their systems are running at peak performance with optimal security, Exchange administrators must understand a variety of external elements, such as storage and hardware characteristics, operating system fundamentals and monitoring, Internet Information Services, Active Directory, Domain Name System, SMTP, and other Internet protocols. With the introduction of new Exchange technologies such as Unified Messaging, continuous replication, and transport agents, as well as ancillary technologies and products such as Windows PowerShell, Windows Rights Management Services, and Office Communications Server, the bailiwick of the Exchange administrator is growing bigger every day. Adding to that is a plethora of new terminology to understand, configure, and manage.

Learning all about the new features, technologies, and protocols used by Exchange Server 2007 can be a daunting task, particularly if you don't have any previous Exchange or messaging experience. Fortunately, the book you're holding in your hands can help you to learn about critical aspects of Exchange 2007, such as the new server role architecture, the administration of recipients, mailboxes, databases, and message queues, secure messaging, and more. Exchange experts and Microsoft MVPs Richard Luckett, William Lefkovics, and Bharat Suneja have packed this book with practical guidance, useful information, and years of knowledge and experience. If you're responsible for one or more aspects of an Exchange 2007-based messaging system, keep this book close, as you'll be referring to it often!

—Scott Schnoll, Principal Technical Writer
Exchange Server Product Team
Microsoft Corporation

Scott Schnoll is a Principal Technical Writer on the Exchange Server Product Team at Microsoft, writing content for Exchange Server 2007. Prior to joining Microsoft, Scott wrote *Exchange Server 2003 Distilled* (Addison-Wesley Professional, 2004) and was the lead author for *Exchange 2000 Server: The Complete Reference* (McGraw-Hill, 2001).

To Marisol, Alex, and Johanna,
who bring meaning to my life and inspire me daily.

—*Richard Luckett*

To my parents,
Krishna and Satpal Suneja.

—*Bharat Suneja*

Acknowledgments

Writing a book, sustaining a career, and spending precious time with family are all desirable goals, but difficult to manage all at once. Over the last year and a half of writing this book, I have stretched the boundaries of all my personal and professional relationships. I would like to acknowledge the individuals who helped make this possible. First, I want to thank my wife, Marisol, and my kids, Alex and Johanna, whose love and support was felt through all the long hours spent writing. I want to thank my business partners, Joe, Tony, and Lance, for their understanding and patience. Thank you to Ashley, Kim, Linde, and Craig at Global Knowledge, and the many instructors, of which there are too many to name, who have supported me during the writing of the book. I want to thank all the wonderful people at McGraw-Hill for their support, particularly Jane Brownlow, Sponsoring Editor, and Jennifer Housh, Acquisitions Coordinator, whose persistence and understanding is very much appreciated. I want to thank my coauthors, Bharat, William, Brad, Nick, and Pat, for stepping up to the plate and delivering such great content. Thank you Rodney and Steve for keeping the book technically sound. Thank you Microsoft Exchange Team for developing such a tremendous messaging application. I want to thank the MVP community, especially the Exchange MVPs. Special thanks to Melissa Travers, the MVP Lead for Exchange Server, for introducing me to Scott Schnoll. And thank you Scott for providing me the opportunity to write this book by introducing me to Jane. Finally, I would like to thank my dad, Joseph, my mom, Barbara, and my other mom, Joan, for blessing me with such a strong foundation to build my life on.

—*Richard*

There are many people involved in the production of books, especially those of a technical nature. I would like to extend my appreciation to the other authors, especially Richard and Bharat. Thank you to Steve and Rodney for picking apart the drafts to help make the book stronger. I would also like to thank the folks at McGraw-Hill, especially Jane and Jennifer, for their abundant patience and tolerance with managing our efforts.

—*William*

Thank you Richard for wanting to write this book with me. I echo your thoughts about the stretching of personal and professional boundaries. First on the list are my wife, Ritu, and my son, Anik, for continuing to support me through the missed meals and weekends that went into this book. Thanks to two excellent ladies from McGraw-Hill—Acquisitions Coordinator Jennifer Housh and Sponsoring Editor Jane Brownlow—for being so patient, persistent, and polite through the missed deadlines. Throughout the E12 TAP and the writing of this book, many members of the Exchange product team provided the kind of support I have never experienced before. The list could easily fill a few pages, but you all know who you are. Thank you for responding to my endless e-mails at all odd hours. In particular, I want to thank David Espinoza for running an excellent TAP program and putting up with me. I also want to thank Scott Schnoll, KC Lemson, Vivek Sharma, Evan Dodds, Greg Thiel, Ayla Kol, Mihai Costea, Chandresh Jain, Mayerber Neto, Chris Davis, Ashish Consul, Ross Smith IV, Kate Follis, and Dave Forrest. Thanks to Steve and my dear friend Rodney Fournier, clustering MVP, for stepping in as technical reviewers, and to fellow Zenpriser Tariq Hamirani for the endless impromptu reviews.

—Bharat

Introduction

Microsoft introduced Exchange Server, their messaging and collaboration platform, over a decade ago. Its popularity, acceptance, and market share have grown with each new version. Today, Exchange Server and its native client Outlook enjoy a larger installed base worldwide than ever before. Along the way, Exchange has shed itself of the dedicated Exchange Directory Service, which evolved as a critical part of the Windows Server operating system as Active Directory. It has flirted briefly with instant messaging and conferencing. It has continued to make strides in scalability, reliability, high availability, and security, while maintaining ease of use and deployment. Exchange Server 2007 was released to manufacturing on December 7, 2006. It provides companies that depend on Exchange as their mission-critical messaging and collaboration platform with a product written natively to take advantage of the power of the 64-bit server platform.

Exchange Server 2007 provides a new level of heightened security features that allow an organization of any size to safely and reliably establish e-mail communications with other messaging systems. New security features provide organizations with greater control over electronic communications, including the ability to regulate e-mail communications using transport rules and to comply with retention requirements using its messaging records management features.

New replication features in their different flavors—Local Continuous Replication (LCR), Cluster Continuous Replication (CCR), and Standby Continuous Replication (SCR)—offer a high-availability solution to fit every budget and requirement. The continued support for clustered implementations using shared storage, dubbed Single Copy Cluster (SCC), ensures existing investments with Exchange clusters can continue to utilize the same type of HA solution. Improved support for Volume Shadow copy Service (VSS) and the ability to move an Exchange database to any server with Database Portability provide additional options for disaster recovery planning.

The new roles-based architecture in Exchange Server 2007 will help organizations design and deploy Exchange Server 2007 with greater flexibility than any other version of Exchange Server before. The Mailbox Server role, Hub Transport role, Client Access Server role, Edge Transport role, and the Unified Messaging server role comprise this new architecture. Administrators can chose to dedicate hardware to each of the five server roles for performance, scalability, and high availability, or combine some server roles to create dependable cost-effective deployments.

Exchange Server 2007 marks the entry of Microsoft in the Unified Communications arena. The Unified Messaging server role not only allows organizations to deliver the unified Inbox for voicemail, e-mail, and faxes, it also speech-enables that Inbox, allowing one to interact with Exchange over the phone. Having one's e-mail read out by an assistant, appointments rescheduled over the phone, or phone numbers dialed without having to remember them, is not a pipedream anymore.

Of all of Exchange Server 2007's features, none generates as much excitement and apprehension, at the same time, as its command-line management functionality. Built on Windows PowerShell, the Exchange Management Shell (EMS) provides powerful new management and automation capabilities to Exchange that have never been available before to a product on the Windows platform. Although the EMS is truly remarkable, resentment came from many quarters because of the lack of equivalent capabilities in the GUI.

Exchange Server 2007 Service Pack 1 (SP1) was released on November 29, 2007, almost a year after Exchange Server 2007. Most organizations have traditionally waited for this landmark in the Microsoft product lifecycle before firming up plans to deploy them. In many ways, Exchange Server 2007 SP1 is a highly anticipated service pack. It adds significant management functionality in the user interface that users sorely missed, and complained about, in the RTM version. It also delivers major new features such as Standby Continuous Replication (SCR), a flexible and low-cost high availability feature designed to provide protection from a site failure, and support for deploying Exchange Server 2007 on Windows Server 2008. The release of Service Pack 1 for Exchange Server 2007 will signify to many organizations that Exchange Server 2007 is now fully production ready, thus producing the green flag to proceed with their upgrades and migrations to Exchange Server 2007.

Who Should Read This Book?

Exchange Server 2007 is different enough from all other versions of Exchange Server that administrators with varied levels of experience will benefit from reading this book. As a reference guide, this book does not have to be read from beginning to end, although that is probably not a bad idea. Whether you are designing a new Exchange 2007 organization, researching advanced features, or just need to know how to create a new mailbox, you will find the information you are looking for in this book. The information in this book is geared toward the intermediate to advanced e-mail administrator. If you are entirely new to Exchange Server and messaging in general, you may want to supplement this book with an earlier McGraw-Hill book, *Exchange 2007 Server Administration: A Beginner's Guide.*

What's in This Book

Microsoft Exchange Server 2007: The Complete Reference is organized into six parts. Each part represents a comprehensive group of chapters closely related to each other. In Part I, "Exchange Server 2007 Fundamentals," the three chapters introduce you to Exchange Server 2007, Active Directory integration, and Exchange 2007 server architecture.

Part II, "Designing and Deploying Exchange Server 2007," is composed of two chapters that cover all manner of Exchange Server 2007 installations, including how to transition or migrate to Exchange Server 2007 from earlier version of Exchange and other messaging systems.

Part III, "Administering Exchange Server 2007," is composed of four chapters that cover the administration of the five server roles. Chapter 6 details how to administer Mailbox Server roles. Chapter 7 details how to administer both the Hub Transport server role and the Edge Transport server role. Chapter 8 details how to administer the Client Access Server role, and Chapter 9 details how to administer the Unified Messaging server role.

Part IV, "Exchange Recipients and Clients," is composed of four chapters that focus on recipient and e-mail client administration. This topic is broad and includes a detailed chapter on how to create and customize recipient objects, including the new resource mailbox objects. The primary thick client, Outlook 2007, and the primary thin client, Outlook Web Access 2007, both have dedicated chapters. Additionally, Chapter 13 explores the new communications and collaboration solutions from Microsoft that integrate with Exchange Server 2007, including Microsoft Office SharePoint Server and Office Communications Server.

Part V, "Security," is composed of four chapters that focus on securing the Exchange Server 2007 organization. Exchange Server 2007 administrative models and the new features for regulatory compliance are covered in the first two chapters. How to encrypt e-mail and prevent spam and viruses with Exchange Server 2007 are covered in the third and fourth chapters of Part V.

Part VI, "E-mail Continuity," is composed of four chapters that focus on implementing and maintaining a highly available Exchange Server 2007 organization. This includes dedicated chapters on disaster recovery, high availability, maintenance and optimization, and troubleshooting.

Covering Exchange Server 2007 in all its breadth and depth in a single book was a significant undertaking. As we wrote this book, additional content was developed that could not be included. To show our appreciation to you for purchasing *Microsoft Exchange Server 2007: The Complete Reference*, we have made additional content available to you on the book's companion web site: Exchange2007tcr.com (http://exchange2007tcr.com). You'll find technology and book updates, errata information, and a bonus chapter on the Exchange Management Shell. We invite you to visit the site and let us know how you like the book.

—Richard —William —Bharat

Exchange Server 2007 Fundamentals

PART

I

Introduction to Exchange Server 2007

E-mail communications and the messaging systems that support their transport and storage, which started as small simplistic text messages stored on electronic post offices with nominal storage capabilities and limited client functionality, have grown and changed over the last 20 years. They have evolved into complex messaging and collaboration systems with e-mail data storage architectures that can scale into terabytes and beyond, and with more client features than the average e-mail user will ever get to know. Driving this evolution has been the shift from e-mail messaging as a mere novelty to e-mail as a critical business and personal communication technology. According to the Radicati Group, there are over 1.2 billion e-mail users worldwide. Insourced messaging systems support approximately 27 percent of these users. That is still 324 million professionally supported e-mail clients. They also estimate that the number of e-mail users worldwide will grow from 1.2 billion in 2007 to 1.6 billion in 2011, at an average annual growth rate of 7 percent over the next four years.

Microsoft's first enterprise e-mail solution, Microsoft Mail (MS Mail), was a fairly average product in the messaging industry. Microsoft's current e-mail solution, Exchange Server, is one of the most commercially successful messaging system, with over 140 million Exchange clients worldwide. From Microsoft Windows for Workgroups Mail, to MS Mail to Exchange 4.0, to Exchange 5.0/5.5 to Exchange 2000, to Exchange Server 2003 and now Exchange Server 2007, you can observe the distinctly different evolution stages in the messaging industry reflected in the e-mail products from Microsoft. Microsoft has proven with Exchange Server 5.5, which has been in some production environments for over eight years, that what they build into their messaging product has true reliability and real staying power. In a sense, Exchange Server 2007 is a window into what technologies will dominate business communications for at least the next two to five years. This chapter will let you peer into that window. This book will open the door, help you understand, and prepare you to take full advantage of Exchange Server 2007.

Demystifying Exchange Server 2007

Are you afraid of what Exchange Server 2007 will mean to your environment? Maybe you just completed the upgrade to Exchange Server 2003 and just a few months later you must contemplate the prospect of Exchange Server 2007. Perhaps you have been running Exchange Server 2003 for a few years now and have become comfortable with it. Marie Curie once said, "Nothing in life is to be feared. It is only to be understood." The good news is that if you have been administering Exchange Server for any length of time, the knowledge you have today is still valid in Exchange Server 2007, and you probably know more about Exchange Server 2007 than you think. You just need to take the mystery of Exchange Server 2007 out of the equation.

The key to demystifying Exchange Server 2007 is to be able to clearly define what it is without oversimplifying. There are enough new features in Exchange Server 2007 to intimidate any seasoned Exchange administrator. While it will take this entire book to do the product justice, some quick insight into Exchange Server 2007 might help you breathe easier and may even get you excited and have you looking forward to deploying the all the new features. The following list should entice you to dig deeper.

- **Built-in security**   Exchange Server 2007 has more built-in features that address the security needs for today's e-mail messaging systems than any other version of Exchange. Even better is the fact that they start working for you out of the box.

- **Client experience**   It doesn't matter where you are, if you are online or offline—your experience with Exchange, from a client perspective, is greatly improved.

- **Administrator experience**   Well-defined server roles, powerful yet easy-to-use tools, and automation galore will have every administrator running to get their hands on Exchange Server 2007.

- **Reduced TCO**   Your C-level decision makers will love the long list of cost savings technologies that are included in the base price of Exchange Server 2007.

Defining Exchange Server 2007

What truly defines Exchange Server 2007 are the core functions it provides that all messaging systems share in common. The ability to transport e-mail, to store e-mail for clients, and to make e-mail readily available to a wide variety of clients in a reliable and secure way are the most common attributes. Exchange Server 2007 does this of course, and much more, as you will soon discover in this book. It is fair to say that the work over the last two years on Exchange Server 2007 has earned Microsoft some bragging rights.

A Brief History of Exchange Server

Why is there not a version 1.x, 2.x, or 3.x of Exchange Server? The reason is that MS Mail for PC Networks was the first enterprise messaging system from Microsoft. The last version of MS Mail released before Exchange Server 4.0 was version 3.x. Interestingly enough, MS Mail support was carried all the way though Exchange Server 2000. Only with the release of Exchange Server 2003 was support finally removed.

Every release of Exchange listed in Table 1-1, including each service pack, has contributed significantly to what Exchange Server 2007 has become. However, three

Name	Version	Release Date
Exchange 4.0	4.0.837	April 1996
Exchange 4.0 (a)	4.0.993	August 1996
Exchange 4.0 SP1	4.0.838	May 1996
Exchange 4.0 SP2	4.0.993	August 1996
Exchange 4.0 SP3	4.0.994	November 1996
Exchange 4.0 SP4	4.0.995	April 1997
Exchange 4.0 SP5	4.0.996	May 1998
Exchange 5.0	5.0.1457	March 1997
Exchange 5.0 SP1	5.0.1458	June 1997
Exchange 5.0 SP2	5.0.1460	February 1998
Exchange 5.5	5.5.1960	November 1997
Exchange 5.5 SP1	5.5.2232	July 1998
Exchange 5.5 SP2	5.5.2448	December 1998
Exchange 5.5 SP3	5.5.2650	September 1999
Exchange 5.5 SP4	5.5.2653	November 2000
Exchange 2000	6.0.4417	October 2000
Exchange 2000 (a)	6.0.4417	January 2001
Exchange 2000 SP1	6.0.4712	July 2001
Exchange 2000 SP2	6.0.5762	December 2001
Exchange 2000 SP3	6.0.6249	August 2002
Exchange 2000 post-SP3	6.0.6487	September 2003
Exchange 2000 post-SP3	6.0.6556	April 2004
Exchange 2000 post-SP3	6.0.6603	August 2004
Exchange Server 2003	6.5.6944	October 2003
Exchange Server 2003 SP1	6.5.7226	May 2004
Exchange Server 2003 SP2	6.5.7638	October 2005
Exchange Server 2007	8.0.685.24 or 8.0.685.25	December 2006

TABLE 1-1   Exchange Version Build Numbers and Release Dates

evolutionary milestones are worth pointing out, in addition to some consistent trends that speak volumes about Microsoft's dedication to improving Exchange Server.

April 1996–Exchange 4.0

Prior to Exchange 4.0, enterprise messaging consisted of storing mail in post offices, which were distributed throughout an organization. This solution worked well in small organizations but was very difficult to scale and support in medium and large organizations. Exchange 4.0 introduced the concept of an X.500 directory-integrated mail system utilizing the X.400 standard for message transport. It also introduced a centralized database model for storing messages and a public folder solution for collaboration. All in all it was a watershed moment in time. The Exchange X.500 directory would eventually evolve into part of what we call Active Directory today.

October 2000–Exchange 2000

With Exchange 2000, Microsoft rocked the Exchange 5.5 install base by rebuilding Exchange Server from the ground up to support SMTP as its primary message transport and relegating X.400 to a secondary status. The Exchange 5.5 directory was superseded by Active Directory, and many administrators struggled to grasp in depth, for the first time, network services like Domain Naming System (DNS), Simple Mail Transfer Protocol (SMTP), and Active Directory (AD), which were no longer optional features but were prerequisites to the deployment of Exchange 2000 Server. In some cases Active Directory was only deployed because organizations wanted to deploy Exchange 2000 Server, even though little was understood about what AD really did and how it could benefit an organization. Exchange 2000 Server also created the collaboration identity crisis for Microsoft.

In Exchange 2000, Microsoft made a key decision in regard to the collaborative functionality that was included. Both Chat Services, and, in particular Instant Messaging were touted as the latest advances in collaboration to be included with Exchange 2000. Ironically, in Exchange Server 2003 Microsoft made an about-face. The new direction removed Chat Services and moved Instant Messaging to the Live Communication Server platform. Then, in a bold move toward the mobile work force, Microsoft integrated the once separate Microsoft Mobile Information Server into Exchange Server 2003. With the release of a number of new mobility features in Service Pack 2 (SP2) for Exchange Server 2003, it is apparent that Microsoft is committed to mobility as the new direction for Exchange collaboration.

December 2006–Exchange 2007

Exchange Server 2007 is the latest milestone in the evolution of Exchange Server. It will undoubtedly be remembered as the version of Exchange that introduced 64-bit computing, 2GB and larger mailboxes as the norm, continuous replication, unified messaging, and the Exchange Management Shell to Exchange Server. While Microsoft will continue to support public folders until 2016, Exchange Server 2007 marks the beginning of the end of public folders.

Messaging vs. Collaboration

The new architecture for Exchange Server 2007 reveals a platform that is heavily focused on message transport, mail storage, and client access and not collaboration—at least not in the sense of collaboration being public folders and instant messaging. While you will see improvements in collaboration, it will be especially noticeable from enhancements in the way in which Exchange Server 2007 interoperates with Office 2007 and Outlook 2007.

The servers that will support the collaborative functions moving forward will not be Exchange Servers. Microsoft Office SharePoint Server and Office Communication Server will likely take center stage when it comes to collaboration. Outlook 2007 and Outlook Web Access (OWA 2007) will provide a single portal to both the messaging and collaboration servers.

Roll Out the Red Carpet: Here Come the New Features

For earlier adopters and messaging geeks in general, there is a long list of exciting new features announced by Microsoft for Exchange Server 2007. These new features run the gamut from Autodiscover to the unified mailbox. We invite you to get to know all of the new features by continuing to explore the various sections throughout this book.

New Features List

Here is a brief description of each of the new features of Exchange Server 2007.

- **Autodiscover**   A web service integrated with Exchange Server 2007 that facilitates clients accessing their mailboxes. It is used to automatically set up accounts in Outlook profiles. It is also used to determine which Client Access Server a remote client should use based on where their mailbox server is located for optimal performance.

- **Availability**   Automatic load balancing of inbound and outbound connections between Hub Transport Servers within an Active Directory site.

- **Built on Active Directory**   The routing topology for Exchange Server 2007 servers is based on the Active Directory site topology. It no longer requires the creation of routing groups to control mail flow.

- **Development**   A new set of web services to access mailbox content on Exchange Mailbox Servers via HTML extends developers' capabilities.

- **Exchange Management Console**   Replacement tool for the Exchange System Manager (ESM). The Exchange Management Console (EMC) is based on Microsoft Management Console (MMC) 3.0 and combines all of the Exchange management tasks into a single graphical interface. That means no more jumping between the ESM and Active Directory Users and Computers (ADUC) to get Exchange administrative tasks done.

- **Exchange Management Shell**   A new command-line interface (CLI) from Microsoft built on the PowerShell technology for advanced administrative tasks that cannot be performed or automated in the Exchange Management Console.

- **High availability for Mailbox servers**   Transaction Log Shipping is now available for Mailbox Server roles in two flavors: Local Continuous Replication (LCR) and Cluster Continuous Replication (CCR). Each creates a second copy of the production database for rapid recovery scenarios. LCR stores the copy on the local server. CCR stores the copy on another server. The Single Copy Cluster (SCC) is the latest implementation for the traditional Exchange Microsoft Cluster Service.

- **Message conversion**   The Hub Transport Server role has the ability to analyze the formatting and encoding of messages and, based on the originator and recipient of the message, make the necessary conversion to prevent formatting errors.

- **Minimization of mail traffic**   Within an organization, least-hop routing is used to determine the best path to a recipient's mailbox. This has a greater potential of reducing traffic than least-cost routing, which is subject to arbitrary administrative constraints. Hub Transport Servers are responsible for determining the least-hop route between Active Directory sites.

- **Performance improvements**   Exchange Server 2007 is a native 64-bit application. Sixty-four-bit computing benefits are visible in the increased memory cache size, increased number of storage groups, and increased number of information stores per server.

- **Recipient resolution**   It has always been possible to designate an expansion server for a Distribution List. This is not as critical to do now that the Hub Transport Servers are site-aware and will use the directory servers that are within the same site for expanding distribution lists.

- **Unified messaging**   For many years unified messaging has been available for Exchange Server from third-party vendors. This technology, which integrates voice messaging, faxing, and e-mail, has also been price-prohibitive for many small- and medium-size businesses. By including unified messaging with Exchange Server 2007, all Exchange organizations can begin to take advantage of this powerful productivity tool.

Client Benefits

Probably the greatest improvements for clients in Exchange Server 2007 will come from the deployment of Client Access Server (CAS) roles in your organization. The same client protocols are still supported as in previous versions: Messaging Application Programming Interface (MAPI), Outlook Web Access (OWA), Internet Message Access Protocol (IMAP), Post Office Protocol (POP), and Remote Procedure Call Over HTTP (RPC-HTTP), now called Outlook Anywhere. However, many changes have taken place, ultimately benefiting the client experience. The features that are integrated with CAS dramatically improve the user's experience. But it's what is under the hood that really revolutionizes how requests from clients are handled by the CAS server. The A-list of benefits includes:

- Even better OWA
- Even better ActiveSync
- Outlook Anywhere, which encompasses:
  - RPC-HTTP
  - Autodiscover
  - Web Services (Free/Busy, Meeting Suggestions, and Out of Office)
  - Offline Address Book
  - Unified Messaging Web service
- Direct SharePoint Access

Administrative Benefits

Exchange administrators will see the most benefits from Exchange Server 2007. A new set of tools that share common business logic will eliminate much of the complexity that existed in Exchange Server 2003. In Exchange Server 2003 some advanced tasks, like delegating administration, required using Active Directory Users and Computers, Exchange System Manager, and DSACLS (dsacls.exe) to complete. This can be accomplished in Exchange

Server 2007 with a one liner from PowerShell. But there are numerous administrative benefits. The A-list of benefits includes:

- Simplified setup that is very fast and intelligent
- Common Business Logic for all administrative tools powered by PowerShell Engine.
  - Exchange Management Shell (EMS)
  - Exchange Management Console (EMC)
  - Exchange Setup
- No more Administrative Groups to manage
- No more system dependency on public folders

What Exchange Server 2007 Is Not

Every version of Exchange that has been released, at its moment in time, had the latest and best technology that Microsoft could integrate. Over time, there have been features like OWA that have grown and evolved and are now counted upon. There have also been features that didn't last past one version, like Instant Messaging. One of the key challenges to administrators each time a new version of Exchange Server is released is getting up to speed not only with the new setup features, but also in understanding what is no longer supported by the latest version. Administrators must then weigh the implications of those changes when integrating the latest version into their existing environments. Some organizations may not be able to go to Exchange Server 2007 based on the removal of configuration of their Exchange organization today.

Where Did That Go?

Another twist to the administrators' quandary is that while they may know exactly how to accomplish a task in Exchange 2000 or Exchange 2003, they will have to relearn how to perform that task in Exchange Server 2007. Here is a Top Ten list of differences that will have to be immediately absorbed by administrators. In order of importance, they are as follows:

1. Exchange System Manager is gone. It was replaced by the Exchange Management Console.
2. Active Directory Users and Computers extensions for Exchange are gone. All recipients are managed in the Exchange Management Console or Exchange Management Shell.
3. Administrative tasks that cannot be performed in the Exchange Management Console must be performed at the command line in the Exchange Management Shell.
4. Front-end/back-end architecture has been replaced by five distinct server roles. These roles must be understood before you can install the first Exchange 2007 server.
5. Exchange Server 2007 cannot coexist with Exchange 5.5; only with Exchange 2000 and Exchange 2003 in native mode.
6. Administrative Groups are gone. Period. Delegated administration is done at the Exchange Server level.

7. Only one Routing Group may exist and that is only used if you have Exchange 2000 or Exchange 2003 servers to connect to. Exchange Server 2007 uses Active Directory sites for its routing topology.

8. SMTP Virtual Servers are no longer visible. This functionality is configured in the Exchange 2007 SMTP Connector and Exchange 2007 Hub Transport Role server properties.

9. ExMerge is gone (we will mourn the loss of our good friend). The **Export-Mailbox** and **Move-Mailbox** cmdlets in the Exchange Management Shell or the Move Mailbox Wizard in the Exchange Management Console will have to be used instead.

10. Recipient Update Service is gone. You must use the **Update-AddressList** and **Update-EmailAddressPolicy** PowerShell cmdlets for manual updates.

Replaced Features

There are even more surprises in store for administrators of previous versions of Exchange. In the next two tables you will find a list of all the features that have been removed from Exchange Server 2007 that existed in Exchange Server 2003. Twenty-six features have some form of alternative or replacement feature.

Removed Feature	Replaced By
Active-Active clustering support	Active-Passive clustering only
Administrative Groups for distributed administration	Universal Security Groups (USGs), distributed administration
CDO for Workflow, which was included with Exchange Server 2003	Windows Workflow Services (WWS)
Clean Mailbox tool	**Export-Mailbox** Exchange Management Shell cmdlet
Exchange Extensions in Active Directory Users and Computers	Exchange Management Console
Exchange Installable File System (ExIFS)	Exchange Web Services or MAPI
Exchange ActiveSync: SMS Always-Up-To-Date	Direct Push Technology
Exchange Web forms	Outlook Web Access Custom Forms
ExProfRe	Autodiscover service
Intelligent Message Filter	Anti-spam agents
Inter-Organization Replication tool	Availability Service for sharing free/busy data across forests (Outlook 2007 clients only)
Link State Routing	Active Directory site-based routing
Mailbox Management Service	Messaging Records Management
Mailbox Recovery Center	Exchange Server Disaster Recovery Analyzer
Message Tracking Center Node and tracking mechanism	Exchange Server Mail Flow Analyzer

PART I

Removed Feature	Replaced By
Microsoft Exchange Server Mailbox Merge Wizard (ExMerge)	**Export-Mailbox** cmdlet or Move Mailbox Wizard
Migration Wizard	**Move-Mailbox** cmdlet
Monitoring and Status Node	Microsoft Operations Manager
Network-Attached Storage	Internet SCSI (iSCSI)
POP3/IMAP4 graphical user interface (GUI) management	Exchange Management Shell cmdlets
Recipient Update Service (RUS)	**Update-AddressList** and **Update-EmailAddressPolicy** cmdlets
Routing Groups	Active Directory sites
Routing Objects	Active Directory site-based routing
SMTP Virtual Server Instances	Exchange 2007 SMTP connectors
URL commands except for free/busy, galfind, navbar, and contents	Exchange Web Services
Workflow Designer, which was included with the Exchange Server 2003 SDK	Windows Workflow Services (WWS)

Decommissioned Features

There are another 26 features that have no equivalent feature moving forward in Exchange Server 2007.

Removed Feature	Replaced By
Active Directory Connector (ADC)	N/A
CDOEXM	N/A
Custom forms	N/A
Editing personal distribution lists	N/A
Event Service	N/A
Exchange WMI classes	N/A
Exchange ActiveSync: S/MIME abilities	N/A
Installing Exchange 2007 into an organization that contains computers that are running Exchange Server 5.5	N/A
Installing Exchange Server version 5.5 into an Exchange 2007 organization	N/A
MAPI Client on and Collaboration Data Objects (CDO) 1.21 on the Exchange Server installation	N/A; can be downloaded and installed separately
Microsoft Exchange Connector for Lotus Notes	N/A
Microsoft Exchange Connector for Novell GroupWise and migration tools	N/A

Removed Feature	Replaced By
Network News Transfer Protocol (NNTP)	N/A
Non-MAPI top-level hierarchies in a public folder store	N/A
Outlook Mobile Access	N/A
Outlook Mobile Access Browse	N/A
Public folder access	N/A
Support for Exchange Server 5.5 in the same forest as Exchange 2007	N/A
Public folder access by using NNTP	N/A
Public folder graphical user interface (GUI) management	N/A
Rules, Post Forms, Monthly Calendar view	N/A
S/MIME Control	N/A
Site Replication Service (SRS)	N/A
X.400 Message Transfer Agent (MTA)	N/A
Transport Event hooks	N/A
Public folder access by using IMAP4	N/A

Deemphasized Features

Microsoft has decided to deemphasize the Exchange features that are on their last legs and are not going to be to replaced or removed at this time. The features that have been deemphasized are as follows:

- Public folders
- Recipient Update Service
- CDO 1.21
- MAPI32
- CDOEX (CDO 3.0)
- Exchange WebDAV extensions
- ExOLEDB
- Store Events
- Streaming backup APIs
- E2K3 VSAPI

Information Workers' Delight

Ultimately what Exchange 2007 must deliver is an improved end-user experience, if Microsoft wants the existing customer base to come back. To extend the reach of Exchange to new customers, Microsoft will need to keep improving and innovating with every release. With the monumental release of Exchange Server 2007, end users, especially information workers, will have a number of new productivity features to celebrate about.

Part IV of this book is a dedicated reference guide for all Exchange Server 2007 Clients. If you want to dig deep into the latest clients for Exchange Server 2007, turn to Part IV. For now, here is a summary of the improvements that are available for Exchange Clients.

Outlook 2007 Improvements

It might be hard to imagine, but there may be more changes to Office and Outlook than there have been to Exchange. At the very least, there is as dramatic a shift in the new experience that users will have with Outlook 2007 as administrators will have with Exchange Server 2007.

From an administrator's perspective the key benefits of Outlook 2007 are

- **New user-friendly User Interface (UI)**   Users who are new to using Outlook will be able to find things easily. Outlook 2007, unlike other Office 2007 applications, has the most similarities with its predecessor, making it easy for long-time users to adapt to.

- **Autoconfiguration**   When a user provides their username, password, and e-mail address to Outlook 2007, it will automatically configure the profile to connect to the proper Mailbox Server. This will eliminate the need for administrators to touch desktops after mailboxes are moved between 2003 and 2007 Servers or even between Active Directory forests, even in the event that the source server (server that the mailbox was originally on) is unavailable to redirect the client.

- **Instant search**   End users who want to find something in their mailbox will have an easier time doing so. The search function is easier to find in Outlook 2007 and the results are tremendously fast. This is due to the new search indexing.

Part IV is dedicated to Exchange clients. Chapter 11 explores all of the new features of Outlook 2007 from the perspectives of those who must deploy and maintain and those who use Outlook 2007.

OWA 2007 Improvements

We have long anticipated the day when the Outlook Web Access (OWA) thin client would be a legitimate replacement for the Outlook thick client. With bated breath we wait with each new release of Exchange and with each Service Pack release if, once and for all, OWA does everything for us that Outlook can.

The fact is that many companies for which web client access fits their business modes, retail for example, have embraced OWA for years. But the rest of the business world tends to use OWA as a secondary client rather than a primary client. With each new improvement to OWA, Microsoft extends the feature set and makes it more enticing to make the switch. With OWA 2007 some much-awaited changes have been made. For more detail on OWA, see Chapter 12, which is dedicated to Outlook Web Access 2007. The following list shows some the latest improvements users will notice. Users will be able to:

- Schedule Out of Office messages and send to internal and/or external recipients
- Search the Global Address List
- Use the Scheduling Assistant to efficiently book meetings

- Access SharePoint documents without a Virtual Private Network (VPN) or tunnel using LinkAccess
- Use WebReady Document Viewing to read attachments in HTML even if the application that created the document is not installed locally
- Access RSS subscriptions
- View content in Managed E-mail Folders
- Retrieve voice mail or fax messages through unified messaging integration

Mobility Improvements

Today there are more cellular phones sold worldwide than there are Personal Computers (PC). As the power of the PC starts to become something that you can hold in the palm of your hand, the palmtop devices of the very near future replace desktop and laptops for the majority of information workers. At least this seems to be the bet Microsoft is making by adding a variety of new features to their product line geared toward the mobile workforce.

- **Search**   Mobile users can search the local device and their entire Exchange mailbox via Exchange Active Sync (EAS).
- **Direct push**   Using a persistent EAS connection, the mobile device receives new or updated e-mail, calendar, contacts, and tasks as soon as they arrive on the server.
- **Numerous devices**   Exchange Server 2007 ActiveSync devices are available from Windows Mobile, Nokia, Symbian, Motorola, Sony Ericsson, Palm, and DataViz.
- **Device security and management**   Policies can be configured to enforce PINs of varying length and strength and to enforce a device wipe of data and applications, should the device be lost or stolen. The policies can be per-user. Device usage can be tracked and managed centrally.
- **LinkAccess**   When a user receives a link to a Windows SharePoint Services site or file share while using a mobile device, Exchange Server 2007 uses LinkAccess to retrieve and display the document.
- **Calendaring and Out of Office**   With Exchange Server 2007, users have many new options when accessing their calendar from a mobile device using Exchange ActiveSync. They can reply to a meeting invitation with a message, forward the invitation to another person, and view acceptance tracking for meeting attendees. Out of Office messages can also be set from the mobile device.

New Unified Messaging

A slam dunk for Microsoft is the inclusion of unified messaging. Unified messaging extends the functionality of e-mail, adding voice messaging and fax messages, by integrating Exchange 2007 with IP Gateways and IP PBX solutions. While unified messaging technology is nothing new in the industry, the high level of integration with Exchange Server 2007, OWA 2007, and Outlook 2007 is unprecedented. The cost savings alone achieved by integrating this with Exchange Server will drive up the usage and popularity of these features. It will not be long before every user in your company can't live without the ability to get their voice messages delivered as e-mails.

Categorical Changes

With any software release from Microsoft, we have come to expect a number of feature additions and enhancements. But every so often there are extreme categorical changes. Earlier we looked at the key milestones in the Exchange product line and identified Exchange 2007 as a true milestone. Here is an introduction to the key architectural changes that make this an evolutionary product release from Microsoft.

Sixty-Four-Bit Computing

Exchange Server 2007 marks the very first time that this application from Microsoft will only be supported on 64-bit hardware. For the last six years, Microsoft has been playing a shell game with the 32-bit computing architecture adjusting to ever-increasing demands being placed on Exchange. The 3GB switch has enabled the Store.exe process to address more User Mode memory. The dedication of disk volumes to transaction logs, information stores, and SMTP queues on expensive disk storage subsystems has prolonged the life of the 32-bit system.

Exchange Server 2003 is the last of the 32-bit mail systems from Microsoft. As we say goodbye to Exchange Server 2003, we welcome an application that is not bound by a 4GB memory threshold, where memory cache sizes are so large that disk I/O is no longer a performance bottleneck. The 64-bit architecture has fostered innovation in Exchange that has been stifled.

Server Roles

Exchange Server 2000 was evolutionary in its architecture in many ways. It was the first native SMTP messaging system from Microsoft. It was also the first version of Exchange Server to depend on Active Directory Services and Internet Information Services (IIS) for both transport and client protocol support. The separation of the storage engine from the Internet client services was the foundation for the front-end/back-end architecture that defined Exchange Server 2000 and 2003.

Exchange Server 2007 does not change the messaging transport, but it does replace the front-end/back-end architecture with a set of predefined server roles that administrators can deploy into a variety of supported topologies (see Table 1-2). Server roles give administrators

Server Role	Description
Mailbox Server	Used for hosting users' mailbox and public folder stores, as well as providing MAPI access for thick-client access
Client Access Server	Provides users with mailbox access through IMAP, POP, Outlook Web Access, and ActiveSync protocols
Hub Transport Server	Handles mail routing and controls mail flow by utilizing Active Directory site information
Unified Messaging Server	Enables user mailbox access through a telephone, as well as enables telephony services such as voicemail, fax, and VoIP capabilities
Edge Transport Server	Provides increased security by placing SMTP services, mail quarantine, and smarthost capabilities on a perimeter network

TABLE 1-2   Exchange Server 2007 Server Roles

a greater degree of control when planning and deploying an infrastructure of Exchange Server 2007 servers.

Continuous Replication

Microsoft has offered two high-availability solutions for Exchange Server. The Microsoft Clustering Services have been available in one form or another since Windows NT 4.0. Exchange Servers in combination with support from various hardware vendors have been clustered as well. Windows Network Load Balancing has been used to provide high availability to Outlook Web Access and all front-end services in Exchange 2000 Server and Exchange Server 2003.

Recent historical events have taught us that Exchange Server high availability is only one part of providing business continuity. Microsoft defines *business continuity* as the ability of an organization to continue to function even after a disastrous event, accomplished through the deployment of redundant hardware and software and the use of fault-tolerant systems, as well as a solid backup and recovery strategy.

In order for Exchange Server to meet continuity requirements, many organizations have turned to third-party software to get beyond the constraints of the Exchange 2003 Standby Cluster solution. For more information on the Standby Exchange 2003 Cluster, see http://technet.microsoft.com/en-us/library/aa996470.aspx?source=rss&WT.dl=0. These solutions make it possible to use clustering as a *hot site* recovery option. To provide hot site failover replication, tools like DoubleTake from NSI and WanSYNC from Computer Associates have been required.

Continuous replication provides Exchange 2007 Administrators with a third high-availability option that will make it possible for the first time in Exchange Server to natively support database replication and failover without the assistance of a third party. Part VI of this book tackles the complex subject of continuity and how it is addressed by Microsoft in Exchange Server 2007. Chapter 18 details continuous replication and other high-availability solutions for Exchange 2007.

Security

The .NET Trustworthy Computing initiative from Microsoft has gone a long way toward helping Microsoft provide a more secure line of products to their customers. Windows Server 2003 and Exchange Server 2003 had a number of security advances as a direct result. It would appear that Microsoft has continued to run with the initiative as Exchange Server 2007 security advances dwarf those made by Exchange Server 2003.

It really should not be a surprise that Exchange Server 2007 should be the focus of many security enhancements. Every corporation or government agency that is subject to regulation compliance has the need to both secure electronic transmission of information and retain electronic communications. Since Exchange has the largest install base of any messaging system, it is subject to the largest amount of scrutiny from compliance officers and auditors. There are two key areas where Exchange Server 2007 distinguishes itself from its predecessors.

Edge Security

Front-end servers in Exchange 2000 and 2003 had the benefit of not having to store any data. This made them a better candidate to place in the perimeter of a network. This was not an ideal situation, however. The front-end servers are still members of the Active Directory domains and therefore required a number of TCP/IP ports to be opened on the internal firewall. Many firewall administrators prohibited Exchange Server 2003 from being placed into the demilitarized zone (DMZ) of their networks because of these port requirements.

Exchange Administrators, in many cases, turned to Microsoft Internet Security and Acceleration Server (ISA Server) as a perimeter solution for Exchange Server. Microsoft also recommends ISA as a more secure perimeter solution for Exchange Server than front-end servers. The downside to ISA as a lone perimeter solution, is that while it can look and act like an Exchange Server to Internet clients, it is not an Exchange Server.

Microsoft has introduced a new server role that has no equivalent in any other release of Exchange Server. The Edge Transport Server is a true Exchange perimeter solution as it does not need to be a member of the Active Directory domain and yet, it is most definitely an Exchange Server that is part of your Exchange Server 2007 organization.

ForeFront

Another area in which Exchange Server has been lacking in is antivirus and spam filtering. Some progress was made when the Intelligent Message Filter (IMF) became integrated with Exchange Server 2003 with the release of SP2. The IMF provides in-house SPAM filtering. But there has been an obvious void in Exchange Server when it comes to antivirus protection. Now available from Microsoft is an antivirus solution for Exchange Server 2007. It is called ForeFront. The antivirus part of ForeFront is, of course, the integration of Antigen, which Microsoft acquired with their acquisition of Sybari back in February 2005.

Part V of this book covers Exchange Server 2007's security features in depth. You can find information on deploying the Edge Transport Servers in Chapter 7.

Unified Messaging and Unified Communications

Unified messaging links together voice and data technologies that have been separated for many years. By adding a new dedicated Unified Messaging Server role, Microsoft has shown its commitment to the merger of voice and data networks. This is illustrated best with the combined features of unified messaging and the new Office Communication Server. In October 2007 Microsoft officially announced its Unified Communications strategy to provide voice and video conferencing as an integrated package. The products in this suite include Unified Messaging and Office Communication Server. Chapters 9 and 13 go into detail on both unified messaging and unified communications.

Paradigm Shift in Management

The PowerShell engine (previously MONAD) was the brainchild of Jeffrey Snover, who is the Windows PowerShell Architect. There are five key design concepts behind the PowerShell with one goal. The goal is essentially to build an intuitive shell that empowers administrators at any skill level. "Administrators" is the key word. The five characteristics that are consistent throughout PowerShell are that it is:

- Interactive
- Composable
- Programmatic

- Production-oriented
- Easy to use

UNIX administrators will find many similarities between PowerShell and the tools that they are familiar with. In fact, many of the individuals who were involved with developing PowerShell have extensive knowledge of UNIX, AS400, and VMS. The level of interactivity in PowerShell was inspired by BASH and KSH. The programmatic sophistication of PowerShell was inspired by Perl and Ruby. The production orientation was modeled after the CS on the AS400 and the DCL on VMS.

Management Architecture

Exchange Server 2007, like earlier versions of Exchange Server, is a showcase for the latest Microsoft technology. The Exchange Server 2007 toolset will likely be the first use of PowerShell that many IT professionals experience. PowerShell is not an Exchange-specific tool, but the Exchange developers have taken full advantage of the PowerShell architecture in order to enhance the Exchange IT professional experience. In Figure 1-1 you can see how the PowerShell architecture is the foundation for all administrative tools. Microsoft Management Console (MMC) snap-ins are built on top of the PowerShell engine. All tasks that can be performed in the UI can be performed from a command line with *cmdlets*, which are .NET object classes, from within the Microsoft Management Shell (MMS). The depth and breadth of the PowerShell can be seen in how advanced programming languages such as .NET can conversely be used to leverage the MMS and MMC cmdlets.

Under the hood, the PowerShell is performing the heavy lifting that would normally require many additional lines of code in a script. Concise cmdlets are created for the majority of the tasks that the administrator will have to perform, making it possible to accomplish complex administrative tasks with a single line of text. Microsoft refers to these simple yet powerful commands as *one-liners*.

FIGURE 1-1
PowerShell
architecture

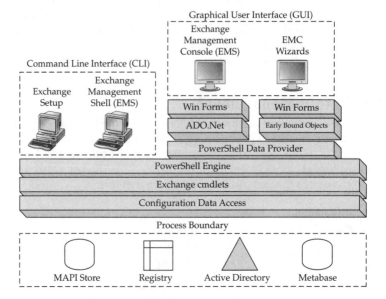

Exchange Management Console

Don't panic! There is still a full-featured GUI for performing Exchange Administrative Tasks. In fact the Exchange Management Console (EMC) may very well be the only tool you will need to administer Exchange Server 2007. So if you are an administrator who loves using the GUI, you can continue to do so (see Figure 1-2). You will also be happy to learn that the EMC is simpler, more flexible, and more powerful than the Exchange System Manager in Exchange Server 2003.

Simplified Navigation

The navigation tree in Exchange 2003 took some getting used to. The MMC in general has some quirks to it that can make administration trying at times. For example, have you ever had to left-click on an object before you can successfully right-click? And have you seen that behavior changes from object to object within the navigation tree? The size of the navigation tree even with a single storage group can be difficult to traverse. Add a few servers and storage groups and you have a quite a bit of navigating to do just to accomplish a single task.

The new navigation tree in the Exchange Management Console is fixed at a predefined size. It will not grow or shrink unless the tree is modified in a future release of Exchange Server. This static tree structure will make it very easy to remember where to go to perform an administrative task. All common administrative tasks are grouped into *work centers*.

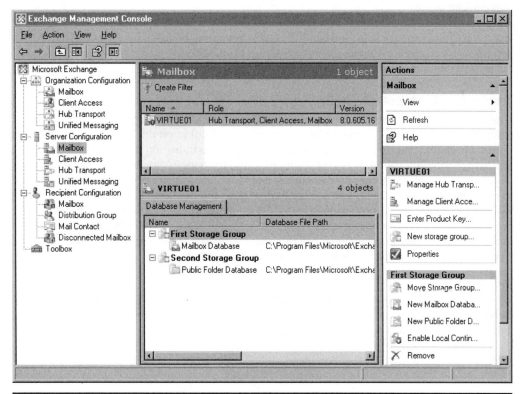

FIGURE 1-2   Exchange Management Console

The four primary work centers are Organization Configuration, Server Configuration, Recipient Configuration, and the Toolbox. As far as the right-clicking anomalies, there is a new Actions pane in the MMC window that displays all of the actions you would normally see if you were to right-click on the active object.

Pickers
When you are configuring objects in the console and you have the option to pick from one or more settings, for example a mailbox store for a mailbox, the picker will always be in an obvious and intuitive location that you will not have to hunt for or expand advanced property sheets to get to.

Wizards
There are at least twice as many new wizards built into the new EMC. Wizards help to make more complex tasks easier to perform with less likelihood of human error.

Rich Filtering
To make the administrative task at hand easier to handle, the results pane of the EMC supports rich filtering. The filters will provide concise results that will allow you to get to the objects you want to administer without having to spend a lot of time manually hunting for an object.

Customized Views
When you are in the middle of a task and are interrupted, your view will be maintained even if you close the console. You can then easily return to the task and pick up where you left off. You can also customize views for various administrative tasks and save a custom filter as the default view.

Exchange Management Shell
The Exchange Management Shell is going to make you look like an Exchange guru. If you have ever used the CMD command-line interface, you should find the Exchange Management Shell easy enough to use. In no time flat you will be able to transition from GUI-based skills into simple one-liners that you can execute from the Exchange Management Shell (see Figure 1-3). It is worth noting that due to development time constraints and a perception that certain tasks were outdated, some administrative tasks did not find their way back into the GUI. For example, you cannot configure IMAP4 or POP3 from the GUI. Some of the initial feedback from administrators suggests that the Exchange Management Console is still underdeveloped. The good news is that all tasks can be done via the Exchange Management Shell. It is in your best interest to at least learn the fundamentals.

Verb-Noun Pairings
Commands (cmdlets) are verb-noun pairings. There are 368 cmdlets just for Exchange Server 2007 (Before installing Exchange 2007 SP1). They are for the most part, in plain English. Can you guess what the following cmdlets will do?

```
get-mailbox
enable-mailbox
move-mailbox
```

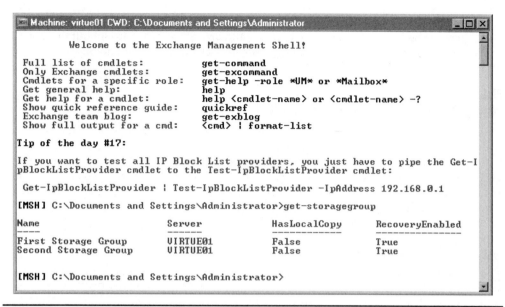

```
Machine: virtue01 CWD: C:\Documents and Settings\Administrator          _|□|×|

            Welcome to the Exchange Management Shell!

Full list of cmdlets:           get-command
Only Exchange cmdlets:          get-excommand
Cmdlets for a specific role:    get-help -role *UM* or *Mailbox*
Get general help:               help
Get help for a cmdlet:          help <cmdlet-name> or <cmdlet-name> -?
Show quick reference guide:     quickref
Exchange team blog:             get-exblog
Show full output for a cmd:     <cmd> | format-list

Tip of the day #17:

If you want to test all IP Block List providers, you just have to pipe the Get-I
pBlockListProvider cmdlet to the Test-IpBlockListProvider cmdlet:

 Get-IpBlockListProvider | Test-IpBlockListProvider -IpAddress 192.168.0.1

[MSH] C:\Documents and Settings\Administrator>get-storagegroup

Name                    Server          HasLocalCopy    RecoveryEnabled
----                    ------          ------------    ---------------
First Storage Group     VIRTUE01        False           True
Second Storage Group    VIRTUE01        False           True


[MSH] C:\Documents and Settings\Administrator>
```

FIGURE 1-3   Exchange Management Shell

Sure you can. If you can think of an Exchange task that you used to do, there is a verb-noun pairing for it. There are only 26 verbs, as shown in the following table:

Add	Clean	Clear	Connect	Copy	Disable	Dismount
Enable	Export	Get	Import	Install	Mount	Move
New	Remove	Restore	Resume	Retry	Set	Start
Stop	Suspend	Test	Uninstall	Update		

Objects and Parameters

Active Directory objects are either filtered or affected by cmdlets. Objects are displayed in columns and rows in the Exchange Management Shell (EMS). In Figure 1-3 you can see that the **Get-Storagegroup** command retrieved and displayed the storage group objects. The object property names appear as column headers. The object values appear in each of the rows. Because no specific server identity was passed in with the command, PowerShell queries the entire domain.

If you need to work with a specific server or you are looking for a storage group with a specific name, an additional parameter must be specified. Parameters are name and/or "argument strings". For example:

```
Get-storagegroup -Server "virtue01"
```

Automate IT

Even with only a basic understanding of the PowerShell, you can begin to automate numerous mundane tasks that would otherwise consume your time. Unlike automation scripts, which have been very popular for the last several years with Exchange, Exchange Management Shell one-liners are easy to create and are safe to run. Throughout this book we will examine the use of the Exchange Management Console for automating administrative tasks.

Exchange Server 2007 Service Pack 1

In the writing of this book we have taken much care to incorporate Service Pack 1 (SP1) features and enhancements. Even to the extent of holding off on the release of the book to make sure that all SP1 updates would be included for your reference. You will find notes on Service Pack 1 in each chapter, and the procedures outlined in this book are based on what you will see when you run the Service Pack 1 version of Exchange Server 2007. That said, here are some excellent reasons to deploy Service Pack 1 as soon as possible in your Exchange 2007 organization.

OWA 2007 Improvements

The first area that the Microsoft Exchange team focused on with the development of Service Pack 1 for Exchange 2007 is "anywhere-access" features. When Exchange 2007 was released back in December of 2006, there were some OWA features that existed in Exchange 2003 but didn't make their way into Exchange 2007. Those have been identified here with "(again)" appended in the list.

- OWA Personal Distribution lists
- OWA Public Folder Accessibility (again)
- OWA Rules Wizard
- OWA Customizable Web Forms
- OWA Custom Address Book Fields
- OWA Recover deleted items (again)
- OWA Monthly Calendar view
- OWA S/MIME support (again)
- OWA Additional Spell check languages

Operational Improvements

Numerous administrative capabilities have been added to the Exchange 2007 tools. New commands are available in the Exchange Management Shell, and new task wizards and object properties are exposed in the Exchange Management Console. But some of the core changes come in supporting Windows 2003 SP2 and Windows Server 2008:

- IPv6
- Windows 2003 SP2 support
- Windows 2008 support
- New and improved PowerShell cmdlets
- Improved Management Console with additional administrative tasks and properties

- Graphical Public Folder Administration (again)
- Client Access Role Proxies to reduce RPCs across WAN
- Unified Messaging and Office Communication Server integration support

Security and Availability Improvements

You will also be able to add security and high-availability features not provided in the RTM version of Exchange 2007, including:

- Mobile remote wipe confirmation
- Information Rights Management prefetching by Hub Transport
- S/MIME for OWA
- Defense Message System (DMS) support
- Standby Continuous Replication (SCR)

There are many more areas in which SP1 increases the functionality of Exchange 2007, as you will discover as you go through the different chapters in this book.

Summary

E-mail communications and the messaging systems, which started as simplistic text messages stored on electronic post offices with nominal storage capabilities and limited client functionality, have grown and changed over the last 20 years. They have evolved into complex messaging and collaboration systems with e-mail data storage architectures that can scale into terabytes and beyond, and with more client features than the average e-mail user will ever get to know. Microsoft's first e-mail solution, MS Mail, was a fairly average product in the messaging industry. Microsoft's current e-mail solution, Exchange Server, is the most commercially successful messaging system, with over 140 million Exchange clients worldwide.

Exchange Server 2007 is the latest milestone in the evolution of Exchange Server. It will undoubtedly be remembered as the version of Exchange that introduced 64-bit computing, 2GB and larger mailboxes as the norm, continuous replication, unified messaging, and the PowerShell to Exchange Server. While Microsoft will continue to support public folders until at least 2016, Exchange Server 2007 marks the beginning of the end of public folders. Exchange Server 2007 provides features for built-in security, client experience, administrator experience, reduced TCO, and more.

Exchange Server 2007 marks the very first time that this application from Microsoft will only be supported on 64-bit hardware. Exchange Server 2007 does not change the messaging transport, but it does replace the front-end/back-end architecture with a set of predefined server roles that administrators can deploy into a variety of supported topologies.

For earlier adopters and messaging geeks in general, there is a long list of exciting new features announced by Microsoft for Exchange Server 2007. These new features run the gamut from Autodiscover to the Unified Messaging Server role. Probably the greatest improvements for clients in Exchange Server 2007 will come from the deployment of Client Access Server (CAS) roles in your organization. Exchange administrators will see the most benefits from Exchange Server 2007. A new set of tools that share common business logic will eliminate much of the complexity that existed in the Exchange Server 2003.

Due to the large number of changes in Exchange 2007, administrators will need to relearn what they already know how to do in some cases. It will also be important that they identify the features that are no longer supported or are deemphasized by Microsoft. And yet there are even more surprises in store. Many features have been removed from Exchange Server 2007 that existed in Exchange Server 2003, while others were deemphasized. The Exchange Management Console (EMC) may very well be the only tool you will need to administer Exchange Server 2007. The EMC is simpler, more flexible, and more powerful than the Exchange System Manager in Exchange Server 2003.

The Exchange Management Shell and the Exchange Management Console are the primary administrative tools for Exchange Server 2007. They are both take advantage the PowerShell architecture. The Exchange Management Console makes common administrative takes easy to do and the and the Exchange Management Shell makes complex administrative tasks possible with less administrative effort.

This book was developed using Exchange Server 2007 Service Pack 1 as the reference environment. You will not have to cross-reference the chapters in this book with external Service Pack 1 documentation. Service Pack 1 is already being considered by IP professionals and industry analysts as a mandatory update. Many organizations have put off their deployment of Exchange 2007 in anticipation of Service Pack 1. With the inclusion of SP1 content, this book provides a one-stop solution for Exchange 2007 information you need to deploy and support Exchange 2007.

Active Directory Integration

The sign of any good system is that it is transparent to the naked eye. Take your car's engine, for example. Do you really think about how the oxygen is mixed with the gasoline at just the right consistency to allow the spark plugs to ignite and fire the pistons in just the right order to cause the crank shaft to turn and deliver power to the axle, ultimately turning your tires to propel your car down the road? The average driver of a vehicle has little to no concept of what is going on under the hood, but any driver knows that if you press down on the gas pedal, the car should go. A good Active Directory design should be as transparent to your end users and in most cases to Exchange administrators as a car's engine is to the driver.

This chapter will open the hood on Active Directory and will show you the key components of Active Directory that are important for you as an Exchange Server 2007 administrator. Knowledge of Active Directory (AD) is an indispensable tool. You will not only have a better understanding of Exchange Server 2007, once you understand AD, but you will also have a greater ability to optimize and troubleshoot your environment. By the end of this chapter you will have the knowledge required to make design decisions that will impact, for better or worse, the experience your end users will have when they access their mailboxes.

Directory Services

Has a nontechnical person ever asked you what a directory service is? If so, were you able to describe to them (in a nontechnical sense) what it is? I have deployed directory services for many years now and oddly enough, I do not take satisfaction in the answers I find myself giving to end users, mostly because of the blank stare I usually receive. In most cases it is simply easier to show someone a benefit of a directory service. An overused, but effective, example is that of the network printer. The dialog goes something like this:

Admin: How do you currently find the printer you want to print to?

User: I walk around or ask around to find the printer that I can print to.

Admin: How do you configure your computer to use that printer?

User: I read the configuration information taped to the front of the printer and then configure a printer on my computer or call the help desk.

Admin: Well, a directory service will allow you to search for a printer based on your printing requirements like color, double-sided, location, and so on… and display a list of printers that meet your specifications. Then it allows you to add the printer to your computer just by selecting it from the list.

User: So what is a directory service?

Admin: Never mind.

No need to get frustrated—remember, the idea of the directory service is for it to be transparent to the end user. Perhaps the best nontechnical definition of a directory service to give to end users is: a *directory service* is a collection of services on the network that makes your life easier by publishing network resources and simplifying searches for those resources to increase your personal productivity.

Distributed Computing

Not long after networks of computers began to exist, the concepts of how to organize the resources on them and facilitate locating resources within a network began to be formulated. One of the earliest directory services ever implemented was actually associated with one of the very first e-mail systems. In the early 1980s at Xerox's Palo Alto Research Labs, a project called Grapevine created a distributed computing environment. The services created in this environment formed one of the earliest directory services. Guess what the primary service provided on the Grapevine network was? It was electronic mail, of course. At the heart of projects like Grapevine we find the true nature of a directory service and the beginnings of our technical definition.

X.500

At the very same time that Xerox was deploying Grapevine, the international standards organizations were working on a set of standards that would ultimately define for us what a directory service is. That set of standards has become commonly known as X.500. There is a long, sordid history to the making of the X.500 standard, but to make a very long story short, it is the tale of two organizations, the International Telecommunications Union (ITU-T) and International Standards Organization (ISO), who combined their resources, over a lengthy period of time, to define a set of standards that we now call ITU-T X.500 and ISO/IEC 9594-1.

NOTE *If you are interested in extreme detail, there is an excellent online book called* Understanding X.500—The Directory *by D. W. Chadwick, which you can find online at http://sec.cs.kent.ac .uk/x500book/.*

To an Exchange administrator, what's interesting to know about X.500 is that X.500 was primarily defined to overcome limitations in early e-mail systems. Specifically it defined a system to resolve addresses for X.400 messaging systems.

Unfortunately, in addressing the name resolution problem inherent in distributed e-mail systems, X.500 presented problems of its own. The very protocols that were defined as part of X.500 (Directory Access Protocol [DAP], Directory System Protocol [DSP], Directory Information Shadowing Protocol [DISP], and Directory Operational Bindings Management Protocol [DOP]) were time-consuming and unwieldy when performing name resolution due to their strict adherence to the Open Standards Interconnections (OSI) model. Because of the lack of performance, there was a very slow adoption of these standards. The OSI model has now been superseded by Transmission Control Protocol/Internet Protocol (TCP/IP). This is not to say that OSI was bad. In fact, there were many benefits to OSI, not the least of which was to get the various proprietary network protocols developers to work on standardizing how computers communicate with each other. The good new is that TCP/IP ultimately led to the development of Lightweight Directory Access Protocol (LDAP), which paved the way for the future of directory services.

Lightweight Directory Access Protocol: LDAP

The very first version of LDAP was not actually called LDAP; it was called Lightweight Directory Browsing Protocol (LDBP). It was not based on an actual Request for Comment (RFC). Initially it was designed to be an alternative to X.500's Directory Access Protocol (DAP) so that a client could browse an X.500 directory on a TCP/IP network. When this protocol was adapted to also be able to make modifications to the directory, it was renamed Lightweight Directory Access Protocol (LDAP). The Internet Engineering Task Force (IETF) further developed and standardized LDAP v2 and subsequently LDAP v3, which is the current version of LDAP (http://tools.ietf.org/html/rfc4510).

LDAP had two things going for it that spelled its instant adoption. First, it worked natively on the TCP/IP protocol stack, which was beginning to dominate computer networks in the early 1990s when LDAP was conceived. The second thing it had going for it was that it was much faster than its predecessors.

Active Directory Services

It was not necessarily an easy decision for Microsoft to develop its own LDAP directory service. After all, Microsoft was a late adopter of the directory services for its flagship operating system Windows Server. Novell Directory Services (NDS), Banyan Street Talk, and various Open Source implementations had a huge head start. This was largely because Microsoft Windows utilized a proprietary network protocol called NetBIOS Enhanced User Interface (NetBEUI) that exclusively used NetBIOS for name resolution. NetBIOS allowed users to browse for resources on the network rather than query an LDAP Directory. Microsoft made the shift to TCP/IP as a default protocol with the release of Windows NT 4.0. Active Directory, Microsoft's LDAP directory for the Windows network operating system, was finally released as part of Windows 2000 Server almost ten years after LDAP was invented.

The First Microsoft LDAP Directory

While it may be true that Active Directory was not available in the early versions of Windows, it is not fair to say that Microsoft did not have a directory service prior to Active Directory. Microsoft has had an LDAP directory since 1996 when Exchange Server 4.0 was released. That's right because Exchange 4.0 was based on the X.400 mail transport standards it required an X.500 directory. By 1996 there were already a number of LDAP directories that resembled X.500 but were actually LDAP directories. What made Microsoft's LDAP directory unique was that it was developed specifically for Exchange Server and NT Domain compatibility.

Since Windows NT Domains provided authentication, account management, and computer management while NetBIOS provided name resolution, the Exchange directory was only needed for the messaging system objects. The Exchange Administrator Tool was created to manage the Exchange Directory. With each release of Exchange Server, improvements were made to the Exchange directory. Exchange 5.5 was the last version of Exchange to have a dedicated LDAP directory independent from the operating system.

Windows 2000 Active Directory Services

The proliferation of routed networks within organizations and the complexity of deploying Windows Internet Naming System (WINS), to provide NetBIOS name resolution in routed networks, spelled doom for NetBIOS as the sole enterprise name resolution solution. The scalability limitations of the Windows NT Domain sealed the fate of NT Account databases. NT Domains were initially limited to 40,000 objects. However, this number did increase to over 100,000 objects by the time NT 4.0 was replaced. NT domains still could not match the scalability of Microsoft's competition. The LDAP directory was the answer to both problems. But where was Microsoft to go to get one? What a stroke of luck that they already owned an LDAP directory. By essentially merging the Exchange directory developers with the Windows development team, Microsoft was able to deliver Active Directory. Or we could say Microsoft's LDAP Directory version 3.0 was born.

The first version of Active Directory Services released with Windows 2000 provided the ability to upgrade from and coexist with Windows NT 4.0 Domains. However, the Active Directory Services eliminated the need for the Windows NT Accounts Databases. Active Directory became the complete network management solution for Windows environments when Active Directory was allowed to take over account management, resource management, and authentication. AD is much more than just a network management solution (as Exchange 2000 Server certainly illustrated). Exchange 2000 Server was not only the showcase for Active Directory Integration; it was the primary reason most early implementers of Active Directory made the switch.

The Windows Server 2000 version of Active Directory added functionality to the Windows environments that had not existed previously.

Windows 2000's Active Directory Key Features

The key features in the first release of Active Directory include:

- Group Policy and the Intellimirror philosophy
- Single Sign-on
- Kerberos and X.509 Certificate Authentication
- Directory-enabled applications
- Scalability (millions of objects per domain)
- Domain Naming System (DNS)

Windows 2003 Active Directory

Windows 2003 Server marked a coming of age for Active Directory. Exchange Server was no longer the only benefactor of an AD-enabled organization. Many other applications and services (from Microsoft and from other software companies) began to integrate with

Active Directory. The extensible schema made it possible for even the most sophisticated solutions, such as Enterprise Resource Planning (ERP) and Customer Relationship Management (CRM), to build on Active Directory as a development platform.

Many organizations that deployed Active Directory 2000 just for Exchange 2000 began to explore the potential of an AD-enabled environment. During these explorations, shortfalls were identified by customers. Microsoft listened and addressed the following items in the release of Active Directory 2003.

Windows 2003's Active Directory Improvements

Improvements in Active Directory made by Windows 2003 include:

- **Active Directory Migration Tool (ADMT)**   ADMT v2 and v3 were enhanced to make migrating from NT, and even other forests, easier and more transparent by adding password migration and other new features.

- **Domain Rename**   Reduces planning time by removing inflexibility. Domains can now be renamed in the event that the organization changes.

- **Schema Redefine**   Increases the flexibility of the schema by allowing previously defined attributes and classes to be disabled. Also, allows incorrectly defined schema elements to be redefined.

- **Group Policy Management Console (GPMC)**   Introduced to facilitate the management of Group Policy objects.

- **Cross-Forest Trusts**   Increases the scalability and flexibility of Active Directory by extending the authentication and authorization facilities to be shared across multiple forests.

- **Software Restriction Policies**   Allows organizations to define what application should and should not be running on computers and enforce those policies.

- **Reduced Replication**   Branch office domain controllers (DCs) do not need to check with group controllers (GCs) to authenticate users. Clients can cache Universal Group Memberships and Active Directory partitions can be configured to control which domain controllers will replicate the partition.

- **Install from Replica**   Domain controllers can be deployed by using a replica of an existing DC, reducing deployment times in environments with bandwidth constraints.

AD vs. Other Directory Services

Active Directory is based on open standards and is 100 percent LDAP v3–compliant. It is still considered by many in the industry to be a proprietary implementation of an LDAP directory. This is probably the biggest complaint you will hear from the competing directory services and their developers. Especially, the Active Directory Service Interfaces (ADSI) interface is a proprietary way in which programmers can interface with Microsoft's Active Directory. Even so, over 70 percent of North American enterprises are running Microsoft's Active Directory.

The desires of both the community at large and Microsoft to see Active Directory be the directory choice for their customers has driven Active Directory services to be even more standards-based. The inclusion of the InetOrgPerson object in the Active Directory 2003 Schema is a great example of this. In a purely Windows environment there is no need

Manufacturer	Directory Name
Microsoft	Active Directory
Novell	eDirectory
Netscape	Netscape Directory Server
Messaging Direct	M-Vault
OpenLDAP Foundation	OpenLDAP
IBM	SecureWay Directory
Sun	Sun One

TABLE 2-1   LDAP Directories

for this object, so it was left out of the Windows 2000 version of Active Directory. But, in a multi-directory environment, the InetOrgPerson object is a key standardization object for synchronizing multiple directories. Microsoft's exclusion of InetOrgPerson and some of their interpretations of LDAP did not bode well in heterogeneous environments. Even now that Active Directory is more compliant than ever, Microsoft still faces the challenge of overcoming the perception that it is a Windows-only directory. This may be an insurmountable challenge as one of the core benefits to AD is its tight integration with the Windows operating systems. In fact, Active Directory will only run on Windows. Table 2-1 lists some of the more prevalent LDAP directories.

Logical Active Directory Components

Now let's pop the hood on Active Directory. To start, the services that make up Active Directory are broken down into two broad categories. The two categories are logical and physical. The logical components to Active Directory allow administrators to easily model their organization. This section will help you understand some of the most commonly associated terms you will hear in an Active Directory environment such as Forest, Tree, Domain, and Organizational Unit.

If you are new to Active Directory, the remainder of this chapter should help you understand the foundation that AD provides to Exchange Server 2007. If you are very knowledgeable about Active Directory, you might want to skip on down to the end of the chapter. There is a section of this chapter called "Active Directory and Exchange Server 2007" that you won't want to miss.

Forests

A *forest* is a single instance of Active Directory. It is often referred to as the only true security boundary in Active Directory. The forest is actually created when the very first domain controller is deployed. Forest is the name given to the collection of services and resources that are maintained by Active Directory. While it may be desirable and typical for an organization to deploy a single forest, there are a number of organizations that have deployed and support multiple forests.

Domains

The *domain* is the primary logical container within Active Directory. It is a logical boundary for administration as well as an actual partition of Active Directory. The very first domain in Active Directory has a special designation as the *forest root* domain. Just like the forest, the forest root domain is created when the very first domain controller is deployed, and it shares the same name as the forest. There are two domain names you must provide when creating a domain. The pre-Windows 2000 name is a NetBIOS name and can be no longer than 16 characters. The actual domain name in Active Directory is based on the dotted DNS nomenclature. So a domain called virtuecorp.com also has a NetBIOS name of VIRTUECORP.

NOTE   *If the registered DNS name for your organization exceeds 16 characters, as many do, be prepared to provide an alternate pre-Windows 2000 domain name.*

Trees

A *tree* is a collection of one or more domains within an Active Directory forest. Trees are contiguous in namespace. What that means is that all domain names within a tree share the same root domain name. The dotted DNS nomenclature is used again to represent the hierarchy of domain. For example, if virtuecorp.com is the root domain, then a child domain would be child.virtuecorp.com. There is no limit on how many child domains you can have in a tree other than the limit that the extra complexity would impose.

It is possible to have more than one tree in a forest, but there is always at least one tree created along with the first domain in the forest. Multiple trees in the forest are distinguishable by two or more root domains with discontinuous namespaces (different root names).

Trusts

Trusts are relationships established between two domains that facilitate authentication and authorization between security boundaries. There are actually multiple types of trusts in Active Directory. This is because there is more than one authentication method supported. Trusts may be one-way or two-way depending on what type of trust they are and how they are configured. A *one-way trust* will allow the accounts in the trusted domain to access resources in the trusting domain. *Two-way trusts* allow accounts in either domain to access resources in the other domain. In the case of Active Directory, this could be any domain in the forest. In Figure 2-1 you can see the various trusts supported in Active Directory.

Intraforest

The default trusts between Active Directory domains are automatic, two-way, and transitive, and they utilize Kerberos. There is nothing required to maintain these trusts. When you add a new domain anywhere in the same forest, a two-way transitive trust will automatically be established. Because of the properties of Kerberos, the trusts are also transitive in nature. Transitivity eliminates the need to create a trust going from all domains to every other domain in the forest. *Transitivity,* simply put, states that if Domain A trusts Domain B and

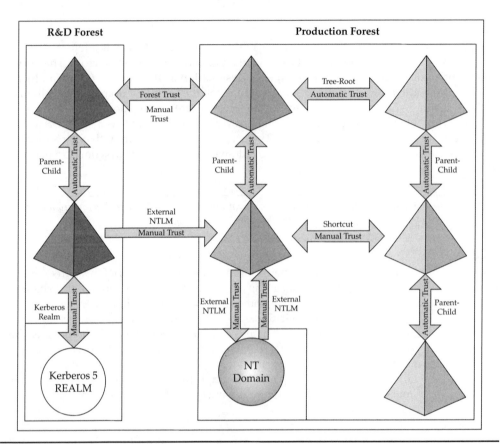

FIGURE 2-1 Active Directory trusts

Domain B trusts Domain C, then Domain A trusts Domain C. The trusts that exist within a forest are referred to as:

- Tree-root trusts
- Parent-child trusts
- Shortcut trusts

NOTE *It is important to understand that the automatic two-way trusts created by Active Directory in the forest do not imply that users have access to any resource they want. They do imply that for any user who is granted permissions to a resource anywhere in the forest, the trusts will be in place to provide the authentication mechanism for accessing that resource.*

Interforest

There are times when the security boundary must be extended to include accounts and resources that reside outside of the Active Directory forest. In these cases there are specific trust relationships that exist for each occasion. When performing migrations from NT 4 Domain to Active Directory it is necessary to create an *external trust*, which is based on the

NT 4 authentication method (NT LAN Manager [NTLM]). External trusts are not transitive in nature and can only be created as one-way. Subsequently, two one-way trusts may need to be established during a migration. Manual external trusts can also be created between specific domains in separate forests.

The newest trust type available in Active Directory is the forest trust. Forest trusts can be one-way or two-way. *Forest trusts* utilize Kerberos as their authentication method and can therefore allow two separate forests to take advantage of transitivity.

CAUTION *Forest trusts are only possible if both forests are running in 2003 mode.*

Forest trusts are powerful allies to Exchange administrators who need to support multiple forests with separate Exchange organizations. Because the forest is the strongest security boundary in Active Directory, the forest trusts additional granular settings not available on any other type of connector. These settings can be leveraged to limit access between forests.

- **Security Identifier (SID) Filtering**   This filter is actually available for external trusts but must be enabled. SID filtering is enabled by default on forest trusts to prevent the passing of SIDs by unauthorized domains.

- **Selective Authentication**   When this mode is selected on a forest trust it will only allow users that have explicitly been given the **Allow to Authenticate** permission. This permission is only available when the forest is running in 2003 Mode.

- **Name suffix routing**   The inbound trust can be configured to allow or exclude inbound connections based on the User Principal Name (UPN) suffix of the user account being authenticated.

Realm

Because Microsoft's implementation of Kerberos is based on MIT Kerberos v5, there are a number of non-Windows environments that can be configured to interoperate with Active Directory. Realm trusts are either one-way or two-way. Transitivity can be enabled or disabled depending on the level of desired interoperability. If you are not familiar with what a Kerberos realm is, you can think of it as an Active Directory domain. Both realms and domains have Key Distribution Centers (KDCs) for creating and associating ticket granting ticket and service tickets. In Active Directory every domain controller is a KDC.

Objects

Ultimately the purpose of Active Directory is to publish, manage, secure, and facilitate finding network resources. This is accomplished with objects. Everything in Active Directory is represented as an object. People, computers, printers, shared folders, and groups, as well as network applications and services, are represented by objects in Active Directory.

An Active Directory object consists of a unique set of attributes. Attributes are not only used to describe each object they are also used to find the objects you are looking for. The more attributes that are populated for an object, the more ways there are to find the object. The directory requires certain attributes to be populated for each object that is created. These are called *mandatory attributes*. Optional attributes do exist. Some are populated automatically. For example, a printer driver may be able to publish information about a specific printer. Still there are many other attributes that must be populated manually.

Organizational Units

There are a number of objects in Active Directory that can contain other objects. Active Directory has some containers, like the Users and Computers containers, that are built in for compatibility with NT Domains. Active Directory has a special container object called an organizational unit (OU). An *organizational unit* is used to group resources together for the delegation of administration or the application of group policy. There is a default OU called Domain Controllers that is used to apply a custom group policy that secures all domain controllers within a domain.

You can think of an OU as a lightweight domain. It has many of the characteristics of a domain without any of the overhead. OUs are also very flexible and can adapt to changes easily. The hierarchical structure of Active Directory, which we have already seen within a forest, can be further subdivided with OU, making a large directory with thousands of objects easier to manage.

Global Catalog

The first domain controller will also be the first global catalog server in the forest. The *global catalog* is an index of every object within the forest with a partial attribute listing of each object. The index is available to all users and applications on the network. The global catalog provides faster results than the domain database does for queries from clients and applications. The global catalog is an essential component to Exchange Server 2007.

In a single-domain forest, the function of a global catalog can be difficult to see. However, in a multidomain forest the necessity of the global catalog become obvious. It is the global catalog that makes a search across multiple domains throughout a forest transparent to end users and applications. Without the global catalog, users would have to know exactly which domain the resource they are looking for is in.

Schema

Active Directory comes with a predefined, but extensible, schema. A *schema,* in the context of Active Directory, is the partition of Active Directory that defines what objects can be created and what attributes each object is composed of. A good way to think of the schema is that it is the blueprint for Active Directory. The schema is made up of an A-Z listing of unique attributes and a hierarchical structure of object classes. *Classes* are the predefined groupings of attributes that distinguish one object type from another. Objects that are child objects in the class hierarchy are referred to as *subclasses.* The user object and the contact object are both subclasses of the person object. The person object is a subclass of Top. Top is the root of the schema hierarchy. There are many classes of objects defined in Active Directory.

All LDAP directories were designed to have extensible schemas. The schema can be extended by administrators that are members of the Schema Admins group by using the Schema Management MMC snap-in. It can also be extended programmatically by Active Directory integrated applications. Exchange 2000 Server, Exchange Server 2003, and Exchange Server 2007 all extend the schema to add attributes and classes to allow Exchange Server to integrate with Active Directory.

Distinguished Names

In a hierarchical namespace like Active Directory, it is possible to have two objects with the exact same name as long as they do not exist in the exact same container. In any size organization this could lead to confusion. Just imagine a large enterprise with multiple domains in their forest where many people share the same name. There must be a way to not only uniquely distinguish each object but also to locate each object in the forest. The RFCs for LDAP define the use of LDAP distinguished names as the solution. The early distinguished names were based on X.500 naming conventions. Today's LDAP directories do much more than X.500 standards originally sought to do. Microsoft has incorporated some of the latest Internet Drafts and RFCs for LDAP into Active Directory. RFC 2247, *Using Domains in LDAP/X.500 Distinguished Names,* was implemented in AD by Microsoft and has made Active Directory stand apart from other directories. By using DNS domain names as containment objects in Active Directory, it is not necessary to map the logical containers in Active Directory to location-based names. In Figure 2-2 you not only see how the logical pieces of Active Directory come together to form a forest, but you can also see how distinguished names are actually formed using DNS domains as containment objects.

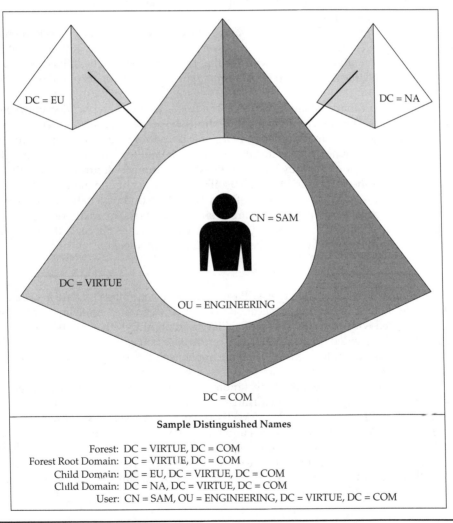

Sample Distinguished Names

Forest: DC = VIRTUE, DC = COM
Forest Root Domain: DC = VIRTUE, DC = COM
Child Domain: DC = EU, DC = VIRTUE, DC = COM
Child Domain: DC = NA, DC = VIRTUE, DC = COM
User: CN = SAM, OU = ENGINEERING, DC = VIRTUE, DC = COM

Figure 2-2   Active Directory distinguished names

Physical Active Directory Components

Behind the logical components of Active Directory is a completely separate layer of physical components. In this section of the chapter, terms like sites, connectors, domain controllers, and replication will be defined. It is important to understand what these and other physical components are and how they relate to each other, in order to optimize the performance and reliability of Active Directory.

Sites and Services

Active Directory *sites* are created to represent areas on your network that have high availability and plenty of bandwidth. A Local Area Network (LAN) would be a good candidate for a site. The scope of a site is defined by subnets. By adding one or more subnets to a site, administrators can control which users and computers will be affected by the site's settings and services.

There is a default first site created by Active Directory when the very first domain controller is deployed. Its scope by default is every subnet in the forest. If you look at the properties of the default first site you will see that there are no subnets defined. When no subnets are defined, the assumption by AD is that you want all subnets to fall within the scope of the site.

There are two primary functions of a site. The first is to control replication between domain controllers. Domain controllers and replication will be described in detail later in this section. The second primary function of a site is to control which domain controller(s) users on a particular subnet in your forest will use by default for authentication and LDAP queries. When a user logs on, they will query DNS for a domain controller. Domain controllers register themselves in DNS. DNS will provide a list of domain controllers to a client based on the site the client is a part of. It is possible to optimize network utilization and improve the client experience if sites are designed properly. An auxiliary function is for the application of group policy. Sites play a huge role in Exchange Server 2007. The role of sites in Exchange Server 2007 will also be detailed later in this section.

Site Links

Once two or more sites are created they will isolate domain controllers that are in different sites from one another. In order for replication to occur between sites, a site link connector must be associated with each site. There is a DEFAULTIPSITELINK that will be used if no other connector is specified for a site. Site links can be based on either Internet Protocol (IP) or Simple Mail Transfer Protocol (SMTP) and are implemented to optimize network utilization of WAN connections.

It is unusual to have a site link connect more than two sites together unless the actual data network is running Asynchronous Transfer Mode (ATM) or Multiprotocol Label Switching (MPLS). It is also unusual for SMTP to be used to for site links. However, if the Wide Area Network (WAN) connection is unreliable, then SMTP will be more resilient to network outages. Just be aware that SMTP requires certificates from a Certificate Authority for security and cannot replicate the entire directory. It is important to create only site links that actually represent WAN connectivity. Creating an invalid site link can have a negative impact on replication.

Domain Controllers

Domain controllers (DC) are the most tangible or physical component to Active Directory. All Windows 2000/2003 *domain controllers* store a read/write copy of the Active Directory domain database. A database is created when the first domain controller is deployed in each domain and then it is replicated to each additional domain controller added to the domain. All objects from each domain are stored in the database. The Active Directory, from a physical perspective, is actually the collection of all of the domain databases in the forest. Domain controllers are essential to Active Directory security. Domain controllers authenticate users and control access to resources in the domain.

Because of the vital role that domain controllers play, it is a best practice to deploy at least two domain controllers for high availability regardless of the organization's size. For optimal performance, you should plan on deploying at least one domain controller per site and configure at least one domain controller in each site to be a global catalog server as well.

Replication

Domain controllers participate in a multimaster replication model in Active Directory. *Multimaster* replication allows changes to be made to all domain controllers. To make sure that all domain controllers in a domain will provide the exact same information to any queries, replication of the changes must take place. Two general types of replication occur in Active Directory. Since domain controllers within a site must be kept up to date with nominal latency, *intrasite replication* is configured to be the fastest replication. Since WAN bandwidth usually comes at a premium, intersite replication is set to occur at slower intervals that can be controlled by administrators.

The default routing topology is generated by the Knowledge Consistency Checker (KCC). The KCC uses a newly revised spanning tree algorithm in Active Directory 2003 to designate which domain controllers will be replication partners. For intrasite replication, a two-way replication ring topology is created. Given enough bandwidth within a site, the KCC will make sure that every domain controller has at least two replication partners and that there are no more than three hops to replicate to any domain controller. The KCC depends on the sites and the site links to determine the intersite replication topology.

Naming Contexts

In order to make the replication more efficient, the domain database is divided into replication partitions called *naming contexts*. There are several naming contexts:

- Schema
- Domain Naming
- Configuration
- Global Catalog
- Application Partitions

The Schema naming context is replicated to all domain controllers throughout the forest. As its name implies, it stores the current schema. The Domain Naming context is replicated to all domain controllers within a domain. It stores the objects that must be associated with only one domain. These objects include Users, Computers, Global Groups, Domain Local Groups, Shared Folders, and others. The Configuration naming context is replicated to all domain controllers throughout the forest. All of the configuration information about services and Active Directory integrated applications within the forest are published in this partition. Exchange Server 2007 configuration information for the entire organization is stored in the Configuration naming context. The Global Catalog naming context is only replicated to domain controllers in the forest that are configured to be Global Catalog servers. Application Partitions are unique. They can be configured by administrators to replicate to only some domain controllers in a domain or to all domain controllers in the forest. A good example of the use of Application Partitions is the enhanced Active Directory Integrated DNS services now available in Windows Server 2003.

Operation Masters

Windows has evolved from a single master Primary Domain Controller (PDC) domain model to the current multimaster domain controller model. To maintain a level of backward compatibility and to further integrate Active Directory with the Windows operating system, Microsoft has developed five Flexible Single Master Operations (FSMO) roles. These roles serve various purposes, but they must have a single domain controller specified for each role. The Domain Naming Master and the Schema Master only need one instance for the entire forest. The RID Master, Infrastructure Master, and PDC Emulator Master roles must have one instance per domain.

Domain Naming Master

The hierarchical structure of the forest is maintained by the Domain Naming Master. This role must be accessible when new domains are added or removed from the forest.

RID Master

For security reasons each domain has a unique ID. Every object in a domain is stamped with the domain identification number. Certain objects are allowed to authenticate against the domain and can be added to access control lists (ACL) to be granted access to resources. These objects are referred to as *security principals*. Security principals need more than just the domain ID; they need a security identifier. Security Identifiers (SIDs) are assigned to Users, Computers, and Security Groups when they are created. A SID is actually the combination of the domain ID and a relative ID. Every domain controller has a unique pool of relative IDs. When the pool of relative IDs runs low, the domain controllers must contact the RID Master to obtain a new pool.

Infrastructure Master

Because each domain is a partition (separate database), the forest must track when objects move between domains. Also, objects that have permissions and settings in multiple domains need to be tracked. The Infrastructure Master keeps track of the interdomain objects. The Infrastructure role also plays a key role by providing a sanity check on the domain database. It does the sanity check by querying the Global Catalog. If the information in the Global Catalog is consistent with the local copy of the database, the check passes. If an inconsistency is discovered, then the Infrastructure Master notifies the domain controllers in the domain. It is important that the infrastructure master is placed on a domain controller that is not the global catalog server; otherwise, a false positive may ensue each time the sanity check is run.

PDC Emulator Master

The name PDC Emulator seems to say it all about this Flexible Single Master Operations (FMSO) role. It is true that PDC Emulation is one of the key functions, but if that were the only function this role would not be necessary in a domain without NT 4.0 Backup Domain Controllers (BDC). Even in a domain running in Windows 2003 Mode, the PDC emulator is necessary. The PDC emulator is the "go-to server" during password change disputes and verifications. The PDC emulator is required for all external trust relationships. The PDC emulator is consistently the busiest domain controller in an active directory domain. Many organizations will actually add extra processing power and memory to the PDC Emulator Master for optimal performance.

Schema Master

The Schema Master role has an intuitive name. It is a role that must be protected on your network. Only members of the Schema Admins group have permission to access this role. Any time the schema is extended, this server must be accessible on the network. Since it only resides on one server in the forest, extra planning may be necessary in order to extend the schema. In the case of Exchange Server 2007, the installation will attempt to extend the schema. If the Exchange administrator does not have sufficient permissions, then setup will fail.

By default, all five of the FSMO roles will be on the very first domain controller that is deployed. It is a best practice to distribute the roles across multiple servers. At the very least, the infrastructure master should be moved off the global catalog server once you have two or more domain controllers.

Kerberos, NTLM, and SChanel

Security is paramount when you are storing vital information for an organization in a directory structure. Microsoft designed Active Directory to be a very secure directory structure. A big part of the security model for Active Directory is authentication. Active Directory is a multiauthentication platform, that supports NTLM, Kerberos, and SChanel Security Support Provider Interfaces (SSPI).

NTLM v1 and NTLM v2

NT LAN Manager (NTLM) attention is a Microsoft proprietary authentication method that has been around since LAN Manager. (If you remember LAN Manager, you have been supporting Microsoft for a long time.) NTLM v1 has a number of vulnerabilities that will put an organization at risk including its weak hashing algorithms. Just ask anyone who has run LOphtCrack. NTLM v2 is much more secure but still has a number of security and performance drawbacks. The obvious reason why it is still supported is for backward compatibility. In fact, it was not until Exchange Server 2003 was released that an Outlook client could actually be configured to only use Kerberos for authenticating to their mailbox. Even then, that is only possible if the client is Outlook 2003. All earlier versions require NTLM.

Kerberos v5

Support for Kerberos v5 was introduced in Windows Server 2000. Ideally all domain authentications would take place exclusively with Kerberos. The good news is that there is broader support today for Kerberos in Windows Server 2003. Microsoft did have some challenges integrating Kerberos v5 in the Windows environment. Microsoft's implementation of Kerberos v5 is based on RFC 1510 and RFC 1964. However, there is no way with the open standard to represent the Microsoft security access token. To support the Microsoft security access tokens, Privilege Access Certificate (PAC) information was added to the authorization data field.

Here are the key reasons why Kerberos is better than NTLM and why Microsoft has standardized on it in Active Directory:

- Symmetric Key Encryption with data encryption standard (DES)/TripleDES is used to secure credentials between the client and the domain controller.
- The ticketing system streamlines and adds security to the authentication process.
- Open Standard facilitates interoperability.
- Public Key Initiation (PKINIT) is supported for certificate-based authentication like Smart Cards and biometrics.
- Mutual authentication allows the client and the resource server to validate each other.
- Impersonation allows services to access resources on behalf of users.
- Authentication forwarding (delegation) allows multitier applications to use clients' credentials even if the application needs to get resources, on different servers, on behalf of the client.

Domain Naming System

Domain Naming System (DNS) is a name resolution service for TCP/IP networks. DNS resolves easy-to-remember Fully Qualified Domain Names (FQDN) like www.microsoft.com to more difficult-to-remember IP addresses. This *forward lookup* is routinely performed for end users. DNS can also be configured to resolve IP addresses to FQDNs. This *reverse lookup* is routinely performed for software applications. DNS uses a hierarchical namespace to make sure that every FQDN is a unique name. This hierarchy is visible in every FQDN. Each dot (".") you see in the FQDN represents a separate level in the namespace. In Figure 2-3 you can see how the Internet DNS namespace is formed. DNS can also be used inside private networks for name resolution. This is often referred to as the *intranet namespace*.

Why AD Requires DNS

Because Windows Server 2003 uses TCP/IP and its default protocol, all applications and services on the network must be able to perform name resolution with DNS. For backward compatibility NetBIOS is supported on TCP/IP networks. The NetBT (NetBIOS over TCP/IP) allows NetBIOS broadcast traffic on the TCP/IP Network, but does not route the NetBIOS traffic between segments. Windows Internet Naming System (WINS) can be installed on a TCP/IP Network to allow NetBIOS name resolution across routed networks. Windows Server 2003 does not require NetBIOS name resolution.

Active Directory requires DNS so that it can publish service location (SRV) records for forest users and computers to find. The Windows operating systems have a built-in DNS

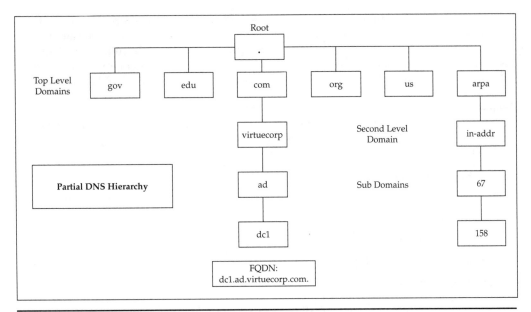

FIGURE 2-3   Internet DNS namespace

client called a *resolver*. Traditionally the resolver would find the IP address of a server that had a resource on it that a client was trying to connect to. Active Directory extends the functionality of DNS by publishing SRV records for services provided by domain controllers. Without DNS no user would be able to find a domain controller to authenticate against. Outlook clients would not be able to find their mailboxes, and users would not be able to find people to send e-mail to using the Global Address List (GAL).

Zones

Traditionally DNS stores information in text files called zones. A *zone* can be composed of one or more contiguous DNS domains. There are three types of zone files in Windows Server 2003 DNS.

- **Primary**   Read/write zone database
- **Secondary**   Read-only replica of a zone database
- **Stub Zone**   Read-only partial replicas of a zone database

Both forward and reverse lookup zones can be created on a DNS server. At a minimum, Active Directory will require a Primary forward lookup zone. The zone must also be configured to support dynamic updates.

A zone that is configured to support dynamic updates will allow computers to register themselves in DNS. All Windows operating systems starting with Windows 2000 and higher are capable of registering themselves and are configured to do so by default. Most client and server computers will only register a single host record and a single pointer record. Active Directory domain controllers must also register Service Location (SRV) records.

Records

Numerous types of records can exist on a DNS Server. Each type of record has a specific purpose. Most records are used in the forward lookup zones. The record types used by Active Directory and Exchange 2007 are:

- **SOA**   Start of Authority
- **NS**   Name Server
- **A**   Host
- **PTR**   Pointer
- **SRV**   Service Location
- **MX**   Mail Exchanger

The Start of Authority (SOA) record is an essential part of each zone. It gives administrators control over Time to Live (TTL) settings. The SOA record is also referenced during zone transfers with other DNS servers to determine if any changes have taken place since the last transfer. Name Server (NS) records are used by DNS servers to identify servers that can perform DNS lookups. If a DNS server doesn't have a zone for a particular DNS query, then the DNS server will search for an NS record in the domain specified in the query so that it can query on behalf of the original client or server. This is a DNS name resolution process known as *recursion*. Host (A) records resolve a Fully Qualified Domain Name (FQDN) to an IP address. This is the most common record you will find in DNS. Every computer in an Active Directory forest should have at least one Host record. Pointer (PTR) Records resolved an IP address to a FQDN. PTR can only be created in a reverse lookup zone. When a user or an application needs to find the FQDN for an IP address, then PTR are used. Service Location (SRV) records are used by all computers in an Active Directory forest to find the domain controllers and other servers that host key services like Kerberos and LDAP. As member computers in a domain, Exchange 2007 Servers are dependant on SRV records. And to be able to send e-mail to organizations outside of the Exchange organization, Exchange Servers must be able to query for Mail Exchanger (MX) records. MX records resolve the domain names after the @ sign in an e-mail address to a host record on the Internet.

Zone Transfers

It is important that at least two DNS servers be deployed in an organization to provide high availability for name resolution. To make sure that both DNS servers are storing up-to-date copies of all records, the zone must be replicated. DNS replicates zones between DNS servers in a process called a *zone transfer*. There are two types of transfers supported in Windows Server 2003 DNS. Authoritative Transfers (AXFR) replicate the entire zone and Incremental Transfers (IXFR) replicate only changes made since the last transfer.

It is possible for a Primary zone to transfer its records to a Secondary zone. Secondary zones can also request transfers from other Secondary zones. There are features built into Windows Server 2003 to optimize and secure zone transfers. The best possible solution for zone transfers in a Windows environment is Active Directory Integrated zones.

Active Directory Integrated Zones

Windows domain controllers that are configured to be DNS servers have the additional benefit of supporting Active Directory Integrated (ADI) zones. ADI zones inherit the benefits of Active Directory. Both Primary and Stub zones can be configured as Active Directory Integrated. By integrating a zone with DNS, it is possible to secure the dynamic updates required by Active Directory. Zone transfers become part of Active Directory replication. All zone records are stored in the Active Directory database and will be backed up when AD is backed up. The DNS Management snap-in for the Microsoft Management Console (MMC) is a graphical administrative tool that makes the administration of DNS easier.

There are new options for ADI zones in Active Directory 2003. The zones are now stored in separate partitions in Active Directory. When integrating a zone with Active Directory, administrators have a choice of scopes in which they want the zone replicated. They can choose to keep the zone on domain controllers in the same domain. They can choose to replicate to all domain controllers within the forest. By default it will replicate to all domain controllers within the domain but not the forest.

NSLOOKUP

DNS name resolution is critical on TCP/IP networks. In the event that DNS name resolution problems occur, NSLOOKUP is one essential tool you should know how to use. NSLOOKUP is a tool built into the Windows 2000 and higher operating systems. Using the built-in DNS client, NSLOOKUP establishes a connection to a DNS server and allows you to perform queries to verify the existence of records in the DNS zones and the name resolution process (see Figure 2-4). Understanding the DNS name resolution process can help you use NSLOOKUP as well.

Active Directory and Exchange Server 2007

Exchange Server, more than any other application, shares a special relationship with Active Directory. Hopefully, this chapter has given you some depth and background to this topic. Exchange Server 2007 represents the third version of Exchange Server to be integrated with Active Directory. Many of the new features of Exchange Server 2007 require updates to Active Directory. A whole new level of dependency exists between the flow of e-mail and the configuration of Active Directory sites.

Schema Changes

Exchange 2000 Server modified the default schema in Active Directory with enough object classes and attributes to nearly double the size of the schema. Exchange Server 2003 and now Exchange Server 2007 have made new contributions to the schema. Exchange 2000 and Exchange Server 2003 used a setup subroutine called Forestprep to import changes into the schema. Exchange Server 2007 calls this process PrepareSchema.

PrepareSchema imports .LDF files from the Exchange Server 2007 source CD. Of the 133 modifications made to the Active Directory schema by Exchange Server 2007 PrepareSchema, only nine are Exchange-specific changes. But PrepareSchema is only one of a number of steps that must be done to prepare Active Directory for Exchange Server 2007. Chapter 4 covers the installation of Exchange Server 2007 and details all of the steps necessary to properly prepare Active Directory.

Functional Levels

Active Directory domains and the Active Directory forest have different functional levels in which they can be set to run. Exchange Server 2007 requires that the domains and the forest be set to run at a specific level prior to installation. The functional levels dictate the topologies supported by Exchange Server 2007 and the features that will be available. The domain modes supported in Windows Server 2003 are:

- 2000 Mixed
- 2000 Native
- 2003 Interim
- 2003 Mode

The forest functional level can be raised from Windows 2000 to Windows Server 2003 once all domains in the forest are raised to 2003 Mode. One of the primary benefits of 2003 Mode to Exchange Server 2007 is improved performance of Active Directory domains. However, from a design perspective the new forest trusts we discussed at the beginning of the chapter make it easier to support multiforest Exchange topologies. In Chapter 3 we will look at how the Exchange 2007 Architecture takes advantage of Active Directory services.

Summary

The sign of any good system is that it is transparent. That explains why most users are not aware of the functions of the directory service. The directory service is a collection of services on the network that makes your life easier by publishing network resources and simplifying searches for those resources to increase your personal productivity. One of the earliest directory services ever implemented was actually associated with one of the very first e-mail systems, which was a project in the early 1980s called Grapevine at Xerox's Palo Alto Research Labs. The services created in this environment formed one of the earliest directory services. The primary service provided on the Grapevine network was electronic mail.

While it may be true that Active Directory was not available in the early versions of Windows, it is not fair to say that Microsoft did not have a directory service prior to Active Directory. Microsoft has had an LDAP Directory since 1996 when Exchange Server 4.0 was released. The Windows Server 2000 version of Active Directory added functionality to the Windows environments that had not existed previously. Windows 2003 Server marked a coming of age for Active Directory. Exchange Server was no longer the only benefactor of an AD-enabled organization. Many other applications and services (from Microsoft and from other software companies) began to integrate with Active Directory.

In order to better understand and work with the logical side of Active Directory, it is imperative that you become familiar with the functionality of terms like forests, domains, trees, trusts, objects, organizational units, global catalog, schema, and distinguished names.

Behind the logical components of Active Directory is a completely separate layer of physical components. It is important to understand what the physical components of Active Directory are and how they relate to each other, in order to optimize the performance and reliability of Active Directory. Some of the physical components are sites and services, site links, domain controllers, replication, operation masters, as well as Kerberos, NTLM and SChanel.

Domain Naming System (DNS) is a name resolution service for TCP/IP networks. DNS resolves easy-to-remember Fully Qualified Domain Names (FQDN) like www.microsoft.com to more difficult-to-remember IP addresses. DNS can also be configured to resolve IP addresses to FQDNs. DNS uses a hierarchical namespace to make sure that every FQDN is a unique name.

Exchange Server, more than any other application, shares a special relationship with Active Directory. Hopefully this chapter has given you some depth and background into this relationship. Exchange Server 2007 represents the third version of Exchange Server to be integrated with Active Directory. Many of the new features of Exchange Server 2007 require updates to Active Directory. A whole new level of dependency exists between the flow of e-mail and the configuration of Active Directory sites.

Exchange Server 2007
Architectural Review

The foundation for the Exchange Server 2007 messaging system architecture is storage and message handling. The features that are built in, on, and around Exchange Server 2007 enhance or take advantage of these two key architectural components. There have been numerous advances in the Exchange Server architecture from Exchange 4.0 to Exchange Server 2007. Some of the biggest changes to the Exchange Server architecture are due to 64-bit computing.

In this chapter, the details of the storage and message-handling architectures are explored. You will be able to see how the new architectures will permanently change the way in which we plan for and deploy Exchange Servers. The features set, now available with Exchange Server 2007, will not only provide a wealth of services to organizations, it will extend what developers do.

Role-based Architecture

Since the first Exchange 4.0 servers were deployed, there has always been the concept of dedicating a server to a specific function or role. The Exchange Performance Optimizer tool (Exchange 4.0 through Exchange 5.5 only) would ask questions about each server's usage just after setup completed so that it could change system parameters and move files to optimize function (or functions) that the server was performing. Mailbox Server, Public Folder Server, Bridgehead Server, and Internet Mail Connector were functions that an Exchange Server could perform. But these were not options that could necessarily be selected during setup. These were post-installation decisions that required manual configurations, which often included disabling services and removing files to enforce a server's role.

The Exchange 2000 Server architecture, and subsequently Exchange Server 2003, introduced the front-end and back-end server roles. This was more than just turning on and off features, however; the architecture itself was split in two. The Store.exe and associated services comprised the back end. The Inetinfo.exe and associated services comprised the front end. The Exchange interprocess communication layer (EXIPC) lay between the front end and back end, allowing them to interoperate. All 2000 and 2003 Exchange Servers are

Exchange Server 2000 and 2003	Exchange Server 2007
Back-end Servers	Mailbox, Hub Transport, Client Access Server Roles combined
Dedicated Mailbox Store Server	Mailbox Server Role
Dedicated Public Folder Store Server	Mailbox Server Role
Dedicated Bridgehead Server	Hub Transport Role
Internet Protocol (SMTP)	Hub Transport Role
Internet Protocols (HTTP, POP3, IMAP4)	Client Access Server Role
Front-end Servers	Client Access Server Role
No equivalent	Edge Transport Server Role
No equivalent	Unified Messaging Server Role

TABLE 3-1   Back-end and Front-end Configurations vs. the New Server Roles

back-end servers out of the box. However, it is possible to electively configure one or more servers as front-end servers. Even with this option, configuring a server to be a front-end server requires a number of additional steps to customize and enforce the server role, including disabling services, moving all mailboxes and mailbox stores, rehoming public folders, and deleting public folder stores.

Based on the functions that dedicated Exchange 2007 servers are used for, Exchange Server 2007 has introduced yet another set of server roles, including new server functions that have never been available prior to Exchange Server 2007. This new modular approach to deploying server roles will make deploying Exchange Server into each unique environment easier (especially for organizations that have complex topologies). In Table 3-1, the back-end and front-end configurations available in Exchange Server 2003 are compared to the new server roles in Exchange Server 2007.

Part III of this book takes a closer look at each of the server roles and provides you with more information on how to properly deploy server roles. This chapter focuses on how the key components of the Exchange Server 2007 architecture are related to server roles.

Storage Architecture

Ultimately, every communication to any Exchange Server 2007 role leads to reading from (or writing to) the database(s) on the Mailbox Server role. The primary storage location in an Exchange 2007 server will be the mailbox store. Microsoft is not encouraging organizations to utilize Public Folder Stores in Exchange Server 2007, but they will be available for organizations that have a need for them. They can be installed on the Mailbox Server role. Another interesting point is the debate over the last several years as to when Microsoft will use a SQL database for Exchange Server data. This is not one of the changes you will find in Exchange Server 2007. The Extensible Storage Engine (ESE) is still being used, but there have been a number of changes to how it is implemented.

Microsoft has essentially three primary goals for Exchange Server 2007 storage:

- Support for larger mailboxes on less expensive hardware
- Reducing disk I/O by taking advantage of 64-bit architecture
- Increasing storage availability

Microsoft has designed the storage architecture to accommodate organizations with an average mailbox size of 1GB and up. Today on average, individual mail items are increasing in size and so are mailboxes. To make these large mailboxes more accessible, the storage architecture now enables features such as content indexing by default. Microsoft has designed the storage architecture to reduce its dependency on disk I/O. The weak link in the I/O chain has always been the physical disk. As data moves back and forth from memory to the database, the disk is always the bottleneck. Less time is spent reading and writing to disk in Exchange Server 2007 translates to less time and money spent optimizing disk I/O. To increase the availability of data, Microsoft has incorporated transaction log shipping into Exchange Server 2007. This will allow the mailbox store to be replicated locally or remotely, and potentially mounted on a separate server in the organization. See Chapter 6 for more detail on the storage architecture.

Mailbox Server Role

At the heart of the storage architecture for Exchange Server 2007 is the Mailbox Server role. The storage redesign for Exchange 2007 will provide you with numerous enhancements to take advantage of when deploying mailbox servers. You can create up to 50 mailbox stores. You can create up to 50 storage groups. Having more mailbox stores and storage groups not only gives you move administrative flexibility, it allows you to dedicate storage groups to individual mailbox stores for easier maintenance and more effective transaction logging. Databases are mounted or dismounted in parallel with one another. This will improve system startup and shutdown times. The deleted item retention for mailboxes has been extended to 14 days. By increasing deleted item retention, Microsoft hopes to decrease the likelihood that you will have to resort to recovering from backup.

Do not confuse the Mailbox Server role with the back-end Exchange server in versions 2000 and 2003. Unlike a back-end server, the mailbox server is not involved with the transport of mail. The architectural components that make up a mailbox server are:

- Store.exe process
- Extensible Storage Engine (ESE)
- Content indexing
- Calendaring
- Enterprise policy
- Mail submission
- Continuous replication (LCR and CCR)

Exchange Databases

Exchange Server 2007 uses the Extensible Storage Engine (ESE) technology for the Mailbox Server role, Hub Transport role, and Edge Transport role. For the Hub and Edge Transport roles, the ESE is only used in a limited fashion to queue mail. The name of the database is MAIL.QUE. The Mailbox Server role makes a more substantial use of the ESE. Each instance of the database is called a mailbox database or a public folder database on the Mailbox Server role.

There have been significant changes in the Exchange 2007 databases. The STM file that was added in Exchange 2000 Server to overcome disk I/O constraints has been removed now that those constraints have been alleviated to a large degree with the adoption of the 64-bit architecture. All "native" content that was placed in the .stm database file is now converted at the time it is submitted to the database rather than being deferred. The Exchange Installable File System (EXIFS), also known as the M: drive, has been completely removed, not just hidden. The benefits of the EXIFS were mostly outweighed by the trouble it caused administrators. Although it virtualized the Exchange databases and represented mailboxes as folders and mail items as files, it led to many unforeseen problems. Exchange Server 2003 removed the logical M: drive to prevent the EXIFS from being accessed by antivirus and backup software, which had the potential to damage the database. With the new Client Access Server (CAS) and the new Web Services running as part of CAS, it is not necessary to have the EXIFS on the mailbox server.

Extensible Storage Engine (ESE)

The Microsoft Exchange Server 2007 ESE is a hybrid Jet database engine. Each version of Exchange Server has seen improvements to the ESE. It is a Balanced Tree (B-Tree) database engine that consists of bidirectional links through multiple tree structures. Microsoft has continued to use the ESE database for Exchange because it is an optimal engine for semistructured data. Exchange Server Mailbox role servers derive a high level of performance from the ESE. There must be a high level of performance when the I/O pattern to mailbox stores is random. On top of the improvements that have gone into the storage design, some changes have been made to the ESE engine itself at the database and logging levels.

Database Changes

To reduce the amount of time the mailbox server spends making reads and writes to the mailbox stores, the following changes have been made:

- Pages increased to 8KB from 4KB.
- Database cache increased from 900MB to unlimited.
- More storage groups added to increase checkpoint depth per store.
- Virtual memory fragmentation eliminated.

Database Cache Size Checkpoint Depth and I/O Coalescing

Checkpoint depth is a measure of the amount of database changes that can be kept in virtual memory prior to being committed to disk. This is directly proportional to the amount of physical RAM that is available to the server. Exchange Server 2003 and earlier versions had very little or no checkpoint depth because the database cache size was limited to 900MB of RAM. The 64-bit architecture allows Exchange Server 2007 to support Very Large Memory (VLM) models. Therefore, the more RAM, the larger the database cache and the deeper the checkpoint depth. By the way, there is no limit set on how large the database cache can be in Exchange Server 2007.

As a side benefit to an increased checkpoint depth, you increase the likelihood that contiguous pages (mail items with attachments spanning multiple pages) can be coalesced when they are written to the database. Technically this could be done in Exchange Server 2000 and 2003, but with the small database cache, it was not likely. Also, the page size in versions 2000 and 2003 was only 4KB, and the maximum commit size to the database was 64KB. In Exchange Server 2007, the page size is 8KB and the maximum commit size is 1MB. The more coalescing that can occur, the fewer disk I/Os that are generated.

Transaction Logging

The Microsoft Exchange database is a transaction-based database. This means that all data committed to the database must first be committed to a transaction log. The primary purpose of a transaction log is to reduce the amount of time completed transactions must wait in memory, and to free up memory for new transactions to occur. An auxiliary function of the transaction logs is as a secondary record of all data in the database itself. From a disaster recovery perspective, transaction logs can be replayed into a restored database from a backup. This allows the administrator to bring the database back to the point of failure.

Significant changes have been made to the transaction logs in Exchange Server 2007, starting with the filenames. Up to Exchange Server 2003, transaction log filenames were sequentially numbered from 00001.log to 99999.log. Exchange Server 2000 appended prefixes E00 to E03 to the beginning to distinguish the storage groups' logs. Many organizations actually reached 99999.log and had to start a new generation of logs within a few years of production use. To extend the life of a set of transaction logs, filenames have been increased to eights digits (E0012345678.log), thus allowing for billions of log filenames. The actual size of the log file is changed from 5MB to 1MB. This facilitates transaction log shipping, which occurs during Local Cluster Replication (LCR) and Continuous Cluster Replication (CCR). It takes one-fifth the time to replicate and ensures that the replica will never be more than 1MB out of sync.

Storage Groups

As mentioned earlier, Exchange Server 2007 can have up to 50 storage groups. Each of the storage groups runs a separate instance of the Jet database engine (ESE). Each storage group has its own set of transaction logs. There is a maximum of 50 databases on a single Exchange 2007 server. This is a dramatic departure from Exchange Server 2003, which is limited to four storage groups and five databases per storage group.

Although you can still create five mailbox databases in a single storage group, it is a best practice to only create one database per storage group. The logic behind this is contradictory to the Exchange 2000/2003 model. In Exchange 2003, for example, it was a best practice to create the maximum number of databases (five) in one storage group before creating any new storage groups. Creating a storage group for one database was considered a waste of the resources allocated to each storage group. The reason for the change in logic is, once again, the 64-bit computing architecture. Now that memory allocation is not a constraint, a different approach to optimization can be taken. By placing a single database in each storage group, you are dedicating system resources to a single database. Specifically, the transaction logging process is optimized. The catch is that to scale the server in this manner there must be a large amount of memory on the mailbox servers. See Chapter 6 for more details on Exchange 2007 storage.

Message Handling

Network engineers like to use the phrase "follow the packet" when they are designing, administering, and troubleshooting data networks. Because when you do actually trace a packet through the network, you discover the interfaces and devices that comprise your network infrastructure. You also discover the true way it behaves, good or bad. E-mail administrators who understand the transport and routing architecture of mail on Exchange Server can also better design, administer, and troubleshoot their messaging systems. Being able to understand what happens behind the scenes when a message is sent from originator to the recipient is a vital skill. Exchange Server message-handling architecture is based on the Simple Mail Transport Protocol (SMTP), so any knowledge you have of SMTP is good. But the Exchange Server 2007 transport architecture is not "simple" by any means.

Two server roles run SMTP and comprise the core message transport. The Edge Transport role and Hub Transport role work together to provide an organization with the complete SMTP transport solution. The Edge Transport role is a locked-down version of the Hub Transport role that can be detached from the organization. The additional security provided by the Edge Transport allows that role to exist in less secure areas of a network, such as the DMZ or perimeter. For security, the Edge Transport will only communicate with the Hub Transport roles on the internal networks. It is the job of the Hub Transport role to process all internal e-mail within an organization. The communications managed by these two roles with all other server roles is called the *transport pipeline*.

The goal of this topic is to provide the details of the transport and routing architecture you need in an easy-to-digest way so that you can create better designs and more affectively administer your Exchange Server 2007 organization. The best way to do this is to examine the transport pipeline and discuss the components that mail passes through along the way. You will find more details about configuring and administering the Hub and Edge Transport server roles later in the book.

Edge Transport Architecture

The core message transport (SMTP) exists on both the Edge Transport and the Hub Transport server roles. Although its functions have not changed with this release of Exchange, SMTP is implemented quite differently in 2007 as compared with previous versions. One of the biggest changes is that a new SMTP stack has been created—MSExchangeTransport.exe. Another process, EdgeTransport.exe, runs in conjunction with it. These new executables allow SMTP to run on the Edge and Hub Transport servers without a dependency on Internet Information Services (IIS). Eliminating IIS from the picture removes one of the primary security concerns faced in Exchange Server 2000/2003 deployments.

The core SMTP functions provided by the Edge Transport include:

- **SMTP Receive**   Accepts and processes inbound connections on port 25 and then places messages into a submission queue.
- **Categorizer**   Resolves recipients and determines the route. Places messages into a destination queue.

- **Remote Delivery**   Queues mail until it can be delivered. Deletes or resubmits undeliverable mail.
- **SMTP Send**   Connects to a remote host and delivers mail.

The extended functionality of SMTP is implemented in the form of *SMTP Receive Agents*. By implementing modular agents as opposed to embedding the functionality into the SMTP stack, Microsoft has created an easy-to-customize transport architecture. Although a number of agents already come with Exchange Server 2007, third-party developers and IT professionals will be able to create and add agents much quicker than ever before.

The key to the adoption of the Edge Transport server role will be EdgeSync, a built-in AD synchronization feature. EdgeSync will allow the Edge Transport role to integrate with the Exchange Server 2007 organization without being a member of Active Directory. The EdgeSync services are run on the computer that has the Hub Transport server role installed. It establishes one-way replication of recipient and configuration information from the AD directory service to the Active Directory Application Mode (ADAM) instance on the Edge Transport server. This is a big step beyond a number of security appliances on the market, even the ones that have LDAP functionality. You can download a complete schematic of the Edge Transport role at http://download.microsoft.com/download/f/f/b/ffb96cba-fc3e-476a-a27a-50d63d36d720/Exchange2007_EdgeTransportRoleArchitecture.pdf.

Hub Transport Architecture

The Hub Transport role also has the core SMTP functionality and a full range of SMTP Receive Agents. But unlike the Edge role, the Hub role was designed to communicate with all Exchange Server 2007 roles and be a member server in Active Directory.

The core transport is enhanced with the following components on the Hub Transport role:

- **MAPI Submit**   Receives inbound encrypted Exchange Remote Procedure Call (ExRPC) connections and places messages in the submission queue.
- **Transport Routing Agents**   Add the Rules, Journaling, and Active Directory Rights Management Services (AD RMS) agents to the Categorizer.
- **Mailbox and Foreign Queues**   Add mailbox server queues and third-party queues to Remote Deliver.
- **Foreign Connectors**   Can add X.400, FAX, VOICE, Lotus Notes, and other connectors.
- **Store Driver**   Sends messages to Mailbox Server roles via outbound encrypted ExRPC connections.

Transport Pipeline: Step by Step

The transport pipeline processes messages in a specific logical order. Once a message has been submitted, a chain of events occurs that usually involves multiple server roles. There is one absolute in the transport pipeline—all messages must be categorized. This means that all messages must go through a Hub Transport server. Figure 3-1 illustrates the transport pipeline.

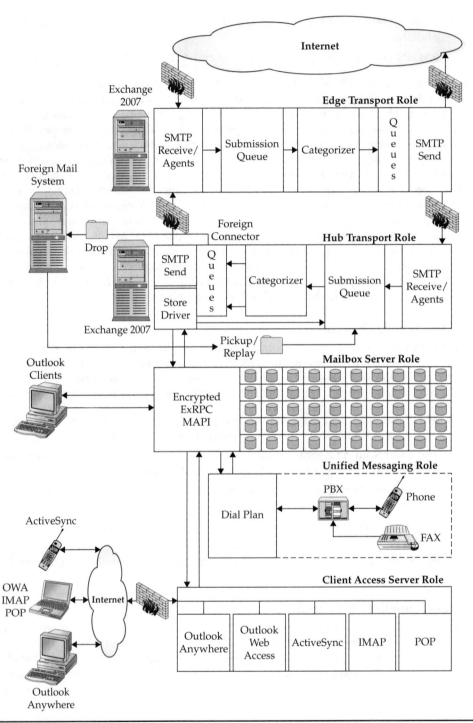

FIGURE 3-1   Transport pipeline

Inbound Mail

The following steps detail the inbound mail flow process:

1. Mail coming from the Internet is accepted by a receive connector on the Edge Transport server.

2. Various agents scan and process the message (antivirus, anti-Spam, and so on).

3. Mail is placed into a submission queue by a receive connector.

4. The Categorizer determines the closest Hub Transport to the destination mailbox (same AD site) and places it in the delivery queue for that server.

5. Mail is sent from the Edge Transport to the Hub Transport server via a send connector.

6. The receive connector on the Hub Transport receives the message, and additional agents scan and process the message for a second layer of protection. This is also essential for protecting internal e-mail that doesn't pass through the Edge.

7. Mail is placed into a submission queue. On the Hub Transport, submissions can be made in one of four ways:

    -   Receive connector

    -   Pick or Replay directory

    -   Store driver

    -   Receive Agent

8. The Categorizer resolves the recipients of the message.

9. The message is routed to the appropriate destination queue (Mailbox Store server).

10. The store driver converts SMTP to MAPI and delivers the message to the mailbox server using encrypted ExRPC communications.

11. Outlook clients use ExRPC to retrieve the mail. All other clients use CAS.

Outbound Mail

When a message is composed in an Outlook client and the Send button is clicked, the message is actually submitted to the mailbox server. OWA, Outlook Anywhere, and Active Sync clients submit to the Client Access Server. POP and IMAP clients can be configured to use either the Hub Transport or Edge Transport server for their SMTP host address, depending on whether the clients are inside or outside of the organization's network. In this example, Outlook is sending the message outbound.

The following steps detail the outbound mail flow process:

1. The Outlook user clicks the Send button and the message is submitted to Mailbox Store role.

2. The store driver converts MAPI to SMTP and submits the message directly to the submission queue on the Hub Transport.

3. The Categorizer resolves recipients. After the recipients are resolved, there are three possible paths:

   - The recipient is on the same mailbox server as the originator or the same AD site (inbound).

   - The recipient is in the same organization but on a different server and possibly another AD site or legacy server (outbound).

   - The recipient is outside the organization (outbound).

4. Mail is placed in the appropriate delivery queue (local or remote).

5. Outbound e-mail is sent via an SMTP send connector to either another Hub Transport in a different AD site, where it then becomes an inbound message, or to an Edge Transport in the perimeter network.

6. Various agents scan and process the message.

7. The message is placed in a submission queue.

8. The message is categorized and placed in a domain-specific remote deliver queue.

9. The Edge Transport's SMTP Send delivers the message outside the organization.

Agents

A single agent API exists in Exchange Server 2007. All agents written for Exchange Server 2007 have full unfettered access to the mail flowing through the transport pipeline. This was somewhat possible in Exchange 2000/2003, but required writing Event Syncs which were somewhat difficult to program. Agents replaced Event Syncs, which are not only easier to program, they are easier to install. Agents can be very powerful and if not carefully tested, they could cause mail flow and security problems. Therefore, you should be careful while implementing new agents.

Events

Agents have predefined actions that are taken against an e-mail when a particular event occurs. Events occur naturally in Exchange Server 2007 all the time. Figure 3-2 illustrates the 17 events that can occur when an e-mail is processed. Thirteen of the events occur every time, and four of them are special events. Figure 3-2 also illustrates the order in which the events fire. All agents depend on the events to be generated prior to taking any action against e-mail. It is important to understand what the events monitor and the sequence of events, if you want to be able to create or troubleshoot agents.

Out of the Box

Microsoft includes a number of agents in Exchange Server 2007. Certain agents specifically run on the Edge Transport role as opposed to the Hub Transport role. It is possible to run the exact same agents on both roles as well. Some agents take actions against a single event. Other agents will take different actions on mail across multiple events. Thirteen agents are built into the Exchange transport stack. Table 3-2 lists the agents and which server they run on.

Transport APIs will be discussed in more detail later in this chapter.

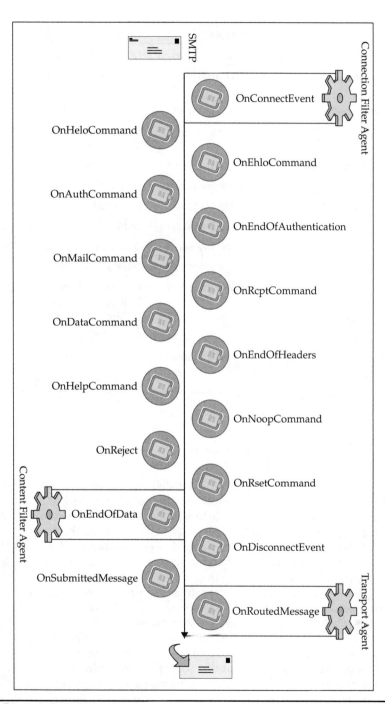

FIGURE 3-2   Events and agents

Agent	Server	Event(s)
Transport Rule agent	Hub Transport	OnRoutedMessage
Journaling agent	Hub Transport	OnSubmittedMessage, OnRoutedMessage
AD RMS Prelicensing agent	Hub Transport	OnRoutedMessage
Connection Filtering Agent	Edge Transport	OnConnectEvent, OnMailCommand, OnRcptCommand, OnEndOfHeaders
Address Rewriting Inbound agent	Edge Transport	OnRcptCommand, OnEndOfHeaders
Edge Rule agent	Edge Transport	OnEndOfData
Content Filter agent	Edge Transport	OnEndOfData
Sender ID agent	Edge Transport	OnMailCommand, OnEndOfHeaders
Sender Filter agent	Edge Transport	OnMailCommand, OnEndOfHeaders
Recipient Filter agent	Edge Transport	OnRcptCommand
Protocol Analysis agent	Edge Transport	OnEndOfHeaders, OnEndOfData, OnReject, OnRsetCommand, OnDisconnectEvent
Attachment Filtering agent	Edge Transport	OnEndOfData
Address Rewriting Outbound agent	Edge Transport	OnRcptCommand, OnEndOfHeaders

TABLE 3-2   Microsoft Transport Agents

Routing Architecture

In the previous section, the transport pipeline was defined. The entire pipeline was illustrated with only two Exchange Server 2007 computers. This section will look at how the routing technologies in Exchange Server 2007 scale to meet the needs of any size organization. The start of the routing story for Exchange Server 2007 begins with the relationship between Hub Transport role and the Mailbox Server role. The two options for deploying these roles are to put them both on the same server and to separate the roles onto separate servers.

A small organization will likely keep the two roles on the same server. As an organization grows in size and begins to require multiple mailbox servers, the mailbox servers' performance can be improved by moving the Hub Transport role to dedicated physical servers. These dedicated servers are sometimes called *bridgeheads*. Modularity is only one of the benefits of the role-based architecture. From a routing standpoint, the new role-based architecture actually translates into less administrative work. The routing process in Exchange Server 2007 is so automated that some Exchange administrators may never have to manually configure mail flow settings anywhere in their organization outside of adding and removing server roles.

Routing Constructs

Being in control is always a good feeling. On a data network, being in control of the bandwidth (which is limited for many organizations) is paramount. The tools to control the bandwidth utilized by Exchange have come in various forms and have evolved from Exchange 4.0 to Exchange 2007. The logical routing boundary evolution is somewhat interesting:

- **Exchange 4.0**   Internet Mail Connector Sites, site connectors, X400 connectors
- **Exchange 5.0**   Internet Mail Connector Sites, site connectors, X400 connectors
- **Exchange 5.5**   Internet Mail Service Sites, site connectors, X400 connectors
- **Exchange 2000**   Routing groups, routing group connectors, SMTP connectors
- **Exchange 2003**   Routing groups, routing group connectors, SMTP connectors
- **Exchange 2007**   AD sites, AD site connectors, Hub Transport roles, send connectors, receive connectors

Many concepts in Exchange 2007 are reminiscent of the early days of Exchange. For example, Exchange has gone back to sites as routing boundaries, but this time they are AD sites not Exchange sites. Another reflection of the past is that up to Exchange 5.5, SMTP only ran on the server where the Internet Mail Service was installed. In Exchange 2007, SMTP only runs on the transport server roles.

The purpose of Exchange sites and routing groups was to group together Exchange servers that existed on one or more LANs and that were interconnected with high-bandwidth, reliable connections. If Exchange servers were separated by low-bandwidth WAN connections, the servers were placed in separate sites or routing groups to prevent mail from flowing over the WAN. The site connectors and routing group connectors were configured to allow mail to flow between the sites or routing groups, and could be configured by administrators to limit the size and type of messages as well as the time of day that the connector would run.

Both sites and routing groups are arbitrary constraints that do not change the nature of the actual data network packet flow. Careful planning was necessary to make sure that the settings in Exchange were congruent with the routing at the data network level. Improperly configuring a site or routing group and the associated connectors could prevent mail flow even if the data network was fine. What was discovered in Exchange 2000/2003 was that all the work had already been done with Active Directory sites when AD was deployed. Turns out adding routing groups was a redundant, superfluous administrative task. So in Exchange Server 2007 routing groups no longer exist. Exchange 2007 now uses AD sites instead.

2007 Routing Rules

Now that Exchange sites and routing groups are gone and there are no more Exchange site or routing group connectors to configure, how does mail get from point A to point B? There are default behaviors (called "rules" for the sake of this discussion) that the Exchange 2007 servers follow when transporting mail though the pipeline. Reviewing these rules will help you understand how Exchange servers figure out how to get mail from point A to point B in Exchange Server 2007.

Rule 1: Direct Relay

The path a message takes on the network should be determined by the routes on the data network, not Exchange. All messages will be sent directly to the destination server unless that server is unavailable.

Rule 2: Stay in Your Site

This rule defines the relationship between the hub and the mailbox servers. The Hub Transport server only delivers mail to mailbox servers that happen to be in the same Active Directory site as the Hub. Conversely, the mailbox server will only submit mail to Hub Transport servers in the same AD site.

Rule 3: Deterministic Route

Once a path has been used between two Exchange Server 2007 machines, they will continue to use that path unless it becomes unavailable. This is called *deterministic routing* and it replaces Link State information used in previous versions of Exchange.

Rule 4: Auto-Connect

As soon as a Hub Transport role is added to the organization, default connectors will be established. When two or more transport servers exist in the organization, both receive and send connectors will exist. Even when transport servers exist in separate AD sites, default connectors will be created to make sure that mail items can flow anywhere in the organization. Note that if only one AD site exists, rule 2 takes care of mail flow.

Rule 5: When in Doubt, Use AD Sites to Reroute

When routing information is required to determine the best path, Exchange 2007 servers will refer to the Active Directory site topology. It is important to note that this is done if a direct path to the target server is not available.

Active Directory Sites

The fact that routing groups are no longer necessary doesn't mean that there is no need for a logical grouping of servers in Exchange 2007. As an Exchange administrator, you may not have to worry about designing an Active Directory site topology. However, it will be a good idea to understand what that topology is in your organization. Exchange 2007 will look for specific information when it queries Active Directory. Sites help Exchange narrow down the search results by site. AD is used by Exchange for far more than just message routing. However, the focus of this discussion is to understand the role that AD sites play in the Exchange 2007 transport architecture.

Active Directory sites define areas of the physical network that have high-bandwidth, reliable connections. Sites are used by AD to determine how Domain Controllers should replicate the Active Directory database and how clients and servers access domain and forest resources. Exchange 2007 transport servers use AD sites to determine the next hop an e-mail must make in the event that a direct relay is not available. Figure 3-3 shows an Active Directory site topology that was designed to accurately reflect the physical network. Notice that there is an Active Directory site for each area of the network separated by WAN connectivity. Also notice that the site links not only reflect the WAN connections, they have costs associated with them that coincide with the link speeds and available bandwidth. These are characteristics of a good AD site design.

Exchange Server 2007 Hub Transport servers are responsible for sending mail between Active Directory sites. Automatic connectors exist by default between all Hub Transport servers

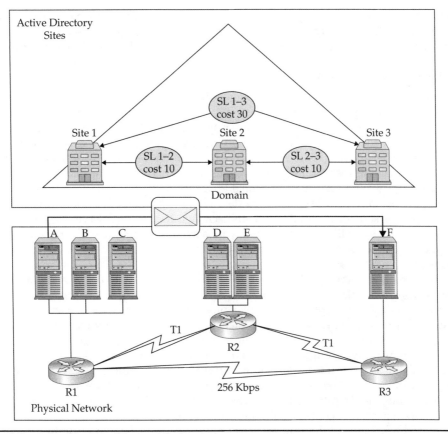

PART I

FIGURE 3-3 Active Directory Sites and Exchange

and their counterparts in other AD sites. Figure 3-3 shows that Hub Transport server A sends an e-mail to Hub Transport server F directly regardless of the physical network or the AD site or site links. Unless the connection fails, AD sites will not be referenced. If the connection does fail and the physical network is unable to reroute the mail itself, Hub Transport A will query Active Directory for an alternate route. In this example, AD would recommend site 2 as the next hop. Server A could then send to Hub Transport D or E as the next hop.

The most important part of this new routing architecture is that once AD sites, site links, and costs have been assigned during the deployment of Active Directory, no Exchange-specific configuration is required.

Management Models

Organizations not only vary in size and complexity, they also vary in how they are administered. Exchange Server has built into its architecture components and tools that allow organizations to customize how administrative tasks get performed and specify who can perform them. The Exchange 5.5 site not only served as a routing boundary, it was also a management boundary. In Exchange 2000 Microsoft introduced the concept of the administrative group as a management boundary. These boundaries were particularly useful when defining which resources a group of administrators had control over—especially in larger environments where different groups of administrators manage different Exchange servers.

Administrative Boundaries

Exchange 2000/2003 had a good thing going with routing groups and administrative groups. When the organization was switched to Native Mode, the routing groups and administrative groups functioned independently from one another. The separation of the logical management boundary and the e-mail routing topology gave a great deal of administrative flexibility that did not exist up to that point. The downside, as we have already mentioned, is that routing groups are really not necessary. The management architecture in Exchange 2007 takes a similar approach on administrative groups.

There are no administrative groups by default in an Exchange 2007-only environment. If Exchange 2007 servers are coexisting with Exchange 2000 or 2003 servers, a single administrative group will be created, along with a single routing group for backward compatibility. These can be removed from the organization once all servers are upgraded to Exchange Server 2007.

The benefit to not having administrative groups may be hard to envision if you are currently using multiple administrative groups. Administrative groups were used in Exchange 2000/2003 to simplify the complex process of delegating administrative tasks. By creating an administrative group and delegating one of three administrative roles, you could quickly isolate groups of administrators and their Exchange servers from one to another. Administrative groups did not make it any easier, however, to delegate custom administrative tasks (roles) to various administrators. For example, if you wanted to give the helpdesk the ability to move mailboxes, you would have to perform seven or more steps using two or more tools. Administrative groups had one major downfall: They did not allow you to move servers between administrative groups.

Microsoft has removed the administrative groups and redefined the administrative roles so that they cover the most common operational tasks that need to be performed by Exchange administrators. Before we detail the new roles, we need to review some common administrative models.

Three Administrative Models

From a top-down perspective, there are essentially three administrative models. Organizations tend to fall into one of the three models. Understanding your organization's current and future model prior to deploying Exchange Server 2007 allows the management architecture to be custom fit to your environment.

Unified Permission Model

The unified permission model is the default model when you deploy Exchange Server 2007. Initially, it is composed of an individual user account that has administrative rights to perform Exchange tasks and Active Directory tasks. A common misconception about the unified permission model is that all administrators must be in a single location or have exactly the same permissions. Although that may be true, it is not a requirement. What makes the unified model "unified" is that there are one or more security groups and all administrators in these groups have rights and permissions to perform administrative tasks in both the Exchange organization and Active Directory forest (see Figure 3-4).

PART I

FIGURE 3-4
Unified permission
model

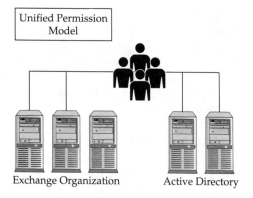

Exchange Organization   Active Directory

Split Permission Model

The reasons to segment Active Directory administrators and Exchange Administrators from one another are numerous. They range from political to technical. When you do this you are implementing a split permission model. Active Directory lends itself to a split permission model as do the Exchange 2007 administrative tools. The database on an Active Directory domain controller is actually partitioned into naming contexts:

- Schema
- Domain
- Configuration
- Global Catalog (only on global catalog servers)

The tools available to administrators only expose certain partitions and even then limit access to only certain properties. While the unified permission model will allow administrators to have permissions in more than one of these partitions, the split permission model will restrict which partitions each administrative group has access to. This is accomplished by creating security groups in AD with no AD permissions, Then granting these groups Exchange Administrative Roles.

You can see in Figure 3-5 that there are three groups of administrators. Each group has been delegated Server Admin roles to their respective server(s).

FIGURE 3-5
Split permission
model

Exchange Organization   Active Directory

Delegated Permission Model

Delegated permission models can be difficult to implement in Exchange because they require the greatest level of customization. You must create security groups and give them only the permission they need to accomplish specific tasks. Microsoft has created two new roles to address this issue: Exchange Server Administrators and Exchange Recipient Administrators (see Figure 3-6). But if further delegation is required it will be necessary to create the custom restrictions.

Exchange Administrative Roles

When Active Directory first came out and Exchange Server 2000 was integrated with it, a new world came into play on the administrative scope. It was possible with Exchange's entire configuration being stored in AD, to use the same tools to administer Exchange and AD. For some environments, such as small and medium-size businesses where there are very few administrators (maybe only one), this was an excellent proposition. However, at the enterprise level (where there are numerous administrators), it is common to have the two administrative jobs split. Having two separate tools for performing these tasks is also beneficial in that it can obscure the tasks you do not want certain administrators performing.

Exchange Server 2007 makes it even easier to split out the administrative functions. All of the Exchange-specific properties are grouped together. This creates a property set that Microsoft calls *e-mail information*. Permissions can be applied to the property set as a single access control entry (ACE). The new administrative roles in Exchange 2007 are possible because of the underlying changes in the Security and Permission models made in Exchange Server 2007 when the/PrepareAD option is executed during setup. Exchange-specific security groups are created in each domain when /PrepareAD is run. These groups have inherent permission to perform Exchange tasks. By delegating a user one of the four administrative roles, you will be adding that user to one or more of the Exchange security groups. Part II of this book covers the planning and installation of Exchange Server 2007 in depth. For additional information on security and permission changes, see Chapter 14.

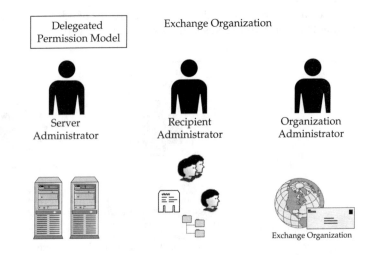

Figure 3-6
Delegated
Permission Model

Exchange Organization Administrators

This role has a corresponding universal security group of the same name in the forest root domain that gives its members full access to all Exchange properties and objects in the Exchange organization. This security group is nested into the local Administrators security group on every Exchange server in the organization, granting the group ownership of all local configuration data.

Exchange Recipient Administrators

This role has a corresponding universal security group of the same name in the forest root domain that gives its members the ability to modify all Exchange properties for all recipients in AD. This includes user, group, contact, dynamic dist list, and public folder objects. Administrators must run setup with the /PrepareDomain option in each domain where recipients reside for this role to function properly.

Exchange View-Only Administrators

This role has a corresponding universal security group of the same name in the forest root domain that gives its members the ability to view the entire organization, but not to change anything.

Exchange Server Administrators (Servername)

This role has two corresponding groups. Delegates of this role will be a member of the Exchange View-Only Administrators universal security group and a member of the local Administrators group on the specific Exchange server that they were delegated. Members will have the ability to view the entire organization, but will be limited to full control of the local server configuration.

Development Platform

The early versions of Exchange Server were not implemented by companies that had demanding in-house application development requirements. Many of these companies chose to go with Lotus Notes instead. Microsoft has struggled to win over these developers. In this attempt over the last decade, Microsoft has released over 42 Application Programming Interfaces (APIs) for Exchange Server. Each API came with the promise of bettering the developers' experience with Exchange Server. One of the more difficult feats for a programmer to pull off is to tie into the Exchange database. Exchange 2000 introduced the Web Storage System, EXIFS, WebDAV, a Work Flow Designer, and many more new ways to interface with the Exchange servers and clients. The Exchange 2000/2003 era saw more migrations from Notes to Exchange than during any of the previous versions of Exchange.

The goal in Exchange Server 2007 is not to only make Exchange a better development platform, but to make it very easy to develop upon. Here are the design goals as stated by Rob McCann (a Microsoft Program Manager for Exchange Server 2007):

- To unify API's with a focus on:
  - Mail transport
  - Exchange management
  - PIM data storage

- To use the same business logic
- To make appropriate architecture choices

API Support Matrix

Some of the biggest changes in Exchange Server 2007 are under the covers, so to speak. Developers need hooks to get into the messaging system, and they depend on Microsoft to provide these hooks with APIs. Although the Messaging Application Programming Interface (MAPI) has been a popular interface, it has a number of limitations that other APIs have allowed programmers to work around. The quality of the APIs directly affects which features Microsoft builds into Exchange and has a direct effect on the third-party providers.

When you examine Table 3-3, pay special attention to the APIs that are not supported in Exchange Server 2007, especially if you have developed or have purchased any applications that were written to use one or more of those APIs. These applications will not function properly unless you maintain an Exchange 2000/2003 server for them to run against.

Web Services

Web Services is a single API in Exchange Server 2007. It replaces various APIs used in previous versions of Exchange. It is a web-based API created to overcome the limitations of some legacy APIs that could not communicate well through the firewall. It takes advantage of the fact that the Exchange 2007 Client Access Servers, Transport Servers, and Unified Messaging Servers all use the same business logic to communicate with the Mailbox Server role. This means that no matter how applications access the store, programmers will not be responsible for maintaining compatibility with numerous clients.

Web Services can be easily leveraged with Visual Studio and .NET. Through Web Services, programmers can access all mailbox data, including mail items, calendars, appointments, public folders, contacts and so on. Web Services is also the first API to provide access to Outlook tasks. Two new Outlook features—Availability Service and Autodiscovery—can be used by programmers through Web Services.

OWA Web Parts

Outlook Web Access (OWA) has been tremendously improved in Exchange Server 2007. Programmers who want to take advantage of the latest features of OWA 2007 can do so easily with very little effort. OWA Web Parts are XML stylesheets that can be imbedded into web-based applications and SharePoint portals for instant access to Exchange data.

Exchange Administrator Benefits

When companies integrate applications that use the new APIs for Exchange Server 2007, they will notice some benefits. Of course in many cases, with a single API the applications should be easier to maintain and be more reliable. Applications will become more secure as well. For example, if you have been working with Exchange Server for some time, you have probably installed and worked with a third-party application that required an account with full access rights to Exchange. This is viewed by most security experts as vulnerability. One of the more noticeable security enhancements for Web Services is server-to-server authentication. This allows an Exchange Server to perform the authentication with reduced access rights and still get the job done, as shown in Figure 3-7.

Application Programming Interface	Exchange 2000/2003 Support	Exchange 2007 Support	Exchange 2007 Alternative API
CDOExM	Yes	No	PowerShell
Queue View	Yes	No	PowerShell
WMI Classes for Exchange	Yes	No	PowerShell
PowerShell Cmdlets	No	Yes	n/a
EDK Gateway	Yes	No	Agent API/Foreign Connectors
Routing Objects	Yes	No	Agent API/Foreign Connector
SMTP Transport Event Sinks	Yes	No	Agent API/Foreign Connector
Agent API	No	Yes	n/a
Foreign Connectors	No	Yes	n/a
CDOSYS	Yes	Yes (deemphasized)	n/a
CDO for Workflow	Yes	Yes	Windows Workflow Foundation/ASP.NET
Workflow Designer	Yes	No	Windows Workflow Foundation/ASP.NET
5.5 Event Service	Yes	No	Windows Workflow Foundation/ASP.NET
EXIFS	Yes	No	Windows Workflow Foundation/ASP.NET
WSS Forms	No	Yes	Windows Workflow Foundation/ASP.NET
MAPI	Yes	Deemphasized	Web Services
CDO 1.2.1	Yes	Deemphasized	Web Services
CDOEx	Yes	Deemphasized	Web Services
ExOLEDB	Yes	Deemphasized	Web Services
WebDAV	Yes	Deemphasized	Web Services
OWA URL Commands	Yes	Deemphasized	Web Services
Store Events	Yes	Deemphasized	Web Services
Web Services	No	Yes	n/a

TABLE 3-3 API Support Matrix

Figure 3-7
Server-to-server
authentication

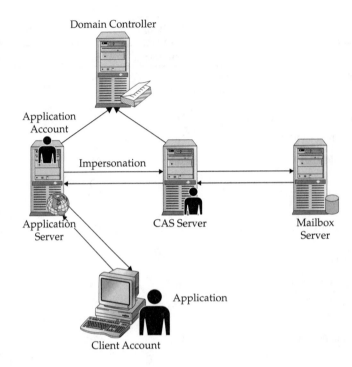

Summary
===

In this chapter we reviewed storage and message handling architectures which form the foundation for Exchange Server 2007. The storage architecture for Exchange Server 2007 has been improved largely in part by the native support for sixty-four bit computing in Exchange 2007. The enhanced database cache creates a new storage dynamic for the Mailbox Server role that improves overall disk I/O. This improvement translates into better response times for end users. The Transport architecture has also been improved. Hub Transport Server Roles and Edge Transport Servers work together in Exchange Server 2007 to provide better performance, reliability, and security. The communications managed by these two roles with all other server roles is called the transport pipeline. To help administrators with organizations of varying sizes and complexity, Exchange Server 2007 introduces a new Administrative Model with support for Unified Permission, Split Permission, and Delegated Administrative models.

PART

II

Designing and Deploying Exchange Server 2007

Installing Exchange 2007

The basic steps required for installing Microsoft Exchange Server 2007 remain the same as they have for the last two versions—prepare the forest, prepare the domain(s), and install the bits. The devil, as they say, is in the details. There are new prerequisites for hardware and software, new considerations for messaging infrastructure design, and new tools to make it all happen.

Pre-installation Review

As we touched on in Chapter 3, many architectural factors influence infrastructure planning. Prior to Exchange 2007 being installed, the infrastructure will have been designed and hardware needs assessed and provisioned. Server locations should all now be mapped out and message routing defined. Bandwidth and storage capacity needs have been determined through historical usage data and current product testing tools such as LoadSim and JetStress. The different server roles for Exchange will have been reviewed and their implementation and coexistence agreed upon.

The next phase of the commitment to Exchange 2007 is the installation. It may involve first testing the product and process in a lab environment, or it may involve installing into a production organization to begin moving some pilot users to the new server. Before the first Exchange 2007 server is to be installed, you need to perform a couple significant steps:

- Prepare the Active Directory (AD) forest.
- Prepare the Active Directory domains and child domains that will host Exchange objects.

For each server that will host Exchange 2007 roles, you have several phases of installation to navigate through:

- Configure and optimize the server hardware and operating system.
- Determine which roles are to be installed.
- Install Exchange Server 2007.
- Work through the post-installation task list.

The post-installation checklist includes "checking for updates." If Exchange 2007 Service Pack 1 (or later) is available but is not streamed into the current installation media, it will be summoned through Microsoft Update at this stage.

Preparing the Server

It is much easier to assemble an appropriate, dependable system prior to establishing its place in the Exchange organization than trying to upgrade an inadequate server after production resources have been deployed to it. Investments in preparation time, allowing for informed decisions in regard to disk and memory configurations, server functionality, and disaster contingencies, can reduce heartache down the road. This is especially true for mission-critical applications such as enterprise e-mail.

System Requirements

Exchange Server 2007, like its predecessors, has fairly significant requirements and expectations of its underlying hardware and software.

Processor

Two primary choices for CPUs are compatible with Exchange 2007:

- A 64-bit processor supporting Intel's Extended Memory 64 Technology (Intel EM64T)
- A 64-bit AMD processor supporting the AMD64 platform

NOTE *Intel's IA64 processors, known as Itanium, are not supported for Exchange 2007, even though Windows 2003 Server has a version for IA64.*

Operating System

Exchange 2007 requires one of the 64-bit versions of Windows 2003 Server:

- Windows 2003 Server 64-bit Standard Service Pack 1 or higher
- Windows 2003 Server 64-bit Enterprise Service Pack 1 or higher
- Windows 2003 Server 64-bit R2 Standard
- Windows 2003 Server 64-bit R2 Enterprise

SP1 *Exchange 2007 Service Pack 1 will require Windows 2003 with Service Pack 2 on the Exchange Server. The domain controllers do not need to be upgraded to Windows 2003 Service Pack 2 in order to install Exchange 2007 Service Pack 1.*

Any of these operating systems may have a Multilanguage User Interface (MUI) language pack installed as well.

Directory Requirements

There are some Exchange 2007 requirements regarding Active Directory as well. The domain controller holding the Schema Master role (by default this role belongs to the first domain controller) must be running Windows 2003 Server with Service Pack 1 or higher.

Also, at least one Global Catalog Server in every Active Directory site where Exchange is to be installed should also be running Windows 2003 Server SP1 or higher.

The Domain Functional level needs to be held at Windows 2000 Server native or higher in every domain that will host Exchange 2007 objects. Finally, if there are any Windows 2000 domain controllers in a domain where Exchange 2007 is to be installed, then Windows 2003 SP1 or higher must be selected using the /DomainController switch from setup.com. Setup will fail if the domain is still in mixed mode. The Domain Functional level is changed in Active Directory Domains and Trusts. Right-click the domain and select Raise Domain Functional Level… to open the windows shown in Figure 4-1. (Note that this change is not reversible.)

There is no 64-bit requirement for the domain controllers specific to Exchange 2007, unless of course Exchange is installed on one of those domain controllers—a practice that, although supported, is discouraged for security and recoverability reasons. Having the 64-bit version of Windows 2003 Server as a domain controller does, however, realize improvements in Active Directory performance.

Obviously, Active Directory is critical for Exchange Server. If AD is not in the best of health, this needs to be addressed prior to introducing Exchange into the mix. Ensuring that Global Catalog Servers are on stable, well-powered and accessible hardware will help ensure Exchange installation success.

Drive Space Requirements

As a bare minimum, Exchange 2007 requires 1.2GB of free space where it is to be installed, in addition to 200MB on the system drive. Also, each Unified Messaging language pack consumes about 500MB of drive space. With the system drive space available these days, meeting these minimums should be trivial. Drives will also have to be formatted with New Technology File System (NTFS).

Memory Requirements

Memory requirements will depend on what server roles are to be installed on individual Exchange Servers. In a standard single-server environment, Microsoft recommends a minimum of 2GB of RAM plus 5MB per user. In addition, memory requirements scale with

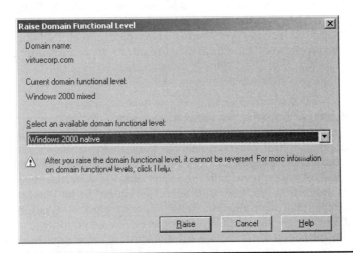

FIGURE 4-1   Raising the Domain Functional level to native for a Windows 2003 domain controller

the number of Exchange 2007 storage groups employed on the server. An additional 2GB of RAM minimum is needed for more storage groups, up to every fourth group added, to improve database caching. Therefore, 2GB of RAM is needed for one to four storage groups, 4GB of RAM is needed for five to eight storage groups, 6GB of RAM is needed for nine to 12 storage groups, and so on.

The move to 64-bit means not having to amend the boot.ini file with the /3GB switch seen in Exchange 2003 deployments with physical RAM of 1GB or more (see Microsoft KB article 823440).

Other Software Requirements

Exchange 2007 uses .NET Framework 2.0, Microsoft Management Console (MMC) 3.0, and Windows PowerShell 1.0, which all need to be installed prior to installing Exchange 2007. Exchange 2007 returns Exchange to its own implementation of SMTP and actually requires that IIS SMTP is not installed for the Hub Transport and Edge roles. Even though Exchange 2007 no longer depends on major services in IIS, such as SMTP and NNTP, there are still some IIS components needed. Other requirements are specific to the server role.

The Mailbox role requires IIS, with the World Wide Web service, and network COM+ access enabled. The Client Access Server (CAS) role needs the World Wide Web service and ASP.NET 2.0 installed also. For the CAS Outlook Anywhere service, the Remote Procedure Call (RPC) over HTTP proxy component needs to be installed on the Exchange server as well. All these additional components for the CAS and Mailbox roles can be added through Add/Remove Windows Components in Add/Remove Programs in the Control Panel on Windows 2003 Server.

The Edge Transport role requires a Windows 2003 Server that is not a member of the AD forest with Exchange 2007. It also requires Active Directory Application Mode (ADAM) to be installed and specific DNS entries configured.

The Unified Messaging (UM) role has more elaborate prerequisites. The UM role installs its own Microsoft Exchange Speech Engine service, which is incompatible with Microsoft's Speech Server. The latter has to be uninstalled first. The UM role also requires Windows Media Encoder 9 Series x64 Edition, the Windows Media Audio 9 Voice codec for x64-based computers (KB 317912), and Microsoft Core XML Services (MSXML) 6.0. The UM roles are not supported in any virtualization application.

Finally, the Windows Installer service must be enabled, and all Exchange 5.5 servers need to be removed from an existing Exchange organization prior to adding any Exchange 2007 servers.

Virtualization

Exchange is not immune from the trend toward server consolidation through virtualization. Virtualization allows multiple independent operating system instances to load and function concurrently on a single physical server. This can translate to significant savings in hardware costs, datacenter space rental expense, and server provisioning time.

The current market leader in virtualization solutions, VMWare, has several products in their line that can host 64-bit Windows 2003 Server. Of course, 64-bit Windows 2003 Server is required for Exchange 2007 in production. These options include VMWare Workstation 5.5 and higher, VMWare Server, and ESX Server. However, Microsoft does not support Exchange 2007 Server in non-Microsoft virtualization solutions. At the same time, Microsoft does not provide a Virtual Server product that can manage 64-bit guest hosts. This is expected to change in the timeframe of Windows 2008 Server, formerly codenamed Longhorn, where virtualization will be built into the operating system. Indeed, virtualization in Windows 2008 is built on 64-bit architecture and has significant enhancements in storage, a common virtual server bottleneck. For lab environments now though, the 32-bit evaluation version of Exchange 2007 on 32-bit Windows 2003 manages quite well as a guest operating system on Microsoft Virtual Server 2005 R2.

Determining Role(s)

As explained earlier in the book, five separate roles can be installed in Exchange Server 2007: Mailbox server, Client Access Server, Hub Transport server, Unified Messaging server, and Edge Transport server. Exchange 2007 does not install the same set of binaries on every server independent of use as previous versions have. A typical installation of Exchange 2007 calls for the roles of Client Access Server, Hub Transport server, and Mailbox server. In addition, the Exchange Management Tools are installed automatically with those roles. A custom installation allows the administrator to choose specific roles for the server. Role requirements are going to be different for each enterprise, as determined through capacity planning, network topology, and policy requirements.

Choosing the Appropriate OS

Exchange Server 2007 installs on the 64-bit version of Windows Server 2003. Windows 2003 ships in Standard and Enterprise versions as well as Web and Datacenter versions. Exchange 2007 does not install on the Web or Datacenter edition. Very early in 2006, Microsoft released a rollup version of Windows 2003, appending an R2 to its name. The Standard and Enterprise versions have different price points and provide different levels of functionality. At that time R2 was released, those without Software Assurance experienced a price of $999 for the Standard version with five Client Access Licenses (CALs) and $3999 for the Enterprise version with 25 CALs. If you do not need more than four CPUs and are not implementing a cluster for this Exchange server installation, then Windows 2003 Standard is sufficient, regardless of whether Exchange 2007 Standard or Enterprise is being deployed.

SP1 *Exchange 2007 Service Pack 1 will require Windows Server 2003 Service Pack 2 on the server where the service pack update is run.*

Windows 2008 Server is currently in beta with an anticipated release very early in 2008. Exchange 2007 cannot install on Windows 2008, nor can there be a Windows 2008 domain controller in the domain where Exchange 2007 is intended to be installed without Exchange 2007 Service Pack 1. This means all Exchange 2007 servers will have to be at the SP1 level prior to the Windows 2008 domain controllers being added. Windows 2008 is scheduled for an early Q1 2008 Release to Manufacturer (RTM) with the launch event scheduled for February 27, 2008, in Los Angeles.

SP1 *Exchange 2007 Service Pack 1 will be required to install Exchange on a Windows 2008 server or in a domain with a Windows 2008 domain controller.*

Installing and Configuring Prerequisite Software

Prior to installing Exchange 2007, there are several software prerequisites as well.

.NET Framework 2.0

Exchange Server 2007 depends on the .NET Framework to establish and maintain Web Services. On Windows 2003 Server R2, the latest version is 2.0 and is available as an optional installation component for Windows in Add/Remove Windows Components accessed through Add/Remove Programs in the Control Panel. For Windows 2003 Server, the .NET Framework 2.0 is an optional component listed in Windows Update or Microsoft Update. It is also available as a redistributable package at the Microsoft Download Center as NetFx64.exe. There is at least one significant security update to .NET Framework 2.0 outlined in Microsoft KB 928365. Though the post-installation task list for Exchange 2007 includes a trip to Microsoft Update, it is not necessary to wait until after Exchange is installed to do so. If .NET Framework 2.0 is already installed, it will appear grayed out on the Exchange installation interface.

Microsoft Management Console (MMC) 3.0

Since its introduction in the Windows NT 4.0 option pack, the Microsoft Management Console (MMC) has provided some semblance of consistency and extensibility to Microsoft administrative interfaces. Exchange 2007 uses MMC 3.0, which allows for richer snap-ins that are .NET based. It also adds the Action pane, which Exchange shows on the right side of the Exchange Management Console. MMC 3.0 is included in Windows 2003 Server R2. For Windows 2003 Server, Microsoft KB 907265 outlines the installation options for MMC 3.0. To verify the version of MMC currently installed, navigate to Start | Run and enter **MMC**. After the Management Console opens, select Help | About Microsoft Management Console to identify the version.

Windows Server 2003 Service Pack 2 installs MMC 3.0, thus meeting this Exchange installation prerequisite.

Windows PowerShell 1.0

The Exchange Management Shell (EMS) installed with Exchange 2007 is an extension of Windows PowerShell. PowerShell needs to be installed prior to Exchange 2007. Microsoft KB 926139 covers the various installation options for Windows PowerShell 1.0.

Localization and MUI   If Windows Server 2003 is installed with an MUI language pack, Windows PowerShell also can be installed with the same language(s). The Windows 2003 64-bit PowerShell installation is available in the following language versions: Chinese Simplified, Chinese Traditional, French, German, Italian, Japanese, Korean, and Spanish. The PowerShell MUI language pack is described in Microsoft KB 926141.

If Windows is running a localized version for German, Spanish, French, Italian, Japanese, Korean, Portuguese, Russian, Chinese Simplified, or Chinese Traditional, the equivalent for PowerShell can be extracted from the localized PowerShell installation package outlined in Microsoft KB 926140. Any other language requires the English version of PowerShell.

Internet Information Services (IIS) and ASP.NET

If the Exchange installation will include the Client Access Server role, IIS and ASP.NET 2.0 need to be installed first. ASP.NET 2.0 is installed with .NET Framework 2.0; however, if IIS is installed after the .NET Framework, ASP.NET may have to be enabled from within IIS. To confirm ASP.NET 2.0 is enabled, open Internet Information Services and expand the server and the folder Web Service Extensions. Select ASP.NET 2.0.50727 and click the Allow button if it is listed as Prohibited.

Microsoft Update

After you install the .NET Framework, MMC, and IIS components, running Windows or Microsoft update will advise of any missing security patches or updates to those components. As mentioned, there is a significant update to .NET Framework 2.0, which will be exposed as a necessary installation from Microsoft Update.

DNS

Domain Name System (DNS) is critical for Exchange organizations, especially for client access and service location. DNS needs to be healthy and available before you implement Exchange 2007. All Exchange servers must be domain members and, as such, will receive an FQDN made up of their hostname and the DNS suffix for the domain when Windows is installed.

Exchange Best Practices Analyzer (ExBPA)—Exchange 2007 Readiness Check

Microsoft introduced the Exchange Best Practices Analyzer back in September 2004, well after the release of Exchange Server 2003. It immediately became an essential utility for the administrator's toolbox. ExBPA has now been included in the Tools section of the Exchange 2007 Management Console.

With Exchange 2007, the ExBPA team has added a new scan to the product—the Exchange 2007 Readiness Check. If this check is not an option in ExBPA, as shown in Figure 4-2, run a

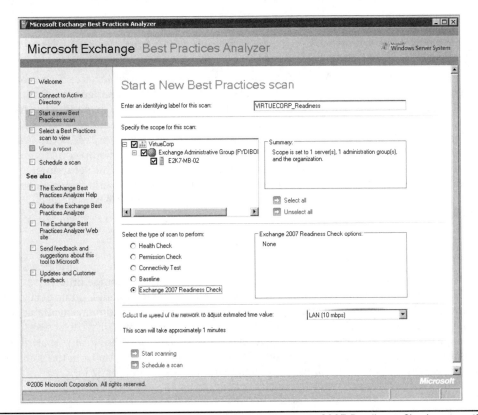

FIGURE 4-2   Exchange Best Practice Analyzer showing the Exchange 2007 Readiness Check scan option

check for updates to bring the version up to date. ExBPA performs many of the same checks that the Exchange 2007 Setup Wizard does in testing for prerequisites and reports on the status of AD and its topology. It alerts the administrator to problem areas and summarizes the installation environment.

Permission and Security Requirements

For preparing Active Directory and installing Exchange 2007 Server there are a few permission requirements. Because the schema for Active Directory is being extended, the account being used to perform that extension must be a member of the Schema Admins group. All other aspects of a fresh Exchange 2007 deployment require the implementer to be a member of the Enterprise Admins group. In addition, the AD account used for the installation also has to be a member of the local administrators group on the Exchange server itself.

Schema updates can be managed independent of the Exchange installation to ensure that operators work with the lowest level of access needed to perform the tasks. Installing Exchange does not need Schema Admin membership after the schema is extended. Accounts used to install the components of Exchange should have the minimum security context needed to complete the task.

After the installation of Exchange, there are new Exchange-specific groups in which membership is required to perform specific tasks. Those are covered in the administration chapters in the book.

Preparing Active Directory

As we covered in Chapter 2, Active Directory has provided directory services for Exchange Server since Exchange 2000. The Exchange-related attributes and Exchange configuration containers are not implemented in AD by default. They are created by extending the AD schema and populated through installation and administration of Exchange.

Setup.exe is the executable for the graphic interface of the Exchange 2007 Setup Wizard. It is the method that most administrators are probably used to using. Setup.com, found in the same place on the Exchange 2007 DVD, is used for the command-line setup interactions we are about to consider. If setup.exe is used from the command line with any switches, it will return a popup declaring, "Setup.exe cannot accept command line parameters. Use setup.com instead."

Preparing for Coexistence

If there are any Exchange 2003 or Exchange 2000 servers in the organization, the first step is to amend permissions in every domain that contains the groups Exchange Enterprise Servers and Exchange Domain Servers. This switch allows the Recipient Update Service to continue working after Exchange 2007 is installed and will reach all domains available to it when it is run. Access control entries (ACE) are assigned as read and/or write access to the Exchange-Information property set for several groups. A *property set* is a group of attributes for assigning permissions by group instead of individually. It can be run from the command line of any Windows 2003 SP1 or higher machine in the forest, 64 bit or 32 bit.

```
>setup.com /PrepareLegacyExchangePermissions:<FQDN>
```

For multiple domain coexistence, the administrator executing this command needs to be a member of the Enterprise Admins group. Removing the domain identifier after the parameter will prepare all domains it has access to over port 389. Figure 4-3 shows the command-line execution of this preparation step.

It is recommended to let these permission changes replicate successfully before running the next step, which is extending the schema. If this step is not run independently, it will be run as part of setup.com /PrepareAD.

Preparing the Schema

On the Exchange 2007 DVD, or the network installation point where it was copied, the schema updates are found in the folder setup\data in the form of LDAP Data Interchange Format (.ldf) files. Updating the schema involves importing these .ldf files into Active Directory. In Exchange 2000 and 2003, it was technically possible to import the .ldf files into Active Directory manually using LDIFDE (Microsoft KB 237677). Manual import of the 100 .ldf files for Exchange 2007 (numbered schema0.ldf through schema99.ldf) is not supported in Exchange 2007. It is both easier and required to simply run Exchange setup.com from the command line with the /PrepareSchema switch shown in Figure 4-4 if the schema is to be extended independent of other steps in the installation of Exchange 2007. During the process, the .ldf files are written to a temp folder on the domain controller and deleted as they are imported into Active Directory. In a typical installation, preparing Active Directory is performed automatically through the Exchange 2007 Setup Wizard, assuming the security context of the individual logged in includes membership in the Schema Admins group.

In some companies, anything affecting Active Directory, especially the schema, may be the responsibility of someone outside of the individuals who may be deploying Exchange 2007. Extending the schema may be performed independently by the Directory Administrator as a member of the Schema Admins group, separate from the Exchange installation, using the /PrepareSchema switch from setup.com. Running setup with the /PrepareSchema switch requires subsequent execution of the /PrepareAD switch.

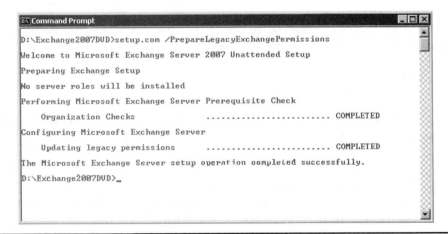

FIGURE 4-3 Exchange 2007 Setup.com with the /PrepareLegacyExchangePermissions parameter

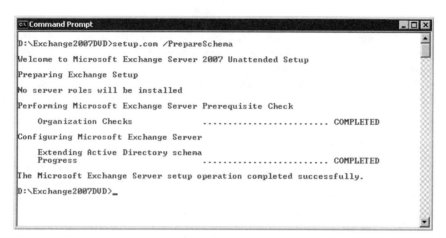

FIGURE 4-4 Preparing the Active Directory schema with setup.com in Exchange 2007

The /PrepareAD switch will perform the duties of the previous switches if they are necessary and not already completed. After the completion of the tasks of previous switches is verified, it creates Exchange universal security groups (USGs) and the Microsoft Exchange System Objects container in Active Directory. It also creates an Exchange 2007 administrative group and routing group for legacy Exchange coexistence. These groups, visible from the Exchange System Manager in versions 2000 and 2003, have specific names that must not be changed, nor can the Exchange 2007 server be removed from them when still supporting Exchange 2000 or 2003 in the organization. These groups are named as follows:

- Exchange administrative group (FYDIBOHF23SPDLT)
- Exchange routing group (DWBGZMFD01QNBJR)

NOTE *The group names chosen had to be sufficiently unique so that no enterprise would choose the same name. The letters chosen are not random, but rather one letter (or number) off going forward for the administrative group and backward for the routing group from EXCHANGE12ROCKS.*

The /PrepareAD switch also requires an Exchange organization name if one does not exist. If an Exchange 2000 or 2003 organization is being joined, one is not required. The syntax, as shown in Figure 4-5, is as follows:

```
>setup.com /PrepareAD /OrganizationName:<OrgName>
```

Exchange 2007 Organization Names

Exchange organization names tend to be basic descriptive top-level titles for the entire set of Exchange servers in the forest. They represent an internal administrative name similar to a NetBIOS domain name for Windows. Organization names have specific limitations of what characters can be used. The Exchange organization name cannot contain the characters listed in Table 4-1.

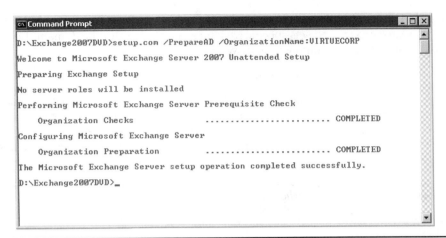

Figure 4-5 Exchange 2007 command-line setup with the /PrepareAD switch for the organization VIRTUECORP

Preparing the Domains

Every domain that will host Exchange 2007 servers or objects needs to be prepared as well. These objects include mail-enabled contacts, mail-enabled users, and distribution groups. Like AD preparation, the Exchange 2007 Setup Wizard will automatically prepare the domain that Exchange is being installed in if this is not done already. Companies may want domain preparation to be complete prior to Exchange installation, or they will

	Description		Description
~	Tilde	{ }	Braces
`	Grave accent	[ ]	Brackets
!	Exclamation mark			Vertical bar
@	At sign	\	Backslash
#	Number or pound sign	:	Colon
$	Dollar sign	;	Semicolon
%	Percent sign	" "	Quotation marks
^	Caret	'	Apostrophe
&	Ampersand	< >	Angle or markup brackets
*	Asterisk	,	Comma
( )	Parentheses	.	Period
_	Underscore	?	Question mark
+	Plus sign	/	Slash
=	Equal sign		Whitespace at beginning or end

Table 4-1 Characters Disallowed in Exchange 2007 Organization Names

just host Exchange objects but not Exchange servers. The /PrepareDomain switch creates Exchange-related groups and sets specific Exchange permissions for the domain. To prepare a specific domain from the command line, we enter the following:

```
>setup.com /PrepareDomain:<domainname>
```

If the <domainname> identifier is omitted, setup assumes the domain within which the command is being run. If you have many domains to prepare, you do not have to do so one at a time. The /PrepareAllDomains switch will add the necessary security groups to all the domains currently in the forest. If new domains are added after that and they are to host Exchange objects as well, they will still have to be prepared.

NOTE   *Setup.com preparation switches have abbreviations as well:*

- *Setup.com /PrepareLegacyExchangePermissions: setup.com /pl*
- *Setup.com /PrepareSchema: setup.com /ps*
- *Setup.com /PrepareAD: setup.com /p*
- *Setup.com /PrepareDomain: setup.com /pd*
- *Setup.com /PrepareAllDomains: setup.com /pad*

If Exchange 2000 or 2003 servers exist in the organization, if different people are to be assigned the different steps in preparation because of security or policy, or if the steps are to be completed over time by choice or network requirements, then the command-line parameters with setup.com should be executed in the order presented in this section.

Verifying That Active Directory Is Prepared

We can verify the setup steps by checking the presence of various attributes or groups in Active Directory.

An easy way to verify that the Active Directory schema has been successfully extended is to check the Exchange schema version point in AD using ADSIEdit. In ADSIEdit, expand the Schema container and the accompanying container therein. In the right pane, scroll down to the CN called ms-Exch-Schema-Version-Pt, as shown in Figure 4-6. If this value is set to 10637, the schema update was successful.

NOTE   *ADSIEdit is part of the Windows 2003 Support Tools, which reside on the Windows 2003 CD. They are not installed by default. They are installed from \support\tools\suptools.msi.*

It may also be necessary to allow for replication time. The same process can be used to verify that the schema updates have replicated by connecting to a different domain controller and isolating the rangeUpper attribute value.

SP1   *Exchange 2007 Service Pack 1 further extends the Active Directory schema. The ms-Exch-Schema-Version-Pt for SP1 is 11116.*

When /PrepareAD is run, it also prepares the domain from which it is run. To verify that the /PrepareAD steps were completed, we can look at Active Directory Users and Computers (ADUC) to see the groups created in that domain. These are shown in Figure 4-7.

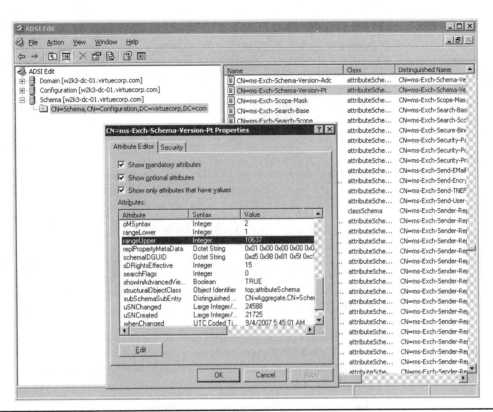

FIGURE 4-6   Verifying schema extensions with ADSIEdit

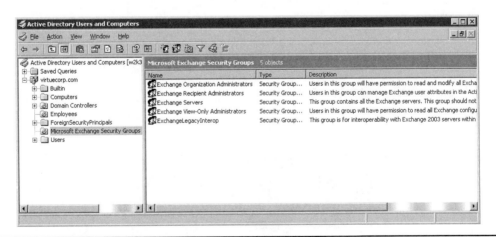

FIGURE 4-7   ADUC confirming the formation of Exchange groups

Verifying That a Domain Is Prepared

We can verify that the /PrepareDomain parameter was successful in a domain by checking the groups formed in ADUC as we did for /PrepareAD. The Exchange Install Domain Servers group should be a member of the Exchange Servers group in the root domain. In ADUC, select the Microsoft Exchange Security Groups object on the left and then double-click the group Exchange Servers in the right pane. The Members tab should include the Exchange Install Domain Servers group, as shown in Figure 4-8.

NOTE   *To see the Microsoft Exchange System Objects container in Active Directory Users and Computers, select View | Advanced Features in ADUC. The Exchange Install Domain Servers group resides there.*

We can also verify permissions on the Manage Auditing and Security Log policy on any domain controller in the domain where setup /PrepareDomain (or setup /PrepareAD) has been run. This policy is found in the Local Policy on a domain controller accessed through the Group Policy editor. On a Windows 2003 domain controller, select Start | Run and then type **MMC** and press ENTER (or click OK). This opens a Management Console template. Now select File | Add/Remove Snap-ins. From the new dialog box, ensure that the Standalone tab is active and then select the Add button at the bottom to show a list of available snap-ins. Select the Group Policy Object editor to activate the Group Policy Object Wizard. Leave the Group Policy Object selected as Local Computer. Click the Finish button and then OK to clear the open windows. Back in the MMC, we can now expand the Local Computer Policy as shown in Figure 4-9 with the path Computer Configuration | Windows Settings |

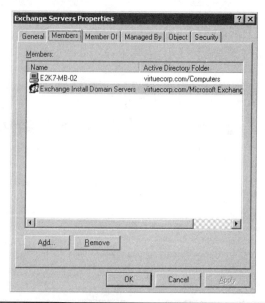

FIGURE 4-8   Members of the Exchange Servers group in ADUC, with the Exchange Install Domain Server group highlighted

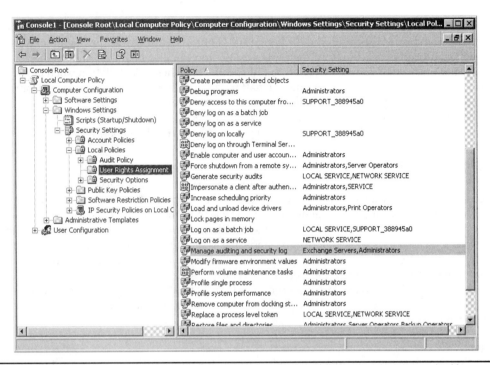

FIGURE 4-9   The Domain Controller Group Policy Object editor showing the permissions on the Manage Auditing and Security Log

Security Settings | Local Policies | User Rights Assignment. Now in the right pane the policy Manage Auditing and Security Log should show Exchange Servers beside the default entry of Administrators, unless previously changed.

Multiforest Considerations

The Active Directory forest is the de facto security boundary for Windows. If Exchange is to be deployed in multiple forests, such as a resource forest, or if separate Exchange organizations have to collaborate more directly through a merger or acquisition for example, then a trust relationship between the two forests must be established. In an Exchange 2007 environment with Outlook 2007, this allows forest-to-forest delegation as well as viewing cross-forest free/busy information. The minimum domain functional level for this cross-forest Exchange functionality is Windows 2003 native, which is a step up from the minimum Windows 2000 native level for installing Exchange 2007 in one forest.

Installing Exchange 2007 Server

There are many scenarios into which an Exchange 2007 server may be deployed. Installing a new Exchange 2007 server in a new organization is the simplest. It is also common to join an existing Exchange 2000/2003 organization. The different scenarios and roles needed determine the type of installation used.

Installation Types

Exchange can be installed with the Exchange 2007 Setup Wizard by running setup.exe or allowing autorun to execute from the DVD. Installation can also be initiated from the command line as well. This is required to call specific switches at installation, such as the switches to prepare AD and the domain. Unattended installations are also initiated from the command line. Setup can also be called from a Windows PowerShell script.

The Exchange 2007 Setup Wizard identifies two types of setup called Typical and Custom. If Exchange 2007 is already installed, the Setup Wizard opens in Maintenance mode.

Typical Installation

A Typical Exchange 2007 installation includes the primary Exchange server roles of Client Access Server, Hub Transport server, and Mailbox server. In addition, a Typical installation will include the Exchange Management Tools. These tools include the Exchange Management Console, the Exchange management help files, and the Exchange cmdlets for the Exchange Management Shell. All the steps in a Typical installation are also in a Custom installation. We will walk through a Custom installation to see the additional steps and options while still covering all the steps for a Typical install.

Exchange 2007 Setup.exe launches the Exchange 2007 Setup Wizard. The wizard shows a checklist broken down into three separate sections. Installing Exchange 2007 is as easy as PIE: Plan, Install, and Enhance.

Plan

The link shown in the Plan area of the setup application simply directs the default browser to the Microsoft TechNet website covering Exchange 2007 documentation. The level of Exchange documentation at Microsoft has improved over the last several versions of Exchange Server.

Install

This section of the wizard covers the primary prerequisites and actual installation of Exchange 2007. If the base server for the installation is Windows 2003 with Service Pack 1, the prerequisites of Windows PowerShell, .NET Framework 2.0, and MMC 3.0 may still be required. Windows 2003 Service Pack 2 includes MMC 3.0, and launching setup.exe will open a window like the one shown in Figure 4-10. As we have shown earlier in this chapter, it is not necessary to wait until setup is launched to install prerequisites.

Enhance

The final section introduces the administrator to additional Microsoft services and applications that can be used in complement with Exchange 2007.

Exchange Hosted Services   Microsoft is trying not to miss the trend toward Software as a Service (SaaS). Exchange Server is solid candidate for an application that can be accessed from a hosted environment instead of maintained in house, especially in an increasingly mobile environment. Exchange Hosted Services can also host a company's MX records and provide message hygiene functionality before the content makes it to the company's Exchange server.

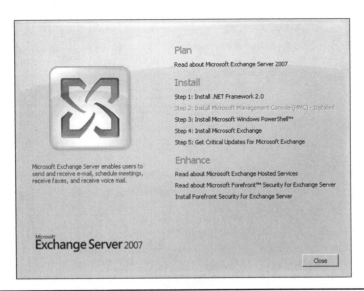

FIGURE 4-10   Exchange 2007 Setup Wizard showing the installation checklist

Forefront Security for Exchange   Forefront Security for Exchange extends the message hygiene functionality to include malware prevention services. In this case, malware is any threat to the network arriving through the medium of e-mail. The addition of Forefront Security is a direct result of Microsoft's acquisition of the popular antivirus solution called Antigen® from Sybari. The Exchange 2007 Setup Wizard provides a link to download Forefront Security. Exchange Enterprise CALs are required to take advantage of Forefront Security for Exchange.

Custom Installation—Graphic Interface

Fulfilling these prerequisites in the Install section allows the administrator to launch the Exchange installation. The interface is different from predecessors, yet very reasonable to use. The first screen introduces Exchange 2007 and the Setup Wizard, as shown in Figure 4-11, even claiming Exchange is the industry's leading unified messaging server. Clicking the Next button will take us to the license agreement.

Throughout the Setup Wizard and the Exchange Management Console, Exchange suggests that the administrator use CTRL-C to copy the window contents. For the license agreement screen, it only presents the offer to print the agreement. Regardless, accepting the license agreement is mandatory to continue the installation.

Clicking Next presents the option to allow error messages to be automatically sent to Microsoft as shown in Figure 4-12. Sending in error reports should be mutually beneficial, giving direction to Microsoft as to where problems may exist and directing the user to resolutions or workarounds if possible. These reports are also fairly secure over HTTPS to a secure facility. The option defaults to No. Depending on your personal preference or your company's policy, you can leave it at that default or change the radio button to Yes.

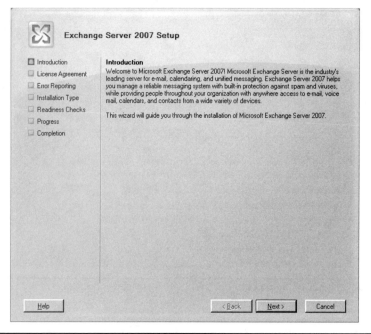

FIGURE 4-11   Exchange 2007 Setup Wizard introduction

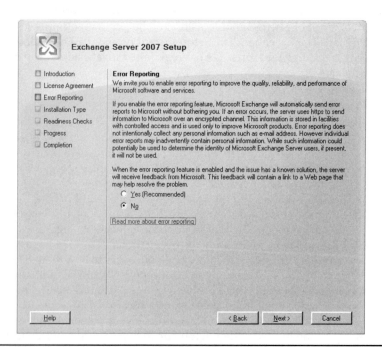

FIGURE 4-12   The Exchange 2007 Setup Wizard's error-reporting option

The next screen provides the option for a Typical installation or a Custom installation. The descriptions themselves are the buttons for selecting the installation type. We will talk about the Custom installation a little later in this chapter. The Typical installation includes the three primary Exchange Server roles and the Exchange Management Tools. The Client Access Server, Hub Transport, and Mailbox roles will all be installed on this server. For a small enterprise this is a very common installation. As shown in Figure 4-13, the administrator can also choose where to install the Exchange binaries, with the default being C:\Program Files\Microsoft\Exchange Server\.

The Custom installation allows the implementer to select the roles to install on this server. Custom installation must also be chosen if a clustered environment is being installed, if the Edge Transport server role is being installed, or if just the Management Tools are needed. Figure 4-14 outlines the different options available for a Custom installation. This is where Custom differs from a Typical installation.

The roles found in a typical installation can be selected from the list or any combination, including the Unified Messaging role and the Exchange Management Tools. If the Edge Transport role is selected, all the other role options become grayed out because the Edge role must be the only role installed and reside on a separate standalone server. The concept of front-end/back-end servers introduced in Exchange 2000 is also applied to the role-based architecture. The Client Access Server role when selected independent of the Mailbox role serves as the front end in Exchange 2007. In Figure 4-14, just below the Edge Transport role option is where Exchange 2007 cluster nodes are selected. The Custom installation provides the choice of Active Clustered Mailbox Role and Passive Clustered Mailbox Role. We will cover the Clustered Mailbox roles in Chapter 19 on high availability.

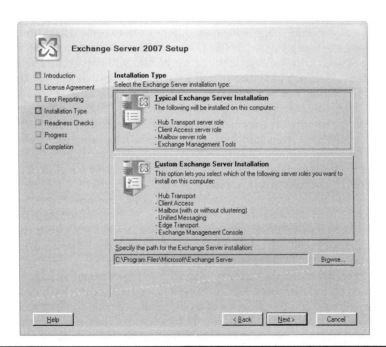

Figure 4-13 Exchange 2007 Setup Wizard's Typical and Custom installation options

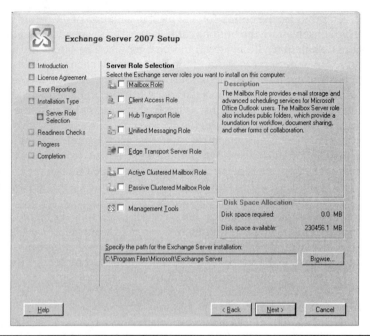

FIGURE 4-14 The Exchange 2007 Setup Wizard's Custom installation options

The Server Role Selection page is the only difference between Custom and Typical installations using the Setup Wizard. If this is a new installation into a forest where Exchange has not been installed before, the Setup Wizard will request an Exchange organization name as shown in Figure 4-15. If we were joining an Exchange 2000 or 2003 organization, there would not be a prompt for a new name; however, setup will request an Exchange 2003 bridgehead server to connect to the Exchange 2007 routing group.

After selecting a reasonable organization name that meets the limitations discussed earlier in this chapter, the administrator has to consider whether the enterprise is supporting any Entourage or legacy Outlook clients on the next screen, shown in Figure 4-16. In this case, *legacy* is any Outlook client earlier than Outlook 2007. Only Outlook 2007 so far can take advantage of the AutoDiscover web service, which is needed for accessing Free/Busy information, Out of Office functionality, and Auto-account creation. Other clients, such as Outlook 2003 and earlier and Entourage, will need to access this information through the use of public folders as in previous Exchange versions. Public folders can be added later if No is selected here. This option is only asked if this is the first Exchange 2007 Mailbox server role in the organization.

The next screen starts the testing for prerequisites. These are similar to the readiness checks performed by the Exchange 2007 Readiness Check scan using ExBPA. Figure 4-17 shows the roles selected and the progress of the readiness checks. To illustrate the type of information the readiness checks return, we omitted some of the prerequisites. Figure 4-18 identifies in the organization check in the user interface that the domain is still in Mixed mode. This failure will prevent the Exchange installation from continuing. There is also a

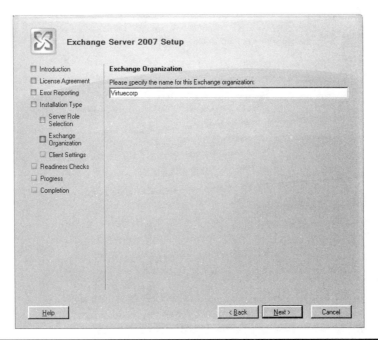

FIGURE 4-15   The Exchange 2007 Setup Wizard's new Exchange organization name option

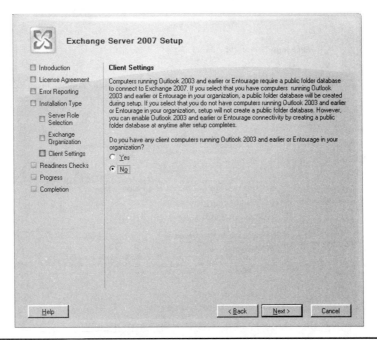

FIGURE 4-16   The Exchange 2007 Setup Wizard's Outlook 2003 and Entourage support with Public Folders option

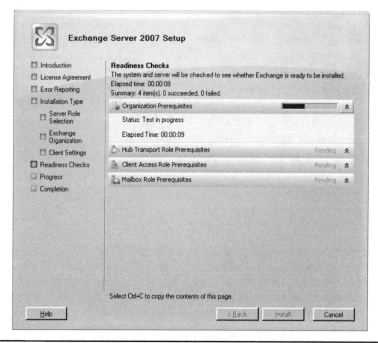

Exchange 2007 Setup Wizard running readiness checks for the selected roles

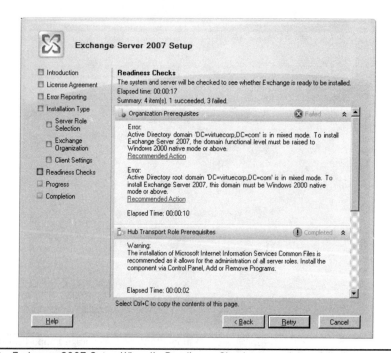

FIGURE 4-18   Exchange 2007 Setup Wizard's Readiness Check prerequisites failed

warning for the Hub Transport that IIS is not installed and is recommended. Microsoft does make it relatively easy to document this output by allowing the result content to be copied to the Clipboard using CTRL-C without having to manipulate the text or the window.

If the World Wide Web service is not installed and running when the Exchange 2007 Setup Wizard is launched, the wizard will have to be closed and restarted because this will return an error in the readiness checks. After the readiness checks are complete, as shown in Figure 4-19, the button formerly labeled Next is now labeled Install. Again, the contents can be copied if necessary, but as you will learn, this has also been logged in the Setup logs.

After you click Install, the wizard displays the progress of the Exchange installation. Figure 4-20 shows the progress of the installation for the organization preparation, which is identified as the Active Directory schema update. If the forest and domain preparation steps were not run from the command line ahead of time, the Exchange 2007 Setup Wizard will walk through the steps for setup.com with the /PrepareAD switch covering the domain in which it is being installed.

Finally, Figure 4-21 reflects the completion of the steps for installing Exchange 2007. The binaries may be in place, but there are a few more things to do to ensure the installation is complete. These are summarized in the post-installation task list, which we cover just a little later in this chapter.

The three most important ones are to enter the Exchange 2007 license key, run Microsoft Update, and then run ExBPA. Currently, Microsoft Update reveals Exchange 2007 Update rollup version 4 released in late August 2007. The rollup patches are cumulative and will also be rolled into Service Pack 1. Exchange 2007 is now installed.

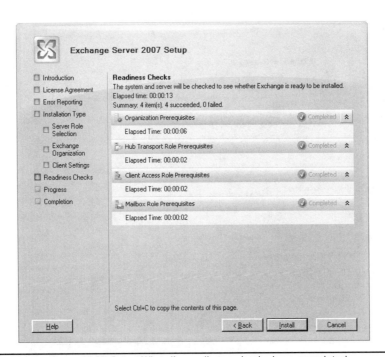

FIGURE 4-19   The Exchange 2007 Setup Wizard's readiness checks have completed

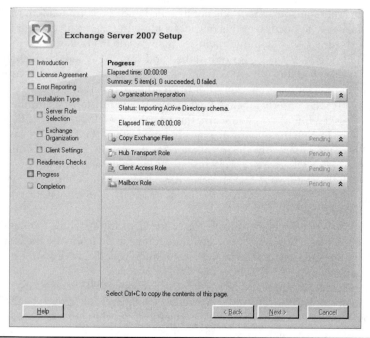

FIGURE 4-20 The Exchange 2007 Setup Wizard's progress for Exchange installation

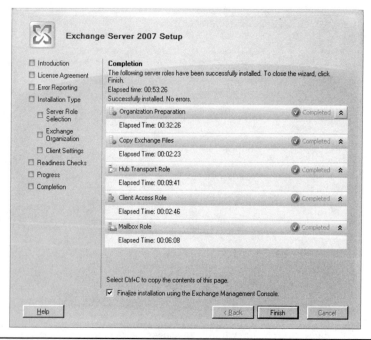

FIGURE 4-21 Exchange 2007 installation complete

ExSetup.exe

After Exchange 2007 is installed, modifying or uninstalling Exchange 2007 requires either the Add/Remove Programs applet in the Control Panel, or ExSetup.exe, which is found in %programfiles%\Microsoft\Exchange Server\bin\. There are several modes for using ExSetup. These are listed from the command line by calling exsetup /help.

- **/mode:Install**   Add a new role to an existing Exchange 2007 Server.
- **/mode:Uninstall**   Remove a role or uninstall Exchange 2007 Server.
- **/mode:Upgrade**   Upgrade an Exchange 2007 Server role.
- **/mode:RecoverServer**   Recover an existing Exchange 2007 server with AD configuration information.

ExSetup is also used to configure an existing server for participation in a clustered configuration and to add or remove Unified Messaging Language Packs. To add the Mailbox role to an existing Exchange 2007 server, ExSetup could be used as follows:

```
>exsetup.exe /mode:install /role Mailbox
```

Management Tools Installation

Some administrators, through preference or corporate policy, use the Management Tools for Exchange installed on their workstation or a management server rather than using RDP through Remote Desktop to the Exchange server. The 64-bit requirement for Exchange 2007 adds some challenges to this strategy because the Management Tools are not immune from this requirement. The Exchange Management Tools also require Microsoft Management Console (MMC) 3.0, .NET Framework 2.0, and Windows PowerShell to be installed prior to the Management Tools being installed.

The Management Tools' only role is installed through setup by selecting only the Management Tools option from the Server Role Selection interface, shown back in Figure 4-14.

Selecting just the Management Tools role installs the following applications:

- Exchange Management Console (EMC)
- Exchange Management Shell (EMS)
- Exchange Help file (exhelp.chm)
- Microsoft Exchange Best Practices Analyzer Tool
- Exchange Troubleshooting Assistant Tool

SP1 *Exchange 2007 Service Pack 1 adds support for the 64-bit versions of Windows Vista and Windows Server 2008 for the Exchange 2007 Management Tools installation.*

Install Exchange 2007 into Existing Exchange 2000/2003 Environment

When Exchange 2007 is installed into an environment where Exchange 2000 or 2003 already exists, setup does a few things differently. Setup will recognize the existing organization in its discovery checks. There are a few components installed that allow Exchange 2007 to coexist with Exchange 2000/2003.

Exchange 2007 does not use routing groups, but rather it depends on Active Directory sites for its routing infrastructure. When Exchange 2007 is installed with the first Hub Transport role into an Exchange 2000/2003 organization, it creates a special routing group called the Exchange routing group (DWBGZMFD01QNBJR), as mentioned earlier. Setup will prompt for an Exchange 2003 bridgehead to connect to this routing group, as shown in Figure 4-22. Only one bidirectional connection is needed to create a single conduit between all the Exchange 2007 servers and the legacy routing topology. This routing group connector is called Interop RGC by default. We will cover the routing group connector in Chapter 5 on transitioning and migrating.

Setup also creates a separate Administrative group called the Exchange administrative group (FYDIBOHF23SPDLT) where the Exchange 2007 servers sit for coexistence purposes. Changing the membership or names of these two groups is not supported by Microsoft.

Additionally, Exchange 2007 setup will also create a universal global group called ExchangeLegacyInterop. This group is granted the permissions necessary to send e-mail from Exchange 2000/2003 to the special Exchange 2007 routing group. The routing and administrative groups for Exchange 2007 are visible in Exchange 2000/2003 Exchange System Manager. Microsoft advises, however, that only the Exchange 2007 tools be used to administer Exchange 2007 servers, whereas Exchange 2003 tools should be used for Exchange 2003.

Provision Server and Delegate Setup

For administrators who are not Exchange administrators for the organization but who may still be needed to install Exchange 2007, Microsoft provides a mechanism for assigning permissions to a group or account to facilitate Exchange installation. Provisioning creates

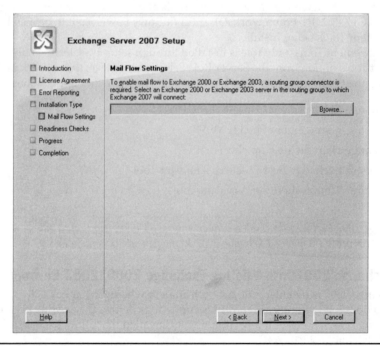

FIGURE 4-22 Exchange 2007 Setup Wizard requesting a routing group bridgehead server

the server object and grants the user or group the minimum permissions needed to install Exchange 2007.

This is accomplished through a pair of parameters in setup.com, as follows:

```
>setup.com /NewProvisionedServer:E2K7-MB-03 /ServerAdmin:VIRTUECORP\Ceriana
```

If no server name is included after the /NewProvisionedServer switch, setup assumes the local server. The /ServerAdmin switch can be a user or a group.

Edge Transport Server Installation

As we mentioned, when doing a custom installation, you have an option to select the Edge Transport role. When you do so, all the other roles become grayed out because the Edge role operates separate from the domain. (Likewise, when other roles are selected the Edge role is grayed out.) Edge Transport servers have the same prerequisites as internal Exchange servers, including the software requirements, such as .NET Framework 2.0 and PowerShell.

Prior to installing an Edge Transport server, you need to add a DNS suffix to the standalone server on which it is to reside.

DNS Suffix and Settings for the Edge Transport Server

Internal Exchange servers are members of an Active Directory domain and dynamically get assigned Fully Qualified Domain Names (FQDNs) and appear in DNS. The Edge Transport server is external to the AD forest and needs to have DNS configured prior to installation.

Edge servers communicate with Hub Transport servers and vice versa, but each does not know about the other by default. They need to be able to use hostname resolution to facilitate message flow. To enter a DNS suffix for the standalone Windows 2003 server that will host the Edge Transport role, right-click the My Computer icon on the desktop (or in the Start menu) and select Properties. In the Computer Name tab, select the Change button followed by the More button to get to the DNS Suffix and NetBIOS Computer Name window, as shown in Figure 4-23. Add the DNS suffix for this server in the box. The DNS suffix is the domain or subdomain name that would appear after the hostname in an FQDN.

The hostname and DNS suffix of the Edge Transport servers need to be published in the internal DNS used by the Hub Transport servers so they can find Edge servers. Likewise,

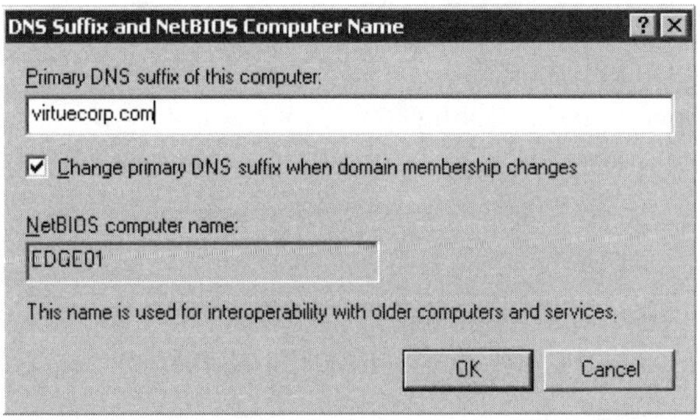

FIGURE 4-23   DNS suffix and NetBIOS name configuration for the Edge Transport server

the names of the Hub Transport servers need to be available in the DNS that is used by internal network interface on the Edge servers. Prior to installing the Edge Transport with setup, test the name resolution between the Edge and Hub transports with nslookup, or ping by FQDN.

Multiple Edge Transport servers may be used for redundancy or for larger enterprises with multiple gateways or capacity requirements. Round-robin DNS could be used as a load-balancing technique for busy SMTP gateways.

Cloning Edge Transport Servers

Edge servers are standalone entities typically deployed in a perimeter network. They do not have a built-in mechanism for sharing configuration information. Microsoft provides a means of "cloning" Edge servers. Really, it is a matter of exporting configurations so that they can be imported on another server. This also represents a means of backing up settings that may have many hours of administrative work invested in them. This is not the same as cloning an installation with disk-imaging software, which is not supported for Exchange servers.

In the scripts folder on the DVD are two PowerShell scripts to assist in moving configuration information from one Edge server to another: ExportEdgeConfig.ps1 and ImportEdgeConfig.ps1. The main section of the first script that identifies what is being exported is an array (called $cloneItems) of cmdlets, as listed here:

- "Get-TransportServer $MachineName"
- "Get-AcceptedDomain"
- "Get-RemoteDomain"
- "Get-TransportAgent"
- "Get-SendConnector"
- "Get-ReceiveConnector"
- "Get-ContentFilterConfig"
- "Get-SenderIdConfig"
- "Get-SenderFilterConfig"
- "Get-RecipientFilterConfig"
- "Get-AddressRewriteEntry"
- "Get-AttachmentFilterEntry"
- "Get-AttachmentFilterListConfig"
- "Get-IPAllowListEntry | where {`$_.IsMachineGenerated -eq `$false}"
- "Get-IPAllowListProvider"
- "Get-IPAllowListConfig"
- "Get-IPAllowListProvidersConfig"
- "Get-IPBlockListEntry | where {`$_.IsMachineGenerated -eq `$false}"
- "Get-IPBlockListProvider"
- "Get-IPBlockListConfig"

- "Get-IPBlockListProvidersConfig"
- "Get-ContentFilterPhrase"
- "Get-SenderReputationConfig"

This is the majority of the configuration content that gets written to an intermediary .xml file to allow for import on another Edge server. You can run the script from the Exchange Management Shell on the source Edge server by specifying an export file as follows:

```
>./ExportEdgeConfig.ps1 -CloneConfigData:"C:\Export\CloneConfigData_edge01.xml"
```

SP1   *The Exchange 2007 SP1 DVD adds a few scripts to the scripts folder. There is only one change to the ExportEdgeConfig.ps1 script. In SP1, the Get-TransportConfig cmdlet is added to the list of $cloneItems. The .xml file needs to be manually moved from the source server to somewhere accessible to the destination server. On the destination Edge Transport server, run the ImportEdgeConfig.ps1 script to capture the same settings exported from the source Edge Transport server. The import can create an answer file for troubleshooting any configurations it deems incompatible with the destination server. In the following example, the filename CloneConfigAnswer.xml is used for the answer file in the command:*

```
>./ImportEdgeConfig.ps1 -CloneConfigData:"C:\Import\CloneConfigData_edge01
.xml" -IsImport $false -CloneConfigAnswer:"C:\Import\CloneConfigAnswer.xml"
```

The export does not include the EdgeSync settings for ADAM and must be configured independently. The ADAM service must also be running for both the export and import of these settings.

Exchange 2007 Service Pack 1 Installation

As of this writing, Exchange 2007 Service Pack 1 has not yet been released, but it is very close and the features in it are set. The first thing of note if you're downloading SP1 from download.microsoft.com or MSDN is the size of the download—over 850MB for the 64-bit version. Service Pack 1 is rolled into the Exchange 2007 RTM product. When Service Pack 1 is released, administrators will be able to run a full Exchange setup from the Exchange 2007 Service Pack 1 DVD or network sharepoint. This is important to meet prerequisites at the time of installation. For example, Exchange 2007 needs SP1 to install on Windows Server 2008. This will not be a problem because SP1 is streamlined into RTM.

Command-line Upgrade or Installation

Setup.com adds a new mode to the switch /mode, which is used to tell Exchange SP1 that it is doing an upgrade from RTM to SP1. The upgrade checks what roles are installed, updates the schema in AD, and installs new binaries for Exchange. For the complete upgrade from the command line, we use the /mode switch as follows:

```
>setup.com /mode:Upgrade
```

The output on a typical Exchange 2007 server is shown in Figure 4-24.

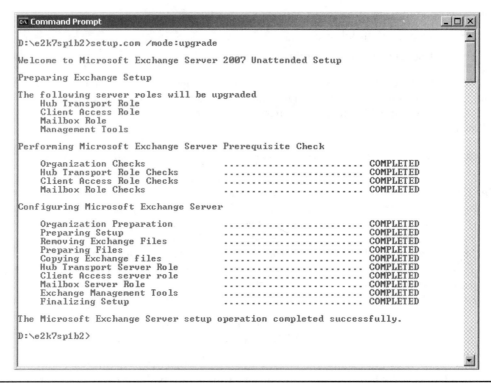

FIGURE 4-24   Exchange 2007 Service Pack 1 upgrade mode installation

All the other prerequisites and steps we considered earlier in the chapter still apply to the Exchange 2007 with Service Pack 1 installation. Full installations performed with the Service Pack 1 media is done just as though it was the original RTM product.

Automated Installations

Not everyone wants to sit and wait for each individual step to complete in setup to proceed to the next one. Automated installations allow Exchange 2007 setup to follow through from start to finish without administrator intervention along the way.

Setup.com–Power Tool

Setup.com run from the DVD (or after installation from the command line) is the Swiss army knife of Exchange 2007 installation modifications. First, setup.com has multiple modes that are listed explicitly using setup.com with the /? switch, as shown in Figure 4-25. The default mode is Install. Also, many parameters are available to specify advanced actions for setup to apply specific settings to.

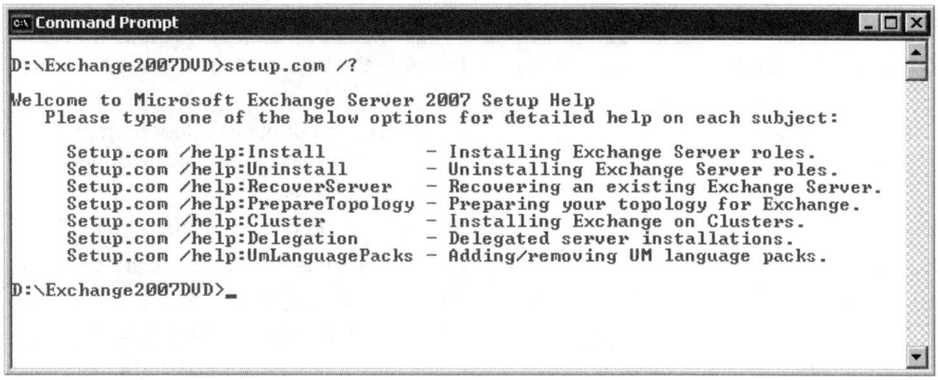

FIGURE 4-25   Exchange 2007 Setup.com command line with the help switch

SP1   *Using setup.com from the Exchange 2007 Service Pack 1 media adds the mode of upgrade to the list assigned to the parameter /mode.*

Many parameters can be implemented with setup.com, as reflected in Table 4-2.

Windows 2008 Server separates the IP address switch for CMS into IPv4 and IPv6 with the switches /CMSIpv4Addresses, /CMSIpv4Networks, and /CMSIpv6Networks.

Setup Switch Name	Abbreviation	Description
/Mode	/m	Runs setup in one of the following modes: Install (default), Uninstall, RecoverServer, PrepareTopology, Cluster, Delegation, or UmLanguagePacks.
/Role	/r	The Exchange Server roles used in conjunction with the /mode parameter. Multiple roles are separated by a comma.
/OrganizationName	/on	Required for the first Exchange server in the forest.
/TargetDir	/t	Destination folder to install the Exchange binaries.
/SourceDir	/s	Source folder for Exchange binaries.
/UpdatesDir	/u	Designated folder for updates to call during installation.
/DomainController	/dc	Used to choose a specific domain controller for setup to contact. Important if not all DCs are at the required OS level.
/AnswerFile	/a	Calls a text file with responses for certain configuration parameters.

TABLE 4-2   Exchange 2007 Setup.com Command-line Switches

Setup Switch Name	Abbreviation	Description
/DoNotStartTransport	–	Prevents the transport service from starting immediately.
/EnableLegacyOutlook	–	Allows creation of public folder storage for OAB and Free/Busy access to legacy Outlook and Entourage clients.
/EnableErrorReporting	–	Sends crash reports to Microsoft silently.
/NoSelfSignedCertificates	–	Disables automatic SSL certificate creation.
/AdamLdapPort	–	Configures a nondefault LDAP port to use for the ADAM instance. The default is 50389.
/AdamSslPort	–	Configures a nondefault LDAP SSL port for use with the ADAM instance. The default is 50636.
/AddUmLanguagePack	–	Adds the Unified Messaging Language Pack for available languages.
/RemoveUmLanguagePack	–	Removes Unified Messaging Language Pack.
/NewProvisionedServer	/nprs	Creates a server object and minimum permissions for delegated installation.
/RemoveProvisionedServer	/rprs	Removes unwanted provisioned servers from AD.
/ServerAdmin	–	User or group to be assigned to the NewProvisionedServer parameter.
/ForeignForestFQDN	–	Creates Exchange universal groups in an external forest, such as a resource forest.
/NewCMS	–	Creates a new clustered mailbox server (CMS). A new CMS can only hold the Mailbox role.
/RemoveCMS	–	Removes a CMS.
/RecoverCMS	–	Pulls CMS information from Active Directory after a reinstall of CMS.
/CMSName	/cn	Names the local CMS server independent of the Windows cluster.
/CMSIpAddress	/cip	Designates the IP address for the CMS.
/CMSSharedStorage	/css	Designates that the CMS uses shared storage.
/CMSDataPath	/cdp	The absolute path to the shared data storage location.

TABLE 4-2   Exchange 2007 Setup.com Command-line Switches *(continued)*

Unattended Installations

Unattended installations of Exchange 2007 are run from the Windows command line using setup.com with specific parameters. For some advanced configurations, an optional answer file can be called during installation. Setup.com is a powerful tool for installing, modifying, and uninstalling Exchange 2007.

Unattended Install Answer File

An answer file for an unattended Exchange 2007 installation is not as comprehensive as the .ini answer file used in Exchange 2003. For Exchange 2007, this is a .txt file covering any combination of the following subset of configuration switches from setup.com:

Setup.com Configuration switches for use in an unattended install answer file	
CMSName	CMSIPAddress
CMSIPAddress	ServerAdmin
CMSSharedStorage	ForeignForestFQDN
CMSDataPath	OrganizationName
NewCMS	DoNotStartTransport
RemoveCMS	UpdatesDir
RecoverCMS	EnableErrorReporting
UpgradeCMS	NoSelfSignedCertificates
EnableLegacyOutlook	AdamLdapPort
CMSName	

PowerShell Installations

No PowerShell cmdlets contribute to the installation process specifically; however, executables, such as setup.com, can be called from a .ps1 file or from PowerShell or the Exchange Management Shell. Configuration of Exchange can be managed through the Exchange Management Shell. With that combination, it is possible to generate PowerShell scripts to automate and provision Exchange 2007 installations.

Finalizing Installations

The post-installation task list mentioned earlier represents some steps to take to finalize an installation. Namely, entering the license key and running ExBPA. In addition to that, it is recommended that you create a Windows and Exchange backup after verifying a successful installation.

Post-installation Task List

After installation using the Setup Wizard, Exchange directs the implementer to a list of tasks to be completed after Exchange is installed. As shown in Figure 4-26, the Exchange Server 2007 Finalize Deployment window in the EMC lists the tasks and configuration settings needed to complete the installation. The content of this list depends on the roles that were installed on this server. This is where the 25-character product key is entered as the first item on the list.

Running the Exchange Best Practices Analyzer (ExBPA)

Running the Exchange Best Practices Analyzer is a recommended step at this point to verify the installation. It's also a way to identify potential configuration or security issues. The ExBPA appears on the Finalize Deployment list as the second task and should be executed

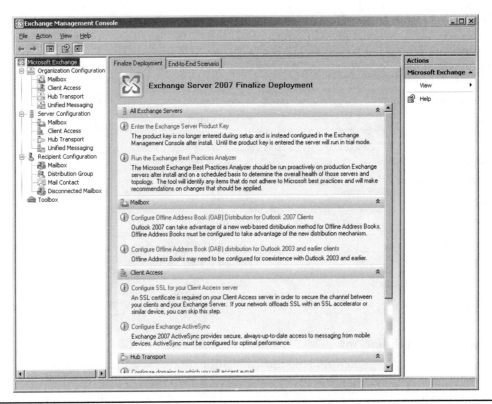

FIGURE 4-26   Exchange 2007 Management Console post-installation task list

on any Exchange 2007 installation. We will cover the ExBPA in more detail in Chapter 21 on troubleshooting.

Verifying Installation Success

After installation has completed, it is a good practice to confirm that intended outcome. There are a few places that an administrator can verify that an installation was successful, and a few tools are available to assist in this process.

Application Event Log

Exchange 2007, being an application running on Windows, reports issues and errors to the Application Event Log. This reporting starts with the setup process. The administrator can check the Application Event Log in Windows to address any warnings or errors if necessary.

Services

The Services applet in Administrative Tools will list the many Exchange Services that are installed by Exchange Server 2007. The Services listed there will depend on the Exchange roles installed on this server, but an administrator comfortable with the list may view them as evidence of a successful installation.

Exchange Setup Logs

By default, Exchange 2007 records setup activities in verbose mode in a pair of text-based log files, which are detailed in the following list. These files reside in %system_drive%\ ExchangeSetupLogs\ and can be parsed for errors that may require attention.

- **ExchangeSetup.msilog**   Reports on the extraction of Exchange binaries from the Microsoft installer files
- **ExchangeSetup.log**   Reports on every step of the installation process in verbose mode by default

The log file can be opened with a text editor and searched by keyword, most notably "error." Microsoft includes a PowerShell script in the scripts folder that allows for easy parsing of the ExchangeSetup.log file for errors. The script is located at \program files\microsoft\ exchange server\scripts\get-setuplog.ps1 and can be used in the following syntax:

```
>Get-SetupLog c:\exchangesetuplogs\exchangesetup.log - error -tree
```

The -error switch returns the errors and warnings only, whereas the -tree option formats the output for presentation in the shell. If the 32-bit evaluation version of Exchange was installed, a warning in the log will appear repeatedly indicating, "The 32-bit version of Exchange 2007 is not supported for production use."

Add/Remove Programs

Once installed, Exchange 2007 will appear in the Add/Remove Programs list, accessed through the Control Panel in Windows. The installation can be changed or removed from here.

Troubleshooting Installation Problems

The tools listed earlier for verifying Exchange 2007 installations are good at alerting the administrator to problems that arise during installation. The most valuable of these tools for troubleshooting is the Exchange setup log. It is verbose in its "play-by-play" of the installation process. If a call is needed to Microsoft Product Support Services (PSS), a copy of that setup log will most likely be requested to assist in troubleshooting. Parsing the setup log for errors will expose the errors and warnings from the installation process.

The most common errors seem to be attributed to missing prerequisites. Both the graphic interface for installing Exchange and the command-line method are good for reporting reasons for installation failures due to missing prerequisites.

Uninstalling Exchange 2007

Sometimes due to downsizing or server consolidation it may be necessary to formally uninstall an Exchange 2007 server or move roles between servers. The modular nature of the various roles makes it easier to add or remove them in an Exchange 2007 environment.

Removing Exchange Server Roles

Just as roles are installed in a somewhat modular fashion, they can be uninstalled in the same manner. Administrators can move the CAS role to another server without disrupting the integrity of the Mailbox role on that server, for example.

There are two mechanisms for modifying roles for an Exchange 2007 server. Add/ Remove Programs in Windows has a button labeled Change when you select the Microsoft Exchange Server 2007 item. This button launches the Exchange 2007 Setup Wizard in Maintenance Mode, as seen in Figure 4-27. The next step allows you to deselect roles you wish to uninstall.

The second option is to use setup.com. (Yes, you can use setup to uninstall items.) After installation, setup.com is located in %programfiles%\Microsoft\Exchange Server\bin, which is placed in the Path environment variable, so setup.com can be run without navigating to its source folder at the command line. Run setup.com or exsetup.exe in the uninstall mode, selecting the specific role(s) to remove, as follows:

```
>setup.com /mode:uninstall /role:ClientAccess,HubTransport,Mailbox
```

NOTE *Just like the parameters for preparing AD, the roles have abbreviations as well that can be used within the command line:*
HubTransport   *HT or H*
ClientAccess   *CA or C*
EdgeTransport   *ET or E*
Mailbox   *MB or M*
UnifiedMessaging   *UM or U*
ManagementTools   *MT or T*

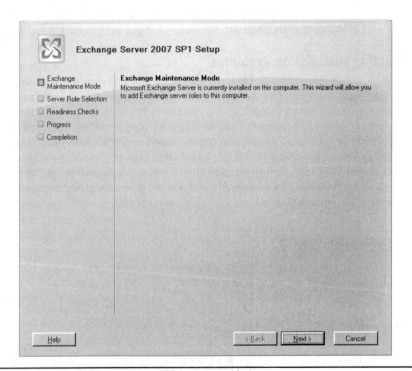

FIGURE 4-27   Exchange 2007 Setup Wizard Maintenance Mode

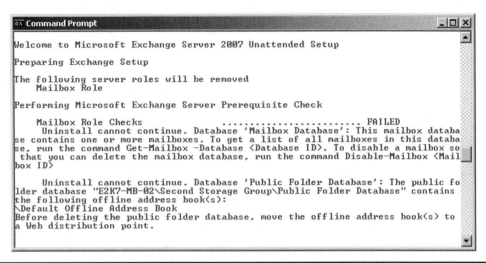

FIGURE 4-28   Exchange 2007 setup fails to remove the Mailbox role.

Removing the Mailbox role requires empty databases. If there are any mailboxes still resident in the databases on the server, the remove action will fail, as witnessed in Figure 4-28. In addition, the Mailbox role maintains the local public folder store if there is one. Any public folders need to be deleted or rehomed to other public folder servers before removing the Mailbox role.

Removing Exchange 2007 from a Server

Much like the options for removing the Exchange roles on the server, there are two ways to completely uninstall Exchange 2007 from a server. First is the standard Add/Remove Programs applet in the Control Panel. Clicking the Remove button with Exchange Server 2007 selected will begin the uninstall process. The Exchange 2007 Setup Wizard launches in Maintenance Mode, as shown in Figure 4-27. Make sure all the check boxes are cleared and then click Next to uninstall.

The second is to run setup.com or exsetup.exe from the command line using the /mode switch with the value uninstall, as shown here:

```
>setup.com /mode:uninstall
```

After uninstalling the server, you can manually delete the database store and associated transaction logs.

Summary

Installing Exchange 2007 is more than just running setup.exe (or setup.com). There are several prerequisites to be aware of and preparation steps to consider. The role-based installation options provide some flexibility in server function. Overall, attention paid to the preparation and installation steps will help ensure a solid dependable Exchange 2007 deployment.

Transitioning and Migrating

There is a practical side to installing Exchange Server 2007 that requires intimate knowledge of your existing environment. In this chapter, we will look at how to take the installation procedures from the previous chapter and apply them to your existing messaging infrastructure so that you can transition or migrate to Exchange Server 2007.

Developing a Roadmap

Understanding where you are today and knowing exactly where you want to be are the two end points of your Exchange Server 2007 roadmap. There are tools that can assist you in documenting the existing environment if you do not already have documentation. There are specific methods for transition or migration to Exchange Server 2007 detailed by Microsoft. The tools and documentation available, however, may not be enough. Although there are a number of documented procedures for transitioning to Exchange Server 2007, business and technical decisions still have to be made that determine not only the path you will take, but also the experience your end users will have during and after the process is complete. These decisions will likely be unique for many environments. To cover all of your bases, you should develop a high-level roadmap that combines your business needs with the appropriate technical procedure.

Existing Environment

Documentation, it seems, is to administrators what Kryptonite is to Superman. It is understandable why documenting is such an unpleasant task. Technology in an IT shop is a moving target. Implementers of the technology are usually busy supporting the solution, so the documentation the company has is usually stored in the head of the person who implemented the solution. Discovery phases in most projects are mandatory because of this. In order to get to a point where all your messaging systems are running Exchange Server 2007, you will have to identify what the current landscape is. More than that, it is necessary to obtain full details on the state of each of the existing messaging servers and the other servers Exchange depends on, such as domain controllers. At a minimum you should run the Exchange Best Practices Analyzer (ExBPA) to help you discover the state of your existing environment (see Figure 5-1). Be sure to download the latest updates to ExBPA. Only versions 2.7 and higher support scanning Exchange 2007.

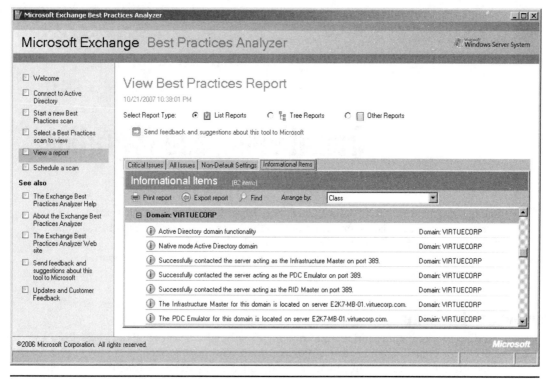

Figure 5-1   ExBPA Informational Items report

For the purposes of getting the most from this chapter, you should know which of the following existing environments you currently have:

- Exchange 5.5
- Exchange 2000
- Exchange 2003
- Mixed Exchange 5.5 and Exchange 2000 or Exchange 2003
- Lotus Notes 5.x, 6.x, or 7.x
- GroupWise
- POP/IMAP

Unfortunately, ExBPA only supports Exchange 2000 and higher. If you are running Exchange 5.5, you should use the Deployment Tools on the Exchange Server 2003 CD and the ExMAP tool from the Exchange Resource Kit, to document your existing environment and use that information to migrate to Exchange 2003 first. Microsoft does not provide a documentation tool for GroupWise, POP, or IMAP, but you can find planning information at Microsoft TechNet that will help you gather the information you will need for a migration. Microsoft does have documentation tools for Lotus Notes that are part of an extensive set of tool for Lotus Notes migrations.

Supported Paths

In the past, with previous upgrade paths from Exchange it has always been possible to do an "in-place" upgrade to the next version of Exchange. For example, if you were running Exchange 5.5, you could upgrade the same server to Exchange 2000. If you were running Exchange 2000, you could upgrade the same server to Exchange 2003. Granted, you could not do an in-place upgrade from Exchange 5.5 to Exchange 2003. However, up until Exchange 2007 you did not have to introduce a new piece of hardware if the hardware you had supported the new version. When you deploy Exchange 2007, you will have to introduce a new server into you environment (see Figure 5-2). Due to the extreme differences in the two architectures for storage, routing, and administration, there is no other way.

As a general rule, you want to choose a path that creates the least amount of disruption for your end users. To minimize human error, you also want to choose a path with the least amount of administrative effort. There are other factors that also influence the path you will define in your roadmap.

Roadmap Path Factors

The paths that are available limit your decisions on how you can go from your existing environment to Exchange Server 2007. But there are clearly two decisions you can make if your existing environment is Exchange 2000 or Exchange 2003. You can choose to transition or you can choose to migrate. Here are some common factors that affect the path you choose:

- The health and stability of the existing environment
- The number of forests or organizations
- The size of the organization
- The size of the mailboxes
- The administrative model

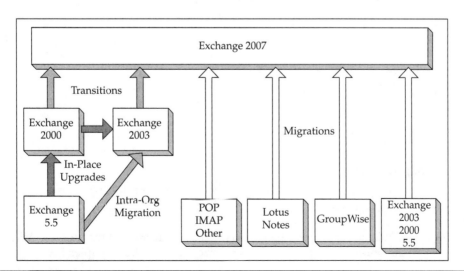

FIGURE 5-2 Paths to Exchange Server 2007

- The impact on users
- The impact on business
- Mergers, acquisitions, or divestitures
- The length of time the transition/migration is expected to take (coexistence)
- The cost/budget

Choosing a Path

Even though in-place upgrades appear to be an attractive way to get from point A to point B, they have their downsides. For instance, any server-related problems that exist tend to be carried over to the new environment. Because Exchange 2007 does not allow in-place upgrades, this will not likely be a problem. But for administrators who like to start with a clean slate when deploying new product, migrations tend to be the most attractive method of "upgrading," even when in-place upgrades were available.

What makes a transition desirable is the limited administrative effort necessary to allow the two versions of Exchange to co-exist together. Transitions allow you to move your mailbox and public folder resources to Exchange 2007 in a process that is virtually transparent to the end-users. There are technical situations where Transitions are not possible. Mergers, acquisitions, and upgrades from non-Exchange messaging systems will require migrations.

Incompatibilities

If you identify an existing feature in your production environment that users depend on that is not compatible with Exchange Server 2007, you must maintain the server that provides that feature. If that feature has an upgrade path, you can incorporate that into your roadmap. Otherwise, you must plan to coexist with the legacy server. Exchange 2000 Server has a number of features that are not compatible with Exchange 2003 or Exchange 2007. If you are running Exchange 2000, the following features will have to be migrated or disabled before you can fully transition to Exchange Server 2007:

- Microsoft Mobile Information Server event sync
- Instant Messaging Service
- Exchange Chat Service
- Exchange 2000 Conferencing Server
- Key Management Service
- cc:Mail connector
- MS Mail connector
- GroupWise connector
- Applications using unsupported APIs (see Chapter 1 for details)
- X.400 connectors

If you are transitioning from Exchange Server 2003, there are still features that Microsoft has chosen to discontinue using or has deemphasized the use of. In Chapter 1 we reviewed these features in detail. Here are a few Exchange Server 2003 features that can have an impact on your roadmap because they are not supported by Exchange 2007:

- Novell GroupWise connector
- Network News Transfer Protocol (NNTP)
- Microsoft Office Outlook Mobile Access
- Inter-Org Replication tool

Required Features

The roadmap you design will reflect the features that are required. Requirements can be desired and/or necessary. There may be a desire to have Unified Messaging, while there is a necessity to have a Hub Transport for messages to be delivered. Review the available features in Exchange Server 2007 and create a list of the ones required for your environment. Use the list of core features in Table 5-1 to help define the path you take.

You should extend this list to include any other requirements you can think of that will impact or influence your ability to transition or migrate.

Coexistence vs. Interoperability

Both transitions and migrations require that two messaging system be integrated together for the duration of the process. Microsoft supports two integration methods: coexistence and interoperability. When a transition or a migration to Exchange Server 2007 takes a lengthy period of time, some special consideration must be made to ensure that users with mailboxes on the legacy e-mail system and the Exchange 2007 server will be able to send/receive mail and collaborate with one another. Coexistence strategies are used for transitions from Exchange 2000 Server or Exchange Server 2003 to Exchange Server 2007, where all Exchange servers

Server Role	Feature	Required (Yes/No)
Client Access Server	Exchange ActiveSync	
	Outlook Web Access	
	POP3/IMAP4	
	Availability Service	
	AutoDiscovery	
Hub Transport Server	Messaging Policy and Compliance	
Mailbox Server	Messaging Records Management	
	Calendaring	
	High Availability (Clustering)	
Unified Messaging Server	Unified Messaging	
Edge Transport Server	Anti-Spam and Antivirus	

TABLE 5-1 Selecting Core Features

reside in the same Active Directory forest. Interoperability strategies must be used during migrations to Exchange Server 2007 from non-Exchange messaging systems, Exchange 5.5, or Exchange 2000/2003 servers that reside in a separate Active Directory forest.

Although a transition will have the least impact on an existing Exchange 2000 or Exchange 2003 organization, the longer the two versions of Exchange coexist with one another, the more obvious the incompatibilities will be. Therefore, it is probably in the best interest of an organization to transition as quickly as is possible and decommission the legacy servers. The size and complexity of an organization are usually the two biggest factors that determine the length of time a transition will take.

A migration will have greater visibility and impact on an existing messaging environment. Integration between two different messaging systems is not as easy or predictable as coexistence is. Migration tools are more complex and vary in their ability to fully migrate user information. Migrations do provide a great deal of flexibility and forgiveness that is not afforded by a transition. There is no "do-over" with a transition. But migration tools can simulate how a migration will go and can be run multiple times if necessary. Due to the nature of migrations, it is likely that they will take longer than a transition will take to get to Exchange Server 2007.

Transitioning and Coexistence

If you have experienced upgrading to a previous version of Exchange in the past, you will be pleasantly surprised at the ease with which you will be able to transition to Exchange Server 2007. Perhaps the most difficult of all upgrades was going from Exchange 5.5 to Exchange Server 2000. The migration term *intra-organization migration* was actually invented to describe the complex process of upgrading from Exchange 5.5 to Exchange 2000 or Exchange 2003. Up to that point the term *migration* was used to describe the process of going from another messaging system to Exchange Server. Although you will find it easier to transition from Exchange 2000/2003 to Exchange Server 2007, there are still some similarities with the intra-organization migration—as well as pitfalls that could lead to errors and failures.

Exchange Topologies

The Active Directory forest topology you support has an impact on how you transition or migrate. There are essentially three forest topologies in which Exchange can be implemented:

- Single forest
- Cross-forest
- Resource forest

Single-forest topologies are the most common. A single forest doesn't necessarily mean simple. However, from an Exchange administrative perspective it is the easiest to support. The majority of Exchange deployments will be transitioning from a single forest to a single forest (same forest).

Active Directory 2003 and higher support enhanced forest modes that Exchange Server can take advantage of. Your organization may currently support a multiforest topology where Exchange mailboxes reside in either multiple forests or where one forest is a dedicated Exchange resource forest. One key feature in particular, called an *inter-forest trust,* can allow two separate forests to authenticate between one another in a transitive nature. The inter-forest trust is only possible if the forests on both sides of the trust are running in 2003 forest mode. In your design for Exchange Server 2007, you may decide to take advantage of these features and transition your existing organization into a cross-forest or resource forest.

One of the characteristics of a cross-forest environment is the need to synchronize recipients. Because each forest maintains separate global catalogs, Exchange cannot display recipients in another forest. Tools do exist to synchronize the Exchange Global Address Book (GAL). Microsoft Identity Integration Server (MIIS) includes a GAL Synchronization tool. The Identity Integration Feature Pack for MIIS includes a lightweight version of the tool that can be downloaded from Microsoft for free. However, it is limited to synchronizing only two GALs. If you are supporting this topology and you wish to maintain it moving forward in Exchange Server 2007, you will need to continue to use the MIIS or the Identity Integration Feature Pack.

Another characteristic of a cross-forest environment is the need to replicate Free/Busy information between Exchange organizations. Outlook 2003 clients and earlier retrieve Free/Busy information for scheduling from public folders. The only tool that can replicate public folders between two Exchange organizations is the Inter-Org Replication Tool. There is specific support for the synchronization of the Free/Busy system folder. If you are currently supporting this tool, you must maintain the Exchange 2003 server it is configured to replicate with in both organizations. There is no support for the Inter-Org Replication Tool in Exchange Server 2007.

If you want to change the forest topology you currently support, it is possible to move recipients between forests. You will find that you have to combine both transition and migration tools to accomplish this.

Resource forest topologies seek to simplify support for multiforest environments. It allows Exchange administrators to host a single Exchange organization from a single forest and then allow user accounts in any number of other forests to authenticate against the "resource" forest. The benefit is that there is no need to synchronize GALs or replicate public folders and Free/Busy information. Exchange Server 2007 makes this topology even easier to support with the addition of a new recipient type called the *linked mailbox.* The linked mailbox simplifies managing the user account/mailbox in the resource forest. There are some known limitations for clients in a resource forest topology that you will want to investigate if you are considering this as a solution for your environment. For example, the Out of Office (OOF) messages do not work properly in this scenario.

Prerequisites for a Transition

The process for installing Exchange Server 2007 is covered in Chapter 4 in depth. Although there is some overlap, these prerequisites are supplemental to what we have already covered there.

Exchange 2007 Readiness Check

By running the Exchange 2007 Readiness Check that is included with the Exchange Best Practices Analyzer, version 2.7 or higher, you can discover other incompatibilities that are not quite as obvious. You will also find that the results of the scan can provide guidance as to how to prepare your organization for a transition (see Figure 5-3).

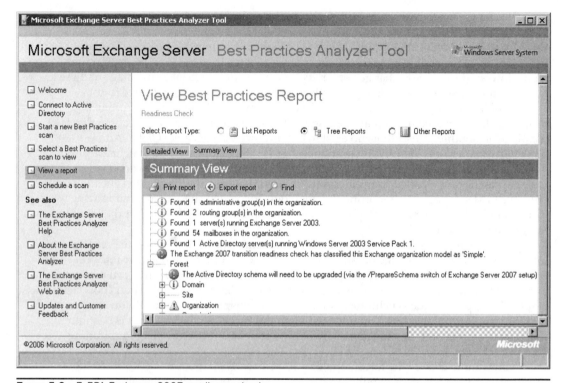

FIGURE 5-3 ExBPA Exchange 2007 readiness check

Active Directory Forest

Before you can introduce an Exchange 2007 Server into an existing Exchange 2000/2003 organization you much meet the minimum requirement in Active Directory. The ExBPA readiness check will perform a thorough sanity check. You will also want to verify the following:

- Windows Server 2003 SP1 or higher Global Catalog and Schema Master Domain Controllers.

- All domain controllers in the forest must be at least Windows 2000 Server or higher. In other words, no NT domain controllers anywhere.

- Domains where Exchange 2007 servers are installed must be 2000 Native Mode.

- Active Directory sites where Exchange 2007 servers are installed must have a Windows Server 2003 SP1 or higher Global Catalog Server.

- Optionally, Setup/PrepareAD can be run prior to deploying the first Exchange 2007 server. It must be run on a system that is a member of the same domain as the Schema Master.

- Domain controllers should be able to pass DCDiag tests.

Here are the steps to follow when verifying/raising the domain functional level:

1. Open Active Directory User and Computers.
2. Connect to the domain in which you plan to install Exchange Server 2007.
3. Right-click the domain name and select Raise Domain Functional Level.
4. Verify that the current level is not Windows 2000 Mixed Mode. If it is, proceed to the next step.
5. Click the drop-down arrow and select Windows 2000 native or Windows Server 2003.
6. Click the Raise button.
7. Click the OK button twice.
8. Close Active Directory Users and Computers.

Legacy Permissions

When the Active Directory schema is extended by Exchange Server 2007, it adds attributes that cannot be seen by Exchange Server 2003 and earlier. In order to make sure that Exchange 2003 can continue to function, the Exchange 2007 setup routine grants permission to certain attributes that must be accessible by Exchange 2000/2003 in Active Directory. If it is necessary to run the schema extensions alone (Setup/PrepareSchema) prior to deploying the first Exchange 2007 Server, it will also be necessary to apply the legacy permissions manually to prevent the Exchange 2000/2003 Recipient Update Service (RUS) from breaking. This can be done by running Setup/PrepareLegacyExchangePermission.

Exchange Server 2007 does not have an RUS service but it does have an RUS API that is called during the creation of each recipient. This enhancement ensures that the attributes an object needs to function exist upon creation and not applied some time later after inception.

Exchange Organization

The existing Exchange organization must meet the following requirements or Exchange Server 2007 setup will fail:

- No Exchange 5.5 servers can reside in the organization.
- Exchange organization must be in Native mode.
- Exchange 2000 servers must have SP3 and the Post-SP3 Rollup.
- Exchange 2003 servers must have SP2.

Here are the steps to follow for verifying/raising Exchange Operation Mode:

1. Open the Exchange System Manager.
2. Right-click the Organization object (Exchange).
3. Select Properties.
4. Verify that the Operation mode is not set to Mixed Mode. If it is, continue with the next step.
5. Click the Change Mode button.
6. Click Yes to confirm the change and OK to close the properties window.
7. Close the Exchange System Manager.

Server Roles

Prior to deploying the first Exchange 2007 server, you must know what server roles you will be deploying, what hardware you will be using, and in which order to deploy each role in.

1. **Client Access Server**   All OWA, Active Sync, RPC over HTTP (Outlook Anywhere), POP3, and IMAP4 clients on Exchange 2003 servers can connect to the first Client Access Server role. This role is also responsible for the AutoDiscovery and Availability services.

2. **Hub Transport Server**   Internal Message Routing topology must be established between the Exchange 2000/2003 routing group and the Exchange 2007 routing group before the mailbox server is installed.

3. **Mailbox Server**   Mailboxes can only reside on the Mailbox Server role. This role must be installed in order to support the transition of both mailboxes and public folders.

4. **Unified Messaging Server**   This role is optional.

The Edge Transport role can be deployed at anytime because it is not part of the Exchange organization. If you already have a messaging security solution at the perimeter of your network, you do not have to deploy an Edge Transport role, but you must configure your Exchange 2007 servers to communicate with that device or service. If you have decided to deploy the Edge Transport server role, you have two basic deployment choices. You can deploy the Edge Transport as an edge security device in your existing organization, or you can deploy it as part of your Exchange Server 2007 deployment. For more information on deploying the Edge Transport server role, see Chapter 7.

Installing Exchange 2007 into an Existing Organization

Again the process for installing Exchange Server 2007 is covered in Chapter 4 in depth. As a review, here are the installation options for Exchange Server 2007:

- GUI installation (Setup.exe)
- Unattended setup (Setup.com)

Most of the changes in the setup routine are in the background when installing the first Exchange 2007 into an existing Exchange 2000/2003 organization. If you are performing a manual installation, you will only see a couple of differences in the GUI installation. If you are planning to perform an unattended setup, you can take advantage of a number of parameters when deploying Exchange 2007 into an existing organization.

GUI Installation

The graphical setup is almost exactly the same as a fresh installation into a pristine environment without a preexisting Exchange organization. The exception is the Hub Transport role. A Typical installation will include the installation of the Hub Transport role. It is also possible to install the Hub Transport separately, but you will need to make sure you install a Client Access Role first.

Here's a review of the GUI installation steps:

1. Place the Exchange Server 2007 media in the server or connect to the source files over the network.
2. Run Setup.exe.
3. Click Next on the Introduction window.
4. Accept the license agreement and click Next.
5. Choose Yes or No on the Error Reporting window and click Next.
6. Choose Typical Install (Exchange will install the three roles in the proper order automatically) and click Next.
7. Click the Browse button on the Mail Flow Settings window, shown next.

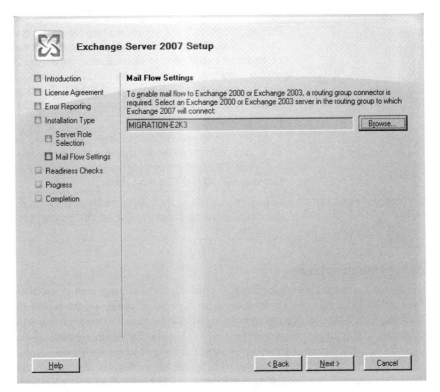

8. Select an Exchange 2003 server that you want the first Exchange 2007 server to connect to, click OK, and then click Next.
9. Verify that all the readiness checks pass and then click the Install button.
10. Click Finish.

The Mail Flow Settings window is the only additional window you will receive in the GUI installation when installing Exchange Server 2007 into an existing organization.

Did you notice what was missing though? Because Exchange 2000 and 2003 both already have public folders, the first Exchange 2007 Server installation will automatically include the /EnableLegacyOutlook parameter, so you will not be prompted during setup.

Unattended Setup

You can run Setup.com to perform the installation of even the first Exchange 2007 server. For it to run successfully and for you to get your desired results, consider the following parameters:

Setup.com Parameter	Transition Considerations
/roles:<roles to install>	Deploy Client Access Role (CA, C) first. Deploy Hub Transport (HT) second. Deploy the Mailbox Role (MB, M) third. Deploy Unified Messaging Role (UM, U) forth.
/DomainController	Exchange Server 2007 setup requires that a Windows Server 2003 SP1 domain controller and Global Catalog be installed in the domain where Exchange Server 2007 will be installed. If you have a mix of 2000 and 2003, DCs use this parameter to specify the 2003 DC. The domain controller that you specify must be in the same AD site as the Exchange server.
/LegacyRoutingServer	If you neglect to specify an Exchange 2000/2003 server as a Legacy Routing Server, the Mail Flow settings will not be configured between Exchange Server 2007 and Exchange 2000/2003 during setup.
/prepareLegacyExchagnePermissions	Should be run manually if /prepareSchema is run to extend the forest schema. Otherwise, it will run as part of the setup routine.

Transitioning Public Folders

The installation of Exchange Server 2007 will create a second storage group, an instance of a public folder database. A replica of the System Configuration public folder is also made on the first Exchange 2007 server. For the remaining public folders that need to transition to Exchange Server 2007, you can do so individually using the Exchange System Manager on an Exchange 2000/2003 server. Although viewing Exchange Server 2007 public folders is limited from the Exchange System Manager, it is possible to select the Exchange 2007 Server public folder database as a replica for each Exchange 2003 public folder. If you intend on deploying a CCR clustered mailbox server, you will need to deploy a nonclustered mailbox server first. The CCR cluster does not support a Public Folder database.

However, there is an easier way. It is possible to replicate all the public folders in a particular Exchange server. You must use the Exchange 2003 SP2 version of the Exchange System Manager (ESM). This is done by right-clicking the Public Folder store and selecting Move All Replicas (see Figure 5-4).

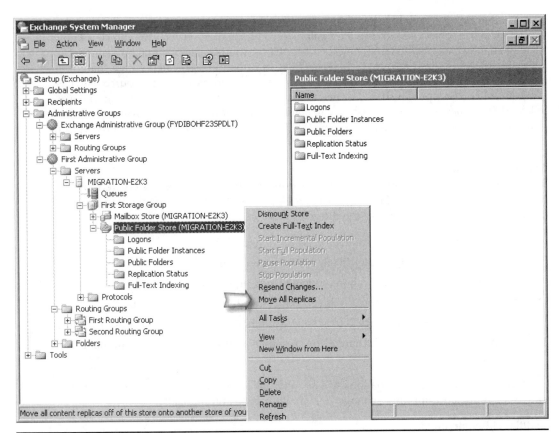

FIGURE 5-4 Selecting Move All Replicas in the ESM

Another easy way to accomplish moving public folders is to use the Exchange Management Shell on the Exchange 2007 server. Microsoft created the script Moveallreplicas.ps1 to perform the same function as the Exchange System Manager:

```
[PS]C:\cd $exscripts
[PS]C:\Program Files\Microsoft\Exchange Server\Scripts>.\Moveallreplicas.ps1
```

It can take some time for the folders to replicate to the Exchange 2007 server regardless of the tool you use. Once replication is complete, the public folder instances on the Exchange 2000/2003 server will be removed. You will not be able to decommission an Exchange 2000/2003 server until all the public folders have been moved. We will explore transitioning public folders in more detail during our discussion of coexistence.

Transitioning Mailboxes

When Microsoft first integrated Exchange Server with Active Directory, they changed what a mailbox is. Prior to Exchange 2000, a mailbox was a separate directory object from an NT user account. In Exchange 2000/2003, a mailbox is a user object with extended attributes.

The positive aspects include being able to choose between assigning an external e-mail address to a user object and giving it a mailbox on an Exchange server. This choice is known as mail-enabling vs. mailbox-enabling the user object. Another use of a mailbox-enabled user object is as a shared resource. The Free/Busy information associated with a shared resource can be invaluable for booking conference rooms and requesting resources such as projectors. The concept of a shared or resource mailbox has existed since Exchange 4.0 was released, but it has never been very easy to configure and administer resource mailboxes. The great news is that in Exchange Server 2007, Microsoft has added more mailbox types to make it easy to create these administered resources objects.

Exchange 2007 Mailbox Types

Exchange 2007 is smart enough to be able to identify what a mailbox was created to do. When you join an Exchange 2007 server to an Exchange 2000/2003 organization, the Exchange 2007 tools will identify the different mailbox types:

- **User mailbox** Mailbox homed on an Exchange 2007 server
- **Shared mailbox** Exchange 2000/2003 resource mailbox
- **Legacy mailbox** Mailbox homed on an Exchange 2003 server
- **Linked mailbox** Mailboxes with accounts in external trusted forests
- **Room mailbox** Exchange 2007 resource mailbox with the "–room" designation
- **Equipment mailbox** Exchange 2007 resource mailbox with the "–equipment" designation

When you move a legacy mailbox or a shared mailbox to an Exchange 2007 server, it is converted to the appropriate Exchange 2007 mailbox type automatically.

Additional Requirements

To prevent errors during the mailbox transitions, you should make sure to address the following requirements.

Permissions The source server permissions (Exchange 2000/2003) are as follows:

- Exchange Administrator
- Member of the Local Administrators Group

The target server permissions (Exchange 2007) are as follows:

- Exchange Recipient Administrator
- Exchange Server Administrator
- Member of the Local Administrators Group

Transaction Logs The most overlooked prerequisite to moving mailboxes is verifying that you can handle the volume of transaction logs on you target server. If you plan to leave circular logging disabled during the transition, you must ensure that the free space on the transaction log drive is 20% greater than the total size of the mailboxes you will be moving. If you do not have that space, you will need to enable circular logging on the target storage group.

Here are the steps to follow to temporarily enable Circular Logging for a transition:

1. Open the Exchange Management Console.
2. Expand Server Configuration and select Mailbox.
3. Choose the target server from the list of mailbox servers.
4. Select the storage group that contains the target mailbox database.
5. Select Properties from the Actions pane.
6. Select the Enable Circular Logging check box and click OK.
7. Close the Exchange Management Console.

It is extremely important that you perform a full online backup of the target database as soon as the mailbox moves are complete. It is equally important to disable circular logging after the moves are complete so that you can use the transaction logs for disaster recovery purposes. To do this, repeat steps 1 through 7, but this time deselect the check box.

Mailbox Cleanup   Have your users clean up their mailboxes. Set a mailbox size goal for your users to get to. Understand that there will be exceptions and those who will refuse to comply. But the majority will likely take some action. If you are able to reduce the mailbox sizes before the move mailbox procedure, it will take less time to move all the mailboxes. Only four threads are spawned during the move mailbox procedure. A single oversized mailbox will consume one of those threads for a large period of time. Try to move all the small mailboxes first and the large mailboxes last, if possible.

GUI Move Mailbox

Transitioning mailboxes from Exchange 2000/2003 to Exchange 2007 is accomplished with Move-Mailbox. Move-Mailbox can be called from the Exchange Management Console (EMC). The EMC is ideal for transitioning a small number of mailboxes. It may also be necessary to use for an administrator who is uncomfortable using the Exchange Management Shell. Note that the Move Mailbox Wizard has been enhanced in Service Pack 1 for Exchange Server 2007. The procedure is slightly different from the RTM version. The most significant change in terms of transitioning and coexistence is the new ability to move mailboxes to Exchange 2000/2003 from Exchange 2007.

SP1   *The Move-Mailbox feature in the Exchange Management Console has been enhanced in SP1.*

Moving mailboxes with the EMC requires the following steps:

1. Open the Exchange Management Console.
2. Expand Recipients Configuration and select Mailbox.
3. Hold down the SHIFT or CTRL key and left-click to select the mailboxes you would like to move.

4. Choose Move Mailbox from the Actions pane.

5. Click the Browse button and select the Exchange 2007 server Storage Group \ Mailbox Database from the server list.

6. Select Skip the corrupted messages. Set the maximum number of messages to skip to 3 (or whatever your tolerance level is) and click Next.

SP1 *The ability to select the domain controller and Global Catalog server was added with Service Pack 1.*

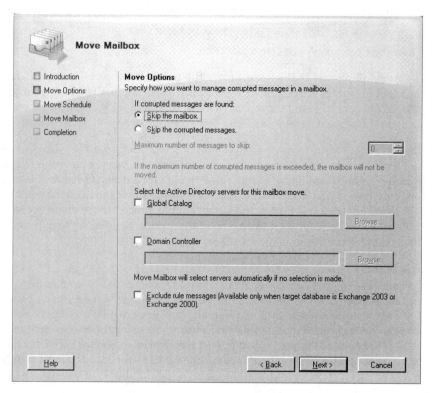

7. Set a move schedule that does not interfere with the users' ability to work. Move the mailboxes "immediately" is the default option. Click Next.

NOTE *It is also possible to set the time limit on the Move Mailbox process. Use this setting to avoid interrupting the backup schedule or normal business work hours.*

8. Verify that the list of mailboxes to be moved is accurate and click Move.

9. Once all the mailboxes have been moved, click Finish.

Command-line Move-Mailbox

It is also possible to perform your entire transition utilizing the Exchange Management Shell (EMS). Although the EMS might be less conducive to moving one or two mailboxes, it is where you will find the most options for going about moving them. When it comes to very large environments, the Exchange System Manager (ESM) is the proper tool to automate moving large batches of mailboxes. The following are examples of how to use the Move-Mailbox command to transition mailboxes from Exchange 2000/2003 to Exchange Server 2007 (see Figure 5-5).

Moving a Single Mailbox   The following cmdlets will move a legacy mailbox to Exchange 2007:

```
[PS] C:\>Move-Mailbox -identity "UserNo2" -TargetDatabase "Migration-E2K7\First
Storage Group\Mailbox Database"
```

Moving an Entire Database

```
[PS] C:\>Get-Mailbox -Database "Migration-E2K3\First Storage Group\Mailbox Store
(Migration-E2K3) | Move-Mailbox -TargetDatabase "Migration-E2K7\First Storage
Group\Mailbox Database"
```

Moving an Entire Server

```
[PS] C:\>Get-Mailbox -Server "Migration-E2K3" | Move-Mailbox -TargetDatabase
"Migration-E2K7\First Storage Group\Mailbox Database"
```

Moving All Exchange 2000/2003 Mailboxes

```
[PS] C:\>Get-Mailbox -RecipientTypeDetails "LegacyMailbox" | Move-Mailbox -
TargetDatabase "Migration-E2K7\First Storage Group\Mailbox Database"
```

```
Machine: Migration-E2K7 | Scope: startup.com                          _ □ ×
[PS] C:\>Move-Mailbox -Identity "UserNo2" -TargetDatabase "Migration-E2K7\First
Storage Group\Mailbox Database"

UserNo2
    Moving messages. Inbox (1/3)
    [ooooooooooooooooooooooo                                           ]

mailbox will be inaccessible until the move is completed.
[Y] Yes  [A] Yes to All  [N] No  [L] No to All  [S] Suspend  [?] Help
(default is "Y"):a
```

Figure 5-5   Moving a mailbox from Exchange 2003 to Exchange 2007 using the EMS

It is possible to increase the number of threads that Move-Mailbox can use (see Figure 5-6). The default is 4. The EMC can only use four, but the EMS can be increased up to 30 if you add the following parameter to your Move-Mailbox command:

```
[PS] C:\>Get-Mailbox -RecipientsTypeDetails "LegacyMailbox" | Move-Mailbox
-MaxThreads 8 - TargetDatabase "Mailbox Database"
```

There is, of course, a reason why it is limited to four out of the box. Increasing MaxThreads too high on a server that cannot handle the additional I/O could cause the server to hang.

Adding the –WhatIf parameter to the end of any of the preceding cmdlets will let you execute the command without actually doing anything to the mailboxes. This could be helpful if you want to make sure the syntax in the command is correct before you try to move thousands of users.

Verifying Mailbox Moves
After the mailboxes are moved to Exchange Server 2007, they will no longer appear as legacy mailboxes in the Recipient Type Details. It is possible to find out more details about how the Move-Mailbox process went (see Figure 5-7). The Application Log in Event Viewer on the target server will display three events for each moved mailbox. Event 1006 is generated when the move has started. Event 1007 is generated when the mailbox has moved. Event 9354 is generated when the mailbox is deleted from the legacy server.

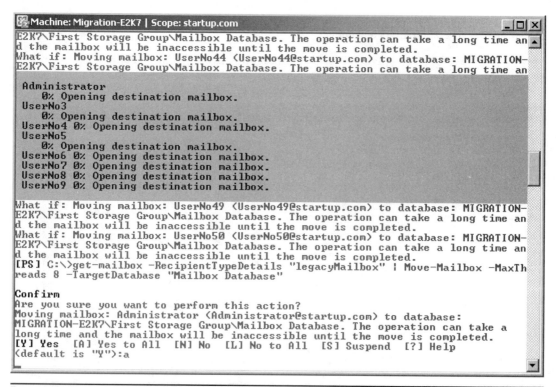

Figure 5-6   Increasing the MaxThreads setting

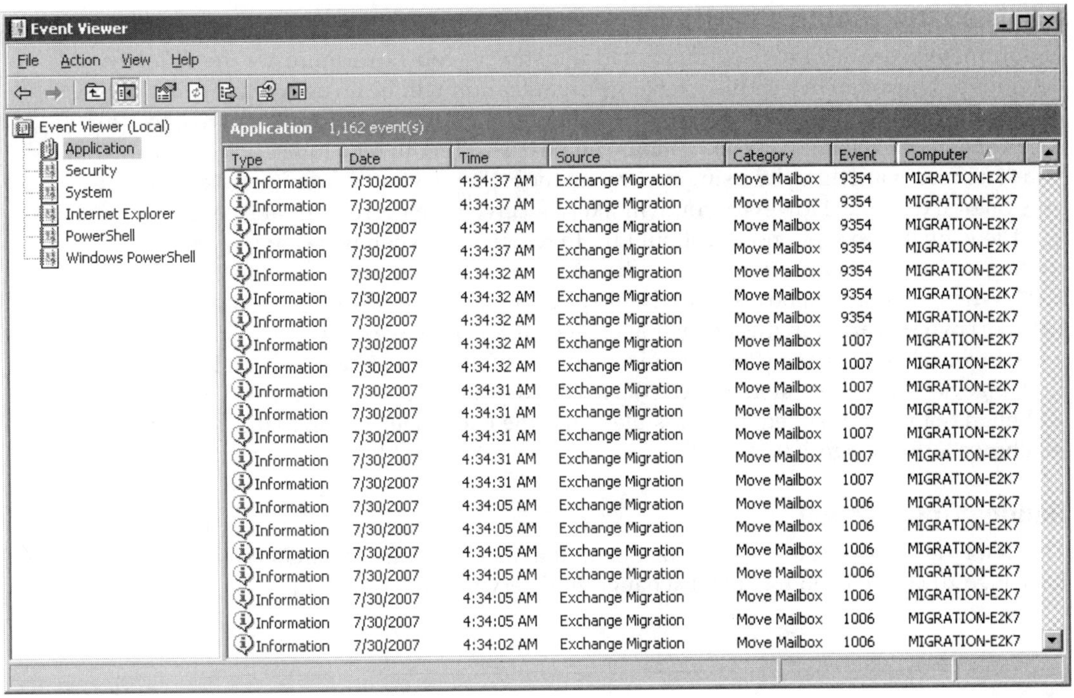

FIGURE 5-7   Move-Mailbox Event Logs

Migration Logs are also created in the %Program Files%\Microsoft\Exchange Server\ Logging\MigrationLogs directory on the target Exchange 2007 server. These logs are helpful because they provide more detail about the process of moving mailboxes than the Event Logs do.

Coexistence

The amount of time it takes you to move all the public folders and mailboxes, combined with the need to maintain legacy Exchange servers for incompatibility reasons, dictates how long your coexistence period will last. You can actually calculate how long your mailboxes will take to move. On average it will take an hour to move 2–4GB (gigabytes) of mail. Your Disk Storage subsystem on the source and target servers, along with the quality and speed of the network that connects them, have the greatest impact on whether you get 2GB or 4GB per hour. Other factors include the maintenance and backup schedules, business hours, and unforeseen events.

It is not as easy to calculate how long you must support an incompatible feature or application. Suffice it to say that you will have to keep an Exchange 2000/2003 server in your organization until you no longer need the incompatible feature. Coexistence during a transition is pretty smooth and very transparent to your users. There are some administrative items that you will need to be familiar with that only apply to coexistence.

Administration During Coexistence

Unfortunately, the need to use different administrative tools to administer the different versions of Exchange in a single Exchange organization will be an aggravating fact of life during coexistence. The basic rule to remember is that you should use the native tool for each version of Exchange. The exceptions can be frustrating to remember. It is not likely that you can break something by using the wrong tool when trying to administer a different version of Exchange. However, you will likely receive many errors upon trying.

There are two exceptions you should try to remember. When working with message routing between the two versions of Exchange, you should use the Exchange 2000/2003 ESM. When moving mailboxes from Exchange 2000/2003, you should only use the EMC or EMS, as covered earlier in this chapter. However, if for some reason you would like to move a mailbox back to Exchange 2003 from Exchange 2007, you must have Service Pack 1 for the Exchange Server 2007 version of the EMC installed or use the Exchange 2003 ESM. Although not recommended, it is possible to use the Exchange System Manager to move mailboxes to Exchange 2007 as well.

Routing Optimization

The first Hub Transport in the organization automatically configures mail flow between Exchange 2000/2003 and the new Exchange 2007 server (see Figure 5-8).

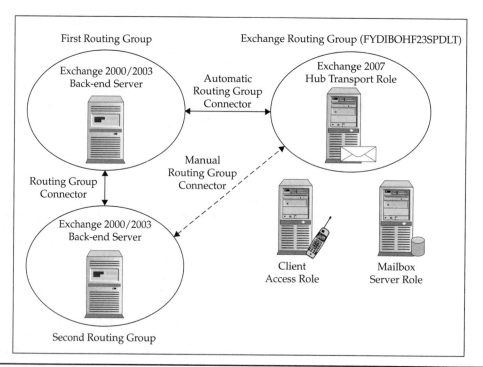

FIGURE 5-8 Coexistence routing topology

Exchange configures a single routing group connector based on the Exchange 2000/2003 server you specified. A single routing group was created for all Exchange 2007 Hub Transport servers regardless of the existing routing topology. This means that mail flow will work between all Exchange Server versions. However, this doesn't necessarily mean it will be optimized. In fact, the more complex the routing topology in Exchange 2000/2003, the more likely it will *not* be optimized. Figure 5-8 shows the default routing topology for a coexistence environment. It also shows how it is possible to set up an additional routing group connectors if it will benefit the organization.

All the configuration changes for coexistence routing must be made with the Exchange System Manager.

Mailbox Delegates

During coexistence, users will be able to continue to delegate access to their mailboxes and calendars. All existing settings will continue to function even after the mailbox or its delegates are moved to Exchange Server 2007. The Exchange Management Shell has the ability to manage delegates for both Exchange 2000/2003 and Exchange 2007 mailboxes. During coexistence, you should try to use the EMS for consistency. For AD permissions, use the Add-Adpermission cmdlet. For Full Mailbox delegation, use the Add-Mailboxpermission cmdlet. For Send on Behalf of rights, use the Set-Mailbox cmdlet.

Resource Accounts

Exchange 2000/2003 resource accounts are still just shared mailboxes even after they are moved to Exchange Server 2007. They will continue to work just as they did before. Meeting requests will be accepted automatically. However, you will need to convert them to room or equipment mailboxes if you want to use the new custom schemas. You can use the Set-Mailbox cmdlet, as follows:

```
[PS]C:\>Set-Mailbox -Identity "Conference Room 2" -Type:Room
or
[PS]C:\>Set-Mailbox -Identity "Projector 2" -Type:Equipment
```

For more details on resource mailboxes, see Chapter 10.

Things That Make Exchange 2007 Go, "Huh?"

Exchange 2000 introduced the concept of address lists to replace the Address Book views in Exchange 5.5 and earlier. Exchange Server 2003 introduced query-based distribution groups to replace home-grown scripts that automatically populated distribution groups. Both of these innovations depend on LDAP queries to produce what we see when we view or send to these objects. Because of changes in Active Directory and Exchange Server 2007, a few configurations are no longer supported. You must update the address lists and query-based distribution groups before they can be used by Exchange Server 2007.

Updating Address Lists

Microsoft dramatically changes the attributes that administrators can choose from to create address list filters. Because of this, it is not possible to modify the existing address lists with the Exchange 2007 tools until they are upgraded to the Exchange 2007 format. If you try to use the EMC, you will receive the following notice:

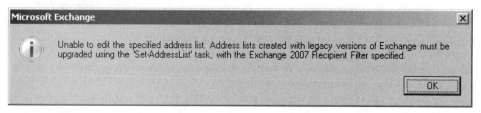

The only way to upgrade the legacy list is with EMS. There are two things that must be done at the same time: You must add a valid Exchange 2007 condition and you must force the upgrade. To do so, run the following command:

```
[PS]C:\>Set-AddressList -Identity "E2K3-List" -IncludeRecipients MailboxUsers -
ForceUpgrade:$true
```

Once this command is run, you will not be able to edit the address list with Exchange 2000/2003 tools.

Query-based Distribution Groups and Non-Universal Groups

Because query-based distribution groups use the exact same filters as address lists, you will have the exact same problem with legacy query-based distribution groups. They will appear as dynamic distribution groups in Exchange 2007 but as a query-based distribution groups in Exchange 2003. Exchange 2007 EMC will gray out the condition options and force you to use the EMS to administer it.

In the following cmdlets an existing query-based distribution group is forced to be upgraded to Exchange 2007 and allow you administer it with the EMC:

```
[PS]C:\>Set-DynamicDistributionGroup -Identity "Users 1-10" -IncludeRecipients
MailboxUsers -ForceUpgrade:$true
```

Exchange 2007 only allows administrators to create universal distribution groups. If you have a number of groups that are global distribution groups, you can still use them. However, you should use the EMC or EMS to convert them to universal groups when possible. The EMS cmdlet is:

```
[PS]C:\>Set-Group -Identity "E2K3-GlobalGroup" -IsUniversalGroup:$true
```

Space Out

Another problem, in a nutshell, is spaces. Exchange 2000/2003 allowed spaces in the Exchange Alias and Display Name attributes for all recipient objects. Exchange 2007 enforces a zero space validation rule on these attributes, which prevents it from reading recipients with spaces in their aliases. All recipients with spaces in the Alias attribute will need to be identified. This can be done by setting up a stored query in Active Directory (see Figure 5-9).

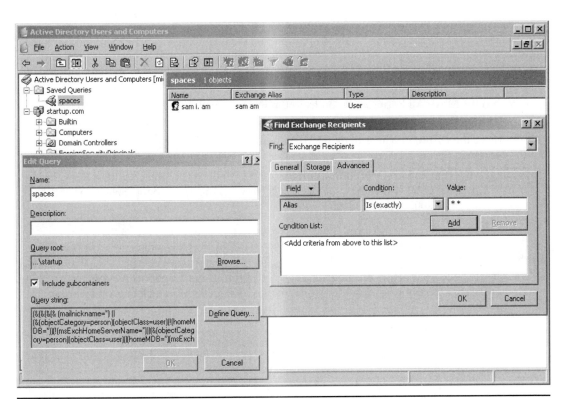

FIGURE 5-9   Query for spaces

The query filter should include all recipient types. The condition you want to specify is an alias with a space anywhere in the name (*sp*). This particular filter will not catch spaces before or after the name, though. In order to find mailboxes whose common names have spaces before and after their names, you can run the following filter:

```
Get-Mailbox | Foreach { Set-Mailbox -Identity $_.Id -DisplayName
$_.DisplayName.Trim() }
```

For more information on recipient validation in Exchange Server 2007, see http://www .exchangeninjas.com/RecipientValidation. If you do not eliminate these spaces you may have trouble moving mailboxes from Exchange 2000/2003 to Exchange 2007, as well as performing other tasks in Exchange 2007 that reference these attributes.

Removing Exchange 2000/2003

The final step in a transition can only be accomplished at the end of coexistence. You can remove an Exchange 2000/2003 server by uninstalling it from the organization once all the mailboxes and public folders have been moved. However, the last Exchange 2000/2003 server in the organization has some special requirements.

Preparing to Remove the Last Exchange 2000/2003 Server

Here are the steps to follow when preparing to remove the last Exchange 2000/2003 server:

1. Move all mailboxes off the last server. This process is described earlier in this chapter in "Transitioning Mailboxes."

2. Run the Move All Replicas option from the ESM on the last public folder database. This process is described earlier in this chapter in, "Transitioning Public Folders."

3. Move the Offline Address Book (OAB) generation to an Exchange 2007 server as shown in Figure 5-10.

    • **EMC**   Expand Organization Configuration | Mailbox | Offline Address Book. Select the OAB you want to move. Select Move in the action pane. Select an Exchange 2007 server and click Move.

    • **EMS**   Use the following command:

    ```
    Move-OfflineAddressBook -Identity "Default Offline Address List" -Server
    Migration-E2K7.
    ```

4. Create Send connectors on the Exchange 2007 Hub/Edge Transport servers to replace SMTP connectors on the last Exchange 2000/2003 server. Details on creating Send connectors can be found in Chapter 7.

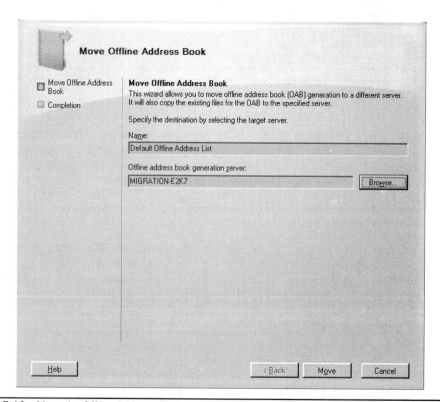

FIGURE 5-10   Move the Offline Address Book

5. Delete the Public Folder Store on the last Exchange 2000/2003 server using the ESM. You do not want to delete the database until after you have moved all public folders and they have finished replicating.

6. Reconfigure the MX record(s) and/or external firewall to point to the Exchange 2007 Edge or Hub Transport server for all inbound mail. Confirm that none of the Exchange 2007 Send connectors are pointing to the last Exchange 2000/2003 server as a "smart host."

7. Test all the Internet protocol services on the CAS role. If there is a firewall such as ISA, make sure it is configured to communicate with the CAS role and not the last Exchange 2000/2003 server. Make sure there are no clients configured to use the 2000/2003 server.

8. Delete any recipient policies that only have Mailbox Manager settings.

9. Delete any Mailbox Manager settings that are configured on recipient polices that apply e-mail address settings.

For more details on removing the last Exchange 2000/2003 server, see the Microsoft TechNet article, "How to Remove the Last Legacy Exchange Server from an Organization," at http://technet.microsoft.com/en-us/library/bb288905.aspx.

Removing the Last Exchange 2000/2003 Server

Here are the steps to follow to actually remove the last Exchange 2000/2003 server:

1. Move the public folder hierarchy using the ESM. Expand the 2003 and 2007 administrative groups. Create a new Public Folders container in the 2007 administrative group. Drag and drop the Public Folders object from the Folders container in the 2000/2003 administrative group to the new Folders container in the 2007 administrative group.

2. Reconfigure the Recipient Update Services to use an Exchange 2007 server.

   • Delete all the Domain Recipient Update Service objects.

   • Configure Recipient Update Server (Enterprise Configuration) to point to an Exchange 2007 server.

3. Use the Add or Remove Programs feature on the Exchange 2000/2003 server to remove Exchange. You will need access to the Exchange 2000/2003 source files, so make sure they can be accessed by the server.

Migrating

As convenient as a transition may be, it is not always practical or possible. This part of the chapter explores various ways you can migrate to Exchange Server 2007 from another messaging system or even another Exchange organization.

Reasons to Migrate

The process of migrating from another messaging system to Exchange Server 2007 can be lengthy and complex. So why would anyone in their right mind do it? In most cases, it is because they have to. The only time someone makes a decision between migrating and

Special Case: Exchange 5.5 to Exchange 2007

There is no support for Exchange 5.5 transitions or coexistence. There is also no support for a direct migration from Exchange 5.5 to Exchange 2007. The supported method is as follows:

- Upgrade from Exchange 5.5 to Exchange 2000 or Exchange 2003.
- Transition from Exchange 2000/2003 to Exchange 2007.
- Alternatively, it is possible to migrate from Exchange 2000/2003 to Exchange 2007.

transitioning is when the existing environment is Exchange 2000/2003 and the original environment was badly configured and unreliable. In such conditions, Exchange administrators actually look forward to migrations as a solution to their administrative woes. In all other cases, migrating is the only way to get to Exchange Server 2007.

Target Organizations

Deploying or identifying a target environment is the first step to a migration. When a merger or acquisition takes place between two organizations, one or both of the organizations may already be running Exchange Server 2007. In this case, there will not be a need to deploy a new Active Directory and Exchange 2007 infrastructure. If, however, you happen to be the administrator looking for a fresh start in a new organization, you have some work to do in setting up a new infrastructure. It would be a good idea to have a firm understanding of Parts I and II of this book to help you design Active Directory and Exchange in the new environment.

The target organization can be built in parallel with the current production environment. This will give you the opportunity to fully test all the functionality before you move the first mailbox.

Migrating Mail Flow

The most difficult task to accomplish in a migration is to maintain and control mail flow while you reconfigure to which servers mail is flowing. This can be particularly complex when you have two organizations that share the exact same SMTP domain name. Unfortunately, this is almost always the case in a migration. That is why it is necessary to reroute mail flow through the new organization before you perform any other migration tasks. If something were to go wrong with mail flow, you can switch back to the original configuration quickly, with one notable exception: If you must reconfigure your MX records as part of the rerouting process, you should be prepared for the change to take up to 48 hours to propagate to all DNS hosts on the Internet.

Here are the steps for rerouting mail flow through your Exchange 2007 organization:

1. Deploy the new infrastructure. Refer to Parts I and II of this book.
2. Test message routing in the new Exchange 2007 organization. Use a nonproduction SMTP domain to test mail flow both inside and outside of the organization.
3. Replace the test SMTP domain with the production SMTP domain.

4. Configure mail flow between Exchange 2007 and the existing messaging system and validate all aspects of internal mail flow between the two mail systems.

   - Create and configure Send connector(s) to send mail from the Edge or Hub Transport servers to the existing messaging system.

   - Create and configure Receive connector(s) to receive mail from the existing messaging system on the Edge or Hub Transport servers.

   - Configure the existing messaging system's SMTP server(s) to forward mail to the Exchange 2007 Edge or Hub Transport servers.

5. Reconfigure the external message flow.

   - Change the MX records and/or the external firewall to point to the Exchange 2007 Edge or Hub Transport server for the production SMTP domain. Note that if your message security is outsourced, you will need to communicate with your service provider to let them know the names and IP addresses of your new Exchange 2007 Transport servers that will be communicating with their service.

   - Reconfigure all internal routes on the both messaging systems to point to the Exchange 2007 Edge server or smart host responsible for external e-mail communications.

6. Clean up and remove connectors and routes when the old messaging system is decommissioned.

Migrating Recipient and Configuration Information

All messaging systems maintain information about their recipients. Some mail systems utilize robust directory services for storing and accessing that information, whereas others use simple text files. Messaging systems typically have proprietary directory services and configurations. Translating the myriad of settings and attributes from one mail system to another would be too difficult, if not impossible, without tools specifically designed to do this. Fortunately, software vendors including Microsoft who know the inner workings of messaging directories have built tools to help with these complex procedures. The good news is that you do not necessarily need to migrate all the directory information. In fact, the tools that are available focus on four key pieces of information:

- User information
- Contact information
- Distribution list information
- SMTP routing information

LDAP Tools

If the source messaging system uses an Lightweight Directory Access Protocol (LDAP) directory, it is possible to run LDAP tools and scripts to export the information you need and then import it into Active Directory. Microsoft has two such tools that you can use:

- **CSVDE**   Comma-Separated Value Directory Exchange
- **LDIFDE**   Lightweight Directory Interchange Format Directory Exchange

FIGURE 5-11   Sample CSVDE import file

CSVDE and LDIFDE are both powerful tools. LDIFDE's format is a bit more complex than CSVDE's. LDIFDE is rarely used for Exchange migrations. CSVDE, on the other hand, is used for migrating contacts and for migrating distribution group members when other migration tools cannot (see Figure 5-11).

When you export a list of contacts with CSVDE, you will export a number of attributes that are not needed when creating new contacts. In Figure 5-11, you can see an example of an import file after the unnecessary values have been removed. You can also see the syntax for the data in the event you want to manually create an import file. Here is a list of the values you need to include in the file:

DN, objectClass, cn, sn, givenName, displayName, proxyAddresses, name, targetAddress, mailNickname

ADMT v3

If the source messaging system uses Active Directory, you can use the Microsoft Active Directory Migration Tool, version 3, to migrate user objects to the target environment. This can be done for Exchange 2000/2003 migrations to Exchange 2007. You can download the "ADMT v3 Migration Guide" from http://microsoft.com/downloads.

GALSync

GAL Synchronization (GALSync) is actually a component of Microsoft Identity Information Server (MIIS) and MIIS Identity Integration Feature Pack 1a. An XML metabase is used to export directory information from the source directory and then import it to the target directory. GALSync is specifically for Exchange to Exchange migrations. The benefit of GALSync is that it can be used for extended interoperability strategies where cross-forest Exchange topologies exist. Rodney R. Fournier writes an excellent blog on GALSync called "Identity Integration Feature Pack (IIFP) – GALSync Unleashed," at http://msmvps.com/blogs/clustering/archive/2004/10/06/15141.aspx.

Migrating Exchange Data

It is possible to migrate an Exchange 2000 and/or Exchange 2003 organization to Exchange Server 2007 with third-party tools or with Microsoft tools. It might be worth looking at third-party tools to see what benefits they can provide you before you decide to use the Microsoft tools. This is especially true if you have a very large enterprise with several terabytes of data to migrate. Another tricky aspect that third-party tools can help you overcome is what to do with your public folders during a migration. There is no native Exchange 2007 tool for migrating public folders. What's more, support for public folders has been deemphasized. Some third-party migration tools are discussed at the end of this chapter. Determine what data you need to migrate and then determine the best tool(s) to help you do it.

Exchange Mailboxes

To move mailbox data between two Exchange organizations, where the target organization is Exchange Server 2007, the source organizations must be Exchange 2000 or higher.

The tool to use is the same as the one used for the transition. Move-Mailbox has the ability to bind to an Exchange 2000/2003 organization and transfer the mailbox data to an Exchange 2007 mailbox server. Currently, there is no support in the Exchange Management Console (EMC) for a cross-org migration.

The following steps illustrate the overall process using the Exchange Management Shell (EMS). What is not shown is that GALSync is crucial to the process to ensure that mail is forwarded from the source organization to the target organization after the Move-Mailbox process is complete. It would be a good idea to have GALSync set up before you embark on your migration. There is no requirement for trust relationships between the forests to get the Move-Mailbox tool to work. What you must have is valid credentials in both organizations, and obviously you need to run the tool from the target environment.

The source server permissions (Exchange 2000/2003) are as follows:

- Exchange Administrator
- Member of the Local Administrators Group

The target server permissions (Exchange 2007) are as follows:

- Exchange Recipient Administrator
- Exchange Server Administrator
- Member of the Local Administrators group

Move-Mailbox Cross-Org

Moving mailboxes from one organization to another organization is more complex than a typical move-mailbox command. The following steps detail the additional requirements to complete the task:

1. Use the Get-Credential command to create stored usernames and passwords for Move-Mailbox to use. Type in the username and password with permissions to the source organization and then do the same for the target organization, as shown next:

   ```
   [PS]C:\> $SourceAdmin = Get-Credential
   [PS]C:\> $TargetAdmin = Get-Credential
   ```

2. Create a Get-Mailbox command to pull the mailboxes you want to move from the source organization. Run the custom Get-Mailbox command you created to verify its results.

    ```
    get-mailbox -DomainController "Migration-E2K3" -Credential $SourceAdmin -Database
    "Migration-E2K3\First Storage Group\Mailbox Store (Migration-E2K3)"
    ```

3. Create a Move-Mailbox command that you can pipe the Get-Mailbox command to. You can specify numerous parameters with the Move-Mailbox command. You might want to create some test accounts to use until you get the results you are looking for.

    ```
    move-mailbox "TestUser" -TargetDatabase "Mailbox Database" -
    SourceForestGlobalCatalog "Migration-E2K3.startup.com" -GlobalCatalog "E2K7-MB-
    01.virtuecorp.com" -DomainController "E2K7-MB-01.virtuecorp.com" -NTAccountOU
    "OU=MigratedUsers, DC=GK,DC=COM" -SourceForestCredential $SourceAdmin -
    TargetForestCredential $TargetAdmin -ReportFile "C:\MigrationLog.xml"
    ```

4. Combine the two into a single cmdlet.

5. Confirm that you want to move all mailboxes by typing A and pressing ENTER.

Depending on the way you have message routing configured between the two organizations, you will either want to leave the account in the source domain or remove it. Use the Get-Help Move-Mailbox -Detailed cmdlet so you can see the options available with the -SourceMailboxCleanupOptions parameter.

For even more examples and information on moving mailboxes between organizations, refer to the excellent blog by Paul MacKnight called, "Exchange 2007 Cross Org Mailbox Migration," at http://msexchangeteam.com/archive/2006/11/02/430289.aspx.

Exchange Public Folders

The only way to use the Microsoft tools is to build your target forest with an Exchange 2003 organization. Then you can transition the organization to Exchange 2007, but leave a server running Exchange 2003 so you can install and run the InterOrg Replication tool. For more information on the InterOrg Replication tool, see the Microsoft Knowledge Base article, "Installing, configuring, and using the InterOrg Replication utility," at http://support .microsoft.com/kb/238573. A less elegant, but effective method to migrate public folder data is to utilize an Outlook client to export the public folders to a .PST file and then import the .PST file content into the new directory. Permissions will not be retained, so you will have to manually apply permission to the migrated public folders.

Migrating from Other Messaging Systems

If you are migrating from another messaging system, you must decide what migration tool you intend to use prior to deploying your target environment. If you plan to use Microsoft's tools and you are not migrating from Lotus Domino 6.x or greater, you will need to incorporate an Exchange 2003 server into your Exchange 2007 organization. The Exchange 2003 migration tools are listed in Figure 5-12.

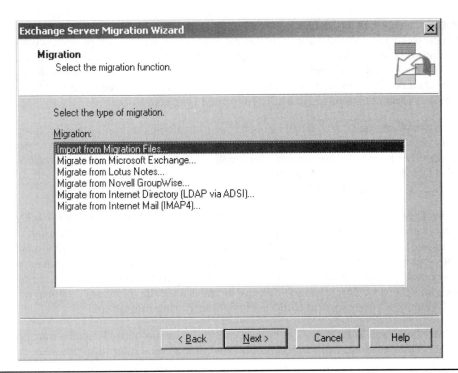

FIGURE 5-12   Exchange Server 2003 Migration Wizard

Microsoft GroupWise Tools

Microsoft has not included a native connector for GroupWise in Exchange Server 2007. At this time Microsoft does not have any plans to develop one. The last connector created by Microsoft for GroupWise was updated to support 6.5 environments. The GroupWise connector combined with the Calendar connector (which are both available as part of the Exchange Server 2003 installation) will allow the two messaging systems to share a single SMTP domain name, address book, and Free/Busy calendar information. The GroupWise Migration tool moves the mailboxes from GroupWise to Exchange Server 2003. After the mailboxes have been moved to Exchange Server 2003, you can then transition the mailboxes to the Exchange 2007 mailbox servers.

For more information on using Exchange 2003 as a pass-through method to migrate from GroupWise to Exchange Server 2007, see the documentation "Interoperating with and Migrating from Novell GroupWise Messaging Infrastructures to Exchange Server 2003," at http://technet.microsoft.com/en-us/library/aa998380.aspx.

Microsoft Transport Suite for Lotus Domino

The Microsoft Transport Suite for Lotus Domino (MTSLD) replaces all previous connectors and migration tools for Lotus/Domino migrations to Exchange. As the name implies, MTSLD is composed of a number of tools that help you plan, deploy, interoperate, and migrate the Lotus Domino environment to Exchange Server 2007 (see Figure 5-13). Note that R5 and earlier versions are not fully supported for coexistence.

Directory Synchronization   A standalone connector is available that can be deployed separately from the message routing connector. The directory connector for Domino will synchronize the address books in both environments by creating contacts for the Exchange mailboxes in the IBM Domino Directory and contacts for the Domino mailboxes in the Microsoft Active Directory. It will also enable SMTP mail flow and Free/Busy calendar sharing.

Directory Migration   The Directory Migration Wizard will walk you through the migration of users from the Domino Directory to Active Directory. As an alternative, you can use the Get-DominoUser command and pipe to the Move-DominoUser command. Optionally, the mailbox can be moved at the same time the object is moved. Groups can be moved with Get-DominoGroup being piped to Move-DominoGroupToAD. It is a good idea to clean out the Domino groups before trying to migrate them because the members do not sync up with the Domino Directory and could lead to errors during migration.

Mail Coexistence and Migration   The biggest change is the use of SMTP as the transport for Exchange–Domino communications and for moving mail. The migration times are faster.

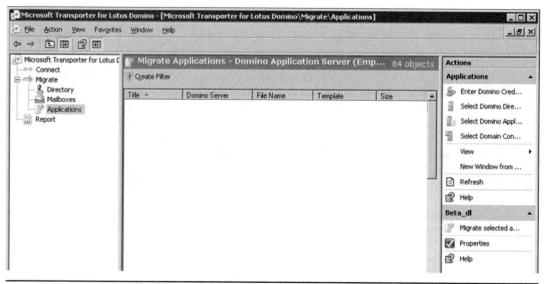

FIGURE 5-13   Transport Suite for Lotus Domino console

The calendar migration uses the iCAL standard, which is more reliable. Migrations can also occur across the WAN, which is very beneficial for Exchange service providers and consolidation projects. The Free/Busy connector for Domino runs on the Exchange 2007 server and communicates with the CalConn Domino task on the Domino server. These two components allow users on both servers to view each other's Free/Busy information when sending out meeting requests.

Once the users' objects have been moved to Active Directory, you can move the mailbox data. To move mailboxes, you can use Get-DominoMailbox and pipe the command to Move-DominoMailbox. For personal data files, you can use the Move-NotesPABToExchange and Move-NotesMailArchiveToExchange commands.

POP3/IMAP

The most effective way to migrate from a POP3 or IMAP4 messaging system to Exchange Server 2007 is a clean cut over. The POP3 client will download each item from the POP server and store it locally. Because many organizations that use POP or IMAP servers actually use Microsoft Outlook as a client for their systems, all a user has to do to migrate is reconfigure their Outlook profile to point to the Exchange 2007 Client Access Server. Alternatively, they can create an Exchange mail account in their Outlook profile that points to an Exchange 2007 mailbox server.

IMAP is a little bit more involved because, unlike POP, IMAP4 clients only download header information from the server until the mail is opened. What that means is that only the mail that the user reads is kept locally on their machine. It is possible to configure IMAP4 clients to download the full message when they connect to the server, though. Therefore, a migration from IMAP would potentially have the additional step of reconfiguring the clients and verifying that they have downloaded all their mail before the reconfiguration. Another option for POP or IMAP server migrations is to leave them running for a period of time to allow users to continue to access their mail from the server but not to allow the server to send or receive any new mail. The clients can be configured with Exchange 2007 as a separate e-mail account in the same Outlook profile.

Third-party Migration Tools

Vendor	Migration Tool
Quest Software	Migration Suite for Exchange Quest Notes Migrator™ Quest GroupWise Migrator Public Folder Migrator for SharePoint
Priasoft	Priasoft Migration Suite for Exchange

TABLE 5-3 Third-party Migration Tools

Summary

It is critical to develop a roadmap for deploying Exchange Server 2007. Documenting your existing environment is the best way to start. Because of the new hardware requirements for Exchange 2007 there are limited ways in which you can upgrade. Since there is no in-place upgrade method, you will need to either transition to Exchange 2007 or migrate to Exchange 2007. If you are not running Exchange 2000 or Exchange 2003 in your current environment you will not be able to transition, you will have to migrate. There is a high level of coexistence between Exchange 2000/2003 and Exchange 2007 that can make administration easier and the end user experience better. When you migrate you will have to determine what level of interoperability you want to support and for how long you want to support them. In this chapter we covered the details of each of these methods as well as various tools that can be used to migrate from non-Exchange messaging systems to Exchange 2007, so that you can make a more informed decision when you lay out your roadmap to Exchange 2007.

PART

Administering Exchange Server 2007

Administering Mailbox Servers

U p to this point in the book we have looked at the fundamentals of Exchange Server 2007 and how to deploy an Exchange 2007 organization. While the deployment of your first Exchange 2007 Servers is critical, that will not constitute the majority of the work you will do with Exchange Server 2007 long term. You will need to take the fundamentals and apply them to the daily operations. Part III of this book is dedicated to the details of administration. Administrative tasks can be categorized by, and coincide with, the five Exchange Server 2007 Server roles. This chapter covers the Mailbox Server role, Chapter 7 covers the HUB and Edge Transport roles, Chapter 8 covers the Client Access Server role and Chapter 9 covers the Unified Messaging Server role.

The Role of Mailbox Servers

E-mail communications systems, including the Exchange Server platform, are store-and-forward systems. Mailboxes are the persistent way-point for messages; therefore, mailbox servers are essential to the operation of any Exchange organization. This chapter focuses on the administration of Exchange Server 2007 mailbox servers, along with supporting concepts.

When you're installing Exchange Server 2007 on a server, the Typical Installation option installs the Mailbox (MB) server role along with the Client Access (CA) and Hub Transport (HT) roles. Custom installations could add the Unified Messaging (UM) role to those or include some subset of those four. For details on installation options for the Mailbox role, see Chapter 4.

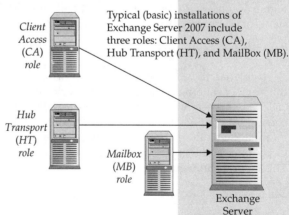

Typical (basic) installations of Exchange Server 2007 include three roles: Client Access (CA), Hub Transport (HT), and MailBox (MB).

Client Access (CA) role

Hub Transport (HT) role

Mailbox (MB) role

Exchange Server

The Continuous Cluster Replication and Single Copy Cluster installation options will force you to dedicate servers to just the Mailbox Server role. If you want to deploy highly available Mailbox Server roles, also see Chapter 19.

Service Architecture

A number of services run on Exchange Server 2007 mailbox servers. If there are other Exchange roles in addition to the Mailbox server role installed, the services that must be running may be different than those for a dedicated mailbox server. It is important to understand the services that constitute each server role. One of the most crucial services is the Information Store Service on the mailbox server.

Introducing the Microsoft Exchange Information Store Service

Figure 6-1 shows the Windows PowerShell with the Get-Service cmdlet used to get the status of all the services whose names include the word "Exchange":

```
Get-Service *Exchange*
```

Note that the Microsoft Exchange Information Store Service (MSExchangeIS) is one of the services running. This service is the heart of the functionality of the Exchange Server 2007 Mailbox server role. This service supports hosting storage groups, the databases they contain, and in turn the mailboxes and public folders those databases contain. To get more information on the status of this service and its dependencies, you can supply its name to Get-Service and then use the Format-List formatter to display more attributes of the service. This is shown in Figure 6-2.

```
Get-Service MSExchangeIS | Format-List
```

This figure shows that the MSExchangeIS service depends on {NtLmSsp, RPCSS, LanmanWorkstation, LanmanServer, EventLog}, which are:

- Windows NT LAN Manager Security services provider
- Remote Procedure Call System Service

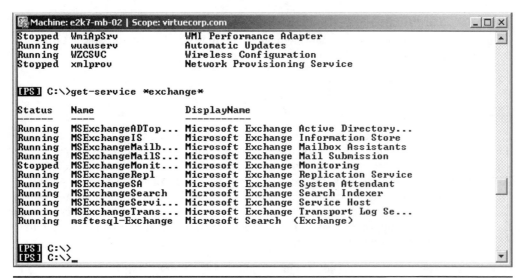

FIGURE 6-1   Exchange Services

- LAN Manager Workstation service
- LAN Manager Server service
- Event Log service

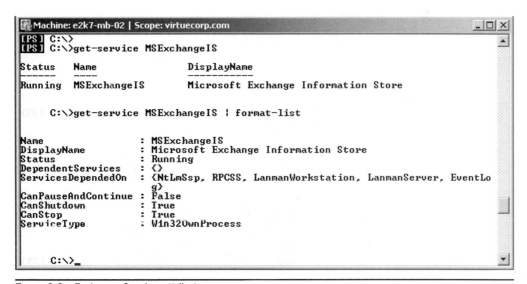

FIGURE 6-2   Exchange Service attributes

The Store.exe Process and Its DLLs

Figure 6-3 shows the tasklist command, which is a regular Windows command not unique to PowerShell. Three forms of tasklist are used here:

```
tasklist /fi "imagename eq store.exe"
tasklist /fi "imagename eq store.exe" /svc
tasklist /fi "imagename eq store.exe" /m
```

The tasklist command may be considered to be similar in some ways to the graphical Task Manager. The first form shows the memory usage; the second form uses the /SVC switch to request that tasklist show the services provided. When tasklist is given the /M switch, it shows the modules of software used by the process (DLLs). Note where several DLLs are used by store.exe to accomplish the job of hosting the Microsoft Exchange Information Store Service in this figure. One of these is called mdbrole.dll, which is a part of the software used to support the Mailbox Database (MDB) role. Another DLL shown in the figure is mdbtask.dll, which also does part of the job.

Starting and Stopping the Microsoft Exchange Information Store Service

The critical part of running store.exe is that it runs smoothly. However, knowing how to start and stop this service may be required for certain preventative maintenance and/or disaster recovery procedures. As with most tasks in Exchange 2007, you can use the Microsoft Management Console (MMC) Services console snap-in or, as a newer approach, you can use Windows PowerShell.

As PowerShell's Get-Help *-Service can reveal, several cmdlets may be used for service control, as shown in Figure 6-4.

```
Machine: e2k7-mb-02 | Scope: virtuecorp.com                          _ □ ×
      C:\>tasklist /fi "imagename eq store.exe"

Image Name                   PID Session Name        Session#    Mem Usage
=========================== ======== ================ =========== =============
store.exe                   2744 Console                  0       81,488 K
      C:\>tasklist /fi "imagename eq store.exe" /svc

Image Name                   PID Services
=========================== ======== =========================================
store.exe                   2744 MSExchangeIS
      C:\>tasklist /fi "imagename eq store.exe" /m

Image Name                   PID Modules
=========================== ======== =========================================
store.exe                   2744 ntdll.dll, kernel32.dll, ExTrace.dll,
                                 MSVCR80.dll, msvcrt.dll, ADVAPI32.dll,
                                 RPCRT4.dll, PSAPI.DLL, AUTHZ.dll,
                                 NTDSAPI.dll, DNSAPI.dll, WS2_32.dll,
                                 WS2HELP.dll, NETAPI32.dll, Secur32.dll,
                                 USER32.dll, GDI32.dll, WLDAP32.dll,
                                 EXRW.dll, ESE.dll, EXCHMEM.dll,
                                 dbghelp.dll, VERSION.dll, jcb.dll,
                                 mdbevent.dll, dsaccess.DLL, WSOCK32.dll,
                                 EPOXY.dll, mdbrole.dll, MDBSZ.dll,
                                 mdbtask.dll, ESCPRINT.dll, MSWSOCK.dll,
```

FIGURE 6-3   Tasklist in PowerShell

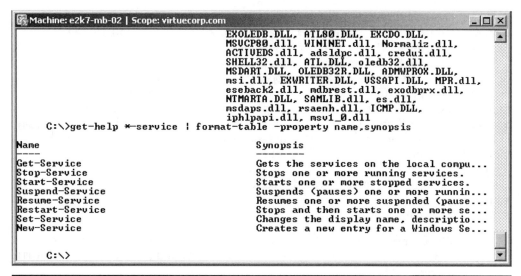

```
EXOLEDB.DLL, ATL80.DLL, EXCDO.DLL,
MSUCP80.dll, WININET.dll, Normaliz.dll,
ACTIUEDS.dll, adsldpc.dll, credui.dll,
SHELL32.dll, ATL.DLL, oledb32.dll,
MSDART.DLL, OLEDB32R.DLL, ADMWPROX.DLL,
msi.dll, EXWRITER.DLL, USSAPI.DLL, MPR.dll,
eseback2.dll, mdbrest.dll, exodbprx.dll,
NTMARTA.DLL, SAMLIB.dll, es.dll,
msdaps.dll, rsaenh.dll, ICMP.DLL,
iphlpapi.dll, msv1_0.dll
   C:\>get-help *-service | format-table -property name,synopsis

Name                             Synopsis
----                             --------
Get-Service                      Gets the services on the local compu...
Stop-Service                     Stops one or more running services.
Start-Service                    Starts one or more stopped services.
Suspend-Service                  Suspends (pauses) one or more runnin...
Resume-Service                   Resumes one or more suspended (pause...
Restart-Service                  Stops and then starts one or more se...
Set-Service                      Changes the display name, descriptio...
New-Service                      Creates a new entry for a Windows Se...


   C:\>
```

FIGURE 6-4   Controlling Exchange Services

The basic way of stopping and starting the MSExchangeIS service would be to use the following Power-Shell cmdlets:

- Stop-Service MSExchangeIS
- Start-Service MSExchangeIS

Mailbox Server Properties

Figure 6-5 shows the Exchange Management Console (EMC) with the Microsoft Exchange | Server Configuration node selected in the navigation pane. The Actions pane (on the right side) shows several ways in which this server may be managed.

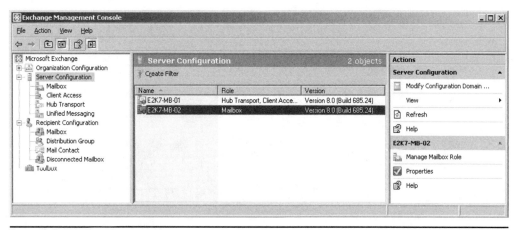

FIGURE 6-5   Mailbox Server actions

Select the server from the list in the middle pane and click the Properties button on the right. Two property sheets may be used for a mailbox server: General and Messaging Records Management. These are shown in Figures 6-6 and 6-7.

The cmdlet Get-ExchangeServer shows information about all Exchange servers in the organization, or just information about a specific server. The basic form that lists all servers and a few basic properties is shown in Figure 6-8, which is followed by the basic properties for one specific server: E2K7-MB-02. The output from Get-ExchangeServer could be sent to a formatter such as Format-List to show many more details, several of which are not visible in the EMC. Also in this figure is a call to the cmdlet Get-MailboxServer, which yields a view of a different set of properties than Get-ExchangeServer. Even though the basic information provided here is not all in the EMC, certainly the additional details provided by Get-MailboxServer | Format-List would exceed the level of detail needed for some administrators.

There are two messages here:

- Multiple interfaces may be used to manage Exchange Server mailbox servers, including the Exchange Management Console (EMC) and the Exchange Management Shell (EMS).

- The EMS provides access to many additional details and actions that are not available in the EMC.

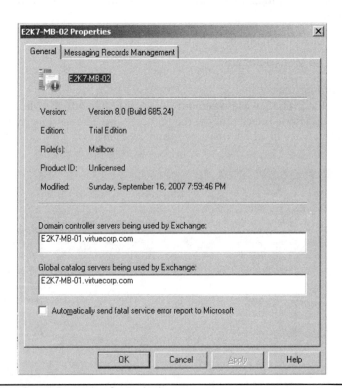

FIGURE 6-6   Mailbox Server Properties General tab

E2K7-MB-02 Properties
General
Messaging Records Management
Schedule the Managed Folder Assistant:
Never Run
Customize...
Never Run
Use Custom Schedule
OK
Cancel
Apply
Help

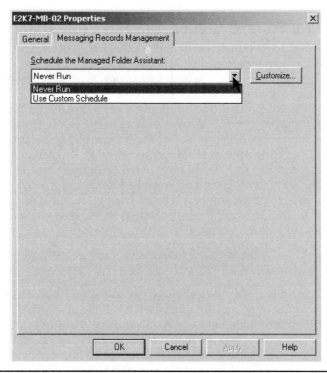

FIGURE 6-7 Mailbox Server Properties Messaging Records Management tab

The great news about this is that each administrator may choose which tool interface is best suited for any given task with which they are faced.

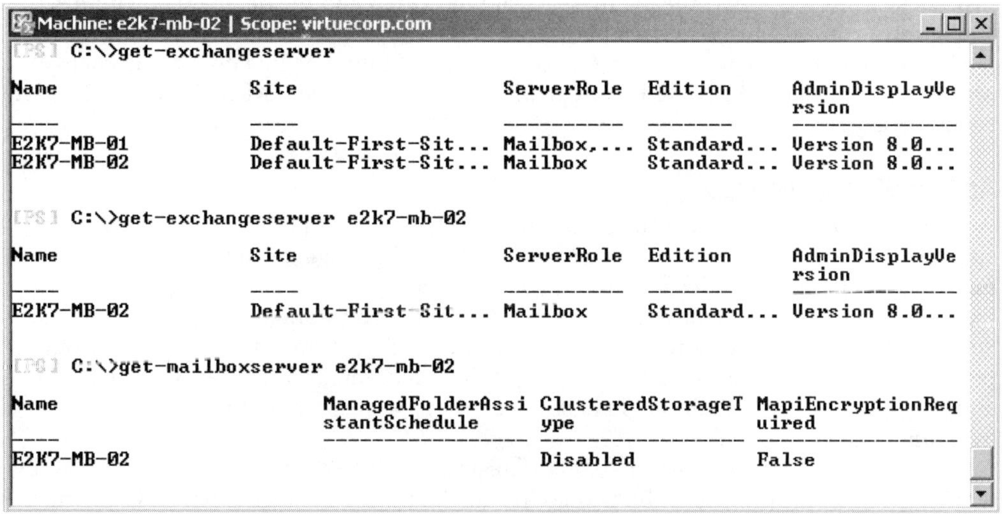

Machine: e2k7-mb-02 | Scope: virtuecorp.com
C:\>get-exchangeserver
Name Site ServerRole Edition AdminDisplayVersion
E2K7-MB-01 Default-First-Sit... Mailbox,... Standard... Version 8.0...
E2K7-MB-02 Default-First-Sit... Mailbox Standard... Version 8.0...
C:\>get-exchangeserver e2k7-mb-02
Name Site ServerRole Edition AdminDisplayVersion
E2K7-MB-02 Default-First-Sit... Mailbox Standard... Version 8.0...
C:\>get-mailboxserver e2k7-mb-02
Name ManagedFolderAssistantSchedule ClusteredStorageType MapiEncryptionRequired
E2K7-MB-02 Disabled False

FIGURE 6-8 Get-ExchangeServer Cmdlet

Storage Architecture: Storage Groups, Log Files, and Databases

The high-level manageable components for mailbox servers are storage groups and databases. Intrinsic in each storage group is a sequence of log files. Although each storage group could support a number of databases (as was done in earlier versions of Exchange Server), the recommended ratio is 1:1.

Exchange Server 2007 Standard Edition supports up to five storage groups and up to five databases, yet a mailbox server may have as little as one storage group with one database. Exchange Server 2007 Enterprise Edition supports up to 50 storage groups and up to 50 databases. These capabilities are favorable for larger capacity deployments when compared with Exchange Server 2003. As such, based on defaults and restrictions in the capacities, Exchange Server 2003 essentially forced a violation of the now recommended 1:1 ratio of databases per storage group, whereas Exchange Server 2007 certainly allows the flexibility of either complying with or deviating from the now generally recommended 1:1 ratio.

Storage Groups

Exchange Server 2007 with the Mailbox server role installed may host a number of message databases, which are most often mailbox databases, but could also include public folder databases. Note that public folder databases are no longer a first-class required feature of Exchange Server. Mailbox databases are therefore the primary reason, and in some deployments the sole reason, to have mailbox servers, which is evident from the name of the server role (Exchange Server 2003 used the name back-end servers, which hosted both mailboxes and public folders). Prior to discussing the details of mailbox database administration, a treatment of storage group administration is in order.

A *storage group* is a collection of one to five databases that share a common set of transaction log files and a checkpoint process. Each database uses a separate data file that accepts transactions lazily committed through the log files. Guidelines for recommended disk subsystems to support the log files of a storage group and the database(s) within a storage group are addressed in two parts: first for the log files, then for each database.

Storage groups may be added, removed, and reconfigured using either the Exchange Management Shell (EMS) or the Exchange Management Console (EMC). Both interfaces will be addressed here.

Adding Storage Groups

When the Mailbox server role is installed on an Exchange Server 2007 server, the default storage group First Storage Group is created. Additional storage groups may be added to a mailbox server, up to the licensing limits, which are no more than five storage groups on Exchange Server 2007 Standard Edition and no more than 50 storage groups on Exchange Server 2007 Enterprise Edition. One motivation for creating more than one storage group per server is essentially disaster recovery, including datacenter portability. Because cache and checkpoint depth are allocated per storage group, performance can be another motivating factor.

As with most Exchange Server 2007 administration, there are two principal methods by which new storage groups may be created in a mailbox server: the graphical user interface (GUI) Exchange Management Console (EMC) and the platform on which EMC is based, the Exchange Management Shell (EMS). Many administrators believe that EMS and its Windows PowerShell foundation are merely a command-line interface (CLI). Yet in reality EMS and PowerShell provide a scriptable platform that may indeed be accessed via a CLI, yet is also used by the EMC GUI (and could be used by other human interfaces).

EMS: New-StorageGroup

The EMS command New-StorageGroup has a self-explanatory name—this command may be used to create a new storage group on an Exchange Server 2007 mailbox server. In the most basic form of the command, two parameters are required, as shown in the following example and Figure 6-9:

```
new-storagegroup  -name  "Virtuous Storage Group" -server  E2K7-MB-01.
virtuecorp.com
```

Note that the current server is not implied—a server designation must be specified explicitly. The name of the storage group must be unique within that server, and the maximum number of storage groups allowed on that server must not be exceeded. Also, a number of options are supplied with default values unless explicitly specified. The get-help new-storagegroup command shows some of these. Figure 6-10 shows the New-StorageGroup cmdlets syntax.

For creating a normal storage group, the syntax from get-help is as follows:

```
New-StorageGroup -Name <String> -Server <ServerIdParameter>
[-CircularLoggingEnabled <$true | $false>] [-HasLocalCopy <$true | $false>]
[-ZeroDatabasePages <$true | $false>] [-CopyLogFolderPath
<NonRootLocalLongFullPath>] [-CopySystemFolderPath <NonRootLocalLongFullPath>]
[-LogFolderPath <NonRootLocalLongFullPath>] [-SystemFolderPath
<NonRootLocalLongFullPath>] [-TemplateInstance <PSObject>] [-DomainController
<Fqdn>] [<CommonParameters>]
```

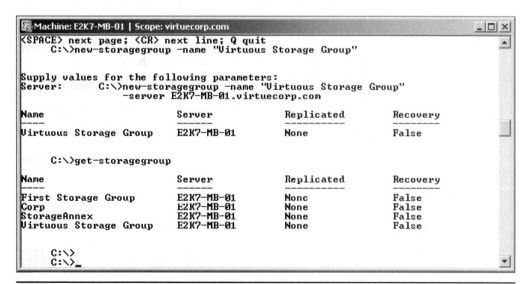

FIGURE 6-9 Creating a New Storage Group

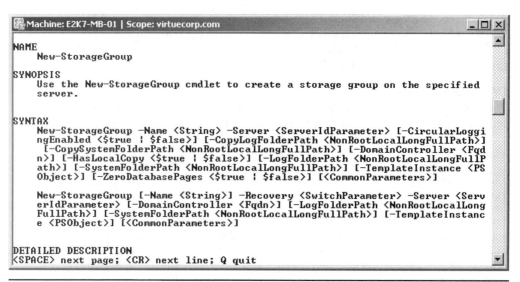

```
Machine: E2K7-MB-01 | Scope: virtuecorp.com                          _ □ ×
NAME
    New-StorageGroup

SYNOPSIS
    Use the New-StorageGroup cmdlet to create a storage group on the specified
    server.

SYNTAX
    New-StorageGroup -Name <String> -Server <ServerIdParameter> [-CircularLoggi
    ngEnabled <$true | $false>] [-CopyLogFolderPath <NonRootLocalLongFullPath>]
     [-CopySystemFolderPath <NonRootLocalLongFullPath>] [-DomainController <Fqd
    n>] [-HasLocalCopy <$true | $false>] [-LogFolderPath <NonRootLocalLongFullP
    ath>] [-SystemFolderPath <NonRootLocalLongFullPath>] [-TemplateInstance <PS
    Object>] [-ZeroDatabasePages <$true | $false>] [<CommonParameters>]

    New-StorageGroup [-Name <String>] -Recovery <SwitchParameter> -Server <Serv
    erIdParameter> [-DomainController <Fqdn>] [-LogFolderPath <NonRootLocalLong
    FullPath>] [-SystemFolderPath <NonRootLocalLongFullPath>] [-TemplateInstanc
    e <PSObject>] [<CommonParameters>]

DETAILED DESCRIPTION
<SPACE> next page; <CR> next line; Q quit
```

FIGURE 6-10   New-StorageGroup cmdlet

Note that only the name of the storage group and the server (the required parameters) were used in the previous example of the Virtuous Storage Group. This implies that values for the other parameters—notably the log folder path, the system folder path, the choice of domain controller, and options such as circular logging and whether to zero out database pages—were assigned default values. In reality, many additional attributes of a storage group may be viewed or tuned. Whereas New-StorageGroup was illustrated in Figure 6-10 to show the table of all storage groups, the full details of a single storage group may be obtained using get-storagegroup -name "Virtuous Storage Group" | Format-list to format the output as a list of attributes as opposed to the default EMS table format as shown in Figure 6-11.

Many of the attributes are Active Directory foundation attributes and don't have a direct effect on the functionality of Exchange Server 2007. Some examples in Figure 6-11 include DistinguishedName, Identity, Guid, ObjectCategory, ObjectClass, WhenChanged, WhenCreated, OriginatingServer, and IsValid. Several attributes are notably the same as the options on the New-StorageGroup command, whereas LogFilePrefix, LogFileSize, LogCheckpointDepth, DatabaseExtensionSize, PageFragment, and others are not exposed in the new-storagegroup interface. A subset of the parameters—mostly those that can be assigned initially when using new-storagegroup—can be assigned or modified later using set-storagegroup and can be viewed using get-storagegroup.

EMC: New Storage Group...

The EMC may be used to create new storage groups as well. This method is merely a graphical shell around the core functionality of the EMS's new-storagegroup command. The New Storage Group Wizard is initiated by selecting a server in the EMC's Microsoft

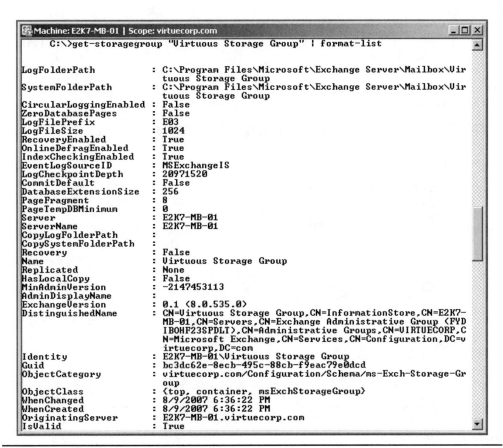

```
Machine: E2K7-MB-01 | Scope: virtuecorp.com                                    _ □ x

          C:\>get-storagegroup "Virtuous Storage Group" | format-list

LogFolderPath              : C:\Program Files\Microsoft\Exchange Server\Mailbox\Vir
                             tuous Storage Group
SystemFolderPath           : C:\Program Files\Microsoft\Exchange Server\Mailbox\Vir
                             tuous Storage Group
CircularLoggingEnabled     : False
ZeroDatabasePages          : False
LogFilePrefix              : E03
LogFileSize                : 1024
RecoveryEnabled            : True
OnlineDefragEnabled        : True
IndexCheckingEnabled       : True
EventLogSourceID           : MSExchangeIS
LogCheckpointDepth         : 20971520
CommitDefault              : False
DatabaseExtensionSize      : 256
PageFragment               : 8
PageTempDBMinimum          : 0
Server                     : E2K7-MB-01
ServerName                 : E2K7-MB-01
CopyLogFolderPath          :
CopySystemFolderPath       :
Recovery                   : False
Name                       : Virtuous Storage Group
Replicated                 : None
HasLocalCopy               : False
MinAdminVersion            : -2147453113
AdminDisplayName           :
ExchangeVersion            : 0.1 (8.0.535.0)
DistinguishedName          : CN=Virtuous Storage Group,CN=InformationStore,CN=E2K7-
                             MB-01,CN=Servers,CN=Exchange Administrative Group (FYD
                             IBOHF23SPDLT),CN=Administrative Groups,CN=VIRTUECORP,C
                             N=Microsoft Exchange,CN=Services,CN=Configuration,DC=v
                             irtuecorp,DC=com
Identity                   : E2K7-MB-01\Virtuous Storage Group
Guid                       : bc3dc62e-8ecb-495c-88cb-f9eac79e0dcd
ObjectCategory             : virtuecorp.com/Configuration/Schema/ms-Exch-Storage-Gr
                             oup
ObjectClass                : {top, container, msExchStorageGroup}
WhenChanged                : 8/9/2007 6:36:22 PM
WhenCreated                : 8/9/2007 6:36:22 PM
OriginatingServer          : E2K7-MB-01.virtuecorp.com
IsValid                    : True
```

FIGURE 6-11 Viewing the attributes of a storage group

Exchange | Server Configuration | Mailbox category and then choosing the New Storage Group... action (see Figure 6-12). As is customary in the EMC, this action may be chosen in a number of ways:

- Using the Action menu
- Right-clicking the server in the Mailbox role list and using the resulting context menu
- Using the link in the Actions pane of the console

To use the most basic form of the EMC New Storage Group Wizard, simply enter a name for the storage group and click the New button. This will run the new-storagegroup command with the appropriate options. Note that the server identity is supplied by EMC to the underlying EMS, because the server was selected prior to choosing the New Storage

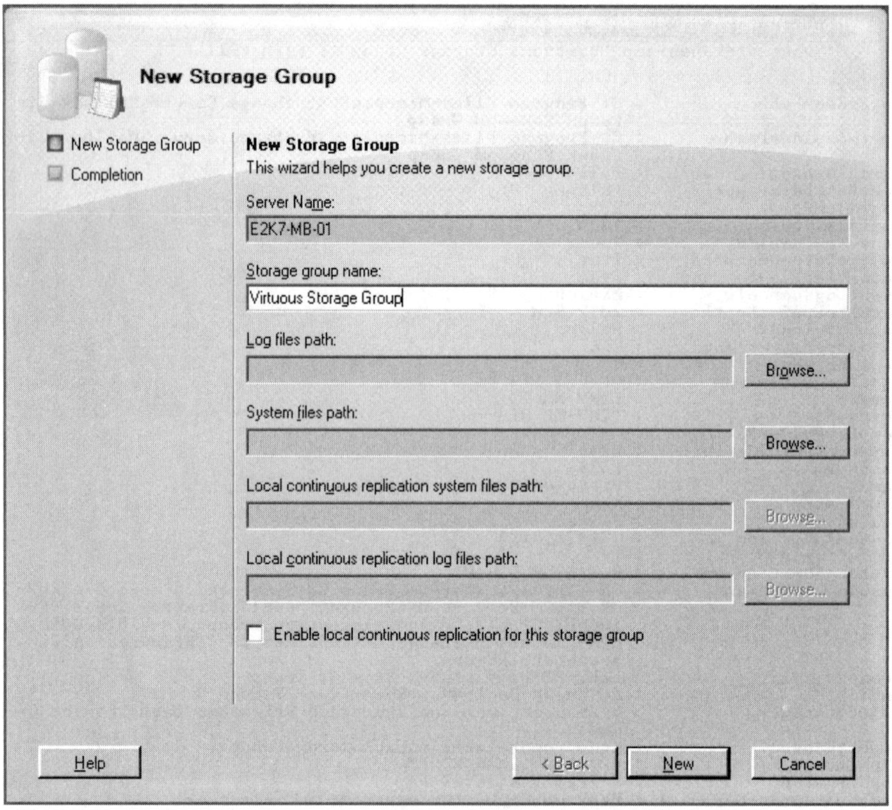

New Storage Group

- ☐ New Storage Group
- ☐ Completion

New Storage Group
This wizard helps you create a new storage group.

Server Name:
```
E2K7-MB-01
```

Storage group name:
```
Virtuous Storage Group
```

Log files path:
```
```
Browse...

System files path:
```
```
Browse...

Local continuous replication system files path:
```
```
Browse...

Local continuous replication log files path:
```
```
Browse...

☐ Enable local continuous replication for this storage group

Help   < Back   New   Cancel

FIGURE 6-12 New Storage Group wizard

Group... action. Regardless of whether this basic (name only) form of the wizard is used or when additional parameters are used (described later in this section), the Completion page of the wizard shows the actual EMS command that was executed by the wizard. Note that not only are the server identity and new storage group name specified, but values for the log folder path and system folder path are also supplied by the EMC to the EMS. Both of these default to the path of the default mailbox folder prefix, plus the name of the storage group as an additional folder level. For example, with C:\Program Files\Microsoft\ Exchange Server\Mailbox\ as the default mailbox folder path prefix, the storage group named Virtuous Storage Group is assigned a log files path of C:\Program Files\Microsoft\ Exchange Server\Mailbox\Virtuous Storage Group, which is also assigned as a system files path. This is shown in the sample Completion page in Figure 6-13.

Alternate paths and Local Continuous Replication (LCR) configuration may also be specified in the New Storage Group Wizard. Click the Browse... button next to either the log files path or system files path to change the corresponding path. Check the box labeled

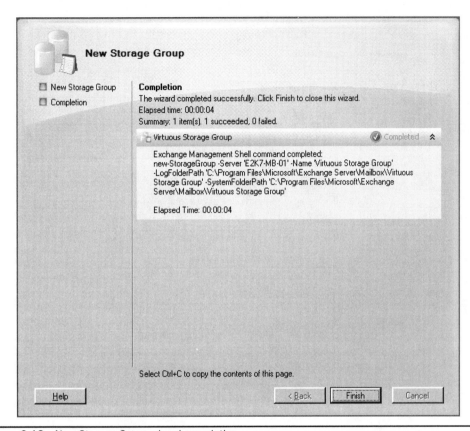

New Storage Group

New Storage Group
Completion

Completion
The wizard completed successfully. Click Finish to close this wizard.
Elapsed time: 00:00:04
Summary: 1 item(s). 1 succeeded, 0 failed.

Virtuous Storage Group   ✓ Completed ☆

Exchange Management Shell command completed:
new-StorageGroup -Server 'E2K7-MB-01' -Name 'Virtuous Storage Group'
-LogFolderPath 'C:\Program Files\Microsoft\Exchange Server\Mailbox\Virtuous
Storage Group' -SystemFolderPath 'C:\Program Files\Microsoft\Exchange
Server\Mailbox\Virtuous Storage Group'

Elapsed Time: 00:00:04

Select Ctrl+C to copy the contents of this page.

Help   < Back   Finish   Cancel

FIGURE 6-13   New Storage Group wizard completion

"Enable local continuous replication for this storage group" to enable Local Continuous
Replication and then be able to specify the log files and system files paths for the copy
(see Figure 6-14).

Note that the EMS command that is run with these values supplied in the wizard will
include the -HasLocalCopy, -CopyLogFolderPath, and -CopySystemFolderPath options, as
shown in the example in Figure 6-15.

EMS: Set-StorageGroup

Some parameters for a storage group can later be changed using the Set-StorageGroup
command; yet other attributes of a storage group are changed using the enable-
storagegroupcopy, disable-storagegroupcopy, and move-storagegrouppath commands. Just
the values that may be assigned using set-storagegroup are described here. Figure 6-16
shows the get-help set-storagegroup syntax.

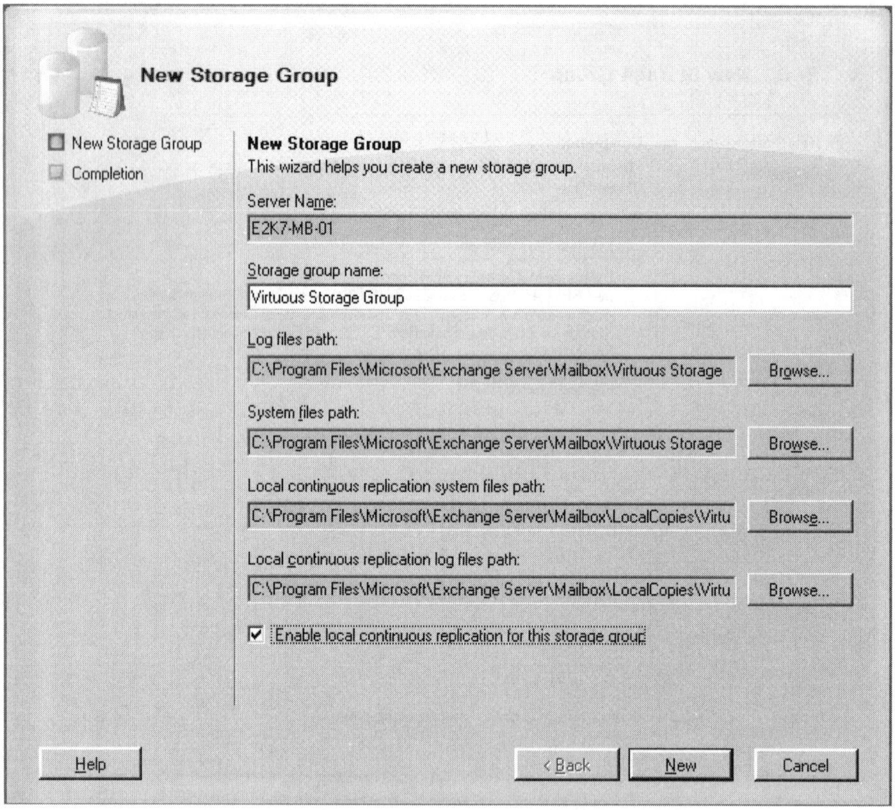

FIGURE 6-14 Enabling Local Continuous Replication with EMC

In the remainder of this chapter, the syntax for the EMS cmdlets will be described using a few variations from what is displayed by Get-Help. As shown in Figure 6-16, the two forms of Set-StorageGroup are mostly the same. The difference between the two forms is in the two methods by which the storage group being reconfigured is specified. The Identity parameter allows various names to be used to identity a storage group, yet the Instance parameter may be used to specify a PowerShell variable that has been previous assigned as a reference to the desired storage group. These two alternate forms are shown next with the logical OR as a vertical bar (|), as is customary in a number of syntax notation methods. In addition, although Get-Help does not indicate this in the figure (but does in the output of Get-Help Set-StorageGroup -Full and in the reality of running the cmdlet), the Identity keyword is actually optional when specifying a storage group identifier as the first parameter. Therefore, as is also the custom in numerous syntax notations, square brackets are used to denote this. Both the vertical bar and square brackets are used in other ways in the regular Get-Help output. Furthermore, in examples in the remainder of this chapter, common parameters such as DomainController are percolated toward the end of our display of the syntax. Therefore, a more concise representation of the Set-StorageGroup syntax is as follows:

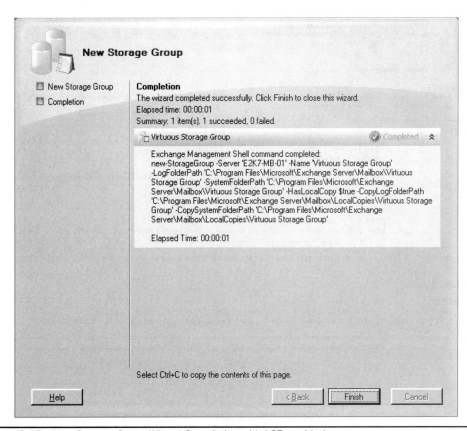

FIGURE 6-15 New Storage Group Wizard Completion with LCR enabled

```
Set-StorageGroup [[-Identity] <StorageGroupIdParameter> |-Instance
<StorageGroup>] [-Name  <String>] [-CircularLoggingEnabled <$true |
$false>] [-ZeroDatabasePages <$true | $false>] [-DomainController  <Fqdn>]
[<CommonParameters>]
```

By comparing the syntax of Get-StorageGroup with that of New-StorageGroup, it becomes evident that only a few of the attributes (also called properties) of a storage group configured at its creation may be later modified by the Set-StorageGroup cmdlet. There are other cmdlets that perform manipulation of other attributes and additional behaviors of storage groups. Furthermore, by comparing the output of Get-StorageGroup | Format-List, as shown in the figure, with the possible parameters of either New-StorageGroup or Set-StorageGroup, another truth may surface: There are many attributes of a storage group that are not normally administratively configurable, but have operating system defaults. In some cases these may be modified via methods other than EMS, such as using the Lightweight Directory Access Protocol (LDAP) to make changes directly in the Active Directory representation of the storage group. This is true not just of storage groups, but most any EMS object class, and it's also true of most object classes in EMS's PowerShell foundation.

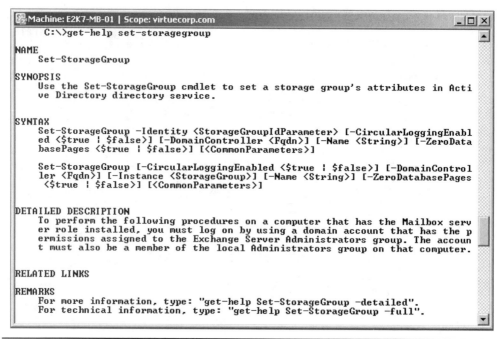

```
Machine: E2K7-MB-01 | Scope: virtuecorp.com                    _ □ ×
       C:\>get-help set-storagegroup

NAME
     Set-StorageGroup

SYNOPSIS
     Use the Set-StorageGroup cmdlet to set a storage group's attributes in Acti
     ve Directory directory service.

SYNTAX
     Set-StorageGroup -Identity <StorageGroupIdParameter> [-CircularLoggingEnabl
     ed <$true : $false>] [-DomainController <Fqdn>] [-Name <String>] [-ZeroData
     basePages <$true : $false>] [<CommonParameters>]

     Set-StorageGroup [-CircularLoggingEnabled <$true : $false>] [-DomainControl
     ler <Fqdn>] [-Instance <StorageGroup>] [-Name <String>] [-ZeroDatabasePages
     <$true : $false>] [<CommonParameters>]


DETAILED DESCRIPTION
     To perform the following procedures on a computer that has the Mailbox serv
     er role installed, you must log on by using a domain account that has the p
     ermissions assigned to the Exchange Server Administrators group. The accoun
     t must also be a member of the local Administrators group on that computer.


RELATED LINKS

REMARKS
     For more information, type: "get-help Set-StorageGroup -detailed".
     For technical information, type: "get-help Set-StorageGroup -full".
```

FIGURE 6-16   Set-Storage Cmdlet

Some of the cmdlets available for managing storage groups are revealed by using Get-ExCommand *storage*, as illustrated in Figure 6-17.

```
Machine: E2K7-MB-01 | Scope: virtuecorp.com                    _ □ ×
       C:\>get-excommand *storage*

CommandType        Name                          Definition
-----------        ----                          ----------
Cmdlet             Disable-StorageGroupCopy      Disable-StorageGroupCopy [-I...
Cmdlet             Enable-StorageGroupCopy       Enable-StorageGroupCopy [-Id...
Cmdlet             Get-StorageGroup              Get-StorageGroup [[-Identity...
Cmdlet             Get-StorageGroupCopyStatus    Get-StorageGroupCopyStatus [...
Cmdlet             Move-StorageGroupPath         Move-StorageGroupPath [-Iden...
Cmdlet             New-StorageGroup              New-StorageGroup [-Name] <St...
Cmdlet             Remove-StorageGroup           Remove-StorageGroup [-Identi...
Cmdlet             Restore-StorageGroupCopy      Restore-StorageGroupCopy [-I...
Cmdlet             Resume-StorageGroupCopy       Resume-StorageGroupCopy [-Id...
Cmdlet             Set-StorageGroup              Set-StorageGroup [-Identity]...
Cmdlet             Suspend-StorageGroupCopy      Suspend-StorageGroupCopy [-I...
Cmdlet             Update-StorageGroupCopy       Update-StorageGroupCopy [-Id...


       C:\>
```

FIGURE 6-17   Cmdlets for Managing Storage Groups

EMS: Move-StorageGroupPath

As was mentioned in the description of Set-StorageGroup, some aspects of a storage group are assigned by New-StorageGroup upon creation of the storage group and may not be later modified using Set-StorageGroup. One such example is the file system path to the database transaction log files and system files for the storage group. These are actually two different paths. In addition, two more paths specify the Local Continuous Replication paths for the storage group. These are moved using the Move-StorageGroupPath cmdlet.

Note that the SystemFolderPath parameter takes a local file system volume path that is fully qualified and not the root of the hierarchy C:\, which is what the data type name <NonRootLocalLongFullPath> indicates. This system folder path is where the system files (for example, E00.chk and tmp.edb) will be stored. If this value is specified to Move-StorageGroupPath, two changes will occur:

- The existing E00.chk and tmp.edb (or similar) files are moved from the old location to the new location
- The configuration of where to store these files in the future for this storage group will be modified.

Note that if the ConfigurationOnly parameter is also included, the copying of the existing files is skipped and only the configuration of the path for future operations of the storage group will be changed. The ConfigurationOnly parameter is of type <SwitchParameter>, which means that it could be given a Boolean value of <$true | $false> (true or false; 1 or 0), yet its mere presence assumes the value of $true.

The value for the LogFolderPath may be the same as or different from the SystemFolderPath, yet they are the same by default. The log folder path is where the temporary log files, two reserved files, and the sequence of log files are stored (for example, E00tmp.log, E00res00001.jrs, E00res00002.jrs, E00.log, and many E0000000001.log files in sequence). Again, the ConfigurationOnly switch allows the cmdlet to skip copying the preexisting log files, reducing the "move" to just changing the path of the storage group without moving the old files.

Similarly, the CopyLogFolderPath and CopySystemFolderPath parameters may be used to specify different values for the attributes by the same name than were originally specified to New-StorageGroup when the storage group was created.

EMS: Get-StorageGroup

The Get-StorageGroup cmdlet reads the configuration of one or more storage groups into memory (RAM) in an object-oriented format that may be used in subsequent operations such as Set-StorageGroup. Yet in its most basic use, Get-StorageGroup will be used to display the current attributes of the storage group(s).

There are four ways of "getting" the storage group or groups. You can specify with the name of an individual storage group with the -Identity parameter. You can get all storage groups from a specific server with the -Server parameter. You can get storage groups from Exchange 2000/2003 servers with the -IncludePreExchange2007 parameter. Or you can show all storage groups in the Organization by not specifying any additional parameter. All the storage groups selected in one of these ways are loaded into RAM. If the output of Get-StorageGroup is not piped to a specific formatter and Get-StorageGroup is also not used in an expression (such as being assigned to a variable), the default formatter Format-Table will be used to display the Name, Server, Replicated, and Recovery attributes (properties) of the storage groups. Explicit use of Format-Table could be employed to control exactly which properties are displayed, or some/all properties could be displayed using another formatter such as Format-List. Figure 6-18 shows a list of nine storage groups on two servers.

An example of the command follows:

```
Get-StorageGroup E2K7-MB-02\EngSG3 | Format-List
```

Although the output of Get-StorageGroup | Format-List is far more than most administrators may care about, the important thing to note here is that more information is lurking under the hood than Get-StorageGroup and many other cmdlets may at first reveal. If any of the elements shown by Format-List prove to be useful for management, then having used Format-List at least once to discover such information would have been worth it. We will not discuss all the attributes of a storage group here.

EMS: Remove-StorageGroup

When all mailboxes have been moved out (or disabled) from all databases within a storage group, you can decommission the storage group by deleting it using the Remove-StorageGroup cmdlet. The syntax is as follows:

```
Remove-StorageGroup [[-Identity] <StorageGroupIdParameter>]
[-DomainController  <Fqdn>] [<CommonParameters>]
```

The Remove-StorageGroup cmdlet may either take an explicit -Identity value of the storage group, which will be removed, or one or more storage groups could be passed along a pipeline to Remove-StorageGroup. Consider these two examples:

```
Remove-StorageGroup E2K7-MB-04\EastwickSG1
Get-StorageGroup -Server E2K7-MB-04 | Remove-StorageGroup
```

In the first example, a single storage group (E2K7-MB-04\EastwickSG1) would be removed, and in the second example all storage groups on the server E2K7-MB-04 would be removed.

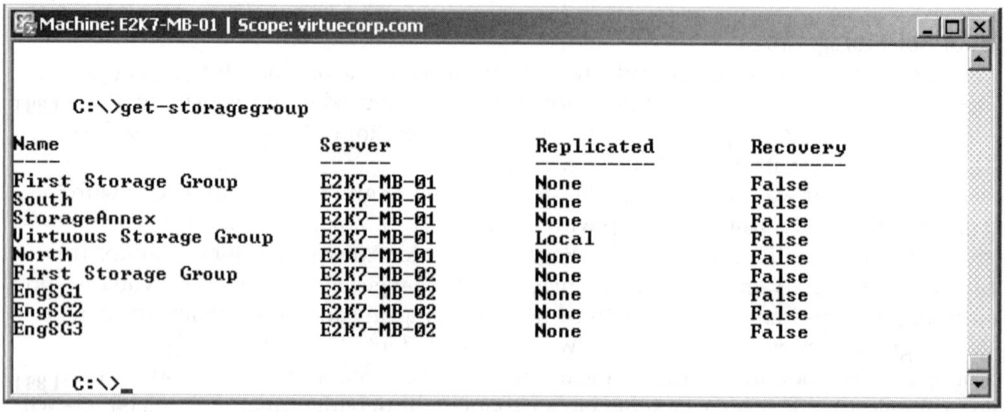

```
Machine: E2K7-MB-01 | Scope: virtuecorp.com                              _ □ X



    C:\>get-storagegroup

Name                        Server        Replicated        Recovery
----                        ------        ----------        --------
First Storage Group         E2K7-MB-01    None              False
South                       E2K7-MB-01    None              False
StorageAnnex                E2K7-MB-01    None              False
Virtuous Storage Group      E2K7-MB-01    Local             False
North                       E2K7-MB-01    None              False
First Storage Group         E2K7-MB-02    None              False
EngSG1                      E2K7-MB-02    None              False
EngSG2                      E2K7-MB-02    None              False
EngSG3                      E2K7-MB-02    None              False


    C:\>_
```

FIGURE 6-18   Enumerating Storage Groups with the EMS

Storage Group Continuous Replication Control

Beside the use of New-StorageGroup or Set-StorageGroup to specify a CopyLogFolderPath and/or CopySystem-FolderPath, the following cmdlets can be use to help manage the functionality of continuous replication (such as Local Continuous Replication) within a storage group:

- EMS: Enable-StorageGroupCopy
- EMS: Disable-StorageGroupCopy
- EMS: Get-StorageGroupCopyStatus
- EMS: Suspend-StorageGroupCopy
- EMS: Resume-StorageGroupCopy
- EMS: Update-StorageGroupCopy
- EMS: Restore-StorageGroupCopy

EMC: Storage Group Properties

The Exchange Management Console (EMC) may be used as a front end to the Get-StorageGroup, Set-StorageGroup, and Move-StorageGroupPath cmdlets. When a mailbox server is selected in the EMC's Microsoft Exchange | Server Configuration | Mailbox category, the bottom of the details pane and the Actions pane will adjust to this context, as shown in Figure 6-19.

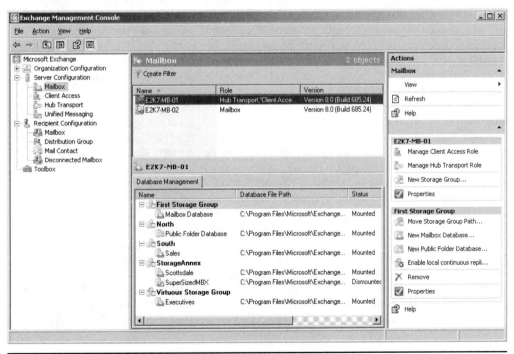

FIGURE 6-19   Enumerating storage groups with the EMC

Figure 6-19 shows the server E2K7-MB-01 selected within the Mailbox category. The Database Management tab at the bottom of the middle of the console shows a list of storage groups hosted by that server and the databases within those storage groups. On the right side, in the Actions pane, are three sets of actions:

- In the Mailbox category, you have the View, Refresh, and Help actions.
- For the E2K7-MB-01 mailbox server, there are buttons to hyperlink to the Manage Client Access Role or Manage Hub Transport Role categories within the console; there is also a link to launch the New Storage Group Wizard and a button to obtain the server's properties.
- For the selected storage group within the server (the First Storage Group in this case) you'll find buttons for the following actions:
  - Moving the storage group path.
  - Creating a new mailbox database within the storage group
  - Creating a new public folder database within the storage group
  - Enabling Local Continuous Replication for the storage group
  - Removing the storage group
  - Obtaining the properties of the storage group

For servers that are dedicated mailbox servers, the set of possible actions will be somewhat smaller (notably there is a lack of hyperlinks for managing other roles because there are no other roles beside the Mailbox role on such servers). An example of this is shown in Figure 6-20 with the mailbox server E2K7-MB-02 selected.

Within the Database Management sheet in a mailbox server's context, the storage groups and databases in the server can be managed. For instance, to obtain the properties of a storage group, select the storage group within that pane and click the Properties button. This is just one method—there are other variations. The properties for the storage group EngSG3 are shown in Figure 6-21.

Only the Name and CircularLoggingEnabled properties of the storage group may be modified on this property sheet by using the name text field at the top or the Enable Circular Logging check box at the bottom of the property sheet and then clicking Apply or OK to commit the changes. The process of obtaining the property sheet utilizes the EMS cmdlet Get-StorageGroup behind the scenes and renders the attributes in the graphical property sheet. Changing the values is like modifying the attributes of variable in EMS, and using Apply or OK performs a Set-StorageGroup on the storage group variable with the accumulated changes. All the data shown on the property sheet, and in the list of storage groups for that matter, is obtained by the fact that the programmers who developed the EMC used the underlying operations we could use in the corresponding EMS cmdlets.

Just as the Move-StorageGroupPath provides separate functionality not included in Set-StorageGroup, in the EMC we use the Move Storage Group Path... button in the Actions pane to launch the Move Storage Group Path Wizard. The pages of the wizard are naturally similar to those in the New Storage Group Wizard; therefore, we'll not reiterate the details here. The Move Storage Group Path Wizard calls the Move-StorageGroupPath cmdlet once the updated path values have been input graphically.

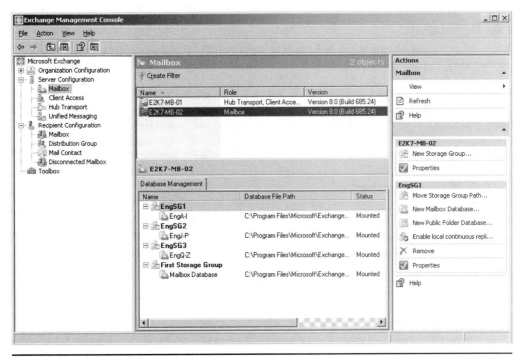

FIGURE 6-20   EMC actions associated with the mailbox role

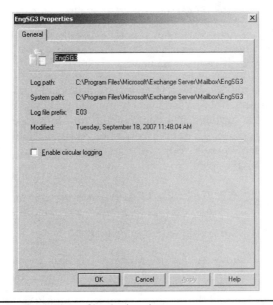

FIGURE 6-21   Storage Group Properties—Circular Logging

Mailbox Databases

Mailbox databases are the heart of Exchange Server 2007. With the Mailbox server role, the reason storage groups exist is to host the mailbox databases. Exchange Server natively allows MAPI access to mailboxes in each database. The reason why Hub Transport servers exist is to relay messages to and from mailboxes in these databases; Client Access servers allow various front ends for MAPI access; Unified Messaging servers allow voice access as well as inbound faxes and voicemail destined for these mailbox databases. This section of the chapter focuses on the mailbox database administration itself, whereas storage group and individual mailbox administration are detailed elsewhere in this chapter.

Adding Mailbox Databases

The default installation of Exchange Server 2007 automatically creates one mailbox database in the First Storage Group, called the mailbox database. In small deployments where the single mailbox database is sufficient, the self-explanatory name is helpful. Although a combination of up to five mailbox databases and public folder databases could be added per storage group, the recommended best practice is to utilize a 1:1 ratio with each storage group hosting just one database. In fact, in order to benefit from Local Continuous Replication (LCR) on the storage group (for the database), there must be only one database per storage group.

EMS: New-MailboxDatabase

The EMS New-MailboxDatabase cmdlet may be used in two ways, with a different form of syntax for each purpose. The first form is used to create a new mailbox database from scratch. The two required parameters are Name and StorageGroup. Note that the StorageGroup parameter may be either literally supplied or piped in from a preceding cmdlet.

```
New-MailboxDatabase -Name <String> -StorageGroup <StorageGroupIdParameter>
[-EdbFilePath  <EdbFilePath>] [-DomainController  <Fqdn>]  [-HasLocalCopy
<$true | $false>] [-CopyEdbFilePath  <EdbFilePath>] [-OfflineAddressBook
<OfflineAddressBookIdParameter>]  [-PublicFolderDatabase
<DatabaseIdParameter>]  [-TemplateInstance <PSObject>] [<CommonParameters>]
```

The -EdbFilePath parameter defaults to %programfiles%\Microsoft\Exchange Server\ Mailbox\<Storage Group name>\<Database name>.edb. Yet when explicitly specified, an alternate value may be supplied. The common parameters supported by New-MailboxDatabase are -Verbose, -Debug, -ErrorAction, -ErrorVariable, and -OutVariable. An example with only the StorageGroup and Name parameters uses the default for the Exchange database (EDB) file path.

```
New-MailboxDatabase -StorageGroup "E2K7-MB-01\First Storage Group" ' -Name
"Marketing Mailboxes"
```

In this example, the EDB file path would effectively be:

```
%programfiles%\ Microsoft\ Exchange Server\ Mailbox\ First Storage Group\
Marketing Mailboxes.edb
```

With the primary instance of the database mounted under P:\Marketing\, the syntax would be:

```
New-MailboxDatabase -StorageGroup "E2K7-MB-01\First Storage Group" ' -Name
"Marketing Mailboxes" -EdbFilePath "P:\Marketing\Marketing Mailboxes.edb"
```

In this example, the EDB file path would effectively be:

```
P:\ Marketing\ Marketing Mailboxes.edb
```

If the path C:\Program Files\Microsoft\Exchange Server\Mailbox\First Storage Group \Marketing\ is the mount point for the Retrieval and Information Database (RAID) volume to be used to house the database for the marketing department's mailboxes, assuming that the $exinstall PowerShell variable is C:\Program Files\Microsoft\Exchange Server\, the following notation could be used to create the new mailbox database:

```
New-MailboxDatabase -StorageGroup "E2K7-MB-01\First Storage Group" ' -Name
"Marketing Mailboxes" ' -EdbFilePath "${exinstall}Mailbox\First Storage
Group\Marketing\Marketing Mailboxes.edb"
```

In this example, the EDB file path would effectively be:

```
%programfiles%\ Microsoft\ Exchange Server\ Mailbox\ First Storage Group\
Marketing\ Marketing Mailboxes.edb
```

Yet, using a variable for the First Storage Group in this example (although any storage group is possible), the EdbFilePath parameter to New-MailboxDatabase is much shorter. The following EMS fragment shows an example of this:

```
$fsg="${exinstall}Mailbox\First Storage Group\"
New-MailboxDatabase ' -EdbFilePath "${fsg}Marketing\Marketing Mailboxes.edb"
```

Going one step further, a handle to the actual storage group (First Storage Group in this example) can be obtained via the Get-StorageGroup cmdlet. Then the LogFolderPath. PathName can be obtained and used as in the previous script. Note that we've included the trailing backslash (\) for the folder path in order to be consistent with the ${exinstall} value's format.

```
$fsgh=get-storagegroup "First Storage Group"
$fsg = $fsgh.LogFolderPath.PathName + "\"
New-MailboxDatabase ' -EdbFilePath "${fsg}Marketing\Marketing Mailboxes.edb"
```

Many more ways of using New-MailboxDatabase in conjunction with other cmdlets, commands, and variables are possible. These few brief examples are intended to illustrate that not all parameters need be literal.

The New-MailboxDatabase cmdlet has another syntax specifically designed for recovering mailbox databases. The only two required parameters are MailboxDatabaseToRecover and StorageGroup.

```
New-MailboxDatabase [-Name <String>] -MailboxDatabaseToRecover
<DatabaseIdParameter> -StorageGroup <StorageGroupIdParameter>
[-DomainController <Fqdn>] [-EdbFilePath <EdbFilePath>]
[-TemplateInstance <PSObject>] [<CommonParameters>]
```

Deleting Mailbox Databases

Although less common than adding new databases, the ability to delete mailbox databases is a necessary function of Exchange Server. All mailboxes within the database should first be move or deleted from the database prior to the deletion of the database itself.

EMS: Remove-MailboxDatabase

The EMS syntax for deleting a mailbox database has only a few parameters, only one of which is required:

```
Remove-MailboxDatabase -Identity <DatabaseIdParameter> [-DomainController
<Fqdn>] [<CommonParameters>]
```

The Identity parameter may be specified as a DatabaseIdParameter, which can be one of the following three types of database identity:

- Globally unique identifier (GUID)
- Distinguished name (DN)
- Mailbox database name

Note that Identity could be piped into the Remove-MailboxDatabase cmdlet rather than explicitly specified in the cmdlet.

For example, the mailbox database name could itself be specified in three forms:

- **Just the database name**   -Identity "SuperSizedMBX"
- **The storage group and database name**   -Identity "StorageAnnex\SuperSizedMBX"
- **The server, storage group, and database name**   -Identity "E2K7-MB-01\ StorageAnnex\SuperSizedMBX"

Alternatively, the GUID or DN could be used as follows:

- -Identity "{d86a09ca-f0cd-4939-ac5a-93385713f33b}"
- -Identity "CN=SuperSizedMBX,CN=StorageAnnex,CN=Information Store,CN=E2K7-MB-01, CN=Servers,CN=Exchange Administrative Group (FYDIBOHF23SPDLT), CN=Administrative Groups,CN=VIRTUECORP,CN=Micros oft Exchange, CN=Services,CN=Configuration,DC=virtuecorp,DC=com"

Both the GUID and DN may be obtained from Get-MailboxDatabase for use with other cmdlets, such as Remove-MailboxDatabase, which itself requires an identity to be explicitly specified or some other selection method used. Therefore, these forms could be used practically to avoid ambiguity with the name forms.

All mailboxes must be either moved, removed, or disabled from a mailbox database prior to the removal of the database itself. For further information on these methods, refer to the discussions of the following cmdlets:

- Move-Mailbox
- Remove-Mailbox

- Disable-Mailbox
- Clean-MailboxDatabase

The first three operate on mailboxes, whereas Clean-MailboxDatabase works with a whole mailbox database to properly disable disconnected mailboxes.

Mounting and Dismounting Databases

Each database within a storage group may be mounted or dismounted, thereby making normal Microsoft Exchange Information Store Service access to the database either possible or not possible, respectively. Databases are automatically dismounted by several other administrative tasks, such as Move-DatabasePath and even New-MailboxDatabase. Mounted and dismounted database states are also referred to as online and offline; therefore, a term such as "offline backup" means that the backup is performed against a dismounted database. Two separate cmdlets are used to mount and dismount Exchange Server 2007 databases.

EMS: Dismount-Database

The EMS syntax for dismounting a mailbox database has only a few parameters, only one of which is required:

```
Dismount-Database -Identity <DatabaseIdParameter> [-DomainController
<Fqdn>] [<CommonParameters>]
```

The Identity parameter may be specified as a DatabaseIdParameter, which is described in the discussion of the Remove-MailboxDatabase cmdlet.

EMS: Mount-Database

The EMS syntax for deleting a mailbox database has only a few parameters, only one of which is required:

```
Mount-Database -Identity <DatabaseIdParameter> [-DomainController <Fqdn>]
[<CommonParameters>]
```

The Identity parameter may be specified as a DatabaseIdParameter, which is described in the discussion of the Remove-MailboxDatabase cmdlet.

EMS: Move-DatabasePath

The EMS Move-DatabasePath cmdlet may be used to change either the regular database path with the EdbFilePath parameter or the continuous replication copy with the CopyEdbFilePath parameter, or both. Only with the ConfigurationOnly parameter specified may this be run successfully on an administrative workstation (to have the full effect, this cmdlet must be run on a mailbox server). The syntax is:

```
Move-DatabasePath -Identity <DatabaseIdParameter> [-EdbFilePath
<EdbFilePath>] [-DomainController <Fqdn>] [-CopyEdbFilePath <EdbFilePath>]
[-ConfigurationOnly <SwitchParameter>] [-Force <SwitchParameter>]
[<CommonParameters>]
```

As with the Mount-Database and Dismount-Database cmdlets, the Identity parameter may be a simple name, GUID, or DN for the database. The normal behavior of Move-DatabasePath is to change the configuration of where the server ought to store this database and also to move the Exchange database (.EDB) file associated with the database. The alternative to this, depending on both parts of the default behavior of this cmdlets, would be to use it to just change the configuration of where the path ought to be and require that the database file manually be moved. Such a manual move has further implications than using this cmdlet to perform both parts of the move. In either scenario, however, great care must be taken to protect the integrity of the database file during the move.

The move cannot take place during a backup, and the database will be dismounted during the move. To quote the Get-Help Move-DatabasePath -full text: "To perform the move operation, the database must be temporarily dismounted, making it inaccessible to all users. If the database is currently dismounted, it is not remounted upon completion." Consider the following pseudo-code (which assumes the value of the Mounted attribute to be valid, which is why the Status parameter is included in the call to Get-MailboxDatabase) for moving a Sales database from its current location to C:\SG2\Sales\Sales.edb:

```
$mbdb = Get-MailboxDatabase Sales -Status
$mustRemountAfterMove = $mbdb.Mounted # assumes valid Mounted status here!
$originalPath = $mbdb.EdbFilePath.PathName
Dismount-Database Sales
Move-DatabasePath Sales -ConfigurationOnly -EdbFilePath C:\SG2\Sales\Sales.edb
Move-Item $originalPath C:\SG2\Sales\Sales.edb
if( $mustRemountAfterMove ){
    Mount-Database Sales
}
```

The database is remounted after the move only if it had been mounted prior to the move. The ConfigurationOnly forms of the cmdlet perform modifications of the appropriate LDAP attribute(s) (for example, msExchEDBFile) for the database on the mailbox server in the Exchange organization. If you're actually using the ConfigurationOnly option, the following warning will be presented:

This operation will skip the safety check and make the change to the Active Directory directory service directly. Do you want to continue? [A] Yes to All [N] No [L] No to All [S] Suspend [?] Help (default is "Y"):

If an attempt to mount the database is performed prior to the database file being moved (for example, Sales.edb), the following warning will result:

At least one of this store's database files is missing. Mounting this store will force the creation of an empty database. Do not take this action if you intend to restore an earlier backup. Are you sure you want to continue? [A] Yes to All [N] No [L] No to All [S] Suspend [?] Help (default is "Y"):

Once a database has been moved and remounted, it should be accessible with all the benefits of the underlying new physical storage location. For example, this method may be used to move from RAID5 to RAID1+0 storage for a mailbox database if such a change entails changing the path. Alternatively, the database could be dismounted, the database copied/moved to the new storage array (for example, RAID1+0 or a larger capacity volume) physically using Move-Item or any other method. Then the old volume could be NTFS dismounted (for example, RAID5) and the new volume NTFS mounted (for example, RAID1+0). Finally, Mount-Database could be used to bring the database back online in Exchange, although the NTFS path has not changed yet the physical storage has. Whichever method is used, it should be clear that the relationship between Dismount-Database, Move-DatabasePath, and Mount-Database is important for changing the underlying storage of an Exchange database.

Managing Disconnected Mailboxes

Disconnected mailboxes are orphaned in the sense that they are still stored in a mailbox database, yet no longer have a user account object in Active Directory associated with them, as illustrated next. This condition can occur when an Active Directory user account has been deleted without the actual mailbox being deleted, or explicitly using the Disable-Mailbox cmdlet. Note that when the Disable-Mailbox method is used, an explicit cleanup task is performed on the mailbox. Thus, this cmdlet may be considered a Disconnect-Mailbox cmdlet, although it is not named that way. For accidental or legacy disconnection causes, the mailbox would not be cleaned up. There are two main choices for how to clean up such mailboxes. First, simply wait for the nightly maintenance tasks to be performed that include such cleanup. Alternatively, the Clean-MailboxDatabase cmdlet could be used to clean one database at a time. Chapter 10 addresses the topic of disconnected mailboxes directly, including Disable-Mailbox, Connect-Mailbox, and other cmdlets such as New-Mailbox and Enable-Mailbox that initially create a mailbox and assert the Active Directory attributes onto a user account object. Note that Remove-Mailbox also disconnects a mailbox cleanly like Disable-Mailbox does, yet actually removes the mailbox from the mailbox database. That, too, falls under the topic of recipient administration. The focus here is on Clean-MailboxDatabase.

Mailboxes are said to be disconnected when a user account
is no longer associated with them.

EMS: Clean-MailboxDatabase

The Clean-MailboxDatabase cmdlet scans a specific mailbox database for all mailboxes and then queries Active Directory for user accounts that correspond with them. The differences between the two sets of results—that is, those mailboxes with no associated user account—may then be cleaned up. The clean operation updates the mailbox database to reflect the disconnected state of these mailboxes. This is not necessary when a clean disconnection has been performed with Disable-Mailbox or when the database maintenance interval has already been run against this database.

```
Clean-MailboxDatabase -Identity <DatabaseIdParameter> [-DomainController
<Fqdn>] [<CommonParameters>]
```

As with other cmdlets such as Mount-Database, the Identity parameter for Clean-MailboxDatabase may be either a simple name, a DN, or a GUID that identifies the database to be cleaned. The DomainController parameter allows the scan of Active Directory to be focused on a specific domain controller. Note that as a scan for all associated user accounts is performed, large mailbox databases with thousands of mailboxes could result in a burst of LDAP activity against the domain controller.

Classically, in Exchange System Manager with Exchange Server 2003, the Run Cleanup Agent action could be run against a specific information store (mailbox database). Because Disable-Mailbox and Remove-Mailbox attempt to cleanly disconnect the mailbox, using Clean-MailboxDatabase or waiting for the nightly maintenance cleanup may be less necessary than in previous versions of Exchange. This typically yields quicker classification of mailboxes as being disconnected. Yet for those occasions when immediate cleanup is desired, Clean-MailboxDatabase offers a convenient method. Use of the common parameter Verbose gives some details on the progress.

Mailbox Database Properties

A number of mailbox database properties are not set with the Mount-Database, Dismount-Database, or Move-DatabasePath cmdlet. Instead, a general cmdlet called Set-MailboxDatabase is used to modify attributes of an existing mailbox database. For retrieving properties of a mailbox database, we have the Get-MailboxDatabase cmdlet. Of course, as is customary with PowerShell, when Get-MailboxDatabase is used without parameters and its output is processed (by default) by the Format-Table cmdlet, it yields a list of available mailbox databases in the Exchange organization.

EMS: Get-MailboxDatabase

Basically four scopes for the EMS Get-MailboxDatabase cmdlet determine which mailbox databases will be retrieved:

- All mailbox databases in the Exchange organization (no extra parameters needed)
- All mailbox databases hosted on a specific mailbox server (using the Server parameter)
- All mailbox databases in a specific storage group (using the StorageGroup parameter)
- A specific mailbox database (using the Identity parameter)

To believe that Get-MailboxDatabase simply retrieves a list of the Name, Server, StorageGroup, and Recovery disposition of each mailbox database in the organization is naive of the power of PowerShell and therefore the Exchange Management Shell. When we remember that Get-MailboxDatabase, in its object-oriented nature actually gets handles to an object representation of those mailbox databases, the greater value of this cmdlet is revealed. With that seed planted for perspective, let's first look at the possible parameters for Get-MailboxDatabase and then briefly investigate some of the deeper truths about our databases that this cmdlet can reveal.

The syntax of Get-MailboxDatabase may be summarized as follows:

```
Get-MailboxDatabase [-Identity <DatabaseIdParameter> |-Server
<ServerIdParameter> |-StorageGroup <StorageGroupIdParameter>]
[-DomainController <Fqdn>] [-IncludePreExchange2007 <SwitchParameter>]
[-Status  <SwitchParameter>] [<CommonParameters>]
```

Note that neither the Server, StorageGroup, nor Identity parameter is required. However, if any is used, only one should be used. With none of these three specified, the scope of the cmdlet is the whole Exchange organization; therefore, all mailbox databases in all storage groups of all Exchange Server 2007 servers with the mailbox server role in the organization will be retrieved. If pipeline input from another cmdlet into Get-MailboxDatabase is provided, a specific set of storage groups, servers, or databases may be specified. Alternatively, any one of the Server, StorageGroup, or Identity parameters could be supplied to Get-MailboxDatabase in order to have it chose the database(s) with which to work.

Getting More Out of the Mailbox Database Configuration

When you're choosing mailbox databases with Get-MailboxDatabase and perhaps other cmdlets in a pipeline, the question after "Which databases?" would typically be "What do you want to do with them?" There are several choices, including but not limited to the following:

- Viewing properties of the mailbox database configuration
- Changing properties of the mailbox database configuration
- Moving mailboxes out of the database to another database
- Mounting, dismounting, or cleaning the mailbox database

Perhaps the most obvious of these is the ability to view properties, because the default formatter shows at least the Name, Server, StorageGroup, and Recovery attributes. Yet using other formatting options reveals that far more attributes are available. The following two formatters may be used to find the available attributes:

```
Get-MailboxDatabase -Status | Format-List | more
Get-MailboxDatabase | Format-Custom >${home}\"My Documents"\all-mdb-custom.txt
notepad ${home}\"My Documents"\all-mdb-custom.txt
```

Note that because the Status parameter is used on Get-MailboxDatabase, the list of properties/attributes will include values (not just empty values with the property names) for the status values that aren't part of the static configuration of each database. The more pager is used to handle medium volumes of output, and it should be sufficient for use with Format-List with a reasonable number of databases. However, without this included in the pipeline, the direct output of Format-List would usually require scrolling in the Exchange Management Shell window to see all the attributes. With Format-Custom and no depth limitation or reduced list of properties, the volume of output may be on the order of megabytes of text (usually hundreds of KB per database displayed). Therefore, the output in this case was redirected to a file and then that file was later viewed using the Windows Notepad application.

```
Get-MailboxDatabase -Status | Format-Table -Property Name,Server,Mounted
```

All four formatters (Format-Table, Format-List, Format-Custom, Format-Wide) accept a number of parameters, such as which properties (attributes) to output. The preceding example illustrates the use of the Property parameter to show the mounted status of all Exchange Server 2007 mailbox databases in the Exchange organization. Note the inclusion of the Status parameter on Get-MailboxDatabase. How would use of the IncludePreExchange2007 parameter change the output? We'll leave that as an exercise for the reader.

EMS: Set-MailboxDatabase

Beside retrieving properties from a mailbox database, a list of one or more mailbox databases retrieved with Get-MailboxDatabase may be used to mount, dismount, or clean collections of databases, and as a context for moving mailboxes, disabling and removing mailboxes, changing quotas, and more. In some cases, simply reconfiguring properties of a mailbox database is necessary. For this purpose, we have the Set-MailboxDatabase cmdlet.

The Set-MailboxDatabase cmdlet provides three ways in which to specify the mailbox databases on which it operates. The most common approach for interactive EMS administrators who work with one database at a time is to use the Identity parameter, for which the actual -Identity keyword may be excluded when the database identity is given as the first parameter. For advanced scripting administrators and programmers who write software such as the graphical Exchange Management Console, the Instance parameter provides a more direct approach to supplying a database reference as a variable. A third approach is to use a pipeline input of one or more databases to this cmdlet, as follows:

```
Set-MailboxDatabase Sales -DeletedItemRetention 21.00:00:00

$execdb = Get-MailboxDatabase Executives -Status

Set-MailboxDatabase -Identity $execdb -DeletedItemRetention 24855.00:00:00

Get-MailboxDatabase | Set-MailboxDatabase -DeletedItemRetention 7.00:00:00
```

Renaming a Mailbox Database

Configuration of mailbox databases is first done using New-MailboxDatabase or a similar technique. In some cases, default values are assumed; yet in other cases (such as the name of the mailbox database), either the New-MailboxDatabase cmdlet requires or the New Mailbox Database Wizard in the Exchange Management Console prompts for and requires such parameters. Changing these values later may be done using Set-MailboxDatabase. The Name parameter allows a mailbox database to be renamed. The previous name may be specified using the Identity parameter either explicitly or implicitly, as follows:

```
Set-MailboxDatabase MBX85258 -Name Scottsdale
```

In this example, the old name of the mailbox database is MBX85258 and the new name of the mailbox database is Scottsdale.

Although we've described the renaming of a mailbox database under a separate heading here, in the EMC the name is viewed/changed on the General property sheet.

Mailbox Database General Settings

Besides the name of a mailbox database, several other attributes may be configured on the General property sheet in the EMC. The values that can be changed are described here. The General property sheet also includes a view of several values that may not be changed directly there, nor are they configurable with the Set-MailboxDatabase cmdlet in EMS. Instead, Move-DatabasePath, Mount-Database, or Dismount-Database must be used. In addition, some Active Directory metadata is revealed: the Modified date/time stamp of the mailbox database configuration object. Again, the focus here is on those parameters for Set-MailboxDatabase that can also be modified via the General properties of a mailbox database in the EMC.

The MountAtStartup parameter may be used to configure a value of $true or $false, thus determining whether the mailbox database will be mounted by the Exchange Information Store Service at startup. Be careful: This is the inverse of the "Do not mount this database at startup" check box on the graphical properties.

All messages stored in this mailbox database may be journaled to a specific recipient. This can be configured with Set-MailboxDatabase's JournalRecipient parameter, as follows:

```
Set-MailboxDatabase Executives -JournalRecipient brad.werner@virtuecorp.com
```

The JournalRecipient parameter accepts any of the valid RecipientIdParameter types, including the following notations:

- GUID
- Domain\Account
- User principal name (UPN)
- LegacyExchangeDN
- Simple Mail Transfer Protocol (SMTP) address
- Name
- Alias

For example, in the previous example where we used the SMTP address brad.werner@virtuecorp.com, we could have used any of the following values:

- 7af6b19c-3643-4d7f-a0e7-e4368a87d762 (GUID)
- VIRTUECORP\Brad Werner (SAM account name: Domain\Account)
- bwerner0147@virtuecorp.com (UPN)
- /o=VIRTUECORP/ou=Exchange Administrative Group (FYDIBOHF23SPDLT)/cn=Recipients/cn=brad.werner (LegacyExchangeDN)
- brad.werner@virtuecorp.com (SMTP e-mail address)

- Brad Werner (Name)
- brad.werner (Alias)

Note that parameter values that include spaces, such as the LegacyExchangeDN and Name parameters, should be enclosed in quotes (for example, "Brad Werner") when used in the EMS. In some cases, the organizational procedure for naming of user accounts and e-mail addresses may dictate that the UPN and SMTP address be the same as one another. However, this example shows different values for those two recipient identifiers. Another approach is to guarantee that these values are different so that internal user names are not "published" as externally useable e-mail addresses as a security consideration.

In order to clear the Journal Recipient attribute of the mailbox database, simply set this parameter to an empty (null) value by using the $null "constant" variable, as follows:

```
Set-MailboxDatabase Executives -JournalRecipient $null
```

The "nightly" maintenance schedule on a mailbox database may be adjusted to run at a specific time period. The default schedule is daily from 1:00 A.M. to 5:00 A.M. in the local time of the mailbox server. The graphical EMC property sheet provides a menu that enables you to choose from the following list:

- Run daily from 11:00 P.M. to 3:00 A.M.
- Run daily from midnight to 4:00 A.M.
- Run daily from 1:00 A.M. to 5:00 A.M. (default)
- Run daily from 2:00 A.M. to 6:00 A.M.
- Use Custom Schedule

The graphical interface has a Customize... button that brings up a 24/7 grid with either 1-hour or 15-minute detail to allow the configuration of variant schedules.

The Set-MailboxDatabase cmdlet has a MaintenanceSchedule parameter that allows you to specify the maintenance schedule. For the Schedule data type, a list of time intervals may be specified, separated by commas. Each of these intervals is specified with a start time, a hyphen (-), and then an end time. Each time is specified as day.hour:minute. Days may be specified either with locale-specific names (or their abbreviations) or with standard Windows (and .NET) integer values. The possible list in a U.S. English locale are shown in Table 6-1. If you're not using 24-hour notation for the hours, am and pm designators (without dots) may be included. Care must be taken with minutes for a few reasons. First, minutes will be rounded down to evenly divisible 15-minute intervals (0, 15, 30, 45). Second, each interval must be at least 15 minutes long. Third, each time interval in the maintenance schedule must be at least 15 minutes apart; otherwise, with the rounding down they'd be adjacent/contiguous anyway.

The default maintenance schedule is daily from 1:00 A.M. to 5:00 A.M., which would be written as follows:

```
Sun.1:00 AM-Sun.5:00 AM, Mon.1:00 AM-5:00 AM, Tue.1:00 AM-Tue.5:00 AM,
Wed.1:00 AM-Wed.5:00 AM, Thu.1:00 AM-Thu.5:00 AM, Fri.1:00 AM-Fri.5:00 AM,
Sat.1:00 AM-Sat.5:00 AM
```

Day of Week Number	Day Name	Day Abbreviation
0	Sunday	Sun
1	Monday	Mon
2	Tuesday	Tue
3	Wednesday	Wed
4	Thursday	Thu
5	Friday	Fri
6	Saturday	Sat

TABLE 6-1   Maintenance Schedule on a Mailbox Database

An abbreviated form of this could be written with numbers for the days and 24-hour time for the hours and then included as the value for the MaintenanceSchedule parameter for the Executives mailbox database, as shown here:

```
Set-MailboxDatabase Executives -MaintenanceSchedule ' "0.1:00-0.5:00,1.1:00-
5:00,2.1:00-2.5:00,3.1:00-3.5:00,4.1:00-4.5:00, 5.1:00-5.5:00,6.1:00-
6.5:00"
```

This may be confirmed by using Get-MailboxDatabase for that database and sending the output to either the Format-List or Format-Custom formatter:

```
Get-MailboxDatabase Executives | Format-List -Property MaintenanceSchedule
```

The format shown by Format-List is compatible with the input format for the MaintenanceSchedule parameter on Set-MailboxDatabase. For a format that includes the duration of each interval in the schedule, consider using the Format-Custom formatter instead, which also happens to reveal programmatically accessible interval parameters for those interested administrators and software developers.

Exchange Server 2007 mailbox servers store changes to the mailbox database in an event history table within the mailbox database itself. A large number of changes to the database will cause a large volume of event history data to be accumulated. The retention period for the entries in this table is configurable in Set-MailboxDatabase, although the EventHistory RetentionPeriod parameter is not revealed in the EMC's graphical property sheets. Like the DeletedItemRetention parameter described in earlier examples, the EventHistoryRetention Period parameter is specified as an EnhancedTimeSpan using the days.hours:minutes: seconds notation. Here's an example of how to change the event history retention from the default of seven days (7.00:00:00) to a new value of 18 hours:

```
Set-MailboxDatabase Scottsdale -EventHistoryRetentionPeriod 18:00:00
```

The value could be confirmed using Get-MailboxDatabase with a nondefault formatter to include the EventHistoryRetentionPeriod, yet because that attribute name can be construed as being a bit long to type, wildcards for the property names to display can be used, as shown next:

```
Get-MailboxDatabase Scottsdale | Format-List -Property *retention*
Get-MailboxDatabase Scottsdale | Format-List -Property *period*
```

Either of the property specifications shown should match the EventHistoryRetention Period. The example that specifies *retention* will likely show MailboxRetention and DeletedItemRetention as well, whereas the *period* notation may just show the desired attribute.

Beside the event history table, other data sets in a mailbox database may be considered metadata or overhead, yet they, too, serve specific purposes. One of these is content indexing. The Full-Text Index Catalog is stored as a collection of files in the folder named "catalogdata-{guidA}-{guidB}" where two GUIDs are used to ensure a unique name for the catalog data, even in a clustered environment. This folder is stored in the same parent folder as the EDBFilePath, as assigned with Move-DatabasePath or originally configured in New-MailboxDatabase. To enable or disable full content indexing using Set-MailboxDatabase, assign a value of $true or $false to the IndexEnabled parameter, as follows:

```
Set-MailboxDatabase Scottsdale -IndexEnabled $true
```

Although this parameter is not included in the graphical EMC, and the default value of $true is usually preferred in most Exchange Server 2007 deployments, knowing how to adjust the value if necessary is useful. Another maintenance procedure for the full-text index catalog of a mailbox database is described in the Exchange Server 2007 Help. For full details, search Help for the topic, "How to Rebuild the Full-Text Index Catalog." We've included an EMS-oriented example of the procedure here:

```
Get-Service *Exchange*
Stop-Service MSExchangeSearch
$scottsdb = Get-MailboxDatabase Scottsdale
$catpath = Split-Path -Parent $scottsdb.EdbFilePath.PathName
Get-ChildItem "${catpath}\CatalogData*" -recurse | Remove-Item
Get-Item "${catpath}\CatalogData*" | Remove-Item
Start-Service MSExchangeSearch
```

This brief example first illustrates how to get a list of the Exchange services by using the Get-Service cmdlet, yet that step is really unnecessary for the purposes of the script. However, it is a good practice to check what services are running initially before blindly stopping or starting them. Next, the Microsoft Exchange Search Indexer Service (MSExchangeSearch) is stopped using the Stop-Service cmdlet. This is the first part of the procedure described in the "How to Rebuild..." Help topic. Then the following four lines of our sample script remove the current catalog(s) for the mailbox database in question. This part of the script could certainly be condensed or simplified—or graphically inclined administrators would probably just remove the folders and their contents in Windows Explorer. Let's walk through the four steps included here.

The purpose of the middle part of the script is to remove all the catalog files and their containing folders that comprise the full-text index catalog for a mailbox database. Once these are deleted and the Search Indexer Service is started again, the full-text index will be rebuilt into a new catalog. To accomplish the deletion of these old catalog files, we first obtain a reference to the mailbox database in question using Get-MailboxDatabase. Then the EdbFile-Path attribute's PathName is obtained in order to use the Split-Path cmdlet to get the parent (containing folder) path of the mailbox database. This parent folder is put in another variable that represents not only the database folder path but also the folder that contains the catalog subfolder(s). There is an assumption in this script regarding having one database per storage group or at least having separate database folders for each database in the storage group. This will be described further after we discuss the next couple steps. The next step uses the path of the database folder and appends the name \CatalogData* in order to select the index catalog folder(s). This is then used as an implicit Path argument to Get-ChildItem, including the Recurse switch to retrieve all the actual index catalog files. This list is sent (piped) to the Remove-Item cmdlet to delete all those that which make up the index catalog. One of the reasons why the Search Indexer Service was stopped prior to this procedure is so that none of those files are exclusively locked for write access so that they can be easily removed. The method of using Get-ChildItem -Recurse | Remove-Item is preferred to simply using Remove-Item -Recurse due to some "quirks" in the latter's behavior. This is followed by a separate explicit step that just uses Get-Item | Remove-Item with the names of the folders themselves. Although the script could be written differently, this should be sufficient for the purposes of the catalog rebuild procedure—that is, once the Search Indexer Service is restarted.

Let's revisit the earlier comment regarding multiple databases in the same folder. First, it's worth noting that in production environments it's generally considered a mistake to have two mailbox databases stored in the same folder (or even the same file system volume/LUN). Furthermore, it's not a best practice to have more than one database per storage group in most situations. There are exceptions. In cases where the same folder holds the .EDB files for more than one database, the $catpath variable in this sample script would refer to the folder for all those databases; therefore, the \CatalogData* suffixed to that path would match the catalogs for all those databases, resulting in a rebuild of the catalogs for several databases, which may not be the desired behavior. In such circumstances, selecting one specific set of catalog files would entail extracting the GUID from the mailbox database, then getting the instance GUIDs and concatenating these with the \CatalogData prefix and hyphens so that the concatenated resultant string identifies one specific database's catalog data folder. The details of such a script are beyond the scope of this chapter.

Finally, after the old catalog files and folder are deleted, the script uses Start-Service to start up the Microsoft Exchange Search Indexer (MSExchangeSearch) Service again. Although that's where the Help topic procedure ends, it could be followed up with sanity checking that the service is running after the start and that new catalog data folders and their constituent files are being created in the appropriate folder.

Another parameter that can be specified to the Set-MailboxDatabase cmdlet is AllowFileRestore, which, like IndexEnabled, also takes a Boolean $true or $false value. The default for the AllowFileRestore attribute of a mailbox database is $false, signified in the EMC's General properties of the mailbox database with the "This database can be overwritten by a restore" check box being unchecked by default.

Mailbox Database Limits Settings

Several attributes of a mailbox database relate to storage limits and deletion settings. Graphically these may be configured in the EMC's Limits property sheet on a mailbox database's properties. Although the settings configured in EMS and EMC at the mailbox database level will act as defaults for everyone in that mailbox database, these could be overridden on an individual mailbox-by-mailbox basis within the database. Under EMC's Recipient Configuration | Mailbox subcategory, the properties of each mailbox may be obtained. On a mailbox's Mailbox Settings property sheet the Storage Quotas properties can be obtained, which normally defaults to "Use mailbox database defaults." Here we will focus on the settings at the mailbox database level. The topic of per-mailbox levels is left to Chapter 10, with the possible exception of how to sanity-check exceptions to the mailbox database configuration.

Seven parameters on Set-MailboxDatabase allow corresponding attributes of a mailbox database to be configured with storage limits and deletion settings. They are listed here in the order in which they appear in the EMC property sheet:

- IssueWarningQuota
- ProhibitSendQuota
- ProhibitSendReceiveQuota
- QuotaNotificationSchedule
- MailboxRetention
- DeletedItemRetention
- RetainDeletedItemsUntilBackup

The IssueWarningQuota attribute of a mailbox database defaults to 1.9GB (1,991,680KB) yet may be set to another specific value or unlimited. Because the units for these limits in the .NET framework are bytes, but the EMC shows them in kilobytes (KB) and the EMS often shows them in either megabytes (MB) or gigabytes (GB), we will take great care to specify or indicate units wherever possible in the discussion of these quotas. Note that these quotas are per mailbox, even when assigned at the mailbox database level. Table 6-2 shows the default quotas in KB, MB, and GB, where 1024 bytes = 1 KB, 1024 KB = 1 MB, 1024 MB = 1 GB, and 1024 GB = 1 TB, as is customary with computing storage and memory capacities (note that times and frequencies in computing still use the international standards with factors of 1000).

Although the KB, MB, and GB values may be interesting when you're using EMC property sheets (or EMS cmdlets such as Get-MailboxDatabase, Set-MailboxDatabase, Get-Mailbox, and Set-Mailbox), two other more important factors should be noted here. For administrators who are used to lower default quotas on Exchange Server 2003 (or earlier), it is worth noting that the 2GB ProhibitSendQuota can easily require several terabytes (TB) of storage when several hundred mailboxes are considered, let alone thousands or tens of thousands.

Quota	KB	MB	GB	% of Send Quota
IssueWarningQuota	1,991,680	1945	1.9	95%
ProhibitSendQuota	2,097,152	2048	2	100%
ProhibitSendReceiveQuota	2,411,520	2355	2.307	115%

TABLE 6-2   Default Quota Limits

Per mailbox database, the database dumpster size and maintenance intervals for garbage collection must be considered as well as log file storage and local continuous replication storage. Perhaps the second most important factor to note with respect to this table is the percentage relationships between ProhibitSendQuota and both IssueWarningQuota and ProhibitSendReceiveQuota. The default warning level is 95% of the send prohibition level, whereas the send/receive prohibition limit is 15% higher than the quota, which just prohibits users from sending messages.

Although it's tempting to say that one could first pick a ProhibitSendQuota value and then just calculate 5% less than that value for the warning level and 15% more than that level for stopping users from sending and receiving messages, there is another heuristic that could be considered. Indeed, the 95% and 115% guard-band could be used as a starting guideline, but a more engineering-wise perspective would include the relationship between the daily send/receive volume of the users with mailboxes in this database. Additionally, the deletion retention settings, managed folder policies, and maintenance interval should also be factored in:

```
$psq = 1024 * 1024 * 1024
$iwq = [int]( $psq * 0.95 )
$psrq = [int]( $psrq * 1.15 )

Set-MailboxDatabase Chandler -IssueWarningQuota $iwq ' -ProhibitSendQuota
$psq -ProhibitSendReceiveQuota $psrq
Get-MailboxDatabase Chandler | Format-List -Property *Quota*
```

This example assumes that the default handling of these parameter value by Set-MailboxDatabase will be in terms of bytes. We start by setting the variable $psq (as in ProhibitSendQuota) to 1GB, again assuming that 1024 * 1024 * 1024 = 1,073,741,824 in units of bytes = 1 GB. Then we set a variable for the IssueWarningQuota $iwq with 95% of the ProhibitSendQuota converted to an integral number of bytes. Converting from a floating point (real) number into an integer is accomplished with the [int] operator in PowerShell. Similarly, $psrq is a variable we'll later use to set the ProhibitSendReceiveQuota to 115% of the ProhibitSendQuota (again, converted to an integer with [int]). Then the example uses Set-MailboxDatabase to assign these values to the appropriate attributes of the Chandler mailbox database. As a sanity check, the quota-related attributes of that database are retrieved; this will include the QuotaNotificationSchedule as well.

Explicit units could also be included for these quotas by taking the concatenation of an integral number of units with the two-unit symbol abbreviation, such as 1GB, 250MB, or 256000KB. There should not be spaces between the number and the units. This may even be done with variables, being careful to delimit the variables and the units by surrounding the variable name in curly braces. Here is an example using KB units rather than bytes:

```
$psq = 2 * 1024 * 1024
$iwq = [int]( $psq * 0.95 )
$psrq = [int]( $psrq * 1.15 )

Set-MailboxDatabase Chandler -IssueWarningQuota ${iwq}KB ' -ProhibitSendQuota
${psq}KB ' -ProhibitSendReceiveQuota ${psrq}KB
Get-MailboxDatabase Chandler | Format-List -Property *Quota*
```

Another type of value may be supplied for these quota limits—unlimited. For that infinite limit, we simply use the string "unlimited" (which is recognized for these quota values). Here's an example:

```
Set-MailboxDatabase Chandler -ProhibitSendReceiveQuota "unlimited"
```

Of course, setting an unlimited quota such as this could have severe negative implications, yet always being able to receive mail may be desired—up to the actual limits of the database. Keep in mind that Unified Messaging treats incoming faxes and voicemail as messages and are therefore subject to these limits, just as classic e-mail messages are.

The quota levels are checked periodically according to a schedule. The EMC graphical interface provides a menu on the mailbox database Limits properties called "Warning message interval." This menu allows you to specify the following choices:

- Run daily at midnight
- Run daily at 1:00 A.M.
- Run daily at 2:00 A.M.
- Use Custom Schedule

Next to this menu is a Customize… button that allows you to change the schedule on a 24/7 hour/day grid, with either 15-minute or 1-hour resolution. The Set-MailboxDatabase cmdlet in EMS allows you to specify the schedule on the QuotaNotificationSchedule parameter using the same notation as described for the MaintenanceSchedule parameter. The default schedule for quota notifications is 1:00–1:15 daily.

Three deletion settings may be configured using Set-MailboxDatabase: the DeletedItemRetention, MailboxRetention, and RetainDeletedItemsUntilBackup parameters. The first two take EnhancedTimeSpan values, whereas the third takes a Boolean value.

Items that are deleted from mailboxes are retained for 14 days (14.00:00:00) by default. The DeletedItemRetention parameter was used in examples earlier in the section to describe how multiple mailbox databases may be configured at once. Again, the notation is dd.hh:mm:ss (days, hours, minutes, seconds), with a maximum of 24,855 days (about 68 years). Note that each mailbox within the database may have its own value specified if the UseData baseRetentionDefaults attribute is $false, in which case the RetainDeletedItemsFor attribute on that mailbox will override the value of DeletedItemRetention on the mailbox database. Note that retention holds may be placed per mailbox as well.

Mailboxes themselves may also be retained after deletion. The default is for 30 days (30.00:00:00), also with a possible maximum value of 24855.00:00:00. The MailboxRetention parameter may be used with Set-MailboxDatabase to assign a different value. No correlated parameter is available on each mailbox.

The final parameter for the mailbox database related to deletion settings is RetainDelete dItemsUntilBackup, which is a Boolean ($true or $false) value associated with the check box "Do not permanently delete items until the database has been backed up" in the Limits sheet of the mailbox database properties in the EMC.

Relationship Between Mailbox Database and Individual Mailbox Limits

The quotas on a mailbox database are a default that is normally assumed by all mailboxes within that database. Each mailbox may override these limits with its own quotas.

EMS could be used to scan all databases, and for each database to search for mailboxes where the limits are different (higher or lower) than the database limits. Furthermore, the mailbox statistics and mailbox folder statistics could be used to show the actual utilization of storage resources per mailbox and then associated with each database. Such scripts or applications are beyond the scope of this chapter, yet the following cmdlets are quite useful in performing such tasks:

- Get-MailboxDatabase
- Get-Mailbox
- Get-MailboxStatistics
- Get-MailboxFolderStatistics
- Where-Object
- Foreach-Object
- Mailbox Database Client Settings

The EMC properties of a mailbox database have a Client Settings sheet you can use to configure the public folder database or offline address book associated with the mailbox database. The EMS may also assign these values using Set-MailboxDatabase and the PublicFolderDatabase or OfflineAddressBook parameters, respectively.

Use the PublicFolderDatabase parameter to configure the public folder database that should be associated with this mailbox database. This is present for backward compatibility with Exchange Server 2003 and earlier versions in which public folders were an essential element of an Exchange organization. Perhaps more importantly, this feature is still included so that even pure Exchange Server 2007 environments may fully support the public folder features expected for Outlook 2003 and earlier versions. If all clients are running Outlook 2007, or OWA or EAS based on Exchange Server 2007, and there aren't other needs for public folders, this parameter does not need to be set on a mailbox database. By default, the value is null ($null). The DatabaseIdParameter accepted by this parameter may be any of the same sort of identifier formats used to specify a mailbox database, yet it must specify the identity of a public folder database.

Use the OfflineAddressBook parameter to configure the offline address book that should be associated with this mailbox database. By default, the Default Offline Address Book is associated with each mailbox database. If this value is changed, another offline address book must be chosen.

Other Parameters for Set-MailboxDatabase

Most of the parameters for the Set-MailboxDatabase cmdlet have been briefly described thus far, and in some cases examples have been provided. A few additional parameters are worth mentioning.

By default, Set MailboxDatabase will automatically choose a domain controller against which to make the changes to the mailbox database(s) configuration. A specific domain controller may be chosen by using the DomainController parameter, which is supported by most of the mailbox database-oriented cmdlets. The format is either a short name or a Fully Qualified Domain Name (FQDN). Use of an FQDN is preferred. Here's an example:

```
Set-MailboxDatabase Chandler -Name CHNDMBX ' -DomainController PHX-DC-01.
virtuecorp.com
```

The common parameters supported by Set-MailboxDatabase are Verbose, Debug, ErrorAction, ErrorVariable, and OutVariable.

Configuring Continuous Replication

Exchange 2007 introduces various levels of high availability for mailbox Servers. Local Continuous Replication (LCR) and Cluster Continuous Replication (CCR) both create copies of the active database. CCR clusters require advanced server configurations. LCR on the other hand can provide any size organization with an affordable high availability solution.

EMS: Enable-DatabaseCopy

Continuous replication, such as LCR, may be configured at the storage group level. The location of replicated database copies may be configured with the CopyEdbFilePath parameter for the New-MailboxDatabase, New-PublicFolderDatabase, or Move-DatabasePath cmdlet. When using LCR, you can use the Enable-DatabaseCopy cmdlet to turn on LCR for the database (assuming that LCR is already enabled on the storage group).

```
Enable-DatabaseCopy [[-Identity] <DatabaseIdParameter>] [-CopyEdbFilePath
<EdbFilePath>] [-DomainController <Fqdn>] [<CommonParameters>]
```

Like Move-DatabasePath -ConfigurationOnly -CopyEdbFilePath, this cmdlet does not move the existing database or any previously used LCR replicas. It does allow configuring the CopyEdbFilePath attribute of the database (mailbox database or public folder database). The seeding and population of the LCR database replica will occur asynchronously to the completion of this cmdlet. This cmdlet merely sets the configuration. It may not be used on clustered mailbox servers because LCR is not supported on clustered mailbox servers.

Managing Mailbox Database Properties

Exchange 2007 mailbox databases properties can be administered by both the Exchange Management Console and the Exchange Management Shell.

EMC: Mailbox Database Properties

The Exchange Management Console (EMC) may be used as a front end to the Get-MailboxDatabase, Set-MailboxDatabase, and Move-MailboxDatabasePath cmdlets. Within a storage group, a database may be created, deleted, or have its configuration viewed or modified.

Earlier in the discussion of storage group management with EMC, we noted that when a storage group has been selected in the EMC, one of the possible actions is to create a new mailbox database. This action launches the New Mailbox Database Wizard, which effective collects parameter values and then invokes the New-MailboxDatabase cmdlet to actually create the database. Similarly, the New Public Folder Database… action may be used to collect data and launch the New-PublicFolderDatabase cmdlet behind the scenes.

Figure 6-22 shows that when a mailbox database has been selected within the storage group in the EMC, the Actions pane provides buttons for access to the following actions:

- Dismount Database (or Mount Database if the selected database is not mounted)
- Move Database Path…

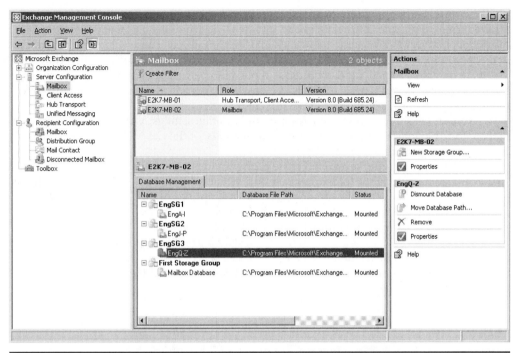

FIGURE 6-22   Mailbox database actions in EMC

- Remove
- Properties

If you've read the descriptions of the EMS Dismount-Database, Mount-Database, Move-DatabasePath, Remove-MailboxDatabase, Get-MailboxDatabase, and Set-MailboxDatabase, perhaps you could guess how these actions in the EMC are performed under the hood. Indeed, the EMC merely collects data or actions in a graphical interface and uses the appropriate EMS cmdlets to perform the requested tasks. If you understand the cmdlets (which is highly recommended), the graphical interface should not be confusing. However, we'll walk through some aspects of the property sheets for a mailbox database to help clarify what's going on.

After selecting a database in the EMC, you can use the Properties action to bring up the mailbox database property sheet. Three tabs and sheets comprise the mailbox database properties in EMC. As a reminder, to select a database in the EMC, first select the Microsoft Exchange | Server Configuration | Mailbox category in the navigation pane on the left. Then, in the middle details pane select the appropriate server in the list at the top, such as E2K7-MB-02 in Figure 6-22. You may have to filter the list of mailbox servers if there are too many in your organization to quickly find the right one by scrolling. Once the server has been selected at the top, find the desired storage group at the bottom, expanding it if necessary, and then choose the database from within the storage group. Now to obtain the properties, once again, just click the Properties button in the Actions pane on the right.

Figure 6-23 shows the properties of the mailbox database EngQ-Z, with the General tab selected. Here, the name, journal recipient, maintenance schedule, automatic mounting restriction, and restore overwrite allowance may be configured. These values are described in the discussion of Set-MailboxDatabase and Get-MailboxDatabase earlier in this chapter. The mailbox database path (and continuous replication path) is shown on the property sheet. To change the path, use the Move Database Path Wizard (the link to it is a button in the Actions pane) or the Move-DatabasePath cmdlet.

The Limits tab shows several storage limits and deletion settings, as depicted in Figure 6-24. Refer to the description of these properties in the sections for the Get-MailboxDatabase and Set-MailboxDatabase cmdlets earlier in this chapter.

The Client Settings tab, shown in Figure 6-25, provides a graphical way to confirm or change which default public folder database and offline address book will be used with this mailbox database. These are also described in the descriptions of the Get-MailboxDatabase and Set-MailboxDatabase cmdlets earlier in this chapter.

Once you understand the nature of mailbox databases and are familiar with the cmdlets for managing them, you may choose to use the EMC for graphical "point-and-click" maintenance of the mailbox database in an Exchange Server 2007 mailbox server. For more advanced administration, scripting, or even custom software for such management tasks, the EMS is recommended.

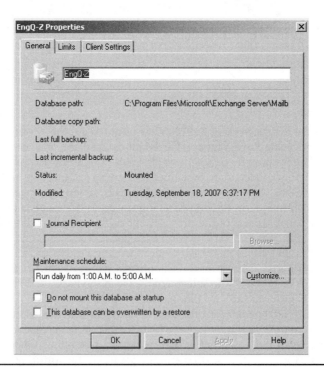

FIGURE 6-23 Mailbox Database Properties General tab

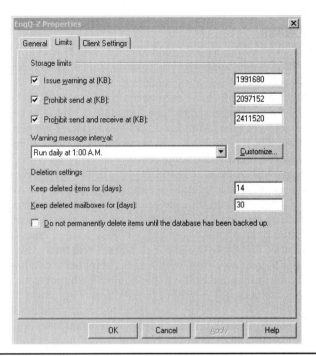

FIGURE 6-24   Mailbox Database Properties Limits tab

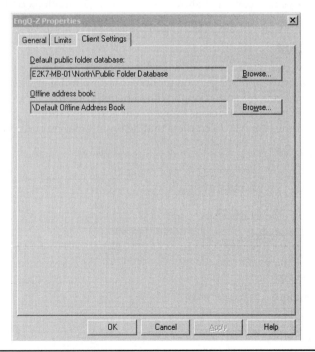

FIGURE 6-25   Mailbox Database Properties Client Settings tab

Public Folder Databases

Public folder databases are very much like mailbox databases. However, instead of mailboxes for individuals, they hold public folders for multiple collaborators to access. Whereas public folders were a significant part of the feature set of Exchange Server 2003 and earlier, with Exchange Server 2007 public folders have become a second-class citizen. Microsoft describes public folder support as a deemphasized feature. Certainly, with the success of Windows SharePoint services and Office SharePoint Server, the need to have Exchange Server also support similar functionality has diminished to some degree. Critical to realizing whether public folders are needed in a given Exchange Server 2007 deployment is the need for backward compatibility with Outlook 2003 and earlier. Yet administrative and management inertia may weigh at least as heavily as end-user and end-user client software conservatism.

In any event, public folders (and thus the public folder databases that host them) are still supported in Exchange Server 2007. Therefore, we'll address their management in two parts. First, public folder database management will be described here. Later in this chapter the management of public folders within those databases will be discussed. The topic of public folder databases is discussed here with respect to mailbox database administration. Therefore, it is highly recommended that you be familiar with that topic first. In other words, there are two reasons for the degree of brevity here. First, due to the similarities with mailbox databases, public folder databases are described relative to mailbox databases, making this section shorter. Second, because public folder databases are a deemphasized feature, the degree of detail is also somewhat deemphasized here as well.

Public folder databases in Exchange Server 2007 have only an .EDB file, as opposed to also having a corresponding streaming database (.STM) file. A public folder database counts against the limit of five databases per storage group, just like mailbox databases do.

Mailbox Configuration

Much of the mailbox configuration is addressed in Chapter 10. However, a few details must be addressed here because their impact on mailbox server administration is critical, and these details are not as much focused on the direct benefit or behaviors allowed by the recipient. Refer to Chapter 10 for details on recipient administration.

Here's a list of some of the EMS cmdlets that deal with mailbox administration:

- Move-Mailbox
- Get-Mailbox
- Set-Mailbox
- Get-MailboxFolderStatistics
- Get-MailboxStatistics
- New-Mailbox
- Disable-Mailbox
- Connect-Mailbox
- Remove-Mailbox
- Restore-Mailbox

- Export-Mailbox
- Enable-Mailbox
- Get-MailboxPermission
- Add-MailboxPermission
- Remove-MailboxPermission

Our focus for mailbox server administration is how these impact the planning and continued operation of mailbox server performance considerations. High availability (although in a large part related to mailbox server load distribution), continuous replication, and clustering are the focus of another chapter. Mailbox permissions are addressed in the Part V chapters on security. Most of the detail with managing individual mailboxes is, once again, in Chapter 10.

EMS: Get-Mailbox

There are five forms of the Get-Mailbox cmdlet, depending on how mailboxes are to be selected. As is typical with other "Get-*" cmdlets, such as Get-MailboxDatabase and Get-StorageGroup, when run with none of the differentiating parameters in these five forms, or even with no parameters at all, the Get-Mailbox cmdlet returns a list of all mailboxes in the Exchange organization. Therefore, in essence, there are six ways to select the set of mailboxes Get-Mailbox gives. Naturally, without a subsequent cmdlet in the pipeline, such as an alternate formatter, the default formatter Format-Table will display the Name, Alias, ServerName, and ProhibitSendQuota attributes of each mailbox. Subsequent cmdlets in the pipeline after Get-Mailbox will generally operate on all resultant mailboxes.

The various sets of mailboxes to be chosen may be selected according to the follow methods:

- All mailboxes in the Exchange organization (no extra parameters needed)
- All mailboxes hosted on a specific mailbox server (using the Server parameter)
- All mailboxes in a specific database (using the Database parameter)
- All mailboxes that match a specific attribute filter (using the Filter parameter)
- All mailboxes with a specific ambiguous name resolution (ANR) match (using the ANR parameter)
- A specific mailbox (using the Identity parameter)

EMS: Set-Mailbox

Running Get-Mailbox | Format-List shows the set of attributes on each current mailbox in the Exchange organization. Even when qualified to display those properties for a single mailbox, it can quickly become clear that mailboxes themselves have many more configurable parameters than mailbox databases, storage groups, and mailbox server objects. In turn, the Set-Mailbox cmdlet offers the ability to configure many mailbox parameters.

Fifteen custom attributes may be assigned to an e-mail recipient such as a mailbox. Coverage of certain parameters fall under the topic of recipient administration, and still other aspects of mailboxes warrant coverage and you will find this additional information in Chapter 15 on Regulatory Compliance and Chapter 17 on AntiSPAM. Additionally, use the Get-Help Set-Mailbox -full cmdlets for a description of all configurable mailbox settings.

Public Folders

Just as mailbox databases contain individual mailboxes, which in turn contain folders with messages (and other items), public folder databases contain top-level public folders that may contain items and subfolders for many users to access. Although some basic cmdlets for public folder database administration have been covered in this chapter, the details of administration of public folders themselves are beyond the scope of this chapter. Only a cursory coverage is included here. Even though the initial release to manufacturing (RTM) version of Exchange Server 2007 had some public folder administration features lacking, Exchange Server 2007 Service Pack 1 (SP1) includes many more administration features for managing public folders. For details, refer to Microsoft's TechNet article titled, "New Mailbox Features in Exchange 2007 SP1," (http://technet.microsoft.com/en-us/library/bb684903.aspx).

Public Folder Management

Although Exchange Server 2007 SP1 includes a graphical Public Folder Management Console, as well as more features within EMC itself for better support of features such as public folder referrals, we will briefly mention some of the EMC cmdlets that may be used to help facilitate public folder management in both the RTM and SP1 versions of Exchange Server 2007. Here's a list of some of the EMS cmdlets for basic public folder management:

- New-PublicFolder
- Remove-PublicFolder
- Get-PublicFolder
- Set-PublicFolder
- Update-PublicFolder
- Update-PublicFolderHierarchy

The first few of these, New-PublicFolder, Remove-PublicFolder, Get-PublicFolder, and Set-PublicFolder, are similar to their mailbox counterparts. Yet, because public folders can be replicated to many servers using content synchronization, the cmdlets Update-PublicFolder and Update-PublicFolderHierarchy are also included to manage features that have no comparable analogy in the world of mailboxes on Exchange Server 2007. See Chapter 13 for more details on the Public Folder Management Console and administering public folders.

Mail-Enabled Public Folders

Indeed, the updated versions after the RTM of Outlook 2007 and Exchange Server 2007 have added public folder access to Outlook and OWA lacking in the RTM versions. Therefore, prior to the SP1 releases, use of an interface such as Outlook 2003 would be required to fully access public folders hosted on Exchange Server 2007 mailbox servers. However, mail-enabled public folders are available in all versions of Exchange Server 2007. Three separate cmdlets allow configuration of the "mail-enabledness" of public folders:

- Disable-MailPublicFolder
- Enable-MailPublicFolder
- Set-MailPublicFolder

Public folders are a powerful feature of Exchange Server 2007 and were heavily used in the Exchange 2000 Server and Exchange Server 2003 environments. When Exchange Server 2007 RTM was released, many organizations who had not yet fully embraced other technologies such as Windows SharePoint Services and Office SharePoint Services were left with the question of what the "deemphasized" nature of the public folder feature in Exchange Server 2007 meant. With Exchange Server 2007 SP1 including greatly enhanced public folder support beyond the RTM version, and with Outlook 2007 following suit, there is again an array of ways to get such functionality, including but not limited to Exchange and SharePoint.

Summary

In this first chapter of Part III we covered the administrative tasks associated the Mailbox Server Role. The services that comprise the Mailbox Server role allow us to store mail and public folder content on the server. Storage groups, Mailbox Databases, and Public Folder Databases can be administered using both the Exchange Management Shell and the Exchange management Console. We looked at numerous cmdlets that allow you to create, remove, delete, and modify these objects on and Exchange 2007 Mailbox Server. A number of advanced Exchange Management Shell cmdlets were also detailed to help you reduce the time it takes to perform administrative tasks on mailbox databases and, that the mailboxes store mail in them. In the following chapters we will take a close look at how to administer the Hub Transport, Edge Transport, Unified Messaging, and Client Access server roles.

PART III

Administering Hub and Edge Transport Servers

E xchange Server 2007 has two explicitly defined transport server roles—the Hub Transport (HT) and the Edge Transport (ET). Besides managing Exchange recipients, managing these transport server roles and the tasks associated with message transport are some of the more important tasks performed by Exchange administrators on a fairly regular basis. This chapter discusses Exchange Server 2007 transport server roles and their associated management tasks.

The Hub Transport Server Role

The Hub Transport server role is a part of Exchange Server 2007's internal messaging topology, responsible for transferring mail and applying policies to messages on route to their destination. Direct comparisons with Exchange Server 2000/2003's Bridgehead Server role are inevitable and not completely out of place. However, the HT performs a number of additional functions besides simply transferring messages.

Before going any further, it's essential that you clearly understand one important behavior of mail flow in Exchange Server 2007: Every e-mail message encounters at least one Hub Transport server in its lifetime. Here's a simplified recap of Exchange Server 2007 message routing functionality:

- Messages between different Active Directory (AD) sites are sent from the source mailbox server to a Hub Transport server in the same site. The HT server routes the message to an HT server in the destination site, which delivers the message to the destination mailbox server.

- Messages to recipients in the same AD site are sent from the source mailbox server to an HT server in the same site, which routes messages to the destination mailbox server. In other words, two mailbox servers do not talk to each other directly, unlike in previous versions of Exchange.

- If a message is sent to a mailbox residing on the same mailbox server as the sender, the message still hops through an HT server before making its way back to the mailbox server. (This is an important part of our message routing recap.)

This may be perceived by many as creating extra network traffic, particularly in the last scenario where the sender and recipient reside on the same mailbox server. However, the capabilities that this behavior makes possible in terms of applying messaging policies to all messages in the transport pipeline are desirable in many organizations. Additionally, it complements the replication features by retaining copies of recent messages in a transport cache and delivering these to the Mailbox server when events such as a failover to a replica database occur.

For environments where these features are not required, and preserving the Exchange Server 2000/2003 mail transport behavior is more important to save on network bandwidth, the HT server role can coexist with the Mailbox (and CAS) server role, except in cases where the mailbox server is clustered. This results in a single server with Mailbox, Message Transport and Client Access (OWA/POP/IMAP/EAS/Outlook Anywhere) functionality, quite similar to single-server Exchange Server 2000/2003 deployments.

The Edge Transport Server Role

The Edge Transport server role is a new member of the Exchange messaging topology. It routes messages between the Exchange organization and external mail systems. As such, it is meant to be a mail gateway, in many ways similar to non-Exchange Message Transfer Agents (MTAs) MTAs such as Sendmail and Postfix, or appliances from vendors such as IronPort and Barracuda that serve as mail gateways in many organizations. Unlike other Exchange server roles that are designed to be domain-joined members of the Exchange organization, the Edge is designed to be a standalone server. Additionally, it is designed to be located in perimeter networks, also known as DMZs (demilitarized zones), a term used for network segments located *between* an external or Internet-facing firewall and the internal firewall. This allays some of the fears of security departments about exposing Windows domain servers to the Internet and locating member servers in perimeter networks.

Nevertheless, the Edge server role can be installed on member servers and located behind firewalls on the internal network, if required.

Unlike its *internal* counterpart (the Hub Transport server role), the ET is *not* a required server role. An organization can expose its internal Hub Transport servers to the Internet, allowing these to directly receive and send external/Internet e-mail. Alternatively, it can continue to use non-Exchange MTAs, such as those mentioned earlier, as its mail gateways for inbound mail and deliver the mail to Hub Transport servers. Whether an ET server becomes a part of your messaging topology will be determined by a number of factors. Unlike the HT role, Exchange does not make it mandatory that you have an Edge Transport server deployed.

Comparing the Hub and Edge Transport Server Roles

Conversations about Hub Transport and Edge Transport server roles often end up in a discussion about the differences between the two roles. Although the general design decisions made by the Exchange product team have been communicated often on the Microsoft website and the Exchange team blog (msexchangeteam.com), a brief feature-by-feature comparison of each is in order so that you can clearly understand what one gains by deploying the Edge Transport server role—or as is often a topic of such discussions, what features are unavailable when one does *not* deploy the Edge Transport server role.

- **Transport rules on the Hub and Edge Transport servers**   Besides the general design considerations, one of the more important differences that does not get as much airplay is the difference in the transport rules functionality. Whereas both the Edge Transport and the Hub Transport can apply transport rules to messages in transit, the Edge Transport server does not have access to Active Directory domain controllers (DCs)/Global Catalog servers that the Hub Transport servers benefit from. This restricts its ability to apply the kind of transport rules that can require Active Directory access, such as rules based on an Exchange recipient or its membership in distribution lists. Instead, the Edge Transport can only use SMTP e-mail addresses. Overall, the transport rules available to the Edge Transport server are for the most part a subset of those available to its domain-joined counterpart—the Hub Transport server. Additionally, the Edge Transport server can use transport rules to deliver messages to the spam quarantine mailbox and to drop SMTP connections.

- **Transport agents**   The Hub and Edge Transport servers also have a small number of distinct transport agents exclusive to them. The Hub Transport sports the Journaling agent and AD Rights Management Services Prelicensing agent. The Edge Transport has the Attachment Filtering agent and Address Rewriting (Inbound and Outbound) agents. Transport rules are applied by the Transport Rule agent on the Hub Transport and by the Edge Rule agent on the Edge Transport server.

Table 7-1 lists the main feature differences between the Hub Transport and Edge Transport server roles.

Feature	Hub Transport	Edge Transport
Required server role	Yes	No
Coexists with other Exchange Server 2007 server roles[1]	Yes	No
Designed to work in perimeter networks (a.k.a. "DMZs")[2]	No	Yes
Designed to work as a standalone (not a domain-joined) server[3]	No	Yes
Requires Active Directory Application Mode (ADAM)	No	Yes
Can send/receive Internet mail	Yes	Yes
Anti-spam agents	Yes[4]	Yes
Safelist Aggregation	Yes	Yes
Attachment Filtering agent	No	Yes
Address Rewriting (Inbound and Outbound) agents	No	Yes
Journaling agent	Yes	No

TABLE 7-1   A Comparison of the Features of the Hub Transport and Edge Transport Server Roles

Feature	Hub Transport	Edge Transport
AD RMS Prelicensing agent	Yes	No
Number of transport rule conditions (a.k.a. "predicates")	26	13
Transport rules based on Active Directory objects such as recipients and distribution groups	Yes	No
Transport rules to apply message classification	Yes	No
Transport rules to apply disclaimers	Yes	No
Transport rules to deliver messages to the spam quarantine mailbox	No	Yes
Transport rules to drop a connection	No	Yes
Sharing of SMTP address spaces (internal relay domains)[5]	Yes	No

[1.] The Hub Transport server coexists with the Client Access Server (CAS), Unified Messaging, and Mailbox Server roles, with the exception of the Clustered Mailbox Server (CMS).

[2.] The Edge Transport server is designed to work in perimeter networks (DMZs), but can be deployed on internal networks as well.

[3.] The Edge Transport server role is designed to be deployed on standalone servers that are not part of an Active Directory domain, but can be deployed on member servers.

[4.] The Hub Transport server role does not have anti-spam agents installed by default. These can be installed using the install-AntispamAgents.ps1 script in the "Exchange Server\Scripts" folder.

[5.] Note: Sharing SMTP address spaces is not a feature as such, but the capability to share address spaces requires a Hub Transport server. It's something the Edge Transport server cannot do because it requires access to Active Directory to look up recipients.

TABLE 7-1   A Comparison of the Features of the Hub Transport and Edge Transport Server Roles (*Continued*)

Common Transport Server Settings

The remainder of this section deals with some of the common settings related to transport servers.

Accepted Domains

When discussing Exchange Server 2007, it is inevitable to start off comparing the functionality provided by components of Exchange Server 2000/2003. If anything, the ability to map a new or changed feature to the functionality in previous versions makes understanding the new features and functionality much easier for those familiar with the previous versions.

A mail host needs to be told what SMTP domains it should accept e-mail for, and also whether it is authoritative for such domains. Additionally, the mail system needs to have recipients with e-mail addresses from such SMTP domains assigned to them. Otherwise, the mail system would not have any place to which to deliver such messages. (Note that specific address space–sharing scenarios are not discussed here.)

In Exchange Server 2000/2003, this was the job of recipient policies. They tell Exchange which address spaces (domains) to accept inbound mail for and to generate e-mail addresses for recipients using those domains.

Exchange Server 2007 splits that functionality into two new features or components—accepted domains and e-mail address policies.

Accepted domains tell Exchange Server 2007 transport servers which SMTP domains to receive inbound e-mail for. The Exchange organization can be authoritative for mail delivery to those domains, or it simply accepts e-mail for them and relays it to SMTP servers outside the Exchange organization. Generally, an Exchange organization is said to be authoritative for a domain if it hosts mailboxes for that domain. In this context, the term *authoritative* also means it is responsible for generating non-delivery reports (NDRs) for those addresses for which a recipient is not found (or if messages cannot be delivered for any other reason).

Default Accepted Domain

By default, Exchange (HT) uses the Fully Qualified Domain Name (FQDN) of the root domain in the Active Directory forest as an accepted domain. The first AD domain set up in the forest is known as the *forest root domain*. Additional accepted domains can be created as and when required. You cannot modify the default accepted domain. However, you can make any other accepted domain the default. To receive inbound e-mail, you need to have at least one accepted domain that is registered with a domain registrar. Setting up Exchange to receive inbound Internet mail is discussed later in this chapter.

NOTE   *The ET is not a member of the domain and does not have access to the FQDN, so the default accepted domain must be designated when you're configuring the ET.*

You can create an accepted domain without having Exchange generate any e-mail addresses using the domain. However, to use a domain in an e-mail address policy, it must exist as an accepted domain first.

Accepted domains should be created on a Hub Transport server. If any Edge servers exist in the topology, it is recommended that you use EdgeSync to have these replicated to ET servers.

To create a new accepted domain using the Exchange console, follow these steps:

1. Expand the Organization Configuration | Hub Transport | Accepted Domains tab.

2. In the Action pane, click New Accepted Domain to start the New Accepted Domain Wizard.

3. On the New Accepted Domain page, enter the following details:

   - **Name**   Enter a unique name for the accepted domain.

   - **Accepted domain**   Enter the SMTP domain name (for example, foo.com).

   - **The default accepted domain type**   This is set to Authoritative but can be changed to Internal Relay or External Relay.

NOTE   *Internal relay and external relay domains are discussed later in this section.*

---

4. Click New and then click Finish to complete the New Accepted Domain Wizard (see Figure 7-1).

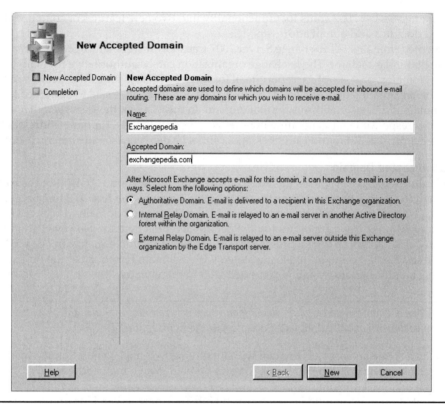

FIGURE 7-1 Creating a new accepted domain using the Exchange console

Here's how to create a new accepted domain using the Exchange shell:

```
New-AcceptedDomain -Name Exchangepedia -DomainName "exchangepedia.com" -DomainType
authoritative
```

The Accepted Domains tab in the Exchange console does not display which accepted domain is the default. In SP1 this has been added to the properties page of accepted domains. The ability to set an accepted domain as the default is also added as a context-sensitive menu choice.

To set an accepted domain as the default using the Exchange console, right-click the accepted domain and select Set as Default. This option does not appear as a choice for an existing default accepted domain.

Use the following command to set an Accepted Domain as the default:

```
Set-AcceptedDomain "Exchangepedia" –MakeDefault $true
```

Note that this command uses the name or identity, not the actual domain name property of the accepted domain.

You cannot remove or modify the default accepted domain. In order to do so, another accepted domain needs to set as the default.

Relay Domains

To understand what relay domains are, it's important that you understand what relaying is. When a mail server receives e-mail for any domains for which it is not authoritative, if it accepts such mail and forwards it either to the mail system authoritative for the domains or to a third mail host, it is said to be *relaying* mail. Relaying is generally perceived as a threat to e-mail security and a major source of spam. However, the security and spam implications are in the context of unauthenticated relaying, or what is commonly known as an *open relay*.

There are legitimate reasons why a server may be configured to relay mail. Remote users who use POP3 or IMAP4 to access their mailboxes need to relay outbound mail to external recipients using an SMTP server. For such remote users, relaying is generally allowed after authentication. Organizations may need to accept and relay mail for domains belonging to subsidiaries, acquisitions, or partners (or for customers in a hosting/service provider scenario). Comparatively, a server configured as an open relay allows unauthenticated relaying to any domain for which it is neither authoritative nor explicitly configured to accept and relay mail for.

By default, Exchange servers are configured to deny relaying to unauthenticated users. In scenarios where an organization needs to relay mail to certain domains, an Accepted Domain (or domains) needs to be created for those domains.

Other than the accepted domains that the Exchange organization is authoritative for, Exchange Server 2007 introduces the concept of external relay and internal relay domains. These specify how mail is relayed for accepted domains.

- **External relay domains**   External relay domains are used to accept inbound e-mail for a domain and relay it to external/non-Exchange SMTP hosts. The external/non-Exchange SMTP hosts in this case may be outside the boundaries of the organization. The Exchange organization does not have any recipients for such domains, so no Active Directory lookups are performed. In topologies with Edge Transport servers deployed, the ET servers receive inbound e-mail and relay it to the responsible mail host(s) for that domain. This is typically done over Send connectors configured for the address space of the relayed domain(s). The external/non-Exchange SMTP host is configured as a smarthost for such Send connectors. Mail for external relay domains is never forwarded to Hub Transport servers in the organization.

  In topologies where no ET servers are deployed, external relay domains work with Hub Transport servers as well, in a similar fashion.

- **Internal relay domains**   Internal relay domains are used in scenarios where the SMTP address space is being shared between an Exchange organization and an external/non-Exchange mail system. The Exchange organization typically has recipients with e-mail addresses from the relayed domains. Additionally, MailContacts with e-mail addresses from that domain may also exist in the organization, perhaps as a result of Directory/Global Address List (GAL) synchronization. In this scenario, Active Directory lookups are performed to determine whether any recipients exist in the organization. If such recipients are found, mail is delivered to them. If no matching Exchange recipients are found in the organization, Hub Transport servers relay mail to the external/non-Exchange SMTP host(s) responsible for the relayed domain, typically over a Send connector configured with the address space of the relayed domain.

New accepted domains that are either external relay or internal relay domains can be created from the Exchange console using the New Accepted Domain Wizard mentioned earlier in this chapter.

Here's how to create a new accepted domain that is either an external or internal relay domain using the Exchange shell:

```
New-AcceptedDomain -Name "ExtRelay-Lefkovics" -DomainName "lefkovics.
net" -DomainType <ExternalRelay | InternalRelay>
```

- **Accepted domains and subdomains**   It is possible to use a wildcard to specify and include all subdomains when creating or modifying an accepted domain (for example, *.lefkovics.net). With an accepted domain thus configured, transport servers in the organization will accept mail for recipients that have an e-mail address from any subdomain (for example, us.lefkovics.net and eu.lefkovics.net). However, a subdomain cannot be used in e-mail address policies unless an explicit accepted domain exists for one (for example, us.lefkovics.net).

E-mail Address Policies

E-mail address policies provide the functionality of generating e-mail addresses for recipients. Together with accepted domains, they are the equivalent of recipient policies (for e-mail addresses) in Exchange Server 2000/2003.

NOTE *Exchange Server 2000/2003 also have recipient policies with Mailbox Manager settings, used to report on or manage the contents of users' mailboxes. These policies are used to accomplish tasks such as purging the Deleted Items folder after a certain number of days. Similar functionality is offered by Managed Folders and Managed Content Settings in Exchange Server 2007.*

You can create additional e-mail address policies using the existing default domain or by adding new Accepted Domains and using them. E-mail address policies consist of three important parameters:

- The e-mail address template to use, which determines how a recipient's properties such as first name, last name, Exchange alias, and so on, are used to create the local part of the address
- The Accepted Domain to use for the domain part
- A recipient filter with which to filter AD recipients

The policy gets applied to recipients returned by the filter. The filtering mechanism ensures you can use different e-mail address policies for different sets of recipients, allowing them to have differently formatted e-mail addresses.

By default, an e-mail address policy is created for the organization using the recipient's *alias* in the local part of the e-mail address and the default accepted domain in the domain part. As mentioned earlier in this chapter, the FQDN of the root domain in the AD forest is used as the default.

The Anatomy of an SMTP E-mail Address

RFC 2821, "Simple Mail Transfer Protocol," and RFC 2822, "Internet Message Format," define the format of an SMTP e-mail address, which is separated into two parts. The "@" character is used to separate both parts of an e-mail address. The part before the @ character is known as the *local part,* and refers to a unique recipient in the mail system. The recipient is generally thought of as a mailbox, but in the context of Exchange Server, it can be a recipient other than a MailboxUser—for example, a MailUser, a MailContact, a distribution group, or a mail-enabled public folder. The part after the @ character is the domain. This can be the fully qualified domain or subdomain of the recipient's mail system.

The following illustration shows an e-mail address and the different characters allowed or disallowed in the local and domain part:

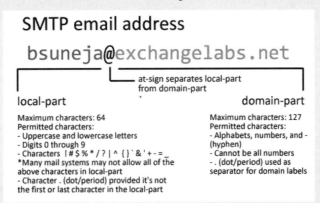

Although RFC 2821 recommends that mail systems accept e-mail addressed to a recipient with a domain literal in the domain part (the domain literal being the IP address of the mail host), Exchange Server 2007 does not allow domain literals to be used in accepted domains or e-mail address policies. Additionally, an e-mail address using a domain literal cannot be added manually to an Exchange Server 2007 recipient.

RFC 2821 has a comparatively permissive definition of the local part. It recommends that the local part be treated as case-sensitive, but for interoperability purposes when comparing e-mail addresses, the use of case-sensitivity is discouraged. The local part should not require the use of non-ASCII characters or ASCII control characters (decimal values 0–31 and 127). The local part has a maximum limit of 64 characters.

The domain part of an e-mail address can be the FQDN of an SMTP host (for example, wormhole.exchangelabs.net) but is generally the domain name (for example, exchangelabs.net). The domain part can have a maximum of 127 characters. Valid characters include ASCII alphabets, numbers, and hyphens (-). The latter, however, should not appear in the beginning or end of the domain part. Note that no other symbols, punctuation marks, or spaces are permitted in the domain part, including the underscore (_) character.

Although it is possible to send outbound e-mail using any properly formatted e-mail address, it is important to remember that inbound Internet mail is dependent on a valid domain name registered with a domain registrar, with an externally accessible Domain Naming System (DNS) zone for that registered domain being available. Recipients should have an e-mail address that uses such a registered domain name in the domain part of the e-mail address. Additionally, to ensure outbound messages are sent using that address, and that this is the address used by Internet senders when replying to e-mail sent by your recipients, the e-mail address should be set as the *default* e-mail address for the recipient. In many cases, the FQDN of the root domain in an AD forest uses a domain that is either not registered with an Internet domain registrar or contains a domain suffix that is not valid in the hierarchy of Internet domains (for example, ExchangeLabs.Local). If recipients have default e-mail addresses that use such *invalid* domain names in the domain part, inbound Internet e-mail cannot be received.

To create a new e-mail address policy using the Exchange console, follow these steps:

1. Expand the Organization Configuration node.

2. Select the Hub Transport node.

3. Select the E-mail Address Policies tab.

4. In the Actions pane, click New E-mail Address Policy to start the New E-mail Address Policy Wizard.

5. In the Introduction page, type a unique name for the new e-mail address policy. Click Next.

NOTE *By default, new policies apply to all recipient types. To have a policy applied to a particular recipient type (such as users with Exchange mailboxes), select the radio button labeled "The following specific types" and then check the boxes for the appropriate recipient types.*

---

6. On the Conditions page, shown in Figure 7-2, select one of the conditions available—Recipients in a State or Province, Recipients in a Department, Recipients in a Company, or Custom Attributes 1 through 15. Click Next.

NOTE *The precanned filters expose a very limited set of recipient attributes that can be used to filter recipients. If the list of attributes does not meet your requirements, or you need to filter based on attributes other than the ones exposed by the precanned filters, you will need to use the Exchange shell to create an e-mail address policy with a custom recipient filter.*

---

7. On the E-mail Addresses page, click the Add button.

8. From the SMTP E-mail Addresses dialog box, select the appropriate e-mail address format from the choices available, as shown in Figure 7-3.

9. To select an accepted domain to use in the EmailAddressPolicy, click Browse. Alternatively, select Specify custom fully qualified domain name (FQDN) for e-mail address. Type a domain that exists as an accepted domain and then click OK to close the dialog box. Click Next.

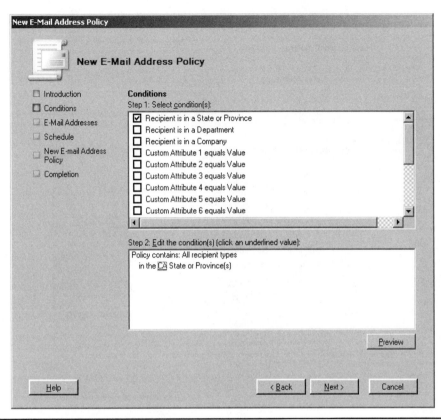

FIGURE 7-2   The Conditions page of the New E-mail Address Policy Wizard exposes a very limited set of recipient attributes available through precanned recipient filters

---

SP1 *In Exchange Server 2007 RTM, the E-mail Address Policy Wizard provides a drop-down control for selecting an accepted domain. In SP1 this has been changed to provide the ability to browse for an accepted domain, and to type an accepted domain directly in a text box.*

NOTE *You cannot create an e-mail address policy for a domain or a subdomain that does not exist as an accepted domain.*

10. On the Schedule tab, click Next to apply the e-mail address policy immediately. Alternatively, you can select At the following time and then specify a date and time for the policy to be applied. Recipients will not get the new e-mail addresses until the policy is applied.

11. On the Configuration Summary page, examine the e-mail address format, the domain selected, and the recipient types selected.

12. Click New to finish creating the new e-mail address policy.

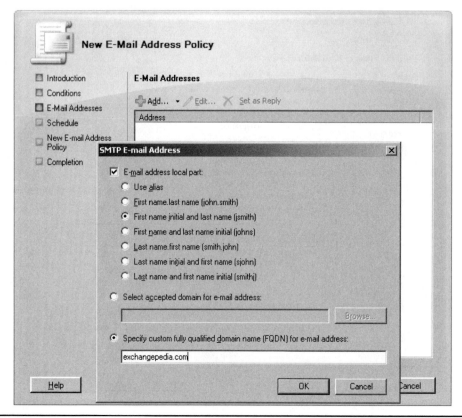

Figure 7-3 Selecting a precanned e-mail address and an existing accepted domain

Here's how to create a new e-mail address policy using the Exchange shell:

```
New-EmailAddressPolicy -Name "EAP-Exchangepedia" -IncludedRecipients UserMailbox
-EnabledEmailAddressTemplates "SMTP:@exchangepedia.com"
```

This command uses a precanned filter to pick up all user mailboxes from the AD forest. E-mail addresses are generated with the users' aliases in the local part. The existing accepted domain exchangepedia.com is used for the domain part.

E-mail address policies allow you to use precanned SMTP e-mail addresses. These include the following common e-mail address formats for the local part:

- Alias
- First name.last name
- First name initial and last name
- First name and last name initial

- Last name.first name
- Last name initial and first name
- Last name and first name initial

If these canned templates do not meet the organizational naming conventions for e-mail addresses, you can use a custom e-mail address using the variables detailed in Table 7-2 for the local part.

A combination of these variables can be used to format e-mail addresses. For example, to use the first name, middle initial, and first three letters of the last name, you can generate the custom e-mail address using the following representation: %g%m%3s.

To generate custom e-mail addresses, you can use the Exchange console (see Figure 7-4). On the E-mail Addresses page in the New E-mail Address Policy Wizard, click the arrow next to the Add button and select Custom Address. In the E-mail address field, type the preceding notation, followed by the @ character and a valid accepted domain. In the E-mail type field, type **SMTP**.

The precanned recipient filters provide a basic and quick filtering mechanism for e-mail address policies and other features that use recipient filters. However, the number and type of conditions available using precanned filters will be inadequate for many deployments. Whereas recipient policies in Exchange Server 2000/2003 allowed the use of Lightweight Directory Access Protocol (LDAP) filters, Exchange Server 2007 comes with a shiny new filter syntax known as OPATH. If you spent a lot of time trying to understand the syntax used by LDAP filters and can list the ldapDisplayname of attributes that can be used natively in them, there's a good chance you may find OPATH and the available number of "filterable" attributes or properties somewhat limiting.

Let's take a look at custom recipient filters and the OPATH filter syntax.

The list of properties that can be used in OPATH filters can be found at http://technet .microsoft.com/en-us/library/bb430771.aspx. It's a subset of the complete list of LDAP attributes associated with a recipient and includes some new properties used by Exchange Server 2007.

Variable	Value	Resulting Local Part for William S. Lefkovics
%g	Given name (first name)	william
%i	Middle initial	S
%s	Surname (last name)	lefkovics
%d	Display name	WilliamLefkovics
%m	Exchange alias	wletkovics
%xs	Use x number of characters of the surname	%3s = lef
%xg	Use x number of characters of the given name	%3g = wil

TABLE 7-2   Variables Used in E-mail Address Templates

FIGURE 7-4
Using a custom
e-mail address

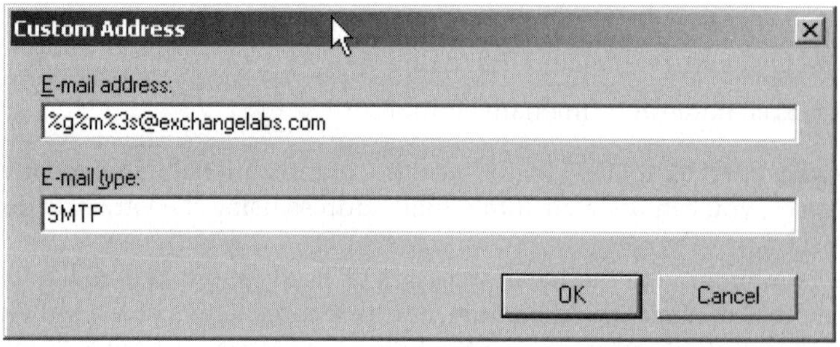

Custom Address   ☒

E-mail address:

%g%m%3s@exchangelabs.com

E-mail type:

SMTP

                                                            OK   Cancel

Armed with this list of filterable properties, let's examine a simple recipient filter based on the recipients' country. We assign the recipients an e-mail address using the first name. last name template.

```
New-EmailAddressPolicy –Name "ExchangeLabs.com" –RecipientFilter "RecipientType
-eq 'UserMailbox' -and Co -eq 'United States'"
-EnabledPrimarySMTPAddressTemplate "SMTP:%g.%s@exchangelabs.com"
```

Not terribly complicated. Instead of using the IncludedRecipients parameter to filter on recipient types, as we do when using precanned filters, we select the recipient types the policy will apply to as part of the RecipientFilter property. Perhaps what may have taken a disproportionate amount of time to come up with the OPATH filter in the preceding example, is the name of the property that holds the value for a recipient's country, commonly referred to as CountryOrRegion in other shell commands, but shortened to Co when used as a filterable property.

Compared to Exchange Server 2000/2003, the way policies apply to recipients has changed:

- Changes made to e-mail address policies are applied immediately. If the changes are made using the Exchange shell, one can actually see the text-based progress bar as the changed policy is applied—a comforting feature that buys one plenty of peace of mind.

- All recipients get evaluated after a new e-mail address policy is created or an existing policy is changed, including a change to its priority value.

- Comparatively, in Exchange Server 2000/2003, recipients falling within the scope of a new or changed policy are acted upon when the policy is applied. Recipients falling out of the scope of a given policy remain unaffected, until the policy that is now applicable to them is updated or applied again.

- The primary e-mail address, used to send e-mail and receive replies, is moved to the proxy addresses attribute when a recipient falls within the scope of a different policy. This allows recipients to continue to receive replies to e-mail sent previously using a different default e-mail address.

What hasn't changed is the fact that out of all the policies applicable to a recipient based on the filter, the one with the highest priority gets applied. Additionally, the *old* e-mail addresses generated by a previous policy stay on as proxy addresses—these do not get removed when a different policy applies to a recipient.

Remote Domains

Remote domains are a group of global settings for message transfer to remote SMTP domains that are not a part of your Active Directory forest, and thus the Exchange organization. Settings such as allowing non-delivery reports, out-of-office messages, automatic replies, and auto-forwarding of messages can be controlled for all external/ Internet mail or for specific domains (see Figure 7-5).

The default remote domain, called Default, is created by Exchange setup for the address space *. As in the case of connectors, the * address space defines all remote domains that Exchange neither has an accepted domain for nor has an explicit (remote domain) setting for.

Additional remote domains can be created for particular domains that require different settings.

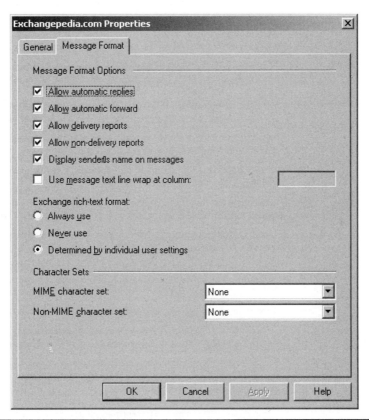

FIGURE 7-5   Remote domains define message format settings for external domains, including settings for auto-forwarding, auto-replies, non-delivery reports (NDRs), out-of-office responses, and so on

CAUTION *Remote domains should not be created for any domain that exists as an accepted domain in the Exchange organization.*

Table 7-3 details all the settings defined by remote domains.

Setting	Description
Character Set	Used for MIME messages that do not have their own character set specified. A list of supported character sets can be found at http://technet .microsoft.com/en-us/library/aa998600.aspx.
Non-MIME Character Set	Character set to be used for non-MIME (text) messages that do not have their own character set defined. A list of supported character sets can be found at http://technet.microsoft.com/en-us/library/aa998600.aspx.
AllowedOOFType	Specifies the type of out-of-office (OOF) messages sent to the domain. Here are the valid values: **None** **External** This is the default value. **ExternalLegacy** Allows external OOFs as well as OOFs set by Outlook 2003 or earlier clients and Exchange Server 2003 or earlier servers. **InternalLegacy** Allows internal OOFs as well as OOFs set by Outlook 2003 or earlier clients and Exchange Server 2003 or earlier servers.
AutoReplyEnabled	Allows automatic replies generated by client e-mail programs to recipients in the remote domain. The default value is $false.
AutoForwardEnabled	Allows client e-mail programs to auto-forward messages to external recipients. The default value is $false.
DeliveryReportEnabled	Allows delivery reports to recipients in a remote domain. Delivery reports can be requested when a message is created. The default value is $true.
NDREnabled	Allows non-delivery reports (NDRs) to recipients in a remote domain. The default value is $true.
MeetingForwardNotificationEnabled	When meeting requests are forwarded to external recipients, the meeting organizer receives a notification. Set this to false to disable notifications. The default value is True.
ContentType	Defines the message format used to send to remote domains. The default is MimeHtmlText.
DisplaySenderName	Enables sending display names to remote domains. The default value is True.
TNEFEnabled	Specifies whether Transport Neutral-Encapsulation Format (TNEF) encoding should be used for message content. The default value is $null, allowing TNEF encoding to be specified by settings like a mail contact or mail user's UseMapiRichTextFormat parameter, the sending user's per-recipient or default Internet message format settings in Microsoft Outlook.
LineWrapSize	Sets the line wrap size for messages to a Remote Domain. The default setting is "unlimited". Valid values include an integer from 0 to 132.

TABLE 7-3   Remote Domain Settings

Out-of-office responses (or OOFs in Exchange lingo) have become a part of accepted and expected business communication since early versions of Microsoft Exchange. Exchange Server 2007 introduces new functionality to restrict their, create different OOFs for internal and external recipients, and schedule OOF start and stop times in advance. These client features are discussed in Chapters 11 and 12. Many organizations and administrators choose to restrict OOFs to external recipients because of concerns related to spam—in other words, responding to spam with an OOF simply confirms that an e-mail address is valid and reachable. OOF responses to external recipients can be turned off by modifying the default remote domain. In organizations where OOFs are viewed as an essential part of business communication, particularly in departments such as Sales and Marketing, they can be turned on for specific external domains by creating a new remote domain for each such domain and enabling OOFs. This approach works in some organizations, where only a few external domains are allowed OOFs, but it may not be practical for a large number of external domains.

Nevertheless, most organizations do prefer to leave OOFs turned on in the default remote domain.

CAUTION *If AllowedOOFType is set to InternalLegacy, recipients in the remote domain receive the internal OOF message. It is recommended not to have the default remote domain (for address space *) set to InternalLegacy. Users may inadvertently set up the internal OOF message to reveal sensitive information or content that may not be appropriate for external recipients.*

Automatic replies and forwards are turned on for the default remote domain. Many organizations prefer to suppress automatic replies, automatic forwards, or both. Automatic forwards can be potentially used to forward e-mail with sensitive or confidential information to external recipients. Both introduce the risk of message loops if the external recipient also responds with an automated response to each received message. Server-generated auto-response messages may be required in many scenarios. Exchange Server 2007 does not have a server-side auto-response feature. These settings in remote domains control only those automatic replies and messages forwarded automatically by the client.

Delivery reports can be requested by clients when creating a message. In Microsoft Office Outlook 2007, this is done from message options by selecting "Request a delivery report for this message." In addition to delivery reports, read receipts can also be requested. Remote domains can be configured to allow or suppress delivery reports. Suppressing these does not have any impact on read reports, which are sent when a user opens a message and is prompted to send one.

Non-delivery reports (NDRs) are sent when an MTA that is authoritative for a domain accepts a message for delivery but cannot deliver it for any reason. RFC 2821 requires NDRs to be sent to a sender if a message cannot be delivered. Due to the ever-increasing volumes of spam, many organizations choose to ignore this requirement defined in the SMTP protocol and suppress NDRs. Suppressing outbound NDRs to remote domains does not provide any protection against reverse NDR attacks your recipients may receive for messages they did not send.

Every once in a while you'll come across users complaining that external recipients get an attachment named winmail.dat with the messages received from your domain. This is because messages are being encoded in Transport Neutral Encapsulation Format (TNEF). TNEF-encoded messages contain the message in plain text, along with a binary "package" that contains various parts of the message. More details about TNEF-encoded messages and the behavior receiving clients display can be found in Microsoft Knowledge Base article (KBA) 241538.

The settings to control TNEF encoding appear in the Exchange rich-text format section of the Message Format tab of a remote domain. The default is "Determined by individual user settings." The corresponding property is called TNEFEnabled and is set to $null. This maintains the setting selected by the user for a particular recipient or message from Microsoft Outlook, or the setting specified in the settings for a MailContact or a MailUser.

Transport Rules

For a long time, the Exchange community demanded the ability to manipulate messages on the server. The Outlook client users' understanding of this, and that of many Exchange administrators, has always been the server-side rules created using Microsoft Outlook that get executed even when the Outlook client is not connected to Exchange server. The Exchange Server 2000/2003 solution for manipulating messages on the server consisted of event sinks. Transport event sinks were used to manipulate messages in the transport pipeline, to accomplish relatively simple tasks such as appending legal disclaimer text to messages. Most antivirus and anti-spam software that work with Exchange also use the hooks to transport events exposed by transport event sinks.

However, for the most part, transport event sinks did not become very popular given the demand for accomplishing the tasks they made possible, primarily because they required intimate knowledge of how the message transport works as well as programming or advanced scripting skills to write the code. An additional limitation was imposed by the SMTP transport, which did not get to see messages originating from and delivered to the local store on an Exchange server, thus never entering the transport pipeline.

With Exchange Server 2007, transport event sinks have evolved into a more complete solution that can be used by most Exchange administrators. Gone is the need to write code—or have any programming or scripting skills at all. Thanks to the new message routing functionality that enables the Hub Transport servers to touch every single message—even those originating from and destined to the same mailbox store on the same server—transport rules can act on every single message sent or received by Exchange recipients.

For more details about transport rules, refer to Chapter 15.

Journaling

Message journaling is a compliance feature that allows a copy of each message to be delivered to a journaling mailbox. In a departure from previous Exchange versions, journaling happens while messages are in the transport pipeline, as opposed to journaling at the store. This allows for more granular journaling capabilities, including journaling all messages, only internal messages, only external messages, and messages for a particular recipient or member of a distribution group. This is yet another reason why routing every message through a Hub Transport server makes more sense.

NOTE *This change from journaling in Exchange 2000/2003 may affect third-party archive solutions that rely on journaling for capturing messages. The administrator should check with third-party vendors to ensure that they can handle the new changes in Exchange 2007.*

Chapter 15 covers message journaling features in detail.

Managing Global Settings

Some transport-related settings can be applied globally to all transport servers in the organization. The RTM version of Exchange Server 2007 did not have any corresponding GUI functionality in the console; these were configured using the shell instead. SP1 sports a new General tab under the Organization Configuration | Hub Transport node that allows these settings to be configured easily (see Figure 7-6).

Let's take a look at these global settings. Table 7-4 lists all the global settings applicable to transport servers that can be configured using both the Exchange console and shell. (Note that some settings can only be configured using the Exchange shell.)

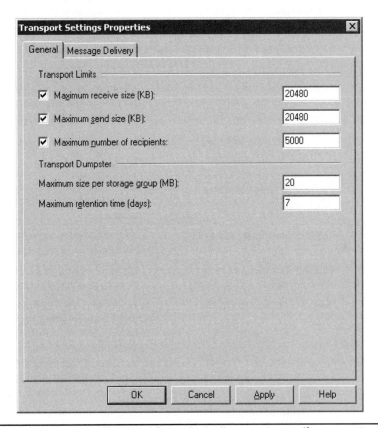

Transport Settings Properties

General | Message Delivery

Transport Limits

☑ Maximum receive size (KB): `20480`

☑ Maximum send size (KB): `20480`

☑ Maximum number of recipients: `5000`

Transport Dumpster

Maximum size per storage group (MB): `20`

Maximum retention time (days): `7`

OK   Cancel   Apply   Help

FIGURE 7-6 In SP1, the Transport Settings I General tab allows you to specify common transport settings related to maximum message sizes and the Transport Dumpster

Console Setting	EMS Parameter	Values
Maximum Receive Size (KB)	MaxReceiveSize	This is the maximum size of a message that can be received by Exchange recipients. This is set to 10,240KB (10MB) by default. The maximum value is 2,097,151KB.
Maximum Send Size	MaxSendSize	Maximum message size that can be sent.
Maximum number of recipients	MaxRecipientEnvelopeLimit	Default is 5000. Maximum is 2147483647.
Transport Dumpster: Maximum size per storage group	MaxDumpsterSizePerStorageGroup	Maximum size of the Transport Dumpster. Default is 18MB. Maximum is 2,097,151MB. Recommendation: 1.5× the maximum message size.
Transport Dumpster: Maximum retention time (days)	MaxDumpsterTime	Maximum time messages should be held in the Transport Dumpster. Default is 7 days. Maximum is 24,855 days.
EMS only	ClearCategories	If set to $true, this clears the message categories.
EMS only	JournalingReportNDRTo	SMTP address which receives journal reports if the journaling mailbox is unavailable.
EMS only	TLSReceiveDomainSecureList	List of domains to receive Domain Secure encrypted e-mail from.
EMS only	TLSSendDomainSecureList	List of domains to send Domain Secure encrypted e-mail to.
EMS only	VerifySecureSubmitEnabled	By default, Microsoft Office Outlook 2007 encrypts MAPI traffic; older Outlook clients do not. When VerifySecureSubmitEnabled is set to $true, it treats all messages submitted using unencrypted MAPI as anonymous. The default is $false.
EMS only	VoicemailJournalingEnabled	Enables journaling of voicemail messages.
EMS only	Xexch50Enabled	Specifies whether X-EXCH50 ESMTP verb should be enabled for backward compatibility with Exchange Server 2000/2003. The default is $true.

TABLE 7-4   Organization-wide Transport Settings

In Table 7-4, the settings related to maximum message sizes that can be sent and received, as well as the maximum number of recipients per message, are self-explanatory.

- **Maximum message sizes**   When setting maximum message sizes, consider the different places in which these can be set:
  - Organizational settings (using Set-TransportConfig or Transport Settings in the console)
  - Send connector (MaxMessageSize)
  - Receive connector (MaxMesageSize)
  - Mailbox and other recipient properties (MaxSendSize and MaxReceiveSize)
  - Global Settings used by Exchange Server 2000/2003
- **Global settings**   When setting up message sizes, it is easy to overlook the role of message size limits set in Global Settings. In Exchange Server 2000/2003, this is done using the Global Settings | Mail Delivery | Properties | Defaults tab. The specific attributes and the corresponding Exchange Server 2007 properties are detailed in Table 7-5.

In Exchange Server 2007 RTM, there was a possibility of the Global Settings conflicting with the organizational settings (configured using set-transportconfig). During upgrades to Exchange Server 2007, if the Exchange Server 2003 global settings were set to No Limit, Exchange Server 2007 changed them to 10240KB, 10240KB, and 5000, respectively. If specific values were specified, they were not modified, resulting in the conflict.

Exchange Server 2007 SP1 changes that behavior. Changes made to organizational limits using the Set-TransportConfig command are automatically applied to global settings as well, thus keeping them in synch.

- **Message sizes and content conversion**   One of the common sources of confusion in previous versions of Exchange is the non-delivery of messages when the message size is apparently lower than that configured in the maximum message size settings. When Internet/MIME messages are converted to MAPI/Exchange format, the message size grows by as much as 30–40%. Additional headers or content such as disclaimers may be added to messages en route to the mailbox. As a result, a message with an original size of 9Mb now exceeds the 10Mb maximum message size limit, thus resulting in a failed delivery. Exchange Server 2007 resolves this issue by adding an X-MS-Exchange-Organization-OriginalSize header stating the original message size when the message enters the Exchange organization. Before the message is delivered, the lower of the current message size, or the original size stamped in the message header, is compared with the recipient's applicable message size limits.

Exchange Server 2000/2003 Attribute	Exchange Server 2007 Property	SP1 Default Value*
delivContentLength	maxReceiveSize	10240
SubmissionContentLength	maxSendSize	10240
msExchRecipLimit	MaxRecipientEnvelopLimit	5000

TABLE 7-5   Maximum Message Size and Recipient Limits in Global Settings

---

TIP *In Exchange Server 2007, the number of recipients in a message is calculated before distribution group memberships are expanded. Each distribution group is counted as one recipient, irrespective of the number of its members. This is different from Exchange Server 2000/2003, where enforcement of maximum recipients per message happens after the Categorizer has expanded distribution group memberships, resulting in each member being counted as a recipient.*

Let's take a look at the settings in the Transport Dumpster section.

- **Transport Dumpster: Maximum Size Per Storage Group**   The Transport Dumpster is used to cache recent messages on Hub Transport servers. In clustered deployments that use Cluster Continuous Replication (CCR), a replica of the mailbox store exists on the passive node. It's logical to expect the replica to not have the most recent transaction log files for a storage group due to replication latency, and also due to the fact that the current transaction log files being written to by the active node are locked or in use and, therefore, cannot be replicated. In the case of a failover, Hub Transport servers deliver messages from this cache to the node that is now active. The Transport Dumpster ensures mailboxes have these recent messages that may be captured in transaction logs that are not replicated to the passive node before a failover.

  The default maximum size of the Transport Dumpster is set to 18Mb. Microsoft recommends the maximum size be configured to 1.5 times the maximum message size that can be received.

- **Transport Dumpster: Maximum Retention Time**   This setting configures the maximum age of messages in the Transport Dumpster. The default value is 7 days, which is also the Microsoft recommendation. This period offers a sufficiently large window to allow an extended Exchange outage without the loss of messages when switching to a replica store.

Next, we look at a few settings that are exclusive to the Exchange shell and need to be configured using the Set-TransportConfig command:

- **ClearCategories**   This parameter determines whether message categories assigned to a message by Microsoft Outlook are cleared during content conversion. By default, this is set to true.

- **JournalingReportNDRTo**   This is an important property that should be configured if you use journaling. It sends non-delivery reports for journaling messages to the specified mailbox. If journaled messages cannot be delivered to the journaling mailbox configured for a particular journaling rule, it makes sense to report this to the appropriate administrators, managers, and/or compliance officers within an organization. By default, this parameter is not configured. This parameter takes an SMTP address for a value.

- **TLSReceiveDomainSecureList**   This parameter lists domains from which received messages should be encrypted using Domain Secure. Domain Secure is an Exchange Server 2007 feature that uses TLS and mutual authentication to encrypt SMTP sessions.

NOTE *When populating the TLSReceiveDomainSecureList parameter with a list of domains, make sure Receive connectors on all transport servers responsible for receiving inbound mail have Domain Secure enabled.*

- **TLSSendDomainSecureList**   This is a list of domains to which outbound mail should be encrypted using Domain Secure mutual authentication.
- **VerifySecureSubmitEnabled**   Microsoft Outlook 2007 uses encrypted MAPI to send messages to Exchange Server; previous versions do not. When VerifySecureSubmit is set to true, it marks all messages received over encrypted MAPI sessions as secure. Messages submitted over nonencrypted MAPI sessions are marked as anonymous. The default value for VerifySecureSubmitEnabled is $false. It is recommended that you use this default setting in environments with previous versions of Outlook.
- **VoicemailJournalingEnabled**   Allows journaling of Unified Messaging voicemail messages. The default is $true.
- **Xexch50Enabled**   Xexch50 is the ESMTP extension used by previous versions of Exchange Server to authenticate and relay certain message properties. The default value is $true.

Managing Connectors

Exchange Server 2007 does not rely on SMTP support provided by Internet Information Services (IIS) in Windows Server 2003, as do its predecessors (Exchange Server 2000 and 2003). Exchange Server 2007 prohibits installation of IIS's SMTP service. Instead, it comes with its own transport stack, provided by the Microsoft Exchange Transport Service (MSExchangeTransport.exe). This has provided Microsoft the opportunity to reshape its support for SMTP, resulting in a smarter message transport.

Exchange Server 2007 supports three types of connectors: Receive, Send, and Foreign connectors. Whereas Receive and Send connectors are meant for SMTP communication, Foreign connectors are used to communicate with non-SMTP messaging systems.

In this chapter, we deal with the operational tasks related to managing connectors.

Managing Receive Connectors

Receive connectors are *protocol listeners*, conceptually similar in many ways to SMTP virtual servers in Exchange Server 2000/2003. They represent a connection point for SMTP clients.

NOTE *The term* SMTP client *is used to refer to a host that connects to an SMTP server to submit a message, irrespective of whether it is an SMTP server (such as an Exchange server) or one running a non-Exchange MTA such as Postfix or Sendmail, or even a computer running an SMTP client such as Microsoft Outlook (in non-MAPI mode), Outlook Express, or Windows Mail.*

For Receive connectors, the connection point is represented by the following:

- An IP address
- A TCP port number
- Remote IP addresses or ranges of IP addresses

The important aspect to note here is that the notion of a unique binding, in the context of SMTP, has changed. An Exchange Server 2000/2003 SMTP virtual server needs to have a unique combination of IP address and port number for it to be able to start. In Exchange Server 2007, the third element of RemoteIPRanges has been added to determine the uniqueness of the binding. The effect: More than one Receive connectors can be bound to the same IP address and port number combination, as long as they have different remote IP ranges.

This allows you to specify a different set of settings for certain remote IP addresses or ranges of IP addresses, while using the same IP address and port combination. Therein lies one of the main differences in the approach taken by Microsoft for Receive connectors, vis-à-vis SMTP virtual servers, in Exchange Server 2000/2003.

Default Receive Connectors

By default, new Hub Transport servers show up with two Receive connectors—the default connector and the client connector.

- **Default connector** The default connector is named Default SERVERNAME. It listens on the default SMTP port (TCP port 25) from all IP ranges (0.0.0.0–255.255.255.255).

NOTE *The default Receive connector on Hub Transport servers is not configured to accept e-mail without authentication. In other words, Hub Transport servers cannot receive inbound Internet e-mail out of the box, unlike Exchange Server 2000/2003.*

- **Client connector** The client connector is named Client SERVERNAME. It is bound to TCP port 587 and listens to connections from all IP ranges (0.0.0.0–255.255.255.255).

Creating New Receive Connectors

New Receive connectors can be created to meet specific requirements, such as allowing unauthenticated relaying for a specific SMTP host, or using another set of a number of parameters that can be configured on Receive connectors, such as receiving larger messages from particular remote SMTP hosts belonging to partners or vendors.

To create a new Receive connector using the Exchange console, follow these steps:

1. Expand the Server Configuration node and select Hub Transport.

2. From the list of Hub Transport servers in the details pane, select the server on which you want to create the new Receive connector.

3. In the Action pane, click New Receive Connector to start the New Receive Connector Wizard, shown in Figure 7-7.

On the Introduction page, provide the following details and click Next:

- **Name** The name identifies the connector.
- **Intended Use** Use the drop-down to select the intended use of the Receive connector. This allows easier configuration of permissions on the connector. Available intended uses include the following:
  - **Internet** Selecting Internet as the intended use type configures the Receive connector to accept unauthenticated e-mail.
  - **Internal** Internal Receive connectors are configured to accept authenticated e-mail from other Exchange servers in the organization.
  - **Client** This option is only available on Hub Transport servers. It allows authenticated connections, typically from Exchange Server users who connect

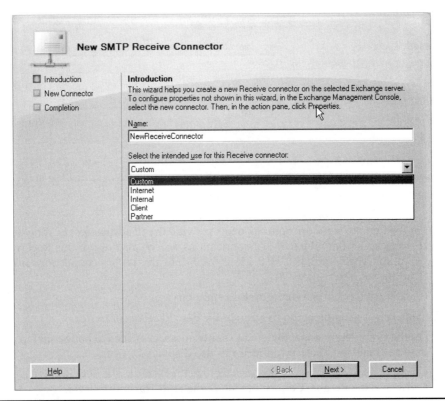

FIGURE 7-7   Selecting the intended use for a new Receive Connector

to it using protocols such as POP3 and IMAP4. Such clients need an SMTP server from which to send outbound mail. Authenticated clients are allowed relaying by default.

- **Partner**   This usage type is meant for creation of a Receive connector that can be configured with specific settings to meet with the requirements for receiving e-mail from partners. The connector is configured to receive e-mail with TLS authentication from domains that are configured to the Domain Secure list of the Receive connector.

- **Custom**   This usage type can be used for scenarios that are not covered by the preceding predefined usage types.

4. On the Local Network Settings page, provide the following settings and click Next:

- **Local IP Address(es) and Port**   Select the IP address(es) and port combination on which the Receive connector will be bound. The default selection is (All Available) for all available IP addresses that are not used by other Receive connectors in a unique IP address/TCP port number/remote IP ranges combination.

- **FQDN**   The FQDN specified here is displayed in the SMTP banner. This parameter is optional. By default, the server's fully qualified name is used.

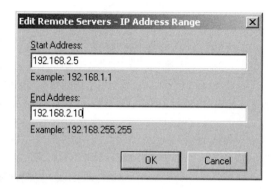

FIGURE 7-8
Remote
IP addresses

5. On the Remote Network Settings page, provide the IP address(es) or range(es) of IP addresses from which SMTP connections will be allowed to this Receive connector. The default is 0.0.0.0–255.255.255.255. This allows connections from all IP addresses (see Figure 7-8).

6. Click Next. Review the configuration summary.

7. Click New to complete the creation of the new Receive connector.

8. On the Completion page, review the status messages. The Exchange shell command used to create the Receive connector is also displayed.

9. Click Finish to exit the New Receive Connector Wizard. The new Receive connector appears in the Receive Connectors tab of the Hub Transport server.

To create a new Receive connector using the Exchange shell, use the following command:

```
New-ReceiveConnector -Name "NewReceiveConnectorName" -Bindings "192.1.1.10:25"
-RemoteIPRanges "0.0.0.0-255.255.255.255"
```

NOTE *Parameters used in this command are the minimum required for the New-ReceiveConnector command. You may need to provide additional parameters to configure the connector to meet your requirements for authentication and other settings.*

Connectors and Permissions

One of the more important aspects of Exchange Server 2007 transport is the permissions on Receive connectors. Outlook users use MAPI to submit messages and are authenticated to gain access to a mailbox. Let's look at the permissions in the context of SMTP communications— for messages submitted to a Receive connector on a Hub or Edge Transport server, and for outbound communication to smarthosts.

By default, all senders submitting messages to the Microsoft Exchange Transport Service are considered to be anonymous senders. During the initiation of the SMTP session, a sender may authenticate with the transport server using a number of methods as shown in Figure 7-9.

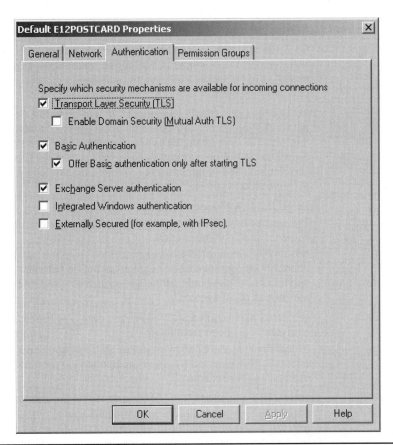

Figure 7-9   Authentication mechanisms available to Receive connectors

---

Tip   *To determine the authentication mechanisms available on a Receive connector, telnet to the Receive connector's IP address/FQDN on the SMTP port and issue the EHLO command.*

Table 7-6 details the types of authentication available for Receive connectors.

The preceding authentication mechanisms establish the identity of a host that connects to a transport server, establishing the sender as a security principal. Based on the identity, different transport-related permissions can be assigned.

Authentication Mechanism	Description
None	No AUTH or LOGIN ESMTP extensions are available. Without authentication, the sender is considered anonymous. Permissions assigned to "NT AUTHORITY\Anonymous Logon" apply to messages submitted by the sender.
BasicAuth	AUTH and LOGIN ESMTP extensions are available. Basic authentication transmits passwords in cleartext. It's best to use this with TLS encryption, by setting the RequireTLS parameter to $true. Using TLS on connectors does not perform verification of the certificates used by either server, unless Domain Secure Mutual TLS authentication is used.
Tls	STARTTLS ESMTP extension is available. The connector can respond with a STARTTLS command to initiate TLS-encrypted communication. Note: When RequireTLS is used on a Receive connector, an unencrypted communication session cannot be established. As such, RequireTLS should not be set up on Receive connectors that are targets of MX records.
BasicAuthRequireTls	The AUTH plus LOGIN ESMTP extensions are only available after TLS encryption has been negotiated. Allows Basic authentication only after the session is encrypted with TLS. This requires TLS as an authentication mechanism (for example, authmechanism Tls, BasicAuthRequireTls).
Integrated Windows	The AUTH + LOGIN + NTLM ESMTP extensions are available. Integrated Windows authentication enables clients to use NTLM. In addition to NTLM, Kerberos authentication can be allowed by setting the EnableAuthGSSAPI property of the Receive Connector to $true. This authentication mechanism is suitable for Receive connectors used by remote IMAP/POP3 clients who need to relay messages after authentication.
ExchangeServer	Allows X-EXPS + GSSAPI for earlier versions of Exchange server, and X-ANONYMOUSTLS for Exchange Server 2007 servers. The latter allows opportunistic TLS sessions using self-signed certificates.
ExternalAuthoritative	Exchange assumes authentication is performed using an external method that it has no knowledge or control of, such as IPSec. Connections from such hosts do not use an authentication method known to Exchange, but the session is treated as an authenticated session. Use this authentication mechanism with care, because it provides the connecting hosts with authenticated access without Exchange being able to confirm whether authentication has actually occurred.

TABLE 7-6   Receive Connector Authentication Options

Let's also take a look at authentication mechanisms available to Send connectors. Send connectors are used to send outbound mail. If delivering mail to Internet hosts by looking up DNS records, the Send connector requires no authentication. Authentication is only available to Send connectors when a smarthost is configured. Generally this is done to route outbound mail through a non-Exchange MTA or an ISP/service provider's mail hosts. Send connectors on Edge Transport servers delivering inbound mail to Hub Transport servers also treat the Hub Transport servers as smarthosts (see Figure 7-10).

NOTE *If Basic authentication is used for outbound mail, with or without TLS, the credentials used are those from the smarthosts' security context. In other words, if an ISP's mail hosts are being used as smarthosts, the security credentials are provided by the ISP. Basic authentication is also the only authentication mechanism that requires credentials to be specified.*

Table 7-7 details the authentication mechanisms available to Send connectors:

Now that you understand these authentication mechanisms, let's take a look at the permissions that can be assigned to the senders:

- **Receive connector permissions**   Receive connectors have a higher number of permissions that can be used to granularly control what each sender can do, as detailed in Table 7-8.
- **Send connector permissions**   Send connectors have a limited set of permissions, as detailed in Table 7-9. Three of the four permissions available control which headers are sent in outbound messages and which ones get removed.

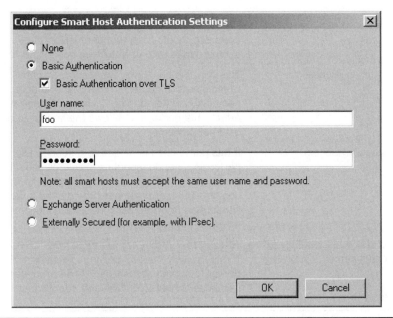

FIGURE 7-10   Authentication settings are available to Send connectors only when a smarthost is configured

Authentication Mechanism	Description
None	Smarthost allows anonymous access with no authentication.
BasicAuth	Basic authentication transmits passwords in cleartext. It's best to use this with TLS encryption, by setting the RequireTLS parameter to $true. If RequireTLS is set to $true, no certificate validation is performed. If multiple smarthosts are configured on the Send connector, all smarthosts should allow the same username and password.
BasicAuthRequireTls	Unlike BasicAuth used with the RequireTLS parameter set to $true, when authentication is set to BasicAuthRequireTls, certificate-validation checks are performed on the certificate presented by the sending host. For this mechanism to succeed, the Certificate Revocation List (CRL) of the CA issuing the certificate presented should be reachable, and the FQDN of the certificate should match the FQDN used as a smarthost on Send connectors.
ExchangeServer	This authentication mechanism is used for internal connectors.
ExternallySecured	When the AuthMechanism parameter is set to ExternallySecured, Exchange assumes authentication is performed using an external method that it has no knowledge or control of, such as IPSec.

TABLE 7-7 Send Connector Authentication Options

Permission	Description
ms-Exch-Smtp-Submit	A sender should have this permission to be able to submit a message to a Receive connector.
ms-Exch-Smtp-Accept-Any-Recipient	This permission allows the sender to submit messages to recipients in domains other than the accepted domains configured in an Exchange organization. In effect, this permission allows the sender to relay to external domains.
ms-Exch-Smtp-Accept-Any-Sender	If this permission is denied to a sender, Exchange performs a sender-spoofing check, disallowing messages where the sender is from an accepted domain. This permission can be denied to anonymous senders on Internet-facing Receive connectors to avoid receiving mail where the sender appears to be from a domain for which Exchange is authoritative.
ms-Exch-SMTP-Accept-Authentication-Flag	This permission allows previous versions of Exchange Server to submit messages from internal senders to Exchange Server 2007 Receive connectors.

TABLE 7-8 Receive Connector Permissions

Permission	Description
ms-Exch-Accept-Headers-Routing	If this permission is not granted, Exchange strips all Received headers from the message.
ms-Exch-Accept-Headers-Organization	If this permission is not granted, Exchange strips all Exchange organization headers—those starting with X-MS-Exchange-Organization—from message headers.
ms-Exch-Accept-Headers-Forest	If this permission is not granted, Exchange strips all Exchange forest headers—those starting with X-MS-Exchange-Forest—from message headers.
ms-Exch-Accept-Exch50	XEXCH50 is an ESMTP verb used by legacy (Exchange Server 2000/2003) servers to transfer messages to other Exchange servers in the organization. This permission allows the use of XEXCH50 verb. MAPI properties of a message such as SCL values are transferred by Exchange Server 2000/2003 servers using the XEXCH50 extension.
ms-Exch-Bypass-Message-Size-Limit	This permission allows submission of messages exceeding the MaxMessageSize configured on the Receive connector.
Ms-Exch-Bypass-Anti-Spam	This permission allows messages submitted in the session to bypass Exchange Server's anti-spam filters.

TABLE 7-8   Receive Connector Permissions (*Continued*)

Permission	Description
ms-Exch-Send-Exch50	If this permission is granted, Send connectors can send the X-EXCH50 ESMTP command to remote servers.
Ms-Exch-Send-Headers-Routing	Equivalent of the Ms-Exch-Accept-Headers-Routing permission on Receive connectors. If this permission is not granted or is denied, all Received headers are removed from outbound messages.
Ms-Exch-Send-Headers-Organization	Equivalent of the Ms-Exch-Accept-Headers-Organization permission on Receive connectors. If this permission is not granted or is denied, all X-MS-Exchange-Organization-headers are removed from messages.
Ms-Exch-Send-Headers-Forest	Equivalent of the Ms-Exch-Accept-Headers-Forest permission on Receive connectors. If this permission is not granted or is denied, all X-MS-Exchange-Forest- headers are removed from outbound messages.

TABLE 7-9   Send Connector Permissions

PART III

These permissions can be retrieved from Receive connectors and Send connectors using the get-adpermission command, as follows:

```
Get-ADPermission "CONNECTOR NAME" | where {$_.extendedrights -ne $null}
```

Permissions can be assigned using the Add-ADPermission command:

```
Add-ADPermission "CONNECTOR NAME" -user "NT AUTHORITY\AnonymousLogon"
-extendedrights ms-exch-accept-headers-routing
```

Permissions can be removed using the Remove-ADPermission command:

```
Remove-ADPermission "CONNECTOR NAME" -user "NT AUTHORITY\AnonymousLogon"
-extendedrights ms-exch-accept-headers-routing
```

Modifying Receive Connectors

The Exchange console allows you to modify basic parameters of Receive connectors, such as the name, protocol logging level, FQDN, maximum message size, local IP address and port, remote IP ranges, authentication, and permission groups.

To configure settings other than the ones just mentioned, you will need to use the Set-ReceiveConnector command from the Exchange shell.

Receive Connector Parameters

Receive connectors come with a wide number of configuration parameters, as detailed in Table 7-10, many of which can only be configured using the Exchange shell.

Allowing Unauthenticated Relaying

Authenticated relaying is enabled by default on Exchange Server 2007 Receive connectors, just as it is in Exchange Server 2000/2003 SMTP virtual servers. Many deployments run into situations where an application server needs to send out notifications, or an SMTP client such as the ones embedded in modern day copiers/scanners need to send out scanned documents or faxes by e-mail. A good number of such applications and devices do not provide authentication features, although there are a fair number that do. The ones that cannot authenticate with Hub Transport servers need to be allowed to relay without authentication.

In Exchange Server 2000/2003, this is a simple task, accomplished by adding the IP address of the SMTP client/host in the list of hosts allowed to relay through an SMTP virtual server. Nevertheless, it is recommended to create a new SMTP virtual server to allow authenticated relaying and to lock it down by only allowing those hosts to connect to it that need to relay.

In a blog post written shortly after Exchange Server 2007 was released, I explained how to set this up in Exchange Server 2007 using a new Receive connector, preferably one with a new IP address (other than the ones used by other Receive connectors). You can use the same IP address/TCP port combination used by another Receive connector, as long as the IP address(es) or ranges specified in the RemoteIPRanges field are different. This allows you to use a single IP address to host multiple Receive connectors for different remote hosts, which is particularly useful in scenarios where one is restricted by the number of IP addresses available internally or by the limited number of external IP addresses provided by an ISP.

Parameter	Description
AuthMechanism	Specifies the authentication mechanisms accepted by the Receive connector. Multiple values can be assigned using a comma as a separator. Values include None, TLS, Integrated, BasicAuth, BasicAuthRequireTLS, ExchangeServer, and ExternalAuthoritative.
Banner	Specifies text to be used in the SMTP banner instead of the standard SMTP banner "220 <Servername> Microsoft ESMTP MAIL service ready at <RegionalDay-Date-24HourTimeFormat> <RegionalTimeZoneOffset>". The banner text specified must start with the SMTP response code 220. To reset the banner to its default, set the value to $null. The Transport service does not need to be restarted when you're changing the banner.
BinaryMimeEnabled	Advertises and allows the use of the BINARYMIME keyword in the EHLO response. If this parameter is enabled, SMTP clients can send binary message data. Requires Chunking to be enabled.
Bindings	Specifies the IP address and port combination on which the Receive connector listens. The default is 0.0.0.0:25, which allows the Receive connector to listen to inbound connections on all available IP addresses not used by other Receive connectors.
ChunkingEnabled	Chunking is an ESMTP extension that allows a client to send binary data to an ESMTP server in chunks using the BDAT command instead of the DATA command used by SMTP. This allows faster transfer of large messages. Valid values include $true and $false.
DefaultDomain	If the SMTP client does not specify a domain name in the MAIL FROM: or RCPT TO: commands, the default domain is used in the domain part to complete the recipient's e-mail address.
DeliveryStatusNoticiationEnabled	When this parameter is set to true, the Receive connector advertises the DSN (Delivery Status Notification) ESMTP keyword when an EHLO command is received, and it provides enhanced DSN functionality specified in RFC 1891. Enhanced DSNs allow easier identification of the types of failure during message delivery. The default is $true.
EightBitMimeEnabled	When this parameter is set to true, the Receive connector advertises the ESMTP keyword 8BITMIME and allows transfer of message bodies encoded using 8BITMIME. Some older messaging systems may not support 8BITMIME-encoded messages.
EnableAuthGSSAPI	If this parameter is set to true, and the AuthMechanism parameter also includes Integrated authentication, it enables the use of Kerberos for authentication. The ESMTP keyword GSSAPI is advertised in EHLO responses, along with NTLM.

TABLE 7-10   Receive Connector Parameters Available Using the Set-ReceiveConnector Command

Parameter	Description
DomainSecureEnabled	Enables Domain Secure mutual TLS authentication. In addition to DomainSecureEnabled being set to $true, the TLSReceiveDomainSecureList and TLSSendDomainSecureList parameters should be configured with the same domain(s), and AuthMechanism on the ReceiveConnector should include TLS. For more details about Domain Secure, refer to Chapter 16.
EnhancedStatusCodesEnabled	When this parameter is set to true, the Receive connector advertises the ENHANCEDSTATUSCODES keyword when an EHLO command is received, and it provides enhanced status codes in DSNs submitted to remote servers.
LongAddressesEnabled	If this parameter is set to false, the maximum size of an SMTP address accepted by a Receive connector is 571 characters. If it's set to $true, e-mail addresses up to 1860 characters long are accepted. This is required to accept long X.400 e-mail addresses encapsulated using the Internet Mail Connector Encapsulated Address method. Setting this parameter to $true also advertises the XLONGADDR ESMTP keyword in EHLO responses and increases the line length of an SMTP session to 8000 characters. Note: This can only be done on Receive connectors on Hub Transport servers.
Fqdn	Specifies the FQDN displayed in the SMTP banner. When the AuthMechanism of a Receive connector includes Exchange Server, the FQDN should not be changed to a value other than the FQDN or NetBIOS name of the Exchange server.
Comment	A text field that can be used to insert administrative notes about particular connectors and their configuration.
Enabled	If this parameter is set to $false, the Receive connector is disabled. The default is $true.
ConnectionTimeout	Maximum time a connection can remain connected, even if active. The default for Hub Transport Receive connectors is 10 minutes. The default for Edge Transport Receive connectors is 5 minutes.
ConnectionInactivityTimeout	Maximum time idle connections can remain connected. The default for Hub Transport Receive connectors is 5 minutes. The default for Edge Transport Receive connectors is 1 minute.
MaxInboundConnection	Another protection mechanism, this parameter specifies the maximum number of concurrent inbound connections a Receive connector accepts and services. The default is 5000. The maximum is 2,147,483,647.
MaxInboundConnectionPerSource	Specifies the maximum number of concurrent connections a Receive connector will accept from one source IP address. The default is 100. The maximum is 10,000. To remove this limit, set the parameter to unlimited.

TABLE 7-10 Receive Connector Parameters Available Using the Set-ReceiveConnector Command (*Continued*)

Parameter	Description
MaxInboundConnectionPercentagePerSource	Specifies the maximum percentage of connections from a single source IP address. The default is 2. The maximum is 100. For Receive connectors receiving inbound mail from a smarthost, set this parameter to 100.
MaxHeaderSize	Specifies the maximum size of an SMTP header a Receive connector will accept in a message. The default is 65,536 bytes (65Kb). The maximum is 2,147,483,647 bytes (slightly less than 2Gb). The default value should be sufficient for most environments.
MaxHopCount	Each SMTP host that receives a message and delivers or forwards it to another host adds a Received header to the message. Too many Received headers may be a sign of a message loop. This parameter specifies the maximum number of hops a message can take, as determined by number of Received headers. The default is 30. The maximum is 500.
MaxLocalHopCount	Maximum number of hops within an Exchange organization, determined by the number of Received headers where the server is local. The default is 8. The maximum is 50.
MaxLogonFailures	Maximum number of logon failures before a connection is closed. The default is 3. The maximum is 10. Setting this to 0 results in a connection never being closed due to authentication failures (resulting in continuing authentication attempts).
MaxMessageSize	Maximum message size that can be received by the Receive connector. The default in SP1 is 10,240Kb (10Mb). The maximum is 2,147,483,647 (slightly less than 2Gb).
MaxProtocolErrors	This is a numerical value that specifies the maximum SMTP errors a Receive connector will allow before closing the connection. The default is 5. The maximum is 2,147,483,647. If this is set to unlimited, an SMTP connection is never closed because of protocol errors.
MaxRecipientsPerMessage	Specifies the maximum number of recipients per message a Receive connector will accept before closing the connection. The default is 200. The maximum is 512,000. The minimum is 1.
MessageRateLimit	This parameter controls the maximum number of messages a sending host can send from a single IP address. This is helpful in protecting Exchange transport from denial-of-service (DoS) attacks. The default for a Hub Transport Receive connector is unlimited. The default for an Edge Transport Receive connector is 600 messages per minute. The maximum is 2,147,483,647.
Name	This parameter specifies the name of the Receive connector. Treat this as a *display name*—it will be visible in EMC/EMS.

TABLE 7-10   Receive Connector Parameters Available Using the Set-ReceiveConnector Command (*Continued*)

PART III

Parameter	Description
OrarEnabled	If set to true, this parameter enables Originator Requested Alternate Recipient (ORAR), a concept from X.400 messaging systems. It allows the sender to specify an alternate recipient in case a message cannot be delivered to the original recipient. An NDR is sent only if the message cannot be delivered to the original or the alternate recipient specified by the sender. If the delivery address is a long X.400 address, the LongAddressesEnabled parameter needs to be set to $true. ORAR is a feature required by the Defense Message System (DMS). For more information, refer to ACP 120 Common Security Protocol (CSP).
PermissionGroups	A permission group is a predefined list of permissions assigned well-known security principals. This parameter specifies who can submit messages to the Receive connector and what permissions they have. For more information on permissions, refer to the earlier section in this chapter titled "Connectors and Permissions."
PipelingEnabled	Pipelining is an ESTMP extension that allows an SMTP client to send requests without awaiting SMTP responses from the server. Pipelining goes with the CHUNKING extension that allows an SMTP client to send chunks of large messages in parallel. Together, PIPELINING and CHUNKING extensions allow for more efficient SMTP communication. When set to $true, the PIPELINING keyword is advertised in EHLO responses.
ProtocolLoggingLevel	This parameter determines whether or not SMTP communication with a Receive connector is logged. The only options available are: **None** This is the default. SMTP logging is disabled by default. **Verbose** This enables SMTP logging.
RemoteIPRanges	This parameter specifies which IP address or IP address ranges can connect to a Receive connector. A single IP address, or a range of IP addresses with a starting IP address and an ending IP address (10.1.2.1–10.1.2.254), can be used. If IP address ranges overlap on multiple Receive connectors, the connector with the most specific range is used. Note: The uniqueness of a Receive connector is determined by a unique combination of the IP address it is bound to, the port number it listens on, and the RemoteIPRanges it can connect to. This is different from SMTP virtual servers in Exchange Server 2000/2003, which only use an IP socket (IP address + port number) to define a unique binding. Multiple Receive connectors can use the same IP address + port combination, if the RemoteIPRanges are different for each.
RequireEHLODomain	If this parameter is set to $true, all SMTP clients are required to provide a domain in the EHLO handshake used to initiate an ESMTP session. Absence of a domain in the EHLO command results in the connection being dropped.

TABLE 7-10   Receive Connector Parameters Available Using the Set-ReceiveConnector Command (*Continued*)

Parameter	Description
RequireTLS	If this parameter is set to $true, all connections to the Receive connector require TLS encryption. This should not be enabled on Receive connectors that are the target of MX records or otherwise receive mail from sources not configured to encrypt sessions using TLS. To selectively enforce TLS for particular domains, consider using the new Domain Secure feature.
SizeEnabled	This parameter determines the Receive connector's behavior for the ESMTP extension SIZE, thus allowing the Receive connector to advertise the SIZE keyword and the SMTP client to declare the message size before sending it. Here are the available options: **Enabled** When the parameter is set to Enabled, the SIZE keyword is advertised in EHLO responses along with the value from the MaxMessageSize parameter. This is the default. **Disabled** The SIZE keyword is not advertised in EHLO responses. The client does not know about the maximum message size. **EnabledWithoutValue** Advertises the SIZE keyword in EHLO responses but does not disclose the value of the MaxMessageSize parameter.
TarpitInterval	By default, SMTP tarpitting is enabled on Exchange Server 2007 Receive connectors. This inserts a delay in SMTP responses sent to SMTP clients when invalid SMTP behavior is seen (for example, sending a message to a recipient that does not exist) or when the RCPT command is used before MAIL. The value is the number of seconds the response should be delayed for. The default is 5 seconds. It can be set to 00:00:00 to disable tarpitting. The maximum value is 10 minutes. Note: Authenticated sessions are never tarpitted. The default value of 5 seconds may be too low and can be safely increased to a higher value (10 seconds recommended) on Receive connectors that receive mail from unauthenticated sources. Setting it too high may result in a higher number of open connections and resource consumption. SMTP tarpitting is covered in detail in Chapter 17.

TABLE 7-10   Receive Connector Parameters Available Using the Set-ReceiveConnector Command (*Continued*)

Also, some network routers or firewalls are able to use only one external IP address to listen for inbound traffic (as is the case with many low-end home/small business router/firewall products). Nevertheless, for security reasons, it is recommended to stick with the unique IP address/port number combination for Receive connectors allowing relaying. Here's how to create a new Receive Connector and allow relaying on it:

1. Create a new Receive connector using the Exchange console, as described earlier in the chapter. Make sure to restrict the RemoteIPRange to the IP address(es) of hosts to which you want to allow unauthenticated relaying. To create the Receive connector, use the following command:

```
New-ReceiveConnector -Name RelayConnector -usage Custom -Bindings
'192.168.1.17:25' -fqdn server.domain.com -RemoteIPRanges
192.168.1.100 -server MYEXCHANGESERVER -permissiongroups
ExchangeServers -AuthMechanism 'TLS, ExternalAuthoritative'
```

NOTE *In this command, substitute the IP address in the –Bindings parameter with the transport server's IP address, and the IP address in the –RemoteIPRanges parameter with the IP address(es) you want to allow unauthenticated relaying to.*

2. Assign permission. Use the following command to assign the ms-Exch-SMTP-Accept-Any-Recipient extended right to anonymous users:

```
Get-ReceiveConnector RelayConnector | Add-ADpermission -User "NT
AUTHORITY\ANONYMOUS LOGON" -ExtendedRights "ms-Exch-SMTP-Accept-Any-Recipient"
```

The preceding method is more secure than assigning the permission group Exchange Servers and using no authentication by specifying ExternalAuthoritative as the authentication mechanism. The latter allows unauthenticated relaying, bypasses anti-spam filters, and resolves display names. More details about both these methods can be found in the blog post titled, "Exchange Server 2007: How To Allow Relaying," at http://exchangepedia .com/blog/2007/01/exchange-server-2007-how-to-allow.html.

Logging SMTP Activity

Exchange Server 2000/2003 used the SMTP support provided by IIS. As a result, SMTP virtual servers used IIS's logging capabilities to log SMTP activity as well. Because Exchange Server 2007 uses its own, it comes with its own logging capabilities, similar to previous versions in some ways, including the fact that by default SMTP logging is turned off. Unfortunately, many administrators new to Exchange discover this after the fact, after problems are reported in mail flow and troubleshooting requires SMTP logs. Lesson number 1 for Exchange administrators dealing with mail flow and transport issues: Turn on SMTP logging.

Exchange Server 2007 uses the notion of distinct Send and Receive connectors, unlike Exchange Server 2000/2003's SMTP connectors, which use SMTP virtual servers as "bridgeheads." As such, the activity of Send and Receive connectors is logged in different protocol logs.

NOTE *Although SmtpReceive and SmtpSend activity is logged separately, there's a single log for all Receive connectors and a single log for all Send connectors.*

Let's take a look at how we turn this on for both.

To enable protocol logging on a Receive connector using the Exchange console, follow these steps:

1. Expand the Server Configuration node and select Hub Transport.
2. Select a Hub Transport server.
3. Select a Receive connector and select Properties.
4. On the General tab, change the Protocol Logging level to verbose.
5. Click OK to close Receive connector properties.

To enable protocol logging on Receive connectors using the Exchange shell, use the following command:

```
Set-ReceiveConnector "Connector Name" -ProtocolLoggingLevel verbose
```

Here's the command to use to enable protocol logging on all Receive connectors that do not have it enabled:

```
Get-ReceiveConnector | where {$_.ProtocolLoggingLevel -eq "None"} | Set-
ReceiveConnector -ProtocolLoggingLevel verbose
```

To enable protocol logging on a Send connector using the Exchange console, follow these steps:

1. Expand the Organization Configuration node and select Hub Transport.
2. From the Send Connectors tab, select a Send connector and click Properties.
3. On the General tab, change the Protocol Logging level to verbose.
4. Click OK to close Send connector properties.

To enable protocol logging on a Send connector using the Exchange shell, use the following command:

```
Set-SendConnnector "Connector Name" -ProtocolLoggingLevel verbose
```

Protocol Log Location   Protocol logs are located in the \Exchange Server\TransportRoles\ Logs\ProtocolLog directory. The Receive connector and Send connector logs reside in the SmtpReceive and SmtpSend subdirectories, respectively. The path is stored in the ReceiveProtocolLogPath and SendProtocolLogPath properties, respectively, of the transport server's configuration. This can be modified using the Set-TransportServer command:

```
Set-TransportServer "SERVER NAME" -ReceiveProtocolLogPath "D:\SMTPLogs\Receive"
-SendProtocolLogPath "D:\SMTPLogs\Send"
```

Controlling Protocol Log File Growth   Exchange Server 2000/2003 rely on SMTP support provided by IIS, which itself provides no control over the growth of log files, except the ability to roll over to a new log file based on time or when a file reaches a particular file size. If left unattended, SMTP logs can accumulate to consume huge amounts of disk space over a period of time. Administrators handle this by archiving or deleting log files manually, or using scripts or batch files running on a schedule to do this task. Exchange Server 2007's Receive connectors provide control over log files and the directories in which they are located. The parameters detailed in Table 7-11 are available.

Parameter	Description
ReceiveProtocolLogMaxFileSize SendProtocolLogMaxFileSize	Maximum file size a single protocol log file can grow to. The default is 10MB.
ReceiveProtocolLogMaxDirectorySize SendProtocolLogMaxDirectorySize	Maximum size of the directory in which the protocol log files are stored. The default is 250MB.
ReceiveProtocolLogMaxAge SendProtocolLogMaxAge	Maximum age of the oldest protocol log file. The default is 30 days (30.00:00:00).

TABLE 7-11 Protocol Log Size and Age Options

NOTE *Besides the maximum file size parameter, which controls the maximum size of a single protocol log file, protocol logs are rolled over every day, regardless of the file size.*

Depending on SMTP traffic volumes in your environment, these seem to be good default values that prevent growth of protocol logs by automatically purging them based on the size of log file directory and the age of the log files.

Protocol Log Fields   In addition to the automated purging, the Exchange team has also utilized this newfound independence from IIS to change the log file format to log data that is more important to Exchange administrators monitoring and troubleshooting SMTP communication. The fields logged are detailed in Table 7-12.

With the addition of a Session-ID field, each SMTP session can be tracked easily in protocol logs. Instead of you having to look at a different log for each instance of an SMTP virtual server, protocol logs are now separated by activity—receive and send. Compared to protocol logs in Exchange Server 2000/2003, Exchange Server 2007 provides more relevant fields, making the logs easier to understand and the troubleshooting process quicker.

To top it all, as you get more proficient with the Exchange shell, you will benefit from the relative agility that comes with being able to search log files using the shell, rather than going through the process of opening a log file in a text editor such as Notepad or importing it in an Excel spreadsheet. There are various ways you can parse, filter, and find relevant information about an SMTP event or session using the shell, including the Get-Content command (provided by the underlying Windows PowerShell) and custom scripts, but these are outside the scope of this chapter.

Field	Description
Date-time	UTC date and time of the protocol event in ISO 8601 format.
Connector-id	Distinguished name (Server\Connector name, not the LDAP distinguishedName) associated with the SMTP session.
Session-id	A unique session identifier (GUID) that is different for each session. Makes it easier to recognize each distinct SMTP session logged.
Sequence-number	Counter for individual SMTP events in a single session. Resets to 0 for every new session logged.
Local-endpoint	Local IP address and TCP port number used.
Remote-endpoint	Remote SMTP host's IP address and TCP port number.
Event	Not related to the events logged in Message Tracking log, these are character representations: + (Connect) - (Disconnect) > (Send) < (Receive) * (Information)
Data	Text information, including SMTP commands and responses.
Context	Additional contextual information associated with an SMTP event.

TABLE 7-12   Fields Logged in Protocol Logs

Back Pressure

Back Pressure is a feature on Hub and Edge Transport servers that monitors resources such as memory consumption by the EdgeTransport.exe and other processes, the number of uncommitted transactions in the queue database, and, most importantly, the amount of free disk space on volumes with the queue database and the queue transaction logs. Under normal circumstances, one does not know about the existence of this feature. However, when resource utilization increases to a level categorized as medium, Back Pressure kicks into action and limits the mail flow to messages sent by senders in authoritative domains. When resource consumption crosses the threshold of high utilization, Back Pressure stops accepting new connections and messages as well as stops mail flow.

My first encounter with Back Pressure, and that of many others, was not very pleasant. It stopped mail flow. When the transport service stops accepting new messages, you can still telnet to SMTP port 25. You are greeted with the following warning:

```
452 4.3.1 Insufficient system resources.
```

The cause: Hard drive space fell below 4GB on the Hub Transport server. With the default Back Pressure limits left unaltered, a fixed amount of free disk space is required on volumes where the queue database resides. For Exchange Server 2007 RTM, this is 4GB. Although this is not too high a bar for free disk space on production servers, you are likely to hit it at some point and have mail flow stopped. In a virtual machines based test environment, where the virtual drives used by VMs are not as large as disk volumes on production servers, one runs into Back Pressure's high-handedness (at least as it exists in RTM) more frequently.

TIP *In SP1, the default Back Pressure limit for free disk space has been lowered to a more realistic 500MB. Mail flow stops if disk space falls below this threshold.*

Back Pressure is configured using parameters in the EdgeTransport.exe.config file (the file has the same name on both Hub and Edge Transport servers), which resides in the \Exchange Server\Bin directory. Although resource monitoring can be disabled by adding the EnableResourceMonitoring parameter or changing it to true in the config file, disabling Back Pressure is not recommended. You can, however, tweak the parameters of what it considers medium or high utilization.

More details about configuring Back Pressure can be found at http://technet.microsoft .com/en-us/library/bb201658.aspx.

If you use monitoring tools or otherwise keep an eye on disk space and memory utilization, you should not run into Back Pressure in normal course. Back Pressure-related events are logged in the Application Event Log on transport servers (look for events 15001–15005 logged by [event source] MSExchangeTransport). Event ID 15002 is logged when resource pressure is constantly high.

Managing Send Connectors

Send connectors are used to route messages for external domains to their next hop, either by using DNS to lookup MX records or by explicitly defining a remote host to deliver messages to, also known as a *smarthost*. As such, they are comparable to SMTP connectors in Exchange Server 2000/2003. Whereas Receive connectors belong to an individual Hub or Edge

Transport server, Send connectors are associated with the Exchange organization and are available to all transport servers in an organization.

By default, no Send connectors are created by Exchange setup. Unlike Exchange Server 2000/2003, which can use the default SMTP virtual server to route outbound messages to the Internet, Exchange Server 2007 organizations cannot route outbound mail without a Send connector.

How do we go about creating Send connectors? There are two ways:

- By manually using the Exchange console or the shell
- By setting up an EdgeSync subscription in topologies where Edge Transport servers are deployed

Use the following procedure to create a Send connector to route outbound mail to the Internet:

1. Expand the Organization Configuration node.

2. From the Actions pane, click the New Send Connector… link to start the New SMTP Send Connector Wizard.

3. On the Introduction page, shown in Figure 7-11, enter the following information and click Next:

    - **Name**   Enter a unique name for the Send connector.

    - **Select the intended use for this Send connector**   The default permissions are assigned on a Send connector based on the usage type. The following usage types are available:

        - **Internet**   Anonymous users can submit messages. No authentication is required.

        - **Internal**   This usage type is selected for connectors used between Exchange Server 2007 Hub and Edge Transport servers, and for connectors to Exchange Server 2000/2003 Routing Groups. Exchange Server Authentication is selected as the authentication mechanism.

        - **Partner**   This usage type is selected to establish mutual TLS authentication with a partner organization.

        - **Custom**   This usage type is selected for connectors used to send messages from a Hub or an Edge Transport server to non-Exchange mail hosts used as smarthosts, to connect two Exchange organizations in cross-forest deployments, and in scenarios where connectors between the Hub and Edge Transport servers are created manually, with no EdgeSync subscription in place. No permissions are assigned by default. No authentication mechanism is selected. Assign permissions and select the authentication mechanism manually.

4. On the Address Space page, click the Add button to add the address space. In the SMTP Address Space dialog box, add the following details:

    - **Type**   The Exchange console does not let you change the address space type. The default is SMTP. To create Send connectors for non-SMTP address spaces, create a Foreign connector using the Exchange shell.

- **Address**   This is the address space (domain) of the destination mail system. You can type a domain (for example, Microsoft.com) or a subdomain (for example, ea.microsoft.com). Wildcards can be used to designate subdomains (for example, *.com for all .com domains or *.microsoft.com for all subdomains of Microsoft. com), but not to complete part of a domain name (for example, *soft.com). For outbound mail to the Internet, type *.

- **Include all subdomains**   Select this check box to include all subdomains of the domain typed in the Address field. If the address includes a wildcard (*), this check box is automatically selected.

- **Cost**   Exchange Server 2007 uses costs to determine the Send connector that has the *best* route to a particular address space. The default cost is 1. The Send connector with the lowest cost is used. However, unlike Exchange Server 2000/2003, Exchange Server 2007 does not check connector availability or fail over between connectors.

NOTE *The address space * is used to indicate all address spaces (domains) for which the Exchange organization is neither authoritative nor has a Send connector with the address space specified.*

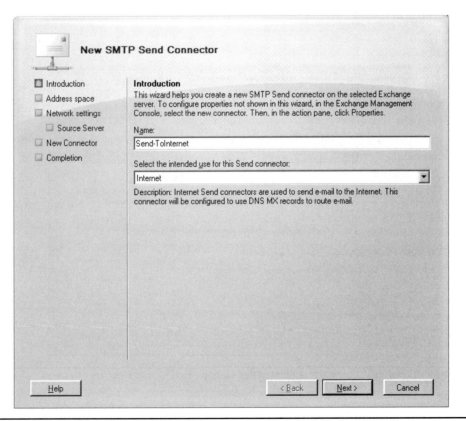

FIGURE 7-11   Creating a new Send connector

5. On the Network Settings page, select how to route outbound mail for the specified address space. Here are the options:

- **Use domain name system (DNS) "MX" records to route mail automatically**
This requires that Exchange be able to resolve Internet domains by using DNS. The server's TCP/IP settings should be configured with valid DNS server(s) that can resolve Internet domains. Name resolution failure will lead to the failure of mail delivery and messages being queued on the server.

- **Route mail through the following smarthosts**   This allows specifying the IP address or FQDN of specific external SMTP hosts, such as those of non-Exchange SMTP servers generally deployed in perimeter networks or those provided by a service provider.

NOTE   *You can add multiple smarthosts on the Network Settings page of the wizard by adding an individual IP address or FQDN, clicking OK, and then clicking the Add button again to add another IP address or FQDN.*

6. If you selected the second option in the previous page to route mail to a smarthost, you are presented with the Configure Smarthost Authentication Settings page, shown in Figure 7-12. Select the appropriate mechanism to authenticate with

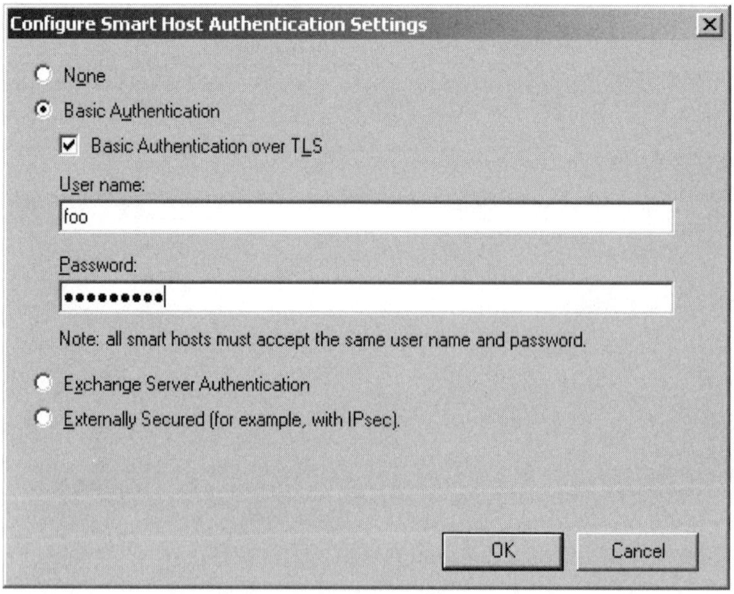

FIGURE 7-12   Configuring smarthost authentication settings on a Send connector

the smarthost(s). If you're using a service provider's SMTP servers (also referred to as *relay servers* or *SMTP relays)*, contact the service provider for authentication settings. Here are the options

- None (no authentication is used)
- Basic Authentication
- Exchange Server Authentication
- Externally Secured (for example, with IPSec)

7. On the Source Server page, verify the connector has the source servers that will be used to route outbound mail for this connector. You can add Hub Transport servers as well as Edge Transport servers that are subscribed to the AD site.

8. Click Next. On the Configuration Summary page, verify all information is entered correctly.

9. Click New to complete creation of new Send connector.

10. On the Completion page, ensure the wizard completely successfully. The Exchange shell command used to create the connector is displayed here.

11. Click Finish to close the New SMTP Send Connector Wizard.

To create a new Send connector using the Exchange shell, use the following command:

```
New-SendConnector -Name "Connector Name" -Usage "Internet" -AddressSpace
"SMTP:*;1" -DNSRoutingEnabled $true -SourceTransportServers "HUB OR EDGE
SERVER NAME"
```

SMTP connectors in Exchange Server 2000/2003 allow you to select a bridgehead server. When selecting a bridgehead server, you are actually selecting from all available SMTP virtual servers on a server. Exchange Server 2007 only allows you to select source transport server(s). All messages routed over the Send connector are sent to the source transport server(s).

Modifying Send Connectors

The Exchange console allows modifying basic parameters of Send connectors such as the name, protocol logging level, FQDN, maximum message size, address space and cost, routing (DNS lookups or smarthost), and source transport servers. These settings can be changed from the properties pages of Send connectors and have been covered in the preceding section.

To configure settings other than the ones mentioned, you will need to use the Set-ReceiveConnector command from the Exchange shell.

Send Connector Parameters

Send connectors come with a wide number of configuration parameters, as detailed in Table 7-13, many of which can only be configured using the Exchange shell.

PART III

Parameter	Description
AddressSpaces	Edge Transport servers can only route to SMTP address spaces. Hub Transport servers can route to non-SMTP address spaces. **Syntax** "Local:SMTP:Zenprise.com;1" **ConnectorScope** You can scope the Connector to the AD site of the Hub Transport server(s) configured as source transport servers by specifying Local. If Local is not used in the address space, the Send connector is not scoped. Hub Transport servers in all AD sites in the organization can use the connector. **AddressSpaceType** For Edge Transport servers, this can only be SMTP. **AddressSpace** Use domain names for SMTP address spaces, including the wildcard (*) to indicate subdomains.
AuthenticationCredential	If authentication credentials need to be specified for a smarthost, use the Get-Credential command to capture credentials in a variable.
Comment	Text comment for configuration notes and such. Enclose the comment in quotes.
ConnectionInactivityTimeout	Maximum time an idle connection can remain open. To specify this parameter, use the time syntax *dd.hh:mm:ss.* The default is 10 minutes.
DNSRoutingEnabled	If this parameter is set to $true, messages are routed using DNS lookups. To route messages to a smarthost, set the value for the smarthost parameter (FQDN or IP address of the smarthost) and set DNSRoutingEnabled to $false.
DomainSecureEnabled	This should be used for specific address spaces if routing using a smarthost. For more details about Domain Secure, refer to Chapter 16.
Enabled	Status of the Send connector. Valid values are $true and $false. If this parameter is not set to $true, a Send connector will not process messages. The default is $true.
ForceHELO	Forces the use of HELO instead of EHLO. Use this on Send connectors for specific smarthosts where the receiving SMTP host does not support Enhanced SMTP (ESMTP). The default is $false.
Fqdn	Use this property to specify an FQDN other than the default domain name to be used in HELO/EHLO commands.

TABLE 7-13 Send Connector Parameters

Parameter	Description
IgnoreSTARTTLS	If a receiving SMTP server offers to start TLS, set this parameter to $true if the use of TLS is not required for that address space. The default is $false (for Send connectors with DNSRoutingEnabled set to $true). This parameter always initiates a TLS negotiation if a STARTTLS command is received.
IsScopedConnector	When set to $true, this parameter scopes a Send connector to the Active Directory site in which the Hub Transport servers (specified as source servers for the Connector) reside. By default, the parameter is set to $false, making the connector available to all Hub Transport servers in the organization.
LinkedReceiveConnector	This parameter specifies the identity of a Receive connector that is linked to this Send connector. All inbound mail received on the linked Receive connector is delivered to a smarthost using this Send connector. Linked connectors can be used in scenarios where all inbound mail is received by an Exchange Server 2007 Receive connector and is delivered to a smarthost for further processing (anti-spam/antivirus and so on), either in-house or at a service provider. Note: To have a particular host or a service provider receive inbound e-mail to be scanned for spam/viruses, the MX record generally needs to point to the in-house smarthost or the service provider's SMTP hosts. Using a linked connector allows you to receive inbound e-mail without redirecting the MX to another host or service provider. This may be required in some deployments, but is not a general practice. To use a linked connector, a Receive connector must be created or already exist. The Send connector is required to use a smarthost. MaxMessageSize should be set to unlimited.
MaxMessageSize	Maximum message size that can be routed over the Send connector. The default is 10MB. This parameter can be specified using bytes (B), kilobytes (KB), megabytes (MB), or gigabytes (GB). Maximum size is 2,147,483,647 bytes (slightly under 2GB). This parameter can be set to unlimited.
Name	Name of the Send connector.
Port	This parameter is used with smarthosts; any TCP port number from 0 to 65535 can be used. The default is 25. Changing this value is not recommended unless specific requirements dictate outbound communication over nonstandard port(s) with particular smarthosts.

TABLE 7-13 Send Connector Parameters (*Continued*)

Parameter	Description
ProtocolLoggingLevel	The default value for this parameter is None. To enable protocol logging, set it to verbose. Protocol logging is discussed earlier in this chapter.
RequireTLS	Specifies whether all messages routed by the Send connector should use TLS encryption. The default is $false.
SmartHostAuthMechanism	Only used when DNSRoutingEnabled is set to $false and smarthosts are specified. Valid authentication mechanisms include None, BasicAuth, BasicAuthRequireTLS, ExchangeServer, and ExternalAuthoritative.
SmartHosts	FQDN(s) or IP address(es) of smarthosts. If FQDNs are used, the Hub Transport server(s) configured as source servers for the Send connector should be able to resolve the FQDNs.
SourceIPAddress	Only valid for Send connectors on Edge Transport servers. You can specify which IP address configured on an Edge Transport server is used. The default is 0.0.0.0 (use any available local address).
SourceTransportServers	Only valid for Send connectors on Hub Transport servers. This parameter specifies the name(s) of Hub Transport servers that can transfer outbound messages using the Send connector. Multiple Hub Transport servers can be specified using commas as separators.
UseExternalDNSServersEnabled	Specifies whether externalDNSServers configured on transport servers using the Set-TransportServer command are used instead of the DNS servers in TCP/IP settings of a server. The default is $false.

TABLE 7-13   Send Connector Parameters (*Continued*)

Managing EdgeSync Subscriptions

As mentioned earlier in this chapter, the new Edge Transport server role in Exchange Server 2007 is designed to be deployed as a standalone (not domain-joined) server in perimeter networks. The Hub Transport servers, which are part of Active Directory domains and thus have access to AD, can periodically replicate information about Exchange recipients and Exchange configuration data required for the configuration and functioning of ET servers. This replication process is called Edge Synchronization, or EdgeSync for short.

The replication is one-way, initiated by HT servers in a subscribed AD site, over an LDAP connection to ET servers. A good question to ask at this point is, Where do the ET servers store this data? It's stored in an LDAP directory on ET servers, called ADAM (Active Directory Application Mode). Think of it as a mini Active Directory. However, unlike the Active Directory instance running on AD domain controllers, it is dedicated to storing application data in LDAP objects.

TIP   When adding new Hub Transport servers to an AD site that has an existing EdgeSync subscription, you're required to remove the existing subscription and create a new one to allow the new Hub Transport servers to participate in the EdgeSync process.

To make this synchronization work, we need to *subscribe* ET servers to HT servers in an AD site. Note that the subscription is not between Edge servers and individual Hub servers, but between individual Edge servers and an AD site. Remember, Exchange Server 2007 message routing is based on AD sites. However, this does not mean that new HT servers joining an already subscribed AD site automatically become part of the EdgeSync subscription. New HT servers added to an AD site do not participate in the EdgeSync process until a new EdgeSync subscription is created that recognizes the new HT servers.

NOTE   Although an AD site can have one or more Edge Transport servers subscribed to it (many to one), an Edge Transport server can be subscribed to only one AD site (one to one). An Edge Transport server with an EdgeSync subscription cannot support more than one Exchange organization.

Before we delve into the specifics of creating a new EdgeSync subscription, an often-asked question when considering the deployment of Edge servers is, What ports do I need to open from my internal network to the Edge servers, and from the Edge servers to my HT servers on the internal network? HT servers communicate with Edge servers over TCP ports 50389 and 50636. The latter of the two is used for LDAP over SSL. The good news: Because this is a one-way process (outbound from the Hub Transport servers to the Edge servers), no additional inbound ports need to be opened on your intranet/internal firewall.

If you cannot use these ports—perhaps because they're already being used by some other application or because the security folks in your IT department believe in security by obscurity and insist on changing the default ports used by all hosts if they can—you can change the ports on which Edge servers listen by using the ConfigureAdam.ps1 script. Use the following syntax to change the ADAM port numbers:

```
ConfigureAdam.ps1 -ldapport:5000 -sslport:5001
```

Substitute the port numbers you want to use instead of ports 5000 and 5001 used in this example.

Next, let's take a look at the EdgeSync subscription process. Here's a list of things to do before you begin the EdgeSync subscription process:

- **Add a DNS suffix to the Edge server**   Unlike member servers and domain controllers, standalone Windows servers do not have a DNS suffix by default. This is done from System Properties | Computer Name tab | Change | More | Primary DNS Suffix of this computer.

CAUTION   Make sure you add the desired DNS suffix before you install the Edge Transport server role. You cannot change the DNS suffix after you install Exchange. To make any changes to the DNS suffix or the computer name, you will need to uninstall Exchange, make the changes, and reinstall Exchange.

- **Ensure the Edge server can resolve the FQDN(s) of HT servers**   This can be accomplished by pointing the Edge server(s) to DNS servers on the internal network, but this requires opening port 53 (TCP and UDP) from the Edge servers to the internal DNS servers. Other alternatives: 1) Replicate the internal DNS zone for the domain to a DNS server in the perimeter network where the Edge servers reside. 2) Create a DNS zone on a DNS server in the perimeter network and create A records for HT servers. 3) Add the FQDNs of HT servers to the HOSTS file on all Edge servers.

- **Ensure the Hub Transport servers can resolve the FQDN(s) of Edge server(s)**   If the Edge server is deployed on a standalone server in a perimeter network, it is likely that no A records exist for such servers in the DNS zones hosted by DNS servers on your internal network. As a result, HT servers cannot resolve the FQDNs of Edge servers by default. You can either create A records for the Edge server(s) on your internal DNS server, or add these to the HOSTS file on HT servers. No points for guessing the former (creating A records) is more efficient.

- **Ensure the NetBIOS name of the Edge server is not too long**   Active Directory only uses the first 15 characters of a NetBIOS name, as documented in KB 909264. When a long NetBIOS name is used on an Edge server (let's say 20 characters), the name used for the EdgeSync subscription gets truncated. This results in failure of the EdgeSync process after completion of the EdgeSync subscription. (At the time of this writing, this needs to be validated through further tests. However, I personally consider this a best practice versus reinstalling the Edge server because someone has decided MYFUNKYNEWEDGESERVER is a great name for the funky new Edge server!)

CAUTION   *When you're creating a new Edge subscription on the Edge Transport server, any accepted domains, message classifications, remote domains, and Send connectors you created manually prior to initiating the subscription are deleted. Any internalSMTPServers defined on the Edge are overwritten.*

TIP   *The security credentials created during the Edge subscription and embedded in the Edge subscription XML file are only valid for a period of 24 hours from the time of creation. Edge subscriptions should be completed on the HT server within those 24 hours. If this is not completed within 24 hours, a new Edge subscription file needs to be generated using the New-EdgeSubscription command on the Edge server.*

Now let's create an EdgeSync subscription. The process is initiated from an Edge server, and is quite simple indeed:

- **Creating an Edge subscription on the Edge Transport server**   Log into an Edge server using an account that is member of the local Administrators group on the Edge server. From the Exchange shell, use the following command to create the Edge subscription XML file:

  ```
  New-EdgeSubscription -FileName "C:\MyEdgeSubscriptionFileName.xml"
  ```

  When you're creating a new Edge subscription on an Edge server, Filename is the only required parameter. The command creates an Edge subscription file in XML format. This file needs to be made accessible to the Hub Transport server in an AD site to complete the subscription process. Any HT server in the site can be used to complete the subscription.

- **Completing the Edge subscription on a Hub Transport server**   Next, let's head over to the HT server to complete the Edge subscription. The Exchange console on internal Exchange servers can be used to complete the subscription as shown in Figure 7-13. Here are the steps to follow:

  1. In the Exchange console, expand the Organization Configuration node | select Hub Transport server.

  2. In the Actions pane, click New Edge Subscription.

     From the Active Directory Site drop-down control, select the AD site to which the Edge Transport server needs to be subscribed.

  3. Click the Browse button next to the Subscription file field and navigate to the path where the Edge subscription XML file created earlier is saved. If you do not have Universal Naming Convention (UNC) access to the Edge Transport server, the file can be transferred by e-mail, FTP, or copying it to removable media.

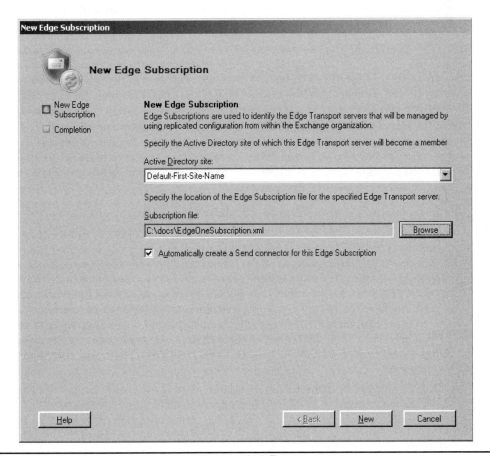

Figure 7-13   Completing an Edge subscription on a Hub Transport server

4. The new Edge subscription automatically creates a Send connector to send outbound Internet mail from the organization to the Edge Transport server. The ET server uses DNS lookups to resolve MX records in destination domains, and it delivers outbound mail. If you do not want the Send connector to be created automatically, uncheck Automatically create a Send Connector for this Edge Subscription.

5. Click the New button.

6. On the Completion page, examine the summary of action taken to ensure it completed successfully.

The Edge subscription is complete!

To complete the Edge subscription using the Exchange shell, use the following command:

```
New-EdgeSubscription -FileName "C:\MyEdgeSubscriptionFile.xml"
```

Let's take a look at what the Edge subscription does:

1. On the Hub Transport server, use the Get-SendConnector command to list all Send connectors. You will see two new Send connectors with names starting with EdgeSync. One of these is for routing outbound mail to the Internet, with the Edge server as the source server. The other one is for inbound mail from the Edge server to the subscribed AD site.

2. On the Hub Transport server, look for Event ID 1000 in the Application Event Log. This information event is logged when an Edge Synchronization operation is completed.

3. On the Hub Transport server, use the command Test-EdgeSynchronization. The output of this command provides the details of the last Edge Synchronization operation and its results, as well as the current synchronization status of recipients, accepted domains, transport servers and their configuration, Send connectors, credentials, and message classifications.

- **Edge synchronization intervals**   By default, the EdgeSync process synchronizes changes to Exchange configuration data every hour. Changes to recipient configuration are made every 4 hours.

  If recipient validation is used on the Edge Transport server(s), messages for nonexistent recipients are dropped or deleted silently. If recipient configuration is not synchronized with the Edge Transport server, it does not have information about new recipients in ADAM. This results in the Edge Transport server not accepting mail for such newly created recipients until the recipient information is synchronized. In environments where changes are made more frequently, you may need to start Edge Synchronization manually or schedule it to run more frequently.

- **Starting Edge Synchronization manually**   When you make changes to the Exchange configuration or recipient data, or need to verify an EdgeSync subscription, you can manually trigger the synchronization process from a Hub Transport server using the Start-EdgeSynchronization command.

Managing Queues

Message queues are temporary holding areas where messages wait to be processed at various stages of message handling and routing.

- **Message Queue database**   In Exchange Server 2000/2003, queued messages exist as files in the Queue folder of the SMTP virtual server, and a logical representation of the messages is held in memory displayed in the Queue Viewer in the Exchange System Manager. In Exchange Server 2007, the Queue folder is replaced by an ESE database, similar to the one used by Exchange's Mailbox and Public Folder databases. The Queue database resides in the \TransportRoles\data\Queue folder in the Exchange Server install path (C:\Program Files\Microsoft\Exchange Server by default).

- **Submission Queue**   All messages submitted to or received by a transport server first enter the Submission Queue. This is the waiting area for newly submitted or received messages, from where they have any transport agents (including anti-spam agents) inspect and possibly act on them, followed by the Categorizer, which resolves recipients and determines their next hop. Under normal circumstances, messages should not have to wait too long here.

- **Mailbox Delivery Queue**   The Mailbox Delivery Queue holds messages to be delivered to mailbox servers in the same AD site. One Mailbox Delivery Queue is created for a set of messages for each mailbox server in the same AD site. If no messages are queued for a mailbox server, no Mailbox Delivery Queue is created.

- **Remote Delivery Queue**   One Remote Delivery Queue is created for all messages for a particular remote destination (that is, for each remote domain). On Hub Transport servers, one Remote Delivery Queue is created for each set of messages for a particular destination AD site.

- **Poison Message Queue**   The Poison Message Queue holds messages that are considered to be harmful to the Exchange server, typically after a server or a connector failure. No attempts are made to deliver messages from this queue—the queue exists in a suspended state.

- **Unreachable Queue**   The Unreachable Queue holds messages that cannot be delivered because a route to the destination is not available, generally resulting from a configuration change to Send connectors such as disabling or deleting a connector or creating a new one for a particular address space that cannot deliver messages to a remote destination or smarthost because of a configuration error. Unlike the Remote Delivery Queue, where an instance is created for every destination domain from which messages exist in the queue when using DNS (MX record lookups) to deliver messages; all messages that cannot be delivered to a remote destination exist in the Unreachable Queue.

- **Managing Queues**   Queues can be viewed and managed from the Queue Viewer utility found in the Toolbox node of EMC, or using the queue management commands from the shell (which we get to in the next few paragraphs). By default, the Queue Viewer connects to the transport server on which the console is started. You can connect to other transport servers by clicking Connect To… in the Action pane.

NOTE *In Exchange Server 2000/2003, all Exchange servers support SMTP and use it to transfer messages to other Exchange servers. SMTP can be disabled on front-end servers if they are not used as bridgeheads or as targets for MX records. Therefore, all servers have message queues that can be viewed. In Exchange Server 2007, mailbox servers (without the Hub Transport server role installed) do not support SMTP, but use Remote Procedure Calls (RPCs) to communicate with Hub Transport servers in the same AD site. Message queues exist only on the Hub Transport and Edge Transport servers.*

To start the Queue Viewer, click the Toolbox link in the EMC and then click Queue-Viewerunder Mail flow tools. The Queue Viewer starts in a separate MMC console. Figure 7-14 shows the Submission Queue, which is always displayed even if it has no messages in it, a queue for the outbound Send connector from the AD site to the Edge Transport server, and a Mailbox Delivery Queue (shown as MapiDelivery under Delivery Type) for the mailbox server LHPOSTOFFICE.

Queues can be in one of four states, displayed in the Status column in the Queue Viewer:

- **Ready** Waiting to be delivered
- **Active** When messages are being transferred to the destination

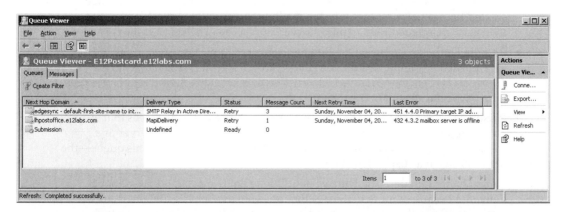

FIGURE 7-14 Managing message queues using the Queue Viewer

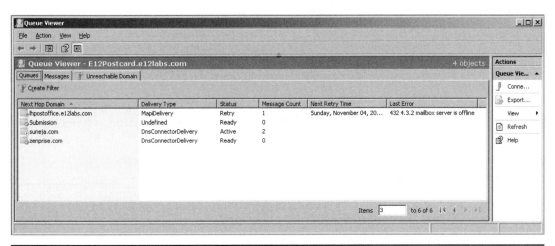

FIGURE 7-14   Managing message queues using the Queue Viewer (*Continued*)

- **Retry**   When one or more attempts to deliver messages to the next hop have failed and the server is waiting for the retry interval to elapse before attempting delivery again
- **Suspended**   The queue has been suspended by the administrator. No further attempts are made until the queue is resumed

A retry attempt can be forced on a queue in the Retry state, awaiting the retry interval to elapse. Queues can be suspended, and those already in that state can be resumed. Messages in a queue can be viewed, and retried, suspended, or resumed individually (or as a group of messages). You can also remove messages from a queue, with or without sending an non-delivery report (NDR) to the sender.

The shell adds an amazing set of capabilities to queue management, including the ability to filter and view queues and messages quickly, as well as take actions on both with relatively little effort. The commands are intuitive, but to document all of them would require a separate chapter. This topic is better suited for a book dedicated to managing Exchange with the shell. Table 7-14 lists the commands available and provides a brief description of what they do.

Each queue has an identity. The *permanent queues* such as the Submission Queue have names; the *temporary* ones, such as those created for remote destinations that can be removed dynamically by Exchange, get a numerical identity. The shell's ability to pipe results from one command to another command makes queue management using the shell a pleasant experience once you become familiar with the process. Here's an example:

```
Get-queue -Filter {NextHopDomain -eq "wormhole.exchangepedia.com"} | Get-Message |
Suspend-Message | Export-Message -Path "C:\ZappedFromQueue" | Remove-Message
```

This command returns the queue where the NextHopDomain is the server wormhole. exchangepedia.com. It also gets messages from the queue, suspends them (a message needs to be suspended before it can be exported), and then finally removes the messages from the queue.

Command	Description
Get-Queue	Gets a list of all queues, with their identity, delivery type (MapiDelivery, Smarthost, and so on), status (Ready, Retry, Active, Suspended), number of messages, and the next hop domain (FQDN of the next hop).
Retry-Queue	Forces an immediate delivery attempt for messages in a queue.
Suspend-Queue	Suspends delivery of messages in a queue.
Resume-Queue	Resumes a suspended queue.
Get-Message	Gets messages in a queue.
Export-Message	Exports a message from the queue to an .eml file.
Suspend-Message	Suspends delivery of one or more messages.
Resume-Message	Resumes delivery of one or more messages.

TABLE 7-14   Shell Commands Used to Manage Queues and Messages

When monitoring or examining queues, look for high number of messages accumulating in a queue and determine the reasons why a particular message (or messages) in a queue cannot be delivered. If you're using a smarthost to deliver outbound messages, depending on the message volume in an environment, a large number of messages can accumulate in a short time due to connectivity or authentication issues with the smarthost. A large number of messages in a Mailbox Submission Queue for a particular mailbox may be the result of the mailbox server being unreachable or the store being unavailable.

Message Tracking

Every once in a while a user will call in enquiring about a message sent by or addressed to him or her that has not been delivered—or delivered with unacceptable delays. This is where Message Tracking comes in. It's an important tool in the Exchange administrator's arsenal used to hunt down messages at every stage—when the user hits Send and a message is submitted to the Exchange mailbox store or when a message from outside the Exchange Organization enters the Exchange transport pipeline.

Message Tracking is enabled by default on Exchange Server 2007, a welcome departure from previous versions, which made one feel quite helpless if discovered after a mail flow incident occurred and required troubleshooting mail flow using the Message Tracking logs. By default, Message Tracking logs are located in the \Exchange Server\TransportRoles\Logs\MessageTracking directory, where "Exchange Server" is the directory in which Exchange Server 2007 is installed. The default configuration also comes with some more helpful parameters set to what appear to be reasonable defaults. The parameters detailed in Table 7-15 can be configured on transport servers for Message Tracking logs.

These parameters can be configured or modified on transport and mailbox servers using the Set-TransportServer and Set-MailboxServer commands, respectively.

Compared to Exchange Server 2000/2003, Exchange Server 2007 allows you to set the maximum file size of a tracking log, and the maximum size the directory can grow to irrespective of time. In environments with a very high volume of messages or when a sudden and sharp spurt is seen in message volume resulting in a tremendous growth of

Parameter	Default
MessageTrackingLogPath	\Exchange Server\TransportRoles\Logs\MessageTracking
MessageTrackingLogEnabled	$True
MessageTrackingLogMaxAge	30.00:00:00 (30 days)
MessageTrackingLogMaxDirectorySize	250MB
MessageTrackingLogMaxFileSize	10MB
MessageTrackingLogSubjectLoggingEnabled	$True

TABLE 7-15   Message Tracking Log Parameters on Transport Servers

tracking logs, this controls the maximum space Message Tracking logs can occupy on the disk volume. Exchange Server 2000/2003 only allow one to configure the maximum age of log files. Additionally, the ability to control the maximum log file size eliminates the instances where you could find yourself dealing with a 300MB tracking log. Large log files are difficult to parse and slow down applications such as text editors or spreadsheets that are commonly used to view them. Besides, it also makes searching such log files difficult from the Message Tracking application.

What I find hard to get terribly excited about is the new Message Tracking GUI interface, located in the Toolbox section of the Exchange console. I find its ExBPA-like wizard interface to be a hindrance and more than mildly annoying when troubleshooting in a hurry (the level of annoyance being dependent on how much of a hurry one is in or what one had for lunch that day).

For those in a hurry—and it seems most Exchange administrators fit this profile— the good news is that the Exchange shell makes tracking messages incredibly easier and faster, provided you are willing to invest some time in understanding how message transport, tracking logs, and the shell work. After using the shell to accomplish tasks such as Message Tracking, it is hard to revert back to the console and deal with its taxing mouse clicks.

Whereas in previous versions of Exchange we are used to seeing all Exchange servers in an organization as a single entity in terms of Message Tracking, and have the ability to track messages end-to-end from any Exchange server in the organization, Message Tracking in Exchange Server 2007 does not quite allow us that luxury. To track messages on an Edge Transport server, you have to log onto the Edge Transport server(s). Edge Transport servers are not part of the Exchange organization as such, and one does not have the luxury of assuming these servers are accessible using RPC. Message Tracking logs generated on Edge Transport servers are not replicated back to Hub Transport servers to enable end-to-end tracking. For this purpose, the Edge Transport servers need to be treated as any other non-Exchange MTAs running as mail gateways, which would otherwise require you to log into those servers and inspect the logs on them.

On the positive side, in environments with Edge Transport servers deployed, you will be using the same interfaces to track messages across your messaging environment and benefit from the familiarity with the Exchange console or shell.

The Microsoft Exchange Transport Log Search service (MSExchangeTransportLogSearch) needs to be started on servers on which you search the Message Tracking logs. On Edge Transport servers, this service is set to start manually. If you do not track messages regularly on Edge Transport servers, you can leave it in its default state and start it from the Services snap-in (services.msc) or from the shell using the following command, before you start tracking messages:

```
Start-Service MSExchangeTransportLogSearch
```

To track messages using the Exchange console, you will need to use the Message Tracking utility located in the Toolbox section of the console. Clicking the Message Tracking button launches the Exchange Troubleshooting Assistant in a separate window. Be confused not, dear Exchange administrator: This is the new tool that allows you to track messages!

Every time the tool starts, it checks for updates. You can cancel the update check by clicking a button, or you can wait for a few seconds until the check is complete and you land on another screen, which generally informs you no updates could be found (unless there are any) and urges you to click another button to go to the Welcome screen.

Here, you can track messages using a number of parameters. In addition to the parameters seen in Exchange Server 2000/2003 (MessageID, Sender, Server, Recipients, Start and End times), the additional parameters that can be used to search for and track messages are EventID, InternalMessageID, Subject, and Reference.

Tip *One reason to like the new Message Tracking tool is the fact that it displays the equivalent Exchange shell command used, just as many Exchange console wizards and dialog boxes do. This is a great tool to learn Message Tracking and its parameters, allowing an easier transition to the shell over a period of time, as one gets more comfortable with it.*

Among these parameters, the one that requires some understanding is EventID. The events detailed in Table 7-16 are logged in the tracking log for a message.

As is clear from this list, all messages have multiple entries in the Message Tracking log, once each for more than one of these EventIDs. If the search is not constrained using one of these EventIDs, or other parameters such as Sender, Recipient, and so on, more often than not one would be looking at a huge set of results. This makes looking for that particular message you want to track like looking for the proverbial needle in a haystack.

Tracking Messages Using the Exchange Shell

Having gone through the Exchange console's Message Tracking tool—and having failed at being able to hide my lackadaisical opinion of it—let's head over to the Exchange shell and do some power message tracking!

The command to use is Get-MessageTrackingLog. Yes, it's a long command to type every single time. Luckily, the shell comes to the rescue with its Tab Completion feature—just enter a few characters of the command and press TAB. The shell will complete the command if enough characters have been typed to uniquely identify the command. If the typed characters match more than one command, you can continue to press the TAB button to have the shell cycle through the commands that match.

I prefer to simply create aliases for such long commands—the one I use for Get-MessageTrackingLog is "track." That allows me to simply use the alias track blah! Here's how to create the alias:

```
New-Alias track Get-MessageTrackingLog
```

EventID	Description
RECEIVE	A message was received and committed to the database.
SEND	A message was sent by Simple Mail Transfer Protocol (SMTP) to a different server.
FAIL	A message delivery failed.
DSN	A delivery status notification (DSN) was generated.
DELIVER	A message was delivered to a mailbox.
BADMAIL	A message was submitted by the Pickup directory or the Replay directory that cannot be delivered or returned.
RESOLVE	A message's recipients were resolved to a different e-mail address after an Active Directory lookup.
EXPAND	A distribution group was expanded.
REDIRECT	A message was redirected to an alternative recipient after an Active Directory directory service lookup.
TRANSFER	Recipients were moved to a forked message because of content conversion, message recipient limits, or agents.
SUBMIT	A message was submitted by an Exchange Server 2007 computer that has the Mailbox server role installed to an Exchange Server 2007 computer that has the Hub Transport server role or Edge Transport server role installed.
POISONMESSAGE	A message is put in the Poison Message Queue or removed from the Poison Message Queue.
DEFER	Delivery of the message is deferred.

TABLE 7-16   Events Logged in Message Tracking Logs

Table 7-17 details the parameters that can be used with the Get-MessageTrackingLog command.

By default, the Get-MessageTrackingLog command returns a maximum of 1000 results. To change the number of results returned, use the optional –ResultSize parameter. To return all results from the available message tracking logs, use –ResultSize unlimited.

Using these parameters, one can search the Message Tracking logs for message(s) sent by william@lefkovics.net to bharat@suneja.com on the 26th of August, 2007, between 10:00 A.M. and 2:00 P.M. with the subject EdgeSync. Here's the command:

```
Get-MessageTrackingLog -Start "08/26/2007 10:00 am" -End "08/26/2007 2:00 pm"
-Sender "william@lefkovics.net" -Recipients "bharat@suneja.com" -MessageSubject
"EdgeSync"
```

Tracking Messages across Transport and Mailbox Servers

As mentioned earlier in this section, the Message Tracking interface in the Exchange console does not allow one to perform end-to-end searches across all transport and mailbox servers in an organization. The shell is a little less restrictive in this aspect, although neither can

Parameter	Description
Start	Restricts the search of Message Tracking logs to entries starting from this date and time. The parameter can be used by itself, or you can specify the End parameter in addition to Start. For example, here's how to start the search from the 26th of August, 2007, at 10:00 A.M.: `Get-MessageTrackingLog -Start "08/26/2007 10:00 am"`

End	Restricts the search of Message Tracking logs to entries ending at this date and time. This parameter can be used by itself, or you can specify the Start parameter in addition to End. To end the search at 2:00 P.M. on 26th August, 2007, use the following command:
	
	`Get-MessageTrackingLog -End "08/26/2007 02:00 pm"`
	
	Here's the command with the start time:
	
	`Get-MessageTrackingLog -Start "08/26/2007 10:00 am" -End "08/26/2007 2:00 pm"`

Sender	This parameter restricts the search to the sender field in Message Tracking logs. Use the sender's SMTP address as a value. `Get-MessageTrackingLog -Sender "william@lefkovics.net"`
Recipients	This parameter restricts the search to the recipient-address field. Use the recipient's SMTP address as a value. Multiple values are allowed using a comma as a separator after each SMTP address. `Get-MessageTrackingLog -Recipients "bharat@suneja.com"`
Subject	This is the message's subject as specified in the Subject: header. The property name in Message Tracking logs is MessageSubject. By default, subject tracking is enabled. Partial values are supported in this field. `Get-MessageTrackingLog -Subject "Exchange shell rocks"`
EventID	EventID is the transport event assigned to each entry in Message Tracking logs. The complete list of EventIDs is provided in the Table 7-16. Each message can have multiple entries in the Message Tracking log, each entry associated with one of the EventIDs. `Get-MessageTrackingLog -EventID "SEND"`
MessageID	MessageID is the unique Message-ID assigned to a message when it is submitted. This value is inserted in the message header and remains constant for the lifetime of the message. This can be used to efficiently track messages across servers and mail systems that handle a particular message. `Get-MessageTrackingLogs -MessageID "E9E9F3275852944E8CBEC6021FAB 137C02468DB87DC1@E12Postcard.e12labs.com"`
InternalMessageID	This is the internal message ID assigned to a message by a particular transport server (Hub or Edge). The same message can have a different InternalMessageID on different transport servers. As such, it is not among the more useful fields used for tracking messages and troubleshooting.
Reference	This field contains additional information about a message. For example, for a NDR, this field will contain the MessageID of the original message that generated the NDR.

TABLE 7-17 Message Tracking Log Search Parameters

search the Edge Transport for reasons mentioned earlier. To search across all transport and mailbox servers in the organization, use the following command:

```
Get-ExchangeServer | where {$_.isHubTransportServer -eq $true -or
$_.isMailboxServer -eq $true} | Get-MessageTrackingLog -MessageID
"E9E9F3275852944E8CBEC6021FAB137C02468DB87DC1@E12Postcard.e12labs.com"
```

That is a lot of typing, indeed! Fortunately, we can get the first half of this command and store it in a variable, as the following command shows:

```
$allServers = Get-ExchangeServer | where {$_.isHubTransportServer -eq $true -or
$_.isMailboxServer -eq $true}
```

Now, we simply need to use the variable $allServers. We can even shorten it further. Remember the ability to assign an alias to a shell command that we used earlier in this section to assign the alias *track* to the Get-MessageTrackingLog command? We can use the variable $allServers and the alias *track* to shorten the relatively long command to the following:

```
$allServers | track -MessageID
"E9E9F3275852944E8CBEC6021FAB137C02468DB87DC1@E12Postcard.e12labs.com"
```

To ensure the variable is available whenever you start an Exchange shell session, you can add it to your Exchange shell profile.

Summary

Exchange Server 2007 has a new SMTP stack native to Exchange and a new message routing model based on Active Directory sites. Although there are similarities to SMTP virtual servers and connectors found in previous versions, plan on spending enough time to understand how the new Send and Receive connectors work, the different parameters for each, the new ways of tracking messages and managing queues, and the many other changes and improvements related to transport servers.

Once you achieve a basic comfort level over time, and you understand the changes, you will find the new transport servers and the functionality they bring a welcome change from the Exchange Server 2000/2003 way of doing things. You may find some limiting factors, as can be expected in a product with the breadth and depth of Exchange and the profound changes this major version brings about. Nevertheless, most discussion I have heard about the transport features relate to the newer ways of doing things, and in the context of RTM, the relative absence of GUI goodness in the EMC, rectified to a great extent by SP1.

PART III

Administering Client Access Servers

The user base is becoming more diverse. Gone are the days when all users were in one central location, all using the same tools to access the same information. Today, we have users with smartphones, users working remotely from home and while traveling, users in remote offices, and those who feel the need to check in while on vacation. With that come many different methods to connect to that information. We arrive at the Client Access Server.

In Exchange 2007, the Client Access Server (CAS) role assumes most of the tasks that were previously handled by front-end servers in Exchange 2000 and 2003. This includes being the point of connection for non-MAPI clients such as Outlook Web Access, Exchange ActiveSync, POP3, IMAP4, and Outlook Anywhere, which was previously called RPC over HTTP/S.

Client Access Server features added in Exchange 2007 include the web distribution of the Offline Address Book (OAB), out-of-office messages, and the Autodiscover and Availability services. The Autodiscover and Availability services are Exchange Web Services that provide for automated client provisioning and send Free/Busy information to Outlook 2007 clients, respectively. The CAS also handles some Unified Messaging (UM) processes.

Deployment Considerations

Although the CAS role does assume some of the features that were in the front-end servers of previous versions, the CAS role works quite differently. In 2003, for instance, the front-end server would accept connections from clients and then direct them to the appropriate back-end server. In 2007, the CAS role handles most of the processing, thus allowing for more efficient operation of the mailbox servers. This allows mailbox servers to handle many more mailboxes.

In medium and large environments, the Client Access Server role may be placed on dedicated hardware, separate from other roles. When that's the case, the CAS role should be the first role you deploy in your Exchange 2007 environment. Also, remember that a CAS machine must be in every site that also holds an Exchange 2007 mailbox server, because the mailbox server relies heavily on the Client Access Servers and communicates with them over Remote Procedure Calls (RPCs).

It is neither recommended nor supported that the CAS role be deployed in a perimeter network. That causes too large of an attack surface due to the sheer number and specificity of the ports you must open to your internal network. The CAS must be deployed on a member server and thus must communicate via RPC to the mailbox servers, among others. Opening that up in your perimeter network will leave you much more prone to attack. The use of SSL certificates to increase security is discussed later in this chapter in the "Autodiscover" section. Additional security is covered in Chapter 14 as well. For even more enhanced security, it is recommended that you use a reverse proxy server in your perimeter network, such as Microsoft's Internet Security and Acceleration (ISA) Server 2006.

IIS Integration

Exchange 2007 makes extensive use of Internet Information Services (IIS). Many of the features based on the Client Access Server utilize IIS in some form. These include Outlook Web Access, Exchange ActiveSync, the Autodiscover service, web-based distribution of the Offline Address Book, and more.

In IIS, we see that several virtual folders are installed when the Client Access Server role is installed on a server. These can be viewed in the IIS Manager snap-in, as shown in Figure 8-1.

These virtual folders and their Exchange-related purpose are listed in Table 8-1.

Outlook Web Access (OWA), which is entirely based on IIS, has been completely revamped for Exchange 2007. As such, Chapter 12 is dedicated to using and configuring Outlook Web Access. The rest of this chapter will focus on other technologies and features associated with Client Access Servers, some of which are also used by Outlook Web Access.

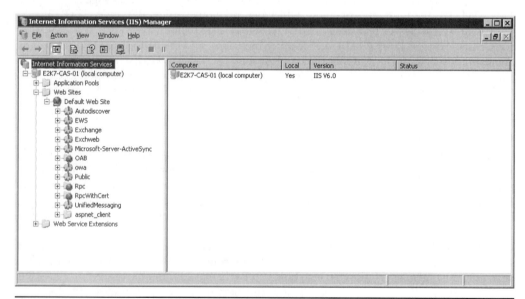

FIGURE 8-1 IIS virtual folders for Client Access Servers

Virtual Folder	Purpose
/Autodiscover	Used by the Autodiscover service for auto-provisioning of clients.
/EWS	Exchange Web Services.
/Exchweb	Used by Outlook Web Access clients connecting to legacy Exchange (2000/2003) mailboxes.
/Exchange	Use by OWA clients connecting to legacy Exchange (2000/2003) mailboxes.
/Microsoft-Server-ActiveSync	Used for ActiveSync with Windows Mobile and supported mobile devices.
/OAB	Used for web distribution of the Offline Address Book (OAB) for Outlook 2007 clients.
/owa	Provides access to OWA clients connecting to Exchange 2007 mailboxes.
/Public	Used by OWA to gain access to public folders.
/Rpc	Used by Outlook Anywhere for remote mailbox access via the full Outlook client.
/RpcWithCert	Used by Outlook Anywhere for secure remote mailbox access via the full Outlook client.
/UnifiedMessaging	Provides access to some Unified Messaging information.

TABLE 8-1   IIS Virtual Folders and Their Purpose in Exchange

Direct File Access

An exciting addition to Outlook Web Access and mobile devices in Exchange 2007 is Direct File Access. This feature provides the ability for end users to gain read-only access to internal files and SharePoint data securely without the need for a VPN client or other additional security measures. Direct File Access allows users to more quickly gain access to critical business information easily, and allows them to be more productive when out of the office or limited to just the OWA client.

Through Exchange management tools, we can grant or deny access to various file resources that users can access through the OWA interface. To do so, we can use the Exchange Management Console:

1. Open EMC and navigate to Server Configuration | Client Access.
2. Highlight your desired Client Access Server in the top part of the results pane.
3. Highlight owa (Default Web Site) in the bottom part of the results pane.
4. In the Actions pane, click Properties.

Notice the two tabs labeled Public Computer File Access and Private Computer File Access as seen in Figure 8-2. These two tabs allow us to configure Direct File Access for the

FIGURE 8-2
Direct File Access
settings in
Exchange
Management
Console

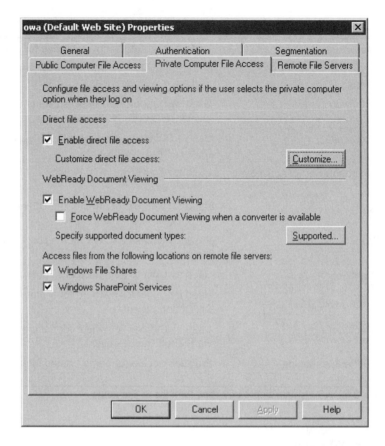

two options users have when connecting via Outlook Web Access: public computers, such as those in libraries or common areas, and private computers, such as those in a user's home or their primary workstation at their desk. The options are the same on both tabs, so I'll just cover the Private Computer File Access tab. A list of those options, including their default settings, is seen in Table 8-2.

Feature	Default Setting
Windows SharePoint Services and Windows file share integration features	Enabled
Block lists	None
Allow lists	None
Document access to Windows SharePoint Services and Windows file shares on unknown servers	Enabled
Windows SharePoint Services and Windows file share document access from public computers	Enabled

TABLE 8-2   Direct File Access Parameters for Windows SharePoint Services and Windows File Shares

Direct File Access is enabled by default for all users. The first check box allows us to disable it entirely. The bottom two check boxes define what kind of resources we can access, including file servers and SharePoint document libraries. To the right of the top check box we have the Customize button, which allows us to configure all other Direct File Access settings. When you open that dialog box, you have the choices of settings that cover:

- What is always allowed
- What is always blocked
- What files the user would have to save to the local machine before opening
- What behavior to use for unknown file types

The configurations for the first three settings all look the same. You have the ability to define both file extensions, such as .bmp, as well as MIME types, such as image/bmp.

To add a new file type to any of the lists, simple enter the file extension or MIME type on the appropriate line and click Add. To remove a file type, highlight it and click Remove. To edit an entry, highlight the desired item and click Edit.

TIP *The Allow list supersedes the Block and Force Save lists. If a file type is listed in Allow and either of the other two lists, the user will be allowed to access the file.*

The last setting gives you the ability to configure what to do with Direct File Access when the user wants to access file types that are not specifically listed in the Allow or Block section. Here, the choices are Allow, Force Save (default), and Save.

We can, of course, also manage Direct File Access from the Exchange Management Shell using the Set-OWAVirtualDirectory cmdlet. In the following example, we'll disable Direct File Access for both public and private computers on the Client Access Server called e2k7-cas-01:

```
Set-OWAVirtualDirectory -identity "e2k7-cas-01\owa (Default Web Site)" -
DirectFileAccessOnPublicComputersEnabled $false -
DirectFileAccessOnPrivateComputersEnabled $false
```

Once we have the feature enabled, we next must configure which Universal Naming Convention (UNC) paths are allowed to be accessed via Direct File Access. From Exchange Management Console, follow these steps:

1. Navigate to Server Configuration | Client Access.
2. Highlight the owa (Default Web Site) virtual folder in the lower half of the results pane.
3. In the Action pane, click Properties.
4. In the Properties dialog box, click the Remote File Servers tab, shown in Figure 8-3.

As with the previous settings, we can set UNC paths of Windows file servers or SharePoint servers that are allowed or blocked, and we can also set the default for servers that don't appear in either list. To allow a specific server to be accessible, click the Allow button and enter the UNC path for the server. Then click Add. If you wish to block a specific server, click the Block button and add the server's UNC path to the list.

FIGURE 8-3
Remote File
Servers
configuration

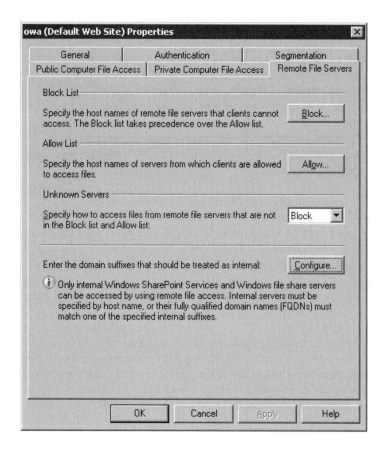

If a server name does not appear in either the Block or Allow list, it's considered Unknown. In the next section down, we can configure the behavior for Unknown servers. The choices are Block and Allow.

Only servers considered internal can be accessed via Direct File Access. Access to servers external to your environment is not possible. To configure what domains are internal for Direct File Access, click the Configure button and add any internal domain namespaces that may house servers to which users will need Direct File Access.

We can use the Exchange Management Shell to make all these configuration changes at one time using the Set-OWAVirtualDirectory cmdlet. Using the same e2k7-cas-01 server as an example, we could use this:

```
Set-OWAVirtualDirectory -Identity "e2k7-cas-01\owa (Default Web Site)" -
RemoteDocumentsAllowedServers "\\dc1" -RemoteDocumentsBlockedServers "\\dc2" -
RemoteDocumentsInternalDomainSuffixList virtuecorp.local,fabrikham.local
```

Note that the internal namespaces are separated by a comma.

WebReady Document Viewing

An alternative to Direct File Access is a new feature called WebReady Document Viewing. This feature allows known document types such as Word, Excel, and Reader files to be displayed within the Outlook Web Access client without needing the associated application to be installed on the local computer. This is possible because the Client Access Server will convert the file to HTML and display it in an Internet Explorer window.

This has some great benefits. First, we have the ability for users to open documents without the expense and administrative effort of installing an application on their computer. Second, the documents can be viewed on public computers that may have safeguards against installing any applications. Third, this alleviates the concern that users would previously be forced to save a file locally first before opening it. With WebReady Document Viewing, documents aren't left behind on public computers and on private computers where confusion can exist over different versions of the same file.

To configure the various options for WebReady Document Viewing, we turn to Exchange Management Console:

1. Open EMC and navigate to Server Configuration | Client Access.

2. Highlight the desired Client Access Server in the upper part of the results pane.

3. Highlight owa (Default Web Site) in the lower part of the results pane.

4. Click Properties in the Action pane.

As with Direct File Access, we configure the appropriate settings in the Public Computer File Access and Private Computer File Access tabs. In the middle of these dialog boxes, we see two settings: Enable WebReady Document Viewing and Force WebReady Document Viewing when a converter is available. The first setting is enabled by default and enables known documents to be viewed directly in OWA. The second setting, when enabled, forces a document to be viewed within OWA first when both WebReady and Direct File Access are enabled.

WebReady Document Viewing has a limit of 5MB for files that it will display in HTML. This is for performance purposes, but can be adjusted. We adjust this limit by editing the registry. To do so, follow these steps on the CAS server:

1. Click Start | Run.

2. Type regedt32.exe and press ENTER.

3. Navigate to HKEY_Local_Machine\System\CurrentControlSet\Services\ MSExchange OWA.

4. Right-click the MSExchange OWA key in the left pane and click New | Key.

5. Name the key **WebReadyDocumentViewing**.

6. Click the WebReadyDocumentViewing key

7. In the right pane, right-click and choose New | DWORD.

8. Call the new DWORD **MaxDocumentInputSize**.

9. Enter the new limit in KB (such as 10000).

10. Close the registry editor.

11. Restart the World Wide Web Publishing Service.

PART III

Remember that the Client Access Server is what does the conversion of the document to HTML for viewing in Outlook Web Access. If you set the preceding limit too high, you will see performance degradation on the Client Access Server.

WebReady Document Viewing in Outlook Web Access does not support the viewing of some specific features of documents that were created using the 2007 Microsoft Office release. WebReady Document Viewing does not support some of the high-end features, such as certain charts or shapes, in files created by applications in the 2007 Microsoft Office release.

POP3 and IMAP4

Support for the legacy POP3 and IMAP4 protocols in Exchange continues in Exchange 2007. POP3 and IMAP4 are used by e-mail clients such as Microsoft Outlook Express, Thunderbird, Eudora and Eudora Pro, and Windows Vista's Windows Mail. Even the full Outlook client can connect to e-mail servers via POP3 and IMAP4. Because Exchange 2007 adheres to the industry standards for these protocols, including RFC 1939 (POP3) and RFC 3501 (IMAP4), any standards-compliant e-mail client should be able to connect to an IMAP4- or POP3-enabled Exchange server. Even Apple's iPhone uses IMAP4 and can access Exchange.

But these antiquated protocols don't allow for many features and shouldn't be used unless absolutely necessary. After all, Exchange supports a plethora of access methods, including Outlook (internally and remotely), Outlook Web Access, and Exchange ActiveSync for mobile devices.

POP3 also only gives you access to your Inbox when connecting to servers. Support for contacts, tasks, calendaring, and out of office (OOF), among other features, are not available. IMAP4 (or Internet Message Access Protocol version 4, rev 1), on the other hand, gives access to individual folders. However, public folder access is no longer available via IMAP4. As with POP3, features such as OOF, meeting request handling, and other rich features are not supported with IMAP.

Configuration

In Exchange 2007, as with Exchange 2003, POP3 and IMAP4 are both disabled by default. However, getting them up and running is quite easy. Although POP3 and IMAP4 are separate protocols, configuration for both is nearly identical, so I've combined them into one section here.

First, you'll need to configure the related Windows services to start automatically on your Client Access Server. To do this, click Start | All Programs | Administrative Tools | Services. To enable the IMAP4 service, find Microsoft Exchange IMAP4 and double-click it. Under Startup Type, change the setting to Automatic as seen in Figure 8-4, and then click Start.

After a few seconds, the service will start. Click OK to close that dialog box. For POP3, do the same for the Microsoft Exchange POP3 service.

As with nearly everything in Exchange 2007, you can also make these changes via the Management Shell. To do so, click Start | All Programs | Microsoft Exchange Server 2007 | Exchange Management Shell. To set the startup type to automatic, type:

```
Set-service MSExchangePop3 -startupType Automatic
```

and then press ENTER. Once that's done, start the service by using:

```
Start-service MSExchangePop3
```

and pressing ENTER.

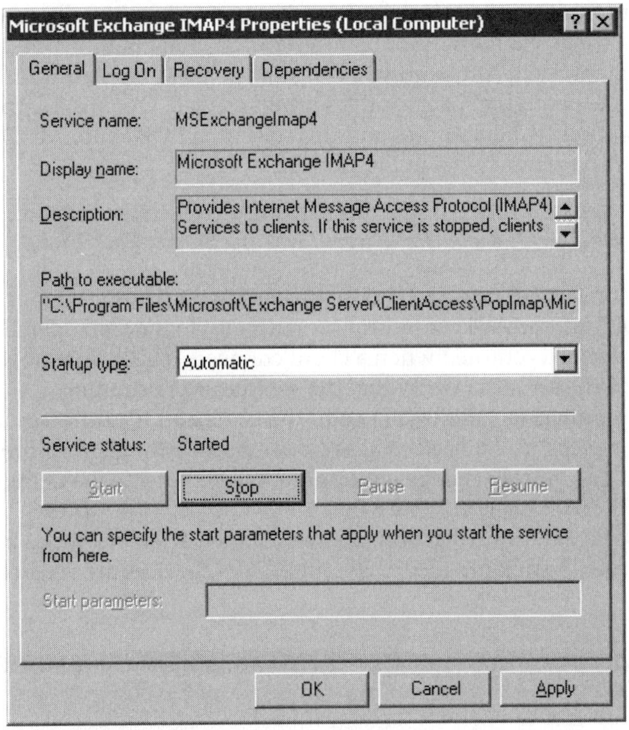

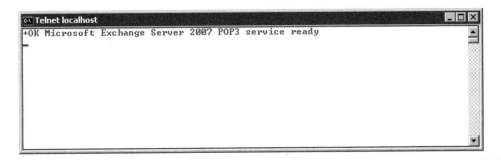

FIGURE 8-4
Enabling POP3 or
IMAP4 services

After a few seconds, the service should be started. If needed, do the same for the IMAP4 service. Note that the IMAP4 service is called MSExchangeImap4. Once you have the services started, test them by making a Telnet connection to them from the server console. Open a command prompt on the Client Access Server and type the following:

```
telnet localhost pop3
```

You should get a reply saying the service is ready, as shown in Figure 8-5. The same process test works for IMAP4. After you confirm that, you can close the connections.

FIGURE 8-5   Telnet results for POP3

Prior to the release of Service Pack 1, you had to manually configure the POP3 and IMAP4 settings via the Set-PopSettings and Set-ImapSettings cmdlets in the Exchange Management Shell. Although you can still use these cmdlets after Service Pack 1, EMC allows us to configure many of the settings as well. Open EMC and navigate to Server Configuration | Client Access and then click the POP3 and IMAP4 tab in the lower half of the results pane, as shown in Figure 8-6.

Sp1 *Managing POP3 and IMAP from EMC is a Service Pack 1 feature.*

Click either service, and choose properties on the right. From here, we can manage most POP3 and IMAP4 configuration settings. On the General tab is the banner string, which is the text returned when a client connects. This was seen when we used Telnet to connect to the server to verify that the services were running.

The Bindings tab allows us to edit the ports and IP addresses used by the POP3 and IMAP4 services. You'll need to allow these ports through your firewall if users will be connecting to your Exchange environment from outside the network. Ports used by IMAP and POP3 can be seen in Table 8-3.

Clicking the Authentication tab, we see the various methods by which users can connect to the server. By default, the POP3 and IMAP4 services are secured, and they accept only

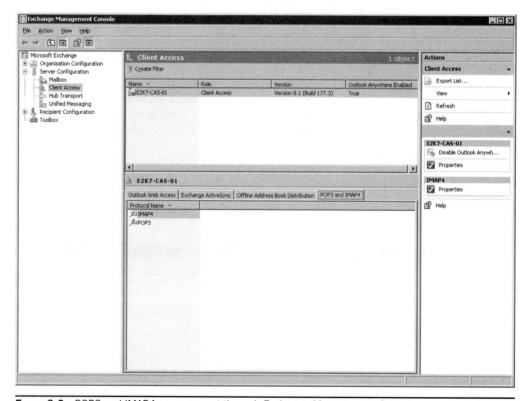

FIGURE 8-6   POP3 and IMAP4 management through Exchange Management Console

Protocol	Port	SSL Port
IMAP	143	993
POP3	110	995
SMTP	25	

TABLE 8-3   Ports Used by POP3, IMAP4, and SMTP

connections that are secured. This requires you either to adjust settings on the Client Access Server or require that your clients use SSL to secure the authentication. Using SSL would be the recommended method because it provides better security.

Note that by default, clients will connect to the Receive connector called Client <servername> on your Hub Transport server. That connector uses port 587 for SMTP. This can be verified in the Exchange Management Console by opening the properties of the connector, located at Server Configuration | Hub Transport in the lower results pane. Click the Network tab to see the port used. Also, verify that Basic authentication is enabled on the Authentication tab. POP3 and IMAP4 require Basic authentication in order to connect.

Once you make changes to your POP3 or IMAP4 configuration, restart the related service from either the Services MMC snap-in or via the Management Shell using the Restart-Service cmdlet:

```
Restart-Service -service MSExchangePop3
```

Once we have the services running, we can focus on the client aspect. POP3 and IMAP4 are enabled by default for all mailbox-enabled accounts. This might not be ideal for your environment, and you may wish to disable access for some users. This can be accomplished via the Exchange Management Console GUI by going to Recipient Configuration | Mailbox and opening the properties of the user, as seen in Figure 8-7.

Click the Exchange Features tab, and from there, you can enable and disable POP3 and IMAP4 access, among other features. You can also use the Set-CASMailbox cmdlet:

```
Set-CASMailbox <username> -ImapEnabled $false
```

or

```
Set-CASMailbox <username> -PopEnabled $false
```

Remember, for any cmdlet that starts with "set-", you can use "get-" to view the current settings. Therefore, we can then verify that POP3 is enabled for the user by using:

```
Get-CASMailbox <username> | fl
```

and looking at the ImapEnabled or PopEnabled fields. Remember, the Management Shell is quite powerful. You can stack commands to process more than one task at a time. For instance, if you wanted to disable IMAP4 for all users on a certain mailbox server, you could use the following:

```
Get-Mailbox -server <servername> | Set-CASMailbox -ImapEnabled $false
```

FIGURE 8-7
User properties

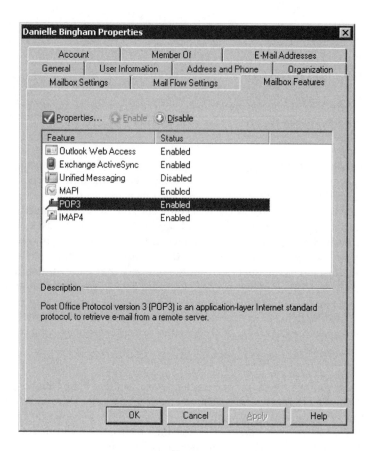

When configuring your POP3 and IMAP4 clients, the format you use for entering user credentials is important. For IMAP4 and POP3, usernames are in the format of domain\username\alias. However, for SMTP, usernames are in the domain\username format. UPN-formatted (or Universal Principal Name) usernames will also work for both. An example would be PRichard@virtuecorp.local.

For more information on configuring the Outlook client, see Chapter 11.

NOTE *POP3 and IMAP clients have to connect directly to a CAS server in the same AD site as their mailbox server. CAS servers do not support cross-site POP or IMAP communications.*

Outlook Anywhere

Outlook Anywhere is the new name for the feature called RPC over HTTP in Exchange 2003. Outlook Anywhere allows a user to use the full Outlook client securely, while outside of your environment—all without the need for a VPN tunnel. Outlook Anywhere works by encapsulating RPC packets inside of HTTP packets and then sending them across the Internet to your Exchange server. Exchange then strips off the HTTP wrapper, leaving just the RPC packets, which are then processed. This can save a lot of configuration headache, as well as allowing the users to use a client they are already familiar with. Also, because it uses HTTP packets, there is no need to open more ports through your firewall. We can further secure this traffic through the use of an SSL certificate. If you're using SSL with Outlook Web Access, you should be able to use the same certificate for both Outlook Web Access and Outlook Anywhere. This will only require that we allow traffic on port 443 though the firewall.

Outlook Anywhere supports the Outlook 2007 and Outlook 2003 clients only. Previous versions of Outlook do not support the Outlook Anywhere feature.

If you have a distributed environment and have Exchange Server 2007 servers in those remote environments, it's recommended that if you're going to use Outlook Anywhere, you enable it on those Client Access Servers in the remote sites so that users can connect directly to a server in their home site.

To use Outlook Anywhere, you need to be running Windows XP SP2 or later, or Windows Vista. Any version of these operating systems will work fine, including Home, Pro, and Ultimate.

Configuration

Configuring Outlook Anywhere on Exchange Server 2007 is a fairly straightforward three-step process.

First, you must install and configure the SSL certificate. Outlook Anywhere requires that the certificate be trusted. If it's not, Outlook Anywhere won't work correctly. I cover installation of certificates in the "Autodiscover" section of this chapter. You'll want to read that section entirely before deciding on an SSL certificate strategy.

Second, install the RPC Proxy Service on your Client Access Server. To do that, follow these steps:

1. Go to the Control Panel and select Add and Remove Programs.
2. Click Add/Remove Windows Components.
3. Highlight Networking Services and click Details.
4. Check the box for RPC over HTTP Proxy as seen in Figure 8-8.
5. Click OK, then Next.
6. When the installation is done, click Finish.

Third, we enable the Outlook Anywhere feature in Exchange. Open Exchange Management Console and navigate to Server Configuration | Client Access. If you have multiple Client Access Servers, click the desired server in the upper half of the results pane. Note that in the upper half of the results pane, Outlook Anywhere Enabled is False. In the task pane on the far right, click Enable Outlook Anywhere. This will start the Enable Outlook Anywhere Wizard, shown in Figure 8-9.

Next, enter the external host name. This will be the host name that users will type in their Outlook client, and it must match the name on the SSL certificate. There are two types of authentication available: Basic and NTLM. Basic sends the authentication credentials in clear text, which can be a security concern. NTLM, on the other hand, encrypts the credentials when sending them. NTLM also will utilize your Windows username and password credentials automatically if you're using a domain PC. This will eliminate the

Figure 8-8
Installing RPC over
HTTP Proxy

Figure 8-8
Installing RPC over
HTTP Proxy

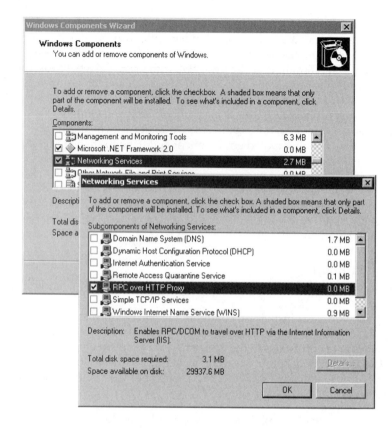

Figure 8-9
Enabling Outlook
Anywhere

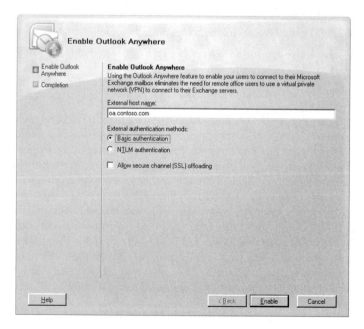

need to enter your username and password every time you open Outlook, as Basic authentication does.

If you'll be using a reverse proxy server (such as ISA 2006) in between the clients and the server, and it will be doing SSL offloading, click the box labeled Allow secure channel (SSL) offloading. Then, click Next. When the process is finished, you'll see the results.

An alternative to using the Exchange Management Console GUI would be to use the Exchange Management Shell and the Enable-OutlookAnywhere cmdlet:

```
Enable-OutlookAnywhere -server <servername> -ExternalHostName
<ExternalHostName> -ExternalAuthenticationMethod Basic -SSLOffloading $false
```

Note that if you still have legacy Exchange servers in your environment, you may get the following error:

Warning: Exchange versions before Exchange 2003 do not support RPC over HTTP; the following servers cannot be enabled:

However, that's a nuisance warning, and generally it can be ignored.

When the wizard finishes, note that it says it can take up to 15 minutes for Outlook Anywhere to be available, as seen in Figure 8-10. Look for event ID entries 3003, 3000, and 2080 in the Application log to verify that it's ready for connections.

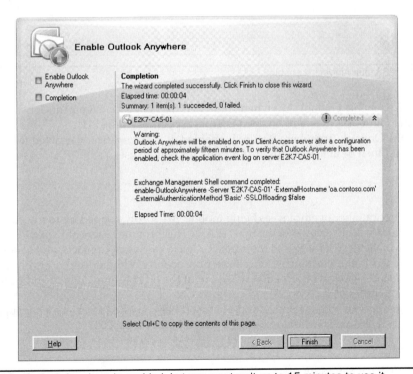

FIGURE 8-10   Outlook Anywhere is enabled, but you must wait up to 15 minutes to use it

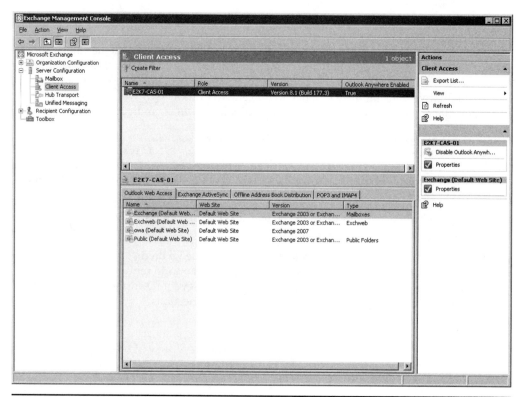

FIGURE 8-11   Outlook Anywhere enabled

After you enable Outlook Anywhere, note that Exchange Management Console now reports that Outlook Anywhere Enabled is True, as seen in Figure 8-11.

Once the Outlook Anywhere feature is enabled, it is automatically enabled for all users. Users should then be able to configure Outlook for remote use.

ActiveSync

With a greater number of employees being mobile, Microsoft stepped up to the plate in Exchange 2003 with Exchange ActiveSync (EAS). This provides users of PocketPC and Windows Mobile devices access to their Inbox, Calendar, Tasks, Contacts, and so on. Via real-time access to these resources, employee productivity is higher, and users have direct access to business-critical information when out of the office—or even in the office but, away from their desk.

In Exchange 2007 this continues, and Microsoft has provided for even better support of remote users. Here are some of the features added in Exchange 2007:

- Exchange Search
- HTML message support
- Support for follow-up flags

- Fast message retrieval support
- Meeting attendee info
- Out-of-office message support
- Password recovery
- Enhanced security
- SharePoint Services and UNC-based document access
- Auto-provisioning through the Autodiscover service

By using a feature called DirectPush, mobile devices can access mail items while keeping bandwidth usage low. When an EAS-compatible device connects to Exchange, it sends what's called a *heartbeat* message to Exchange. This is basically a ping, telling the server, "Hey, I'm here." It is used to create a persistent connection with the Exchange server. After a while, (generally between 15 and 30 minutes) if the device hasn't received any notifications from the server, the device sends another heartbeat. However, if the mailbox changes during the interval between heartbeats, such as a new message arrives, the server will send a notification to the device. If the device is still online and receives a notification that a change has occurred, it will begin a synchronization and get any new messages. This is actually more of a pull method than a push method, so the DirectPush moniker has more of a marketing aspect.

Exchange ActiveSync sends its traffic over port 443 using the SSL certificate installed on the Exchange server, so you don't have to open additional ports on your firewall. In order for EAS to work correctly, however, the certificate must be trusted by the device. The recommended method is to use a commercial SSL certificate to avoid additional administrative effort. If the certificate is not trusted by the device, Exchange Active Sync will not work. I discuss in the "Autodiscover" section of this chapter the various certificate combinations, the pros and cons of each, and the configuration for them.

ActiveSync Mailbox Policies

A great feature of Exchange 2007 is the ActiveSync policies. These policies can be used to push various configuration parameters to the devices. You can have multiple policies and apply them to individual users as requirements dictate. For example, if your Management group needs to be able to access e-mail attachments, but other users shouldn't, you can specify a separate policy for the management staff and configure it accordingly.

To create or edit EAS policies, we go into the EMC under Organization Configuration, and click Client Access. In the results pane, we see the default policy. Open it by double-clicking it. Inside, through the first two tabs, we see the standard settings we can set on each policy. Those basic policy settings and their default values can be seen in Table 8-4.

CAUTION *When specifying the Minimum Password setting, verify that all affected devices support that minimum password length. Some devices, such as the Palm® Treo™, support passwords up to four characters. Setting a policy higher than what the device supports will lock out the user.*

Although that's an impressive list of basic settings, the extended Exchange ActiveSync policy settings are even more robust. Moving to the third tab, Sync Settings, we can control how data is synced and retained on the devices. These settings can be tweaked to optimize the bandwidth usage, which, in turn, will help conserve battery life. They will also help keep data costs low when roaming. These sync settings can be seen in Table 8-5.

Setting	Description	Default
Allow non-provisionable devices	Allows older devices (those that do not support EAS policies, such as Windows Mobile 5.0 without the Messaging and Security Feature Pack applied) to connect to Exchange 2007 by using Exchange ActiveSync.	True
Allow simple password	Enables or disables the ability to use a simple password such as 1234.	False
Alphanumeric password required	Requires that a password contains numeric and nonnumeric characters.	False
Attachments enabled	Enables attachments to be downloaded to the mobile device.	True
Device encryption enabled	For Windows Mobile 6.0 devices this controls the storage card encryption on the device.	False
Password enabled	Enables the device password.	False
Password expiration	Enables the administrator to configure a length of time after which a device password must be changed.	Unlimited
Password history	Sets the number of unique passwords a user must use before an old password can be reused.	0
Policy refresh interval	Defines how frequently the device checks the Exchange Server for changes to the Exchange ActiveSync policy.	Unlimited
Maximum attachment size	Specifies the maximum size of attachments that are automatically downloaded to the device.	Unlimited
Maximum failed password attempts	Specifies how many times an incorrect password can be entered before the device performs a wipe of all data.	4
Maximum inactivity time lock	Specifies the length of time a device can go without user input before it locks.	15 minutes
Minimum password length	Specifies the minimum password length.	4
Password recovery	Enables the device password to be recovered from the server.	Disabled
UNC file access	Enables access to files stored on Universal Naming Convention (UNC) shares, commonly known as Windows File Shares.	Enabled
WSS file access	Enables access to files stored on Microsoft Windows SharePoint Services sites.	Enabled

TABLE 8-4   Configuration Settings in ActiveSync Policies

Setting	Description	Default
Include past calendar items	Select the date range of calendar items to synchronize to the device. Available options include: • All • Two weeks • One month • Three months • Six months If you need to specify other options, use the Exchange Management Shell to configure this setting.	All
Include past e-mail items	Select the date range of e-mail items to synchronize to the device. Available options include: • All • One day • Three days • One week • Two weeks • One month If you need to specify other options, use the Exchange Management Shell to configure this setting.	All
Limit message size to (KB)	Limit the message size that can be downloaded to the device. When this setting is enabled, specify a maximum message size in KB.	Unlimited
Allow synchronization when roaming	Enables the mobile device to synchronize when the device is roaming. Disabling (clearing this check box) prevents the device from synchronizing when the device is roaming and data rates are traditionally higher.	Disabled
Allow HTML formatted e-mail	Enables HTML-formatted e-mail to be synchronized to the device. If this check box is not selected, all e-mail is converted to plain text before synchronization. (Note: Use of this setting does not affect whether the device will receive a message.)	Enabled
Allow attachments to be downloaded to the device	Enables attachments to be downloaded to the device. Users must select the attachment within the e-mail on the device in order to download the attachment. If this check box is cleared, the name of the attachment is visible within the e-mail message. However, the attachment cannot be downloaded to the device.	Enabled
Maximum attachment size (KB)	Specify a maximum size for attachments downloaded to the mobile device. When this setting is enabled, enter a maximum attachment size in KB. Also, when this setting is enabled, attachments that are larger than the specified size cannot be downloaded to the device.	Unlimited

TABLE 8-5   ActiveSync Profile Sync Settings

PART III

NOTE *All settings accessed on the Device and Advanced tabs of an ActiveSync policy are premium features of Exchange ActiveSync. For these features to apply, the users' mailboxes require an Exchange Enterprise Client Access License (CAL).*

In the last two tabs, Device and Advanced, we can set additional parameters on the devices, including what features to enable/disable, allowed and blocked applications, and so on.

Creating a New ActiveSync Mailbox Policy

Creating a new policy is quite easy, and only takes a few steps using the Exchange Management Console:

1. Navigate to Organization Configuration | Client Access.
2. In the Actions pane, click New ActiveSync mailbox policy.
3. On the New ActiveSync Mailbox Policy page, enter a name in the Mailbox policy name box.
4. Select one or more of the optional check boxes as seen in Figure 8-12.
5. Click New to finish creating your mailbox policy.
6. Click Finish to close the New ActiveSync Mailbox Policy Wizard.

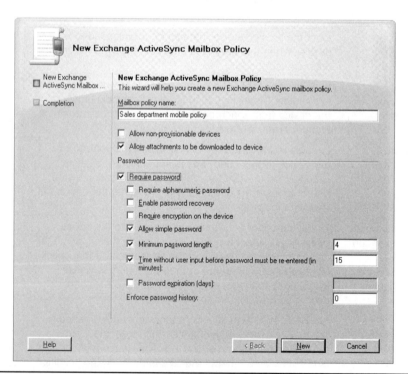

FIGURE 8-12 Creating a new ActiveSync Mailbox Policy

Once the policy is created, we can open it up and edit the rest of the settings, such as the sync settings, the device, and advanced settings.

Using the Exchange Management Shell, we can configure all parameters in one command using the New-ActiveSyncMailboxPolicy cmdlet:

```
New-ActiveSyncMailboxPolicy -Name '<policy name>' -DevicePasswordEnabled $false -
AlphanumericDevicePasswordRequired $false -MaxInactivityTimeDeviceLock 'unlimited'
-MinDevicePasswordLength $null -PasswordRecoveryEnabled $false -
DeviceEncryptionEnabled $false -AttachmentsEnabled $true
```

That will create a new policy with all the default settings. All policy settings can be specified using EMS. Use the following to see all the available parameters with the New-ActiveSyncMailboxPolicy cmdlet:

```
Get-Help New-ActiveSyncMailboxPolicy
```

If you want your newly created policy to be the default policy applied to all users who aren't explicitly configured for a policy, you can right-click the policy in EMC and choose Set As Default. If you're using the EMS instead, you can specify -IsDefaultPolicy $true in your cmdlet parameters.

Assigning Policies to Users

Once the policies are created and edited to your liking, you can assign them to users. If a user is not explicitly assigned an EAS policy, they will get the default policy, as mentioned previously. If, however, you need to assign different policies to different users, follow these steps:

1. Navigate to Recipient Configuration | Mailbox.
2. In the results pane, right-click the user who you want to assign to a policy and then click Properties.
3. In the user's Properties dialog box, click Mailbox Features.
4. Click ActiveSync and then click Properties.
5. Select the Apply an ActiveSync mailbox policy check box.
6. Click Browse to view the Select Exchange ActiveSync Mailbox Policy dialog box.
7. Select an available policy as seen in Figure 8-13, and then click OK three times to apply your changes.

From the EMS, we can also assign a user to a policy using the Set-CASMailbox cmdlet:

```
Set-CASMailbox <UserName> -ActiveSyncMailboxPolicy(Get-ActiveSyncMailboxPolicy
"Policy Name").Identity
```

Because we can stack commands in EMS, we can assign all users to a policy using:

```
Get-Mailbox | Set-CASMailbox -ActiveSyncMailboxPolicy(Get-ActiveSyncMailboxPolicy
"Policy Name").Identity
```

which would be much more convenient than modifying the users one at a time if there are a lot of them.

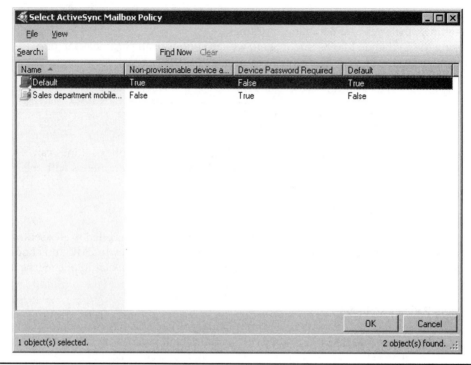

FIGURE 8-13   Selecting an Exchange ActiveSync mailbox policy

Because ActiveSync is enabled by default for all users, it can sometimes be difficult to find out who is actually using an EAS-compatible device. Fortunately, we can use the Exchange Management Shell to find out. We just use the Get-CASMailbox cmdlet:

```
Get-CASMailbox | where {$_.HasActiveSyncDevicePartnership} | select Name
```

This is much easier than it was in Exchange 2003!

Remote Wipe

Although we can assign passwords to help keep devices secure, there are times when devices are lost or stolen. Having a device in the wild that holds your companies' proprietary information can be unnerving. Fortunately, we can take matters into our own hands and remotely wipe the device. And, even better, we can give this capability to the end user.

When a mailbox-enabled user has an ActiveSync device tied to their mailbox, they can manage it through Outlook Web Access by following these steps:

1. Log onto Outlook Web Access.
2. Click the Options link in the OWA toolbar in the upper-right part of the screen.
3. Click the Mobile Devices link on the left.

NOTE *The Mobile Devices link is only visible if the Exchange feature ActiveSync is enabled on the user's account.*

From here, the user can see their devices listed. Note that only devices that have synchronized with Exchange at least once will be visible in the list.

If a user needs to wipe a device because it has been lost, they simply choose the device and click the Wipe All Data From Device link at the top.

SP1 *When the user clicks Wipe All Data From Device, the link will then change to Cancel Wipe Request…. If the user decides to cancel the wipe request, it must be done quickly, because once the device begins to wipe the data, it cannot be canceled.*

Once a device has been cleared, the user will receive an e-mail stating that the Remote Device Wipe operation has completed successfully.

SP1 *The confirmation e-mail is a Service Pack 1 feature.*

If a user wants to remove the device from their list, such as when they change devices or following a wipe request, the user highlights the device and clicks Remove Device From List near the top. This removes all remnants of its partnership from the server, including any sync data. It also terminates any remote wipe activity.

This task can be performed from the Exchange Management Shell using the Remove-ActiveSyncDevice cmdlet:

```
Remove-ActiveSyncDevice -Identity:<email address>\<device name>
```

and then confirming the "Are You Sure?" prompt.

Of course, we can also see the status of a device via the Exchange Management Shell using the Get-ActiveSyncDeviceStatistics cmdlet:

```
Get-ActiveSyncDeviceStatistics -mailbox <user name>
```

This cmdlet allows us to monitor the remote wipe status. In the output of Get-ActiveSyncDeviceStatistics are three parameters of interest: DeviceWipeRequestTime, DeviceWipeSentTime, and DeviceWipeAckTime. When the user sends a remote wipe command to the device, the timestamp is placed in the DeviceWipeRequestTime parameter. Once the server actually sends the command to the device, the DeviceWipeSentTime receives a timestamp. And, finally, when the device receives and acknowledges the command, the DeviceWipeAckTime receives a timestamp. By monitoring these parameters, we can see the status of a remote wipe request.

If the device is recovered after it has been remotely wiped, it can be reused, but must be removed from the device list in OWA and then added back in. If it's not removed from the list, the device will continue to wipe itself. This is by design as part of Exchange security. Also, removing the device partnership without performing a remote device wipe does not delete data on the device.

PART III

Recover Password

Because we can use EAS policies to require passwords on devices, we need a way to recover passwords should users forget and lock themselves out of their devices. Again, we give this capability to the user in Exchange 2007. From Outlook Web Access, the user can request a recovery password in just a quick series of steps:

1. Log into Outlook Web Access.
2. Click Options in the OWA toolbar in the upper-right part of the screen.
3. On the left side, click Mobile Devices.
4. Select the appropriate device.
5. Click Display Device Password.

This will display a device password that can then be entered into the device to unlock it.

From the administrative side, we can also display the recovery password and other information in both the Exchange Management Console and the Exchange Management Shell. From the EMC, go to Recipient Configuration | Mailbox. Right-click the user's account and choose Manage Mobile Device. The various device statistics, including recovery password, will be displayed in the resulting screen. From this screen, you can also remove the device partnership, as well as perform a remote device wipe.

As with the Exchange Management Console, we can use the Exchange Management Shell to view the recovery password. We do this by viewing the Get-ActiveSyncDeviceStatistics results if we use the –ShowRecoveryPassword parameter like this:

```
Get-ActiveSyncDeviceStatistics -Mailbox <mailbox name> -ShowRecoveryPassword $True
```

Autodiscover

In Exchange 2007, a new component brings about some long-sought-after features. The Autodiscover service provides access to various information via Exchange Web Services. But the most popular is the autoprovisioning of Outlook 2007 and mobile devices running at least Windows Mobile 6. That's right! Administrators won't have to manually configure Outlook 2007 for users, nor will we have to resort to creating scripts, transforms, or Group Policy objects to do it for us! Not only that, but if the user's Exchange information changes, Autodiscover makes sure to notify Outlook of the changes. All of this is done transparently to the user.

When you install the first Client Access Server in an Exchange 2007 environment, a new virtual folder is created in the IIS Default Web Site called Autodiscover (see Figure 8-14).

This virtual directory is what handles requests for Autodiscover information from Outlook 2007, Outlook Web Access 2007, and Windows Mobile clients. Previous versions of Outlook, OWA, and Windows Mobile do not support Autodiscover. For each Client Access Server you install, a Service Connection Point (SCP) object is added to Active Directory, and it contains the URLs of all Autodiscover services in the forest. When a user starts Outlook 2007 for the first time, Outlook queries the SCP for a URL to use to gather Autodiscover information from. The SCP provides those Autodiscover URLs in XML format, and Outlook then contacts those URLs over HTTPS for configuration information. The Autodiscover service provides the information, and Outlook is then able to configure itself for the user. To see this process, look at Figure 8-15.

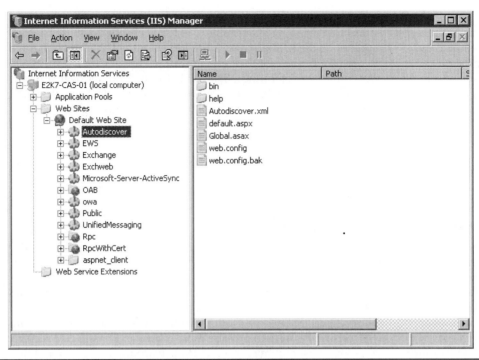

FIGURE 8-14   Autodiscover virtual folder

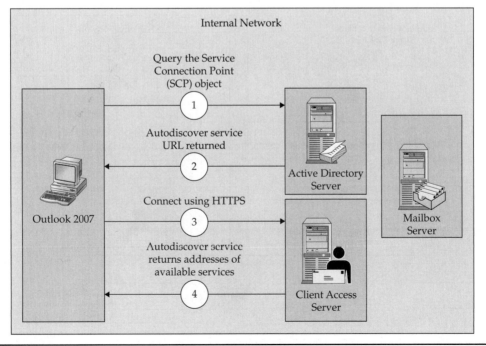

FIGURE 8-15   Autodiscover process by machines within the network

The process is a bit different when the user is outside of your environment. This is because the Service Connection Point is not available to external clients. So, these clients then attempt to make a connection to the Autodiscover URL. When Outlook 2007 is configured for the first time, it will prompt the user for their e-mail address. It will then use the SMTP domain from that e-mail address to determine a likely URL for the Autodiscover service. As shown in Figure 8-16, and using virtuecorp.com as an example of an SMTP domain name, Outlook 2007 clients will look for Autodiscover information in the following order:

- https://virtuecorp.com
- https://autodiscover.virtuecorp.com
- http://virtuecorp.com
- http://autodiscover.virtuecorp.com

Autodiscover Service and SSL Certificates

When the Client Access Server is installed, it automatically generates and installs a self-signed Secure Sockets Layer (SSL) certificate using the host name of the Client Access Server. This allows clients to connect to the Autodiscover service using a secured connection. Exchange also uses that host name to assemble the URLs used by the various Exchange Web Services.

However, most organizations that expose Outlook Web Access to the Internet will install a third-party, trusted SSL certificate in IIS to provide more robust and hassle-free security. Without doing so, OWA users must first bypass a certificate warning dialog box and that can cause user confusion and frustration. Once a trusted certificate is installed that OWA

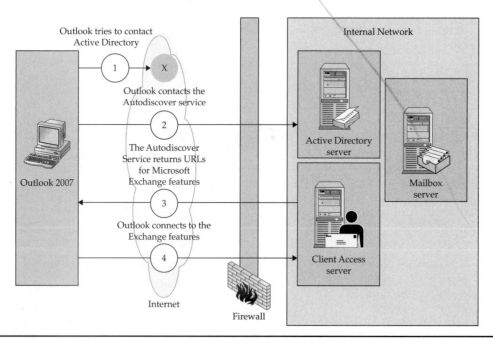

FIGURE 8-16 Autodiscover process by machines outside of the network

problem goes away, but Outlook 2007 users will begin to see a certificate warning popup, like the one shown in Figure 8-17, when they launch Outlook that reads
The name of the security certificate is invalid or does not match the name of the site.
This prompt occurs because Outlook is attempting to get information from the Autodiscover service, but the Common Name (CN) of the certificate that's installed now no longer matches the FQDN that is stored in all the following objects:

- The Service Connection Point (SCP) object for the Autodiscover service
- The Exchange Web Service (EWS)
- The Offline Address Book (OAB) Web Service
- The Unified Messaging (UM) Web service

When Exchange is installed, the NetBIOS name is stored in those objects in a format similar to https://NetBIOS_name.virtuecorp.com/autodiscover/autodiscover.xml.
When the certificate is replaced, that no longer matches. There is a variety of ways to tackle this.
Configuration requires three major steps:

1. Determine the best SSL certificate strategy.
2. Use split-brain DNS if desired.
3. Configure URLs for access.

For the SSL certificate strategy, the following six methods work:

- Use a Subject Alternative Name SSL certificate
- Use separate websites, IP addresses, and certificates for OWA and Autodiscover
- Redirect Autodiscover to your OWA address
- Use one certificate and use a unified name for all web services
- Use an Outlook hotfix on all clients
- Use the original certificate and not external Autodiscover

There are positives and negatives to each of these methods, and I've listed them in Table 8-6.

FIGURE 8-17
Outlook 2007
certificate warning

Method	Pros	Cons
One SSL certificate that is valid for multiple DNS names (or Subject Alternative Names)	Simple configuration. Requires: • One certificate • One website • One public IP	Cost of additional DNS names for SSL certificates can be more expensive. Not all Certificate Authorities support Subject Alternative Certificates. See KB article 929395 for a list.
Two single-name SSL certificates (one specifically for Autodiscover)	Two single-name certificates may be less costly than a certificate with multiple names.	Complex configuration. Requires: • Two websites • Two public IPs • Two single-name SSL certificates Difficult to load balance two sites.
One single-name SSL certificate with a second HTTP redirection website	Requires one single-name SSL certificate.	Complex configuration. Requires: • Two websites • Two public IPs Difficult to load balance two sites. An additional dialog box is displayed to the Outlook users asking if they trust the redirected URL.
One single-name SSL certificate for Autodiscover and OWA using Autodiscover name (autodiscover .virtuecorp.com)	Simple configuration. Requires: • One website • One public IP • One single-name SSL certificate	Users may have a hard time remembering and adjusting to using a new name.
One single-name SSL certificate with DNS SRV lookup	Simple configuration. Requires: • One website • One public IP • One single-name SSL certificate	Not all DNS hosting providers support DNS SRV records. An additional dialog box is displayed to the Outlook users asking if they trust the redirected URL. Requires Outlook 2007 client-side hotfix 939184. Requires all users have Outlook 2007.
Self-signed certificate	Simple configuration. Requires: • One website • One public IP	External Autodiscover won't work. Users will see a certificate prompt when using OWA. ActiveSync won't work correctly.

TABLE 8-6   Various Autodiscover Configurations

As mentioned earlier, when you install Exchange, it creates a self-signed SSL certificate with a CN that matches the NetBIOS name of the server. This won't have the desired effect when connecting externally, so we turn to commercial SSL certificates.

In previous versions of Exchange, you could install a certificate that matched the address your users would use for Outlook Web Access (such as mail.virtuecorp.com), and life was good.

In Exchange 2007, it's a little more complicated. First, we have the URL for OWA, then we have the URL for Autodiscover and its related services. Because a website in IIS can only have a single certificate, we have to choose how we want to make this work. As mentioned in Table 8-6, various certificate solutions include the following:

- You can use what's called a Unified Communications Certificate, also known as a Subject Alternative Name certificate (or SAN certificate, for short). This is the preferred method because it keeps everything within one website in IIS and uses a single certificate. This makes it easier to administer.

    One problem with SAN certificates is that not all Certificate Authorities (CAs) can provide them. See http://support.microsoft.com/kb/929395 for information on which CAs handle Subject Alternative Name certificates. The other problem is that SAN certificates are considerably more expensive than traditional certificates. Often up to ten times as much. For smaller companies, it might not be feasible to purchase a SAN certificate.

- You can split the Autodiscover virtual directory out from the default website and give it a website of its own. This would allow you to use one certificate for OWA and one for Autodiscover, each with its own Common Name (CN). This requires an additional IP address to be configured in IIS, as well as the additional setup for multiple websites.

- Use the same name for both Autodiscover and Outlook Web Access. With this method, users would go to https://autodiscover.domain.com/owa for OWA and would use https://autodiscover.domain.com for Autodiscover. Only a single SSL certificate is required. Users would need to adjust to going to autodiscover.domain.com/owa for OWA, and that may cause confusion.

- Redirect Autodiscover using an IIS redirect. This requires additional setup, and the users still get a prompt when using Outlook asking whether they trust the redirected website.

- Use the same URL for OWA and Autodiscover. This would mean your users would use https://autodiscover.virtuecorp.com/owa for Outlook Web Access and https://autodiscover.virtuecorp.com for Autodiscover and Outlook Anywhere. This method works fine, but users might not be able to grasp that OWA URL if they are already using a different one, such as https://mail.virtuecorp.com/.

- Use the original self-signed certificate. Internally, Autodiscover will work fine. Externally, users will be prompted with a certificate warning. Additionally, mobile users may not be able to use ActiveSync on their mobile devices because the certificate is not trusted.

As you can see, there are many options and each brings its own pros and cons. Once you've decided which path to pursue, you can set out to get it configured. In the remainder of this section, I'll cover the various configurations.

Subject Alternative Name Certificates

Subject Alternative Name certificates allow you to specify several names on one certificate. This allows you to use the one certificate for multiple purposes, and it's a perfect fit for securing Autodiscover. Once you've chosen a Certificate Authority, you'll need to determine all the Subject Alternative Names that you need to register. Here's an example:

- mail.virtuecorp.com
- virtuecorp.com
- virtuecorp.local
- autodiscover.virtuecorp.com
- e2k7-cas-01.virtuecorp.local
- e2k7-cas-01

The NetBIOS name of the server is not technically required. There are no ill effects from adding internal names, but they are not necessary. Having them in the certificate may be beneficial if you wish to avoid using split-brain DNS, or use some internal URLs such as https://e2k-cas-01/owa without getting a certificate warning. Note that some Certificate Authorities limit how many names can be provided, so check their requirements before creating your certificate request.

After you have the list of names that will need to be listed on the certificate, you can use the New-ExchangeCertificate cmdlet to create a certificate request. Here's an example:

```
New-ExchangeCertificate -domainname mail.virtuecorp.com, virtuecorp.com,
virtuecorp.local, autodiscover.virtuecorp.com, e2k7-cas-01.virtuecorp
.local, e2k7-cas-01 -Friendlyname virtuecorpinc -generaterequest $true
-keysize 1024 -path c:\certrequest.req -privatekeyexportable $true
-subjectname "c=US, o=Virtuecorp Inc, CN=virtuecorp.com"
```

Pay special attention that the –subjectname option is correct. The "c" parameter must be the correct country. The "o" parameter must be the registered owner of the domain name specified in the "cn" parameter. Some Certificate Authorities will query that WHOIS information when validating your certificate request. If the owner and domain name don't match, your certificate won't be generated.

The New-ExchangeCertificate command will generate a certificate request file you can then submit to your preferred commercial CA. In the preceding example, the file is c:\certrequest.req. Use this file when requesting an SSL certificate from your chosen Certificate Authority.

Importing and Enabling a SAN Certificate

Once the certificate request is processed and you receive the certificate from your commercial Certificate Authority, save it to your server. Next, you need to install it onto your default website. SAN certificates don't get installed using the IIS Admin Console like conventional single name certificates. Instead, we must use several commands in the Exchange Management Shell.

First, you have to import the certificate using the Import-ExchangeCertificate cmdlet:

```
Import-ExchangeCertificate -path <path to cert file>
```

When the certificate is imported, it will supply you with the thumbprint. Copy the thumbprint because you'll need it again for the next command.

Next, you'll need to enable the certificate so that Exchange can use it for both IIS purposes, such as Autodiscover and OWA, and for TLS encryption when communicating with other servers. As with most cmdlets, the Enable-ExchangeCertificate cmdlet allows you to specify several parameters at one time instead of being prompted for them. The first is the –services parameter, which allows you to supply a list of services you wish to use the certificate for. The choices are IIS, POP3, IMAP, SMTP, and UM. You can specify more than one (or all of them) in the –services parameter, as follows:

```
-services IMAP, POP, UM, IIS, SMTP
```

However, only specify the services you are using and that are enabled. This would typically be at least SMTP, IIS, and UM.

Next is the -thumbprint parameter, which specifies the certificate you wish to use. The thumbprint was displayed when you imported the certificate, and it looks something like D8CFBDCF7E4809A048DF6C85005DB521E2D2CEEA. If you missed the thumbprint, use the Get-ExchangeCertificate cmdlet to display it again.

With those two parameters together, we enable the certificate using the following:

```
Enable-ExchangeCertificate –services IMAP, POP, IIS, UM, SMTP -thumbprint
D8CFBDCF7E4809A048DF6C85005DB521E2D2CEEA
```

Once those commands are done, your certificate is installed, enabled, and ready for use.

Before we configure the Autodiscover URLs, create a host record for "autodiscover" in your public DNS that points to your Client Access Server (via the firewall).

Enabling Multiple Websites

An alternative method to a Unified Communications Certificate, or SAN certificate, is to put the Autodiscover virtual folder in its own website and secure it with its own certificate. This allows you to use a friendlier name for OWA, such as mail.virtuecorp.com, while using the recommended format, such as autodiscover.virtuecorp.com, for the Autodiscover service. The caveat here is that you'll need two certificates—one for the default website and one for the Autodiscover website. It also requires that you assign another IP address to the Client Access Server, as well as forward traffic for that IP address through your firewall and to the server. This essentially doubles your administrative duties, but may be worth the savings over a SAN certificate. To create another website, follow these steps:

1. Assign another IP address to the server's network connection.

2. Open IIS Manager.

3. Right-click Web Sites, choose New | Web Site, and then click Next.

4. On the Web Site Description screen, set the description as Autodiscover and click Next.

5. On the IP Address and Port Settings screen, choose the new dedicated IP address to this website.

6. Verify the default port is set to 80.

PART III

7. Leave the host header field blank and then click Next.

8. On the Website Home Directory screen, set the path to the same directory as your default website, which should be c:\inetpub\wwwroot. Then click Next.

9. On the Web Site Access Permissions screen, accept the default permissions, click Next, and then click Finish.

Once you've created the additional website, you can tell Exchange to create a new Autodiscover virtual folder in it and to populate it with the required files. From the Exchange Command Shell, run the following command:

```
New-AutodiscoverVirtualDirectory -WebSiteName AutoDiscover -BasicAuthentication
$true -WindowsAuthentication $true
```

Note that the WebSiteName parameter is case sensitive.

Go back to IIS Manager, confirm the creation of your new Autodiscover virtual directory. You can delete the Autodiscover virtual directory from the default website, but it's not necessary and there is no additional risk by leaving it there. Finally, make sure your external DNSs have A or CNAME records for the following:

- mail.virtuecorp.com pointed to the external IP of Default Web Site. This is for OWA

- autodiscover.virtuecorp.com pointed to the external IP of the Autodiscover website

Conventional Single-name Certificates

If you choose to use conventional single-name certificates, the process to request and install them is nearly identical to previous versions of Exchange. For this, we use the Internet Information Services (IIS) Manager snap-in.

Here are the steps for creating a certificate request and installing an SSL certificate:

1. Open Internet Information Services Manager.

2. Right-click Default Web Site and choose Properties.

3. Click the Directory Security tab and then click Server Certificates. The Web Server Certificates Wizard will start. Click Next.

4. On the Modify Current Certificate Assignment screen, choose Remove the current certificate. Click Next.

5. On the summary screen, click Next.

6. On the Completing the Web Server Certificate Wizard screen, click Finish.

7. Restart the wizard.

8. On the Server Certificate screen, select Create a new certificate. Click Next.

9. In the Delayed or Immediate Request screen, select Prepare the request now, but send it later. Click Next.

10. In the Name and Security Settings screen, give the certificate a descriptive name, leave the security level at 1024, and click Next.

11. On the Organization Information screen, enter the name of your organization. This is the name that will appear in your certificate, so it should match the legal name of your organization. For the Organizational Unit, enter a department or location.

12. On the Your Site's Common Name screen, enter the FQDN of your web server. This is important, and it must be the address that will be publicly available, such as autodiscover.virtuecorp.com.

13. On the Geographical Information screen, enter the state in full.

14. Enter the location you would like the Certificate Request File to be created. This will be the file you'll send to the Certificate Authority, so remember where you placed it and what you called it. Then click Next.

15. On the Request File Summary screen, verify that everything is correct and then click Next.

16. The certificate request has now been created, and you can send it to the Certificate Authority.

Adding a Single-name SSL Certificate to IIS

Once you've received the certificate from the Certificate Authority, you need to install it in IIS so that it's available:

1. Open Internet Information Services Manager.

2. Open the Properties Default Web Site.

3. Click the Directory Security tab and then click Server Certificates.

4. You will see the Pending Certificate Request screen. Choose the option Process the pending request and install the certificate. Click Next.

5. On the Process a Pending Request screen, browse to the certificate you received from the Certificate Authority. Click Next.

6. You should now see the Certificate Summary screen. Verify everything is correct and then click Next.

Once that's completed, we must enable the certificate for Exchange. First, we must determine the thumbprint for the new certificate. To do that, use the Get-ExchangeCertificate cmdlet, which will display all certificates and their corresponding thumbprints. Copy the thumbprint for the certificate you just installed.

Next, we enable the certificate in the same manner as the SAN certificate using the Enable-ExchangeCertificate cmdlet and specifying the desired services and thumbprint:

```
Enable-ExchangeCertificate -services IMAP, POP, IIS, UM, SMTP -thumbprint
D8CFBDCF7E4809A048DF6C85005DB521E2D2CEEA
```

Remember, when using single-name certificates and separate websites for OWA and Autodiscover, you'll need to purchase and install a certificate for each website and enable them accordingly.

Split-Brain DNS

Split-brain DNS is where you have two DNS services serving up different information for the same zone. In most instances, split-brain DNS is used to provide internal IP address resolution using public names, such as mail.virtuecorp.com. Externally, your public DNS would resolve the name to a public IP address, but internally, your Active Directory DNS would resolve that name to the internal IP address of your Client Access Server.

Split brain DNS has another benefit besides just Autodiscover. When you use it, your users can use the same URL for OWA whether they are inside or outside of your network, and they won't receive a certificate error. Having the same namespace for all URLs will make administration easier and reduce confusion.

Installing and configuring DNS is outside the scope of this book, and is not detailed here. However, once you have split-brain DNS configured with a forward lookup zone for your SMTP domain name, you just need to create an A record in that zone called Autodiscover that points to the internal IP address of your Client Access Server.

Changing Autodiscover URLs

The last step in configuring Autodiscover is to make the required changes to the various Autodiscover service URLs using the Exchange Management Shell. This includes the following:

- Autodiscover
- Exchange EWS
- Offline Address Book
- Unified Messaging

Microsoft recommends using something like autodiscover.domain.com when configuring these services. Because we included that in our certificate request, we can configure the URLs accordingly.

Modifying the Autodiscover URL in the Active Directory Service Connection Point (SCP)

First, record the existing Autodiscover URL using the Get-ClientAccessServer cmdlet in case you need to restore it later:

```
Get-ClientAccessServer | fl
```

Save the results to a text file. Note that this single command will list information for all Client Access Servers in your organization. When looking at the results, note that the AutoDiscoveryServiceInternalUri looks something like https://e2k7-cas-01.virtuecorp .local/autodiscover/autodiscover.xml. We only need to change the domain name part of the URL.

To modify the Autodiscover URL, use the Set-ClientAccessServer cmdlet. Here's an example using https://autodiscover.virtuecorp.com as the name on our certificate:

```
Set-ClientAccessServer -Identity e2k7-cas-01 -AutodiscoverServiceInternalUri
https://autodiscover.virtuecorp.com/autodiscover/autodiscover.xml
```

Modifying the InternalUrl and ExternalUrl Attributes of the Exchange Web Services

As with the Autodiscover URL, record the existing settings in case you need to restore them later, as follows:

```
Get-WebServicesVirtualDirectory | fl
```

Save the results to a text file. Note that this will list information for all Client Access Servers in your organization. Then use the Set-WebServiceVirtualDirectory cmdlet to change both the InternalUrl and ExternalUrl parameters, such as this:

```
Set-WebServicesVirtualDirectory -Identity "e2k7-cas-01\EWS (Default Web Site)" -
InternalUrl https://autodiscover.virtuecorp.com/ews/exchange.asmx -ExternalUrl
https://autodiscover.virtuecorp.com/ews/exchange.asmx
```

Modifying the InternalUrl and ExternalUrl Attributes for a Web-based Offline Address Book

Again, record the existing settings in case you need to restore them later:

```
Get-OABVirtualDirectory | fl
```

Save the results to a text file. Pay special attention to the fact that the InternalUrl uses HTTP, and not HTTPS, by default. Because the Offline Address Book is distributed using the Background Intelligent Transfer Service (BITS), it cannot use a self-signed certificate. If a certificate is used, it must be a commercially trusted certificate. Note also that this command will list information for all Client Access Servers in your organization. Assuming we're using a trusted certificate, we can use Set-OABVirtualDirectory to set the InternalUrl and ExternalUrl parameters. Here's an example:

```
Set-OABVirtualDirectory -Identity "e2k7-cas-01\oab (Default Web Site)" -
InternalUrl https://autodiscover.virtuecorp.com/oab -ExternalUrl
https://autodiscover.virtuecorp.com/oab
```

Modifying the InternalUrl and ExternalUrl Attributes of the Unified Messaging Web Service

Lastly, we change the InternalUrl and ExternalUrl attributes for the unifiedmessaging virtual folder. Record the existing settings in case you need to restore them later:

```
Get-UMVirtualDirectory | fl
```

Then use the Set-UMVirtualDirectory cmdlet to make the necessary changes:

```
Set-UMVirtualDirectory -Identity "e2k7-cas-01\unifiedmessaging (Default Web Site)"
-InternalUrl https://autodiscover.virtuecorp.com/unifiedmessaging/service.asmx -
ExternalUrl https://autodiscover.virtuecorp.com/unifiedmessaging/service.asmx
```

These changes need to be made on all Client Access Servers in your environment. Fortunately, you can run them all from one Exchange Management Shell session by just changing the -Identity value in the commands.

Once all the previous tasks are complete, you can publish a new A record in your external DNS called Autodiscover and point it to the public IP address used by your Client Access Server.

The Last Solution: Using DNS SRV records

Microsoft has released a hotfix for Outlook 2007 that will allow Outlook to search an additional DNS record when attempting to locate the Autodiscover service. This hotfix also requires some additional configuration at the server level. Information on the hotfix is available at http://support.microsoft.com/kb/939184.

PART III

Essentially, the hotfix enables Outlook 2007 to query a DNS SRV record as a last resort of locating the Autodiscover service. Because the Service Connection Point (SCP) provides the information when users are internal, the SRV method is only needed for external Autodiscover.

In your public DNS, remove any host or CNAME records you may have created for Autodiscover.

Next, create a DNS SRV record using the following information:

- **Service**   _autodiscover
- **Protocol**   _tcp
- **Port number**   443
- **Host**   mail.virtuecorp.com

The host parameter should be configured as the name listed in your single-name certificate. This is usually your OWA address, such as mail.virtuecorp.com.

If your external DNS is Windows DNS, the steps would be as follows:

1. Open the DNS Management MMC snap-in.
2. Expand Forward Lookup Zones.
3. Locate and right-click the external DNS zone and then click Other New Records.
4. Click Service Location (SRV).
5. Enter the parameters by using the required values.
6. Click OK.

Once this record is created and your Outlook 2007 clients have the aforementioned hotfix installed, they will check the SRV record if the normal process fails. Here's an example:

1. https://virtuecorp.com/Autodiscover/Autodiscover.xml. This fails.
2. https://autodiscover.virtuecorp.com/Autodiscover/Autodiscover.xml. This fails.
3. http://autodiscover.virtuecorp.com/Autodiscover/Autodiscover.xml. This fails.
4. Autodiscover uses DNS SRV lookup for _autodiscover._tcp.virtuecorp.com, and then "mail.virtuecorp.com" is returned.
5. Outlook then posts a request to mail.virtuecorp.com/Autodiscover/Autodiscover.xml and successfully gets Autodiscover information.

Of course, this requires that all external users are using Outlook 2007 and that you install the hotfix on all external machines.

As you can see, the Autodiscover service is quite complex, but there is a lot of flexibility in how it can be configured to best fit your environment. Once configured, it allows for easier setup and management of Outlook clients, as well as provides more complete information.

Availability Service

In previous versions of Exchange, Free/Busy information was stored in a public folder called the Schedule+ Free/Busy system folder. Clients such as Outlook could then query that public folder for calendar information for other mailboxes.

In Exchange 2007, that information is now accessed as part of an Exchange Web Service called the Availability service. When an Outlook 2007 or Outlook Web Access 2007 client needs to query availability information, it contacts the Availability service URL given to it as part of the Autodiscover exchange. The Availability service then queries the destination mailbox, retrieves the information, and sends it to the scheduling user.

With the new Availability service, you get better, more up-to-date information than with public folders because you don't have replication or latency issues, and you're getting the information from the mailbox itself in real time. The information is always up to date.

Legacy versions of Outlook still use public folders for Free/Busy information, but the two methods can coexist in an Exchange 2007 environment. Remember when you were installing Exchange 2007 and it asked if you had legacy versions of Outlook? If you answered "no," then the related public folders were not created because Outlook 2007 and OWA 2007 don't need them. If you answered "yes," then Exchange setup created an instance of those public folders so that legacy Outlook clients can work.

Outlook 2007 users now have a far more granular opportunity to share their information. Unlike previous versions of Outlook and Exchange, users can specify individuals and/or groups and assign calendar sharing permissions to each. Those permissions, as seen in Figure 8-18, include:

- Share nothing (no access to anything)
- Share Free-Busy information
- Share more detailed info, including subject, location, and time
- Full calendar information

This allows others in, say, your department to be able to see what is on your schedule, and for everyone else to just see if you're busy.

In Outlook 2007, you can attach the calendar to an e-mail message by clicking the Calendar button in the ribbon. The user has the option to send just availability (Free/Busy) information, limited information, or full details, as seen in Figure 8-19.

Cross-site Considerations

When a user attempts to schedule an event with users in other Active Directory sites, the scheduling users' Client Access Server contacts the Client Access Server in the remote site. The CAS box in the remote site then looks up the information either in the users' mailbox (Exchange 2007 mailbox) or in the public folders (legacy Exchange mailbox) via MAPI. Once it has that information, it sends it back to the original Client Access Server over HTTPS, which then sends it to the scheduling user.

PART III

Figure 8-18
Outlook 2007
calendar sharing
options

How the Availability service gets information is dependent on where the source and destination mailboxes reside. Table 8-7 shows how information is retrieved.

To verify that Availability is working and properly configured, we can use the following Test-OutlookWebServices cmdlet and optionally specify a user:

```
Test-OutlookWebServices -identity user@virtuecorp.com | fl
```

Figure 8-19
Outlook 2007
Free/Busy
information added
to an e-mail
message

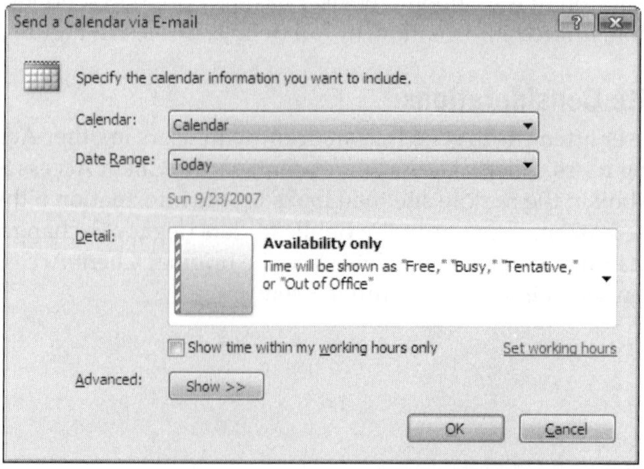

Client	Source Mailbox	Target Mailbox	Free/Busy Retrieval Method
Outlook 2007	Exchange 2007	Exchange 2007	The Availability service reads Free/Busy information from the target mailbox.
Outlook 2007	Exchange 2007	Exchange 2003	The Availability service makes HTTP connections to the /public virtual directory of Exchange 2003 mailbox.
Outlook 2003	Exchange 2007	Exchange 2007	Free/Busy information will be published in local public folders.
Outlook 2003	Exchange 2007	Exchange 2003	Free/Busy information will be published in local public folders.
OWA 2007	Exchange 2007	Exchange 2007	OWA 2007 calls the Availability service API, which reads Free/Busy information from the target mailbox.
OWA 2007	Exchange 2007	Exchange 2003	OWA 2007 calls the Availability service API, which makes an HTTP connection to the /public virtual directory of Exchange 2003 mailbox.
Any	Exchange 2003	Exchange 2007	Free/Busy information will be published in local public folders.

TABLE 8-7   Availability Service Data Retrieval

Many of the issues that pop up in the Test-OutlookWebServices results are certificate related, such as an incorrect URL. For information on the various output parameters that you might see, refer to Table 8-8.

Cross-forest Free/Busy Information Considerations

If you need to have Free/Busy information available to other forests in a cross-forest scenario, where the other forest is not Exchange 2007, you will need to verify that the information is replicated between the forests. For Outlook 2007/Outlook Web Access 2007 users to see the Free/Busy information of Exchange 2003 users in the other forest, use the Add-AvailabilityAddressSpace cmdlet to configure the Availability service. You only need to run it once as part of your Exchange 2007 setup:

```
Add-AvailabilityAddressSpace -ForestName:<forest name such as
fabrikham.com> -AccessMethod:PublicFolder
```

Now let's suppose the two forests are Exchange 2007. If a user in site A requests Free/Busy information for a user in site B, the Availability Service in site A sends a proxy request to the Availability service in site B, gathers the response, and returns the results.

If the two forests have an established trust, the Availability service can request information for a specific user. Additionally, users can specify cross-forest accounts when settings calendar permissions. This allows the user to grant the same granularity of rights as those within the same forest.

PART III

ID	Type	Message
1000	Error	If no Autodiscover URL(s) are available – None on the SCP objects and the autodiscover.domain.com and domain.com are registered.
1001	Warning	Autodiscover can only be connected over a non-SSL connection.
1002	Warning	Supplied a contact's target address to Test-OutlookWebServices.
1003	Information	The e-mail address to be used for Autodiscover.
1004	Error	CLR reports a RemoteCertificateNameMismatch and the server name is not on the SSL certificate.
1005	Error	Other SSL errors, but can also be the same as 1004.
1006	Warning/ error/success	Autodiscover was contacted but returned an error/garbage/worked (depending on Type). (Reports the status for Autodiscover.)
1007	Information	The caller specified a Client Access Server. Test-OutlookWebServices will only use the specified CAS server.
1010	Error	Cannot figure out the identity provided to the task.
1011	Warning/Error	Availability Service threw a warning/error (depending on Type) for a specific Free/Busy response.
1012	Warning	Test-OutlookWebServices did not understand all the XML returned by Autodiscover. Usually, this means there was a change to the Autodiscover protocol but Test-OutlookWebServices was not updated.
1013	Error	An unknown web exception happened while contacting a URL. Possibilities include name resolution issues for the name(s) supplied for some web services.
1017	Error	Usually a certificate error, such as a mismatch, or a missing certificate.

TABLE 8-8   Common Events for Test-OutlookWebServices

When the two forests do not have an established trust, the conventional Free/Busy information is all that is available.

Summary

As we've seen in this chapter, the Client Access Server role has many features. The Exchange Team did a great job of giving us more granular control over the parameters of the server, and the ways that users can access information. With new methods such as WebReady Document Reading and Direct File Access, and streamlined features such as Outlook Anywhere, the physical boundaries of a business are no longer a boundary to doing business. By incorporating new features such as Autodiscover service, Availability service, ActiveSync policies, and others, administrators can streamline the deployment of devices and clients more easily.

Administering Unified Messaging Servers

The new Unified Messaging server role in Exchange Server 2007 extends the functionality of your Exchange messaging infrastructure, allowing it to transmit and store more than just traditional e-mail. As more established communication solutions (voice and fax) find a new life on IP networks, a new means of storing and facilitating access to the information is required. The Unified Messaging (UM) server role provides that capability natively in your Exchange 2007 organization. From a user's perspective, Unified Messaging provides easy access to voice messages, faxes, and e-mail in way that was simply not possible before Unified Messaging. This chapter will help you understand what Unified Messaging is by describing the voice, fax, and e-mail technologies that the Unified Messaging role supports. And, to help you with your implementation of Unified Messaging, this chapter details the process of deploying the Unified Messaging server role and the steps to configure and administer the UM server and UM clients.

Understanding Unified Messaging

Before you plan for and implement Unified Messaging, you will want to become familiar with the technologies you will be working with. Voice and fax technologies are traditionally analog technologies, whereas e-mail has always been a digital technology. Because of the vast difference between the analog world and the digital world, the ability for the average organization to merge the technologies only came about circa 1997. The first environments to adopt technology to send digitally encoded voice communications were the telecom companies. This was done to improve the quality of voice communications across long distances (long-hauls) and to reduce the cost of those connections. Today a number of commercial solutions provide digitally encoded voice communications. These technologies and associated protocols are generally referred to as *Voice over Internet Protocol*, or *VoIP*. VoIP is allowing organizations to unify their communications infrastructures. Microsoft Exchange 2007 Unified Messaging does utilize VoIP. Unified Messaging is only part of an overall Unified Communications strategy. Although Unified Communications refers to the new digital forms of voice, fax, and more, a Unified Messaging solution is the storage and retrieval solution for the digitized voice, fax, and e-mail messages. E-mail systems such as Exchange are attractive back-end solutions for centrally storing (unifying) all types of messages that a knowledge worker uses.

A Brief History of Unified Messaging

The introduction of Unified Messaging to Exchange could not have happened at a worse time. In 1999 Microsoft laid out their first strategy for supporting Unified Messaging on the soon-to-be-released Exchange 2000 Server, code-named Platinum. Vendors such as Lucent were lining up to take advantage of Microsoft's improvements to their storage system to handle the additional load of voice and fax data. Studies from analysts such as the Radicati Group showed that companies that used Unified Messaging technologies could regain up to 30 minutes a day in individual user productivity and save 70% in administrative costs by replacing the traditional voicemail and faxing solutions with the existing messaging infrastructure.

So why has it taken so many years for Unified Messaging to really start taking off? Well, in 2000 when Unified Messaging would have flourished, IT departments had to stand back and rethink the adoption of untested technologies due the burst of the dot-com bubble. However, it is not entirely fair to blame this on the economy alone. There are other reasons as well, including the slow adoption of digital-based voice communications (VoIP) solutions due to cost and quality-of-service issues. The slow adoption of Unified Messaging has not hindered the development of communication technologies. And UM has taken on new life in 2007 with the inclusion of support for Unified Communications and Unified Messaging in Microsoft Exchange 2007 and Office Communications Server 2007. For more details on Office Communications Server 2007, see Chapter 13.

Voice Primer for Exchange Administrators

Voice and e-mail technologies not only differ in how they work, they differ in how they are administered. Perhaps the most difficult part of deploying a Unified Messaging solution is bridging the knowledge gap between the voice system administrators and the Exchange administrators. When the voice system administrators in an organization do not understand Exchange and the Exchange administrators do not understand the voice systems, it does not necessarily help to bring the two together on a Unified Messaging project. One side or the other is going to have to give in and learn the other technology so there is common ground. Because this book is written for the Exchange 2007 administrator, the following will serve as a primer for voice communication systems. This primer only covers the information and terminology that is essential to know in order to implement a Unified Messaging server role. You should supplement this information with the documentation provided by your voice system's vendor. Each vendor will likely have proprietary technology that falls outside the scope of this chapter.

Voicemail is the primary voice system that the Exchange Unified Messaging Server role replaces. Call management still requires a Private Branch Exchange (PBX). Voicemail is commonly associated with PBXs, which are premise-based (business) phone systems. Voicemail was a feature created from necessity. Voicemail was conceived and demonstrated in the 1970s, many years before it became commercially viable. The first commercial solutions did not appear until the 1980s, when a product called VMX was successfully adopted by many big name companies. It was limited in its ability to work with only internal voice messages, and provisioning new users and making changes were very difficult. A company called Octel really brought voicemail to the masses in the 1990s. Although legacy PBXs have the ability to forward calls to other extensions, they do not have the ability to prompt a caller to leave a voicemail or convert the caller's voice to a digital format. Prior to voicemail systems, calls had to be routed to phone extensions where dedicated operators resided. A number of companies filled this niche for many years by providing organizations with call-answering services. In fact, when voicemail systems began to rise in popularity, the telecom companies were prohibited by federal regulations from using voicemail systems in order to prevent them from putting the call-answering services out of business. When this restriction was eliminated in the mid 1980s, all the carriers began to offer voicemail solutions.

Voicemail systems were designed to mimic e-mail systems. They provide storage and retrieval mechanisms for voice messages. The voicemail solutions digitize the messages left by callers and then replay the messages back to the intended recipients. Integrating a PBX with the corporate e-mail system is a logical evolution for voicemail. For a voice messaging system to work properly, it must be able to communicate with the PBX and send and receive signals to the PBX and signals to desktop sets (phones) via the PBX. Prior to Exchange Server 2007, e-mail systems did not have native voicemail capabilities. Prior to Exchange 2007, leaders in the voice industry provided the only Unified Messaging solutions that could store voice messages on an Exchange server.

PBX/Voicemail Architecture

A PBX allows a few inbound phone lines to be used by a large number of people within an organization by managing and logging each call. The PBX is also used by the voicemail solution in the process of storing and retrieving voicemail. Many organizations, and possibly yours, will need to connect Exchange 2007 Unified Messaging to a legacy PBX. Figure 9-1 shows how the legacy PBX and legacy voicemail systems interoperate.

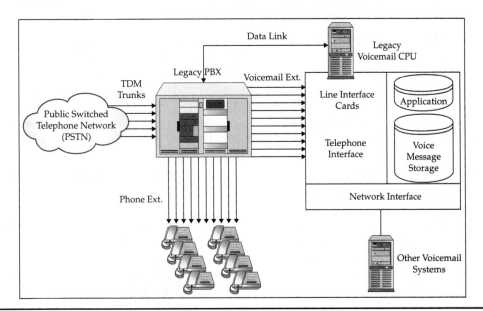

FIGURE 9-1 Legacy PBX and voicemail

The following walkthrough of the inbound voicemail process will help you understand how the legacy PBX and voicemail systems are integrated:

1. An inbound call from the PSTN comes across a TDM trunk.

2. The PBX routes the call to the specified extension.

3. When there is no answer after an administrative-defined number of rings, the call is forwarded to a voicemail extension.

4. PBX sends a command across the data link to the voicemail CPU, to prompt the inbound call with the target's voicemail message.

5. The voicemail CPU instructs the telephone interface to answer the call.

6. The CPU application plays the voicemail prompt and the application-specific prompts.

7. The CPU application listens for any keystrokes from the caller. The voice message is digitized from the incoming analog voice stream. Then, when the caller hangs up or specifies the end of the voice message, the CPU application stores the voice message.

8. When the call is complete, the voicemail system sends a command to the PBX via the data link to turn on the Message Waiting Indicator for that phone extension.

A similar process ensues when a person checks their e-mail. The key to a sophisticated voicemail system is in the application's ease of use. Is it easy to navigate the voice prompts? Does the application provide a range of playback and storage options? The best systems do that—and then some.

Voice System Terminology

We have already used some voice system terminology that may seem like a foreign language to an Exchange administrator. Reviewing the following comprehensive list of voice system terms will help you during your deployment of Unified Messaging:

- **Public Switched Telephone Network (PSTN)**   A term that represents the worldwide collection of publicly available phone networks run by private corporations and governments. One connotation of the term implies the circuit-switching (legacy) portion of the public network. However, today the PSTN is a combination of both circuit-switching and packet-switching technologies.

- **Private Branch Exchange (PBX)**   Voice system that enables companies to manage incoming calls by sharing a small number of outside phone lines among many internal extensions.

- **Time-Division Multiplexing (TDM)**   TDM is used to allow multiple connections to exist on the same circuit-switched network. The PSTN still contains many circuit-switched networks.

- **Trunk**   A connection that consists of multiple individual TDM-based links, aggregated to increase the overall bandwidth.

- **VoIP trunking**   A way of providing scalable long-haul phone connections using high-bandwidth WAN connections to interconnect PBXs in a corporation through VoIP gateways. This concept is used at the carrier level for the logon hauls between PSTNs. H.323, SIP, Media Gateway Control Protocol (MGCP), and Inter-Asterisk Exchange (IAX) are some of the supported trunking protocols.

- **Message Waiting Indicator (MWI)**   PBXs that support voicemail systems that support MWI signaling requests to allow individual phone extensions to know that there is a message wafting for them on the voicemail system.

- **Interactive Voice Response (IVR)**   IVR extends the functionality of a voicemail system by allowing the application to understand voice requests and dial tones (DTMF) from callers. Microsoft UM has a built-in IVR.

- **Quality of Service (QoS)**   A protocol used on IP networks to set the priority of data packets used by bandwidth-sensitive applications such as VoIP.

- **Call Forward No Answer (CFNA)**   A setting on a PBX designed to forward mail to a legacy voicemail system. Can be configured to forward calls to a VoIP gateway instead.

- **Voice over Internet Protocol (VoIP)**   A general term used to describe various methods of digital voice communications across an IP network.

- **VoIP gateways**   Network devices that connect local PSTNs that use TDM circuit-switching to an IP-based packet-switching backbone. These devices are required to connect Exchange 2007 Unified Messaging servers to legacy PBX systems.

- **Session Initiation Protocol (SIP)**   SIP is used as a means for an IP phone to establish a connection to a VoIP gateway or Digital PBX (call manager). SIP is also used by the VoIP gateway to connect to the Exchange UM server.

- **Real-time Transport Protocol (RTP)**   Protocol for creating and transmitting the data packets that contain audio and or video communications. RTP is used after SIP establishes a session.

- **Uniform Resource Identifier (URI)**   Used by SIP to uniquely identify each client.

- **Digital Set Emulation (DSE)**   A feature of some VoIP gateways that emulates digital phone sets, so the PBX views the gateway as different phone sets on the same hunt group and handles the connections and requests (transfer/receive call) as a phone set.

- **Hunt group**   Also known as *hunting*, a hunt group is a method of forwarding calls from a single inbound number to a group of extensions. The three methods of hunting are circular, linear, and most-idle.

- **Pilot number**   Phone number assigned to a hunt group for inbound calls.

- **T1 Channel Associated Signaling (CAS)**   Used by some legacy PBXs to transmit control signaling data between the PBX and the voicemail system on the same channel as the data.

- **T1 Q Signaling (Q.SIG)**   Q Signaling is an ISDN-based protocol. Used by some legacy PBXs to transmit data between the PBX and the voicemail system. Also used for PBX-to-PBX interoperability.

- **Integrated Services Digital Network (ISDN)**   A dedicated WAN connection between an Internet or telecom provider and a subscriber. Can be used for voice or data.

- **Basic Rate Interface (BRI)**   A method of provisioning a dedicated ISDN line for voice communications or data communications. This configuration consists of two B channels for voice or data and a D channel for signaling information. Used for small business and home users.

PART III

- **Primary Rate Interface (PRI)**   A method of provisioning a dedicated T1 or E1 for voice or data communications. T1 PRI has a maximum capacity of 23 B channels for voice or data and one D channel for signaling. E1 PRI has a max of 30 B channels on ISDN circuits, for voice or data and one D channel for signaling. Used for large enterprises.

- **B channel**   Bearer channel with a data rate of 64 kilobits per second (Kbps). Each B channel could classically bear the TDM digital form of one analog voice call. For data purposes, multiple B channels may be aggregated for greater combined data rates.

- **D channel**   Delta channel for signaling changes, status updates, and command initiation associated with the B channels that are provisioned along with the D channel. For BRI, the D channel is 16 Kbps whereas for PRI the D channel is 64 Kbps (like a B channel).

- **T.38**   A standard for supporting fax communications. It specifies how to send an audio packet through a data network, similarly to G.711. T.38 describes the process of converting analog connections from the telephone company to the PBX into encoded voice between the PBX and VoIP gateway. Exchange UM supports T.38.

- **Simplified Message Desk Interface (SMDI)**   A legacy method for a phone system to provide voice messaging systems with the information necessary to process incoming calls. Usually communicated across a dedicated data link cable.

- **Audio codec**   A computer program that compresses as well as decompresses digital audio data according to a given audio file format. Voicemail systems do not require the same frequency range or quality as music audio codec.

- **Speech compression**   Specialized audio codec for voice files. Early speed compression codecs include G.711 A-Law and G.711 mu-Law (µ-Law) pulse-code modulation (PCM). The most widely used speed compression method today is Code Excited Linear Prediction (CELP). This can be seen in standards such as GSM and WMA. Decisions on which codecs are used affect the quality and performance of a voice messaging system.

- **Dual-tone Multifrequency (DTMF)**   A standard that defines the sound frequencies generated when each key is pressed on a phone. This is also commonly referred to as *touchtone inputs*. DTMF is used by voicemail systems to allow callers to navigate Auto Attendant menus and subscribers to retrieve messages from the system.

- **Telephone user interface (TUI)**   The voicemail interface available from a standard analog, digital, or cellular telephone.

- **Voice User Interface (VUI)**   A voicemail system that can interpret voice commands has a Voice User Interface that parallels the telephone user interface. The VUI depends on the Automatic Speech Recognition (ASR) service to interpret speech input from a caller.

- **Automatic Speech Recognition (ASR)**   A feature of Unified Messaging that allows an Outlook Voice Access user to move through the mailbox menus by using voice commands.

- **Text to Speech (TTS)**   The component of the Unified Messaging architecture that reads e-mail, voicemail, and calendar items, and plays the menu prompts for callers.

Exchange Unified Messaging Features

Exchange 2007 Unified Messaging is more than a substitute for an existing voicemail system. Besides the basic voicemail functionality that can be expected of any voicemail system, the following unique features make Exchange's UM Server attractive:

- Outlook Voice Access
- Outlook Calendar Access
- Directory and Personal Contacts Access
- Outlook and OWA Voicemail Form
- Auto Attendant

Outlook Voice Access

A phone system is recognizable to most people by the phones used to place calls. Today this includes analog phones, digital phones, cellular phones, satellite phones, and VoIP phones. The keypad interface we are familiar with using to place calls, accept calls, and check for messages is called the telephone user interface (TUI). Exchange 2007 Unified Messaging extends the phone user interface to include voice commands and voice menus. This additional interface is called the *voice user interface (VUI)*. Microsoft refers to both interfaces from the Exchange 2007 UM server as simply *Outlook Voice Access (OVA)*. It makes sense then that the primary Unified Messaging client will still be phones.

The only command that cannot be entered by voice is the subscriber's PIN. Currently OVA only supports the English language for voice commands. But it can be customized to support phonetic version of users' names that do not sound like they are spelled. A text-to-speech engine is built into the UM server to allow e-mail message to be read from a users mailbox. The text-to-speech feature is available for languages other than English, including Portuguese (Brazilian), Dutch, French, German, Italian, Japanese, Korean, Mandarin Chinese, Spanish, and Swedish. This feature is smart enough to know which one to use based on the content of an e-mail.

Outlook Voice Access allows a phone to be a Unified Messaging client. A UM-enabled user can call into their company's UM server and access the following:

- Voicemail
- E-mail
- Calendar
- Contacts
- Meeting requests
- Out-of-office messages settings
- Security settings
- Personalization settings

To secure access to voicemail, Exchange associates a personal identification number (PIN) with each subscriber. Although this is an attribute on the user object, it is not the same as the user's password. Users can change their PINs on their own without administrative assistance.

Outlook Calendar Access

UM phone users can connect to their calendars and listen to their upcoming schedule. Appointments can be added, modified, or cancelled by phone. Responses can be made to meeting requests. In fact, it is also possible for a subscriber to notify other participants of a meeting that they are running late by sending an "I'll be late" message from their phone. This has been one of the more popular demonstrations that Microsoft is using to bring awareness to Unified Messaging at technical conferences and sales events.

Directory and Personal Contacts Access

Because UM is integrated with Active Directory and Exchange, UM clients have additional contact lookup capabilities. The Global Address List, which contains all Exchange recipients in Active Directory, and Outlook contacts, which are stored in each user's mailbox, are fully accessible to the UM clients. Using a keypad on a phone or a voice command, users can search for a contact. Once a contact has been found, the user can use the contact's phone number to send a voicemail, place a call to one of their listed numbers, or just listen to their contact information, such as the business address.

Outlook and OWA Voicemail Form

Although Unified Messaging has transformed what a phone can be, it has also transformed what an e-mail client can be. In fact, the line has been so blurred between the two that it no longer matters if you use a phone or a computer for any form of messaging. It is simply a matter of preference and convenience. Unified Messaging extends the functionality of the e-mail client by adding a new form specifically for voicemail messages in a user's mailbox. The new form provides a number of options for reviewing voicemails from Outlook and Outlook Web Access. Because voicemails contain audio, the voicemail form contains controls similar to a media player, allowing users to perform the following tasks:

- Play a voicemail on speakers/headphones
- Stop a voicemail
- Pause a voicemail
- Play voicemail on a telephone
- Add and edit notes

The voicemail form is only compatible with Outlook 2007 and Outlook Web Access 2007, as shown in Figure 9-2 from one of Microsoft's Virtual Hard Drives (VHD). To obtain the Exchange Server 2007 SP1 VHD go to http://www.microsoft.com/downloads/details .aspx?FamilyID=43621a8f-12fb-4e7c-bb38-lcbb6ef272c5&DisplayLang=en. If an incompatible client receives a voicemail, it will appear as an attachment to an e-mail. The attachment can be played back with windows Media Player or another audio player.

Auto Attendant

Today's global economy opens opportunities for businesses to serve customers around the globe. Both small and large businesses alike are dependent on having a phone system that can respond to calls on a 24/7 basis in order to maintain good customer relationships and

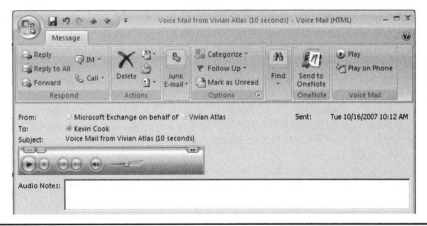

FIGURE 9-2   Outlook 2007 voicemail form

participate in the global marketplace. The Auto Attendant in the Exchange Unified Messaging Server allows an organization to do the following:

- Create customized menus
- Define custom greetings
- Add holiday schedules
- Provide help with searching the voice directory
- Provide help with connecting to a user's extension
- Provide help with searching the directory for a specific user
- Define an operator extension

Each of these are voice prompts stored as WAV files that take the place of a dedicated person answering inbound phone calls. The Auto Attendant can respond to input from a caller. The input could be in the form of DTMF from a keypad or speech inputs from the caller. The best part is, the Auto Attendant never has to go home.

Exchange Unified Messaging Architecture

The Exchange Unified Messaging architecture is quite different from the legacy voicemail systems. There are three major components in the architecture: Microsoft Exchange Unified Messaging Service, Unified Messaging Worker Process, and the Speech Engine Services. Figure 9-3 details the architecture.

In terms of running processes on the UM server, the architecture is based on two executables: UMservice.exe and SpeechService.exe. The executable UMService.exe spawns UMWorkerProcess.exe and is responsible for voice and fax message access and storage in the

Exchange 2007 mailbox store. The executable SpeechService.exe spawns the SESWorker.exe worker process and is responsible for DTMF, ASR, and TTS. The UM Worker Process Manager starts each of the UM worker processes defined for the UM server and monitors their activity. The UM Worker Process Manager is responsible for directing inbound calls to the correct UM worker process. Each UM worker process works with the speech worker process to process all requests made to the UM server. Communications to and from the UM server are established using SIP over TCP. This is different from many other VoIP solutions from other vendors. Most other vendors use SIP over UDP. The UM server listens for communications on port 5060 (unsecured) and port 5061(MTLS). Service Pack 1 allows the UM server to listen to both ports simultaneously. The worker processes listen for communications on TCP port 5056 and 5066 (unsecured). Service Pack 1 allows the worker processes to listen on 5057 and 5058 for secure connections. The RTP traffic that carries voice input from an IP gateway will use UDP ports 1024–65535. The UM worker process also contains a fax service provider that uses UDTL and the T.38 protocol to receive inbound faxes.

SP1 *Service Pack 1 improves the security of the UM architecture by extending support for secure connections.*

Microsoft Unified Messaging cannot communicate directly with a legacy PBX. It is necessary to use an IP gateway device between the Unified Messaging server and the legacy PBX. However, if an organization has deployed an IP PBX, there is a chance an IP gateway

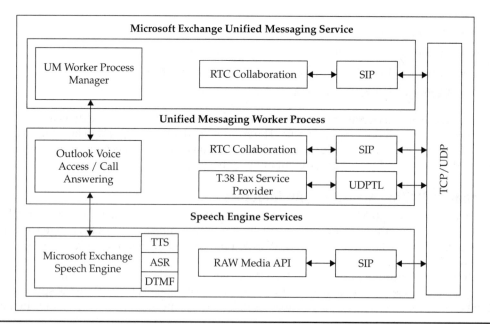

Figure 9-3 Exchange 2007 Unified Messaging architecture

is unnecessary if the IP PBX is compatible with the Exchange 2007 Unified Messaging server. Figure 9-4 shows how the Exchange Unified Messaging server integrates with both types of PBXs. Note that the connection from the IP PBX to an IP gateway device is necessary if Exchange 2007 does not support the IP PBX.

The "Inbound Call Handling" and "Retrieving Messages with OVA" sections illustrate how the IP PBX and the legacy PBX integrate with the Exchange 2007 Unified Messaging server.

Inbound Call Handling

The inbound call handling steps performed by the UM server role:

1. An external caller dials a UM user's phone number on the PSTN.

2. The UM user's office phone rings for a preset number of times.

3. The legacy PBX routes the call to the IP gateway or the IP PBX establishes a direct VoIP connection to UM server.

4. The IP gateway identifies an available UM server. Once the UM server is determined, the voice input is converted to VoIP: SIP and RTP.

5. The UM server queries AD to determine the mailbox server of the recipient by filtering for a user with the extension specified by the caller.

6. The UM server plays the user's greeting, encodes the voice message, and attaches it to an e-mail.

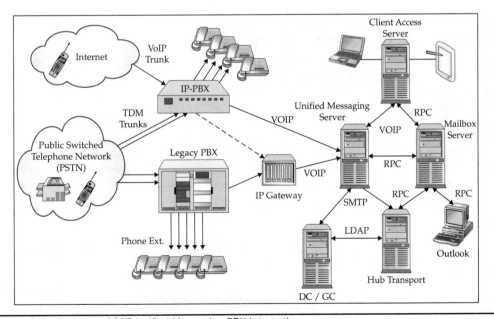

FIGURE 9-4 Exchange 2007 Unified Messaging PBX integration

7. The UM server sends the message to a Hub Transport server.

8. The Hub Transport server in the same Active Directory site as the user's mailbox server submits the voicemail/e-mail to the database where the user's mailbox data is stored.

Retrieving Messages with OVA

The process to retrieve a voice mail from the UM server role:

1. The UM user dials a preconfigured OVA call-in number from the PSTN.

2. The legacy PBX routes the call to the IP gateway or the IP PBX establishes a direct VoIP connection to UM server.

3. OVA requests the user's extension number and PIN.

4. OVA queries AD to determine which mailbox database belongs to the UM user and to validate the PIN.

5. The UM server waits for input from the user. When a request for a message is made, the appropriate menu of options is presented.

6. If the user request that the message is read, the Text-To-Speech engine will read the mail header and content (it cannot read the attachments to the e-mail).

7. The UM server retrieves the message from the Mailbox server role and plays the voice message.

For more details on PBXs, see "PBX and IP Gateways vs. IP PBXs" later in this chapter.

Deploying Unified Messaging Servers

The Unified Messaging role can be installed as a standalone server role. It can also be installed with the Hub Transport, Client Access Server, and/or Mailbox server roles, but not clustered Mailbox server roles. Dedicating hardware to the Unified Messaging server will make it easier to properly size the hardware required for your environment. Microsoft's deployment of Unified Messaging servers in North America supports 30,000 users on only five dedicated Unified Messaging servers. To deploy Unified Messaging in your Exchange 2007 environment, you need to carefully consider a number of factors from the number of Unified Messaging users, and the type of features you will provide them to the voice codec you select. For more information on the requirements and processes for installing Exchange Server 2007, see Chapter 4.

Hardware

Consider the hardware requirements for the UM server role. Table 9-1 shows the recommended processor and memory configurations from Microsoft.

Resource	Minimum	Recommended	Maximum
Processor	One core	Four cores	Four cores
Memory	2GB	1GB per core	4GB

TABLE 9-1 Unified Messaging Serve Role Processor and Memory Requirements

As a general rule of thumb and a default limit, a single Unified Messaging server can support up to 100 simultaneous connections for phone calls and 100 for inbound fax connections. The server can be configured to support twice that number of connections for phone calls and faxes, respectively, but the hardware would need to be scaled up to support that load. It is suggested that if you need to scale a Unified Messaging server for more than 100 connections that you add more Unified Messaging server roles to your organization. If you need to adjust the number, you can change it to a value between 0 and 200. You will need to use cmdlets like these:

```
[PS]C:\>Set-UmServer -Identity OCS-EX1 -MaxCallsAllowed 70
and
[PS]C:\>Set-UmServer -Identity OCS-EX1 -MaxFaxCallsAllowed 60
```

Microsoft recommends that you configure a Unified Messaging server role with four processor cores to support the processor intensive conversion of voice messages to digital files. Disk requirements are nominal because there is no critical data stored on the Unified Messaging server, expect during the processing of voice and fax messages. The factor that impacts scalability the most is the size of the voicemail messages. Voice messages can vary in size depending on the codec used by the IP gateway and Exchange 2007. The Exchange Unified Messaging server role supports WMA, GSM 0.610, and PCM G.711. Each codec has different storage formats. WMA generates .wma files whereas the others generate .wav files. The longer the voice message, the larger the file attachment will be when it is delivered to the recipient's mailbox. Choosing a codec that keeps the size of long messages down, while keeping the integrity of the voice message, is essential to UM's performance. Next to WMA, GSM 06.10 has the best compression, but GSM uses an 8-bit sampling rate whereas WMA and G.711 use a 16-bit rate. The bit rate directly impacts the quality of the voice message (16-bit is better than 8-bit). WMA is a Microsoft proprietary codec and is the recommended codec as long as the IP gateway UM connection supports it as well.

If you use WMA, you can anticipate supporting up to 60 concurrent calls on each of your Unified Messaging servers and 75 concurrent calls if you use GSM. With that in mind, Microsoft estimates that it is possible to support a minimum of 2000 users and a maximum of 10,000 users per server, depending on the volume of messages and the length of the messages. It is important to note that a user who is making an inbound call to leave a voicemail (unauthenticated user) actually uses fewer resources on a Unified Messaging server than a user who calls in to check their voicemails (authenticated user) via OVA.

Deployment Process

The size of an organization and the complexity of the existing phone system affect the amount of time the deployment of Unified Messaging will take. The process of deploying Unified Messaging in an organization is custom built by administrators to meet the organization's needs. However, there are some lessons you can learn from what others have already deployed for Unified Messaging. For example, Microsoft documented their deployment of Unified Messaging in a showcase article titled, "Using Exchange Server 2007 for Unified Messaging." They devised a deployment process that allowed them to not only implement Unified Messaging, but also to integrate with a variety of PBXs and migrate off of the third-party Unified Messaging solutions that they have been using for many years. Here are the high-level phases to the process they utilized:

- **Preparation phase**   Install the Exchange UM server, configure the PBX, and gather all the required data for installation: IP addresses, hunt group, and operator numbers. Identify test users group.

- **Procurement phase**   Procure the gateway, cables, patch panels, interface cards, and other hardware.

- **Gateway installation and configuration phase**   Install IP gateways. Configure, test, and validate the installation.

- **UM server integration phase**   Configure the IP gateway with the UM partner servers with which the IP gateway can communicate.

- **Testing phase**   Use a test account and detailed checklists to test and verify that all UM components are operational.

- **Pilot number and production rollout phase**   Create a pilot number to use with the PBX and IP gateway. Verify that when the pilot number is dialed that the PBX forwards it to the IP gateway with call details. After successful testing, roll out UM services to users.

- **User support and education phase**   Live testing with test user group. Document any issues that arise during live testing. Make changes to configurations as necessary. Communicate changes to the users along with timeframes and options. Provide documentation with step-by-step procedures for user self-service, such as PIN resets.

Unified Messaging Coexistence and Migrations

When you have an established voicemail system or Unified Messaging system, you will have to determine how and when the transition to Exchange 2007 Unified Messaging will occur. Among the factors to weigh are the connectivity, signaling integration, and PBX requirements for each site as well as the IP gateway options. Because existing solutions may have more or fewer features than Exchange 2007 Unified Messaging, it may be necessary to keep some of the legacy components around to support your current service levels. Some of the additional considerations are:

- PBX integration
- IP gateway selection
- Consolidation
- Fax integration
- System monitoring
- Security

Table 9-2 can be used to help you evaluate how you should transition. The options are to stage your migration or to perform an overnight migration.

Migration Considerations	Overnight	Staged
All hardware must be implemented at once.	X	
Hardware can be deployed over time.		X
User migration can occur in phases.		X
Requires configuration and testing.	X	X
User education required prior to migration.	X	
User support and education occurs in line with migration.		X
Can monitor system capacity and performance for design miscalculations before they reach critical mass.		X
Allows periodic issue resolution.		X
Can pilot with smaller set of users.		X

TABLE 9-2   Overnight Migration vs. Staged Migration

PBX and IP Gateways vs. IP PBXs

Unified Messaging server roles are deployed as part of the Exchange 2007 Server deployment. The Unified Messaging role need only be added with the default configurations during the server installation. However, before the UM server can be configured to receive calls, a VoIP solution must be in place. Two VoIP solutions are supported by the Unified Messaging role with the RTM version of Exchange 2007. You can have a legacy PBX connected to an IP gateway or you can use a supported IP PBX. In short, a three-step process is used to integrate UM with a VoIP solution: Install the UM Server role, install and configure the IP gateway with the legacy PBX or install an IP PBX, and then configure the UM Server role to use the IP gateway or IP PBX.

Legacy PBX and IP Gateways

Legacy PBXs vary greatly. Your choice of an IP gateway should be based on its support for the legacy PBX. The critical features that need to be supported by the IP gateway are:

- **Line provisioning type**   T1 PRI CAS trunk, T1 PRI, ISDN BRI, individual voice lines.
- **Signaling integration**   SMDI, Q.SIG, or digital set emulation (DSE). Q.SIG and DSE have built-in signaling integration. T1 CAS requires SMDI for signaling.
- **Line call plan**   Settings on the PBX that define the supported call scope. This can be as broad as worldwide and as limited as internal calls only.
- **Hunt group/pilot number**   If existing hunt groups and pilot numbers are in place from an existing solution, consider whether you want to reuse voicemail numbers or create new ones.

Vendor	IP Gateway	Supported Protocols
AudioCodes	MediaPack 114/8 FXO	Analog with In-Band DTMF Analog with SMDI
AudioCodes	Mediant 1000	T1/E1 Q.SIG
AudioCodes	Mediant 2000	T1/E1 CAS T1/E1 Q.SIG
Dialogic	PIMG80PBXDNI	Digital Set Emulation
Dialogic	PIMG80LS	Analog with In-Band DTMF Analog with SMDI
Dialogic	TIMG300DTI, TIMG600DTI	T1 CAS T1/E1 Q.SIG

TABLE 9-3   Supported IP Gateways

It is important to review the, "PBX Configuration Notes – Tested by Microsoft or Gateway Vendor Partners," at http://www.microsoft.com/technet/prodtechnol/exchange/pbx-partners.mspx to locate the configuration notes document for the PBX and IP gateway that you will be using. These documents are created by the vendor specifically to show how to configure their devices to work with your PBX. Reviewing the capabilities of these documents prior to purchasing an IP gateway is recommended so you can make an informed decision. The supported IP gateways are listed in Table 9-3.

IP PBX

The IP PBXs that are supported by Exchange 2007 Unified Messaging Server are few and far between. However, the list is expected to grow as adoption of Unified Messaging increases. The key to their integration is support for SIP over TCP. Table 9-4 lists the currently supported IP PBXs.

PBX Manufacturer	PBX Model/Type	Minimum Software Version
Avaya	Avaya Communication Manager	V2.0
Cisco	CallManager	5.0, 5.1
Interactive Intelligence	Customer Interaction Center	2.4
Mitel	3300 CXi, CX/MXe	7.1 UR2
Nortel Networks	CS 1000 (a.k.a. CS1K)	5.0

TABLE 9-4   Supported IP PBXs

Configuring Unified Messaging Servers

After the PBX has been integrated with an IP gateway or an IP PBX has been deployed, you will need to integrate the Unified Messaging server with the IP gateway or IP PBX. Although a number of administrative tasks can be performed from the Exchange Management Console (EMC), you may want to review the cmdlets available for administering the Unified Messaging servers and UM users from the Exchange Management Shell (EMS) shown in Table 9-5.

Integrating Unified Messaging servers with a VoIP solution requires a minimum number of configurations performed in a specific order. These steps should be performed after the gateway and legacy PBX or IP PBX have been tested and are functioning:

1. Create a dial plan.

2. Create a UM IP gateway.

3. Create a UM mailbox plan.

4. Create a UM hunt.

5. Create UM dialing rules.

6. Assign UM dialing rules to the dial plan and to the mailbox policy.

7. Generate GAL Grammar.

Following this procedure will guarantee that you have meet the prerequisite(s) for each step you are performing in sequence.

Get-UMActiveCalls	New-UMDialplan	Disable-UMAutoAttendant
Get-UMAutoAttendant	New-UMAutoAttendant	Disable-UMIPGateway
Get-UMDialplan	Set-UMServer	Enable-UMIPGateway
Get-UMHuntGroup	Set-UMAutoAttendant	Enable-UMMailbox
Get-UMIPGateway	Set-UMMailbox	Enable-UMAutoAttendant
Get-UMMailbox	Set-UMMailboxPolicy	Enable-UMServer
Get-UMMailboxPIN	Set-UMMailboxPIN	Remove-UMHuntGroup
Get-UMMailboxPolicy	Set-UMIPGateway	Remove-UMAutoAttendant
Get-UMServer	Set-UMDialplan	Remove-UMIPGateway
New-UMIPGateway	Test-UMConnectivity	Remove-UMDialplan
New-UMHuntGroup	Disable-UMMailbox	Remove-UMMailboxPolicy
New-UMMailboxPolicy	Disable-UMServer	

TABLE 9-5   Unified Messaging Cmdlets (Service Pack 1)

Dial Plans

A UM dial plan defines a link from the telephone extension number of a user to the corresponding UM-enabled mailbox. Regions around the world have different access numbers and extension patterns. Dial plans allow you to specify unique dialing rules for different locations in your organization. UM dial plans store the configuration information necessary to communicate with the telephony system in Active Directory. Each UM dial plan has an associated UM mailbox policy.

SP1 The New Dial Plan Wizard is enhanced in SP1. This allows you to configure the URI type and VoIP security level.

Creating a Dial Plan

Use the following steps to create a new Dial Plan:

1. Open the Exchange Management Console with an administrator account that has the Exchange Organization Administrator role.

2. Expand Organization Configuration and select Unified Messaging.

3. Select New UM Dial Plan in the Actions pane.

4. Type the name of the dial plan in the Name field, as shown next.

5. Enter a value that matches the number of digits in your users' extensions in the field Number of digits in extension numbers. The default is 5.

6. Select the option in the URI Type drop-down list that is recommended by your IP gateway or IP PBX vendor. The options are:

   - Telephone Extension (Default)
   - E.164
   - SIP URI

7. Choose a security method from the VoIP security drop-down list. The options are:

   - SIP secured
   - Unsecured (default)
   - Secured

8. Click New.

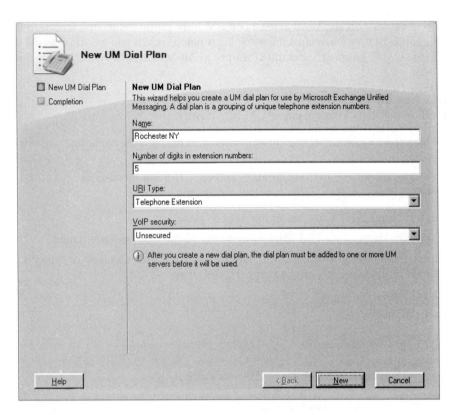

9. Click Finish.

As an alternative to the EMC, you can also use the New-UMDialplan cmdlet in the EMS, like in this example:

```
[PS]C:\>New-UMDialplan -Name "Rochester NY" -NumberofDigits 5
```

If you do not choose a URI type or a VoIP security option, the default values will be used.

UM IP Gateway

The IP gateway must be identified in the UM IP gateway object configuration for the UM server to be able to communicate with it. It is possible to configure the UM IP gateway object in Active Directory to use an IP address or the Fully Qualified Domain Name (FQDN) of the physical IP gateway device. If you use the FQDN, there must be a corresponding DNS host (A) record so that the UM server can resolve the FQDN to an IP address. This address is used by the Session Initiation Protocol (SIP) to establish each session between the IP gateway and the Unified Messaging server. Integrating voice with a data network does increase its exposure to data network vulnerabilities. For additional security, the Unified Messaging server is configured with a list of trusted SIP peers. If a SIP connection attempt is made from an untrusted SIP peer, the connection attempt will be blocked and a 1187 event will be logged.

After configuring the UM IP gateway object, you can associate it with the UM dial plan you created first. Be sure to verify that there is a UM server configured for the UM dial plan.

The UM IP gateway will also need at least one UM hunt group associated with it so that it knows the range of user extensions it covers. Fortunately, when you associate a UM dial plan with the UM IP gateway, a default UM hunt group will also be created if one does not already exist.

Creating a New UM IP Gateway

Use the following steps to create a new UM IP Gateway:

1. Open the EMC with an administrator account that has the Exchange Organization Administrator role.

2. Expand Organization Configuration and click Unified Messaging.

3. Click the UM IP Gateways tab.

4. Select New UM IP Gateway in the Actions pane.

5. Type the name of the UM IP gateway in the Name field, as shown next.

6. Type the IP address for the UM IP gateway in the IP Address field or type the FQDN in the Fully qualified domain name (FQDN) field.

7. Click New.

8. Click Finish.

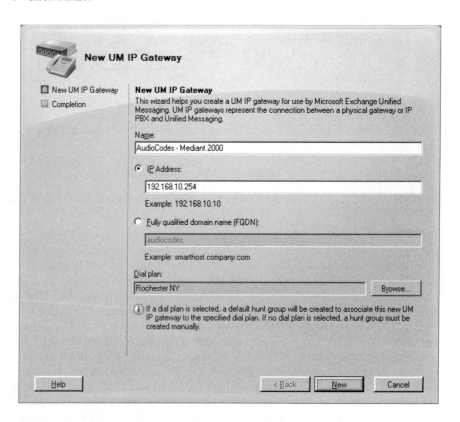

As an alternative to the EMC, you can also use the New-UMIPGateway cmdlet in the EMS, like in this example:

```
[PS]C:\>New-UMIPGateway -Name "AudioCodes-Mediant 2000" -Address 192.168.10.254
```

UM Mailbox Policy

Configuring each and every mailbox with the common settings, such as PIN lengths and dialing restrictions for the various locations, would be tedious and could lead to inconsistent or even invalid configurations. The UM mailbox policy object allows you to apply settings to groups of UM-enabled mailboxes in a consistent way. A default mailbox policy is created when you create a new UM dial plan. You can chose to leave the default settings, customize the default policy, or create a new policy to link to the UM dial plan. You will need to configure the UM mailboxes to use the custom UM mailbox policy.

Creating a New UM Mailbox Policy

Use the following steps to create a new UM Mailbox Policy:

1. Open the EMC with an administrator account that has the Exchange Organization Administrator role.

2. Expand Organization Configuration and click Unified Messaging.

3. Select the UM Mailbox Policies tab in the Work pane.

4. Select New UM Mailbox Policy in the Actions pane.

5. Type the name of the UM mailbox policy in the Name field, as shown next.

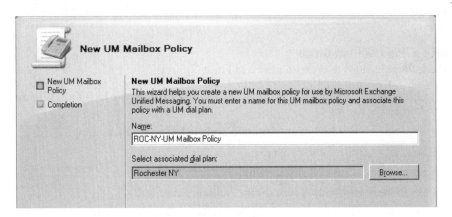

6. Click Browse, select a UM dial plan to associate with the mailbox policy, and click OK.

7. Click New.

8. Click Finish.

As an alternative to the EMC, you can also use the New-UMMailboxPolicy cmdlet in the EMS, like in this example:

```
[PS]C:\>New-UMMailboxPolicy -Name "ROC-NY-UM Mailbox Policy" -UMDialPlan
"Rochester NY"
```

UM Hunt Group

The UM hunt group is an Active Directory object used to represent an actual hunt group on a PBX. From the perspective of a UM servers deployment, the UM hunt group links a pilot number (inbound call number) to a specific UM dial plan. An administrator can specify a specific pilot number by assigning a custom hunt group to a dial plan. Additionally, the dial plan will need to be associated with one or more UM servers. The UM hunt group itself is created for a specific UM IP gateway object. It is also possible to create more than one UM hunt group per UM IP gateway. These objects work together in the following order:

1. The IP gateway initiates a session with the UM server by using SIP.

2. The SIP header includes the pilot number.

3. The UM server verifies that the number in the SIP header is part of a particular hunt group.

4. The associated UM server accepts the call.

Two parameters in a UM hunt group can be configured: the UM dial plan and the pilot identifier or pilot number. You will add the UM hunt group to the UM IP gateway that you previously created and then specify the UM dial plan you want to link to. Finally, specifying a pilot number and creating the new UM hunt group allows the UM server to begin accepting inbound calls.

Creating a New UM Hunt Group

Use the following steps to create a new UM Hunt Group:

1. Open the EMC with an administrator account that has the Exchange Organization Administrator role.

2. Expand Organization Configuration and click Unified Messaging.

3. Select the UM IP Gateways tab.

4. Select an existing UM IP gateway.

5. Select New UM Hunt Group in the Actions pane.

6. Type the name of the hunt group in the Name field, as shown next.

7. Click Browse, select the UM dial plan you want to link to, and then click OK.

8. Type the number of the pilot identifier for the hunt group and then click New. (Be sure to enter in the correct pilot number because you cannot change this number without removing and then re-creating the hunt group.)

9. Click Finish.

As an alternative to the EMC, you can also use the New-UMHuntGroup cmdlet in the EMS, like in this example:

```
[PS]C:\>New-UMHuntGroup -Name "ROC-HG" -PilotIdentifier 12700 -UMDialplan
"Rochester NY" -UMIPGateway "AudioCodes - Mediant 2000"
```

UM Dialing Rules

The default settings on the Unified Messaging server do not allow UM-enabled users to dial outbound calls to any phone numbers that are not defined as part of the organization. In fact, users are limited to making calls only to UM-enabled users configured to use the same UM dial plan.

Outdialing is a term used to describe the call-handling process that occurs when a UM-enabled user makes a call to an external phone number. Outdialing requires the following configurations:

- Dialing group rules
- Dialing rule entries
- Dialing restrictions

To enable outdialing for UM-enabled users, you must perform the following tasks:

- Configure the UM IP gateway to allow outgoing calls
- Create dialing rule groups/entries
- Configure dialing restrictions on the UM mailbox policy

As a Unified Messaging administrator, you will need to create appropriate dialing rules and properties for each location in your organization if you are going to allow outdialing. When you create a dialing rule entry, you will simultaneously be populating one of the two types of dialing rule groups: in-country/region rule groups or international rule groups. A dialing rule entry is used to define the telephone numbers and number masks for in-country/region and international calls that can be made by UM-enabled users who are associated with a UM mailbox policy. Each dialing rule determines the types of calls that users within a dialing rule group can make. However, you must correctly configure the dial rule entry with a valid number mask and a dial number. After you create a dialing rule group and define the appropriate dialing rule entries on the Dialing Group Rules tab, you must add the appropriate dialing rule groups from the UM dial plan to a UM mailbox policy on the Dialing Restrictions tab.

Creating a Dialing Rule Entry

Use the following steps to create a new Dialing Rule Entry:

1. Open the EMC with an administrator account that has the Exchange Organization Administrator role.

2. Expand the Organization Configuration and click Unified Messaging.

3. Select the UM Dial Plans tab and then select a UM dial plan to edit.

4. Click Properties in the Actions pane.

5. Select the Dialing Rule Groups tab, click the Add button under In-Country/Region Rule Groups or International Rule Groups.

6. Provide the following information, as shown in the next illustration.

    - **Name**   Select the name of an existing dialing rule group, or create a dialing rule group and type the name of the dialing rule group.

    - **Number mask**   A number mask is used to limit the outgoing telephone numbers it will dial for a user. An example of a valid number mask is 91585xxxxxxx. This example will limit the user to just calls made to the 585 area code in the U.S.

    - **Dialed number**   Your IP gateway vendor will expect to see numbers in a specific format. Use the Dialed number field to define in which format the number should be, especially if it is different from the numbers obtained by the Unified Messaging server. An example of a valid dialed number is 9xxxxxxx.

    - **Comment**   Type a description of the dialing rule entry.

7. Click OK to save your changes.

As an alternative to the EMC, you can also use the Set-UMDialPlan cmdlet in the EMS, like in the following examples.
For an in-country/region rule group:

```
[PS]C:\>Set-UMDialPlan -Identity "Rochester NY" -ConfiguredInCountryOrRegionGroups
US-NY-ROC, 91585xxxxxxx, 9xxxxxxx, "Valid Numbers for Rochester NY Office"
```

For an international rule group:

```
[PS]C:\>Set-UMDialPlan -Identity "Rochester NY" -ConfiguredInternationalGroups
"International, 901144*, 901144*, International Calls"
```

If you have complex dialing rules and a large number of dialing plans to configure, you may want to create a **.csv** file with the **Name,NumberMask,DialedNumber,Comment** headings and use the following cmdlet to import the file:

```
[PS]C:\>Set-UMDialPlan "Rochester NY" -ConfiguredInCountryOrRegionGroups
$(IMPORT-CSV C:\CustomDialingRules\InCountryRegion.csv)
```

Assigning UM Dialing Rules to a Mailbox Policy

The final step to enable outdialing is to assign the UM dialing rules to the appropriate UM mailbox policies. Until this is done, the outdialing settings do not affect the UM-enabled users.

Once the rule groups are assigned, their settings will apply to the UM-enabled users configured to use that specific mailbox policy.

Configuring Dialing Restrictions on UM Mailbox Policy

Use the following steps to configure Dialing Restrictions on a UM Mailbox Policy:

1. Open the EMC with an administrator account that has the Exchange Organization Administrator role.

2. Expand the Organization Configuration and click Unified Messaging.

3. Select the UM Mailbox Policies tab and then select a UM mailbox policy to edit.

4. Click Properties in the Actions pane.

5. Select the Dialing Restrictions tab.

6. Click the Add button for in-country/region rule groups or international rule groups.

7. Select one of the rule groups you created previously from the list of rule groups and then click OK, as shown next.

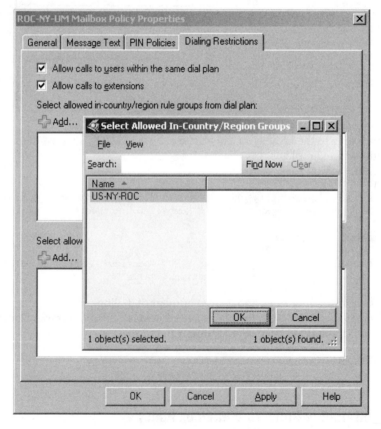

8. Click OK to save the change and close the Mailbox Policy Properties window.

Generating GAL Grammar

Exchange 2007 Unified Messaging server roles include the English language pack by default. This provides grammar files used by the Unified Messaging server speech engine to recognize words and phrases that a caller might use to interact with Automatic Speed Recognition (ASR). The grammar files also define what options are available to a caller. When the Exchange Unified Messaging servers are deployed, they generate the grammar files based on default settings. The default settings will work fine the majority of the time, but Microsoft recommends that grammar generation be performed manually under the following circumstances:

- When you complete a new installation of the Unified Messaging server role
- After creating a new UM dial plan, UM Auto Attendant, custom address list, or custom distribution list
- After creating UM-enabled users
- After modifying a UM dial plan
- After modifying a UM Auto Attendant

By default, grammar generation occurs every day at 2:00 A.M. The schedule can be modified with Set-UMserver in the EMS. To make sure that the very first users of the Unified Messaging services are able to connect without errors, you should plan on running the executable galgrammargenerator.exe as the last step in the deployment process before allowing users to access the Unified Messaging servers. The grammar files are updated when:

- Unified Messaging servers join a UM dial plan
- Default or custom update schedules occur
- The file galgrammargenerator.exe is manually run

The galgrammargenerator.exe tool should be used to force an update when changes occur in the organization that affect the users' ability to find other recipients. As a side benefit, the tool can be used to repair missing or corrupted grammar files. Table 9-6 lists all the possible switches available with the tool.

Switch	Description
-d <dialplan>	Creates a grammar file for a specified UM dial plan.
-g	Generates the grammar file.
-l	Generates a grammar file for a distribution list.
-o	Generates a log file. The default path is \UnifiedMessaging\Temp.
-p	Preloads all generated grammars into the Microsoft Speech Server platform.
-s <UMserver>	Creates a grammar file for each UM dial plan to which the specified Unified Messaging server belongs.
-u	Creates or updates DTMF maps for users who are enabled for UM and who are not enabled for UM.
-x	Defines the speech filter list that is used in XML format.

TABLE 9-6   Galgrammargenerator.exe Parameters

The recommended command to issue after the initial deployment of a Unified Messaging Server is:

```
Galgrammargenerator.exe -s <UMserver>
```

Unified Messaging Users

Exchange 2007 Recipient Administrators have the ability to mailbox-enable user objects that exist in Active Directory. When a Unified Messaging server role is deployed into an Exchange 2007 organization, the Exchange Recipient Administrator role also has the ability to enable Unified Messaging for existing mailbox-enabled users. After the users' mailboxes are enabled for UM, e-mail, voicemail, and fax messages can be delivered to their Inboxes. A wide variety of clients can take advantage of the unified mailbox, including Outlook 2007, Outlook Web Access, Windows Mobile with Exchange ActiveSync, and telephones.

Once you become more familiar with Unified Messaging concepts and the Exchange Management Shell, you can administer UM users exclusively from the command line with the following four cmdlets:

- Enable-UMMailbox
- Disable-UMMailbox
- Get-UMMailbox
- Set-UMMailbox

It is probably best to start administering UM-enabled users with the Exchange Management Console to become more familiar with them.

UM-Enabling Users

An Active Directory user object is arguably the most significant object in the directory. Exchange 2007 greatly extends the definition of what a user object is. With the release of Service Pack 1 for Exchange, which includes additional enhancements for Unified Messaging, user objects will now be able to support integration with not only Unified Messaging but also Office Communications Server. Organizations that choose to integrate Exchange 2007, Unified Messaging, and Office Communications Server as a VoIP solution will take full advantage of the latest enhancement to the user object in Active Directory made by Service Pack 1. For more on Office Communications Server and Unified Messaging integration, see Chapter 13.

SP1 *When you enable a user for Unified Messaging, SP1 provides the ability to add a SIP or E.164 address along with the required phone extension number.*

There is an administrative gotcha when you configure a new UM-enabled user with a SIP or E.164 address: You will no longer be able to change the user address with the Set-UMmailbox cmdlet. You can configure the new Unified Messaging proxy address (EUM) with the EMC on the E-Mail Addresses tab on the user's Mailbox Properties page.

UM-Enabling a User's Mailbox Using the EMC

Use the following steps to UM-Enable a user's mailbox:

1. Open the EMC with an administrator account that has at least the Exchange Recipients Administrator role.

2. Expand Recipient Configuration.

3. Select the user mailbox to enable for Unified Messaging.

4. Click Enable Unified Messaging in the Actions pane.

5. Click the Browse button, select a UM mailbox policy for this user, and then click OK.

6. Configure the following PIN settings for the user, as shown next:

   - Automatically generate PIN to access Outlook Voice Access (default)
   - Manually specify PIN
   - Require user to reset PIN at first telephone logon

7. Click Next.

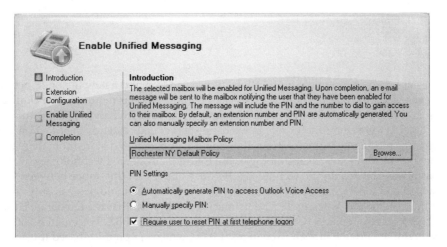

8. Configure the options on the Extension Configuration page, as shown in the next illustration.

   - **Automatically generated mailbox extension**   Only available if the Business field on the Address and Phone tab in the user's properties are populated.

   - **Manually entered mailbox extension**   If you have a dial plan that is configured to use E.164 or SIP as the URI type, you must manually enter a mailbox extension for the user.

   - **Automatically generated SIP resource identifier**   This option will be available if the user you are enabling for Unified Messaging is associated with either a SIP URI or E.164 dial plan.

   - **Manually entered SIP resource identifier**   This option will be available if the user you are enabling for Unified Messaging is associated with either a SIP URI or E.164 dial plan.

9. Click Next.

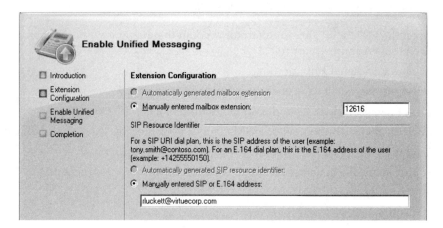

10. Click Enable.

11. Click Finish.

Summary

As more established communication solutions (voice and fax) find a new life on IP networks, a new means of storing and facilitating access to the information is required. The Unified Messaging server role provides that capability natively in your Exchange 2007 organization. The new Unified Messaging server role in Exchange Server 2007 extends the functionality of your Exchange messaging infrastructure, allowing it to transmit and store more than just traditional e-mail. Voice and fax technologies are traditionally analog technologies, whereas e-mail has always been a digital technology. Because of the vast difference between the analog world and the digital world, the ability to merge the technologies has only come about in the last decade. Voicemail is the primary voice system that the Exchange Unified Messaging server role replaces. Call management still requires a PBX. Voicemail is commonly associated with the Private Branch Exchanges (PBXs), which are premise-based (business) phone systems. Exchange 2007 Unified Messaging is more than a substitute for an existing voicemail system. Besides the basic voicemail functionality that can be expected of any voicemail system, there are unique features that make Exchange's UM server attractive. The key features that make Exchange's UM solution stand out are:

- Outlook Voice Access
- Outlook Calendar Access
- Directory and Personal Contacts Access
- Outlook and OWA Voicemail Form
- Auto Attendant

IV PART

Exchange Recipients and Clients

Administering Recipients

The term *recipient* is used in Exchange Server documentation to refer to an Exchange object that can receive e-mail. In other words, the object is "mail-enabled." (More on mail-enabled vs. mailbox-enabled a bit later in the chapter.) Administrators in many organizations spend a good part of their day managing recipients. This includes tasks such as the creation and modification of user accounts and mailboxes, e-mail addresses, distribution lists, and their related parameters.

Exchange Takes Over Recipient Management: Goodbye RUS!

Exchange Server 2007 takes a considerably different route to recipient management than its recent predecessors (Exchange Server 2000 and 2003) did. Yet, in a manner of speaking, it comes back full circle to the path taken by earlier versions of Exchange. Recipients are now managed from Exchange, using either the Exchange console or the Exchange shell.

When greeted with this change in behavior of a fairly important task performed frequently by administrators, many resent the fact that the Active Directory Users and Computers (ADUC) console can no longer be used to perform recipient management tasks. However, this does not mean Exchange has lost its tight integration with Active Directory, as many administrators are prompted to ask. Nor is recipient information stored within Exchange. It is still stored in the same familiar Active Directory location—the domain naming context—and besides the addition of new attributes to facilitate newer features such as Unified Messaging (UM), very little has changed.

It is important to consider the possible motivations that drove the product teams to divorce recipient management from ADUC, in what appears to be a step back to the Exchange 5.0 days. The prime reason for this move—and this is little more than my humble opinion and input from interactions with the product team—is the fact that the Recipient Update Service (RUS) in Exchange Server 2000/2003 was the cause of a disproportionate number of support calls to Microsoft's Customer Support Services (CSS; formerly known as *Product Support Services*, or *PSS*). For those not very familiar with RUS, it is a component of the System Attendant in Exchange Server 2000/2003 that watches Active Directory for the creation of new objects or the modification of existing ones, and it applies recipient policies to the new and modified recipients. Without going into too much detail about the numbers and types of issues faced by administrators when dealing with RUS, let me summarize by saying the demise of RUS is greeted by high-decibel shrieks by some Exchange folks, and deliberately visible sighs of relief by others.

NOTE *Is RUS gone, really? The Recipient Update Service, as known to mankind (or at least as known to the vast majority of Exchange administrators), no longer exists. However, the RUS component does exist under the hood, and it performs a much smaller number of tasks, such as helping out the System Attendant with information from e-mail address policies, address lists, and so on. Most importantly, it does not sit there watching AD, it never reads recipients information, and it never writes anything to AD.*

The other more important benefit in this tradeoff is the elimination of wait time after provisioning recipients. It was the job of RUS to watch for changes to Active Directory, and although set to Always Run, it did so at its own leisurely pace, coming across as someone who was never happy with their job. As a result, administrators had to wait for what appeared to be random amounts of time for recipients to be provisioned. Some administrators like to kill idle time by checking a newly created recipient's properties, to determine if RUS has processed it and generated e-mail addresses and Exchange attributes for it. That is a thing of the past—with RUS gone, recipient provisioning happens almost instantly, the moment you click the New button in the New Mailbox Wizard in the console (or enter the corresponding shell command). I rather like this newfound nimbleness.

Finally, the inevitable discussion—the role of the mighty Exchange shell (a.k.a. EMS or Exchange Management Shell) in recipient management. From the early days of Exchange Server 2007 (then known by its codename E12 or Exchange12), I have frequently witnessed, and sometimes participated in, heated discussions about GUI management consoles vs. managing from the command line. For all its one-liner goodness, the shell is not likely to become the preferred way of creating one-off recipients. That job is better done by the GUI wizards in the Exchange console, unless you are so used to the shell, are totally smitten by it, have the required brain cycles and memory cells to remember the syntax, or have enough time to spare looking at command help within the shell or online. Somewhere between the early betas of Exchange Server 2007 and the countdown to RTM (release to manufacturing, a milestone used by Microsoft to mark the end of the development cycle for a product and its release to manufacturing for products that are shipped on media such as CDs/DVDs), I fell into one or more of these categories. However, I assure you I will not let that get in your way.

Nevertheless, it is important to realize many recipient management tasks can only be performed from the shell. Given the granular recipient management control Exchange Server 2007 provides the administrator, and the number of recipient parameters exposed, it is virtually impossible to present a GUI dialog box or a wizard to configure every one of these parameters. Making the shell your friend will pay off if you manage more than a handful of Exchange recipients.

Most tasks in this chapter illustrate how to accomplish a task using both approaches— the console and the shell. Additionally, some quick tips and one-liners show you how to do more with the shell.

Which Tool Do I Use to Manage Recipients?

As you begin your Exchange Server 2007 deployment, which is likely to be a move from an earlier version of Exchange (Exchange Server 2000 or 2003 in most cases), one question you will need to answer is, Where do I manage recipients from? As mentioned previously, the Exchange Server 2000/2003 way involves using the Active Directory Users and Computers (ADUC) console, enhanced by the COM objects or DLLs installed by Exchange (2000/2003) Management Tools. During the time that Exchange Server 2007 coexists in an environment with Exchange 2000/2003, you have the option of using Exchange Server 2003 tools to manage mailboxes residing on Exchange Server 2007 servers.

However, such mailboxes get marked as legacy mailboxes and therefore are limited in functionality.

A good rule of thumb is to use the Exchange Server 2007 console or shell to manage recipients, except for mailboxes residing on Exchange Server 2000/2003 servers, which can be created using the ADUC console on a server or workstation with Exchange Management Tools (for Exchange 2000/2003) installed.

Some of the common tasks we look at in the rest of the chapter include creating and managing mailboxes or mailbox-enabled users, mail-enabled users, contacts, distribution groups, and dynamic distribution groups, and resource mailboxes.

The Exchange Recipient Bandwagon

Before you start creating a mailbox or a mailbox-enabled user, you need to understand the difference between a user that is mailbox- or mail-enabled and one that is neither mailbox- nor mail-enabled, as well as other types of recipients.

- **Mailbox-enabled user**   A mailbox-enabled user is an Active Directory user object that has a mailbox residing on an Exchange server. The mailbox itself is nothing but a pointer to a bunch of folders in an Exchange information store, designated by a unique Globally Unique Identifier (GUID). The Exchange Server 2007 term for a mailbox-enabled user is UserMailbox.

- **Resource mailbox**   This term used for a user mailbox used for a resource such as a conference room or other facility, or resources such as projectors and other equipment. Creating a mailbox for such resources results in those resources being visible in the Address Book in Outlook, and because the resources are mailbox-enabled user accounts, with their own calendar and availability (Free/Busy) information, users in your organization can "reserve" them by inviting them to meetings. In most organizations where Exchange is deployed, you are likely to find users habituated to this resource reservation process. Exchange Server 2007 improves on the resource mailbox concept by explicitly defining resource mailboxes as such, and further segmenting them as room or equipment mailboxes.

- **Linked mailbox**   A linked mailbox is used in cross-forest topologies. In such topologies, the Exchange server resides in one AD forest, known as a *resource forest.* A mailbox is created for a disabled user account in that forest. The account that accesses the mailbox resides in a different forest, commonly referred to as a *user forest.* A user forest is trusted by a resource forest to enable access to resources.

NOTE *In topologies where Exchange servers reside in a source forest and a target forest, when mailboxes are moved from the source forest to the target forest (a process known as a cross-forest mailbox move), a disabled user account is automatically placed in the target forest. Exchange Server 2007's Move Mailbox Wizard and the move-mailbox shell command enable you to move a mailbox between two trusted forests. More details about cross-forest mailbox moves can be found later in this chapter.*

- **Mail user**   A mail user, known as a *mail-enabled user* in previous versions, is an Active Directory user object that does not have a mailbox residing on an Exchange server (at least not in the Exchange organization in the same Active Directory forest), but does nevertheless have an e-mail address defined. This e-mail address resides in a mail system that is external to the Exchange organization—it can be an Exchange organization in some other Active Directory forest, an e-mail account hosted by an ISP, or even a free web-based e-mail system such as Hotmail, Yahoo!, or Gmail. The important thing to remember about mail users is that they are user objects and therefore have the ability to log onto the domain. The term *security principal* is used for objects that can show up in security permissions (a.k.a. *Access Control Lists,* or *ACLs)*. Mail users are security principals.

- **Mail contact**   Just like mail-enabled users, mail contacts are objects in Active Directory that have an external e-mail address—one hosted outside the Exchange organization, as explained previously. However, unlike mail-enabled users, contacts are not security principals. In other words, they can neither log onto the domain or be authenticated, nor can they be assigned permissions to any resources. As such, Mail Contact objects are merely a way of making an external recipient show up in Exchange's address lists, including the Default Global Address List (GAL), thus saving users the effort involved in having to remember frequently used e-mail addresses and entering these manually when sending e-mail.

- **Distribution group**   Distribution groups are groups that are mail-enabled—they have an e-mail address (and a fef other Exchange attributes). Sending a message to the group's e-mail address results in "expansion" of the group, and the message is delivered to members of the group. Just like contacts, distribution groups are not security principals. In other words, they cannot have permissions to access resources.

- **Dynamic distribution group**   One of the issues with distribution groups has long been the management costs they bring along with them—the user requests or business processes that mandate the addition or removal of recipients from distribution groups based on their current work status, department, location, and so on. One solution to reducing such group management tasks is dynamic distribution groups. Rather than defining group membership by adding recipients as members of the group, the membership of dynamic distribution groups is controlled using user attributes, defined by LDAP filters in Exchange Server 2000/2003 and OPATH filters in Exchange Server 2007. The filters are similar to those used by other components of Exchange such as EmailAddressPolicies (or recipient policies in Exchange 2000/2003) and address lists.

> **Distribution Groups and Security Groups: What They Mean in Exchange Server 2007**
>
> The term *distribution group*, at least in the Active Directory and Exchange Server 2000/2003 context, has meant a mail-enabled group that is not a security principal. In other words, it cannot be assigned permissions on resources. When creating a new group in the Active Directory Users and Computers console, you can choose to create either a distribution group or a security group. Both types of groups can be mail-enabled. In essence, this allows mail-enabled security groups to function like distribution groups.
>
> Exchange Server 2007 uses the term *distribution group* for mail-enabled groups. These can be either mail-enabled distribution groups or security groups that are mail-enabled. This is where the Exchange Server 2007 Management Tools seem to be a little out of step with Active Directory (besides the change in common Exchange and AD terms such as *mail-enabled user* to *mail user* and *contacts* to *mail contacts*).
>
> When creating a new "distribution group" in Exchange Server 2007, you can specify whether the group is a security or distribution group (from the Active Directory perspective) by specifying the group type.
>
> However, it has been a general recommendation—and certainly one I have professed for a long time—that there's a reason security and distribution groups exist and it's therefore not a good idea to use security groups for e-mail functions by mail-enabling them. Exchange Server 2007's use of the term *distribution group* for mail-enabled groups, whether distribution or security groups, may come across as a little confusing for those used to the Active Directory and Exchange Server 2000/2003 definitions.

Like distribution groups (non-dynamic), messages sent to the e-mail address of the dynamic distribution group is received by all its "members." However, when the membership of such a group is expanded, Exchange queries Active Directory with the filter and gets back recipients matching the filter. Depending on the recipients' attributes, the query returns the most up-to-date set of recipients matching the filter. This reduces administration costs for maintaining group memberships, and is particularly useful for creating groups such as All Users, All Employees, All-Marketing, or All-Users-In-United-States.

In addition to these recipients, there is at least one more type of recipient you should know about—a mail-enabled public folder. This is a public folder with an e-mail address defined, and therefore the ability to receive e-mail.

Creating a Mailbox

When creating a new Exchange mailbox, either you create the underlying user account at the time of mailbox creation or you mailbox-enable an existing user account that is not mailbox- or mail-enabled. Let's go through the process of creating one using both the Exchange console and the shell.

To create a new mailbox using the Exchange console, follow these steps:

1. In the Exchange console, expand the Recipient Configuration container.
2. In the Action pane, click New Mailbox. This starts the New Mailbox Wizard, shown in Figure 10-1. Alternatively, you can right-click the Mailbox leaf object under Recipient Configuration node and select New Mailbox.

PART IV

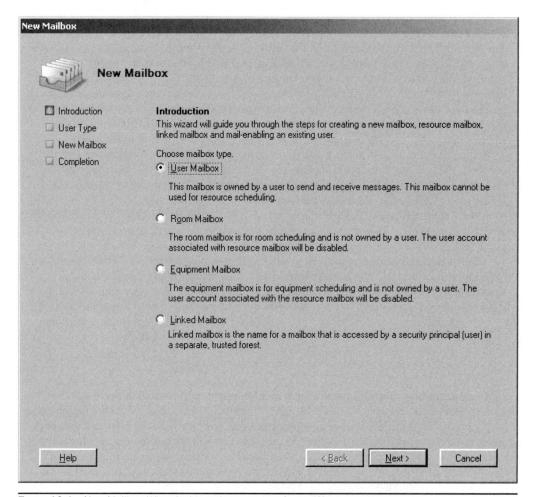

FIGURE 10-1   New Mailbox Wizard with option to select from different mailbox types

3. On the Introduction page, select User Mailbox and click Next.

4. On the User Type page, select New User. The Existing Users option allows you to browse existing users in Active Directory that can be mailbox-enabled. In SP1, multiple users can be selected and mailbox-enabled simultaneously using the wizard.

5. In the User Information dialog box, fill out the necessary details, such as first name, last name, logon name, and so on.

NOTE *The Organizational Unit field displays the Active Directory container or OU in which the new user account will be created. By default, new users are created in the Users container. If you want to create the user in an OU, select the OU by clicking Browse. Once created, users can be moved between containers and/or OUs using ADUC.*

6. Click Next. On the Mailbox Settings page, you are prompted to complete the Exchange-related attributes listed next:

- **Alias**   By default, the alias field is populated with the same value as the user's logon name. This can be modified.

- **Server**   This allows the selection of an Exchange server on which the mailbox can be located.

- **Storage Group**   This allows the selection of a storage group on the Exchange server selected in the Server field.

- **Mailbox Database**   This allows the selection of a mailbox database from the selected storage group.

- **Managed Folder Mailbox Policy**   This allows the selection of a Managed Folder Mailbox Policy, if you have any defined. Managed Folder Mailbox Policies allow configuration of message retention and journaling features and are covered in Chapter 15. This is optional.

- **Exchange ActiveSync Mailbox Policy**   Exchange ActiveSync Mailbox Policies define a group of settings related to Exchange ActiveSync (EAS) for mobile access to the mailbox. This is optional.

7. Click Next. The New Mailbox page presents a configuration summary for verification. You can click the Back button to step back through the different pages and change any fields if you need to. To create the mailbox, click New.

8. The Completion page displays the result of the New Mailbox Wizard. The Exchange shell command that was used to create the mailbox is displayed.

TIP   *Commands displayed by the wizard can be copied to the clipboard using the key combination* CTRL-C *and pasted into your own notes for reference. This provides a great way of learning shell commands and observing the correct syntax and values used. It is a well-thought and valuable learning tool.*

9. Click Finish to close the wizard.

Creating a New Mailbox in Exchange Shell

If you completed the preceding steps to create a new mailbox using the Exchange console, the final step displays the shell command used to create a new mailbox. The command used has a lot of parameters, many of which are required to create a new mailbox, as shown next:

```
New-Mailbox -Name 'Jim Murphy' -Alias 'jmurhpy' -OrganizationalUnit
'e12labs.com/Users' -UserPrincipalName 'jmurhpy@e12labs.com' -SamAccountName
'jmurhpy' -FirstName 'Jim' -Initials '' -LastName 'Murphy' -Password
'System.Security.SecureString' -ResetPasswordOnNextLogon $false -Database
'CN=Mailbox Database,CN=First Storage
Group,CN=InformationStore,CN=E12Mailman,CN=Servers,CN=Exchange Administrative
Group (FYDIBOHF23SPDLT),CN=Administrative Groups,CN=E12Labs,CN=Microsoft
Exchange,CN=Services,CN=Configuration,DC=e12labs,DC=com'
```

Although this command uses a lot of parameters to create a new mailbox, you can create one using far fewer parameters, as shown in the following example. Before we start creating a new mailbox, it is important to capture the password for the new mailbox in a secure fashion. This is done using the following shell command:

```
$password = Read-host -AsSecureString
```

This command results in a prompt to enter a password. The password entered at the prompt is masked using asterisk (*) characters, so the password is not visible at the command line when entered.

With the password captured in the variable $password, we can proceed with creating the new mailbox using the following command:

```
New-Mailbox -Password $password -Name "Jim Murphy" -UserPrincipalName
jmurphy@e12labs.com -OrganizationalUnit Users -Database "Mailbox Database"
```

As seen here, the new-mailbox command only requires the parameters password, name, userprincipalname, organizationalunit, and database.

Creating a Mailbox for an Existing User Account

The procedure in the previous section shows you how to create a new mailbox and an Active Directory user account. This is useful when no user account exists for the new mailbox. To create a new mailbox for an existing user account (also called "mailbox-enabling" an existing account), select Existing Users in step 4 in the preceding example and select the existing user account in Active Directory. To mailbox-enable an existing account using the Exchange shell, use the following command:

```
Enable-Mailbox -Identity "Axel Foley" -Database "Mailbox Database"
```

As seen here, the command to enable an existing user account requires even fewer parameters than the one to create a new mailbox (with a new user account).

Bulk-Creation of Mailboxes

One of the more popular posts on the Exchangepedia Blog describes how to create mailboxes in bulk using a CSV file as input. The post can be found at http://exchangepedia .com/blog/2006/11/exchange-server-2007-bulk-creation-of.html.

Here is the procedure explained in brief:

1. Create a CSV file using a spreadsheet or a text editor, with the following columns:

   ```
   Alias,Name,UPN
   ```

   Add data for the new mailbox-enabled accounts in a row, as follows:

   ```
   User_One,User One,userone@yourUPNsuffix.com
   User_Two,User Two,usertwo@yourUPNsuffix.com
   User_Three,User Three,userthree@yourUPNsuffix.com
   ```

   Save the file in CSV format (let's call it CreateRecipients.CSV).

2. In the Exchange shell, capture the password you want to use for all accounts as a secure string:

```
$password = Read-Host -AsSecureString
```

Enter the password. It will be masked using * characters.

3. Create mailbox-enabled users using the following command:

```
Import-CSV CreateRecipients.CSV | foreach {new-mailbox -alias
$_.alias -name $_.name -userPrincipalName $_.UPN -database "Mailbox
Database" -org Users -password $Password}
```

This command imports the CSV file, and it treats each row after the header as a new record. The ForEach command goes through every instance (row) from the CSV file and creates a new mailbox in the database "Mailbox Database," using the password captured in step 2.

Similarly, the procedure to bulk-enable existing users (who are not mailbox-enabled) is outlined in another post on the blog, titled "Exchange Server 2007: Bulk mailbox-enabling users using Exchange shell," at http://exchangepedia.com/blog/2006/12/id-written-about-how-to-bulk-create.html.

Removing Mailboxes

Mailboxes can be removed from the Exchange console by right-clicking a mailbox-enabled user and selecting Remove. Note that this not only removes the mailbox, but also removes the user account from Active Directory. A more appropriate term to describe this is *Delete User*. To remove a mailbox using the Exchange shell, use the following command:

```
Remove-Mailbox "Adam Smith"
```

In either case, both the console and the shell warn you about the action you are about to perform and require a confirmation. The warning states clearly that the action will remove the user account and mark the mailbox for removal.

Really Removing a Mailbox: Mailbox-Disabling a User Account

To simply remove the mailbox, and not the attached user account, select Disable from the console when right-clicking the mailbox-enabled user. To do the same from the shell, use the disable-mailbox command.

Creating Mail Users

Whereas there are separate nodes under the Recipients container for Mailbox, Mail Contact, and Distribution Group objects, there is no separate container for mail users. These are displayed under the Mail Contact node. To create a mail user using the Exchange console, follow these steps:

1. Expand the Recipients node and select Mail Contact.

2. In the Action pane, click the New Mail User link to start the New Mail User Wizard.

3. On the Introduction page, select the New User radio button (default) to create a new mail user. (To mail-enable an existing user account, select Existing user and click Browse. This presents a list of user accounts in Active Directory that are neither mailbox-enabled nor mail-enabled.)

PART IV

4. Enter the following user details:
   - First name
   - Middle initial
   - Last name
   - User logon name (user principal name)
   - Password (and password confirmation)
   - User must change password at next logon (optional)

5. On the Mail Settings page, click the Edit button to add the user's external e-mail address. Click OK to close the SMTP Address dialog box. Click Next.

6. On the New Mail User page, verify the displayed parameters.

7. Click New to complete creation of the new mail user. You can copy the Exchange shell command displayed in the wizard using the CTRL-C key combination.

8. Click Finish to exit the New Mail User Wizard.

To create a new mail user using the Exchange shell, use the following command:

```
New-MailUser -Name 'Joe MailUser' -Alias 'jmailuser' -OrganizationalUnit
'e12labs.com/Users' -UserPrincipalName 'jmailuser@e12labs.com' -SamAccountName
'jmailuser' -FirstName 'Joe' -Initials '' -LastName 'Contact' -Password
'System.Security.SecureString' -ResetPasswordOnNextLogon $false -
ExternalEmailAddress 'SMTP:jmailuser@somedomain.com'
```

To mail-enable an existing user, use the following command:

```
Enable-MailUser -Identity "Joe MailUser' -Alias 'jmailuser'
-ExternalEmailAddress 'SMTP:jmailuser@somedomain.com'
```

Removing a Mail User

Removing a mail user is similar to removing a mailbox. In the Exchange console, select the mail user. In the Actions pane, select Remove Mail User to remove the mail-enabled user account. To simply remove the mail-related attributes (or in other words, to mail-disable the account), select Disable Mail User.

Here's the Exchange shell equivalent to remove a mail user:

```
Remove-MailUser -Identity "Joe MailUser"
```

And here's the command to remove Exchange-related attributes:

```
Disable-MailUser -Identity "Joe MailUser"
```

Creating a Mail Contact

To create a mail contact in the Exchange console, follow these steps:

1. Expand the Recipients node. Select Contact.

2. In the Actions Pane, select New Mail Contact.

3. On the Introduction page, select the New Contact radio button. (To mail-enable a contact already existing in Active Directory, select the Existing contact radio button and click Browse. This presents a list of existing contacts in Active Directory that have not been mail-enabled). Click Next.

4. On the Contact Information page, enter the appropriate information in the following fields:

   - **First Name**
   - **(Middle) Initials**
   - **Last Name**
   - **Name**   This field is populated automatically using the First Name, (Middle) Initials, and Last Name fields.
   - **Alias**   This field is automatically populated using the First Name, (Middle) Initials, and Last Name fields.
   - **External e-mail address**   The default e-mail address type that can be entered after clicking the Edit button is SMTP. To enter a Lotus Notes, Novell GroupWise, or X.400 address, click the drop-down arrow next to the Edit button and select Custom Address.

5. Click Next. On the New Mail Contact page, examine the parameters for the new mail contact.

6. Click New. The Exchange shell command used to create the new mail contact is displayed in the Completion dialog box. To copy the command to the clipboard, you can use the CTRL-C key combination.

7. Click the Finish button to exit the New Mail Contact Wizard.

   To create a new mail contact using the Exchange shell, use the following command:

```
New-MailContact -ExternalEmailAddress 'SMTP:jcontact@somedomain' -Name
'Joe Contact' -Alias 'JoeContact' -OrganizationalUnit 'e12labs.com/Users'
-FirstName 'Joe' -Initials '' -LastName 'Contact'
```

Mail Contacts and E-mail Addresses

After creating a mail contact, you will notice that it has received an e-mail address from your domain. The default EmailAddressPolicy also applies to mail contacts (and mail users). As a result, these objects also get an e-mail address from your domain(s), created by the policy. The external e-mail address of Mail Contact and Mail User objects is stored in the ExternalEmailAddress parameter of the object, which maps to the targetAddress LDAP attribute. This allows Mail Contact and Mail User objects to be able to receive inbound e-mail with an e-mail address from your domain, and Exchange is able to route messages to the correct external e-mail address.

Removing a Mail Contact

To remove a mail contact using the Exchange console, select the mail contact and click the Remove link in the Actions pane. This deletes the object from Active Directory.

To remove a mail contact using the Exchange shell, use the following command:

```
Remove-MailContact -identity "Joe Contact"
```

To mail-disable a contact using the Exchange console, select the mail contact and click the Disable Mail Contact link in the Actions pane. This removes the contact's Exchange attributes, without deleting the object from Active Directory.

To mail-disable a mail contact using the Exchange shell, use the following command:

```
Disable-MailContact -identity "Joe Contact"
```

Creating Distribution Groups

Before we get into the creation of distribution groups, it is important to take note of the new management quirks of Exchange Server 2007 mentioned in the sidebar "Distribution Groups and Security Groups: What They Mean in Exchange Server 2007."

Here's how to create a new distribution group using the Exchange console:

1. Under the Recipient Configuration node, select Distribution Group.

2. In the Actions pane, select New Distribution Group. This starts the New Distribution Group Wizard.

3. On the Introduction page, select New Group. (To mail-enable a group that already exists in Active Directory but isn't mail-enabled, select Existing group).

4. On the Group Information page, enter the appropriate information into following fields:

   - **Group Type**   Select between a distribution group and a security group. Regardless of which group type is selected, the remaining steps of the wizard are the same.

   - **Organizational Unit**   Like in most new object wizards, the default is set to the Users container. This can be changed to another container or OU by clicking the Browse button and selecting it.

   - **Group Name**

   - **Group Name (pre-Windows 2000)**   This is automatically generated.

   - **Display Name**   This is automatically generated. By default, this is the same as the group name.

   - **Alias**   This is automatically generated.

5. Click Next. On the New Distribution Group page, review the parameters of the new group. To create the group, click New.

6. On the Completion page, verify that the group was created successfully. The dialog box also displays the Exchange shell used to create the new distribution group. This can be copied to the clipboard using the CTRL-C key combination.

7. Click Finish to exit the New Distribution Group Wizard.

> **New Distribution Groups Cannot Receive Internet E-mail**
>
> In Exchange Server 2007, new distribution groups do not receive Internet e-mail by default. To enable them to receive Internet e-mail, go to the group's properties in EMC, select the Mail Flow Settings tab, click Message Delivery Restrictions, uncheck Require that all senders are authenticated, and then click OK twice to close the group's property pages. Alternatively, use the following shell command:
>
> ```
> Set-DistributionGroup "Group Name" -RequireSenderAuthenticationEnabled $false
> ```
>
> When creating new distribution groups using the Exchange shell, you can include the –RequireSenderAuthenticationEnabled parameter in the New-DistributionGroup command with a value of $true to make it a one-step process.

NOTE *Regardless of the Group Type setting selected—Security or Distribution—Exchange Server 2007 only creates groups with a universal scope—that is, universal distribution or security groups. Although it was possible to create and mail-enable global and domain local groups in Exchange Server 2000/2003, this created issues with expansion of such groups in a multidomain environment. The group membership of global groups is not replicated to a Global Catalog server in other domains of the Active Directory forest. This results in messages not being delivered to all users, and the sender not getting a non-delivery report (NDR) for the same. The message simply disappears into some black hole, never to be heard from again. The use of universal distribution groups was recommended before Exchange Server 2007, but never enforced by Exchange Management Tools or Active Directory. Exchange Server 2007 enforces this.*

To create a new distribution group using the Exchange shell, use the following command:

```
New-DistributionGroup  -Type Distribution –sAMAccountName HumanResources
–Name HumanResources –OrganizationalUnit "Distribution Groups"
```

NOTE *Using the container name (CN) of an OU or container as shown in the preceding example works if you do not have more than one OU or containers with the same CN. If that's not the case, the shell is now faced with an ambiguous object—it is not unique in the environment. Because the shell lacks the intelligence of being able to read your mind and determine whether you meant, say, the Sales OU that's a child of the N. America OU, or the one under the EMEA OU, it is forced to greet you with an error. Using a more specific name such as "YourDomain .com/N. America/Sales" makes the shell's job easier.*

Adding Members to a Distribution Group

Creating distribution groups without adding any members allows these groups to do a fine job of pretending to be real recipients. They don't have the capability to store messages addressed to them anywhere, unlike mailboxes and public folders. Therefore, any messages sent to such groups do a great disappearing act. The senders do not get an NDR because delivery is never attempted! Having seen instances of some folks happily sending messages to such memberless distribution groups, and later receiving requests to be able to retrieve such messages—"Surely, it cannot disappear completely, it must be somewhere!"—it's a good idea to populate groups with members, or at least one member, after creating them.

Interestingly, the ability to add members to distribution groups is not restricted to the Exchange console—this can be done using Active Directory Users and Computers as well, should you so desire. In either tool, members can be added from the Members tab of the group's properties.

NOTE *Only Exchange recipients (that is, Active Directory objects that are mailbox- or mail-enabled, such as users, contacts, public folders, and other distribution groups) can be added as members of distribution groups.*

To add members to a distribution group using the Exchange shell, use the following command:

```
Add-DistributionGroupMember "Human Resources" -Member User1,User2,User3…
```

Creating Dynamic Distribution Groups

As discussed earlier in this chapter, dynamic distribution groups are distribution groups that have their membership determined dynamically every time an e-mail is sent to them. This determination is based on a recipient filter used by Exchange to query Active Directory for recipients. Like most recipient management tasks in Exchange Server 2007, creation of dynamic distribution groups is made possible using Exchange tools—that is, the console and the shell. A new filtering mechanism has been added to the mix—OPATH filters, also used by address lists/GAL. The ability to use LDAP filters directly has been removed.

Before we dive into the creation of dynamic distribution groups, here are some rules of thumb for using them, and some questions answered:

- **What kind of groups are dynamic distribution groups ideal for?** Small distribution groups with mostly static group membership do not really benefit from dynamic distribution groups. The ideal targets are groups that change frequently, and groups with a fairly large number of members—such as All Users. Let's take an "All Employees" or "All Company" distribution list for instance. As an administrator, have you ever received complaints of some users not receiving e-mails to the All Company distribution list? Did this happen because the user was not made a member of the Western Region Sales group, which was a member of the N. America Sales group, which was a member of the Worldwide Sales group, which was a member of the All Company group? What if the user would have automatically been added to the Western Region Sales group, based on the user's location (San Francisco, California, for instance) and department (for example, Sales)? Going back to your Active Directory 101 class, and the preceding group membership pattern, which group would make the best candidate for being a dynamic distribution group? The All Company group probably consists of a number of smaller groups, and is mostly static. So is Worldwide Sales, unless your company is on a furious growth path, and adding country offices and sales departments every other day. The number of groups that are members of the N. America Sales group isn't going to change much, unless your sales territories are remapped or a major geographical change takes place in the country. That leaves the Western Region Sales group—and other groups at that level.

These are the ones where membership may change on a more frequent basis. Rule of thumb: You gain nothing by creating a dynamic distribution group for groups with a small number of members that don't change much.

- **What attributes can I use to filter on?** Technically speaking, any attribute can be used to filter recipients. The attribute must be part of the partial replica—in other words, it must be replicated to a Global Catalog (GC). Like most database queries, Active Directory/LDAP queries perform better if an indexed attribute is used.

- **What if the attribute I want to filter on does not get replicated to a Global Catalog?** You can modify an attribute's properties in the Active Directory schema to make it replicate to GCs, using the Schema Management snap-in or other AD tools or scripts.

CAUTION *Adding a new attribute to be replicated to the Global Catalog will result in a full synchronization of the Global Catalog if the AD forest functional level is not set to Windows Server 2003. This may be of concern in large environments, depending on the number of Global Catalog servers and the available bandwidth.*

- **What if the attribute I want to filter on is not indexed?** You can change the AD schema to mark an attribute to be indexed (and replicated to the Global Catalog) using the Active Directory Schema snap-in or other LDAP tools or scripts (see Figure 10-2). Note that changing an attribute to be indexed and/or included in the Global Catalog will trigger a full synchronization of the Global Catalog if the forest functional level is not Windows Server 2003.

FIGURE 10-2
Modifying an AD attribute to be indexed and replicated to the Global Catalog

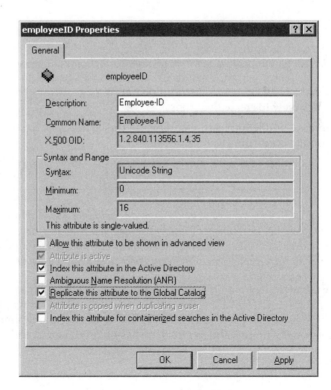

To create a dynamic distribution group using the Exchange console, follow these steps:

1. Select Recipient Configuration in the console tree.

2. In the Actions pane, click New Dynamic Distribution Group (DDG). This starts the New Dynamic Distribution Group Wizard.

3. On the Introduction page, complete the following details:

   - **Organizational Unit**   By default, the Users container is selected. To change it, click Browse and select the OU or container in which you want to create the group.

   - **Group Name**   Type in a group name.

   - **Alias**   The alias is generated automatically and is the same as the group name.

4. Click Next.

5. On the Filter Settings page, define the filter that will be used to *determine membership* of this group. Unlike static distribution groups, which store group membership in the Members attribute, dynamic distribution groups query Active Directory and get a list of recipients using the defined filter.

6. On the Conditions page, shown in Figure 10-3, you can select one of the conditions from the list. This includes State or Province, Department, Company, and Custom Attributes 1 through 15. Not selecting any condition will result in all recipient types defined in the scope of the previous page being returned. For instance, if you selected all users with Exchange mailboxes, not selecting a condition will return all user mailboxes.

NOTE   *The Exchange console restricts you to a small list of attributes that can be used to define the filter for a Dynamic distribution group. The Exchange shell allows creation of Dynamic distribution groups using a wider set of filterable attributes or properties.*

7. On the New Dynamic Distribution Group page, review the configuration summary. Click New to create the group.

8. In the Completion page, examine the task status. The Exchange shell command used to create the group is displayed.

9. Click Finish to exit the New Dynamic Distribution Group Wizard.

TIP   *Clicking the Preview button allows you to preview the recipients that are returned using the filter defined. It's a good idea to go through this list of recipients returned by the filter and ensure the filter picks up the recipients you want. When you're adding new recipients, it is important to populate relevant attributes such as Department that are used for dynamic distribution groups, to ensure all such newly created recipients will be returned by the filter conditions of the group.*

The Exchange shell provides more flexibility in creating dynamic distribution groups. The command parameters allow the creation of DDGs either using precanned filters, just like the console, or using a custom OPATH filer in the RecipientFilter property. The parameters used with precanned filters are easy to understand and similar to the ones seen in the console.

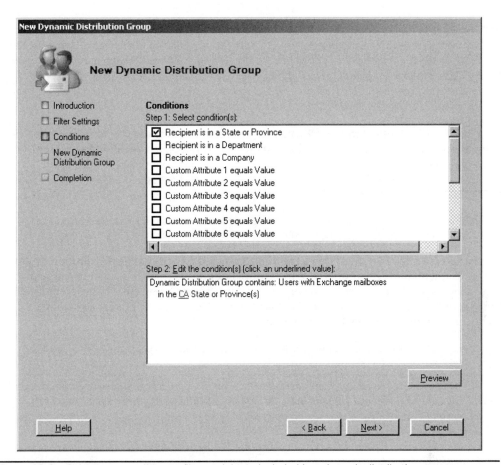

FIGURE 10-3   Selecting a condition to filter recipients included in a dynamic distribution group

NOTE   *When a DDG is created using a precanned filter such as the preceding, the RecipientFilterType property of the group is set to Precanned. You can modify the filter for such groups from the console, and you can also preview the list of recipients that the filter will return. When you use a custom OPATH filter, this is set to Custom. You cannot create groups with custom filters from the Exchange console, nor can you preview the recipients returned or modify the filter from the console.*

The following command creates a new DDG called "Sales" in the Distribution Groups OU. The precanned filter includes all user mailboxes from the Sales department:

```
New-DynamicDistributionGroup -Name "Sales" -IncludedRecipients
MailboxUsers -OrganizationalUnit "MyDomain.com/Distribution Groups"
-ConditionalDepartment "Sales"
```

TIP *For objects that use LDAP filters, such as dynamic distribution groups, EmailAddressPolicies, and address lists/GAL, Exchange Server 2007 uses the new OPATH filter syntax. Under the hood, this is converted to the familiar LDAP filters most Exchange 2000/2003 administrators are used to. This maintains a degree of compatibility for coexistence with Exchange Server 2000/2003. You can view this converted LDAP filter of a DDG by looking at the LdapRecipientFilter property of the group: Use Get-DynamicDistributionGroup "Sales" and select LdapRecipientFilter.*

Dynamic distribution groups with custom recipient filters allow you to filter recipients using properties that are not included in the precanned filters. In the following example, we create a new dynamic distribution group that filters on the server property of a mailbox. The group will include all mailboxes that are hosted on an Exchange server called E12Postcard:

```
New-DynamicDistributionGroup -name "E12Postcard-Mailboxes" -OrganizationalUnit
"e12labs.com/Distribution Groups" -RecipientFilter {ServerName -eq "E12Postcard"}
```

As noted earlier, Exchange stores the filter type used for a dynamic distribution group in the RecipientFilterType property of the group. For groups created using a precanned filter, this is set to 'pre-canned'. Likewise, for groups created using custom recipient filters, this is set to 'custom'. To get a list of all dynamic distribution groups using a custom recipient filter, use the following command:

```
Get-DynamicDistributionGroup | where {$_.RecipientFilterType -eq 'custom'}
```

NOTE *After creating the group, if you check the recipient filter property of the new group, you will find that OPATH automatically includes the appropriate filter string to exclude Exchange's system and CAS mailboxes. For the group created in the preceding example, the filter modified by Exchange looks like this:*
(servername –eq 'e12postcard' –and –not (Name –like 'SystemMailbox{') –and –not (Name –like 'CAS_{*'))*

To view the recipients that get filtered by a custom recipient filter requires use of the shell, using the following commands:

```
$DDG = Get-DynamicDistributionGroup "DDG Name"
Get-Recipient -filter $DDG.RecipientFilter
```

TIP *The use of LDAP filters in Exchange Server 2000/2003 address lists, recipient policies, and dynamic distribution groups exposed a large number of recipient attributes, providing a rich filtering mechanism. Exchange Server 2007's use of the OPATH filter changes this—only a subset of attributes are available as filterable properties to OPATH. A list of such filterable properties can be found in the document "Filterable Properties for the -RecipientFilter Parameter" (http://technet.microsoft.com/en-us/library/bb738157(EXCHG.80).aspx in Exchange Server 2007's online documentation. When working with OPATH filters, use the list in this document to determine which properties can be used.*

Disconnected Mailboxes

When a mailbox is disabled in Exchange, the association between the Active Directory user account and the mailbox is removed. Now the mailbox exists independent of the user account, which is known as a *disconnected mailbox*. In Exchange Server 2000/2003, such mailboxes continued to show in the mailbox database view, with a red X superimposed on the mailbox icon, and little else to distinguish them as disconnected. Additionally, the process of marking them as disconnected only occurred as part of the mailbox management process, which is scheduled to run every night.

Exchange Server 2007 provides a home to such orphaned mailboxes, in the Disconnected Mailbox node under Recipient Management, as shown in Figure 10-4. This makes it easier to determine which mailboxes are disconnected. Additionally, newly disconnected mailboxes show up quickly under this node, not subject to the nightly mailbox management process anymore.

Reconnecting a Disconnected Mailbox

The console provides a new Connect Mailbox Wizard to reconnected disconnected mailboxes. To connect a disconnected mailbox, use the following procedure:

1. In Exchange console, expand the Recipient Configuration | Disconnected Mailbox node.

2. Select the disconnected mailbox.

3. In the Actions pane, click Connect to start the Connect Mailbox Wizard.

4. In the Introduction dialog box, select the type of mailbox (user, room, equipment, or linked mailbox) and then click Next.

5. The console provides an easy way of connecting a disconnected mailbox to a matching user. Select the Matching user radio button and click Browse. Exchange looks for any user accounts that match the name on the disconnected mailbox. If the matching/original user account for this mailbox has been deleted or disabled for administrative reasons, you can reconnect the mailbox to any other account that is not mailbox- or mail-enabled. To do this, select Existing user.

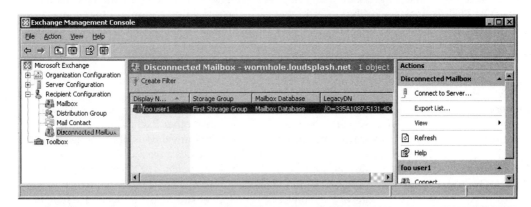

FIGURE 10-4   Disconnected mailboxes are displayed separately in the EMC.

6. The Alias parameter can be changed, if required.

7. The wizard also allows assigning a Managed Folder Mailbox Policy and an Exchange ActiveSync mailbox policy to the mailbox. Select the appropriate policies if you need to apply these.

8. Click Next.

9. On the Connect Mailbox page, examine the configuration summary.

10. Click Connect. This completes the process.

11. On the Completion dialog box, note the shell command used to reconnect the mailbox.

12. Click Finish to exit the Connect Mailbox Wizard.

To reconnect a disconnected mailbox using the Exchange shell, you need to be able to get the GUID of the disconnected mailbox. This can be done by querying Exchange for accounts that have been disconnected, using the following command:

```
Get-MailboxStatistics | where {$_.DisconnectDate -ne $null} | select
displayname,disconnectdate,identity | fl
```

The identity parameter of disconnected mailboxes has the GUID. Once you have this GUID—a fairly large alphanumeric value—you can reconnect the mailbox using the following command:

```
Connect-Mailbox -Identity '"c86ced6b-02bc-4be8-a4d6ab701433" -Database
"Mailbox Database" -User "foouser1" -Alias "foouser1"
```

If the account still exists in Active Directory and it is not mailbox- or mail-enabled, Exchange can select it for you, using the following command:

```
Connect-Mailbox -Identity "c86ced6b-02bc-4be8-a4d6ab701433" -Database
"Mailbox Database"
```

As seen in this command, we did not have to specify a user account to connect the mailbox to. Note that if the user already has been mailbox-enabled, a new mailbox with a new GUID already exists for that user. In that case, the preceding command to reconnect the orphaned mailbox to that user will not work. You will need to specify another user account to connect the mailbox to.

Moving Mailboxes

Every once in a while an administrator will need to move mailboxes, either from one mailbox store to another on the same server or to a mailbox store on another Exchange server. Moving mailboxes is also a common way of migrating between different versions of Exchange server. With a new mailbox server installed, moving mailboxes provides a way to migrate to another version of Exchange server with minimal downtime, moving batches of a few mailboxes at a time. This reduces the risk of upgrading an Exchange server to a newer version, which was possible with previous versions of Exchange but is no longer supported between Exchange Server 2000/2003 to Exchange Server 2007, because of the platform differences between these versions. (Although not currently supported, in-place upgrades may be supported in future versions of Exchange server, where the platform differences of 64-bit vs. 32-bit processors, Windows Server operating systems, and Exchange Server may not exist).

Yet other scenarios where mailbox moves may be required include the mailbox store being taken offline for reasons such as performing offline maintenance, and changes to the storage subsystem or the server hardware being implemented. Again, as in the scenarios involving migrations to newer versions of Exchange or to newer server hardware, mailbox moves also lower the risk and guarantee minimal downtime in cases of such maintenance operations being undertaken. Rather than imposing unwanted downtime on users during such maintenance operations, moving mailboxes to other available mailbox stores on the same server or a different server allows continued availability of messaging services to the affected users. As such, mailbox moves help your messaging department or IT organization to meet any Service Level Agreements (SLAs) by providing continued availability during maintenance operations.

Exchange Server 2007 and Outlook 2007's Autodiscover functionality further ensures that such mailbox moves cause less pain to affected users by making these moves transparent to users. No changes need to be made to users' Outlook/MAPI profiles, which automatically get redirected to the new location where their mailboxes reside, using the Autodiscover functionality.

Although most mailbox moves happen within the same Exchange organization, which spans an Active Directory forest, there are also cases where mailboxes need to be moved across AD forests, to another Exchange organization. Exchange Server 2007 provides the functionality to move mailboxes easily across an AD forest, between two different Exchange forests.

To move a mailbox from one mailbox store to another on the same server is no different than moving a mailbox to a mailbox store on another server in the same organization. To do this using the Exchange console, use the following procedure:

1. Expand the Recipient Configuration container and select Mailbox.

2. Select the mailbox (or mailboxes) that needs to be moved.

3. In the Actions pane, click Move Mailbox to start the Move Mailbox Wizard.

4. On the Introduction page, select the mailbox store, the storage group, and the server you want to move the mailbox to. Click Next to continue.

5. On the Move Options dialog box, select how corrupted messages should be handled during the move. Here are the options:

   • **Skip the mailbox** This option instructs the Move Mailbox Wizard to skip moving a mailbox if any corrupted messages are detected in it.

   • **Skip the corrupted messages** This option instructs the Move Mailbox Wizard to skip moving any corrupted messages and move the mailbox.

   • **Maximum number of messages to skip** If the option to skip corrupted messages is selected, this option sets a maximum number of corrupt messages that can be skipped before stopping the move mailbox process for that mailbox. Leaving the field empty instructs the wizard to skip all corrupt messages in that mailbox.

6. Click Next to continue.

7. On the Move Schedule dialog box, the wizard can be scheduled to run immediately or at a scheduled date and time in the future. This provides the ability to schedule mailbox moves after hours, when the users are less likely to be impacted by such a move.

PART IV

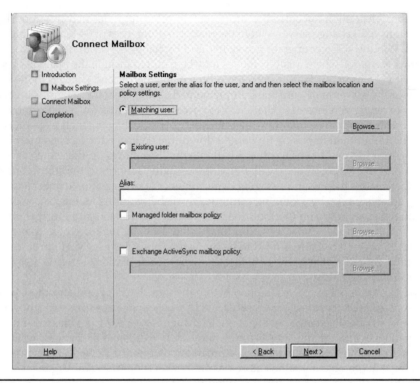

Connect Mailbox

- Introduction
  - Mailbox Settings
- Connect Mailbox
- Completion

Mailbox Settings
Select a user, enter the alias for the user, and and then select the mailbox location and policy settings.

○ Matching user:

[   ] Browse...

○ Existing user:

[   ] Browse...

Alias:

[   ]

☐ Managed folder mailbox policy:

[   ] Browse...

☐ Exchange ActiveSync mailbox policy:

[   ] Browse...

Help   < Back   Next >   Cancel

Figure 10-5 Selecting a mailbox server, storage group, and mailbox database to move a mailbox to

Additionally, should the Move Mailbox Wizard encounter any issues or otherwise continue running for a long period of time—perhaps because you selected very large mailboxes to be moved or selected more mailboxes than the after-hours window during which you want to complete the move mailbox process—it can be instructed to stop after a set period of time. This is done by selecting the check box "Cancel tasks that are still running after (hours):" and entering a numerical value in hours. The value defaults to 8 hours.

8. Click Next to continue.

9. On the Move Mailbox page, examine the summary information displayed, including the mailbox(es), the storage group, the mailbox store, and the server you want to move the mailbox to.

10. Click Move to continue the move.

If you scheduled the move to occur immediately, the wizard begins the move process. If scheduled to move at a later time, the wizard begins a countdown and will start the move at the scheduled time. One drawback the ability to schedule mailbox moves at a later time brings with it is the inability to close the dialog box and the console, or to log off the session, until the move has completed. The ability to close the dialog box and perhaps have the scheduled mailbox move appear in the Actions pane or another suitable location in the console is missing.

Cross-Forest Mailbox Moves

Exchange Server 2007 allows moving mailboxes from one AD forest and Exchange organization to another. This is invaluable in different scenarios such as cross-forest deployments and consolidating or splitting Exchange orgs when companies reorganize, merge, get acquired, or split.

To move mailboxes across Exchange orgs, a trust needs to exist or be created between the two AD forests that contain the orgs. The move can only be accomplished from the Exchange shell. The user account used to perform the move needs to be delegated the Exchange Administrator role in the source forest where the mailbox resides, and the Exchange Server Administrator role in the destination forest where the mailbox will be moved. Additionally, the account should be a member of the local Administrators group on the destination server.

Some additional considerations for cross-forest mailbox moves:

- The move-mailbox command requires at least one domain controller running Windows Server 2003 in both the source and destination forests.

- A cross-forest mailbox move results in a mailbox move and the creation of a disabled user account in the destination forest if one doesn't already exist. The user account is not moved from the source forest.

- The legacyExchangeDN attribute of the account in the destination forest points to the user account in the source forest. As such, only the account in the source forest can be used to access the mailbox. The move-mailbox process is not a substitute for tools such as the Active Directory Migration Tool (ADMT v3.0), which can move the account from the source forest to the destination forest.

- In scenarios where directory synchronization tools such as Microsoft Identity Integration Server (MIIS) are used to create contacts for users from the source forest; such existing contacts are replaced by a disabled user account.

- Items in the *dumpster* (used by the deleted item retention feature) are not moved unless the mailbox is allowed to be merged using the AllowMerge parameter.

To move mailboxes across two forests, use the following procedure:

```
$SourceCredential = Get-Credential
```

Enter credentials for the account from the source forest with appropriate permissions:

```
$TargetCredential = Get-Credential
```

Enter credentials for the account from the destination forest with appropriate permissions:

```
Move-Mailbox -TargetDatabase "Target Server\Target Storage Group\Target
Database"  -Identity "Joe User" -GlobalCatalog GC1.DestinationForest.com
-SourceForestGlobalCatalog GC2.DestinationForest.com -NTAccountOU
"OU=OUName,DC=DestinationForest,DC=com" -SourceForestCredential
$SourceCredential -TargetForestCredential $TargetCredential
```

Managing Mailboxes

Newly created mailboxes have a default set of parameters configured at the time of creation or inherited from Global Settings applicable to the organization or from the mailbox database on which the mailbox is located. Every so often, various parameters of a mailbox are required to be configured differently from others in the organization or on the same Exchange server or mailbox store. This can be easily accomplished from the Exchange console and shell. For the rest of this section, we will take a look at the Exchange-specific properties of mailboxes, ignoring the common user parameters exposed by Active Directory. Properties that are common to mailboxes and other types of recipients are discussed later in this chapter under the "Managing Recipients" section.

Mailbox Features

Exchange Server 2007 allows granting or denying mailbox access using particular protocols or access methods such as MAPI access, Outlook Web Access (OWA), Exchange ActiveSync (EAS), and Unified Messaging (UM).

To enable or disable mailbox features using the Exchange console, follow these steps:

1. Select the mailbox from the Recipient Configuration | Mailbox node.

2. In the Actions pane, click the Properties link.

3. In mailbox properties, select the Mailbox Features tab, as shown in Figure 10-6.

Figure 10-6
The Mailbox Features tab allows you to control specific client access methods.

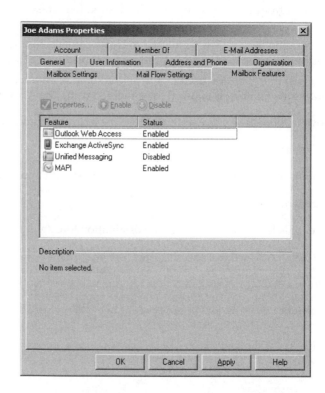

4. Select a mailbox feature to enable or disable. The following mailbox features are available from this tab:

- **Outlook Web Access**   OWA allows access to a mailbox using a web browser.

- **Exchange ActiveSync**   EAS allows access to a mailbox using the ActiveSync protocol used by mobile devices such as those running the Windows Mobile operating system.

- **Unified Messaging**   Unified Messaging allows access to UM features such as Auto Attendant, voicemail, and Outlook Voice Access.

- **MAPI**   MAPI is the protocol used by Microsoft Outlook clients.

In addition to these features, the shell allows the enabling/disabling of POP3 and IMAP4 access. All mailbox features except Unified Messaging can be configured using the Set-CASMailbox command:

```
Set-CASMailbox "Joe Adams" -OWAEnabled $false -MobileSyncEnabled $false
-MAPIEnabled $true -PopEnabled $false -ImapEnabled $false
```

Besides enabling IMAP and POP access, the Set-CASMailbox command allows a number of client access–related features for the preceding protocols, such as enabling or disabling Outlook Anywhere (RPC over HTTP) and Outlook Cached Mode, blocking particular versions of Microsoft Outlook, allowing OWA access to features such as Calendar, Contacts, Notes, and Search Folders, and so on. A list of the options available using the Set-CASMailbox command is available in the online documentation at http://technet .microsoft.com/en-us/library/bb125264(EXCHG.80).aspx.

NOTE *If the preceding link does not work or has been changed, search for "Set-CASMailbox" using a search engine to be directed to the current location of this document.*

By default, all mailbox features or protocols such as OWA, MAPI, EAS, POP3, and IMAP4 are enabled, with the exception of Unified Messaging. To enable Unified Messaging, a Unified Messaging Policy and a telephone extension number need to be assigned to a mailbox. This is done using the Enable-UMMailbox command:

```
Enable-UMMailbox "Joe Adams" -UMMailboxPolicy "Test UM Policy" -Extensions 4567
```

NOTE *A Unified Messaging Mailbox Policy does not exist by default. Unified Messaging functionality, including Unified Messaging Mailbox Policies, are covered in Chapter 9.*

To generate lists or reports of users with particular features enabled or disabled, you can use the pipelining and filtering capabilities of the Exchange shell. For example, to get a list of all mailboxes with Outlook Web Access disabled, use the following command:

```
Get-CASMailbox | where {$_.OwaEnabled -eq $false}
```

Managing Mailbox Settings

Mailbox settings control settings related to Messaging Records Management and mailbox storage quotas.

PART IV

Messaging Records Management

Compliance features for a mailbox include Managed Folder Mailbox Policy and Retention
Hold. Mailboxes can be assigned a Managed Folder Mailbox Policy, covered in detail in
Chapter 15.

To assign a Managed Folder Mailbox Policy to a mailbox using the Exchange console,
follow these steps:

1. Select the mailbox from Recipient Configuration | Mailbox node.

2. In the Actions pane, click the Properties link.

3. From the Mailbox Settings tab, select Messaging Records Management and click
   Properties. This opens the dialog box shown in Figure 10-7.

4. Check the option Managed folder mailbox policy.

5. Click the Browse button to select a Managed Folder Mailbox Policy and click OK.

6. Click OK to close the mailbox properties dialog box.

In the following example, we assign the Managed Folder Mailbox Policy
"Policy-DeletedItems90Days" to Joe Adams' mailbox:

```
Set-Mailbox "Joe Adams" -ManagedFolderMailboxPolicy "Policy-DeletedItems90Days"
```

Note *The Managed Folder Mailbox Policy needs to exist or be created before you use the preceding
command to assign it to a user.*

Messaging Records Management can be turned off for a particular mailbox in cases
where the mailbox may not be used for a period of time, such as when a user is on vacation.
This is called Retention Hold. Start and end dates can be specified when enabling Retention
Hold to make the hold effective for a particular period.

To enable Retention Hold for a mailbox using the Exchange console, follow these steps:

1. Select the mailbox from the Recipient Configuration | Mailbox node.

2. In the Actions pane, click the Properties link.

3. From the Mailbox Settings tab, select Messaging Records Management and click
   Properties.

Figure 10-7
Assigning a
Managed Folder
Mailbox Policy
to a mailbox

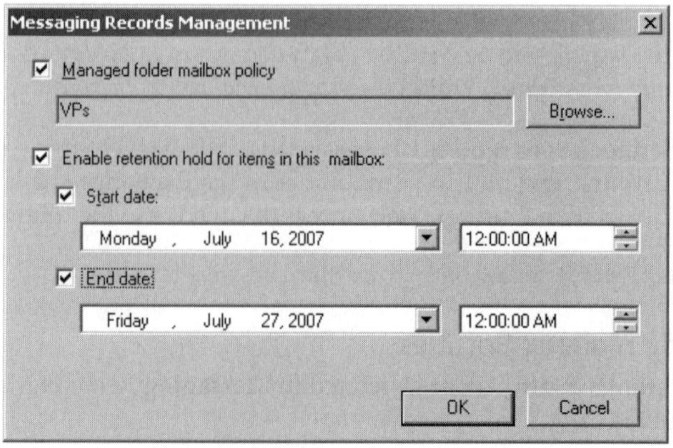

4. Check the option Enable retention hold for items in this mailbox.

5. Optional: Check Start date and enter a particular start date and time when you want the Retention Hold to begin. Check End date and enter a particular end date and time when you want it to end.

6. Click OK twice to close the mailbox properties dialog box.

To enable Retention Hold on a mailbox using the shell, use the following command:

```
Set-Mailbox "Joe Adams" -RetentionHoleEnabled $true -StartDateForRetentionHold
"7/16/2007" -EndDateForRetentionHold "7/27/2007"
```

NOTE *If a time is not specifically entered for either the start or end date for Retention Hold, it is scheduled to begin and end at 12:00 A.M. Optionally, a specific time can be entered with the start and/or end dates.*

Mailbox Storage Quotas

Storage quotas are an important tool for managing mailbox and mailbox store sizes. These prevent runaway growth of both mailboxes and mailbox stores, and they also prevent situations where mailboxes are "attacked" by a deluge of messages, perhaps of a large size, which can make the mailboxes (and thus the mailbox store) grow quickly to very large sizes. If left uncontrolled, a mailbox store can quickly grow to consume a large amount of free disk space, potentially resulting in a situation where the disk volume runs out of free space. When this happens, the mailbox store is dismounted. Whether intentional or not (or resulting from a virus or worm outbreak), this can effectively result in a denial of service, and therefore should be considered a security issue.

Mailboxes on a mailbox store inherit the mailbox quota limits configured on the store. Ever so often, you may need to configure individual mailboxes with limits that are either higher or lower than the mailbox limits on the mailbox store on which they reside.

Three different mailbox quota limits can be configured for a mailbox:

- **Issue Warning Quota**   The Issue Warning Quota is the first quota limit a mailbox can reach. When a mailbox reaches this limit, Exchange issues a warning message to the mailbox, without impacting the user's ability to send or receive messages. As such, it can be thought of as a "soft" quota.

- **Prohibit Send Quota**   When the mailbox size reaches the Prohibit Send Quota, Exchange stops the user from sending messages. The user does continue to receive inbound messages, though.

- **Prohibit Send and Receive Quota**   This is the final frontier, the largest size to which a mailbox can grow. When the mailbox reaches this limit, a user can neither send nor receive new messages. As such, this can be thought of as a "hard" quota or limit.

To configure a mailbox to bypass the mailbox storage quotas on the mailbox store using the Exchange console, follow these steps (as shown in Figure 10-8):

1. Select the mailbox from the Recipient Configuration | Mailbox node.

2. In the Actions pane, click the Properties link.

3. From the Mailbox Settings tab, select Storage Quotas and click Properties.

4. By default, the option "Use mailbox database defaults" is checked. To configure the mailbox to bypass the mailbox store default, uncheck this box.

5. To configure the Issue Warning Quota, check Issue warning at (KB). Type a value in the corresponding field.

TIP *All these values are in kilobytes. It is not uncommon for an administrator to mistakenly configure these limits much lower than intended for the simple reason that because storage capacity has grown so rapidly in the last few years, we have stopped using kilobytes as a storage unit and are now more used to megabytes or gigabytes instead. Setting these limits from the Exchange shell allows the flexibility of specifying these larger units of storage. An example of using storage units like megabytes follows.*

6. To configure the Prohibit Send Quota, check Prohibit send at (KB). Type a value in the corresponding field.

7. To configure the Prohibit Send and Receive Quota, check Prohibit send and receive at (KB). Type a value in the corresponding field.

NOTE *If "Use mailbox database defaults" is unchecked and no values are provided for the three mailbox storage quota limits, the mailbox will effectively have no mailbox storage quotas applied, resulting in an unlimited mailbox size.*

8. To change the deleted item retention period for the mailbox, uncheck the option Use mailbox database defaults. Optionally, modify the default value in the field Keep deleted items for (days).

CAUTION *When "Use mailbox database defaults" is unchecked, deleted items will be deleted permanently once the number of days configured in the corresponding field elapse. It is generally a good idea not to permanently delete items until the mailbox store has been backed up successfully. This is done by checking Do not permanently delete items until you back up the database. This is unchecked by default if you uncheck Use mailbox database defaults.*

9. Click OK to close the Storage Quotas dialog box and then click OK to close the Properties dialog box.

To set mailbox storage quotas using the Exchange shell, use the following command:

```
Set-Mailbox "Joe Adams" -UseDatabaseQuotaDefaults $false -IssueWarningQuota
250Mb -ProhibitSendQuota 275Mb -ProhibitSendReceiveQuota 300Mb
```

NOTE *When using the shell to set the quota limits, you can use either of the three storage units—kilobytes, megabytes, or gigabytes. When you use megabytes, the technical definition of a megabyte is used, which is 1024 kilobytes. Similarly, when you use gigabytes, the technical definition of a gigabyte is used, which is 1,048,576 kilobytes or 1024 megabytes.*

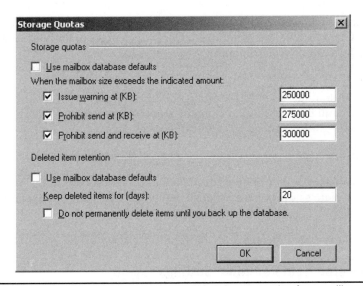

FIGURE 10-8 Modifying mailbox storage quotas and deleted item retention for a mailbox

Reporting on Mailbox Quotas and Mailbox Sizes

The Exchange shell provides a quick way of reporting on mailbox quotas and the actual mailbox sizes. Here's how to get a list of all mailboxes where the quotas are set not to inherit from the store:

```
Get-Mailbox | where {$_.UseDatabaseQuotaDefaults -eq $false} | sort name |
select Name,IssueWarningQuota,Prohibit*
```

The Get-MailboxStatistics command provides information similar to what Exchange Server 2000/2003 administrators are used to seeing when a store is expanded in those Exchange versions. To get a list of all mailbox sizes and their storage quota status (whether the actual mailbox size is above or below the storage quota), follow these steps:

```
Get-MailboxStatistics | sort DisplayName | ft
DisplayName,TotalItemSize,StorageLimitStatus
```

This command outputs the actual size of the mailbox in bytes. Though useful, it has been a long time since we measured or reported using this lowly unit of measuring storage/memory—even kilobytes for that matter. To convert the values to megabytes, use the following command:

```
Get-MailboxStatistics | sort DisplayName | ft
DisplayName,@{expression=$_.TotalItemSize.value.ToMb()};label="Size
(Mb)"},StorageLimitStatus
```

Note that the StorageLimitStatus parameter displays the mailbox status. This can be BelowLimit, indicating the mailbox size is below the IssueWarningQuota. If the mailbox size exceeds the IssueWarningQuota but is below the ProhibitSendQuota, the status is IssueWarning. On exceeding the ProhibitSendQuota, it changes to ProhibitSend. Finally, if it exceeds the ProhibitSendReceiveQuota, also known as the *hard quota limit*, no messages can be sent or received from the mailbox. The StorageLimitStatus displays the status as MailboxDisabled.

This allows us to filter based on the StorageLimitStatus parameter. For instance, here's how to get a list of all the packrats in an organization who refuse to delete any mail and let their mailbox sizes grow past the ProhibitSendReceiveQuota:

```
Get-MailboxStatistics | where {$_.StorageLimitStatus -eq "MailboxDisabled"}
```

Similarly, mailboxes can be filtered based on the values IssueWarning, ProhibitSend, and BelowLimit. Here's how to get a list of all mailboxes where the StorageLimitStatus is not BelowLimit:

```
Get-MailboxStatistics | where {$_.StorageLimitStatus -ne "BelowLimit"}
```

Modifying Deleted Item Retention Settings

In the following example, we modify the deleted item retention settings for Joe Adams' mailbox to bypass the mailbox store defaults, set the retention period to 27 days, and retain deleted items until the store is backed up:

```
Set-Mailbox "Joe Adams" -UseDatabaseRetentionDefaults $false -
RetainDeletedItemsFor 27.00:00:00 -RetainDeletedItemsUntilBackup $true
```

To get a list of mailboxes with custom deleted item retention settings, use the following command:

```
Get-Mailbox | where {$_.UseDatabaseRetentionDefaults -eq true} | Select
Name,RetainDeletedItemsFor,RetainDeletedItemsUntilBackup
```

Mail Flow Settings

Mail flow settings control delivery options, message size restrictions, and message delivery restrictions. Of the three, message size restrictions and message delivery restrictions are available for recipients other than mailboxes as well. These are covered later in this chapter. Let's take a look at the delivery options.

NOTE *Because the following settings are quite easy to configure in the Exchange console, step-by-step instructions on how to configure these are not provided. The matching shell commands are provided, however.*

Send On Behalf

The Send On Behalf permission allows a recipient to send messages on behalf of a particular recipient. Such permissions are commonly required to be granted on executive mailboxes to executive assistants. When composing messages, executive assistants can populate the From field in Outlook to send a message on behalf of an executive. A message sent in such a manner will clearly indicate the message was sent by User B on behalf of User A. This is different from the Send As permission, which allows User B to impersonate User A, thus making it appear that the message was actually sent by User A instead.

Let's assign the Send On Behalf permission on Dixie Baker's mailbox to Joe Adams:

```
Set-Mailbox "Dixie Baker" -GrantSendOnBehalfTo "Joe Adams"
```

Forwarding Address

In many cases, it is required to redirect inbound mail for a particular recipient to another recipient. Messages can be redirected transparently, without the mailbox for which mail is being forwarded getting a copy. Alternatively, messages can be delivered to that mailbox, and a copy can be sent to an alternate recipient by checking the option Deliver message to both forwarding address and mailbox.

NOTE *Inbound mail can be forwarded to Exchange recipients such as mailboxes, distribution groups, and mail-enabled public folders. To forward a copy to an external recipient, create a mail contact for the external e-mail address and modify the delivery options for the original recipient to forward to the mail contact. It is generally not advisable to forward mail to external e-mail addresses because this may result in mail loops being created, where the external e-mail address could generate some form of auto-response to forward a message back to the original recipient, which in turn forwards that message back to the external address. Additionally, such auto-forwarding may result in inadvertently forwarding sensitive e-mail messages outside the organization, potentially in violation of any existing policies restricting it.*

To forward mail for Dixie Baker to Joe Adams' mailbox using the Exchange shell, use the following command:

```
Set-Mailbox "Dixie Baker" -ForwardingAddress "Joe Adams"
```

TIP *To specify the identity of Exchange recipients in shell commands, you can use the recipients' e-mail addresses (for example, Set-Mailbox "Dixie Baker" –ForwardingAddress jadams@e12labs .com). You can also use a mail contact's external e-mail address in the command. However, if the e-mail address does not exist, the shell will gladly display an "object not found" error.*

To deliver a message to Dixie Baker and send a copy to Joe Adams as well, use the following command:

```
Set-Mailbox "Dixie Baker" -ForwardingAddress "Joe Adams" -
DeliverToMailboxAndForward $true
```

Maximum Recipients (per Message)

The Maximum Recipients field allows limiting the maximum number of recipients a mailbox can send messages to. It's important to note that in Exchange Server 2007 this no longer prevents sending a message to large distribution groups because group expansion happens after maximum recipients limit is checked. If a message is sent to more than the number of recipients allowed by Maximum Recipients, Exchange returns the message as undeliverable, with the following error code:

```
#550 5.5.3 RESOLVER.ADR.RecipLimit; too many recipients ##
```

Note *The Maximum Recipients per Message setting on a mailbox bypasses the value of maximum recipients in the transport configuration (MaxRecipientEnvelopeLimit).*

Here's how to set the maximum number of recipients on a mailbox using the Exchange shell:

```
Set-Mailbox "Dixie Baker" -RecipientLimits 50
```

Message Size Restrictions

Message size restrictions allow you to set individual sending and receiving message sizes for a mailbox. When you set this in the Exchange console, the storage unit used is kilobytes. When you're using the Exchange shell, the storage unit defaults to *bytes*, but the unit can be specified in kilobytes, megabytes, or gigabytes.

Here's how to set the maximum send and receive message sizes using the Exchange shell:

```
Set-Mailbox "Dixie Baker"-MaxSendSize 15Mb -MaxReceiveSize 1Gb
```

Note *Message size limits can be set in many different places—on the entire organization, on Send and Receive connectors, on recipients, and so on. These are covered in Chapter 7. When you're troubleshooting mail flow problems related to message sizes, it is important to know about and examine all the message size settings that can be configured.*

Message Delivery Restrictions

Message Delivery Restrictions settings are used to specify who can send messages to a mailbox, or who is prohibited from sending to it. By default, a mailbox (and all other types of Exchange recipients) accept mail from all senders.

A recipient can also be restricted to receiving mail only from authenticated senders via the option Require that all senders are authenticated.

Caution *Requiring senders to be authenticated prevents a recipient from receiving Internet mail.*

In the following example, we configure Dixie Baker's mailbox to receive mail only from Dmitri Daiter:

```
Set-Mailbox "Dixie Baker" -AcceptMessasgesOnlyFrom "Dmitri Daiter"
```

Next, we configure her mailbox to reject messages from Ilan Raab:

```
Set-Mailbox "Dixie Baker" -RejectMessagesFrom "Ilan Raab"
```

Finally, here's how to configure a mailbox to receive mail only from authenticated senders:

```
Set-Mailbox "Dixie Baker" -RequireSenderAuthenticationEnabled $true
```

E-mail Addresses

The functionality exposed by the E-mail Addresses tab is no different from its equivalent in Active Directory Users and Computers in Exchange Server 2000/2003. A recipient can have

---

**Preventing a Recipient or Group of Recipients from
Sending and Receiving Internet Mail**

Setting the –RequireSenderAuthenticationEnabled parameter to $true prevents a
recipient from receiving mail from unauthenticated senders, including Internet senders.
However, there is no equivalent setting to prevent a user from sending outbound mail
to an Internet recipient. In Exchange Server 2000/2003, an SMTP connector (for address
space *) could be configured with delivery restrictions for a recipient or a group, to
make this possible. In Exchange Server 2007, this can be accomplished using transport
rules. This is discussed in a blog post titled, "HOW TO: Prevent a user from sending
and receiving internet mail," at http://exchangepedia.com/blog/2007/07/how-to-
prevent-user-from-sending-and.html.

---

more than one e-mail address. Exchange applies E-mail Address Policies to recipients and
generates the e-mail addresses defined in the policy. The E-mail Addresses tab, shown in
Figure 10-9, enables creating additional e-mail addresses for a recipient, removing an
existing e-mail address, and setting a particular SMTP address as the default e-mail address
for the recipient.

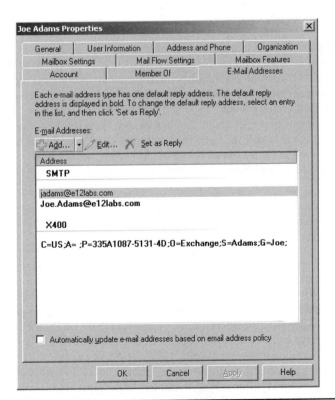

Figure 10-9 The E-mail Addresses tab in the Exchange Management Console can be used to add,
remove, or modify e-mail addresses and to set the default e-mail address.

To add an additional e-mail address for a recipient using the Exchange System Manager, use the following procedure:

1. In the recipient's properties pages, select the E-mail Addresses tab.
2. Click Add.
3. Type the SMTP e-mail address (for example, AltAddress@yourdomain.com).

NOTE *Clicking the Add button opens the dialog box for SMTP addresses, the default type of e-mail address. To add addresses other than SMTP e-mail addresses, click the drop-down arrow next to the Add button and select Custom Address.*

4. Click OK to exit the Properties dialog box.

TIP *When you're adding additional e-mail addresses for a recipient, the Exchange console and shell allow e-mail addresses for domains that the Exchange organization is not responsible for. However, simply adding additional e-mail addresses does not ensure that a recipient will be able to get e-mail for those addresses or domains from the Internet. Domains used in recipients' e-mail addresses should exist as accepted domains in the Exchange org. Additionally, to receive Internet mail for a domain, it is recommended to have MX records in the domain's DNS zone hosted on an Internet-accessible DNS server.*

Adding an e-mail address using the shell isn't a *one-liner*, unlike many tasks accomplished from the shell. The recipients' EmailAddresses property, which maps to the proxyAddresses LDAP attribute, is a multivalued property. When adding or removing a single value from multivalued properties, one needs to ensure the existing values are not overwritten—which is exactly what happens if you use the Set-Mailbox "Joe Adams" –EmailAddresses newaddress@domain.com command. Nevertheless, the shell does make it possible to accomplish this task using three short lines, compared to the hundreds of lines of script code many of us found ourselves writing or using until lately.

Here's how to add an additional e-mail address using the Exchange shell:

```
$Mailbox = Get-Mailbox "Joe Adams"
$Mailbox.EmailAddresses += newaddress@e12labs.com
$Mailbox | Set-Mailbox
```

Here's what we're doing: In line 1, we get Joe Adams' mailbox in a variable called $Mailbox. In line 2, we add the new e-mail address to the EmailAddresses property (held in the variable $Mailbox). Note the syntax used. In line 3, we dump the properties of the variable (which holds all properties of the mailbox, with the EmailAddresses property changed) and pipe it to a Set-Mailbox command. This commits the change to the mailbox.

Similarly, to modify a distribution group, you would use Get-DistributionGroup and Set-DistributionGroup commands instead of Get-Mailbox and Set-Mailbox. To modify a mail contact, you would use Get-MailContact and Set-MailContact.

Public folders break away from this pattern—instead of Get-PublicFolder and Set-PublicFolder, the Get-MailPublicFolder and Set-MailPublicFolder commands are used. Although a tad confusing initially, the former commands are used to work with the public folder, whereas the latter (Get/Set-MailPublicFolder) commands are used to work with

Exchange Server, Outlook, and Additional E-mail Addresses

Whereas Exchange server gladly receives e-mail addressed to any of a recipient's e-mail addresses, replying to an e-mail or sending a new message always results in the default e-mail address being used. This is also true when replying to a message that was originally received on an e-mail address other than the recipient's default e-mail address. Additionally, when composing an e-mail in outlook, if any of the sender's e-mail addresses are entered in the From: field in Outlook, it automatically gets resolved to the default e-mail address. This has been a long-standing annoyance of users and administrators alike, one that may get resolved in a future refresh of both Microsoft Outlook and Exchange server applications. Till then, users and administrators will have to resort to workarounds offered by third-party utilities like IvaSoft's ChooseFrom, or by creating additional mailboxes for additional e-mail addresses and allowing the user Full Mailbox Access and Send As permission on the additional mailboxes created for this purpose.

the public folder's corresponding Active Directory object, which actually holds e-mail addresses for mail-enabled public folders.

Changing the Default E-mail Address

The E-mail Address Policy applicable to a particular recipient determines which address is designated as the default e-mail address for a recipient. If a recipient has more than one SMTP address, the default e-mail address is displayed in bold type in the E-mail Addresses tab. It can be changed using the following procedure:

1. From the a recipient's properties pages, select the E-mail Addresses tab.
2. Select the check box "Automatically update e-mail addresses based on e-mail address policy" to uncheck it.
3. Select the e-mail address that should be set as the default e-mail address for the recipient.
4. Click the option Set as Reply.
5. Click OK to close the properties pages.

NOTE *The Set as Reply button in the E-mail Addresses page is grayed out until the recipient is removed from the scope of EmailAddressPolicies by checking Automatically update e-mail addresses.... This removes the possibility of an administrator changing the default e-mail address of a recipient, only to discover minutes later that it reverted to the earlier default e-mail address, thanks to the policy being applied again. Also note that removing a recipient from the scope of policies does not remove any existing e-mail addresses generated by policies or added manually.*

To change the default e-mail address using the Exchange shell, use the following command:

```
Set-Mailbox "Joe Adams" -EmailAddressPolicyEnabled $false
-PrimarySmtpAddress jadams@e12labs.com
```

Managing Send As and Full Mailbox Access Permissions

An Exchange recipient can be allowed the Send As permission for another recipient in the organization. This allows the recipient to impersonate another recipient when sending a new message by populating the From field in Microsoft Office Outlook. The Full Mailbox Access permission allows a user to access another user's mailbox. Exchange Server 2007 SP1 allows you to manage both Send As and Full Mailbox Access permissions from the EMC, as shown in Figure 10-10.

Managing Distribution Groups

Distribution groups share many common settings with mailbox users and other recipients:

- **Controlling who can send to a distribution group** It is important to control who can send messages to large distribution groups such as All Employees, or to important or sensitive distribution groups depending on business requirements. This can be controlled using Message Delivery Restrictions settings from a group's properties—the functionality is similar for all recipient types and is illustrated earlier in this chapter.

NOTE *By default, all new distribution groups are set to receive e-mail only from authenticated users.*

Some settings are unique to distribution groups. Let's take a quick look at these.

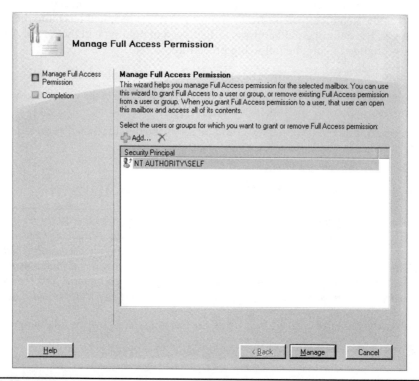

FIGURE 10-10 Managing the Full Mailbox Access permission from the EMC

- **Designating a group manager**   Distribution groups can be assigned a manager. The group can be configured to have the recipient configured as the manager receive delivery reports. The manager can also manage group membership.

- **Expansion server**   Distribution groups are generally expanded by the Hub Transport server that receives a message addressed to such as group. Expansion of distribution groups, particularly those with a very large number of members, can have an adverse effect on the performance of a Hub Transport server when many messages are sent to such large distribution groups. This can be avoided by configuring a group with an expansion server that has adequate resources to perform the task, as shown in Figure 10-11.

- **Out-of-Office Messages**   If your users often send messages to large distribution groups, quite frequently they will be greeted with plenty of "out-of-office" messages from members of the group who find it important to inform senders that they are either at home sick, out of the country on a business trip, or on a beautiful beach in Maui enjoying a Mai Tai. Given the love-hate relationship most Exchange administrators have with OOFs, and the fact that most users cannot live without them, Exchange Server 2007's new OOF features are a welcome relief. One OOF feature that does not get as much attention is how Exchange Server 2007 treats OOFs for distribution groups.

FIGURE 10-11
The Advanced tab of a distribution group's properties allows you to set an expansion server, hide the group from address lists, and control out-of-office messages and NDRs.

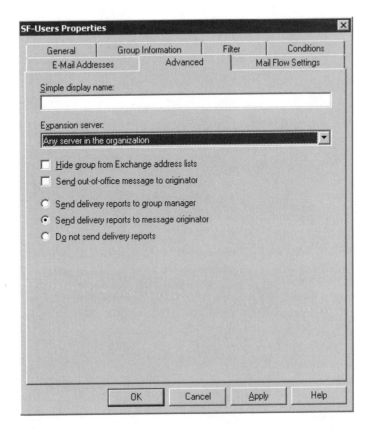

- **Delivery reports**   Although it may be important for senders to know about message delivery issues for messages sent to some distribution groups, it can be an annoyance to receive delivery reports from other, more casual distribution groups. Delivery reports can be controlled so they are sent to the sender, to the manager of the group, or not sent at all.

Summary

In Exchange Server 2007, the Exchange product team took a major decision to move recipient management back to Exchange server. Although administrators will initially find this change disruptive to their recipient management workflow, it does come with numerous benefits – the least of which is, not having to deal with the Recipient Update Service. The new administration and automation functionality provided by the Exchange Management Shell is also a major leap forward in lowering the cost of managing recipients, and managing Exchange servers in general.

So long, Exchange extensions for Active Directory Users and Computers – thou shalt be missed!

Outlook 2007

For years Microsoft has revered Outlook and Exchange as being "Better Together." This slogan continues to describe what can be accomplished when using Microsoft Office Outlook 2007 and Microsoft Exchange Server 2007 together cohesively. There are many new features in Outlook that can improve worker productivity and many that require or impact Exchange Server as well. Security is always something that software developers seek to improve, and Outlook 2007 adds a few features to enhance messaging security.

Feature Overview

Whether Outlook is installed as part of the Microsoft Office 2007 System or as a standalone Personal Information Management application, there are several updates to Outlook and its user interface. This is especially true of the toolbar on the various forms used by Outlook in addition to many new features.

New Office 2007 Ribbon

With each new version of Office, the number of commands and tools accessed through the menu and toolbar system has grown significantly. Personalized menus introduced in Office XP helped keep drop-down menus under user control, but the toolbar could not continue to support the growing number of features in its Office 2003 and earlier form. The Office 2007 Ribbon toolbar has been introduced as an adaptive solution for the toolbar. Contextual options are presented to the user depending on what form they are using, such as a new e-mail message or new task form. There is no "classic mode," so migrating to Office 2007 will require that users become familiar with the ribbon. Most Office applications have a single ribbon, but Outlook with its many forms has 19 ribbons. Figure 11-1 shows the ribbon for a new e-mail message.

Word 2007 Is the Standardized Editor

In previous versions, Outlook maintained multiple message composition editors for the different message formats. Outlook 2007 depends solely on Word 2007 as its e-mail editor. There has been some grumbling over weaker HTML and CSS support for content rendering with the embedded Word version, but the single editor should simplify Outlook while allowing some of the advanced formatting features and styles of Word 2007.

FIGURE 11-1   The Outlook 2007 Ribbon toolbar for the new e-mail message form

Word formatting is accessible in the text areas of tasks, contacts, and calendar items, as well as e-mail messages. This unified editor also eases the burden of Outlook programmers somewhat because there is greater consistency across the application.

Autodiscover Service

The Autodiscover service is actually an Exchange 2007 web service created when the Client Access Server (CAS) role is installed. It is consumed by Outlook 2007 as well as Windows Mobile 6 devices. It publishes configuration information that allows clients to establish Exchange connectivity automatically. When the CAS role is installed, it creates Service Connection Point (SCP) objects in Active Directory. When Outlook 2007 is launched for the first time, it queries AD for the SCP information and then locates the CAS and retrieves the Autodiscover.xml file from which its profile is automatically configured. We discuss Auto Account configuration with the Autodiscover service later in this chapter. Previous versions of Outlook are not able to benefit from the Autodiscover service.

Autodiscover information is maintained in an .xml file dynamically generated by the Client Access Server and stored in the following default locations:

- https://virtuecorp.com/autodiscover/autodiscover.xml
- https://autodiscover.virtuecorp.com/autodiscover/autodiscover.xml

The standards-based .xml file could be manually maintained and updated but still needs to keep the name autodiscover.xml. For most organizations, allowing the Autodiscover service control of this file is all that is needed. Outlook 2007 uses the Autodiscover service to find services such as Availability services, Unified Messaging (UM), and the Offline Address Book (OAB). In addition, the Availability service returns Free/Busy and out-of-office (OOF) information.

Cross-forest Improvements

Outlook 2007 also uses the Autodiscover web service to assist in cross-forest information sharing. This includes improvements in cross-forest mailbox moves and mailbox delegation. Free/Busy, OOF, and Outlook 2007 sharing requests, which are invitations for others to access a specific non–e-mail folder in the sender's mailbox, also can be sent cross-forest. Figure 11-2 shows an Outlook 2007 sharing request for a user's calendar. Autodiscover calls on the Availability service, which as a web service does not need to be in a trusted forest for organizational-level content. A trust is needed for more granular information on an individual's Free/Busy information, however.

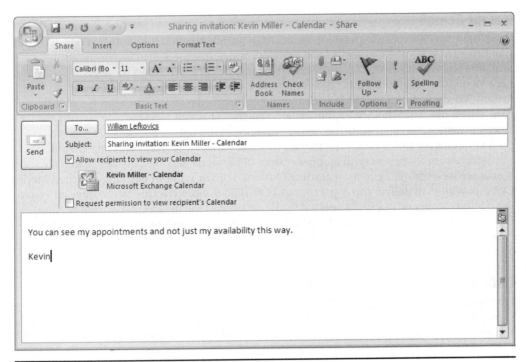

FIGURE 11-2   Outlook 2007 Calendar sharing request message

Reduction of Network Traffic

Outlook 2007 has improved caching for better performance. Shared folders, such as calendars, are cached locally to reduce calls to the server for that data. When accessing another user's shared folder, Outlook downloads a copy to the local machine, allowing the user to work with cached data, even when offline. Outlook 2007 with Exchange 2007 also enhances Cached Exchange Mode with partial-item download when messages in the Inbox are changed using another source. Instead of synchronizing the entire message after an existing message is changed through another client, like in Outlook Web Access (OWA), Outlook 2007 in Cached Exchange Mode will only bring sections of the message where the changes were applied across the wire to the local copy.

Network traffic is also reduced relative to previous versions when the Exchange mailbox quota is reached. When a user's mailbox reaches its quota, where policy dictates that sending new messages is prevented, the user is now blocked from sending at the client level. The message does not travel across the wire to the Exchange server first.

Productivity Enhancements

There are many changes to Outlook—some significant and others subtle—that impact the productivity of users.

Instant Search

Users have become more dependent on localized search functionality, and Outlook 2007 can take full advantage of Microsoft's local search product. Instant Search is automatically available when Outlook 2007 is installed on Windows Vista. Windows XP users will have to have Windows Desktop Search 3.0 or later (3.01 as of this printing) installed to benefit from Instant Search. If Windows Desktop Search is not installed on XP, a line atop the middle pane will show "Click here to enable Instant Search." This will send the user to the Desktop Search download at Microsoft. The classic Advanced Find option previously found in context menus for folders has been moved to Tools | Instant Search | Advanced Find.

Searches are more powerful and faster than in previous versions. Instant Search also works across all current clients, including Outlook with or without Exchange Cached Mode, Outlook with mail delivery to a .pst file, and OWA 2007. Search terms can be queried across the mailbox store and not just a specific folder, or even at the desktop level from within Outlook. Users can have the search output highlight their search terms in a color of their choosing, as shown in Figure 11-3. The status of the index can also be checked from the Tools | Instant Search menu.

To-Do Bar

Outlook 2007 organizes calendar items, tasks, and items flagged for follow-up into the convenient, retractable To-Do Bar. In the past the Task folder was underutilized because it resides in a window separate from the Inbox. The To-Do Bar brings immediate tasks to the

FIGURE 11-3
Instant Search options in Outlook 2007 with Windows Desktop Search

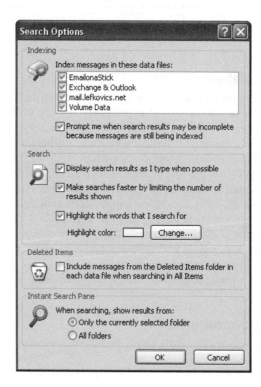

e-mail view and just about every other folder view as well, the exception being the Calendar view. The To-Do Bar is fixed to the right side of the interface, but how content is displayed within it can be somewhat customized. A default configuration is shown in Figure 11-4, but the user can control the size of the Date navigator, Appointment list, and Task list, as well as whether those items are even displayed in the To-Do Bar.

FIGURE 11-4
Outlook 2007
To-Do Bar with
calendar and
task entries

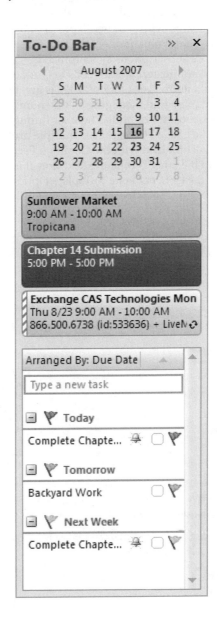

Integrated RSS

RDF Site Summary or Real Simple Syndication (RSS) has become an important mechanism for gathering information or staying up-to-date on site changes, news updates, and blog entries. There were a few third-party utilities that successfully integrated RSS with Outlook 2003, such as IntraVNews and NewsGator. RSS aggregation is now built into Outlook 2007. The list of RSS subscriptions in Outlook can also be synchronized with the Common Feed List (CFL), which is shared with Internet Explorer and programmatically accessible by other applications, such as SharePoint. Indeed, the first time Outlook 2007 is started it will ask the user if they want those subscriptions synchronized.

The interface for administering RSS feeds in Outlook is found in Tools | Account Settings, as shown in Figure 11-5. Outlook 2007 is great for managing a small number of RSS feeds, but some users may find managing a large number to be better handled by a separate RSS aggregator. RSS feeds can be added here, or through Internet Explorer if the feeds are synchronized with the CFL. If the user has multiple profiles on the same login and the RSS feeds are set to be synchronized with the Common Feed List, the feeds added in one profile will also be added to the other profile the next time it is accessed. To check whether Outlook is configured to use the CFL, navigate to Tools | Options. From the Other tab, select the Advanced Options button. Then look for a check box item that reads "Sync RSS feeds to common feed list."

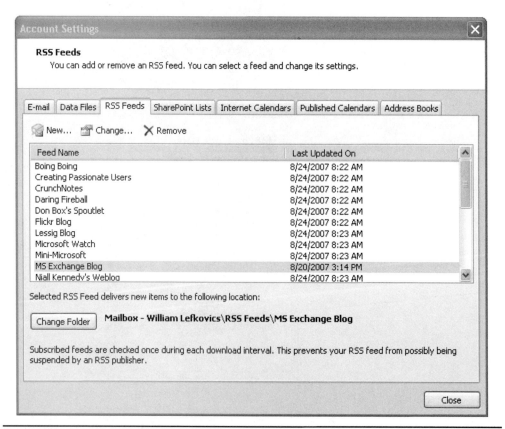

Figure 11-5   Outlook 2007 RSS feeds in Tools | Account Settings

There are a few options to configure with RSS on a per-feed basis. Figure 11-6 shows the window that opens when the user selects the Change button with a feed selected from the list in the Account Settings window. By default, Outlook 2007 does not download enclosures with RSS feed content, which are analogous to attachments in an e-mail message. Because feeds are polled by Outlook and delivered to the mailbox on Exchange through the client, the active server-based SMTP antivirus scanner will not scan these attachments. Either client or store scanning is used to scan RSS feed enclosures. With or without enclosures, a fair number of active RSS feeds can fill up a mailbox quite quickly. Store size may also grow unnecessarily if many users are subscribed to the same feeds. Both the Outlook user and Exchange administrator need to be aware of these potentially disruptive scenarios and use monitoring and mailbox management best practices.

Finally, the Outlook 2007 Import and Export feature adds the ability to export a user's RSS list to an Outline Processor Markup Language (.opml) file or import feeds from an .opml file. When importing from an .opml file, the user can select the desired RSS subscriptions from the list of feeds in that .opml. If Outlook is not configured to use the CFL, the user can still import feeds from the CFL through the Import and Export window as well.

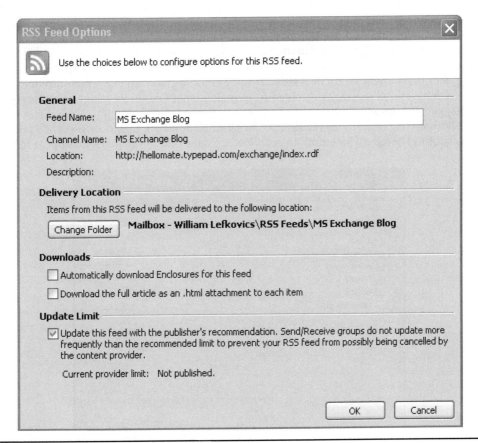

FIGURE 11-6   Outlook 2007 RSS Feed Options screen

Color Categorization and Follow-up Flags

There is a small-yet-important change to categorization. The colors formerly used when assigning a follow-up flag have been expanded to 25 and moved to the Categories option. Some colors on the palette do not have enough contrast between them, and it may be difficult for some users with accessibility issues, such as color blindness, to discern the difference. These categories can be personalized by renaming them. In addition, they can be assigned shortcut keys, up to 11. Color categorization can be applied to almost any Outlook item. Messages, tasks, contacts, and calendar items can all be assigned a colorized category, making them more easily recognizable, manageable, and searchable for the user. A common use of categories might be to assign one color for personal items and a different color for items pertaining to a supervisor or a project. Figure 11-7 shows the category options from Actions | Categorize | All Categories with some sample categories, some with assigned shortcut keys. Rules can be used to assign color categories to new messages, and categories can be a useful search parameter for Instant Search. Search folders, introduced in Outlook 2003 and still present in Outlook 2007, can be created based on categories as well.

Color category selections are stored in the users' default mailbox storage location, which with Exchange 2007 should be the mailbox on the server. In previous versions, category information was stored in the local Registry. This means categories now roam with the user. Group Policy with the Outlook administration template (outlk12.adm) can be used to standardize categories for Outlook 2007 clients; however, only the text, and not the color, is configurable. Group Policy can also control whether categories are included with messages arriving in users' mailboxes from other users. Allowing categorization across the enterprise is more useful when categories are consistent among users. An example of that benefit might be a standardized color applied against a position field in Active Directory. All messages received from management could be assigned a category and flagged red, for example.

Follow-up flags are still available in Outlook 2007; however, they now present a relative intensity of red based on time until their follow-up date. Follow-up items do appear in the

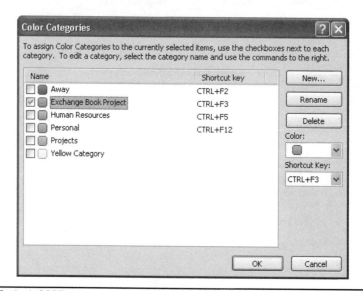

FIGURE 11-7   Outlook 2007 category options with sample categories

To-Do Bar as though they were tasks to better remind the user, as evident in Figure 11-4 earlier in this chapter. This feature, if well used, can return productivity value.

Improved Out-of-Office Settings

When using Outlook 2007 with an Exchange account, Out of Office (OOF) adds a couple new features. The interface, shown in Figure 11-8, is accessed through Tools | Out of Office Assistant. When "Send Out of Office auto-replies" is selected in the Out of Office Assistant, the user can then schedule when OOF should be used in advance. That in itself should reduce those OOF messages received for days after the person has returned to the office. In addition, separate OOF responses can be sent in response to messages from internal senders versus messages originating outside of the Exchange organization. For example, it may be more suitable to provide more information to coworkers than outside sales representatives. OOF messages also can be composed in HTML instead of plain text, as shown in Figure 11-8. When OOF is enabled, an icon in the bottom right of the Outlook 2007 interface both advises the user of the OOF status and provides a quick launch to the Out of Office Assistant and a quick way to disable OOF. These options are not available in POP and IMAP accounts.

The Out of Office Assistant does depend on the new Availability web service and the Autodiscover service on Exchange 2007, as covered in Chapter 8 as well as elsewhere in this chapter. The Autodiscover service provides the address for the Availability service, which in turn provides the URL for Outlook 2007 OOF. That URL is typically https://<exchange_server_fqdn>/EWS/exchange.asmx.

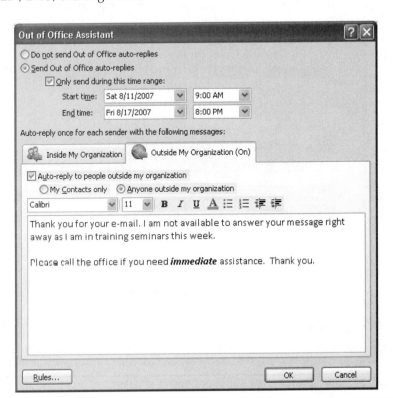

FIGURE 11-8 Outlook 2007 Out of Office reply setup scheduled for external senders

Scheduling and Calendar Improvements

Outlook 2007 improves several aspects of the calendar and scheduling. The Outlook 2007 calendar adds a new Week view highlighting a typical business week instead of a standard calendar week. In addition, tasks are integrated into the Calendar view as well. The To-Do Bar is not visible in the Calendar view; however, tasks are not shown on the bottom of the frame below the calendar when in Day or Week view. Tasks can be dragged to places on the calendar to allocate a specific time for them. This task and calendar integration increases exposure for the often underutilized tasks feature for Outlook. When multiple calendars are open, their contents can be viewed as in previous versions (side by side) or, new in Outlook 2007, overlaid one atop the other to more readily identify deltas. Figure 11-9 shows a busy Calendar view with tasks in different colors.

For scheduling, when changes are made to existing appointments, the attendees are sent an update with the changes highlighted. They do not need to accept a new invitation to facilitate the meeting change. Also, with the Availability service and Exchange 2007, there is no longer a dependency on public folders and associated replication delays, especially when retrieving Free/Busy calendar information across forests, for example.

FIGURE 11-9   Outlook 2007 basic Calendar view with appointments and tasks

Multiple Calendar Overlay

In previous versions of Outlook, where a user is permitted to view another user's calendar or create additional calendars, multiple calendars could be positioned side by side for comparison. An example is shown in Figure 11-10. Outlook 2007 allows for calendars to be placed over one another easily, thus visually exposing mutual availability for the calendar owners. There is an arrow at the top of the second calendar in Figure 11-10. Clicking that arrow merges the view of the two calendars, as witnessed in Figure 11-11. One calendar is presented in full color, with secondary calendar entries ghosted to show the different source. This overlay of calendars can be shown with more than two calendars, but after a few the screen can be very busy.

Internet Calendars

Internet Calendaring, or iCal, has been an IETF standard for many years and is outlined in RFC 2445. Outlook 2007 adds the ability to subscribe and display Internet Calendars. Internet Calendars are accessed in the tab labeled Internet Calendars in Tools | Account Settings.

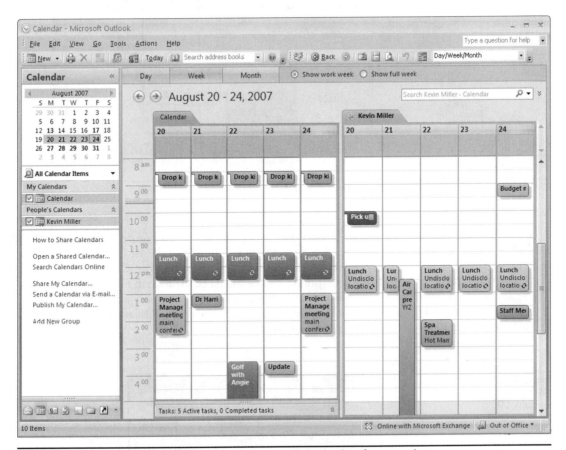

FIGURE 11-10   Outlook 2007 Calendar view with two parallel calendars for comparison

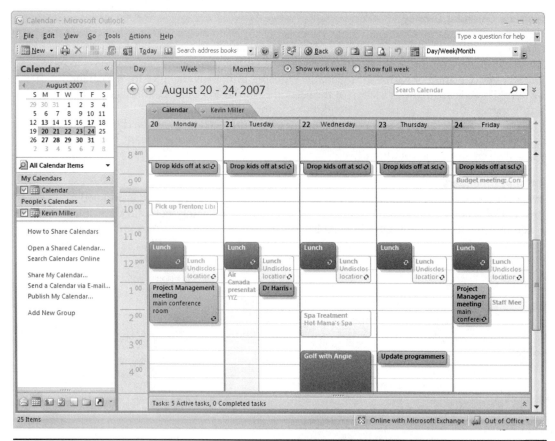

FIGURE 11-11   Outlook 2007 Calendar view with two calendars overlaid for quick comparison

A URL is needed in the form of webcal://<server>/<calendar_name>.ics. Figure 11-12 shows an iCal URL for adding a U.S. Holidays calendar to Outlook 2007 as an Internet Calendar.

There are a few configuration options for iCal subscriptions. Selecting the iCal account in Tools | Account Settings opens the Subscription Options dialog box shown in Figure 11-13. The iCalendar account can be for the individual on the specific computer only and cannot travel with the profile. Like RSS enclosures, iCal subscriptions can come with attachments. In the Subscription Options dialog box, attachments can be blocked.

FIGURE 11-12
Adding an iCal to
Outlook 2007

New Internet Calendar Subscription

Enter the location of the Internet Calendar you want to add to Outlook:

webcal://ical.mac.com/ical/US32Holidays.ics

Example: webcal://www.example.com/calendars/Calendar.ics

[Add]   [Cancel]

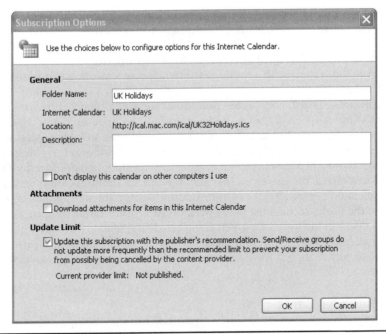

FIGURE 11-13   Outlook 2007 Internet Calendar subscriptions options

Publishing Calendars

The context menu on an Outlook 2007 calendar has the option Publish to Internet. Calendars can be published to Office Live Online or to a WebDav server to share with others. After that has been completed, the Shared Calendar tab in Tools | Account Settings will list the calendars.

Increased Room for Outlook Rules

In previous versions of Exchange Server, Outlook rules had to be contained in a single 32KB RPC packet. This meant that the number of rules was somewhat limited. With Unicode formatting introduced in Outlook 2003, even fewer rules fit in that 32KB limit. Many people met this limitation over the years and had to play words games to get the total bytes of their rules down in order to fit more within the 32KB limit. Finally, this limit has been doubled to 64KB by default, but expandable per mailbox to 256KB. In the Exchange Management Shell, the command to set the Rules Quota on a mailbox would be the following:

```
>Set-Mailbox "William.Lefkovics" –RulesQuota 256KB
```

Unified Messaging and Instant Messaging Integration

One of the most significant changes in Exchange going to version 2007 is the addition of Unified Messaging (UM) technology. This will be covered in greater detail in Chapter 13, but it is important to recognize changes for the end users. UM features are somewhat integrated with Outlook 2007 through the add-in UmOutlookAddin.dll in the Trust Center, which is shown later in this chapter in Figure 11-17. Voicemail and inbound faxes can be directed to users' Inboxes just as messages with attachments. When calling into the voicemail system, a user can initiate actions that send information to other mailboxes. For example, a user can use voice to have the system send a message to attendees of a meeting to advise them that the user will be late.

Instant Messaging is also part of the communication convergence. Presence information can be seen in Outlook when "Display online status next to a person name" is selected in Tools | Options | Other in Outlook. If the sender is not offline, an Instant Message can be called in reply from Outlook. Outlook 2007 integrates with Windows Live Messenger, MSN Messenger, and Windows Messenger, but is especially useful when deployed with Office Communicator, which is the preferred IM client for Office Communication Server 2007 and Live Communication Server 2005. For Office Communicator, the individuals do not have to be included in the user's contact list to see their presence information. Figure 11-14 shows presence awareness in the form of a green circle beside the sender through Outlook 2007. Office Communicator can also integrate with the phone system, alerting the user of new calls or automatically changing the user's presence status to unavailable while their phone is engaged.

Electronic Business Cards

eBusiness cards in Outlook 2007 are simply a rendering of contact information to take the form of a classic paper-based business card. In addition to the standard contact information, eBusiness cards can include logos or photos and can take on company colors as well as match stationery. They can also pull content from external sources such as SharePoint.

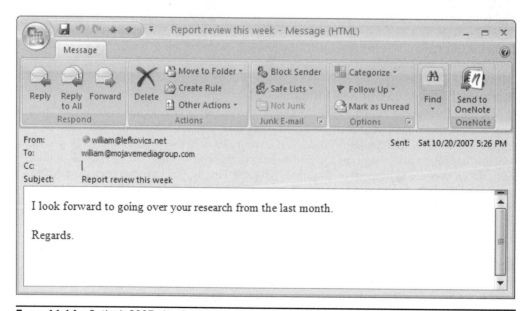

FIGURE 11-14 Outlook 2007 showing presence awareness of the message sender

Security Enhancements

Microsoft continues to work to improve security and message hygiene in Exchange and Outlook, both separately and together.

Outlook E-mail Postmark

In an ongoing effort to reduce spam—or more accurately reduce legitimate e-mail being tagged as spam—Microsoft has added a new feature called an *e-mail postmark.* By default, outbound messages in Outlook 2007, when used with Exchange 2007, are given a postmark based on the characteristics of that message. The postmark is created as a pair of custom SMTP X-headers followed by a sample puzzle algorithm output:

```
>x-cr-puzzleid: {24B75461-3B63-4C9E-91F0-D9A3733C075F}
>x-cr-hashedpuzzle: ANCj ASoD B9Wr D64F GeSW G7HL G8Wb HO5P H7VP IsHi NCIV
```

This unique presolved puzzle or fingerprint uses a little bit of resources to compile and slows outbound e-mail slightly. If the recipient uses Exchange 2007 or another mail system capable of validating these client e-mail postmarks, the chances of a message being classified as junk mail can be reduced. The Exchange 2007 Content Filter will decrease the Spam Confidence Level (SCL) value assessed for the message. Spammers do not tend to spoof postmarking because of the resource cost when sending e-mail in the quantities that spammers need to send. Validation of Outlook e-mail postmarks can be toggled off at the Exchange 2007 server using the Exchange Management Shell.

E-mail postmarks are not applied when the recipients are all within the organization, the message has been encrypted, or it has been restricted through digital rights policy. The postmark feature can be toggled off in Tools | Options | Preferences | Junk E-mail at the bottom of the Options tab.

Message Classifications

Outlook 2007 and Exchange 2007 offer another security and management mechanism in the form of message classification. Classifying e-mail content is a way of describing a message for the purposes of meeting regulatory compliance or confidentiality policies. Unfortunately, message classification is not operational by default and requires some administration to implement. Message classification provides only an informational label to the messages; however, Exchange 2007 Transport rules can be created based on an assigned classification to assist with internal ethical walls for message flow.

When Exchange 2007 is installed, it creates a script repository with some very useful Exchange Management Shell scripts. One script contains basic message classifications for Outlook and Exchange and is by default located at:

```
>c:\program files\microsoft\exchange\scripts\Export-OutlookClassification.ps1
```

To export those classifications to an .xml file, we execute the PowerShell script as follows:

```
>Export-OutlookClassification.ps1  > <path>\OutlookClass.xml
```

PART IV

The path to the folder level must exist; the script will not create the path if it does not. OutlookClass.xml creates several default classifications and their descriptions:

```
<?xml version="1.0" ?>
<Classifications>
     <Classification>
          <Name>A/C Privileged</Name>
          <Description>This message is either a request for legal advice from an
attorney or a response by an attorney to a request for legal advice. It should be
treated confidentially, should only be sent to people with a need to know, and
should only be forwarded by an attorney.</Description>
          <Guid>d74dbde8-4cb0-4043-ae4b-2a1b5686c9dc</Guid>
          <AutoClassifyReplies/>
     </Classification>
     <Classification>
          <Name>Attachment Removed</Name>
          <Description>A system-generated classification to inform users that an
attachment was removed from this message.</Description>
          <Guid>a4bb0cb2-4395-4d18-9799-1f904b20fe92</Guid>
     </Classification>
     <Classification>
          <Name>Company Confidential</Name>
          <Description>This message contains proprietary information and should
be handled confidentially.</Description>
          <Guid>19e795ab-f38c-4d55-a009-0a3ad32ffc1f</Guid>
          <AutoClassifyReplies/>
     </Classification>
     <Classification>
          <Name>Company Internal</Name>
          <Description>This message contains sensitive information that should
only be delivered to internal recipients.</Description>
          <Guid>f93fcaf3-00b6-4bfe-a84b-40e78f498560</Guid>
          <AutoClassifyReplies/>
     </Classification>
     <Classification>
          <Name>Partner Mail</Name>
          <Description></Description>
          <Guid>030e9e2f-134b-4020-861c-5bfc616f113d</Guid>
     </Classification>
</Classifications>
```

The .xml file reveals the default categories of A/C Privileged, Attachment Removed, Company Confidential, Company Internal, and Partner Mail. Using the EMS, administrators can add their own classifications as well. The cmdlet New-MessageClassification can create the label and a description for the new classification. Exchange will automatically generate a new GUID for the classification. An example of this cmdlet in use might be as follows:

```
>New-MessageClassification -Name "Complete Exchange 2007" -DisplayName
"Exchange2007" -SenderDescription "McGraw Hill Exchange Book Project"
```

Figure 11-16 shows the new classification this command added to the default offerings.
The .xml file must be stored in a location accessible to Outlook 2007 at startup. A network share location would prevent it from being used offline. The .xml file can be pushed out to Outlook 2007 client workstations in a login script, through Group Policy, SMS, or another

desktop management solution. The same applies to the subsequent Registry entry that is required for each Outlook 2007 workstation that is to send e-mail using message classification. The Registry values tell Outlook where to retrieve and load the .xml file so it can make the message classifications available to the user interface. The Registry changes can be manually entered or saved and distributed as a .reg file, as follows:

```
Windows Registry Editor Version 5.00

[HKEY_CURRENT_USER\Software\Microsoft\Office\12.0\Common\Policy]
"AdminClassificationPath"="<path>\\OutlookClass.xml"
"EnableClassifications"=dword:00000001
"TrustClassifications"=dword:00000001
```

The result should appear in the Registry as it does in Figure 11-15. Note that the message classification configuration is user specific and does not roam with the user. The name of the .xml file is arbitrary as long as the value in the Registry matches the actual name and path in the file system.

The other message classification cmdlets are listed next:

```
>Get-MessageClassification
>Remove-MessageClassification
>Set-MessageClassification
```

After exporting the PowerShell script to an .xml file, customizing the .xml file, pushing the .xml file to the Outlook 2007 clients, and pushing out the Registry changes on those Outlook clients, the user can now apply message classifications to messages, as shown in Figure 11-16. Because this Registry entry uses the HKEY_CURRENT_USER, all Outlook profiles generated for this user will have the classifications available for use.

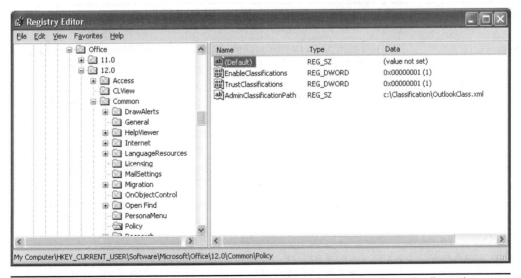

FIGURE 11-15   Windows Registry on the Outlook 2007 workstation showing the .xml policy path

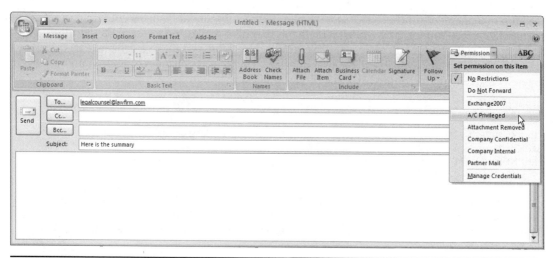

FIGURE 11-16   Applying message classification to a new message in Outlook 2007

In Exchange 2007, every message passes through a Hub Transport server. At the Hub Transport, the administrator can implement message transport rules that can act upon message classifications for compliance or other company policy.

Trust Center

Under the Tools menu in Outlook 2007 is the Trust Center option. This interface consolidates several client-side security features for Outlook, as described in Table 11-1.

Trust Center Category	Description
Trusted Publishers	Authors of macros, ActiveX, add-ins, or any other application extension trusted by Outlook through a reputable and current digital signature.
Add-ins	This is a summary of add-ins for the local installation of Outlook. Figure 11-17 shows the Exchange Unified Messaging add-in UnOutlookAddin.dll highlighted.
Privacy Options	These options control user connectivity with Microsoft in various forms—from online help access to participation in Microsoft's Customer Experience Improvement program.
E-Mail Security	Allows configuration of personal encryption and digital signatures as well as forcing plain text for inbound messages.
Attachment Handling	Controls previewing of attachments in the reading pane and allowing replies with changes to attachments.
Automatic Download	Controls whether Outlook downloads images in HTML content in messages, RSS, and other sources.
Macro Security	Disables or configures warnings for macros.
Programmatic Access	Allows the configuration of alerts when another application attempts to access the address book or send an e-mail on behalf of the user.

TABLE 11-1   Outlook 2007 Trust Center Configuration Options and Descriptions

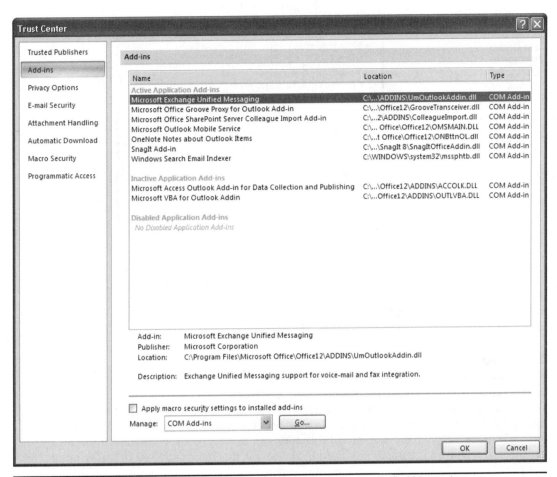

PART IV

FIGURE 11-17   Outlook 2007 Trust Center showing the add-in for Exchange Unified Messaging

Figure 11-17 shows the Trust Center window opened to the Add-Ins page. Highlighted is the Unified Messaging add-in used by Outlook 2007 to better use the new Unified Messaging components of Exchange 2007.

Document Attachment Preview

Outlook 2007 now allows the preview of certain attachments within the preview pane. In this setting, Outlook maintains security without the need to open the full associated application. The various Office system data files will readily show in the preview pane in this manner, but other applications may need to have an application previewer installed to view their files. Adobe added previewer functionality in their free Adobe Reader in version 8.1 released earlier in 2007. The attachment needs to be selected for the preview to be shown in the preview pane.

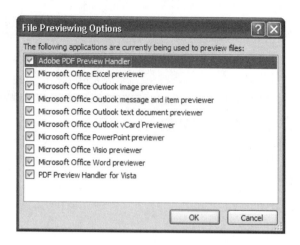

Attachment previewing can be toggled on or off in the Outlook 2007 Trust Center in the Attachment Handling section. Individual attachment types for which a previewer is available can be enabled from there as well. The list of previewers available for a typical Office 2007 installation is shown in Figure 11-18.

Safelist Aggregation

In Outlook, the user can maintain whitelists and blacklists of addresses for anti-spam filtering consideration. These are called the safe senders list, safe recipients list, and blocked senders list and, historically, have been a client-side feature. Safelist aggregation is a server-initiated collection of safe senders and safe recipients lists from Exchange users saved in Active Directory. From there, the safelist collection can be read by the Hub Transport role or synchronized with an Edge server with ADAM. Moving this information to an earlier point in the message hygiene flow reduces resources spent filtering messages at the server level that the recipient has deemed safe as a message sender as well as reduces the occurrences of false positives. In Outlook 2007, the safelists are accessed through Actions | Junk E-Mail | Junk E-mail Options. Figure 11-19 shows the Safe Senders tab with some sample addresses. Safelist aggregation is discussed in more detail in Chapter 17.

Auto-Encryption

Exchange 2007 installs with a set of certificates for encryption. Wherever possible in message flow, Exchange encrypts content automatically. Transport Layer Security (TLS) is used between Exchange servers in the organization, and RPC encryption is in place from Outlook to Exchange and Exchange to Outlook. In addition, if an external SMTP server supports TLS, Exchange will force encryption opportunistically. When possible, message communication is auto-encrypted for transport.

NOTE *Transport encryption is not the same as message encryption. The message is encrypted in transport; it is not encrypted in the information store.*

PART IV

FIGURE 11-19
Outlook 2007
Safe Senders tab
in the Junk E-mail
Options dialog box

Managed E-mail Folders

Exchange 2007 introduces managed folders for compliance and retention requirements. Through Exchange, an administrator can provision mailbox folders in client mailboxes with specific retention and expiration parameters and manage them centrally. In Outlook 2007, a managed folder does not appear any different from a normal e-mail folder.

The Managed Folder Assistant in the Exchange Management Console allows the creation and configuration of managed folders for the enterprise. Then a Managed Folder Policy is created to which managed folders can be added. Finally, Managed Folder Policies can be applied to users or groups. The managed folders functionality is covered in more depth in Chapter 18 on regulatory compliance.

Mailbox Cleanup

Mailbox Cleanup is an administrative improvement, but also a security enhancement because it may be part of a compliance or archival policy. In Outlook 2007, the Mailbox Cleanup command under the Tools menu opens a window where, much like the Trust Center, several options have been consolidated. In this case, the options involve the maintenance of users' mailboxes. Figure 11-20 shows the different categories of the Mailbox Cleanup window, each described in Table 11-2.

Mailbox Cleanup Feature	Feature Description
View Mailbox Size	This button opens a window showing the size in KB of each folder in the mailbox. This view helps identify the distribution of mailbox content by volume.
Find items by size or age	This is a preset query to return a list of items older than a chosen age or items greater than an input size. These are likely best suited for archival or deletion.
AutoArchive Settings	AutoArchive allows mailbox maintenance by automating the archiving of content of a specific minimum age to a personal folders file (.pst).
Empty Deleted Items	Simply empties the Deleted Items content. In addition, a button returns the value of the Deleted Items folder only.
Conflicts	If there is any conflicting content, where messages of the same ID think they are the right one, or offline synchronization resulted in multiple messages, conflicts can be resolved through this option.

TABLE 11-2 Mailbox Cleanup Options in Outlook 2007

FIGURE 11-20
Outlook 2007
Mailbox Cleanup
window

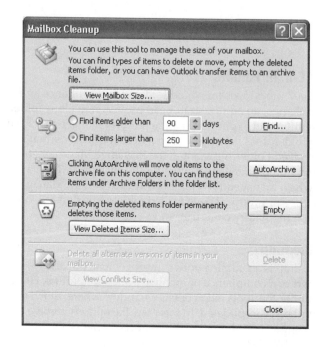

Deploying Outlook 2007

Most Outlook installations in business are part of full Microsoft Office System deployments. Many of the tools available for deploying and customizing Outlook 2007 also apply to Office 2007.

System Requirements

Outlook 2007 requires Windows XP Service Pack 2 or greater with a minimum of 256MB of RAM and a CPU running at 500 MHz or more. Those minimums double if Outlook is deployed with Business Contact Manager. In addition, Vista has greater resource demands as well, which will bring the RAM requirement up to 1GB at least. About 2GB of free hard drive space is necessary for the Local Installation Source files. The Office Source Engine (oso.exe) copies the compressed installation files to the hidden folder \MSOCache\All Users and calls Windows Installer to install from that point.

Deployment Options

Microsoft provides several mechanisms for customizing Office 2007 installations. Companies may opt for third-party offerings to manage Office upgrades, such as Altiris Client Management (now Symantec), or installations across the network. Alternatively, they may already have systems in place to manage application rollouts. Of course, administrators can always just copy the CD to a network share and run setup.exe from there manually.

Office Customization Tool (setup /admin)

When you run Office 2007 setup.exe with the /admin switch, it starts the Office Customization Tool (OCT). OCT replaces the Custom Installation Wizard (CIW) from the Office 2003 Resource Kit. OCT has two main functions—to create configuration files (.msp) for Office deployments and to generate Outlook profile files (.prf) for profile configuration.

Figure 11-21 shows the four main sections of the OCT as Setup, Features, Additional Content, and Outlook, as detailed in Table 11-3, and it shows Outlook profile settings configured in the right pane. In the Modify User Settings under the Features section, administrators can configure Outlook with many of the same settings accessible through the menus in Outlook after it is installed.

OCT Section	Description
Setup	Configures installation location, first-run scripts, and product key control. License acceptance, previous version uninstall, and high-level security settings are also configured here.
Features	Set installation state for components and configure user settings. The user settings are analogous to menu operations in Outlook, such as the various tabs in Tools I Options.
Additional Content	Here the administrator can add files or make Registry changes. The OCT can be used to deploy message classifications, for example.
Outlook	Outlook warrants its own section for profiles and account settings, such as cached exchange mode.

TABLE 11-3   Office Customization Tool Sections and Their Description

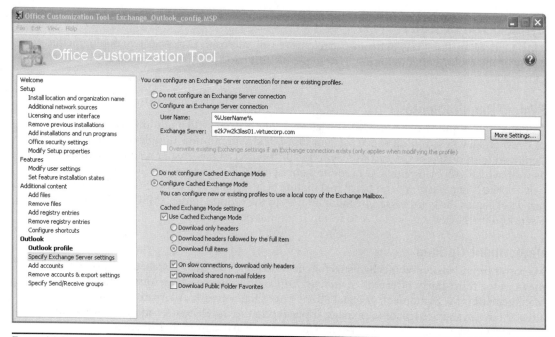

FIGURE 11-21   Office Customization Tool with the Features section showing Exchange Server Settings

OCT can provision customized profiles and even allow for export of profile information to .prf files. Outlook has its own section in the OCT where profile and account information can be entered. After configuring Outlook account information in the Outlook section, navigate to Remove accounts & export settings. Here, you'll find a button labeled Export Profile Settings. This will save the configuration as a .prf file, which can be redistributed to configure Outlook profiles. OCT can also configure Cached Exchange Mode settings and Offline Address Book configuration.

The OCT allows administrators to configure specific settings for their deployments and generate an .msp file to accompany installations. After configurations are made, using File | Save will allow the administrator to name the .msp file. The .msp file gets placed in the Updates folder in the Office 2007 installation source location. Appropriate files in this folder will get run after the core installation of Office. The OCT only establishes customized Office settings at installation; it does not enforce those settings as policy.

Config.xml

The config.xml file is read at the start of installation of Office 2007 to apply specific configuration information to the installation, including the 25-character serial key. It replaces the old setup.ini information file from previous versions. Config.xml does have some overlap with the OCT but is used in different places. If both a setup customization file (.msp) and config.xml are used simultaneously, the latter takes precedence. Primarily, config.xml would be used in conjunction with Group Policy for software deployment, but can also be referenced running Office setup.exe manually as well when it resides in the same folder as setup.exe. Running Office setup with the /config switch further allows the administrator to define an alternate path to the config.xml file.

There are many elements and attributes configurable with setup and config.xml. These pertain to Office 2007 as a whole and are beyond the scope of this book.

Group Policy Objects (GPO)

Office 2007 can also be distributed to workstations using Group Policy's software installation mechanism. Config.xml is required for GPO software deployment of Office; however, when Office is deployed using GPO, only a subset of the options is read by setup. Table 11-4 outlines the four config.xml options used in a GPO installation of Office 2007. Any other options defined in config.xml would be ignored.

Outlook 2007 GPO Settings   The first thing needed to distribute Office 2007 through GPO is the 2007 Office System Administrative Templates (ADM). This set of templates is downloaded from Microsoft.com. Within that set of administrative templates is the Outlook template called outlk12.adm. After opening the Group Policy Management console, navigate to the Group Policy Objects container beneath the domain object. A right-click on the desired policy will allow us to click Edit, which opens the Group Policy Object Editor. In Figure 11-22, the policy name is Windows Clients. Right-clicking the Administrative Templates object offers an Add/ Remove Template option. Navigate to the outlk12.adm template from the expanded Office 2007 templates download. Now the policy includes settings relevant to Outlook 2007 in a container called Microsoft Office Outlook 2007 under Administrative Templates, beneath the User Configuration heading. Figure 11-22 also shows some of the Outlook 2007 related options in the GPO policy after the Outlook administrative template is applied. These settings might look familiar because they are very similar to the options presented in the OCT. These settings will be applied to clients with the rest of the policy.

Office 2007 GPO Software Installation   Office 2007 is installed through the Computer Configuration container. Right-click the Software Installation object under the Software Settings folder and select New | Package. This allows us to navigate to the appropriate .msi file for deployment. Normally, this is the path to a network share where the Office 2007 installation files have been copied. Note that GPO is looking for a Microsoft installer package and not setup.exe. For example, in Office 2007 Enterprise, this is located at \Enterprise.WW\ EnterpriseWW.msi. Once this file is selected, the package Properties window will appear,

Config.xml option	Description
INSTALLLOCATION	Fully quallfied installation path on the destination workstation.
OptionState	Configures installation options for different Office features.
PIDKEY	The 25-character volume license key.
Add Language / Remove Language	Add or remove a language from the installation.

TABLE 11-4   Office 2007 config.xml Options Used in a GPO-driven Installation

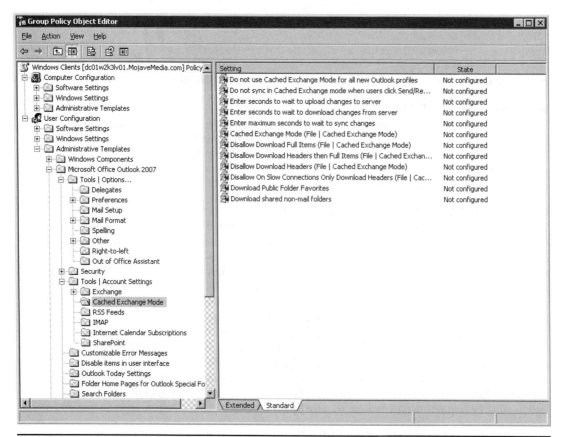

FIGURE 11-22   Group Policy Objects Policy with Outlook 2007 Administrative Template add-in showing some Outlook configuration settings

offering customization opportunities for the installation. Office 2007 is assigned to workstations and not published. The administrator can define what application, if any, is being upgraded. Also, any Microsoft installation transform files (.mst) to customize the installation are associated with the installation package in the Modifications tab of the Properties window. Figure 11-23 shows the Office 2007 Enterprise package added to assigned packages for deployment under the Computer Configuration container.

The next time the remote computer is restarted and the policy is applied, Office 2007 Enterprise will be installed, referencing any properly located and formatted customizations.

System Management Server 2003 R2

SMS 2003 is still a flexible option for deploying software solutions. Office 2007 is no exception, especially when combined with Office 2007 deployment tools such as the OCT. SMS can create specific installation packages that get pushed out to the client when resources are free

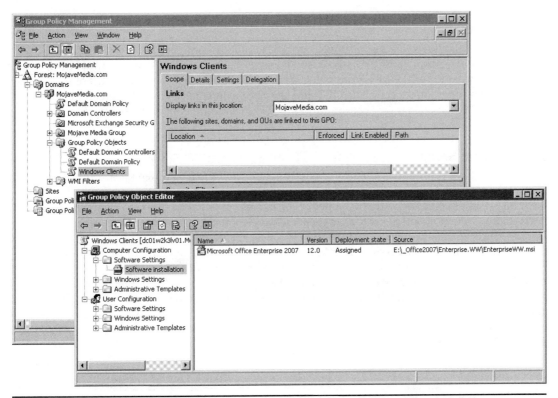

FIGURE 11-23   Office 2007 Enterprise package assigned through Group Policy software installation

to do so, and schedule a silent or interactive installation of the package. The OCT is used to customize the installation. SMS can also be used to push out service packs and other updates that maintain the software well after initial installation.

Microsoft Solution Accelerator for Business Desktop Deployment (BDD) 2007

BDD 2007 is a system rather than a product. It consolidates best practices from a variety of deployment methods and products into one end-to-end pathway. It can be used with or without SMS to create installation packages for different workstation configurations, of which Office 2007 may be a part.

Microsoft Office Migration Planning Manager (OMPM)

This is a set of planning and testing tools specific to Office 2007 migrations. One thing OMPM does is assess migration implications for Office files such as Excel, Access, and Word. Conversion utilities can mass-migrate those files to current versions. OMPM will confirm that Outlook 2007 supports Outlook 2003 files for Unicode personal folders (.pst) and offline folders (.ost). Older versions of Outlook will need to have personal folder content migrated to the Unicode format for use in Outlook 2007.

Configuring Profiles

Outlook 2007 still allows users or administrators to manually configure profiles through the Mail program in Control Panel. In 64-bit Vista, you may have to enable 32-bit Control Panel programs in order to see the Mail option in Classic View. Profile creation can be part of the deployment or upgrade process. The OCT and GPO both allow for user profile creation at installation with supplementary configuration files such as config.xml and the .msp file from OCT.

Auto Account Setup

Creating Outlook profiles has generally required using an Office resource kit utility (or several), visiting workstations, customizing install images, or providing painstakingly clear instructions complete with the name for the Exchange server for users to create their own profiles. The first options at the very least required some administrator time, whereas the last one often resulted in too many help desk calls. Profile creation in Outlook 2007 is simpler than in any other version. The Autodiscover web service will query Active Directory to retrieve the corresponding user alias and the name of the appropriate Exchange server, or even the POP3 or IMAP4 server. Autodiscover is automatic for domain-joined workstations, but on computers that are not members of the domain users can still just enter their e-mail address and domain credentials. Figure 11-24 shows the Auto Account Setup credentials needed on a workstation that was not a member of the domain in which Exchange 2007 is installed.

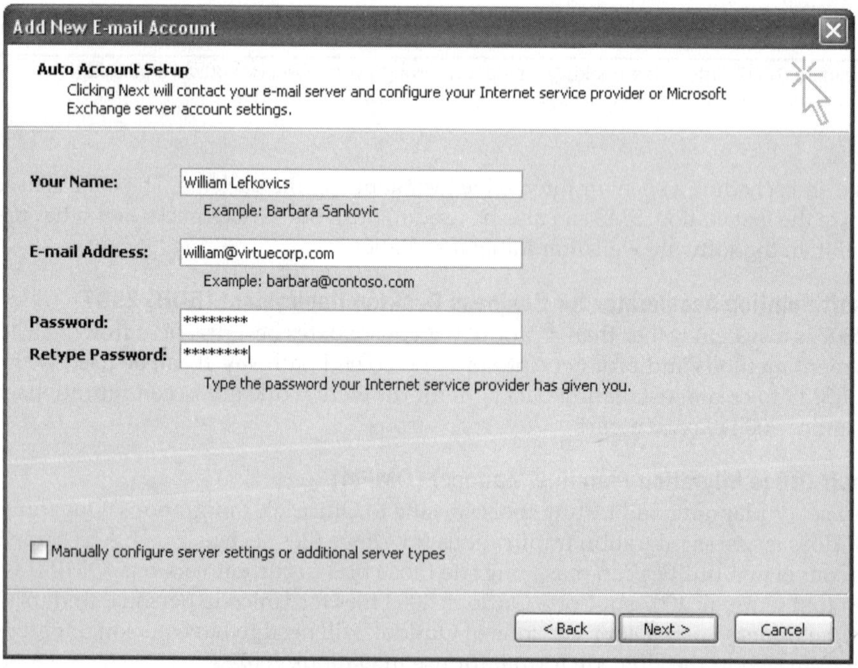

Figure 11-24   Outlook 2007 Auto Account Setup input form

Autodiscover Internal versus External

Autodiscover uses the domain in which the server is a member. If the workstation is not a domain member, it uses the domain provided with the SMTP address on the Auto Account Setup form in Figure 11-24 to query Active Directory. For external locations, Outlook will also use the SMTP domain to formulate a standardized URL as one of the following:

https://<smtp_domain>/autodiscover/autodiscover.xml
https://autodiscover.<smtp_domain>/autodiscover/autodiscover.xml

A host record needs to be added to the external DNS zone for the Autodiscover service. There is more coverage on the Autodiscover service in Chapter 11 covering Client Access Servers.

Testing Auto Account Configuration

CTRL-right-clicking the Outlook icon in the task bar will open a pop-up menu. Selecting the Test E-mail AutoConfiguration option opens a window to help troubleshoot the Autodiscover service and identify the specific URLs that it returns for the different services. Figure 11-25 provides the output of that test showing the URLs for the Availability service, OOF, OAB, and UM. From the Exchange Management Shell, the Web services can also be tested as follows:

```
>test-OutlookWebServices
```

Outlook Profile Files (.prf)

Outlook Profile files (.prf) are configuration files used in creating or updating Outlook profiles. The format for .prf files has not changed; it remains the same as in Outlook 2002 and 2003.

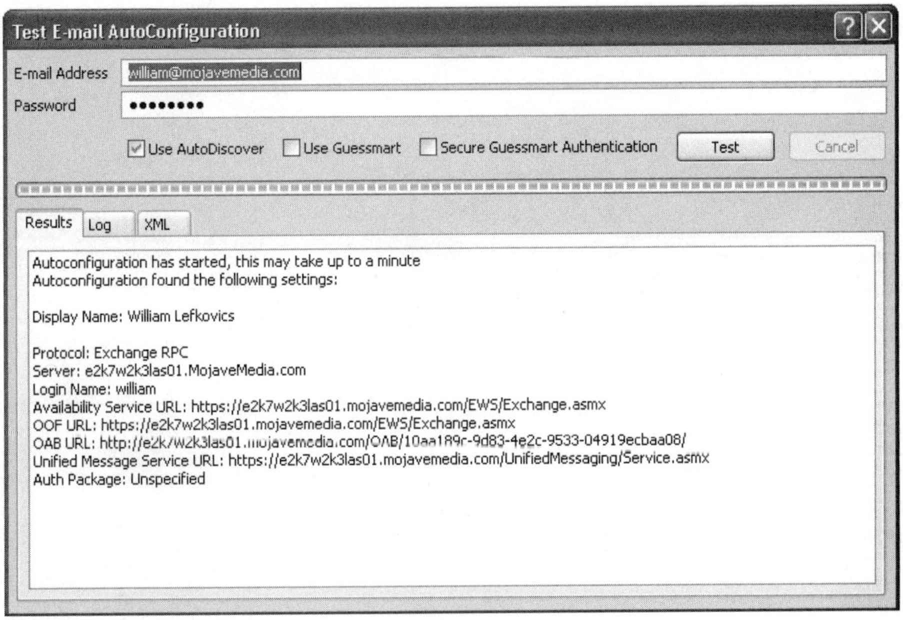

FIGURE 11-25   Outlook 2007 Test E-mail AutoConfiguration output

The Office Customization Tool provides the easiest method for creating new .prf files. After configuring profile settings as desired, you can use OCT to export that information to a .prf file from the Remove accounts & export settings option, as shown in Figure 11-26.

There are a few ways to update profiles in Outlook 2007 using .prf files. Profiles are intrinsic to the .msp files created with OCT, so before you create the .msp file, a .prf file can be imported if needed. Outlook.exe also has an /importprf switch, which when run will silently update the local profile. A separate switch will prompt the user. Here's the syntax for those options:

```
>outlook.exe /ImportPRF \\servershare\outlook.prf
>outlook.exe /PromptImportPRF \\servershare\outlook.prf
```

The OCT can make Registry updates as well, configured under the Additional Content option. A Registry change can be made so Outlook thinks it is running for the first time. Two keys need to be removed, then one added to have Outlook implement a .prf on startup:

Delete:
HKEY_CURRENT_USER\Software\Microsoft\Office\12.0\Outlook\Setup\First-Run
HKEY_CURRENT_USER\Software\Microsoft\Office\12.0\Outlook\Setup\FirstRun
Add a DWORD value ImportPRF with the string showing the path to the .prf file:
HKEY_CURRENT_USER\Software\Microsoft\Office\12.0\Outlook\Setup\

These profile changes are, of course, in the user context on the workstation. If the workstation is shared, the same process would be used for secondary Outlook users on that machine.

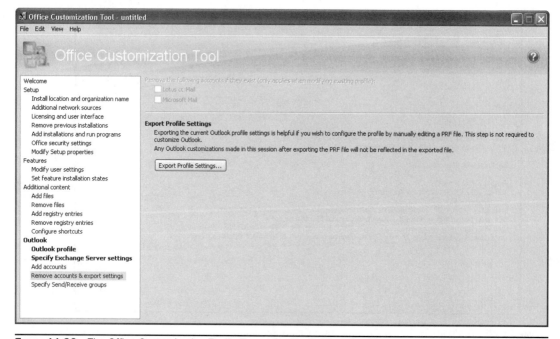

FIGURE 11-26   The Office Customization Tool's Export Profile Settings function

Additional Outlook Configurations

Some settings for Outlook and Exchange may not be employed in all environments.

Cached Exchange Mode

First introduced in Outlook 2003, Cached Mode is still a valuable client configuration. A local copy of the user's mailbox is maintained and kept synchronized with the Exchange mailbox while available. The primary function and benefit of Cached Exchange Mode is a more fluid user experience through poor or often disruptive connectivity between the client and the Exchange server, but it is required for offline folders and for local junk mail filtering. Cached Exchange Mode is configurable as part of the deployment with the tools mentioned earlier, including OCT, as shown in Figure 11-27. This also appears as a check box on the client in the Outlook account settings that can be changed at any time.

In Exchange 2007, the administrator can force the use of Cached Mode on a mailbox, so that any MAPI profile created against that mailbox in Outlook 2003 or 2007 has to use Cached Mode. This is accomplished with the Exchange Management Console using a command such as the following:

```
>Set-CASMailbox "William Lefkovics" -MAPIBlockOutlookNonCachedMode $True
```

With the Set-CASMailbox cmdlet, the administrator can also block the use of Outlook Anywhere or older versions of Outlook.

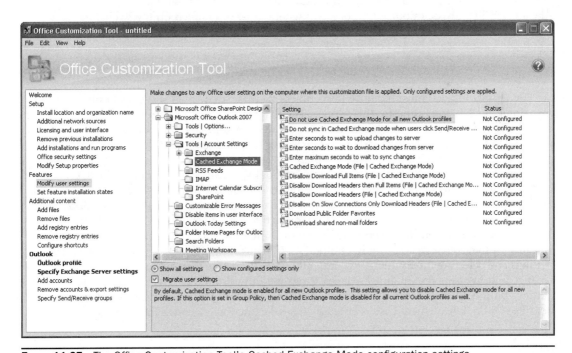

FIGURE 11-27   The Office Customization Tool's Cached Exchange Mode configuration settings

Outlook Anywhere

Outlook 2003 and Exchange 2003, with some specific requirements, introduced RPC over HTTPS as a means of accessing Exchange securely through a firewall without a VPN. Exchange 2007 and Outlook 2007 rename this method of access to Outlook Anywhere and make configuration much simpler. Outlook Anywhere can be configured as part of a deployment using OCT or GPO, and of course can also be implemented after installation. Microsoft recommends that Outlook Anywhere users also be configured with Cached Exchange Mode as well, for a better user experience when connectivity is less than ideal. Outlook must be installed on Windows XP SP2 or later, including versions of Vista.

You have a few prerequisites to complete before configuring Outlook Anywhere on Exchange 2007:

- Install a valid SSL certificate from a CA Outlook can trust
- Install the Windows RPC over HTTP proxy component on Exchange
- Enable Outlook Anywhere using EMS or EMC on an Exchange 2007 server

The SSL certificate for Outlook Anywhere needs to be valid and issued by a trusted Certificate Authority, independent of the self-issued certificates Exchange uses by default. If a third-party certificate is being used for OWA and ActiveSync, it can also be used for Outlook Anywhere. After the SSL is in place, the Windows RPC over HTTP proxy component needs to be implemented on the Exchange server hosting the Client Access Server role. This is found by navigating to Control Panel | Add/Remove Programs | Add/Remove Windows Components and expanding Networking Services and selecting RPC over HTTP Proxy. Initially, Outlook Anywhere must be enabled on the Exchange 2007 CAS server shown in Figure 11-28 or by using EMS as follows:

```
>Enable-OutlookAnywhere -SSLOffloading <$True|$False> -ExternalHostname
<fqdn> -ExternalAuthenticationMethod: <Basic|NTLM>
```

SSL Offloading will most likely be false, unless there is a dedicated server or appliance managing the SSL processing for this service. The External host name setting is often a descriptive name, such as oa.virtuecorp.com or owa.virtuecorp.com. Microsoft recommends using NTLM, Cached Exchange Mode, and an SSL certificate provided by a trusted third-party Certificate Authority.

After that, client configuration can be done manually, or can be pushed out using OCT or GPO. For OCT, the Outlook category has a container called Specify Exchange Server Settings, where the administrator can configure an Exchange Server connection. The More Settings button by the Exchange Server name opens the window shown as Figure 11-29. This is directly analogous to the options shown in Outlook when changing the Account Settings for the Exchange account. In Outlook itself, navigating through Tools | Account Settings and selecting the Exchange account allows us to change the configuration. The Change button opens the Change E-Mail Settings window. From there, we select the More Settings button, then the Connections tab. At the bottom is the Outlook Anywhere check box. The Outlook Anywhere URL is entered after selecting the Exchange Proxy button.

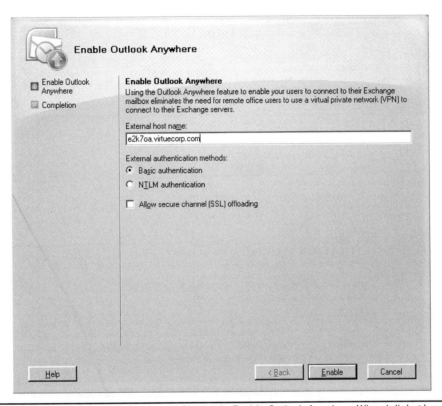

FIGURE 11-28   The Exchange Management Console's Enable Outlook Anywhere Wizard dialog box

Internal versus External Outlook Anywhere
When external URLs are different from internal ones, Microsoft recommends implementing an SSL certificate that allows multiple host names on the same certificate, called a Subject Alternative Name Certificate.

Troubleshooting Outlook Anywhere from Outlook
Outlook 2007 provides a couple ways to verify that the connectivity to the CAS server is using RPC over HTTP in Outlook Anywhere. One way is to start Outlook.exe with the /rpcdiag switch. You can also CTRL-right-click the Outlook icon in the task bar, which will reveal a context menu where you can select Connection Status, which will report on Outlook-Exchange connectivity.

Offline Address Book (OAB)
In previous versions of Exchange Server, the Offline Address Book maintains a special system folder in the public folder store called OFFLINE ADDRESS BOOK, where clients pulled the OAB at regular intervals. With the introduction of Cached Mode, and Offline mode before it, there could be a lot of time before changes in the directory made their way

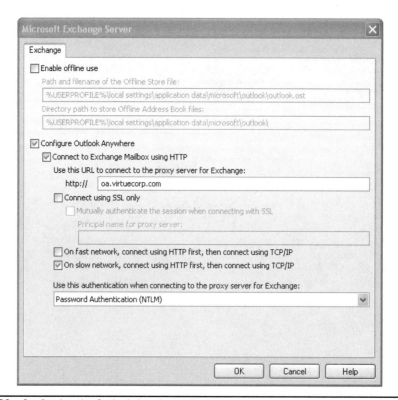

FIGURE 11-29   Configuring the Outlook Anywhere client

to the client. For example, OABs could be rebuilt once per day and Cached Mode clients might retrieve the OAB once per day. In that scenario, a person added to the directory may not appear in a user's version of the GAL for a day or two.

We are now at version 4 of the OAB, and the different version and distribution points do not allow us to freely move OABs between Exchange 2003 and 2007. A hotfix is provided in Microsoft Knowledge Base Article 922817 when moving the OAB server from Exchange 2007 to Exchange 2003. Exchange 2007 eliminates the need for public folders moving the OAB to IIS, accessible by Outlook 2007 through HTTP and the Background Intelligent Transfer Service (BITS). If the organization is still supporting older versions of Outlook, then both the HTTP and the Public Folder options will have to be utilized. Outlook 2007 can use either one.

The OAB is created by a service called OABGen on an Exchange server with the Mailbox role installed, but it is provided to clients through the Client Access Server (CAS) role. The Exchange File Distribution Service is responsible for moving the OAB to the CAS server. In a single-server environment, this is the same machine. OAB distribution can be based on any CAS server or servers in the organization. Outlook 2007 depends on the

Autodiscover service, which runs on a CAS server to learn and return the closest URL from the CAS servers hosting OABs. Figure 11-25 (earlier) shows the URLs provided through the Autodiscover service to Outlook 2007 clients, including the OAB URL.

Custom Outlook Forms

The Organization Forms Library from Exchange 2003 is gone from Exchange 2007 because it was a system folder in the public folder store. If Exchange 2007 is installed with a public folder store, administrators can still create the organizational forms library folder as they did in Exchange 2000 and 2003. Moving forward, Office Forms Server and InfoPath will provide developers with Office and Outlook custom forms resources and repositories.

InfoPath 2007 Integration

If installed, InfoPath 2007 enjoys full integration with Outlook 2007. InfoPath forms can be embedded into e-mail messages. If a form is requesting user input, recipients can complete the form and return it to the sender. This can be used as a means of gathering information—from expense reports to employee surveys. After the message is returned to the sender, the form can be exported to various formats, including an Excel spreadsheet or a web page.

Windows SharePoint Services v3

Another application integration benefit of Outlook 2007 is how data can be shared with SharePoint services. With lists and libraries, Outlook can render data stored in SharePoint, and Outlook can store and share content with SharePoint. In addition to calendars, contacts, tasks, and discussion lists, Outlook 2007 features such as the To-Do Bar and eBusiness cards can also incorporate data retrieved from SharePoint. Access to SharePoint List content is initiated from SharePoint, and when a user is subscribed to a SharePoint list, it is managed from within Outlook 2007 through Tools | Account Settings | SharePoint Lists.

The potential for integration with applications such as SharePoint and InfoPath is rather unlimited in terms of sharing and accessing information and is, therefore, beyond the scope of the chapter.

Programming Outlook and Exchange

Coding applications for Outlook and Exchange in the past has involved a potpourri of APIs and languages. The commitment to Word as the editor and renderer of message content provides a single interface for programmatic message manipulation. Exchange 2007 consolidates many APIs to Web services, which will simplify Outlook programming for Exchange Server as well.

Summary and Resources

For several versions of Exchange Server now, we have seen a complementary, parallel release of Outlook and Office. The 2007 versions fit together well and add several compelling features. A few were introduced in this chapter. Microsoft Office 2007 has just entered the beta version for Service Pack 1. Initially, there does not appear to be any significant changes for Outlook 2007 SP1 beyond what was covered here. Outlook 2007 offers the greatest return of features when employed with Exchange Server 2007. Some of the features that are only available when Outlook 2007 and Exchange 2007 are deployed together include:

- Autodiscover
- Availability service
- Unified Messaging
- Separate Internal and External Out of Office Assistants
- Managed folders
- Partial Item Change Download
- Message classification
- HTTP-based Offline Address Book (OAB)

Outlook 2007 has a vibrant user community, almost half of which does not use Exchange Server. Some of the resources for Outlook information, assistance, and content include:

- http://www.outlook-tips.net
- http://www.outlookcode.com
- http://www.slipstick.com

For e-mail-based peer discussion forums specific to Outlook, there are a couple of Yahoo! Groups forums that have been around almost a decade:

- http://groups.yahoo.com/group/outlook-users
- http://groups.yahoo.com/group/outlook-dev

For additional information on integrating Exchange, Outlook, SharePoint, and InfoPath, here are a couple of books to consider:

- *How to Do Everything with Microsoft Office InfoPath 2003,* by David McAmis
- *Microsoft Office SharePoint Server 2007: The Complete Reference,* by David Sterling

Outlook Web Access 2007

Starting with Exchange 5.0, Microsoft has offered browser-based access to mailboxes and public folders on Exchange Server message stores. In spite of its name, Outlook Web Access (OWA) does not provide web access to Outlook, but rather web access to much of the same Exchange and mailbox content as the full Outlook client provides. OWA in Exchange 2007 has been rewritten to maintain the goal of being a feature-rich complement to the full Outlook client—and for some even a comparable alternative. However, because of this complete rewrite and accompanying time constraints, some of the features that users had been accustomed to were not included in the initial release of Exchange 2007 RTM. One of the main areas of focus for OWA (as well as other areas, such as the Exchange Management Console) for Exchange 2007 Service Pack 1 has been feature parity with Exchange 2003 OWA.

The New Outlook Web Access

As mentioned, there seems to be a directive at Microsoft to make OWA resemble the rich Outlook application as much as possible—both in appearance and set of features. With the many changes inherent to Exchange 2007 itself, this has its own requirements and challenges. This version is more than just a facelift on OWA 2003. OWA 2007 is one of, if not *the* premier browser interface for corporate messaging and calendaring.

Although OWA 2007 is an advanced, feature-rich browser application, it is not Outlook 2007. Many components have not been translated to the browser experience. These include the To-Do Bar, offline use (Cached Exchange Mode, Offline Address Book), access to .pst files, multiple calendar display, and data import and export.

OWA Components

OWA 2007 is an ASP.NET web application installed with the Client Access Server (CAS) role on Exchange 2007. ASP.NET forms the requirement for .NET Framework 2.0. As a web application, OWA also needs Internet Information Service (IIS) with the WWW service running. OWA 2007 is a complex AJAX application and depends on current capable browsers for the premium experience. Internet Explorer 6 or higher is required for the OWA 2007 premium experience.

OWA Installation

In Exchange 2003, OWA was automatically installed with every Exchange server by default. In Exchange 2007, OWA is a component of the Client Access Server role and therefore is only installed on CAS servers. If the prerequisites for the Client Access Server role are met on the Exchange server, there are no special requirements for installing OWA. It will be accessible with the installation of the CAS role. We will look at configuration and administration later in this chapter.

Outlook Web Access Light

Microsoft supports the premium OWA client on Internet Explorer. For all other browsers, they provide OWA Light. In Exchange 2003, the options were called Premium and Basic, but the principle was the same. Users on non-Windows operating systems, such as Linux or Mac OS X, using non-Internet Explorer browsers can use OWA Light to access Exchange content. OWA Light works well on Mozilla Firefox 1.8 and higher, Opera 7.54 and higher, Safari 1.2, and Netscape Navigator 7.1 and higher.

Figure 12-1 shows OWA 2007 Light in Firefox 2.0.0.4 on a Novell SuSE Linux workstation.

OWA Light shows solid improvement in accessibility features, including better color contrast management and more effective screen reader output, which is not really possible to include in the more complex interactive experience of the premium client. OWA Light also consumes less bandwidth in client-server communications, so it may be a better choice when connectivity is restricted.

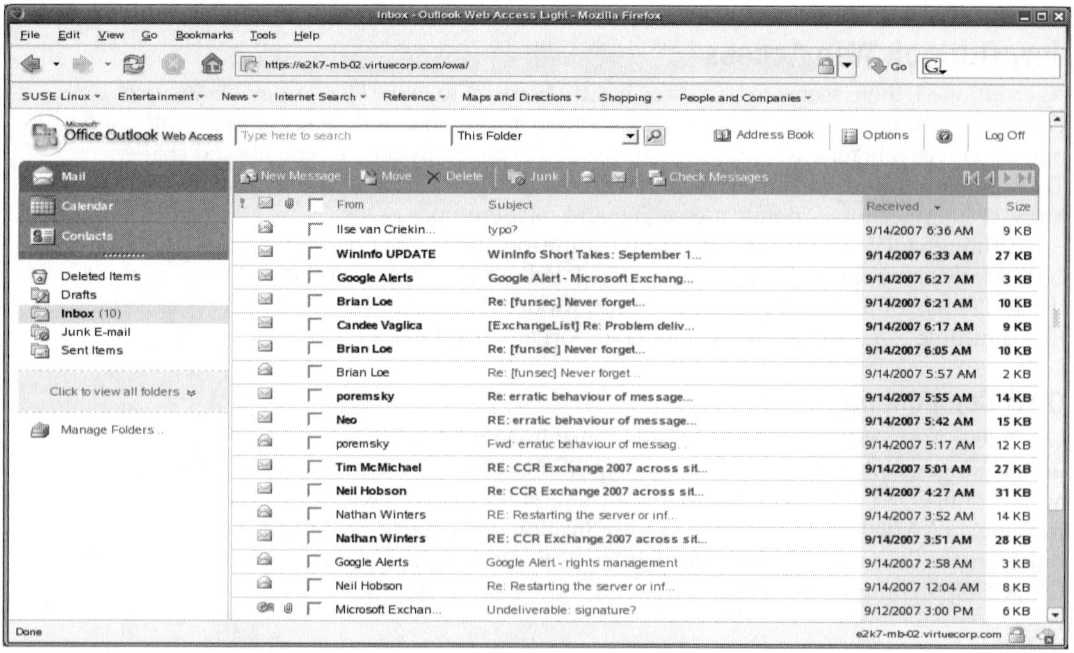

FIGURE 12-1   OWA 2007 Light in Firefox 2.0.0.4 on Novell SuSE Linux Workstation 10

OWA Premium Client Experience

Many Exchange customers have grown to use OWA frequently while they are away from the office or even in the office. Some even use it as their primary e-mail client for work. As stated earlier, OWA continues to try to match its Outlook client counterpart as much as possible in appearance and with the features it offers. This is only plausible when Internet Explorer 6 or later is used. Older Internet Explorer versions and other browsers, whether on Windows or other operating systems, will defer to OWA Light. As OWA and Outlook approach homogeneity, the user experience is improved for users who move back and forth between the options.

OWA is enabled by default and can be disabled (or enabled if already disabled) on a per-user basis in Mailbox Properties in the Exchange Management Console. Figure 12-2 shows the Mailbox Features tab with the option to disable or enable specific mailbox features, including Outlook Web Access.

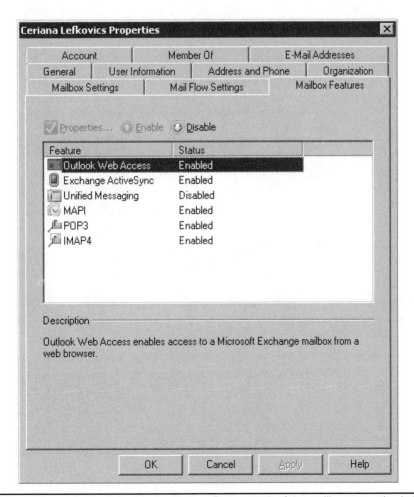

FIGURE 12-2   OWA enabled by default in the Mailbox Features tab of the mailbox properties in EMC

A lot of improvements have been made to OWA for Exchange 2007 over its predecessors. The following features described in this section apply to the Premium experience only.

Logon Screen

The first point of entry for users into the realm of OWA is the logon screen. It is simple and clean, with configurable username formatting. The default is domain\username. Figure 12-3 shows the logon screen. Here, the user makes an important determination for their session. They must select whether they are accessing OWA through a public computer or a private computer. The upcoming security section discusses this feature in more detail.

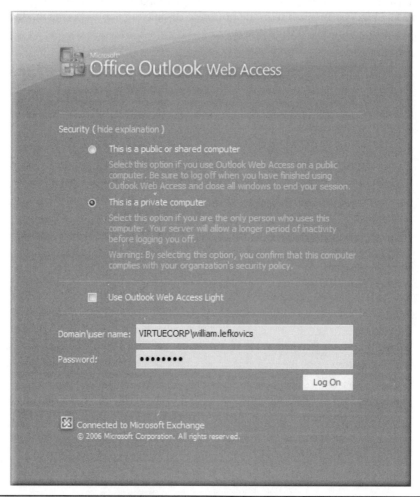

FIGURE 12-3   OWA 2007 logon screen

If this is the first logon, a second screen is shown where the user can assign the language in which to render the OWA interface, independent of the operating system language. This screen is shown in Figure 12-4.

Interface and Navigation

The navigation pane on the left side of the OWA 2007 interface resembles the Outlook client. It is somewhat customizable in that it the width can be controlled. The option buttons closely resemble those of the full Outlook client, as you can see in Figure 12-5.

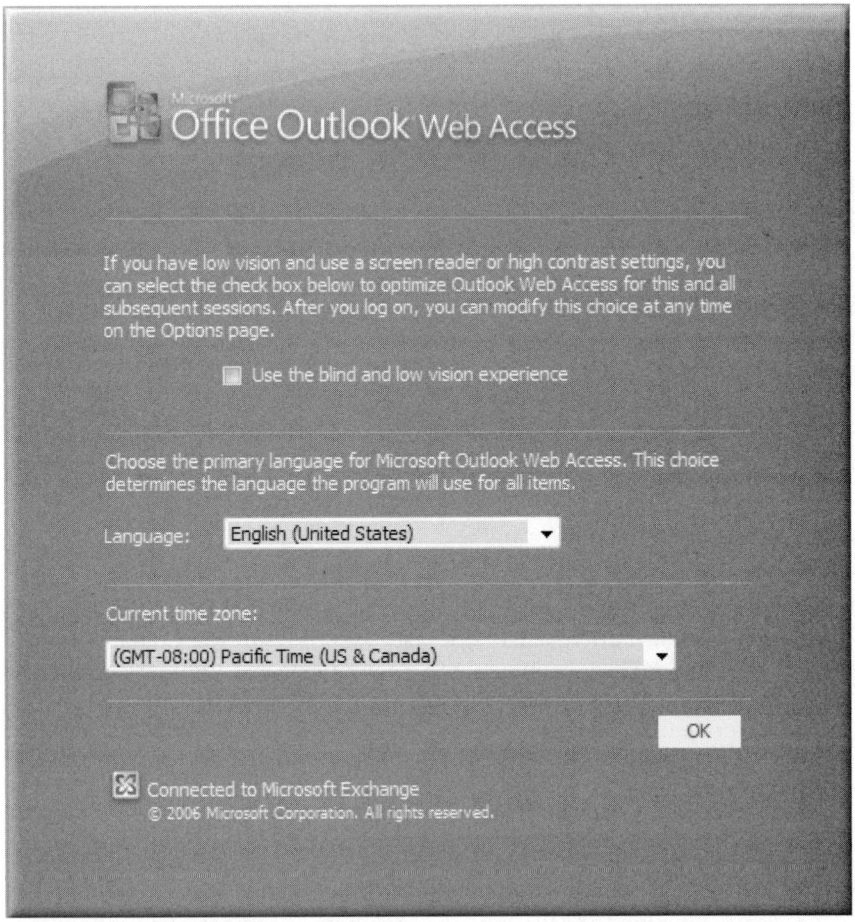

FIGURE 12-4 OWA 2007 language preference configuration at first logon

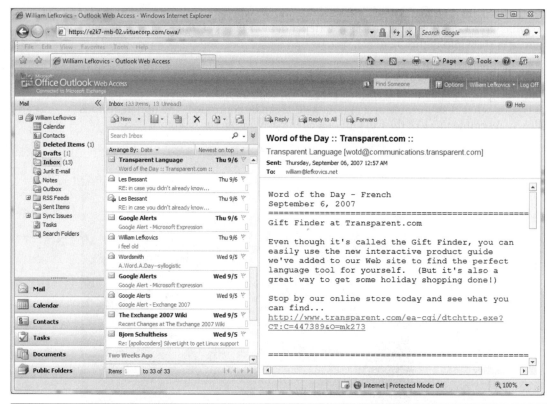

FIGURE 12-5   OWA 2007 main Inbox view

The calendar provides different views based on duration and renders different colors of assigned categories as the Outlook client does (see Figure 12-6). The Contacts view, shown in Figure 12-7, includes the list of contacts and a comprehensive summary of information on each contact, including a picture if one was added. All the interfaces add a clean look and feel to the user experience.

Responsiveness

A big improvement, though one that can easily be overlooked, is the overall responsiveness of OWA 2007. It is really designed to bring the user experience to a level usually reserved for client-side applications and not web browsers. This responsiveness contributes to the client experience resembling the full Outlook client. Some users may forget they are actually in a web browser.

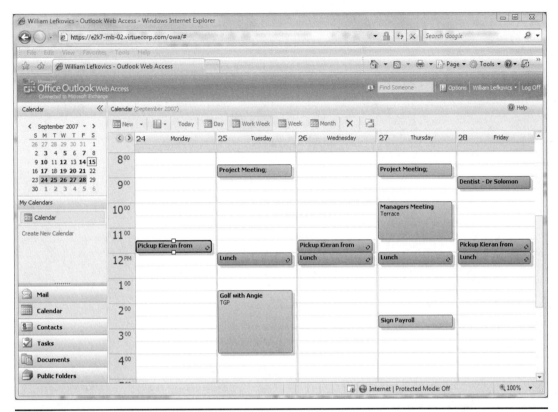

FIGURE 12-6   OWA 2007 main Calendar view

Automatic Folder Updates

In previous versions of Exchange, updates to the mailbox, such as the arrival of new e-mail messages, was not always a timely experience. OWA 2007 keeps the user current without requiring them to initiate a refresh or to click the Check Messages button.

Autocomplete Functionality

When you enter names in the address fields, OWA 2007 exercises one of its new features (long available in Outlook). OWA maintains an Autocomplete cache based on the input experience of the user, as shown in Figure 12-8. This cache is stored on the server and is pulled down when the user accesses OWA. So, unlike Outlook, the OWA 2007 Autocomplete cache travels with the user.

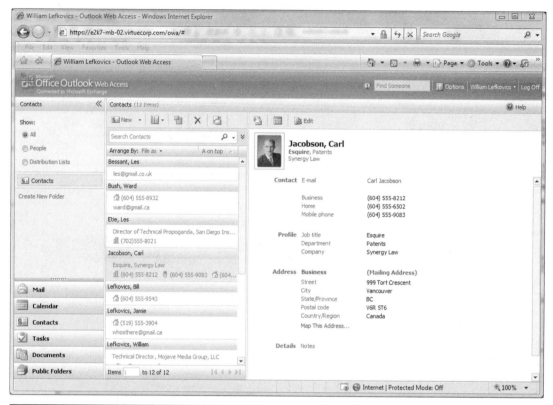

FIGURE 12-7   OWA 2007 main Contacts view

Our tests with Exchange 2007 SP1 installed placed 52 addresses in the Autocomplete cache, which had negligible impact on performance and definitely boosted the client experience. We did not identify an upper limit to the number of names allowed within the OWA Autocomplete cache. Like Outlook's Autocompete feature, the user can use the arrow keys to move up and down the listed items and can also delete individual entries.

Calendaring Improvements

Both the presentation and the functionality of the calendar in OWA 2007 have changed significantly.

Scheduling Assistant

The ability to reconcile people, resources, and free time has been greatly improved in OWA 2007. The new Scheduling Assistant works much the same as the full Outlook client.

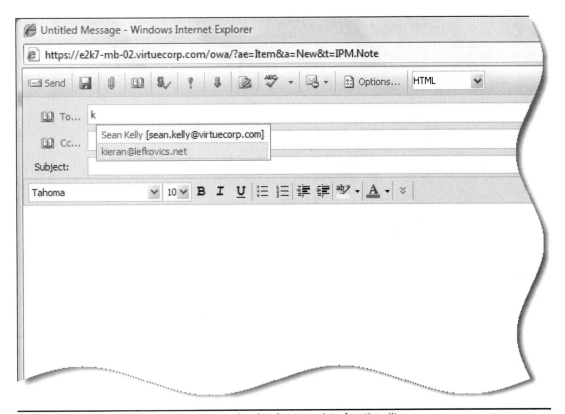

FIGURE 12-8   OWA 2007 new mail message showing Autocomplete functionality

Previously in OWA the user could only retrieve the next available time slot for meeting with others. The Scheduling Assistant can include resources and locations as well as suggest meeting times and even rate the potential meeting times as great, good, or poor. Figure 12-9 shows the Scheduling Assistant at work.

Return of the Month View
Exchange 2007 SP1 brings back the OWA Month view. Users with many meetings scheduled may not find this view too useful, but the demand to have this feature in OWA has been great. Figure 12-10 shows a Month view from OWA 2007 SP1.

SP1 *OWA 2007 in Service Pack 1 brings back the Month view to OWA.*

WebReady Document Viewing
Analogous to Outlook 2007 and the document preview handlers that allow Outlook to render certain documents in the preview pane, OWA 2007 can render certain documents as HTML.

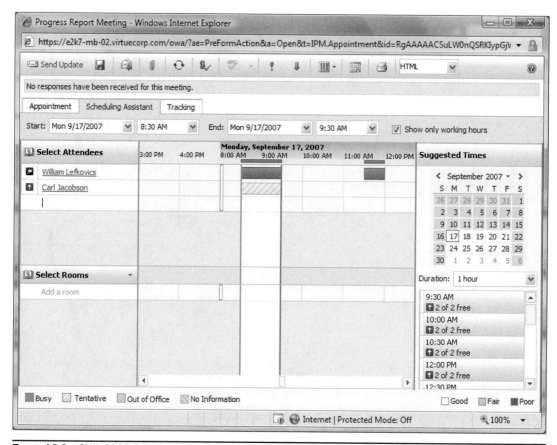

FIGURE 12-9   OWA 2007 Scheduling Assistant

Unlike Outlook 2007, OWA 2007 and its WebReady document viewing functionality is not open to third-party developers. There is no mechanism for companies to create their own WebReady document viewing handlers.

When you view a message with a compatible WebReady document file attached to the message in OWA 2007, a text link appears next to the attachment that reads "Open as Web Page," as shown in Figure 12-11. Clicking that link opens a new window in which the converted document is rendered as HTML. There are a few benefits to having OWA use HTML to render such documents. First, if the user is accessing OWA from a kiosk that does not have the associated applications installed, the user can still view the content of the attachment. OWA also removes the HTML version of the attachment from the local cache when the user logs out, or when the user's session times out, to help ensure that the document does not remain resident on a shared computer.

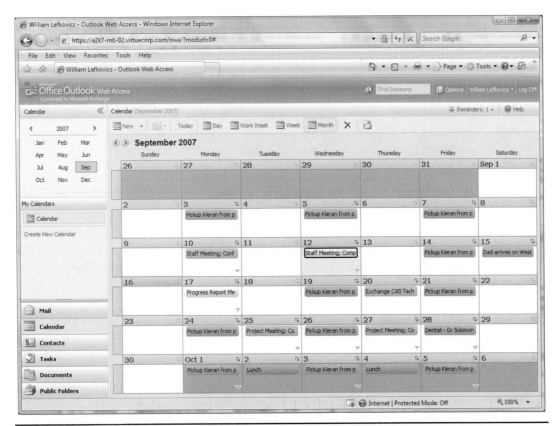

FIGURE 12-10   OWA 2007 monthly calendar view

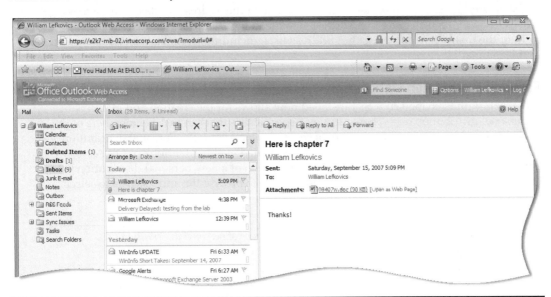

FIGURE 12-11   OWA 2007 WebReady document viewing option

Document Type	Extension
Microsoft Word documents	.doc and .docx
Microsoft Word templates	.dot
Rich text format	.rtf
Microsoft Excel spreadsheets	.xls and .xlsx
Microsoft PowerPoint Presentations	.ppt and .pptx
Microsoft PowerPoint slide shows	.pps
Adobe PDF documents	.pdf

TABLE 12-1   Document Types Supported for OWA 2007 WebReady Document Viewing

By default, through Service Pack 1, OWA 2007 is able to convert the document types listed in Table 12-1.

SP1 Exchange 2007 Service Pack 1 adds the Office 2007 file formats of .docx, .xlsx, and .pptx to the list of supported WebReady document viewing file types by default.

Browsable Address Book

In previous versions of OWA, the user was able to query an address book, but they were not able to view the contents of the address book. Even a wildcard query returned a limited number of entries. OWA 2007 now allows users to browse the address book to select individuals to send messages to, as reflected in Figure 12-12.

This window is created either by selecting one of the address fields of a new message (To, CC, or BCC) or selecting the Address Book icon beside the search field at the top right of the main OWA screen. Other address lists, including Contacts, can be navigated in this manner.

Personal Distribution Lists

OWA 2007 with Exchange 2007 SP1 installed now allows for the creation and maintenance of personal distribution lists. These are client-specific lists that can include members of the Global Access List (GAL) and members of the user's local contacts. Personal distribution lists are stored in the user's Contact folder. Lists created in either Outlook or OWA are available to each other. Figure 12-13 shows the creation of a new personal distribution list in OWA with members selected. Again, the user is able to browse the address lists to select members and not just submit a blind query.

SP1 OWA 2007 now supports the creation and maintenance of personal distribution lists.

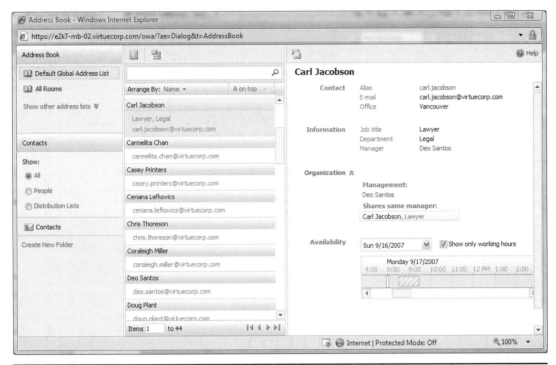

FIGURE 12-12   Browsing the Global Address List in OWA 2007

SharePoint and Document Shares

OWA 2007 now allows access to file shares either through a SharePoint Document Library or through a standard Windows folder share. With the Documents option selected, the user can enter a "file location" in the form of a Universal Naming Convention (UNC) path for Windows shares or the SharePoint Services server. Figure 12-14 shows a path to a Windows share that opens the share folder called Data, while Figure 12-15 shows the files and folders accessible in the share called Office 2007.

Improved Search

OWA 2007 uses the same back-end search mechanism as Outlook—namely, the Microsoft Exchange Search service on the Exchange server. The search functionality in Exchange is improved over previous implementations as a result of its complete rewrite. Searching on the server is now more associated with the Information Store Service. If resources from other sources are in demand, the Search service will release resources it is using.

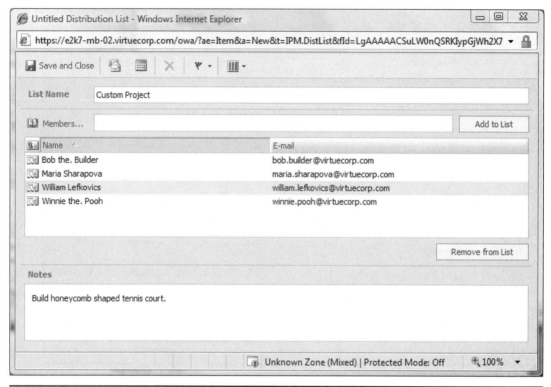

FIGURE 12-13   Creating a personal distribution list in OWA 2007

During peak server usage, Search will not consume unnecessary resources. Mailboxes have their own associated search index, including text-based attachments such as Word and Excel, and content is indexed upon arrival rather than on an independent schedule. The index, therefore, remains more current for use.

FIGURE 12-14
Using the Open
Location dialog
box to access
documents in
OWA 2007

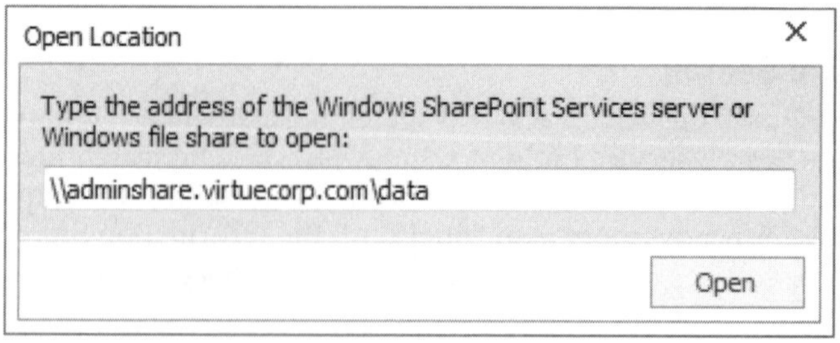

Open Location	✕
Type the address of the Windows SharePoint Services server or Windows file share to open:	
\\adminshare.virtuecorp.com\data	
	Open

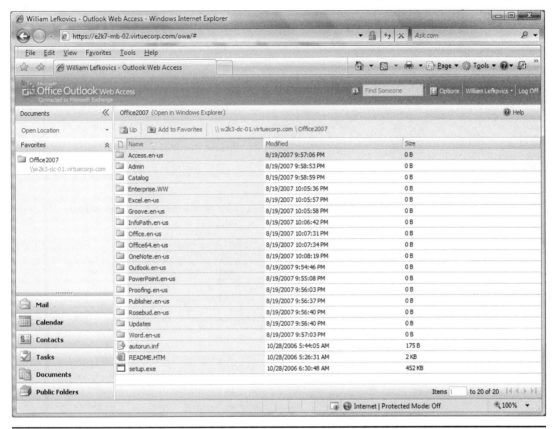

FIGURE 12-15   OWA 2007 Windows folder share shown with remote file access

The user interface for entering search keywords is found in the same place in OWA as Instant Search in the full Outlook client—atop the central pane in the interface when the reading pane is specified as the default vertical setting. Figure 12-16 shows a search using the OWA Search function.

Change Password

In previous versions of Exchange, implementing the web-based Change Password functionality involved using IIS Manager to create a Change Password web page. This feature was launched from OWA Options, though. The Change Password feature is still launched from within the Options section of OWA 2007, but the interface is now intrinsic to the OWA interface, as evident in Figure 12-17. The previous requirement of SSL remains.

Other Minor Changes to OWA 2007

Many lesser changes to OWA 2007 will also be well received. These likely will not be deal makers or deal breakers in regard to Exchange 2007 adoption, but they may add to the long list of reasons for migrating.

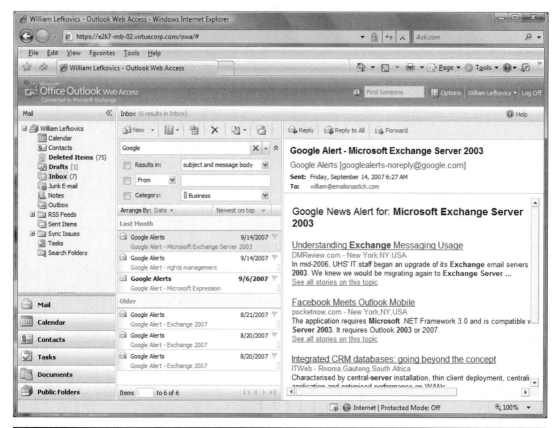

FIGURE 12-16 OWA 2007 Search function

Mailbox Size Limit Notification
In OWA 2007, simply moving your mouse over the mailbox name in the top left of the OWA 2007 interface will show a pop-up listing the current size and any size limitation placed on the mailbox. The size is not divided into folders, as we see in the Outlook 2007 client, but it does inform the user how close they may be to having automatic sending, or receiving restrictions placed on them as a result of their mailbox size exceeding their quota.

Viewing Internet Message Headers
The full SMTP header information for an inbound message in OWA 2007 is now easily accessed. With a message open, selecting the Header Information icon to the left of the Print icon will initiate a pop-up with the full Internet headers.

HTML Message Creation
Even though it is a web application, previous versions of OWA only allowed for plain-text messages to be created. With a browser as the local application used for e-mail, received

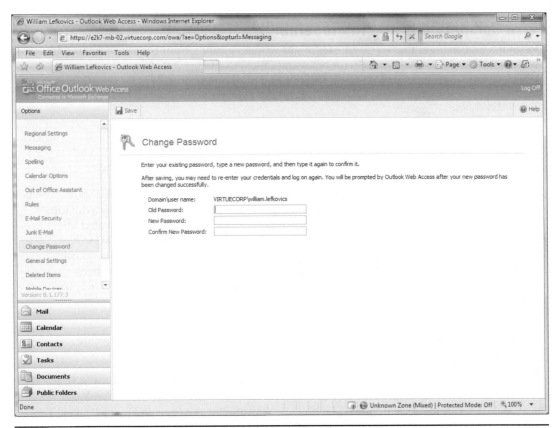

FIGURE 12-17   The Change Password feature in OWA 2007

HTML messages were rendered fine, but composing new messages did not allow for a rich message experience. OWA 2007 adds HTML composition to new e-mail messages.

Open Another User's Mailbox

In previous OWA implementations, the option to open another user's mailbox to which permissions had been assigned or delegated required entering the full URL to the mailbox in a browser window. OWA 2007 brings this function into the user interface. At the top right of the OWA Premium interface, OWA shows the mailbox username. The little triangle located there opens a drop-down window where the user can add the username of another mailbox. The Open button will launch a new browser window to access the delegated mailbox. If the correct permissions are not in place, the user will see the error, "You do not have permission to open this Mailbox. Contact your Exchange Administrator for access or for further information."

Backward Compatibility and Interoperability

One of the first changes that an OWA user might witness moving from Exchange 2000/2003 to Exchange 2007 is the default URL for accessing OWA. Exchange 2007 keeps the "legacy" virtual directories from older Exchange versions and adds a new one:

- /exchange
- /exchweb
- /public
- /owa

The first three directories in this list are for accessing Exchange 2000/2003 mailbox servers. Previously, a user would have entered http://<servername>/exchange as a default URL for accessing OWA. OWA 2007 updates this path to a new default URL, located at https://<servername>/owa. If the user's mailbox still resides on an Exchange 2003 server, they can still access their mailbox through the CAS role server, but should continue to use the legacy URL https://<servername>/exchange. Alternatively, if all users have been moved to an Exchange 2007 mailbox server and they are used to the legacy OWA URL, IIS can redirect the /exchange resource to the new /owa URL.

SP1 *Service Pack 1 adds support for the /public virtual directory. Users can now access public folders through OWA.*

As we have discussed in earlier chapters, the front-end/back-end topology for OWA has given way to the new Exchange roles of CAS and Mailbox servers. When the CAS role is installed on a separate server from the Mailbox role, it can serve as a front end to the back-end mailbox servers of Exchange 2000, 2003, and 2007. It will redirect OWA requests as needed, effectively serving as a front end for legacy mailbox servers. Exchange 2000/2003 will render its legacy OWA even though the front end is an Exchange 2007 CAS box. If the CAS role is installed on a server with the Mailbox role, it cannot serve as a front-end server for Exchange 2000/2003 back ends. In addition, using an Exchange 2003 front-end server to access Exchange 2007 mailboxes is not supported.

Administration of OWA for Exchange 2007 and Exchange 2000/2003 should be kept separate where possible. The rule of administering Exchange 2007 with Exchange 2007 tools and Exchange 2000/2003 with Exchange 2000/2003 tools extends to Outlook Web Access configuration and administration.

OWA Configuration and Administration

Many tools are available to administer OWA settings. Exchange-specific functionality is configured with the Exchange toolset, but because OWA is a web application, some configuration may require web tools such as IIS and web configuration files.

Exchange Management Console (EMC)

Many Exchange-specific OWA configuration settings can be maintained through the EMC. OWA is installed with the CAS role, so within EMC, OWA settings are accessed through the

Server Configuration section on servers where the CAS role is installed. After you select the Client Access Server role under the Server Configuration section in the left pane of the EMC, the middle pane will show the available servers and the CAS services below. In Figure 12-18, the server with the CAS role installed is listed on the top, and the Outlook Web Access tab is selected below, reflecting the available virtual directories for that server.

In a pure Exchange 2007 organization, we would only see the virtual directories applicable to 2007; however, if this is a mixed environment, the virtual directories for Exchange 2000/2003 will also be listed here. Exchange 2007 actually creates the legacy virtual directories in IIS, but they are empty and not listed in the EMC in a pure 2007 organization. They should also be managed with Exchange 2000/2003 tools. The default virtual directory is called \owa\. In the Properties window of the \owa\ virtual directory, we find most of the configuration options available through the EMC. The General tab of the Virtual Directory Properties dialog box identifies the Exchange server and shows the internal and external URLs, if configured, for accessing OWA for this directory (see Figure 12-19).

The Authentication tab shows the different types of authentication available for OWA. The default is forms-based authentication (FBA), as shown in Figure 12-20. Under FBA, the administrator can also configure how the user will need to enter their credentials. When a change is made here, it is reflected in the text prompt beside the user input in the logon screen. The default is "domain\user." Whenever the switch is made to or from forms-based authentication, IIS needs to be restarted or IISReset /noforce needs to be run from the command line or the EMS.

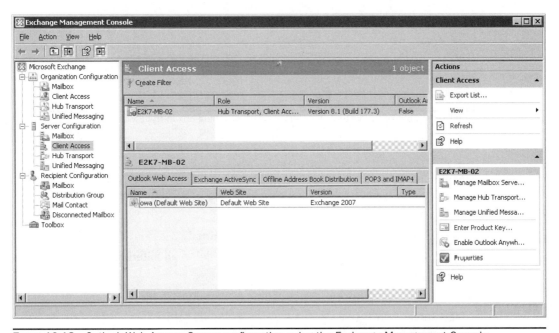

FIGURE 12-18   Outlook Web Access Server configuration using the Exchange Management Console

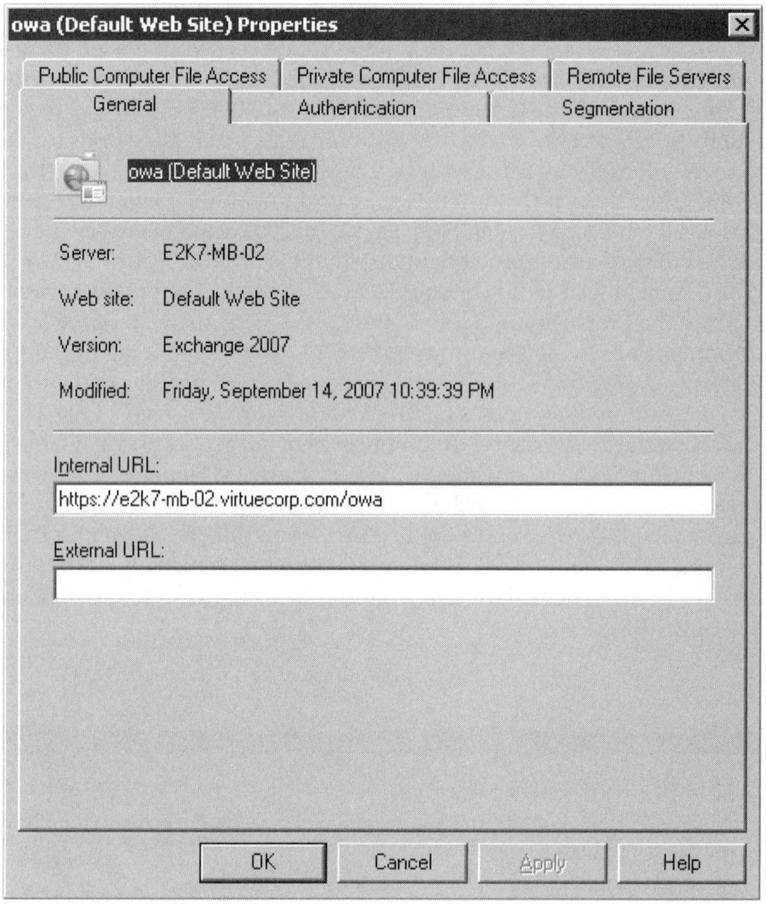

FIGURE 12-19   The General tab of the Virtual Directory Properties dialog box in the EMC

The Segmentation tab lists all the independently enabled features for OWA 2007 specific to the virtual directory. This means we can toggle on or off any of the following in this list of features:

- All Address Lists
- Calendar
- Change Password
- Contacts
- E-mail Signatures
- Exchange ActiveSync Integration

- Journal
- Junk E-mail Filtering
- Notes
- Premium Client
- Public Folders
- Recover Deleted Items

- Reminders and Notifications
- Rules
- Search Folders
- S/MIME

- Spell Checker
- Tasks
- Theme Selection
- Unified Messaging Integration

SP1 Exchange 2007 Service Pack 1 adds Public Folders, Rules, Recover Deleted Items, and S/MIME to the list of features in the Segmentation tab of the Virtual Directory Properties dialog box in the EMC.

These segmentation settings are specific to the virtual directory, so the features enabled or disabled will apply to all users who access OWA through that specific virtual directory. These settings are also all enabled by default. The first few are visible in Figure 12-21.

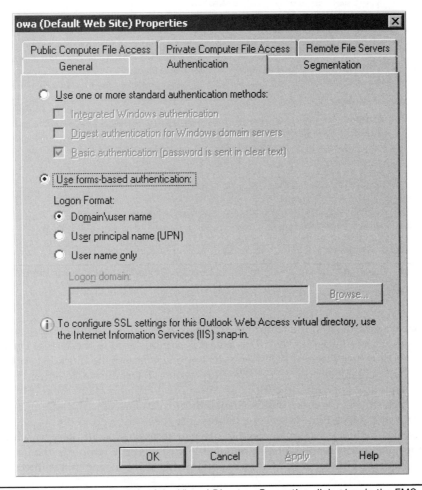

FIGURE 12-20   The Authentication tab of the Virtual Directory Properties dialog box in the EMC

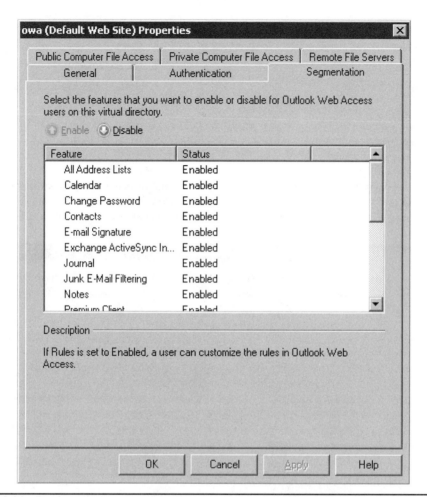

FIGURE 12-21   The Segmentation tab of the Virtual Directory Properties dialog box in the EMC

Earlier we talked about the feature of accessing SharePoint document libraries and Windows file shares through OWA. This access is administered in the Virtual Directory Properties dialog box. Figure 12-22 shows the buttons to access the Block list and Allow list of servers available for file access. The third setting determines a default access for computers not listed on either the Block or Allow list. In combination, these settings control which servers the users of this virtual directory can access. The administrator can set the default to block remote servers, listing only those allowed in the Allow list. Alternatively, the Block list can be used to prevent access to specific servers while the balance remains available. Finally, remote file access is only remote to the user, not the network of the OWA server. That is, the remote file server is one that is internal to the

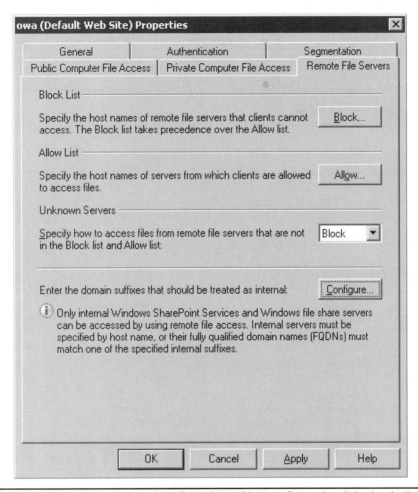

FIGURE 12-22   The Remote File Servers tab of the Virtual Directory Properties dialog box in the EMC

network, and the Remote File Servers tab allows you to enter the FQDN of domains that should be treated as internal for the purpose of this type of access.

It should be apparent that allowing file access through a remote mail client such as OWA could be a security issue. The Allow and Block lists allow the administrator to lock this access down on a broad scale. Figure 12-23 shows entries in a Remote File Server Block list.

As you saw earlier in the chapter, the logon screen provides the opportunity for the user to select whether they are accessing OWA through a public computer that is shared by others or a private computer, such as their company laptop. This decision can be important because different levels of service and access can be assigned this value of public or private access.

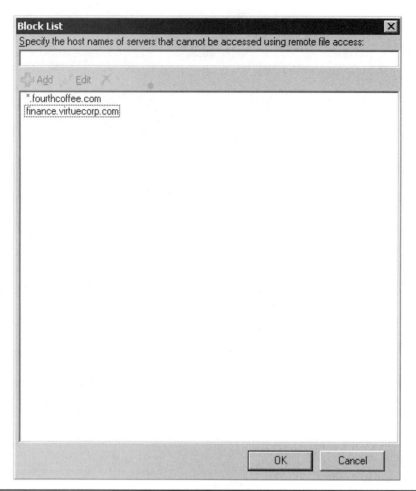

FIGURE 12-23   A Remote File Server Block list in OWA 2007

Figure 12-24 shows the settings available for Public Computer File Access should the user select Public when they log onto OWA. The Private Computer File Access tab has the same options as the Public tab. The administrator can enable or disable remote file access and WebReady document viewing independently for access from public or private computers. In addition, remote file access can be limited to Windows shares or SharePoint document libraries, or both can be enabled.

Exchange Management Shell

Like many other areas in Exchange, the EMS provides the most granular administrative access to Exchange configuration. The main management cmdlet relevant to OWA, Set-OWAVirtualDirectory, controls virtual directory property settings, most of which you saw using the EMC in the previous section. This cmdlet controls many settings

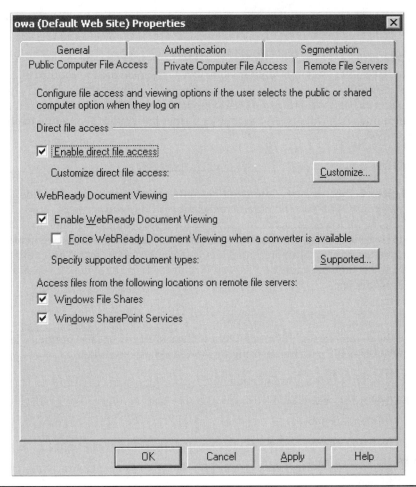

FIGURE 12-24   The Public Computer File Access tab of the Virtual Directory Properties dialog box in the EMC

governing OWA 2007 for users. It is the Swiss Army knife of OWA configuration. To get the list of parameters available with this versatile and important cmdlet, enter the following in the EMS:

```
>Get-help Set-OWAVirtualDirectory
```

In addition to the Set- verb, there is also the following:

- **New-OWAVirtualDirectory**   Creates new virtual directory for use in web access
- **Remove-OWAVirtualDirectory**   Deletes a specific virtual directory
- **Get-OWAVirtualDirectory**   Returns the configuration parameters of the requested virtual directory

The cmdlet Set-OWAVirtualDirectory is the most-used cmdlet for OWA server-side administration in Exchange 2007.

Test-OWAConnectivity

This is a special cmdlet used in troubleshooting OWA. It can be used to confirm that OWA is working on a specific CAS role or domain controller or throughout the Exchange organization as a whole. It even has a -WhatIf parameter to report the ramifications of suggested changes to the configuration. We will discuss this cmdlet further in Chapter 20 covering maintenance and optimization.

Set-CASMailbox

Whereas Set-OWAVirtualDirectory is the main cmdlet for server administration of OWA, Set-CASMailbox is the primary administrative cmdlet for the user side of Outlook Web Access. Numerous OWA-specific parameters can be called with the Set-CASMailbox cmdlet. These are all toggle switches to enable or disable specific OWA functionality for a mailbox, and not surprisingly they are analogous to the list shown in the Segmentation tab, which controls the functionality presented by OWA on the server side. This cmdlet also can be used as a full switch to enable or disable OWA altogether. The syntax for disabling OWA for a user is as follows:

```
>Set-CASMailbox <username> -OWAEnabled $false
```

Each of the parameters in this cmdlet follow the same $true | $false options. Here is the full list of OWA-specific parameters from the Set-CASMailbox cmdlet:

- OWAActiveSyncIntegrationEnabled
- OWAAllAddressListsEnabled
- OWACalendarEnabled
- OWAChangePasswordEnabled
- OWAContactsEnabled
- OWAEnabled
- OWAJournalEnabled
- OWAJournalEnabled
- OWAJunkEmailEnabled
- OWANotesEnabled
- OWAPremiumClientEnabled
- OWAPublicFoldersEnabled
- OWARecoverDeletedItemsEnabled
- OWARemindersAndNotificationsEnabled
- OWARulesEnabled

- OWASMimeEnabled
- OWASearchFoldersEnabled
- OWASignaturesEnabled
- OWASpellCheckerEnabled
- OWATasksEnabled
- OWAThemeSelectionEnabled
- OWAUMIntegrationEnabled
- OWAUNCAccessOnPrivateComputersEnabled
- OWAUNCAccessOnPublicComputersEnabled
- OWAWSSAccessOnPrivateComputersEnabled
- OWAWSSAccessOnPublicComputersEnabled

Internet Information Services (IIS) Manager

Because OWA is still a web application, the IIS Manager is required to administer the web server components of OWA. With the IIS Manager, the administrator can control the security settings and properties of the websites and their virtual directories. IIS is used to make a new certificate request for a virtual directory when a third-party SSL certificate is installed.

Redirect or Shorten the OWA URL

A common question that arises for administrators involves the ability to use a simplified URL for their client base. Control of the website URL is managed in the virtual directory properties in IIS. Figure 12-25 shows the settings to redirect the legacy /exchange address to the default URL for OWA 2007 with the /owa at the end. The URL can be shortened as well so users can omit the /owa part altogether. This is accomplished through the same interface, but you select the check box beside "A directory below URL entered" and change the URL in the Direct To field to https://owa.virtuecorp.com. It is even possible to place a shortcut on users' desktops to the OWA URL through logon scripts or a Group Policy Object so they need not remember the syntax at all.

Managing Virtual Directories

Though visible and accessible through IIS, the virtual directories as they pertain to Exchange properties are managed from the EMS and EMC. Even the addition of SSL certificates, which can be accomplished through IIS, can also be implemented using the EMS and the New-ExchangeCertificate cmdlet.

Registry Editor

The Registry Editor (regedt32.exe or regedit.exe) is used to a lesser extent than in Exchange 2003, but there still are settings controlled by Registry keys that require direct manipulation of the Registry.

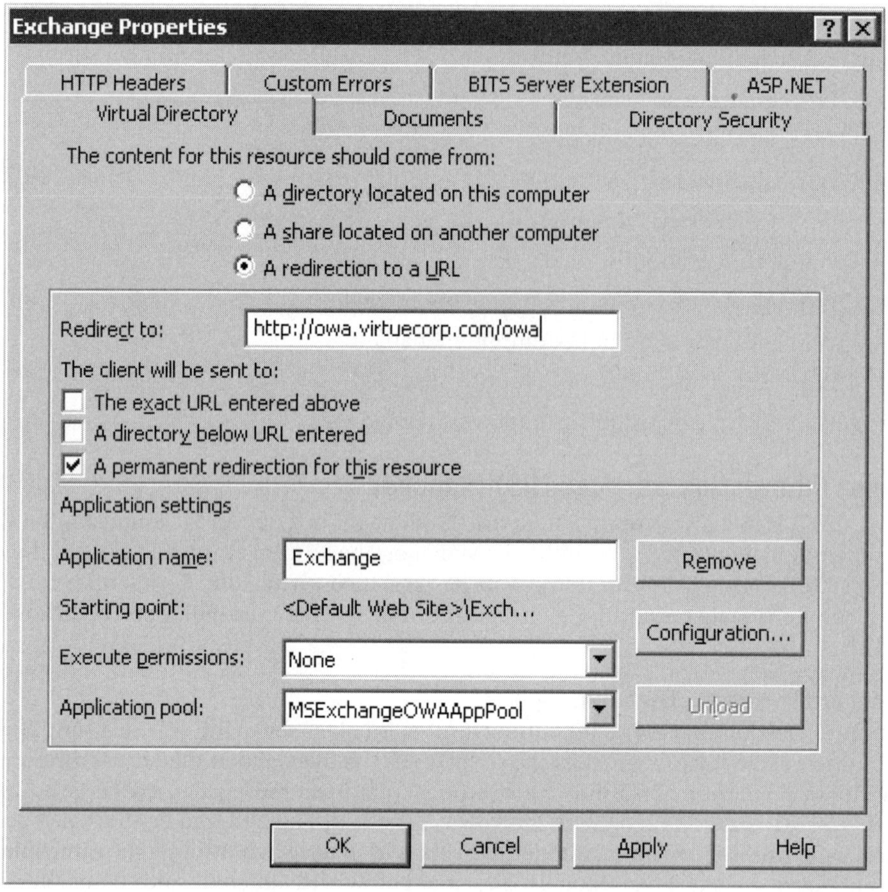

FIGURE 12-25   IIS Manager Redirect /exchange to /owa for OWA 2007

In addition, Registry changes can be implemented by alternative means, such as scripting the execution of a .reg file to update the Registry. OWA timeout settings can be configured directly through the Registry, for example. OWA has its own folder in the Registry where custom configuration entries reside, as shown in Figure 12-26.

web.config

Certain settings specific to ASP.NET are controlled by editing the related web.config file using a standard text editor, such as third-party application assemblies not located in the appropriate folder for OWA. There is a web.config file for each of the Exchange web services in IIS, including Autodiscover, ActiveSync, UM, and OWA. Web.config is a standard XML file that most administrators will not need to change.

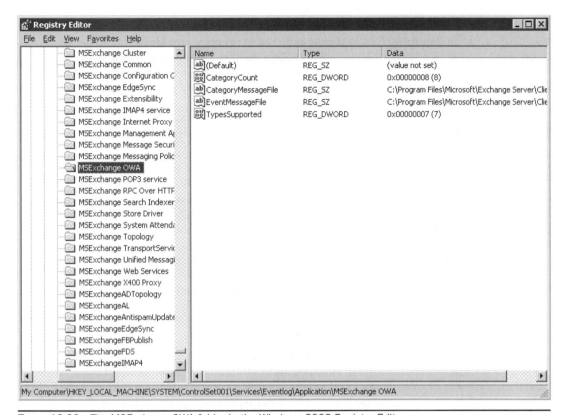

FIGURE 12-26   The MSExchangeOWA folder in the Windows 2003 Registry Editor

OWA Security Features

With each new release of a product, Microsoft is acutely aware of security. You might say
they are constantly being reminded of it. OWA 2007 security is optimized with the use of
Internet Security Accelerator (ISA) Server 2006.

OWA and ISA: Better Together

OWA 2007 can benefit from the versatile perimeter security product known as ISA 2006. ISA
remains a 32-bit application, so it cannot run directly on Exchange 2007, which requires 64-bit
in production. This includes the Edge Server role, which seems a good fit for ISA coexistence
otherwise. ISA can serve as a reverse-proxy inspecting HTTP/HTTPS packets prior to
forwarding them on to the CAS server. In addition, ISA can provide authentication services
for OWA, in which case the OWA authentication type is changed to basic from the default
forms-based authentication.

Microsoft Forefront Security

Available only with Enterprise CALs, Microsoft Forefront Security provides a comprehensive defense solution for Exchange 2007 as a whole. Because it is a server-controlled solution, OWA 2007 still benefits from any antivirus, malware protection, and message hygiene solution implemented in front of Exchange. We will cover Microsoft Forefront Security a little more in Chapter 19.

Public versus Private Computer

As mentioned earlier, the user makes an important determination during logon. They select whether they are accessing OWA with a public or private computer. In this case, the use of "public" really means a workstation that is beyond the control of the user at some time, even a shared home computer. A private computer is one that is used solely by the user. The administrator can determine features that apply to private computers yet are not exposed to connections from workstations deemed as public. Also, there are inherent traits associated with each type of connection by default.

A private computer is assumed to be more secure and therefore more generous with settings such as timeout values. A logon using the private computer selection enjoys a longer period of inactivity before a request to reauthenticate is issued by OWA. The default timeouts are 15 minutes for a public computer and 480 minutes on a private computer.

Secure Sockets Layer

Microsoft Exchange 2007 generates its own default security certificates when it is installed. These do work fine in a default setting. However, unless they are specifically trusted by each workstation accessing OWA, the user will receive a warning pop-up much like the one shown in Figure 12-27. In Internet Explorer 7, the address bar will also display the URL with a background color of red as a means of alerting the user that the certificate does not meet all the trust requirements. A third-party issued and trusted certificate can be installed in its place.

FIGURE 12-27
Untrusted
certificate
warning in
OWA 2007

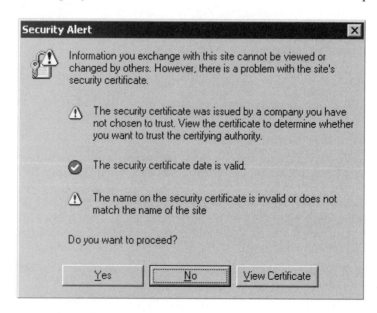

OWA 2007 also requires SSL by default. This means that the user will have to use HTTPS and not HTTP to gain access to OWA. If the user misses the *S*, the error message will read as follows:

HTTP Error 403.4 - Forbidden: SSL is required to view this resource.

Advanced Features

There are several features that many administrators may not need to change, but may apply to specific situations.

Segmentation

We described the settings available on the Segmentation tab earlier in this chapter, as part of the Virtual Directory Properties dialog box. A common question asked by administrators is how to restrict OWA, which is available to all mailbox-enabled users by default. This is done through segmentation. In Exchange 2003, OWA segmentation was managed mostly through Registry entries. In Exchange 2007, it is managed through the Set-OWAVirtualDirectory cmdlet for the OWA server and the Set-CASMailbox cmdlet for the user. The latter sets the necessary values in the msExchMailboxFolderSet attribute in the user object in Active Directory.

GZip Compression

In situations where bandwidth throughput provides the bottleneck for OWA performance, increasing GZip compression can improve overall performance. Additional resources are required on the server to compress the bits more before they go across the wire, so sufficient resources are needed on each end to accommodate an increase in compression. By default, GZip compression is set to Low on all the virtual directories. This value can be changed to Off, High, or Error using the EMS, as follows:

```
>Set-OWAVirtualDirectory -identity "<Virtual_Directory_Name>" -GzipLevel <Off |
Low | High | Error>
```

Setting the default virtual directory GZip compression level to High on the Exchange server with the CAS role installed would be accomplished as follows:

```
>Set-OWAVirtualDirectory -identity "owa (Default Virtual Directory)" -GzipLevel
High
```

Like most virtual directory changes, IIS needs to be restarted. This is easily done with the following command:

```
>iisreset /noforce
```

Web Beacons

Web beacons are bits of HTML that require a call to a remote web server in order for the browser or e-mail client to fully render the content. They are often in the form of 1×1 pixel .gif files. They may even hold hazardous code or specifically confirm the recipient e-mail address of the message in which they are embedded. Web beacons may also be used in legitimate e-mail newsletters as well as ill-intentioned junk mail senders. If an e-mail client is set to automatically retrieve HTML content that is not specifically intrinsic to the message, the remote server hosting the .gif file can log the success rate or the overall exposure of the e-mail message. Like its Outlook counterpart, OWA 2007 can block the application from polling remote servers for HTML content. This setting is configured using the EMS as follows:

```
>Set-OWAVirtualDirectory -identity "<Virtual_Directory_Name>" -
FilterWebBeaconsAndHtmlForms <UserFilterChoice | ForceFilter | DisableFilter >
```

The FilterWebBeaconsAndHtmlForms parameter has several properties. The UserFilterChoice offers the end user the option to block web beacons. The ForceFilter option will block remote HTML calls regardless of what the client attempts. And finally, DisableFilter stops the server from actively preventing remote web server access for HTML e-mail content. A sample command granting users the option on the default virtual directory on the local Exchange server with the CAS role installed might look like the following:

```
>Set-OWAVirtualDirectory -identity "owa (Default Virtual Directory)" -
FilterWebBeaconsAndHtmlForms UserFilterChoice
```

Customizing OWA

Outlook Web Access in Exchange 2007 maintains its customizable interface through its Exchange 2007 rewrite. It is a web application, after all. There are a few places and mechanisms for customizing the user experience. The logon, logoff, and language selection pages can be customized. In addition, themes of varying complexity can be made available or enforced for the users.

Logon and Logoff Screens

Both the logon and logoff screens are formed through the combination of .gif files and Cascading Style Sheet (.css) files. The easiest way to customize the logon screen is through the simple manipulation of these files to accommodate different colors and fonts. CSS files can control the presentation of web pages in many ways. In customizing the logon and logoff screens, the primary attributes in logon.css that administrators might want to amend are the background color, the text color, and the color of the dividing lines in the page. These can be changed to match corporate colors, for example. The .gif files will need to be changed or re-created in a graphic-editing application.

Here's a list of the set of files that form both the logon and logoff pages:

- logon.css
- lgnbotl.gif
- lgnbotm.gif
- lgnbotr.gif
- lgnexlogo.gif
- lgnleft.gif
- lgnright.gif
- lgntopl.gif
- lgntopm.gif
- lgntopr.gif

Language Selection Page

If OWA is being run for the first time, it will ask the user to confirm the language to be used. As mentioned earlier, OWA 2007 allows for a different OWA language than that of the operating system.

OWA Themes

Although making changes to the logon and logoff screens is a good way to show a brand as the first and last thing the user sees during their OWA session, it is possible to customize the entire OWA experience. Microsoft uses the concept of themes for OWA presentation. Two themes ship with Exchange 2007. The default is named Seattle Sky, with an alternative called Carbon Black. Service Pack 1 for Exchange 2007 adds two new themes to the mix.

SP1 *With Exchange 2007 SP1, Microsoft adds two OWA themes—a brown Zune theme and a green-and-black Xbox 360 theme.*

The files for the default theme are held in the folder under %ProgramFiles%\Microsoft\Exchange Server\ClientAccess\owa, which is the local path for the \owa\ virtual directory in IIS. Microsoft puts the default theme into a folder called "base" under \owa\current\themes\base. These files consist of .gif files, .css files, and an .xml file as a name placeholder for the theme.

Additional themes are placed in their own folders under the \themes folder. When a new theme is selected in OWA by the user, the files are pulled from the theme folder and any missing files are drawn from the \base folder. The administrator could, therefore, implement a "theme" where OWA uses a different logo on the main page. The new theme may only have one file for the logo in its own folder, then the rest of the theme will be composed of files drawn from the \base folder appearing as the default theme called Seattle Sky.

Summary

Microsoft continues to improve Outlook Web Access while making the user experience more like the full Outlook client. Although there is still no offline use for OWA, it can provide companies with a viable alternative to Outlook or just a complementary means of connecting users to their mailboxes and the office while away from their desks.

PART IV

13

Unified Communications and Collaboration

B efore there was an Internet that linked the world together with digital electronic communications, the largest networks were the analog telephone and telegraph systems. If you have had the opportunity to see the Blue Man Group, you were probably introduced to the largest network in the world—this is, of course, the plumbing network. Lots of bandwidth in plumbing, but much worse items than spam exist there. Therefore, plumbing is not very good for communications. The good news is that even in its relatively short lifespan, the Internet, which is excellent for communications, has grown larger and has become faster and cheaper to use. The Internet is, in essence, the Wild Wild West of the twenty-first century. One of the key things the Internet has done for computer networks has been to facilitate and extend people's ability to communicate with one another, breaking down many barriers along the way. As the Internet has evolved, so have the ways in which people communicate. So many fantastic developments in human communication have occurred in the last 10 to 20 years. As an e-mail administrator, you are at the heart one of the most revolutionary ways in which humans have ever been able to communicate.

The next stage in the evolution of the Internet is being referred to as Web 2.0. The next generation of business professionals entering the workforce are bringing their knowledge of the Web 2.0 communication tools from the Internet to within the corporate walls. Many organizations are struggling with how to incorporate the new technology that is being demanded. The instantaneous nature of many of the latest means of communications are antiquating e-mail communications, the same way e-mail antiquated interoffice memos and postal services. Organizations are looking at how this can be done and are looking for a vendor that not only has a solution, but provides a complete vision and a detailed roadmap for achieving this. Microsoft's vision is called Unified Communications, and its roadmap consists of Exchange 2007 and Office Communications Server 2007. SharePoint is their solution moving forward for collaboration. Although an in-depth discussion of Office Communications Server 2007 and Microsoft Office SharePoint Server are outside the scope of this book, it is important to examine the technologies they provide for communication and collaboration that relate to Exchange 2007.

All for One, and One for All

For the last 11 years, Microsoft has explored various ways to integrate communication technologies into a single platform. The Exchange Server application was introduced as a messaging and collaboration system, implying that it did more than just distribute e-mail. The very first form of collaboration in the product was *public folders*. Every version of Exchange up to Exchange 2003 has included public folders in the default installation. In Exchange 2000, Instant Messaging and Chat services were added. In Exchange 2003, Instant Messaging was moved to the Live Communication Server, and Chat Services went away. However, mobile services which were part of the Mobile Information Server (MIS) were integrated into Exchange 2003. The year 2007—and the suite of Unified Communication servers Microsoft has released in 2007—marks a new direction in Microsoft's communication and collaboration platform strategy. Figure 13-1 shows the evolution of communication methods over the last decade and how they relate to the Exchange Server application.

Unified Messaging and Collaboration go together hand and hand, but a line has been drawn between messaging and collaboration in the form of separate platforms. Exchange 2007 and the Office Communication Server comprise the messaging solution. The other half of the next generation of communications is collaboration and content management, also known as *knowledge management*, and it is decidedly Microsoft Office SharePoint Server (MOSS). For more detail on Unified Messaging, see Chapter 9.

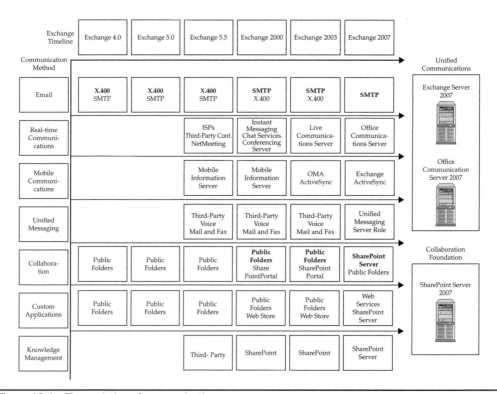

FIGURE 13-1 The evolution of communication

Microsoft Messaging

The industry as a whole coincides with Microsoft in terms of the separation of collaboration and messaging technologies. However, the new Web 2.0 functionality depends on both. The messaging solutions include both: voice and messaging. The hardware and software technologies include Voice over IP (VoIP), Instant Messaging (IM) with presence information, videoconferencing, and Unified Messaging (voicemail/fax/e-mail). By merging these technologies into a unified solution, the concept of messaging takes on a whole new meaning.

Microsoft sees their messaging solution as a software-based solution that can bring the promise of unified communications to any organization. The applications provided by Microsoft for on-premise deployment include the following:

- Microsoft Exchange Server 2007
- Microsoft Office Outlook 2007
- Microsoft Office Communications Server 2007
- Microsoft Office Communicator 2007

Microsoft also hosts the following services for businesses that lack the expertise to deploy and support the messaging infrastructure:

- Microsoft Exchange Hosted Services
- Microsoft Office Live Meeting 2007

Today's Knowledge Worker

When a person communicates with another person in an organization electronically, they have two choices typically: phone and e-mail. Traditionally, for an IT department, these are two incompatible communication networks that are supported by administrators with very different skill sets. For the last seven or so years, vendors such as Nortel and Cisco have been supporting the fledgling world of voice communications over IP, also known as VoIP. Unlike traditional voice solutions, VoIP does not depend on the PSTN (Publicly Switched Telephone Network). VoIP phones are not dependent on an analog handset. In fact, VoIP phones are dependent on the data network and digital handsets. When a company integrates VoIP into their infrastructure, they can turn their phones into network devices and turn computers into phones. Office Communication Server, in combination with Office Communicator, can turn a computer into a phone and allow all users within a corporation to be able to find and connect with each other in multiple ways. When Exchange is tied into the traditional voicemail systems managed by an organization, a person's Inbox can transform into a voicemail repository, allowing voicemail to be retrieved and managed in many different ways. Inbound fax capabilities are built into the Exchange Unified Messaging role, allowing faxes to be delivered to user's mailboxes as well.

With all the options available today for your organization's knowledge workers, the big debate is whether these options improve productivity or hinder it. Although statistics show low numbers in terms of adoption, there is no doubt these technologies are here to stay, and organizations will risk competitiveness if they do not start looking seriously at how to implement these latest communication technologies.

One other consideration about the blending of traditional phone and voicemail data networking and electronic messaging is that this not only is creating a new breed of knowledge worker, but is demanding a new breed of administrator as well. The writing is on the wall for us who are Exchange administrators: Start learning more about voice technologies and digital call management solutions from vendors so that we will be able to assist our organizations in the event that they move forward with a Unified Communication strategy.

Business Subcultures

Organizations that implement this technology are looking to allow their knowledge workers to be more productive. But that requires more than just dynamic communication tools. Workers need to be able to collaborate and access information no matter where they are or where the information resides in an organization. In the early 1990s a movement called Knowledge Management began. Some of the earlier adopters included large technology companies such as Motorola. Today, the technologies that make information available are referred to generically as *content managing systems.*

On the Internet, Wikipedia, MySpace, and Filckr are shaping the future of social networks. Some organizations have begun to see the benefits of implementing similar technologies geared for business. IT departments have begun to use wikis for projects and application support. Business units are beginning to set up team blogs and intranet portals for sharing and collaborating ideas and information. Really Simple Syndication (RSS) technology allows information to be syndicated both inside and outside the organization with partners and customers. Content management of various data silos in an organization brings business intelligence to an entirely new level.

In a way, the Web 2.0 technologies are bringing the concepts of virtual communities into the business world. Business subcultures can be built around projects and can form organically, allowing a business to be very nimble when it comes to change management. Microsoft has provided public folders in Exchange Server for collaboration, but is starting to put an emphasis on SharePoint Server 2007 as their collaboration platform and deemphasizing public folders. Both public folders and SharePoint allow knowledge workers to collaborate, but only SharePoint will allow adopters to take advantage of the latest content management technologies. In the remainder of this chapter you will be introduced to Office Communications Server, Exchange public folders, and Microsoft Office SharePoint Server in an attempt to help you determine which of these technologies delivers the communications and collaboration your organization requires.

Anywhere, Anytime, from Any Client

Although the 20-something age group in a company may embrace the latest technology, how will the remainder of the company adopt it? The answer may ultimately be training, but other aspects determine how quickly adoption will take. End user familiarity with the product or technology makes the adoption process much quicker. The cool thing about a lot of the new technology is that it can be utilized with very little retraining. If you can use a phone, use Outlook, and navigate a website, you can take advantage of this technology. A good communications and collaboration architectural design will make the adoption of the technology go much smoother. The best part of the new technology is that once someone uses it and sees the benefit of using it, they will be hooked and will begin to discover the intricacies on their own or through peer interaction.

Nothing sells this technology better than the "anywhere, anytime, from any client" aspect of Unified Communications. Assume for a minute that you have already deployed Exchange 2007, Office Communication Server, and SharePoint Server 2007. A VIP in the company is traveling to a meeting at a customer's site. He needs to review an e-mail in relationship to the meeting but does not have access to his computer. He calls into his mailbox via the Unified Messaging server in Exchange 2007. He requests that the e-mail be read to him by the Exchange server. After listening to the e-mail, he determines that an additional technical person should attend the meeting. He requests an additional attendee on the same phone connection to Exchange. The invitation is sent to the new attendee. When the VIP arrives at the client site and gets online, he sets up a Live Meeting via the Office Communications Server so that the technical person can join the conference from a remote location. The remote attendee connects to the conference using the link sent to her via the Office Communications server. The Live Meeting room has voice and video capabilities, allowing for a dynamic collaborative experience created on the fly.

Microsoft Office Communications Server (OCS)

If the organization you are working for determines that real-time communications are essential to productivity, it is likely that the first technology they will want to incorporate is a premise-based Instant Messaging solution. Microsoft has been indecisive on which application this technology should be integrated with. In Exchange 2000, they included Instant Messaging but then removed it in the very next version. For those who deployed Exchange 2000 with Instant Messaging, there was a required migration of data to Live Communication Server before moving to Exchange 2003.

In Live Communication Server 2005 (the last version of LCS), administrators will need to migrate to Office Communication Server 2007 if they want to take advantage of not only the enhanced presence information, but also the integrated conferencing capabilities. You will want to evaluate a number of features of Office Communication Server before your deployment so that you can deploy the appropriate components and clients. Table 13-1 shows the available features and what components of OCS are required to support it.

Technical Overview

The Office Communication Server architecture is similar to Exchange's architecture in that each component of the OCS architecture is broken into server roles, as detailed in the following list:

- **Front-end server(s)**   The Office Communications Server 2007 (Standard edition or Enterprise edition) front-end server is responsible for the following tasks:
  - Handling signaling among servers and between servers and clients
  - Authenticating users and maintaining user data, including all user endpoints
  - Routing VoIP calls within the enterprise and to the PSTN
  - Initiating on-premise conferences and managing conference state
  - Providing enhanced presence information to clients
  - Routing Instant Messaging (IM) and conferencing traffic
  - Managing conferencing media
  - Hosting applications
  - Filtering spim (unsolicited commercial IM traffic)

Feature	OCS Server Role / Client
Instant Messaging and enhanced presence	OCS Standard or Enterprise Server / Office Communicator (2005 or 2007).
On-premise web conferencing	OCS Standard or Enterprise Server / Office Communicator 2007 and Conference add-in for Outlook.
A/V conferencing	OCS Standard or Enterprise Server / Office Communicator 2007, Live Meeting 2007, and Conference add-in for Outlook.
Address book server	OCS Standard or Enterprise Server.
Archiving and call detail records	Archiving and DCR Server.
External users access, federation, and/or public IM connectivity	Access Edge Server and HTTP reverse proxy / Office Communicator (2005 or 2007).
Web conferencing with external access	A/V Edge Server / Office Communicator 2007 and Live Meeting 2007.
IM and presence via web browser	Communicator Web Access Server / Communicator Web Access (IE or compatible web browser).
Enterprise Voice (VOIP)	Mediation server with a basic media gateway, basic hybrid media gateway, or advanced media gateway and the A/V Edge Server / Office Communicator 2007 or Office Communicator 2007 Phone edition.

TABLE 13-1 OCS Feature Requirements

- **Web Conferencing Server**   Manages conference data collaboration, including native support for Microsoft Office PowerPoint presentations, Microsoft Office document sharing, white boarding, application sharing, polling, Q&A, compliance logging, annotations, meeting summaries, handouts, and various multimedia formats. The Web Conferencing Server uses PSOM (Persistent Shared Object Model), a Live Meeting protocol, for uploading slides to a meeting. The Web Conferencing Server can reside either on the front-end server (Standard edition and Enterprise edition consolidated pool) or on a separate physical computer (Enterprise edition expanded pool).

- **Web Components Server**   Includes roles that utilize Internet Information Service (IIS).

- **A/V Conferencing Server**   Provides multiparty IP audio and video mixing and relaying, including Microsoft RoundTable, by using industry-standard RTP (Real-time Transport Protocol) and RTCP (Real-time Transport Control Protocol). The A/V Conferencing Server can reside either on the front-end server (Standard edition and Enterprise edition consolidated pool) or on a separate physical computer (Enterprise edition expanded pool).

- **Archiving and CDR Server**   Provides a solution for archiving IM conversations and group conferences and for capturing usage information related to file transfers, audio/video (A/V) conversations, application sharing, remote assistance, meetings, and conferencing servers in call detail records.

- **Access Edge Server** Validates and forwards SIP signaling traffic between internal and external users. Access Edge Server is the new name for what was known in Live Communications Server 2005 as the Access Proxy.
- **Web Conferencing Edge Server** Enables data collaboration with external users.
- **A/V Edge Server** Enables audio and video conferencing and A/V peer-to-peer communications with external users who are equipped with the Office Communicator 2007 client. Peer-to-peer communications traverse between the clients and do not go through the A/V Conferencing Server.
- **Communicator Web Access Server** Provides IM and presence to users who are connecting either from within the corporate network or over the Internet using one of the many supported web browsers. The Communicator Web Access Server components are deployed as part of a Live Communications Server 2005 SP1 deployment. For users, there are no client components to install; all that is required is a web browser and network connectivity to the Communicator Web Access server.
- **Director** Authentication of inbound traffic is performed by the Director or the front-end server. A Director can be a dedicated Office Communications Server 2007 Standard edition server or Enterprise pool.
- **Mediation Server** Provides signaling and media translation between the VoIP infrastructure and a basic media gateway. A Mediation Server also links Office Communications Server with a PBX in both the departmental deployment and PBX integration topologies.

The protocols used by the OCS servers and clients have been improved upon since Live Communication Server 2005. Table 13-2 lists the protocols used by OCS.

Figure 13-2 shows a sample topology that illustrates how the components fit within the OCS architecture.

Protocol	Primary Use
Session Initiation Protocol (SIP)	Internal server-to-server communications and server-to-Office communicator. Also used by Access Edge Server for external IM connectivity.
Transport Layer Security (TLS)	HTTPS connections to Web Conferencing Server.
Multiplexed Transport Layer Security (MTLS)	Remote user access and federation services.
Secure Hyper Text Transport Protocol (HTTPS)	Communications to front-end servers.
Distributed Component Object Model (DCOM) and Remote Procedure Calls (RPC)	Used to move OCS-enabled users and make WMI calls.
Persistent Shared Object Model (PSOM)	Communications between Live Meeting clients and Web Conferencing Servers.
RTP/RTCP	Audio and video conferencing.
Simple Traversal of UDP through NATs (STUN)	Audio and video conferencing though an A/V Edge Server.

TABLE 13-2 OCS Protocol Descriptions

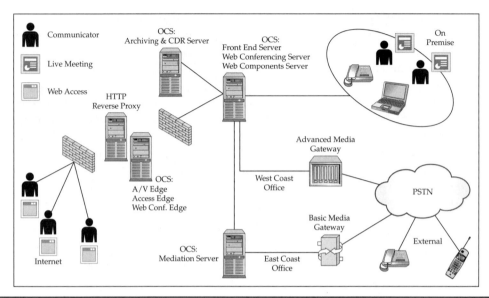

FIGURE 13-2 OCS Architecture

Standard vs. Enterprise

There are two versions of Microsoft Office Communication Server: Standard and Enterprise. Both support the exact same features. Where the two products differ is in how they support the following:

- High availability
- WAN connectivity
- External user access
- Enterprise Voice

The Standard edition is full featured and easier to deploy because the various roles are consolidated as part of the installation. A single Standard edition server can support up to 5000 users. It is not, however, a good choice for organizations with little or no tolerance for service outages, because the Standard edition is a single point of failure. When the WAN topologies become more complex and the number of users at different sites in a company get to be over 100 users, multiple servers will need to be deployed. The Standard edition does not scale as well as the Enterprise edition does. When it comes to external users, the Standard edition will not be able to do this on its own; it will require at least a single Edge server. An additional server will have to be added for Enterprise Voice, too.

The Enterprise edition assumes that the server roles will be deployed onto different servers to optimize performance and to provide high availability. An Enterprise edition topology can scale to up to 125,000 users. The role-based architecture lets you customize your deployment to match your specific needs. The Enterprise edition requires a separate server for the back-end SQL database. This allows pools of OCS servers to centrally manage presence information across the enterprise and prevents a failed front-end server from taking out the presence information.

OCS System Requirements

Many factors are involved in determining your system's requirements. It is important, just like it is with your Exchange servers, to identify the way in which your users will use the OCS features. Consider the number of Instant Messaging (IM) clients, both internal and external. Consider the number of concurrent audio/video conferencing sessions that will take place. How many connections will there be with the native Live Meeting client, and how many will there be with Web Access? Will there be a large number of small conferences, or a small number of large conferences? What will be the total bandwidth consumed by all your connected users? For more on capacity planning for OCS servers, see the Office Communication Server Planning Guide at http://www.microsoft.com/downloads/details .aspx?FamilyID=723347C6-FA1F-44D8-A7FA-8974C3B596F4&displaylang=en.

OCS Clients

Here's a list of the clients that can be used with Office Communications Server:

- Office Communication 2005 (IM and basic presence only)
- Office Communicator 2007 (IM, group IM, multimode conferencing, enhanced presence)
- Office Live Meeting (on-premise web conferencing)
- Communicator Web Access (browser-based IM and enhanced presence)
- Outlook with Conferencing add-in

The client requirements published by Microsoft are detailed in Table 13-3. This should give you an idea of what each user will need to have a good experience with Instant Messaging and video and data conferencing.

The bandwidth requirements for each client will depend greatly on how they use the Office Communication server and Office Communicator. Table 13-4 can help you plan bandwidth for all your users as well as help you determine the end users' experience.

Office RoundTable is a new videoconferencing device being released by Microsoft. It will allow an entire room to be included in a videoconference.

Administering OCS Users

After Office Communication Server has been successfully deployed in your organization, there is still a fair amount of work required to configure your user accounts before they can use any of the OCS features. None of your users will be enabled for OCS by default.

PART IV

Client Dependencies	Minimum Requirement
Display resolution	Required: Super VGA 800×600. Recommended: Super VGA 1024×768 or higher.
Operating system	Windows Vista 32-bit operating system. Microsoft Windows XP Professional with Service Pack 2.
Computer/processor	Data and voice: 500 MHz or higher processor, Intel Pentium-compatible. Video: 1 GHz or higher. Microsoft Office RoundTable communications and archival system: 1.8 GHz or higher.
Memory	512MB of RAM.
Install free space	1.5MB.
Video memory	Video card with 64MB of RAM (video RAM, or *VRAM*) and Microsoft DirectX application programming interface.
Telephony	Microphone and speakers, headset with microphone, or equivalent device.
Video	Video camera or Office RoundTable device.
Security	Administrator privileges or, in Windows Vista Standard User Mode, administrator credentials.
Other requirements	Microsoft Office Outlook 2002, 2003, or 2007 and Microsoft Exchange Server are required for Outlook integration options.

TABLE 13-3   Client Requirements

You not only will have to enable them to use OCS, you will have to configure which of the features they will be able to use. In order to administer users, you must be a member of the RTCUniversalUserAdmins security group. You must also perform these tasks from a machine that has the Office Communications Server 2007 administration tools installed.

Bandwidth Requirements	Minimum	High-Quality
Data	56 Kbps	56 Kbps
Voice	50 Kbps	80 Kbps
Video	50 Kbps	350 Kbps
Office RoundTable	50 Kbps	350 Kbps

TABLE 13-4   Client Bandwidth Requirements

Here are the steps to follow to enable user accounts:

1. Log onto your management machine.
2. Click Start | Run, type **dsa.msc**, and click OK.
3. Navigate to the Organization Unit (OU) with the user account(s) you want to enable.
4. Right-click the user account and then select Enable users for Communications Server, as shown next.

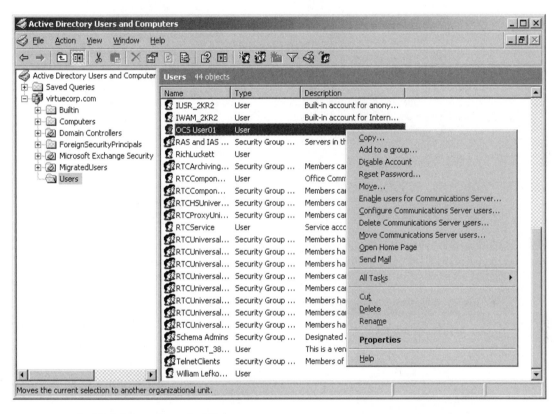

5. Click Next when the Welcome page appears.

6. On the Select Server or Pool page, shown next, select the appropriate target from the list and then click Next.

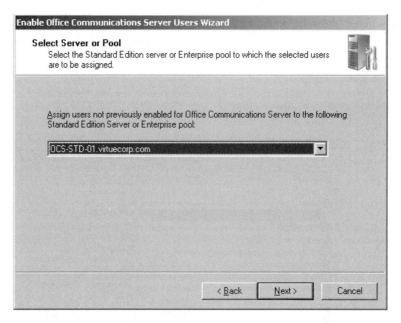

7. Choose one of the options on the Specify Sign-in Name page, shown here. (If you have not mailbox-enabled the user account, do *not* choose the option to generate the Serial Interface Protocol (SIP) address from the user's e-mail address.)

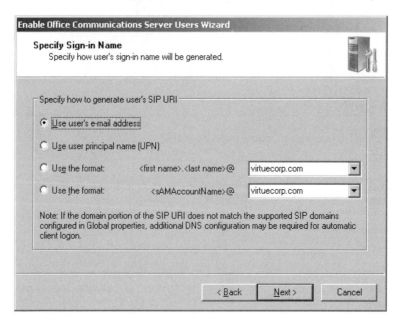

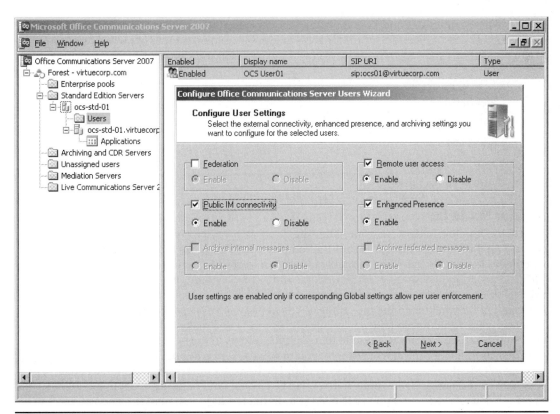

FIGURE 13-3   Configuring user settings

After you enable the account(s) for OCS, you will need to configure the user settings. This can be done from the OCS enhanced version of ADUC, or it can be done in the Office Communications Server 2007 administrative tool. Figure 13-3 shows the configuration options via the OCS 2007 administrative tool. The options that are available depend on which features you have deployed and which features were configured to be available in the Global Settings.

Public Folders

Because public folders have been Microsoft's de facto answer for collaboration for users from 1996 to 2006, it stands to reason that a number of organizations running Exchange have taken advantage of public folders. Many of them rely heavily on public folders for sharing critical business information. Perhaps the greatest dependencies on public folders come from organizations that have built custom public folder applications.

Public folders use the Microsoft Exchange storage and transport to create a repository for a wide variety of content. In its simplest form, a public folder can be thought of as a file server because of the way it stores files in a central location. But it is how the information gets there in the first place and how it is ultimately managed and retrieved that makes it a true collaborative solution. The client for accessing public folders is Outlook, which uses the MAPI protocol to access the repository. Some of the common uses for public folders include:

- Document sharing
- Calendars
- Custom workflow applications
- Project tasks lists
- Discussion groups
- Outlook contact lists

To Be or Not to Be

The future of public folders is certain. They are going away. Microsoft is committed to supporting them until at least 2016, but the company does not make any commitment on whether that means they will be available in future releases like they are in Exchange Server 2007. The smart money says bet on SharePoint and .NET programming if you need to invest in developing custom business applications. We will take a close look at SharePoint Server at the end of this chapter. In the meantime, if you already have a vested interest in public folders or you would like to take advantage of them until you make a decision regarding SharePoint, you can certainly continue to use public folders in the near term.

There are a few technical reasons why you may have kept a Public Folder database even if you don't use public folders for collaboration. The first is your transition from Exchange 2000/2003 to Exchange 2007. Public folders will be created automatically. Even if you do not transition from an earlier version of Exchange to Exchange 2007, you may still need public folders. If you tell Exchange 2007 during setup that you are still supporting Outlook 2003 and earlier clients, it will create a storage group and a Public Folder database just for storing the system folders that contain Free/Busy availability information and the offline address books required by Outlook 2002/2003 clients. Finally, you will need to maintain public folders in Exchange 2007 as long as your custom applications depend on them.

Public Folder Administration

The RTM version of Exchange 2007 does not come with a graphical tool for administering public folders. Some of the advanced features of public folders were not kept around either, such as multiple public folder trees. The core administrative tasks for public folders were kept intact (see Figure 13-4). However, they were relegated to the Exchange Management Shell, which for many Exchange administrators is the equivalent of them not existing at all. A few more public folder cmdlets were added with Service Pack 1.

SP1   *The Public Folder Management Console was added in Exchange 2007 Service Pack 1.*

In terms of making public folder administrators' lives easier, Service Pack 1 does include a graphical administrative tool called the Public Folder Management Console (PFMC), shown in Figure 13-5. This additional tool will undoubtedly be appreciated by those of you who have hundreds, if not thousands, of public folders and do not have time to master the Exchange Management Shell before the move to Exchange 2007.

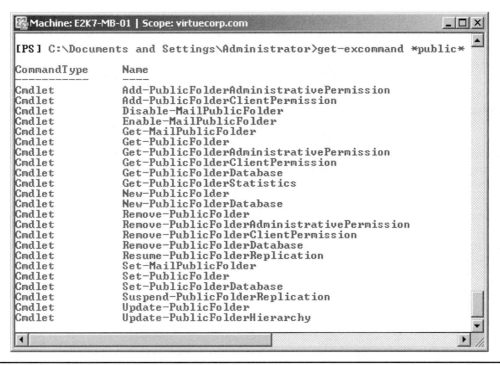

Figure 13-4   Public folder cmdlets (Service Pack 1)

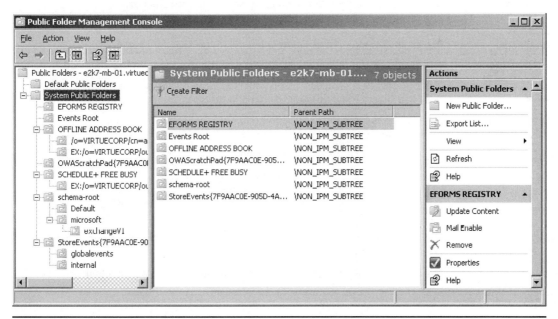

Figure 13-5   The Public Folder Management Console

The hierarchal nature of public folders lends itself to a graphical administrative tool. Using the PFMC, administrators will be able to manage both public folders and system folders. New folder creation can be controlled at the top level with a new administrative role called the Exchange Public Folder Administrator role, which was also added as part of SP1. Like its predecessor the Exchange System Manager (2000/2003), the PFMC is good at creating a folder structure and managing replication, but it doesn't let you specify the type of public folder you want to create or how you want to delegate permissions.

Public folder administrators can use the Exchange Management Shell to delegate the initial permission for a top-level public folder. Delegates can use Outlook to further delegate access rights to public folders. In order to create top-level public folders, you will need the Exchange Public Folder Administrator role. For more information on delegating Exchange administrator roles, see Chapter 14. Exchange administrators can assign delegate access rights using the Add-PublicFolderAdministratorPermission cmdlet. One of the most popular features of public folders is its granular client access model. A number of predefined combinations of client access rights are available that allow you to assign roles easily to mailboxes and/or security distribution groups. The individual access rights are listed in Table 13-5.

The preconfigured roles that can be applied using the Add-PublicFolderAdministrator Permission cmdlet or Outlook are described in the Table 13-6.

Client Access Right	Description
CreateItems	The client has the right to create items within the specified public folder and send e-mail messages to the public folder if it is mail-enabled.
CreateSubfolders	The client has the right to create subfolders in the specified public folder.
DeleteAllItems	The client has the right to delete all items in the specified public folder.
DeleteOwnedItems	The client has the right to delete items that the user owns in the specified public folder.
EditAllItems	The client has the right to edit all items in the specified public folder.
EditOwnedItems	The client has the right to edit the items that the user owns in the specified public folder.
FolderContact	The client is the contact for the specified public folder.
FolderOwner	The client is the owner of the specified public folder. The user has the right to view and move the public folder, create subfolders, and set permissions for the folder. The user cannot read items, edit items, delete items, or create items.
FolderVisible	The client can view the specified public folder, but cannot read or edit items within the specified public folder.
ReadItems	The client has the right to read items within the specified public folder.

TABLE 13-5   Public Folder Client Access Rights

User Access Role	Permissions
Author	CreateItems, ReadItems, FolderVisible, EditOwnItems, DeleteOwnItems
Contributor	CreateItems, FolderVisible
Editor	CreateItems, ReadItems, FolderVisible, EditOwnItems, EditAllItems, DeleteOwnItems, DeleteAllItems
None	FolderVisble
Non-EditingAuthor	CreateItems, ReadItems, FolderVisible
Owner	CreateItems, ReadItems, CreateSubfolders, FolderOwner, FolderContact, FolderVisible, EditOwnItems, EditAllItems, DeleteOwnItems, DeleteAllItems
PublishingAuthor	CreateItems, ReadItems, CreateSubfolders, FolderVisible, EditOwnItems, DeleteOwnItems, DeleteAllItems
PublishingEditor	CreateItems, ReadItems, CreateSubfolders, FolderVisible, EditOwnItems, EditAllItems, DeleteOwnItems, DeleteAllItems
Reviewer	ReadItems, FolderVisible

TABLE 13-6 Public Folder Client Access Roles

Public folder administrators depend greatly on the delegates to manage the permissions of the subfolders created under the administratively defined top-level folders. Because the delegates tend not to be administrators, they will manage access to public folders using Outlook. Figure 13-6 shows the Permissions tab of a public folder in Outlook 2007.

FIGURE 13-6
Outlook 2007
public folder
Permissions tab

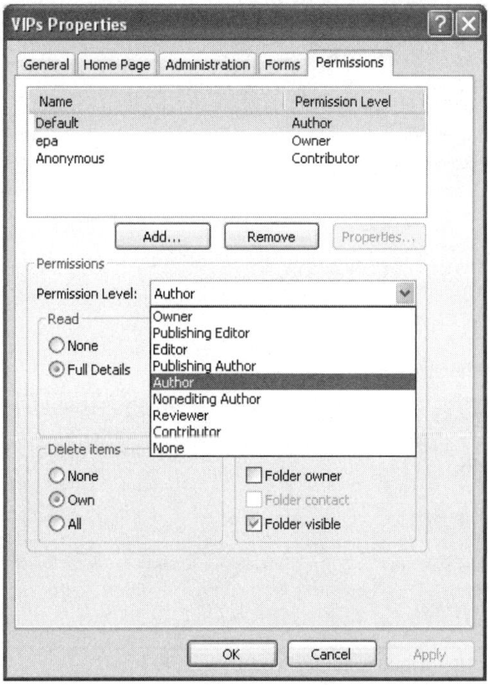

Outlook or Outlook Web Access 2007 SP1 clients can be used to create public folders when you want to customize the content of a public folder. The custom folder options include Calendar Items, Contact Items, InfoPath Form Items, Journal Items, Mail and Post Items, Note Items, and Task Items. Whereas Outlook will allow you to choose from any of these options in the Folder Contains field when creating a new folder, Outlook Web Access will limit the choices, as shown in Figure 13-7.

SP1 *The RTM version of OWA 2007 does not support access to public folders, let alone the creation of new public folders. Exchange 2007 Server Pack 1 adds the ability to do both from OWA 2007.*

Public Folder Replication

Public folders are specialized mailboxes that store data in a separate database from users' mailboxes so that the data can be logically organized into a hierarchal structure called the *public folder tree.* The most outstanding feature of public folders is the ability to replicate content between databases on different Exchange servers, even across various WAN connections. This important feature of public folders still sets it apart from other collaboration solutions, including SharePoint Server. Being able to create replicas of folders allows administrators to create fault-tolerant collaborative solutions. Having multiple instances of a public folder can also improve the client experience when local instances are created for users. It is also possible to replicate public folders between Exchange 2007 and Exchange 2000/2003 public folder servers.

The two components to public folder replication are Active Directory (AD) and the Exchange Information Store. Active Directory replicates all public folder objects and their

Figure 13-7   Creating a public folder with OWA 2007 SP1

associated attributes to all other domain controllers in a domain, and all Global Catalogs keep a copy of all public folder objects from all domains in the forest. The Exchange Information Store is responsible for creating and replicating the public folder tree to all Exchange servers with a Public Folder database. The Exchange Information Store is also responsible for replicating the content of public folders to their replica servers. Because all Public Folder databases contain read/write copies of the database, a change can take place on any server. Replication latency and a lack of content management make public folders too prohibitive for collaboration that depends on document/records management.

Public Folder database objects store the default settings for storage limits, deleted item retention, and the replication interval used by individual public folders. In order to create a replica of a folder, you will have to use the Exchange Management Shell Set-PublicFolder-Replicas cmdlet or the new Public Folder Management Console to configure specific folders. With the PFMC, you can use the Replica tab in the properties for a public folder to specify one or more replica servers.

Microsoft Office SharePoint Server

Microsoft Office SharePoint Server (MOSS) is to public folders what Office Communications Server is to Exchange's mailboxes. For now, it is a supplement to extend an enterprises' ability to collaborate in new and more effective ways. In the future, that may change. At least for the foreseeable future there is no end of life for e-mail support from Microsoft. Ultimately, the rate of adoption and acceptance of MOSS by organizations will determine the lifespan of Exchange public folders. It is obvious to see why Microsoft has made the decision to promote SharePoint as the public folder replacement when you look at what features SharePoint offers above and beyond anything you can do with public folders.

Web 2.0 Gets a Business Suit

Windows SharePoint Server is, at its heart, an IIS web server. Many of its features are business versions of what is commonly known as Web 2.0. The industry has dubbed the features found in SharePoint Server and similar solutions from third parties as *Enterprise 2.0 Services*. SharePoint Services allows centrally stored information to be managed, and ultimately presented, using a wide variety of services.

Features Overview

The features that make SharePoint Server an integral part of an organization's communication and collaboration roadmap include the following:

- **Document management**   Offers check-in and check-out features with built-in version control.
- **Office 2007 integration**   Each Office application has the potential to be a MOSS client.
- **Change alerts**   Individuals and teams can be notified when pertinent information changes.
- **Traditional collaboration (public folders replacement)**   Includes calendars, contacts, task lists, and various other types of lists.

PART IV

- **Interactive collaboration**   Includes discussion boards, surveys, and reports.
- **News subscriptions**   Collections of RSS feeds that are relevant to a team.
- **Enterprise Search**   The indexing of all corporate data silos brings relevant information to teams and individuals.
- **Reporting**   Provides business intelligence information or key performance indicators (KPIs) in the form of dashboards and reports.

Out of the box, SharePoint Server has built-in site templates to help you rapidly support your organization's requirements. The templates available in the Enterprise edition are broken into four categories: Collaboration, Meetings, Enterprise, and Publishing. Table 13-7 lists all the templates.

Technical Overview

Microsoft Office SharePoint Server 2007 has introduced the following new deployment and management features in order to improve the administrator and programmer experience with SharePoint Services:

- Three-tier administration model with delegation tools
- Centralized configuration management with automatic propagation of configuration settings to all servers in a farm

Template Category	Templates
Collaboration	Team Site Blank Site Document Workspace Wiki Site Blog
Meetings	Basic Meeting Workspace Blank Meeting Workspace Decision Meeting Workspace Social Meeting Workspace Multipage Meeting Workspace
Enterprise	Document Center Records Center Personalization Site Site Directory Report Center Search Center with Tabs Search Center
Publishing	Publishing Site Publishing Site with Workflow News Site

TABLE 13-7   SharePoint Site Templates

- New administrative GUI that represents multiserver (farm) topologies
- New compliance features for policy enforcement, auditing and logging, and item-level access control
- Document lifecycle management with a Records Repository site that can enforce labeling, auditing, and retention periods
- Restricted administrator access to prevent administrators from viewing sensitive content
- Volume Shadow Copy Service (VSS) backups are now supported
- New site migration tools
- Improved support for MOM
- Host header mode supports multiple DNS domain names for a single application
- Support for server renaming using the Stsadm RenameServer command
- Improved credential management for service accounts
- New network configuration options for Alternate Access Mapping (AAM), pluggable authentication, and SQL Server authentication
- Improved support for custom applications

Deployment Options

SharePoint Server is composed of three server roles: application server, front-end web server, and database server. You can choose to deploy Microsoft Office SharePoint Server as a standalone server or as a server farm. All three server roles will be installed automatically if you choose the Basic installation options, thus creating a standalone configuration that cannot be made part of a server farm. Furthermore, it is extremely limited in its ability to scale. A Basic installation will only support one CPU and a maximum database size of 4GB. The Basic installation will install and use SQL Server 2005 Express edition. Choosing the Basic installation options is the easiest way to deploy a standalone server. However, if you want to use the SharePoint server in production for anything beyond testing out the product, you will need to perform an Advanced installation. If you want to use a single SharePoint server that is not limited and can be a member of a farm later on, you will need to choose the Advanced installation option (see Figure 13-8) and then select "Complete— Install all components. Can add servers to form a SharePoint farm" from the custom options.

SharePoint Requirements

SharePoint Server has the following requirements:

- Windows Server 2003 with SP1 or later and all critical updates (Standard, Enterprise, Datacenter, or Web edition can be used)
- A Standard or Enterprise product ID key
- Internet Explorer 6.0 (with all service packs) or Internet Explorer 7.0

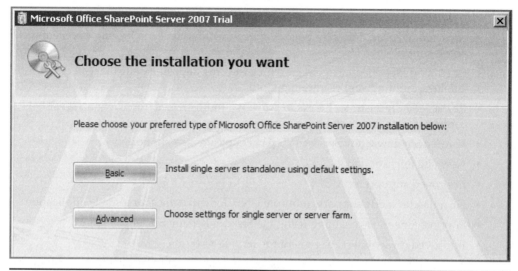

FIGURE 13-8   Selecting the SharePoint Installation Type

- Internet Information Services (IIS) 6.0
  - WWW
  - SMTP
  - Common files
- Microsoft .NET Framework 3.0 with ASP.NET 2.0 enabled
- SQL Server 2000 SP3a, Microsoft SQL Server 2005 SP1, or later
- SQL Server 2005 Analysis Services SP1 or later

For details on hardware requirements and sizing the SharePoint servers for a SharePoint server farm, see, "Determine hardware and software requirements (Office SharePoint Server)," at http://technet2.microsoft.com/Office/en-us/library/bd99c3a9-0333-4c1c-9793-a145769e48e61033.mspx?mfr=true.

Integrating MOSS and Exchange

You can use Microsoft Office SharePoint Server to send e-mail alerts and notifications to collaboration team members by configuring the outbound mail setting to connect to an SMTP host. SharePoint can also be configured to receive inbound mail. Inbound mail requires the SMTP protocol stack that comes with IIS 6.0. SharePoint can deliver mail to document libraries and other SharePoint sites, which streamlines the collaboration greatly.

Although IIS 6.0's SMTP works fine for sending and receiving e-mail, it is not secure as or integrated with Exchange 2007. In fact, there is nothing easy about integrating Exchange 2007 with SharePoint's SMTP. This is a bit surprising considering SharePoint is going to replace public folders, which are tightly integrated with Exchange. A good whitepaper titled,

"How to configure Incoming Email Enabled Libraries in MOSS2007 RTM using Exchange 2007 in an Active Directory Domain," can be downloaded at http://www.combined-knowledge.com/Downloads%202007.htm. Here's a high-level summary of the steps you will need to take:

1. Create an OU in AD for MOSS recipient objects.

2. Create an MX record for the SMTP domain used by the SharePoint server and point it at the SharePoint server's A record.

3. Install and configure IIS 6.0's SMTP service on the SharePoint server (if it has not already been installed). Allow it to receive e-mail from the Exchange 2007 Hub Transport server(s).

4. Use the SharePoint Central Administrator tool to configure the following:

    • Incoming e-mail settings

    • The Directory Management Service

    • The incoming e-mail server display address

    • Save e-mail servers

5. Create a mail-enabled feature such as a Document Management Library on a SharePoint team site.

6. Verify that contacts were created in AD by the SharePoint Directory Management Service.

7. Create a Send connector in the Exchange 2007 organization to route mail to the SharePoint server's IP address as a smart host.

8. Configure the Windows SharePoint Service Timer to be able to delete objects from the SMTP drop folder to prevent duplicate e-mails.

Public Folder Migration Tools

Microsoft does not currently have any tools for migrating public folders to SharePoint Server. However, some third-party vendors do offer migration tools. Table 13-8 lists these vendors' tools.

Vendor's Product	Link
AvePoint's DocAve 4.1 Migrator for SharePoint	http://www.avepoint.com/products/sharepoint-migration
Quest Software's Public Folder Migrator for SharePoint	http://www.quest.com/public-folder-migrator-for-sharepoint/

TABLE 13-8 Public Folder–to–SharePoint Migration Tools

Unified Voice (Unified Messaging and Enterprise Voice)

At the beginning of this chapter, we discussed how the new Web 2.0 collaboration methods depend on the integration of communication technologies that are traditionally separated from each other. In Chapter 9, we discussed the introduction of Unified Messaging (UM) into the Exchange 2007 architecture, which extends the traditional nature of the e-mail system to include voicemail and faxes. This certainly falls into the category of Web 2.0. Unfortunately, it is not possible with the RTM version of Exchange 2007 to integrate Unified Messaging with Office Communication Server. With the release of Exchange 2007 Service Pack 1, it is now possible to extend the functionality of Exchange 2007 once more by integrating the functionality of Unified Messaging and Office Communication Server 2007 Enterprise Voice.

SP1   *SP1 adds support for integrating Unified Messaging and Office Communication Server 2007 Enterprise Voice.*

Office Communications Server 2007 Enterprise Voice—once integrated with Exchange 2007 Unified Messaging—uses the Unified Messaging server role for voicemail, call notifications, Auto Attendant services, and subscriber access. Communications Server 2007 Enterprise Voice has specific integration points that make the two applications compatible. Table 13-9 shows the Unified Messaging and Enterprise Voice components that integrate together.

The combination of location profiles, server pools, and front-end servers allows Office Communication Server to function as a software-based IP PBX. Exchange 2007 Service Pack 1 and higher allow the Unified Messaging role to establish connectivity to Office Communication Server and use it as an IP gateway for voice communications. Of course, OCS has a number of benefits over a third-party IP gateway appliance. It is actually mutually beneficial to both products to be integrated.

UM Component	OCS Enterprise Voice Component	Description
Unified Messaging Dial Plan object (SIP URI only)	Enterprise Voice location profile	This is an SIP-only relationship. The name of each location profile must match the forest FQDN of the SIP URI dial plan.
Unified Messaging IP gateway	Office Communications Server 2007 pool and front-end server	The combination of the OCS 2007 server/pool and a front-end server functions as an IP PBX to the UM server. A UM IP gateway is specifically configured to communicate with the OCS 2007 server/pool.
Unified Messaging Hunt Group object	N/A	Multiple UM Hunt Group objects can associate with a single UM IP gateway. The UM IP gateway associates with multiple UM dial plans. The UM dial plans associate with corresponding Enterprise Voice locations.

TABLE **13-9**   UM and OCS Integration Points

Office Communication Server Enterprise Voice Dependencies

The following Office Communication Server Enterprise Voice features are dependent on UM DialPlan, UM IPGateway, and UM Hunt Groups objects to function properly.

- **Location profiles**   A set of normalization rules used to translate telephone numbers for a location. The location name and UM DialPlan's FQDNs need to be identical.
- **Phone number normalization**   A process of converting number strings that are entered in various formats into the E.164 format. For more information on E.164, see http://searchnetworking.techtarget.com/sDefinition/0,,sid7_gci1094695,00.html.
- **Phone usage records**   Used to assign call permissions to users. Depends on the voice policy for call routing.
- **Voice policies**   Collections of phone usage records that are assigned to one or more users. Can be configured as a global policy for all users or as a special policy for individual users.

OCS Call Routing

Unified Messaging depends on an IP gateway or IP PBX to allow callers to leave voicemails and to provide UM-enabled users (subscribers) to access their voicemail. When OCS Enterprise Voice is deployed with Unified Messaging, the following Enterprise Voice call-routing components handle the phone-based communications with Unified Messaging:

- **Inbound Routing component**   Handles incoming calls based on preferences specified by Enterprise Voice clients.
- **Outbound Routing component**   Handles calls that are placed by subscribers to VoIP, PSTN, or mobile networks. This component looks up the target number in the RTC database. If there is a match to a SIP Uniform Resource Identifier (URI), the call is routed through all SIP endpoints for that user.

Enterprise Voice Services

The Set Up Routing for Office Communications Server 2007 option, during OCS Enterprise Voice installation, adds the following services necessary for integrating OCS with Unified Messaging:

- **Address Book Service**   Converts user telephone numbers that are replicated from AD to the RTC database to E.164 format. The converted numbers are used to create the contacts for Enterprise Voice.
- **Enterprise Services**   Performs reverse number lookup on the target telephone number of each incoming call, matches that number to the SIP URI of the destination user, and sends the call to that user's SIP endpoints.
- **Translation Service**   The application responsible for translating the dialed number into an E.164 number based on the normalization rules defined by the administrator.
- **User Replicator**   Replicates user telephone numbers from Active Directory to the RTC database.

Working Together

As mentioned earlier, both UM and OCS Enterprise Voice benefit from integrating the applications. Microsoft defines the following four scenarios in which it is possible to use both applications together:

- Call notification
  1. User 1 calls User 2. User 2 does not answer the call.
  2. User 1 hangs up.
  3. User 2 receives an e-mail message in their Exchange 2007 mailbox that User 1 called.
- Leaving a voice mail message
  1. User 1 calls User 2.
  2. User 2 does not answer the call.
  3. Because User 2 has not configured call forwarding to another telephone number, the call from User 1 is diverted to the voicemail for User 2.
  4. User 1 is invited to leave a voice message.
  5. The greeting that was previously recorded by User 2 is played.
  6. User 2 receives a voicemail message recorded from User 1.
- Subscriber access
  1. User 2 dials into a subscriber access number and accesses their Exchange 2007 mailbox to check for voice messages.
  2. User 2 can listen to the e-mail or voicemail messages or access their calendar.
  3. After listening to the voice message from User 1, User 2 decides to return the call from User 1.
  4. User 2 accesses the options menu and uses the callback option to place a call to User 1.
- Auto Attendant
  1. User 1 does not know the extension number for User 2.
  2. User 1 dials into a telephone number that is configured on a UM Auto Attendant.
  3. The welcome greeting and prompts that are configured on the Auto Attendant are played to User 1.
  4. User 1 uses the directory search feature to locate User 2 in the directory and places a call to the extension number for User 2.

Office Communication Server extends the reach of the Unified Messaging mailbox to additional technologies, including Instant Messaging (IM), enhanced presence, and audio/video conferencing.

Integration Process Overview

Because of the complexity of integrating Unified Messaging and Office Communication Server Enterprise Voice, there are numbers of steps that must be performed in a specific order. The following provides an overview of the integration process:

1. Create a UM SIP URI dial plan that maps to an OCS location profile. Use the Get-UMDialPlan cmdlet to obtain the FQDN of a SIP URI dial plan so that this can be used when the location profile is created.

2. Install a valid server certificate on the UM server(s). It is a best practice to use a standalone UM server so that there are no certificate conflicts between Exchange 2007 server roles.

3. Encrypt the VoIP traffic by configuring the SIP URI dial plan as SIP secured or Secured.

4. Add UM servers to the SIP dial plan.

5. Add Enterprise Voice SIP addresses to UM-enabled mailboxes.

CAUTION *UM-enabled mailboxes associated with SIP URL dial plans that use OCS as an IP gateway lose the ability to receive inbound faxes. This is due to a limitation of the mediation server used by OCS Enterprise Voice.*

6. Run the exchucutil.ps1 script from the Exchange Management Shell to perform the following tasks:

   - Grant Office Communications Server permission to read Exchange UM Active Directory objects
   - Create a UM IP Gateway object for each server/server pool running Enterprise Voice
   - Create an Exchange UM hunt group for each gateway

7. Create location profiles.

8. Assign location profiles to servers or server pools.

9. Deploy and configure media gateways and mediation servers.

10. Define telephone usages, voice policies, and outbound call routes.

11. Configure the users for Enterprise Voice services.

12. Run the ocsumutil.exe command to create the contact objects for subscriber access and for the Auto Attendant.

You can view and configure the Office Communications Server voice properties using the Office Communications Server 2007 Management Console, as shown in Figure 13-9.

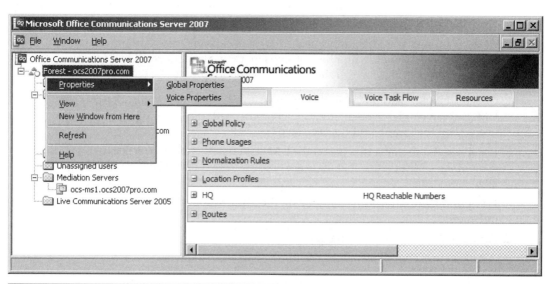

FIGURE 13-9   Office Communication Server 2007 Voice Properties

Summary

Before there was an Internet that linked the world together with digital electronic communications, the largest networks were the analog telephone and telegraph systems. One of the key things the Internet has done for computer networks has been to facilitate and extend people's ability to communicate with one another, while breaking down many barriers along the way. As the Internet has evolved, so have the ways in which people communicate. The next evolution of the Internet is being referred to as Web 2.0.

For the last 11 years Microsoft has explored various ways to integrate communication technologies into a single platform. The Exchange Server application was introduced as a messaging and collaboration system, implying that it did more than just distribute e-mail. The year 2007, and the suite of Unified Communication servers Microsoft has released in 2007, marks a new direction in Microsoft's communication and collaboration platform strategy.

Public folders have been around since 1996, so it is acceptable to think that a number of organizations are taking advantage of public folders. Public folders use the Microsoft Exchange storage and transport to create a repository for a wide variety of content. But it is how the information gets there in the first place and how it is ultimately managed and retrieved that makes it a true collaborative solution.

Microsoft Office SharePoint Server (MOSS) is to public folders what Office Communications Server is to Exchange's mailboxes. For now, it is a supplement to extend an enterprises' ability to collaborate in new and more effective ways. The rate of adoption and acceptance of MOSS by organizations will determine the lifespan of Exchange public folders.

Unified Messaging extends the traditional nature of the e-mail system to include voicemail and faxes. With the release of Exchange 2007 Service Pack 1, it is now possible to extend the functionality of Exchange 2007 once more by integrating the functionality of Unified Messaging and Office Communication Server 2007 Enterprise Voice.

V
PART

Security

Administrative Models

Approximately 97 billion e-mails are sent every day. According to IDC analysts, 40 billion of those daily e-mails are spam. It stands to reason that unsolicited e-mail poses a considerable threat to business communications and productivity. E-mail-borne viruses pose another serious threat to e-mail security. These threats are not usually directed at your Exchange organization specifically, but they are part and parcel to communicating on the Internet. There are other threats that are not as random, such as mail bombs and other denial-of-service attacks, that can affect your origination. Threats can also be personal in nature, such as harassing e-mails. History has shown us that the worst threats will most likely come from within your organization. Before you can protect your Exchange organization, you must look at e-mail security from a "Defense in Depth" perspective. Defense in Depth is a strategy used by information security professionals that has its roots in military defense. This strategy delays an attack by creating multiple barriers that an attacker must overcome. The more barriers, the stronger the defense is. Part V of this book is dedicated to all e-mail security topics and how to configure Exchange Server 2007 to provide secure e-mail communications. This chapter details the different Exchange administration models and how to implement them. Chapter 15 details the subject of regulatory compliance. Chapter 16 details e-mail item and transport security, and Chapter 17 details antivirus and anti-spam solutions.

Active Directory and Exchange Permissions

Additional efforts have been made by the Microsoft Exchange team to separate the permissions required to administer Exchange from the permissions required to administer Active Directory in Exchange Server 2007. This separation of permissions makes it easier than ever to delegate administrative tasks without compromising security. The goal of a good administrative model design is to grant only enough permission for an administrator to do their job and nothing more.

Active Directory Naming Contexts (Partitions)

The average administrator only needs to know that the Active Directory Domain database stores Exchange objects and attributes. Senior Exchange administrators and architects will

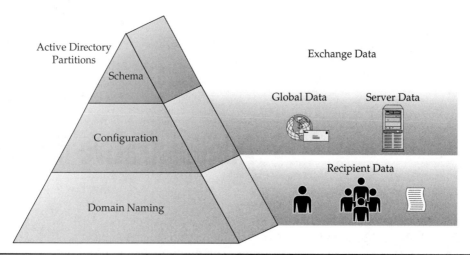

Figure 14-1   Exchange Data in Active Directory

benefit in knowing where Exchange objects and attributes are stored in Active Directory (AD) (see Figure 14-1).

Every domain controller in an Active Directory domain stores a copy of the schema. The schema defines what objects can be created and what attributes are mandatory or optional to populate. The schema is extended by Exchange so that Active Directory can store Exchange data. The actual data is not stored in the schema partition. As Figure 14-1 shows, Exchange data is stored in the Configuration and Domain Naming context. Different permissions are required to access each partition in Active Directory.

Exchange Data

Three Exchange data types are stored in Active Directory, as detailed in the following list. They are separated from each other by partitions and permissions.

- **Global data**   Data that applies to the entire Exchange organization. Global information such as the organization name, Receive domains, and Send connectors are stored in the Configuration partition.

- **Server data**   Data that applies to a specific Exchange server. Server information such as server role, storage groups, databases, and storage limits are stored in the Configuration partition.

- **Recipient data**   Data that applies to a specific Exchange recipient. Users, contacts, distribution groups, and other Exchange-enabled recipients' information are stored in the Domain Naming partition.

Exchange 2007 Permission Changes

Earlier versions of Exchange also separated the Exchange permissions from the Active Directory permissions, but administrators had difficulty taking advantage of that separation.

Exchange 2000/2003 administrative groups were used to create logical areas of administration. As long as you knew what your administrative model was before your servers were deployed, and it rarely (if ever) changed, you could easily implement administrative groups. But if you needed to move a server from one administrative group to another administrative group, you had to uninstall the server and reinstall it in the other administrative group. For organizations that did not need more than one administrative group, there was a lack of specificity when performing delegation tasks. The administrative roles defined in Exchange 2000/2003 were ambiguous at best. Few administrators really understood the difference between the Exchange Administrator and the Exchange Full Administrator roles. Probably the most confusing to an organization with a split administration model was the use of Active Directory Users and Computers for Exchange recipient management.

To improve upon what was started in Exchange 2000/2003, the Exchange 2007 administrative model has the following features:

- **New administrator roles** New roles were designed to be intuitive like the built-in groups for Active Directory administrators.

- **Separate Exchange tools for Recipient administration** The Exchange Management Console and Exchange Management Shell were designed specifically for Exchange administration. They include the ability to perform both system and recipient administrative tasks. ADUC is no longer used for Exchange administrative tasks.

- **Exchange property sets** To delegate recipient administration in Exchange 2000/2003, it was necessary to manually modify individual ACLs on directory objects. Now it is only necessary to modify a single property set. Microsoft does this automatically during the installation of Exchange 2007.

Administrative Model Comparison

The Exchange 2007 permission model is extremely flexible. It is possible to have a single person perform both Exchange and Active Directory administrative tasks. It is also possible to have a group of administrators perform just Exchange tasks and a separate group that performs Active Directory–related tasks. This is known as an *Exchange split permission model*. It is also possible to break down the tasks that the Exchange administrator performs and assign different permissions or roles to different groups. *This* is known as the *Exchange delegated permission model*.

Unified Permissions

The default model in Exchange 2007 is a Unified permission model. In this model, Exchange administrators have the ability to modify the organization, server, and recipient data and perform Active Directory administrative tasks. The word *unified* in the context of administrative models does not necessarily imply that administrators are all in the same physical location, although that could be the case. It is possible to have a unified permission model where the administrators are in many different geographic locations. What makes them "unified" is their collective ability to perform all administrative tasks equally without limitation. In a unified model, all administrators share the responsibility for administering the entire organization. This is accomplished by adding all administrator accounts to a single security group in Exchange Server 2007 that is nestled into active directory security groups as well.

Split Permission Model

The opposite of a unified model of course is a split one. The larger and more complex an Exchange organization gets, the more difficult it becomes for a single person to administer. Although a unified model would certainly allow many administrators to support the complexity, it assumes that all administrators are capable and can be trusted with that level of permissions. Larger organizations with a number of administrators with varied skill sets and geographically distributed Exchange servers tend to split administration. Other factors in split administration include politics, geographical locations, and project budgets.

Exchange 2007 supports the decentralized administrative model with a split permission model. The most common area of administration that is decentralized is recipient administration, because it constitutes the majority of the day-to-day administration of Exchange. Also, most recipient administration tasks are often entrusted to junior administrators and the helpdesk team.

Exchange 2007 Property Sets

The key to the split permission model is the use of the Exchange property sets to delegate permissions. Exchange 2000/2003 also had property sets, but they included non-Exchange attributes. This presented problems for delegating administration because it gave additional and unnecessary permissions when used. Exchange 2007 solves this problem by creating two entirely new property sets that only contain Exchange-specific attributes. The first comprehensive property set is the Exchange Information property set, which is listed here:

altRecipient	altRecipientBL	attributeCertificate
authoring	authOrigBL	autoReply
autoReplyMessage	deletedItemFlags	delivContLength
deliverAndRedirect	deliveryMechanism	delivExtContTypes
dLMemberRule	dLMemDefault	dLMemRejectPerms
dLMemRejectPermsBL	dLMemSubmitPerms	dLMemSubmitPermsBL
dnQualifier	enabledProtocols	expirationTime
extensionAttribute1	extensionAttribute10	extensionAttribute11
extensionAttribute12	extensionAttribute13	extensionAttribute14
extensionAttribute15	extensionAttribute2	extensionAttribute3
extensionAttribute4	extensionAttribute5	extensionAttribute6
extensionAttribute7	extensionAttribute8	extensionAttribute9
extensionData	folderPathname	formData
forwardingAddress	heuristics	hideDLMembership
homeMDB	homeMTA	importedFrom
internetEncoding	kMServer	language
languageCode	mailNickname	mAPIRecipient
mDBOverHardQuotaLimit	mDBOverQuotaLimit	mDBStorageQuota
mDBUseDefaults	msExchADCGlobalNames	msExchALObjectVersion
msExchAssistantName	msExchConferenceMailboxBL	msExchControllingZone
msExchCustomProxyAddresses	msExchELCExpirySuspensionEnd	msExchELCExpirySuspensionStart
msExchELCMailboxFlags	msExchExpansionServerName	msExchExternalOOFOptions
msExchFBURL	msExchHideFromAddressLists	msExchHomeServerName
msExchIMACL	msExchIMAddress	msExchIMAPOWAURLPrefixOverride
msExchIMMetaPhysicalURL	msExchIMPhysicalURL	msExchIMVirtualServer
msExchInconsistentState	msExchLabeledURI	msExchMailboxFolderSet
msExchMailboxGuid	msExchMailboxOABVirtualDirectoriesLink	msExchMailboxSecurityDescriptor
msExchMailboxTemplateLink	msExchMailboxUrl	msExchMasterAccountHistory

msExchMasterAccountSid	msExchMaxBlockedSenders	msExchMaxSafeSenders
msExchMDBRulesQuota	msExchMessageHygieneSCLJunkThreshold	msExchMobileAllowedDeviceIDs
msExchMobileDebugLogging	msExchMobileMailboxFlags	msExchMobileMailboxPolicyLink
msExchOmaAdminExtendedSettings	msExchOmaAdminWirelessEnable	msExchOriginatingForest
msExchPfRootUrl	msExchPFTreeType	msExchPoliciesExcluded
msExchPoliciesIncluded	msExchPolicyEnabled	msExchPolicyOptionList
msExchPreviousAccountSid	msExchProxyCustomProxy	msExchPurportedSearchUI
msExchQueryBaseDN	msExchQueryFilterMetadata	msExchRecipientDisplayType
msExchRecipientTypeDetails	msExchRecipLimit	msExchRequireAuthToSendTo
msExchResourceCapacity	msExchResourceDisplay	msExchResourceGUID
msExchResourceMetaData	msExchResourceProperties	msExchResourceSearchProperties
msExchServerAdminDelegationBL	msExchTUIPassword	msExchTUISpeed
msExchTUIVolume	msExchUMAudioCodec	msExchUMDtmfMap
msExchUMEnabledFlags	msExchUMFaxId	msExchUMListInDirectorySearch
msExchUMMaxGreetingDuration	msExchUMOperatorNumber	msExchUMPinPolicyAccountLockoutFailures
msExchUMPinPolicyDisallowCommonPatterns	msExchUMPinPolicyExpiryDays	msExchUMPinPolicyMinPasswordLength
msExchUMRecipientDialPlanLink	msExchUMServerWritableFlags	msExchUMSpokenName
msExchUMTemplateLink	msExchUMUnmergedAttsPt	msExchUseOAB
msExchUserAccountControl	msExchUserCulture	msExchVersion
msExchVoiceMailboxID	oOFReplyToOriginator	pOPCharacterSet
pOPContentFormat	protocolSettings	publicDelegatesBL
replicatedObjectVersion	replicationSensitivity	replicationSignature
reportToOriginator	reportToOwner	securityProtocol
submissionContLength	supportedAlgorithms	targetAddress
telephoneAssistant	unauthOrig	unauthOrigBL
unmergedAtts		

A second, smaller but equally important property set is the Exchange Personal Information property set:

msExchMessageHygieneFlags	msExchMessageHygieneSCLDeleteThreshold
msExchMessageHygieneSCLQuarantineThreshold	msExchMessageHygieneSCLRejectThreshold
msExchSafeRecipientsHash	msExchSafeSendersHash
msExchUMPinChecksum	

Administrative Roles

An administrative *role* is a combination of permissions that, when applied to an object, allows specific tasks to be performed. New roles have been created in Exchange 2007 to replace the Exchange 2000 roles as shown in Table 14-1.

The Exchange Full Administrator role is replaced by the Exchange Organization Administrator role. The Exchange Administrator role is replaced by the Exchange Server Administrator role. The Exchange View-Only Administrator role remains the same in name and function, but it is implemented differently. The Exchange Recipient Administrator role is new in Exchange 2007. The Exchange Public Folder Administrator role is only available in Exchange 2007 SP1 and higher.

When either the first Exchange 2007 server is installed or Setup /PrepareAD is run, a new Organizational Unit called Microsoft Exchange Security Groups is created. Additionally, five universal security groups are then created in the Microsoft Exchange Security Groups OU, as shown in Figure 14-2.

Through a careful strategy of nesting the groups, Microsoft provides the bulk of permissions to the Exchange 2007 roles. Table 14-2 shows the inter-relationships of each of the security groups.

The Exchange Server Administrator and the Exchange Public Folder Administrator roles do not have exclusive security groups. When a user or group is delegated these roles, they will be made a member of one or more of the Exchange security groups.

Exchange Organization Administrator

The Exchange Organization Administrator role has full control over all objects and their associated properties in the Exchange 2007 organization. This is the highest level of

Exchange 2000/2003 Roles	Exchange 2007 Roles
Exchange Full Administrator	Exchange Organization Administrator
Exchange Administrator	Exchange Server Administrator
Exchange View-Only Administrator	Exchange View-Only Administrator
	Exchange Recipient Administrator
	Exchange Public Folder Administrator

TABLE 14-1   Exchange 2000/2003 vs. Exchange 2007 Roles

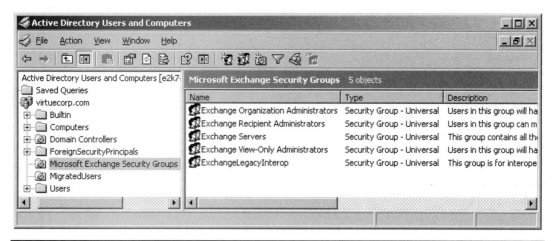

FIGURE 14-2   Exchange 2007 Security Groups

permission you can give to a user or group. Once you have delegated the Exchange Organization Administrator role to a user account, the user will be able to do the following:

- Configure all organization-wide settings, including Send connectors, Receive domains, address lists, managed folders, ActiveSync policies, remote domains, Edge subscriptions, E-mail Address Policies, UM dial plans, and UM policies stored in the Configuration partition in Active Directory.

- Read all recipient object attributes in the Domain Naming partition of the Active Directory forest.

- Write all recipient object Exchange-specific attributes in the Domain Naming partition of the Active Directory forest.

- Have full control of all server-specific configuration settings on the local machine and in the Configuration partition in Active Directory.

Group Name	Members	Member Of
Exchange Organization Administrators	Administrator (the account used to install Exchange 2007)	Administrators* Exchange Recipient Administrators
Exchange Recipient Administrators	Exchange Organization Administrators	Exchange View-Only Administrators
Exchange Servers	Exchange 2007 Servers Exchange Install Domain Servers	N/A
Exchange View-Only Administrators	Exchange Recipient Administrators	N/A
ExchangeLegacyInterop	Exchange 2003 Servers	N/A

TABLE 14-2   Exchange 2007 Security Group Nesting

> **Exchange 2007 Creates a Security Hole When Installed on a Domain Controller**
> If you install Exchange 2007 on a domain controller, the Organization Administrator
> role will become a member of the Built-in Administrators group in the domain. This
> will give the Exchange Organization Administrator role full control of all domain
> controllers in the domain. If, however, you install Exchange 2007 on a member server,
> the organization administrators will become members of the local administrators group
> on the server and not the domain.

Exchange Public Folder Administrator

The Exchange Public Folder Administrator role grants access to the new Public Folder
Management Console tool and the underlying PowerShell PF-management cmdlets. When
granted this new Exchange Administrator role, a user will be able to do the following:

- Create and manage top-level Public Folder objects
- Run the public folder management commands in the EMS
- Administer public folders with the Public Folder Management Console

SP1 *Public folder administration features have been added in SP1.*

Exchange Recipient Administrator

The Exchange Recipient Administrator role is new to Exchange. Although this has certainly
been a desirable role to deploy, doing so has been a manual procedure in previous versions
of Exchange. Once you have delegated the Exchange Recipient Administrator role to a user
account, the user will be able to do the following:

- Read all recipient object attributes in the Domain Naming partition of the Active
  Directory forest
- Write all recipient object Exchange-specific attributes in the Domain Naming
  partition of the Active Directory forest

There is a catch to this role. Exchange recipient administrators can only read and write
the attributes of recipients in domains where the Setup /PrepareDomain switch has been
run. This is not an issue in domains where Exchange 2007 servers have been installed.
However, it is a concern in domains where there are no Exchange servers and there is an
increased likelihood that Setup /PrepareDomain has not been run. The recipients that can
be created and modified by a recipient administrator are:

- Users
- Contacts
- Distribution groups (universal)
- Dynamic distribution lists
- Public folders

PART V

Exchange View-Only Administrator

The Exchange View-Only Administrator role, as its name implies, allows its delegates to view objects in the Exchange organization. In Table 14-2 you can see that this role is significant and that the two other roles depend on it. The Exchange Organization Administrators group is a member of the Exchange Recipient Administrators group. The Exchange Recipient Administrators group is a member of the Exchange View-Only Administrators group. The Exchange View-Only Administrator role can be thought of as the minimal role required for performing Exchange-related tasks. Specifically, once you have delegated the Exchange View-Only Administrator role to a user account, the user will be able to perform the following tasks:

- Read the entire Exchange organization tree in the Configuration partition of the Active Directory forest
- Read every recipient object's attributes in the Domain Naming partition of the Active Directory forest

Exchange Server Administrator

The Exchange Server Administrator role is used to restrict a delegate's access to a specific Exchange server. This granularity was missing in previous versions of Exchange, which depended on administrative groups or Exchange sites as administrative boundaries. What is also very nice about this role is that if the administrative model changes, it is easy to change the membership of the Exchange Server Administrator role to match. Once you have delegated the Exchange Server Administrator role to a user account, the user will be able to do the following:

- Control all server-specific settings, including storage groups, databases, storage limits, retention settings, CAS settings, Hub Transport settings, and Unified Messaging settings on the local server and in the Configuration partition in Active Directory

Simply making a user or group a delegate of the Exchange Server Administrators group is not enough to grant these permissions. You must also manually add the user or group to the local Administrators group on the Exchange 2007 server. The following warning appears after you delegate the Exchange Server Administrator role:

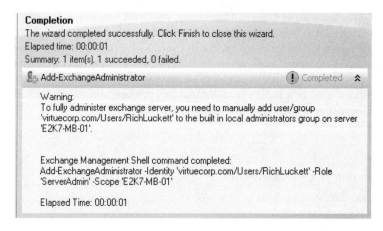

Exchange Server Administrators cannot perform Recipient administrative tasks or organization configuration tasks.

Delegating Permissions

In order to delegate permissions, you must first be an Exchange organization administrator. You can use the Exchange Management Console (EMC) or the Exchange Management Shell (EMS). Both tools will allow you to view existing Exchange administrators, add new Exchange administrators, and remove Exchange administrators. Although Microsoft offers administrative roles, it may also be necessary to create custom delegation models.

Responsibilities and Roles

Before you jump in and start adding administrators, it may be a good idea to spend some time defining the responsibilities that each administrator has in your organization. This is usually referred to as *roles and responsibilities.* I have intentionally reversed the two words in the heading, because the roles have already been defined by Microsoft. Your challenge is to carefully define what you want each administrator to be able to do (their responsibilities) and then associate that with one of the Microsoft Exchange roles. For some mental exercise, let's look at the following three scenarios:

- **Scenario 1: Small Organization**

    You are the administrator for a small organization. Active Directory is a single forest and single domain. You have a single Exchange 2007 member server with 50 mailboxes. What administrative model would you implement? How would you implement that model?

- **Scenario 2: Medium Organization**

    You are the administrator for a medium-size organization. Active Directory is a single forest and single domain. There are two Active Directory sites called East and West. You have two Exchange 2007 member servers with 200 mailboxes on each server. One server is in Los Angeles, and the other is in New York City. The company has a helpdesk that needs to be able to create mailboxes for users and manage distribution groups. You are responsible for all other Exchange administrative tasks. What administrative model would you implement? How would you implement that model?

- **Scenario 3: Large Organization**

    You are the administrator for a large multinational organization. Active Directory is a single forest with four domains in a single tree. The domain names are virtuecorp .com, eu.virtuecorp.com, na.virtuecorp.com, and sa.virtuecorp.com. There are three Active Directory sites called EU, NA, and SA. Each domain has dedicated Exchange administrators responsible for their servers and recipients. At the EU and NA sites are three tiers of administration: helpdesk, client support, and server support. The SA site only has two administrators, and they perform all Exchange administrative tasks for their servers and recipients. All administrators defer to you when there is a task they cannot perform. What administrative model would you implement? How would you implement that model?

Roles and Responsibilities Matrix

To be able answer the questions in these three scenarios, you first need to examine what the responsibilities are. See how a roles and responsibilities matrix can help you solve the three scenarios.

Scenario 1 Matrix:

Task/Responsibility	Group	Role Assignment
Administer the entire Exchange organization	You	Exchange Organization Administrator

Scenario 2 Matrix:

Task/Responsibility	Group	Role Assignment
Administer the entire Exchange organization	You	Exchange Organization Administrator
Create mailboxes	Helpdesk	Exchange Recipient Administrator
Manage distribution groups	Helpdesk	Exchange Recipient Administrator

Scenario 3 Matrix:

Task/Responsibility	Group	Role Assignment
Administer the entire organization	You	Exchange Organization Administrator
Administer the NA servers	Server Support	Exchange Server Administrator
Administer the NA recipients	Helpdesk Client Support	Exchange Recipient Administrator
Administer the EU server	Server Support	Exchange Server Administrator
Administer the EU recipients	Helpdesk Client Support	Exchange Recipient Administrator
Administer the SA site	SA Admins	Exchange Server Administrator Exchange Recipient Administrator

Manage Administrative Roles

Once you have a roles and responsibilities matrix to work with, you can begin to delegate administrative tasks. Whenever possible, you should delegate to security groups and not individual user accounts. So, the first step should be to create the groups to which you will delegate the role(s). Another best practice, in line with the Defense in Depth security strategy, is to create separate administrator accounts for each of your administrators. They should have two accounts: one user account for using e-mail and running productivity suite applications and a different account for performing Exchange administrative tasks. Only make administrator accounts, not personal accounts, as members of the security groups you create for delegation purposes.

Adding the Exchange Administrator Role Using the EMC

When you are ready to delegate an Exchange role to a user or group, you can use the Exchange Management Console, as follows:

1. Log on as an account with Exchange Organization Administrator permissions.

2. Click the Organization Configuration container. This will display the existing Exchange administrators.

3. Click the Add Exchange Administrator link in the Actions pane. The Add Exchange Administrator Wizard, shown here, should appear.

4. Click the Browse button, select the user or group you want to make an Exchange administrator, and click OK.

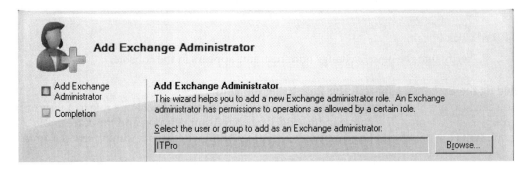

5. Select the radio button next to the role you want to assign, as shown next, and click the Add button.

Select the role and scope of this Exchange administrator:

- ○ Exchange Organization Administrator role
- ○ Exchange Public Folder Administrator role
- ○ Exchange Recipient Administrator role
- ○ Exchange View-Only Administrator role
- ◉ Exchange Server Administrator role

NOTE *If you select Exchange Server Administrator role, you will also need to add one or more servers before you can continue, as shown here.*

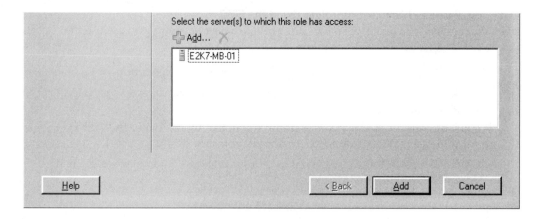

6. Click Finish.

7. Verify that the new Exchange administrator appears in the console.

Adding the Exchange Administrator Role Using the EMS

You can also use the Exchange Management Shell to delegate an Exchange role to a user or group, as shown next. The command is Add-ExchangeAdministrator, and the correct role name syntax in the EMS is OrgAdmin, PublicFolderAdmin, RecipientAdmin, ServerAdmin, or ViewOnlyAdmin.

```
[PS] C:\>Add-ExchangeAdministrator -Identity "ITPro" -Role ServerAdmin
-Scope "E2K7-MB-01"
```

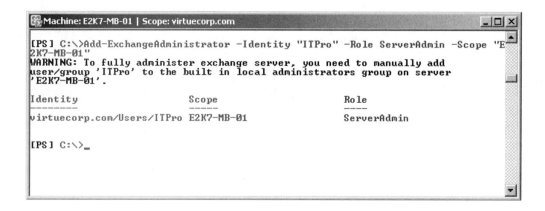

Viewing Exchange Administrators Using the ESM

If you want to view all the Exchange administrators in your organization from the Exchange Management Shell, you can issue the following command:

```
PS] C:\>Get-ExchangeAdministrator
```

The Get-ExchangeAdministrator command will generate a list of all the administrators in the organization, as shown in the following example:

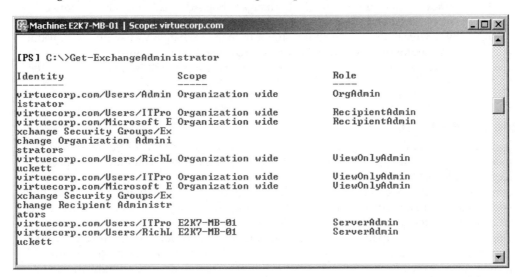

Removing an Exchange Administrator

To make changes to the administrative model, you may also need to remove Exchange administrators from a role. This can be done with both the Exchange Management Console and the Exchange Management Shell.

Here are the steps using the Exchange Management Console:

1. Log on as an account with Exchange Organization Administrator permissions.

2. Click the Organization Configuration container. This will display the existing Exchange administrators.

3. Click the Exchange administrator you want to remove and then click the Remove link in the Actions pane.

4. When the following warning appears, click Yes to confirm.

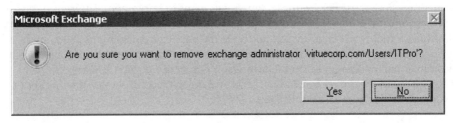

Before you remove an Exchange administrator using the Exchange Management Shell, it is a good idea to understand all the roles the administrator has been assigned. Because there can be more than one role, you will need to specify which role you want to remove the administrator from. The role name syntax is identical to that for Add-ExchangeAdministrator (OrgAdmin, PublicFolderAdmin, RecipientAdmin, ServerAdmin, and ViewOnlyAdmin):

```
PS] C:\>Remove-ExchangeAdministrator -Identity "ITPro" -Role OrgAdmin
```

If you remove administrator from the Exchange Server Administrator role, you must also specify the scope. Be careful not to remove an administrator from a dependency role. For example, if you were to remove an administrator from the Exchange View-Only Administrator role and administrator was still a member of the Exchange Server Administrator role, the account would no longer function properly. Warnings will appear if this happens in both the EMC and the EMS.

Advanced Delegation

Although the flexibility and specificity of the new Exchange Server 2007 permission model makes it easy to implement and support a split permission model, you may have special requirements that the Microsoft-defined roles cannot satisfy. The Exchange organization administrator may have full control over the configuration of all Exchange objects, but unless additional permissions are granted, it is not possible to actually create and delete the objects. At a minimum, the administrator would also need to be a member of the Windows Account Operators security group in each domain. In some cases, it is not more permission but less permission that is required. An extreme example would be an Exchange hosted service provider. In a hosted Exchange environment, it is necessary to delegate administration to each customer being hosted in the same Exchange organization. This level of specificity is not inherent in Exchange. However, it is possible to get that granular with your permission delegation.

Active Directory administration is broken down into two categories: service management and data management. Service management tasks include adding and removing servers, performing backups and restores, managing security policies, and designing and maintaining the infrastructure. Data management tasks include user account, computer account, and group object management. Unless your Exchange administrators will need to manage the Active Directory infrastructure as well as Exchange, you should be able to limit your Active Directory delegation to the data management category.

Designing an OU Structure

Active Directory delegates administration of data at two levels. You can delegate at the domain level or at the Organizational Unit (OU) level. Using domains to delegate control is sometimes necessary. For example, when you want to implement different password policies for different groups of users, multiple domains are necessary. It is necessary to use multiple domains when you want to divide the service management tasks, such as between groups of administrators. However, using OUs to delegate control over objects is often more desirable than creating additional domains. Keep in mind that OUs are objects in a domain. They give you the ability to group objects and delegate control over them without the overhead of extra domain controllers.

Designing the OU structure is the logical part of the process of creating a delegation model. The overall process flow is as follows:

1. Determine the roles and requirements.
2. Plan the OU hierarchy.
3. Assign roles to administrators.
4. Document the model.

If you want to be able to specify the scope of delegation further than Exchange 2007 provides out of the box, you will need to delegate at the OU level. The Exchange 2007 roles are applied at the domain level so that the permissions will be inherited by all subcontainers. You use OUs so that the permissions you set will be limited to the OUs and the object classes you apply them to. Creating a roles and responsibilities matrix like the one earlier in this chapter is the very first step. Once you have accomplished that, you can begin to create an OU structure based on how you want to do administrative delegation.

Let's use the large organization example from earlier in the chapter. Here is a sample OU structure that could be created for the administrative model:

- VirtueCorp.com
  - Delegation
- EU.VirtueCorp.com
  - Recipients
  - Exchange Servers
- NA.VirtueCorp.com
  - Recipients
  - Exchange Servers
- SA.VirtueCorp.com
  - Recipients
  - Exchange Servers

Because this example already has four domains, it is not necessary to create an OU for each group of administrators. In each domain an OU is created for managing user accounts with mailboxes and other recipient objects. A separate OU is created for managing the Exchange Server computer objects. The Delegation OU in the forest root domain can be used to manage the security groups that will need to be created to delegate permission to each of the child domains. Managing the groups in the forest root will prevent the administrators in the child domains from being able to modify the groups' membership.

Applying Custom Permissions Using the EMS

The next step is to apply the custom permissions (roles) to the OU structure. The Exchange Management Shell includes the command Add-ADPermission. This is the recommended method of applying custom Exchange permissions to Organizational Units in Active Directory. Other tools that can be used are ADSI Edit and DSACLS. This discussion, however, will be limited to Add-ADPermission. For more information on ADSI Edit, see the article, "How to Use ADSI Edit to Apply Permissions," (http://technet.microsoft.com/en-us/library/aa997502.aspx). For more information on DSACLS, see the article, "How to Use Dsacls.exe in Windows Server 2003 and Windows 2000," (http://support.microsoft.com/kb/281146).

The first permission that must be applied is the Exchange View-Only Administrator role. None of the custom permission you will see in this discussion will work without it. The following is an example of what the VirtueCorp administrator would run in the Exchange Management Shell to delegate the ability to mail-enable and mail-disable recipients, manage e-mail addresses, and display names for all users, groups, and contacts contained in the Recipients OU:

```
[PS]C:\>Add-ADPermission -Identity "ou=Recipients,dc=EU,dc=VirtueCorp,dc=com "
-User "VirtueCorp\EU Helpdesk" -AccessRights ReadProperty, WriteProperty
-Properties Exchange-Information, Exchange-Personal-Information,
legacyExchangeDN, displayName, adminDisplayName, displayNamePrintable,
publicDelegates, garbageCollPeriod, textEncodedORAddress, showInAddressBook,
proxyAddresses, mail

[PS]C:\>Add-ADPermission -Identity "ou=Recipients,dc=EU,dc=VirtueCorp,dc=com "
-User "VirtueCorp\EU Helpdesk" -AccessRights GenericRead
```

Unfortunately, these commands alone will not allow the EU helpdesk to manage dynamic distribution groups. The admin can additionally run the following commands to include dynamic distribution groups:

```
[PS]C:\>Add-ADPermission -Identity "ou=Recipients,dc=EU,dc=VirtueCorp,dc=com "
-User "VirtueCorp\EU Helpdesk" -AccessRights GenericAll -InheritanceType
Descendents -InheritedObjectType msExchDynamicDistributionList

[PS]C:\>Add-ADPermission -Identity "ou=Recipients,dc=EU,dc=VirtueCorp,dc=com "
-User " VirtueCorp\EU Helpdesk " -AccessRights CreateChild, DeleteChild
-ChildObjectTypes msExchDynamicDistributionList
```

Because Exchange 2007 applies e-mail addresses differently from Exchange 2000/2003, it is necessary to grant the recipient administrator the rights to update the Address Lists and Email Address Policies. To do this, the admin would run the following:

```
[PS]C:\>Add-ADPermission -Identity "CN=Address Lists Container, CN=VirtueCorp,
CN=Microsoft Exchange,CN=Services,CN=Configuration, DC=VirtueCorp,DC=com" -User
"VirtueCorp\EU Helpdesk" -AccessRights WriteProperty -Properties
msExchLastAppliedRecipientFilter, msExchRecipientFilterFlags

[PS]C:\>Add-ADPermission -Identity "CN=Recipient Policies,CN=Virtuecorp,
CN=Microsoft Exchange,CN=Services,CN=Configuration,DC=VirtueCorp,DC=com"
-User "VirtueCorp\EU Helpdesk" -AccessRights WriteProperty -Properties
msExchLastAppliedRecipientFilter, msExchRecipientFilterFlags
```

Note that the Address List and Email Address Policy permissions are applied to the forest root domain, not the child domain. Although a copy of the Configuration partition exists on all domain controllers in every domain, the scope is forest-wide. This is in contrast to the Domain Naming partition, which is unique in each domain.

As a final step in the delegation model, the admin should carefully document all the custom roles and how they are applied to the domain and OU structure.

Coexistence Permissions

If you are transitioning from Exchange 2000/2003 to Exchange 2007, the Exchange 2007 setup /PrepareLegacyExchangePermissions routine will run to update the Exchange 2003 recipient permission structure. Specifically, it grants the Exchange Domain Servers and Exchange Enterprise Servers security groups in Exchange 2000/2003 read and write access to the Exchange 2007 Exchange-Information property set.

When you perform custom delegation during coexistence, you must additionally specify the following permissions on the Exchange 2007 administrative group in order for the Exchange 2000/2003 Recipient Update Service to work properly:

```
Add-ADPermission -Identity "CN=Exchange Administrative Group (012345678912345),
CN=Administrative Groups,CN=VirtueCorp,CN=Microsoft Exchange,CN=Services,
CN=Configuration,DC=Contoso,DC=com" -User "VirtueCorp\EU Helpdesk"
-InheritedObjectType ms-Exch-Exchange-Server -ExtendedRights ms-Exch-Recipient-
Update-Access -InheritanceType Descendents
```

Additional Tools

If your organization requires complex permission models, it may not be able to manage them with the tools Microsoft provides. Many large institutes and hosted service providers turn to third-party software developers to meet their needs. Quest Software has a powerful tool called ActiveRoles (http://www.quest.com/activeroles-server). Microsoft provides separate tools for hosting providers called Hosted Messaging and Collaboration (HMC), which was just recently updated to support Exchange 2007 and SharePoint (http://www .microsoft.com/technet/serviceproviders/default.mspx). The Microsoft Identity Integration Server (MIIS) can be used to manage complex permission structures between two or more Active Directory forests and an Exchange organization.

Summary

A good administrative model will limit the abilities of individual administrators to just the tasks necessary to complete their jobs. Active Directory and Exchange Server 2007 provide a flexible permission model and the tools for defining an organization's administrative model. The Exchange 2007 administrative roles are preconfigured in Exchange 2007 by applying permissions to a set of new Exchange 2007-specific universal security groups. The roles are:

- Exchange Organizational Administrator
- Exchange Public Folder Administrator (SP1 or higher)
- Exchange Recipient Administrator
- Exchange View-Only Administrator
- Exchange Server Administrator

Although companies that host Exchange 2007 for their customers may find it necessary to use a third-party tool to manage Exchange permissions and delegate administrative tasks, the average organization will likely find Exchange 2007 delegation possible to accomplish using the tools provided by Microsoft that were covered in this chapter.

By taking the steps required to limit the permissions your users need, you have already begun to secure your Exchange environment. The next three chapters will help you continue down that path.

Regulatory Compliance

Because e-mail is a critical part of your business, it is probably safe to assume that some (if not most) of the decisions that have had significant impact on the success or failure of your organization have been communicated via e-mail. This has an impact on the application of e-mail to regulatory compliance standards, because many require the retention of any and all communications in an effort to protect sensitive data, prove the security of said data, or simply be able to provide the content of the communication to a requesting party. In this chapter, we will look at the regulations that impact your environment, the compliance features supplied by Exchange Server 2007, and how to implement the features that will help ensure your Exchange environment is within compliance.

It is also important to note that although not every environment will initially appear to be subject to compliance standards, many countries (including the United States) have federal mandates requiring businesses to be prepared for electronic discovery, which will require organizations to know where data is and be able to retrieve it. Additionally, we do recommend that you read this chapter because the features discussed in this chapter still have application to organizations simply seeking to better utilize messages and their content for historical use after their original intent.

A Regulatory Compliance Overview

For many organizations, the topic of compliance seemingly does not apply; it is for public companies, healthcare organizations, or government agencies. Although there are compliance standards that apply to all those examples, there are plenty of other "best practice" standards that seek to align technology objectives with business objectives and are "self-governing" in that the organization itself drives the goal of being "compliant" with the standards that exist. Even so, those regulated standards that may not apply to an organization provide useful guidelines for establishing enforced security, defined processes, and provable results. Let's take a look at each type of compliance standard and how it impacts e-mail.

Regulatory Standards

Most externally imposed standards (such as those imposed by government or regulatory bodies) evolve out of the need either to protect a particular sensitive data set or simply to prove that the imposed standards of security are in place and are being continually enforced.

If you think about these two positions, the only difference is that one is trying to protect a specific data set whereas the other is trying to protect everything, both by putting practices and policies in place that ensure the needed protection. These standards are regulated by some governing body outside the organization; it is often the government (as in the case of Sarbanes-Oxley, which applies to companies publicly traded on United States stock exchanges) or by a governing body, often industry specific (as in the case of the Payment Card Industry standard, which seeks to protect credit card-holder information held by companies processing any kind of cardholder information).

Here is a list of a wide variety of compliance standards across the globe. Note that this is most definitely not a comprehensive list; it is merely designed to demonstrate the global application of regulatory compliance.

Jurisdiction	Standards
United States	Federal Rules Of Civil Procedure (FRCP) Sarbanes-Oxley (SOX) Health Insurance Portability and Accountability Act (HIPAA) Gramm-Leach-Bliley Act (GLBA) Securities and Exchange Commission (SEC) Rule 240 Title 21 Code of Federal Regulations (CFR) Part 11 Federal Information Security Management Act (FISMA) Payment Card Industry (PCI)
Canada	Canadian Sarbanes-Oxley (CSOX) Personal Information Protection and Electronic Documents Act (PIPEDA)
India	Indian Information Technology Act, 2000 Indian Evidence Act (Amended by Indian IT Act) Securities and Exchange Board of India (SEBI) Clause 49 of Listing Agreement
Mexico	eCommerce Act
South America	Data Protection Acts – Argentina, Chile, and others
United Kingdom	Data Protection Act (DPA) Freedom of Information Act (FOI)
European Countries	Basel II – European Union Data Protection Acts – Germany, Spain, France, Italy, Belgium, Portugal, Austria, Sweden, Finland, Ireland, and many others
South Korea	eCommerce Act
Hong Kong	Personal Data (Privacy) Ordinance
Japan	Japanese Sarbanes-Oxley (J-SOX)
Australia	Privacy Act

Best-Practice Standards

Unlike regulatory standards that keep organizations under the constant threat of being audited by the governing body, best-practice standards are completely self-governed, where an organization adopts an industry-recognized standard set of business practices to make IT more efficient, more secure, and more aligned with the overall business objectives of the organization. Usually the scope of these standards spans far beyond just the use and security of data, but because the protection of sensitive data is a part of these standards, there is equal application to your Exchange environment.

Here is a list of some of the most widely accepted best-practice standards that are self-imposed by organizations around the world.

Standard	Description
Information Technology Infrastructure Library (ITIL)	Developed by the British Office of Government Commerce, ITIL focuses on the delivery of high-quality IT services through establishing defined processes.
Control Objectives for Information and related Technology (COBIT)	Developed by the Information Systems Audit and Control Association (ISACA), COBIT focuses on IT governance where control requirements, business risks, and technical considerations are brought together to establish proper policies and procedures.
International Organization for Standardization (ISO) / International Electrotechnical Commission (IEC) 27002:2005	Formerly known as ISO 17799, this standard was originally published by the British Standards Institute as BS 7799 to establish security standards to be used by the British government.
Federal Information Security Management Act (FISMA)	Although a regulatory standard for United States government agencies, many organizations outside of the government use FISMA as their own standard of security.

You may be wondering how these best-practice standards apply to e-mail, which has become the primary method of business-to-business communication, even over voice. Any transaction, business deal, agreement, or the like that your organization has processed most likely has pertinent related information stored in one or more e-mails. Now add in the fact that standards are in place that seek to protect data from improper use either by mandating procedures or policies that control the access to and use of said data or by being able to prove compliance after the fact by allowing examination of the data in question. So the issue becomes the data within your e-mails—who has access to it, who reads it, and was it protected from inappropriate access.

Let's take a look at how the technologies built into Exchange can assist you in making the e-mail aspect of your organization compliant.

Exchange Server 2007 Compliance Features

Exchange Server 2007 touts more compliance-applicable features than previous versions, and those features that existed in previous versions have been significantly improved to provide better application to compliance standards. Here's a list of the features we'll discuss in this chapter:

- **Retention**   Exchange can be configured to retain needed messages as well as delete unneeded messages.

- **Messaging Records Management**   Policies can be defined that move, copy, delete, or strip attachments from stored messages on a per-folder, per-mailbox basis.

- **Journaling**   Copies of messages (either at a mailbox database or at the per-mailbox level) can be made to a designated recipient.

- **Transport rules**   Messages can be automatically classified, moved, copied, forwarded, or stripped of their attachments while en route.

- **Message classifications**   Classifications assist in identifying messages for later use by Transport rules, message searches, or archiving solutions.

Let's look at each of these features and see how it assists with compliance.

Retention

Retention of e-mail is the first (and simplest) method of achieving some level of compliance to a standard; retained e-mails can be used to prove your organization's compliancy. For example, if you worked for a healthcare company and needed to prove that no information about Mr. Jones left the organization, it would be possible (although not easily feasible) to search the entirety of your message stores for "Jones" and see by perusing the resultant set of messages whether Mr. Jones's information had been inappropriately sent outside the organization.

We've seen some organizations take the stance that they want to keep everything in order to prove their compliancy. We've also seen others that utilize a policy that all e-mail should be deleted after 30 days (and no backups are kept beyond 30 days either). How can this be? It's quite simple: The compliance standards are so vague in defining their implementation that the organization itself is usually able to interpret how to apply these standards. Fortunately, Exchange allows either goal to be met.

Like in previous versions of Exchange, each mailbox store has its own settings to specify how Exchange should retain messages, even after they're deleted by the user as well as after mailboxes are deleted by an administrator.

To view and specify retention settings for a given mailbox store in the Exchange console, follow these steps:

1. Expand Server Configuration.

2. Select the Mailbox node.

3. Select the mailbox store you want to manage.

4. In the Actions pane, click Properties and select the Limits tab (see Figure 15-1).

5. Under the Deletion Settings section, specify the number of days individual items (messages, appointments, and so on) should be retained (even after being deleted), the number of days a deleted mailbox should be retained, and whether Exchange should continue to retain both deleted items and mailboxes until a backup has been performed to preserve the data.

To specify the retention settings using the Exchange shell, use the Set-MailboxDatabase command, as follows:

```
Set-MailboxDatabase -Identity <Mailbox-Store-Name> -DeletedItemRetention <Days>
-MailboxRetention <Days> -RetainDeletedItemsUntilBackup <$true | $false>
```

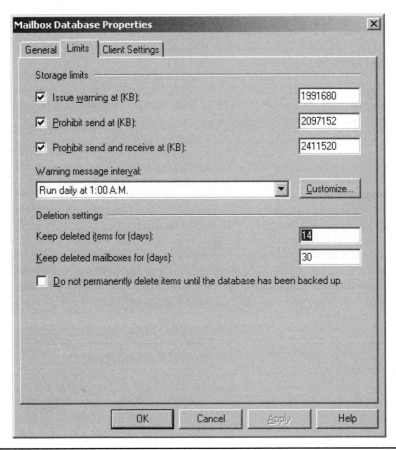

FIGURE 15-1   Setting the retention limits for a mailbox store

In addition to telling how long Exchange should retain messages, you can also establish how long until Exchange should delete messages using a new feature called *Messaging Records Management.*

Messaging Records Management

Exchange Server 2007 has a few new features to manage the retention (or lack thereof) of messages and their content. Exchange administrators can now establish size quotas for mailbox folders, specify that message content be moved or deleted after a period of time, and even extend the retention of messages, if desired. These settings provide the flexibility to only retain desired content while removing unneeded content, which makes retrieval of important information either very easy (in the case of retaining only data related to compliance) or impossible (in the case of deleting all information after a specified period of time).

PART V

The following is the process of establishing Messaging Records Management:

1. Define the folders within a mailbox that are to be managed (whether default folders or custom folders).
2. Establish the content settings for the folders being managed.
3. Create Mailbox Policies that combine the various managed folders and their content settings.
4. Apply the appropriate Mailbox Policy to each user's mailbox.

We'll walk through each step in the following sections.

Defining Managed Folders

A managed folder within a mailbox is one that can have its content managed by Exchange. Specifying a folder as being "managed" in and of itself does nothing; it is simply the first step in defining those folders that Exchange *can* manage. The default folders in a user's mailbox are marked as being "managed" (as shown in the Exchange console by expanding Organization Configuration, selecting Mailbox, and then clicking the Managed Default Folders tab) with the ability to specify comments to Outlook clients when folders are selected (this feature allows the user to be notified of the purpose of a folder or what content is appropriate).

NOTE *A special folder called Entire Mailbox exists on this tab to manage all folders within the mailbox with the same managed settings.*

The Managed Custom Folders tab can be used to create additional standardized folders to be managed within each user's mailbox. To create a custom managed folder from within the Exchange console, follow these steps:

1. Expand Organization Configuration and select the Mailbox node.
2. Select the Managed Custom Folders tab.
3. In the Actions pane, click New Custom Managed Folder to start the wizard.
4. On the New Managed Custom Folder pane of the wizard, provide a name for the object, a name for the folder to be viewed in Outlook, a storage limit for this folder and any subfolders, and an optional comment to be displayed when the folder is viewed within Outlook (see Figure 15-2).

Here's how to create a new custom managed folder from the Exchange shell:

```
New-ManagedFolder -Name '<Folder-Object-Name>' -FolderName '<Folder-Name>'
-StorageQuota '<size>' -Comment '<Comment-Viewed-In-Outlook>'
```

Establishing Managed Content Settings

Once the folders to be managed are defined, the content management actions must be specified for each. You can utilize the managed folders as part of a content management policy by establishing the managed content settings for the organization. It is important to note that the content settings are not based on the folder within a mailbox, but are focused on the content type. This way, Exchange can address old voicemails, calendar entries, faxes,

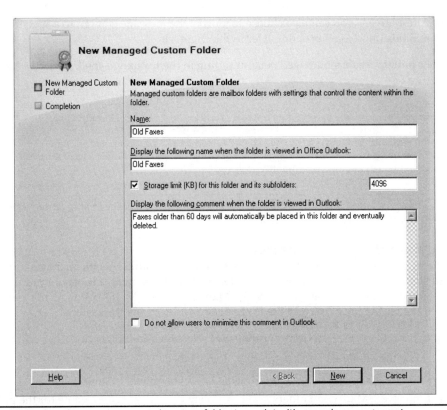

FIGURE 15-2 Creating a new managed custom folder to assist with records management

notes, and such appropriately, regardless of where in the user's mailbox they reside. To specify these settings from within the Exchange console, follow these steps:

1. Expand Organization Configuration and select the Mailbox node.
2. Select the Managed Default Folders tab.
3. Select the folder you want to apply settings to.
4. In the Actions pane, select New Managed Custom Settings.
5. In the wizard, provide a name and then select the message type (which is determined by the message class), the retention period duration and start criteria, and what action to take once the retention period is reached.

TIP *Be careful of your choices when selecting what action to take. Exchange can move the item to the Deleted Items folder (where it may be deleted on the closing of Outlook or possibly retrieved by the user), delete it but allow recovery (where it can be recovered using the Recover Deleted Items option in Outlook), permanently delete it (in which case, you can't get it back and the default retention times no longer apply), mark it as being past the retention limit (in which case it will show up in strikethrough gray in Outlook), or move it to a managed folder (which is where the custom managed folders come into play).*

6. Alternatively, you can also choose to journal the message content to a specified mailbox (more on journaling later in the chapter).

Here's how to create a managed custom setting in the Exchange shell:

```
new-ManagedContentSettings -Name 'Organization Fax Retention Policy'
-FolderName 'Inbox' -RetentionAction 'MoveToFolder' -AddressForJournaling
'pennywiseresort.local/Users/Journal-Mailbox' -AgeLimitForRetention
'60.00:00:00' -JournalingEnabled $true -MessageFormatForJournaling
'UseTnef' -RetentionEnabled $true -LabelForJournaling 'Journaled Managed
Content' -MessageClass 'IPM.Note.Microsoft.Fax*' -MoveToDestinationFolder 'Old
Faxes' -TriggerForRetention 'WhenDelivered'
```

NOTE *Although a given folder can have multiple content settings, there can only be one setting specified per content type.*

Creating Managed Folder Mailbox Policies

Now that it has been determined what to do with content within specific managed folders, the next step is to create combinations of folders so that the content settings for multiple folders can be applied to a user with a single Managed Folder Mailbox Policy. To create a Managed Folder Mailbox Policy in the Exchange console, follow these steps:

1. Expand Organization Configuration and select the Mailbox node.
2. Select the Managed Folders Mailbox Policy tab.
3. In the Actions pane, click New Managed Folders Mailbox Policy.
4. In the New Managed Folders Mailbox Policy Wizard, specify a name for the policy and add the managed folders (both default and custom are available for selection).

Here's how to create a Managed Folder Mailbox Policy in the Exchange shell:

```
new-ManagedFolderMailboxPolicy -Name 'Policy-Name' -ManagedFolderLinks
'Folder-Name1',' Folder-Name2'
```

The next step is to apply a policy to a mailbox. By doing so, the Managed Folder Assistant (an Exchange process that both creates any needed managed folders, as well as takes content setting actions on those folders) will know which folder(s) in a given mailbox are under management. It can then look up the content settings for the folder(s) and take the actions specified. To assign a policy to a mailbox using the Exchange console, follow these steps:

1. Expand Recipient Configuration and select the Mailbox node.
2. Select the desired mailbox and in the Actions pane and click Properties.
3. Select the Mailbox Settings tab.

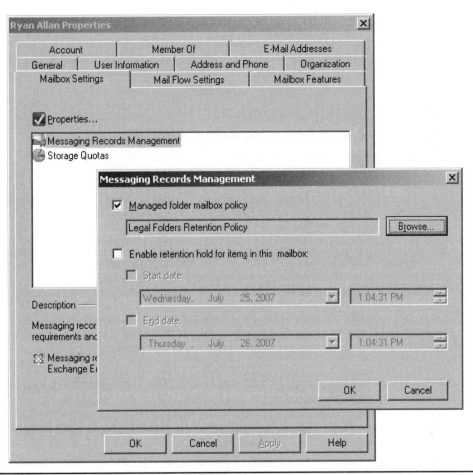

FIGURE 15-3   Select the appropriate policy for a selected mailbox

4. Choose Messaging Records Management and click the Properties button.
5. Select the Managed Folder Mailbox Policy check box and browse for the appropriate policy (see Figure 15-3).

To assign a policy to multiple mailboxes using the Exchange shell, use the Get-Mailbox command with the appropriate filter in place and then pipe the output through the following command:

```
Set-Mailbox -ManagedFolderMailboxPolicy '<Policy-Name>'
```

Journaling

Both retention and Message Records Management assist compliance needs by retaining only desired message content. Journaling takes this concept of retaining messages up to the mailbox

---

Disabling Messaging Records Management

There may come a time when the content settings need to be temporarily disabled, as in the case of someone on vacation, maternity leave, and so on. Exchange allows you to suspend the content management of managed folders in a given mailbox either indefinitely or for a specified duration. Within the Exchange console, follow these steps:

1. Expand Recipient Configuration and select the Mailbox node.
2. Select the desired mailbox and in the Actions pane, click Properties.
3. Select the Mailbox Settings tab.
4. Choose Messaging Records Management and click the Properties button.
5. Select the Enable Retention Hold for Items in This Mailbox check box. (Do *not* uncheck the Managed Folder Mailbox Policy check box because this will permanently disable Messaging Records Management.)
6. If known, specify a starting and ending date and time. This way, the Managed Folders Assistant will know to skip this mailbox during the specified period.

Here's how to suspend Messaging Records Management from the Exchange shell:

```
Set-Mailbox -Identity '<mailbox-name>' -RetentionHoldEnabled <$true | $false> -
StartDateForRetentionHold <value> -EndDateForRetentionHold <value>
```

---

and even the mailbox store level through retaining copies of sent and received messages for a designated recipient. Exchange Server 2007 has two types of journaling available:

- **Standard journaling**   Exchange copies all sent and received messages on a per–mailbox database basis for a specified recipient.
- **Premium journaling**   When coupled with an Enterprise Client Access License (CAL), Exchange can copy messages with a higher level of granularity in regard to the messages journaled and the individual mailboxes that participate in journaling.

With both types of journaling, Exchange uses a special process, the Journaling Agent, to read the appropriate journaling configuration, watch for the messages that meet the basic criteria, and send copies of those messages to the specified recipient. To verify the existence and status of the Journaling Agent, use the Get-TransportAgent command in the Exchange shell. If the agent is not enabled, run the following command in the Exchange shell:

```
Enable-TransportAgent -Identity "Journaling agent"
```

Standard Journaling

This default level of journaling takes place on a per-mailbox database level. Each mailbox database must be configured to journal messages to a designated recipient. To configure journaling within the Exchange console, follow these steps:

1. Expand Server Configuration and select the Mailbox node.
2. Select the desired mailbox database.
3. In the Actions pane, click Properties.
4. On the General tab, select the Journal Recipient check box and browse to select a recipient.

Journaled messages sent to an Exchange mailbox are accessed simply by configuring Outlook to open the Journal mailbox (presuming appropriate permissions to the mailbox have been established).

Premium Journaling

As previously mentioned, standard journaling is not a great option by itself when you're seeking to retain messages for compliance purposes. This is because standard journaling makes a copy of every message, whether pertinent to an organization's compliancy or not. In contrast, premium journaling is accomplished on a per-mailbox and/or per-distribution group basis. Additionally, three message scopes are applied to further isolate only those messages that should be journaled, as listed here.

Journaling Scope	Captured Messages
Internal	Those sent to and from internal mailboxes.
External	Those sent from or to an external address.
Global	Both internal and external messages.

Selecting a Journal Recipient

Exchange Server 2007 supports mailboxes, distribution groups, and contacts as journal recipients. There are a few considerations to take into account when selecting an appropriate journal recipient.

- **Storage**   Standard journaling copies every message sent from and received by all mailboxes residing on the configured mailbox database. Although there is no way for us to predetermine how much space is required, it should be considered at the very least that the journal recipient location will be double the size of the mailbox database (assuming journaling is turned on from day one).

- **Security**   Because journaling is most likely enabled to support a compliance effort, the destination recipient should exist within the grasp of your organization's security. (In other words, don't journal to a Gmail.com mailbox!)

- **Access**   Once journaled, the copied messages will presumably, at some point in the future, need to be looked at. The recipient host system needs to facilitate appropriate access for auditors, legal counsel, and so on.

Consulting the legal counsel of your organization would be in order should journaling become part of the compliancy plan.

Unlike standard journaling, which runs on the mailbox server where the mailbox database resides, premium journaling runs on all Hub Transport servers. Exchange uses journaling rules to define which messages a Hub Transport server should journal. To create a journaling rule in the Exchange console, follow these steps:

1. Expand Organization Configuration and select the Hub Transport node.

2. Select the Journaling tab.

3. In the Action pane, click New Journal Rule.

4. In the New Journal Rule Wizard (shown in Figure 15-4), provide the following information:

   - A name for the rule
   - The recipient to journal messages to
   - The scope of the journal rule
   - The mailbox or distribution group to journal messages from

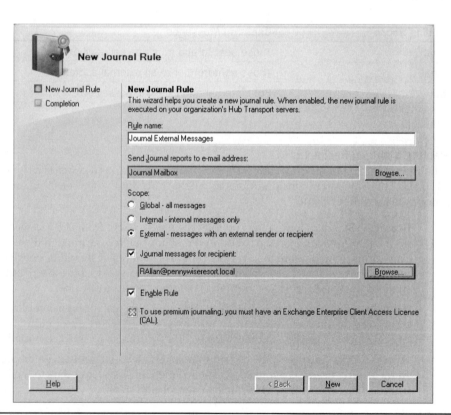

FIGURE 15-4   Creating a journal rule

Here's how to create a journal rule from the Exchange shell:

```
new-journalRule -Name 'Journal External Messages' -JournalEmailAddress '<Journal-
Mailbox>' -Scope '<External | Internal | Global>' -Enabled <$true | $false> -
Recipient '<Journaled-Recipient>'
```

Journal Reports   Premium journaling also provides an additional level of detail to each journaled message in a journal report. When a message is journaled with premium journaling, instead of you just seeing a copy of the journaled message, the original message is placed into a journal report as an attachment with the content of the journal report providing additional detail about the original message, including the following information (when appropriate):

- Sender SMTP address
- On-behalf-of SMTP address
- Message subject
- Message ID
- To recipients
- Cc recipients
- Bcc recipients
- Forward-to recipients (if specified on the original recipient)

When a message is sent while premium journaling is in effect, a journal report is created for each recipient. Therefore, if a message is sent to a distribution group with three members, and one of the members has a fourth recipient specified in their mailbox settings as a forward-to address, four journal reports will exist in the Journaling recipient's mailbox.

Transport Rules

Transport rules are a fantastic feature of Exchange Server 2007 that assists with meeting compliance requirements. The concept of the Transport rule is as follows: On Hub Transport and Edge Transport servers, an agent exists that has a set of rules that define specific message criteria and actions to be taken on those messages. Transport rules can perform actions such as the following:

- Modify the message subject
- Send a copy of the message to a specified recipient
- Redirect the message
- Append a disclaimer to the message
- Drop the message

Transport rules can recognize messages that should be acted upon using criteria such as these:

- Recipients
- Sender/recipient combination
- Message classifications
- Presence of specific words

- Presence of specific text patterns (think "V1agra")
- Attachments
- Importance

The application to compliance is six-fold:

1. Identify the message as pertinent to the compliance standard (based on sender, recipient, subject, attachment, or message body).
2. Tag the message as being pertinent to compliancy (could be via message classification or altering the subject or message body).
3. Notify appropriate persons in the organization (such as legal counsel or an auditor) to the presence of the message and/or recipients of the message using disclaimers.
4. Retain a copy of the message without user intervention (via adding a To, Cc, or Bcc recipient).
5. Depending on the organization's stance, delete either important or unimportant messages as they relate to compliancy.
6. Keep compliance-related messages inside the organization.

Rules Agents

As stated previously, there are two rules agents in use within Exchange Server 2007. The Transport rules agent runs on Hub Transport servers. The rules defined will protect message content being sent and received both inside and outside the organization. Creation and management of Transport rules is not focused on a specific Hub Transport server; it is an organization-wide configuration, shared by all Hub Transport servers. Because the Hub Transport rules are stored in Active Directory, replication of rules is automatic, facilitating each Hub Transport server to be enforcing the same rules. Edge Transport servers have their own Edge rules agent. The purpose of this agent is different from the Transport agent; the Edge rules agent is working to keep unwanted messages out of the organization by utilizing a number of indicators for potential spam or malicious messages, such as the following:

- Message subject
- Attachment name
- Presence of specific text patterns
- Message header values

Creation and management of Edge rules is done on the server hosting the Edge Transport role and is not replicated to any other servers.

Building a Rule

The process of creating a Transport rule and Edge rule essentially is the same, with the only difference being the presentation in the Exchange console. To create a rule, follow these steps:

1. Expand Organization Configuration and select Hub Transport (on an Edge server, simply select the Edge Transport node).
2. Select the Transport Rules tab.

3. In the Actions pane, select New Transport Rule to start the wizard, shown in Figure 15-5.

4. Provide a name and optionally a comment.

5. Select the conditions that define a message as meeting the rule criteria.

6. Select the actions the server should take.

7. Select the exceptions to the conditions (optional).

Transport rules can also be created within the Exchange shell using the new-TransportRule command.

Message Classifications

It is often difficult to identify which messages are applicable to compliance needs. The Transport rules assist by being able to test message content for certain criteria and then prepending the subject or stamping on a disclaimer, but that only helps when applicable messages perfectly meet the criteria established in a Transport rule.

Message classifications allow users to self-identify messages related to compliance, legal, a particular topic, and so on. The user experience is a simple one—once the feature is enabled, a simple drop-down listing the available message classifications can be used in Outlook 2007 and in Outlook Web Access to tag the message, making it easy to search for in the future.

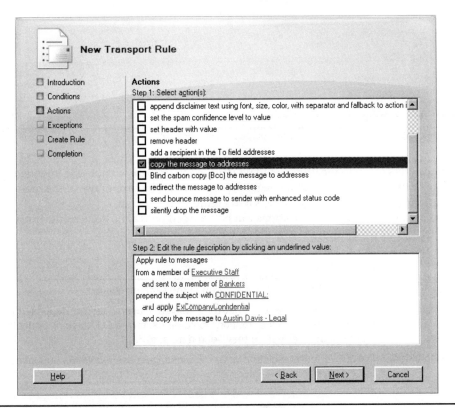

Figure 15-5   Create Transport Rules that assist with compliancy

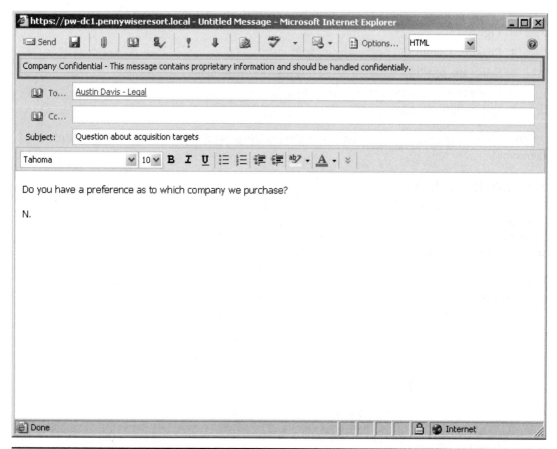

FIGURE 15-6   Message classifications identify the purpose of a message.

Within the message, classification metadata is added to properly denote the intended audience of the message (such as the legal department) or the proper use of the message (such as "for internal use only"), as shown in Figure 15-6.

Additionally, message classifications can be stamped onto a message using Transport rules. The message classification provides the following information:

Field	Description
Display Name	The classification name displayed in the Outlook client.
Sender Description	Describes to the sender what the message classification is supposed to be utilized for. This information would be used by an Outlook or Outlook Web Access user before they send a message.
Recipient Description	Describes to the recipient what the message classification is supposed to be utilized for. This information would be used by an Outlook or Outlook Web Access user when they open a message.
Locale	Creates a locale-specific version of the message classification.

A message classification, once assigned, stays with the message for the life of that message, unless it is stripped out by a Transport rule or by setting another message classification. To retain specific initial classifications, you can assign each message classification a priority value so that one classification cannot overwrite another. For example, if you had a classification of "SOX-Related – Never Delete," and you wanted to ensure the classification was never overwritten, you could set the priority of that classification to a value of Highest (the possible values are Highest, Higher, High, MediumHigh, Medium, MediumLow, Low, Lower, and Lowest, with a default value being Medium). Setting the priority is accomplished via the Set-MessageClassification command in the Exchange shell using the DisplayPreference parameter.

Deploying Message Classifications

The following default message classifications come out of the box: A/C Privileged (that is, attorney/client), Company Internal, Company Confidential, Partner Mail, Originator Requested a Receipt, and Attachment Removed. Although these are useful, there will probably be the need to add classifications. Remember, classifications don't just need to be used for compliance purposes; there are dozens of other uses. Here are some examples:

- To automate journaling/archiving via a Transport rule that copies classified messages to a specific mailbox.

- A message classified automatically by an Edge rule as having inappropriate content (based on the presence of swear words and such in the message body) would have a recipient description that reminds recipients of corporate policies regarding the appropriate use of the e-mail system.

- Messages classified as being part of a particular project could be more easily found at a later date.

There are plenty more, but those are just a few use cases for message classifications. Creating a new message classification is only done using the Exchange shell, as follows:

```
New-MessageClassification -Name <name> -DisplayName <display name> -
SenderDescription '<sender-description-text>' -RecipientDescription '<recipient-
description-text>'
```

Thus, creating a message classification to denote messages that are only to be viewed by members of the executive staff would be created by running the following command:

```
New-MessageClassification -Name 'ExecutiveStaff' -DisplayName 'Executive Staff
Only' -SenderDescription 'This message contains information that is only to be
viewed by members of the Executive Staff.' -RecipientDescription 'This message
contains information that is only to be viewed by members of the Executive Staff.
If you are reading this and are not a member of the Executive Staff, you must
delete this message immediately.'
```

Once the appropriate message classifications are created in Exchange, Outlook Web Access clients can use them immediately without any configuration. Outlook 2007 clients (previous versions of Outlook do not support message classifications) need to be individually configured to use message classifications. Although it may seem odd that Outlook 2007 clients do not automatically support message classifications, this is by design to protect the integrity of the classifications. If everyone in the organization could mark a message "Company Confidential," the classification itself would lose its meaning. Configuring an Outlook 2007 client involves three steps:

1. Exporting the message classifications from Active Directory
2. Placing the message classifications file on the client
3. Modifying the client's Registry to utilize the message classifications file

Exporting the Message Classifications   Exporting the message classifications is done using a mixture of Exchange shell commands and a script that ships with Exchange Server 2007:

```
"<identities of classification>" | Get-MessageClassification | .\Export-Out-
lookClassification.ps1 > path\classifications.xml
```

NOTE *The script Export-OutlookClassifications.ps1 is found in the \scripts subfolder of the Exchange installation folder.*

This will export the designated message classification(s) listed into an XML file using the following format:

```
<?xml version="1.0" ?>
<Classifications>
      <Classification>
            <Name>Company Confidential</Name>
            <Description>This message contains proprietary information and should
be handled confidentially.</Description>
            <Guid>19e795ab-f38c-4d55-a009-0a3ad32ffc1f</Guid>
            <AutoClassifyReplies/>
      </Classification>
</Classifications>
```

Copying the Classifications File   The XML file needs to be copied to a folder on the client—the path will be used in the last step.

Modifying the Local Registry   The Registry path HKEY_CURRENT_USER\Software\Microsoft\Office\12.0\Common\Policy will need to be created and with the following Registry entries:

Registry Value Name	Type	Data
EnableClassifications	REG_DWORD	1
TrustClassifications	REG_DWORD	1
AdminClassificationPath	REG_SZ	<path to classifications file>

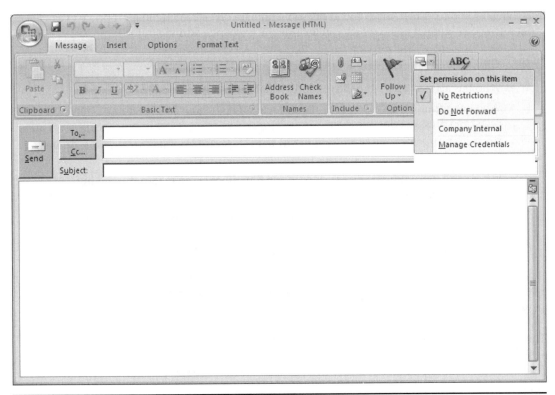

FIGURE 15-7   Outlook 2007 supporting message classifications

Once this is complete, Outlook 2007 will support the message classifications listed in the XML file, as shown in Figure 15-7. Remember that all users utilizing the same classifications will need to have them installed locally as part of the classifications XML file.

Other Compliance Considerations

Now that you've seen the various features of Exchange that apply to compliance, let's take a step back out of the technology and address some of the issues surrounding Exchange and compliance.

Implementing Access Control

It's all well and fine to implement the compliance-related features of Exchange—retaining specific e-mails, moving others to special folders, journaling mailboxes, and so on—but those technologies are only a part of the larger plan to be able to prove compliance. So think about the proving part: It most likely involves an auditor or someone from the legal department searching for and reading e-mail, and at the same time involves keeping inappropriate eyes from seeing confidential data. (which can include the Exchange administrator!)

Determining appropriate access—who, how much, when, and so on—needs to be a part of the compliance plan. This includes the following:

- Who has access to user mailboxes, individual folders, and so on?
- Who has administrative access to manage retention and journaling settings, Transport rules, and message classifications?
- What ethical walls need to be established to keep protected data from inappropriate eyes?
- Where will journaling be directed to (internal mailboxes, an external archiving system, and so on)?
- Who has access to journal mailboxes (assuming the journal recipient is an internal mailbox) or the external archiving system?
- Are messages only being read by the intended recipient?

So it now becomes clear that compliance is not just about turning on the Exchange features, but looking at Exchange as a whole and developing a comprehensive plan for compliance. Most of these issues are addressed by making simple proactive decisions about who will have access, documenting the access, and periodically auditing the access controls to ensure nothing has changed. The establishment of ethical walls is accomplished using a combination of Transport rules, message classifications, and distribution groups. Ensuring only intended recipients read e-mail is done using message encryption.

Ethical Walls

If you're unfamiliar with the concept, an *ethical wall* is simply an enforced logical separation of individuals or departments. Transport rules can be used to create an ethical wall via the following steps:

1. Create distribution groups for the sets of mailboxes that should remain on either side of the ethical wall.
2. Ensure the appropriate message classifications exist to identify only those messages that should not be crossing the wall.
3. Create a Transport rule that checks to see if the message has the appropriate message classification *and* is being sent between the two distribution groups, as shown in Figure 15-8.
4. If necessary, create a second Transport rule with a higher priority that automatically sets the message classification based on sender and message content.

Message Encryption

Exchange has supported for years the ability to encrypt messages so that only the intended recipients can read them. This is done using public/private key pairs (more on this in Chapter 16), where the message is encrypted using the recipient's public key and decrypted

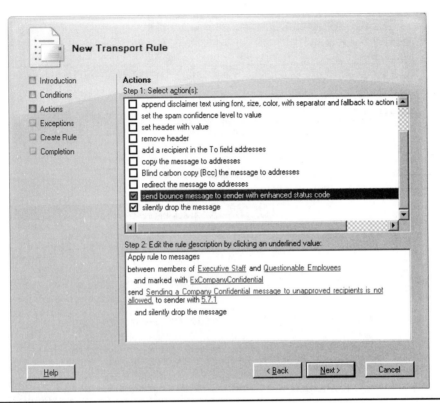

FIGURE 15-8 Creating an ethical wall using a Transport rule

using the matching private key. Within an organization this is relatively easy with Exchange 2007, but in the case of sending messages outside the organization (as in the case of an insurance company communicating with a hospital about a patient and their care), both parties need to obtain the public keys from the individuals they will be communicating with in the foreign organization. This can be accomplished by having each sender digitally sign a message sent to the foreign organization. The digital signature contains the public key of the sender, which can be imported by trusting the Certificate Authority. An example is shown in Figure 15-9.

Once imported, messages sent to that same individual can be easily encrypted within Outlook, as shown in Figure 15-10. The sender will need to obtain the public key for each recipient they wish to encrypt messages to.

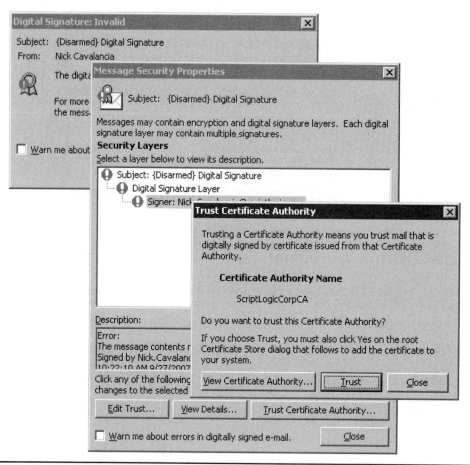

FIGURE 15-9   Trusting the foreign Certificate Authority

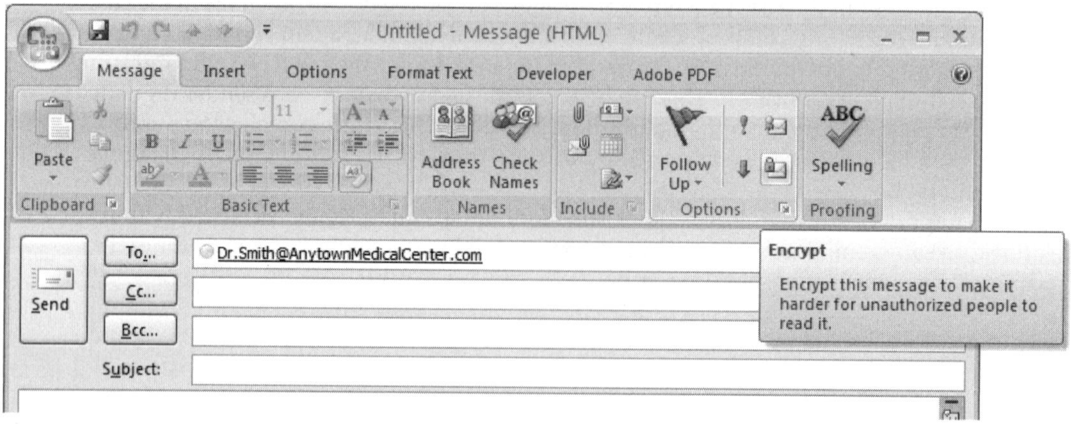

FIGURE 15-10   Encrypting messages in Outlook

Summary

Compliance standards require the protection of sensitive data that may exist within an e-mail. Exchange Server 2007 not only provides you the means to automatically and manually identify messages applicable to a compliance standard using message classifications, but also the ability to automate the management, retention, and journaling of applicable messages. Depending on the standards that apply to you, as well as the interpretation your organization has for the compliance standards verbiage, Exchange Server 2007 provides a flexible architecture to ensure your e-mail environment is in compliance.

Securing E-mail

With each version of Exchange Server—and indeed most software products that arrive on the market—emphasis is given to improved security. Exchange 2007 does not deviate from that trend. Improvements can be found in several aspects of security as well as the ease of deploying overall security. In accordance with their own Trustworthy Computing initiatives, Microsoft has worked to make Exchange 2007 secure—from deployment to administration and all the communication in between. You will see that almost all communication between servers and between the clients and servers has been secured through encryption mechanisms. Securing e-mail in Exchange 2007 has been taken seriously from start to finish—from corporate e-mail policy to employing the technological solutions available with the product.

Security as an Exchange Philosophy

Security should be a state of mind or even a way of life, not an inconvenience. Every aspect of a messaging infrastructure needs to be considered a potential point of failure when maintaining a secure network. At the same time, a secure e-mail system also depends on network security. We used to install Exchange Server and then spend time working through security checklists to harden the server to be secure. Exchange 2007 is created from the ground up to be secure by design, secure through deployment, and secure by default.

Data Path Security

By default, all data transported in an Exchange organization is secured. Client access, including Outlook Web Access (OWA), ActiveSync, and Outlook Anywhere, is secured by a Secure Sockets Layer (SSL) certificate. Traffic between Exchange servers is encrypted using mutual Transport Layer Security (TLS). Also, Outlook 2007 client traffic is secured through Remote Procedure Call (RPC) encryption and encrypted Messaging Application Programming Interface (MAPI) submission.

Outlook 2003 can also use this encryption, but it is not set by default. It is specific to each account and subsequently is configured from within Tools | Account Settings. In the Account Settings window, select the option View or Change existing e-mail accounts. Then select Change | More Settings. Under the Encryption area in the Security tab, check the box by the option Encrypt data between Microsoft Office Outlook and Microsoft Exchange, as shown in Figure 16-1.

FIGURE 16-1 Outlook account settings for encrypting data between Microsoft Office Outlook and Microsoft Exchange

An enterprise using all the functionality of a Microsoft Exchange organization with diverse clients will see many different authentication and encryption methodologies in play, depending on what point-to-point communication is occurring.

Role-Based Installation

In previous versions of Exchange, the entire core Exchange product was installed for each server, with the exception of the Management Tools, which could be installed separately. By dividing Exchange up into the five roles, administrators can now install only the roles needed for each server. This in itself reduces the potential attack surface by reducing the installation code and active applications by default.

Patch Management

Security updates and patches seem almost inevitable in software applications. Exchange itself is not immune from patches, although they are infrequent. A good messaging infrastructure will accommodate a mechanism for testing and deploying crucial patches to messaging applications and the underlying operating system in a timely manner.

Microsoft added Exchange to Microsoft Update (not Windows Update) for Exchange 2003. Exchange 2007 administrators should establish a policy of implementing updates for Exchange servers as part of their network patch management process, whether it is a centralized software approach, such as Microsoft Windows Server Update Services, or a manual system for servers.

In addition, administrators need to manage urgent updates to third-party applications on Exchange servers, including monitoring, reporting, antivirus, and anti-malware solutions.

Given the mission-critical nature of most messaging systems, automatic updates should be set to download only for manual installation or another manual setting (such as notification only) to allow for the testing of patches before formal deployment. Not all scenarios are tested when a security patch or application update is created, so it is especially important for systems such as Exchange 2007 to ensure minimal interruption in patching.

Principle of Least Privilege

When working on networked systems, the authenticated user should not maintain greater privileged access to network resources than is needed to perform their required duties. Users should not be enabled for POP3 access if POP3 access is not required for them to access their e-mail. This principle is of course true also for Exchange administration. I have seen administrators performing day-to-day business activities using office productivity applications logged in with a user account with Exchange Enterprise Administrator and Domain Administrator permissions. I have also seen companies that set up separate accounts for administration by adding an *e* in front of Exchange administrator usernames and a *w* in front of Windows administrator usernames. Of course, these accounts with elevated permissions would not have mailboxes associated with them, thus further reducing the chances of message-borne malware executing under administrator privileges. These accounts are only accessed via RDP to the individual servers or to a dedicated administration server. These administrators do not have to log out of their normal user account to perform administrator-level tasks.

As we covered in earlier administration chapters, Exchange 2007 introduces administrator roles in the form of security groups to help segment administrative tasks as follows:

- Exchange Organization Administrators
- Exchange Recipient Administrators
- Exchange View-Only Administrators
- Exchange Server Administrators
- Exchange Public Folder Administrators

SP1 *Exchange 2007 Service Pack 1 adds the new security group Exchange Public Folder Administrators, which allows enterprises to assign public folder administration to specific administrators without allowing access to other areas of Exchange.*

User accounts assigned to these groups of course inherit the permissions to perform the functions related to their descriptive universal security group names. They are all global roles themselves, except the Exchange Server Administrators role, which allows delegation of administration to one or more specific Exchange servers.

Exchange 2007 and Perimeter Networks

Exchange topology contributes to overall e-mail security. Many companies utilize at least one DMZ or perimeter network where security-related processing can be performed with less risk to the internal network. For messaging, SMTP relay and message hygiene services are often maintained in a perimeter network. As we have repeatedly mentioned, Exchange 2007 introduces server roles for more granular server deployment. A significant role pertaining to e-mail security is the Edge Transport server role (see Figure 16-2).

Deploying an Edge Transport server in your Exchange topology is not required; however, Edge is designed to bring protection beyond a basic smarthost or relay server because it integrates effectively with Active Directory through Active Directory Application Mode (ADAM). An Edge Transport server handles the external SMTP connections and message hygiene functionality, thus limiting the exposure of your internal network to external threats.

Security Configuration Wizard

The Security Configuration Wizard (SCW) was introduced with Windows Server 2003 Service Pack 1 and helps to minimize the potential attack surface of Windows servers. SCW is installed through the Add/Remove Programs applet in Control Panel. It is listed in Add/Remove Windows Components on Windows 2003 servers with Service Pack 1 installed. Custom SCW policies can be created based on specific Windows Server roles. This is especially valuable if many servers are performing the same duties. SCW uses an .xml template as a starting point, which can be customized for your servers.

In the \scripts folder in the Exchange Server installation path is a pair of Exchange 2007 Server templates that can lock down unnecessary services and ports on servers running Exchange 2007. One template, Exchange2007Edge.xml, is for the Edge Transport Server role, and the second, Exchange2007.xml, is for the rest of the Exchange roles. The Exchange 2007 templates are not immediately recognized by the SCW and have to be manually registered

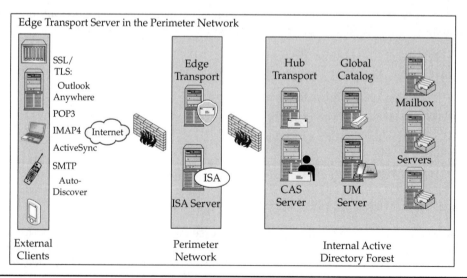

FIGURE 16-2 Basic Exchange 2007 topology with an Edge server in the perimeter network

on each server to be assessed by the SCW. For Exchange 2007 servers with the Client Access, Hub Transport, Mailbox, and Unified Messaging roles, the command-line syntax would be as follows:

```
>scwcmd register /kbname:Ex2007KB /kbfile:"%programfiles%\Microsoft
\Exchange Server\scripts\Exchange2007.xml"
```

This command must be run from the %windir%\system32 directory to avoid an "Access is Denied" error. With the Exchange 2007 template registered, the SCW is accessed through the Administrative Tools folder. Running the SCW introduces the Welcome to the Security Configuration Wizard screen, shown in Figure 16-3.

SCW can create a new secure server policy template or be used to edit and apply an existing one. Figure 16-4 shows the configuration option in the Security Configuration Wizard before it assesses the current services, applications, and ports on the server.

The wizard checks the machine and asks the administrator for changes in the different configuration categories, such as applications, ports, services, and server roles. The latter is shown in Figure 16-5. When the SCW is run, it can make a more complete assessment if applications that are needed on the server are running.

FIGURE 16-3 The Welcome to the Security Configuration Wizard screen

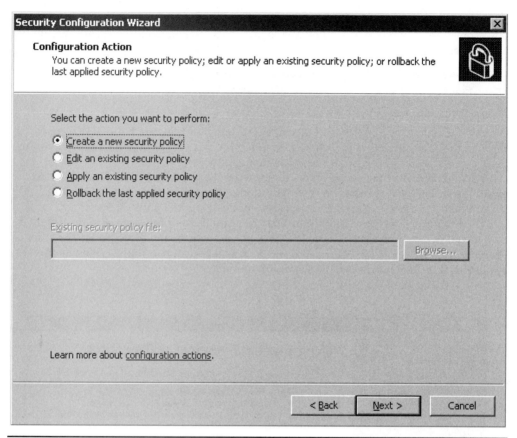

FIGURE 16-4   Security Configuration Wizard policy action

If this Exchange server has the Edge Transport role installed, a couple manual entries must be performed. We have to tell SCW that the Edge Transport server uses the ports 50389 and 50636 for ADAM and EdgeSync communication. Now completing the SCW will generate a security policy file we can use for other servers. It will disable unnecessary services and restrict unneeded ports.

The SCW is not a mandatory security measure, but with the Exchange templates it can be very useful in reducing the potential attack surface of Exchange 2007 servers. The SCW will also confirm changes before implementing them, and in the end the administrator can choose to save the policy to apply it at a later time. Finally, if unexpected results prevail, running the SCW again provides the ability to roll back the last policy applied as a configuration option, as shown previously in Figure 16-4.

Data Storage Security

Securing e-mail does not just require security for messages in transit, but also demands consideration for storage as well. Where security concerns exist, administrators should know all the places where e-mail can and should be stored in the enterprise. If an archival solution is in place, that storage should be secured by access control and possibly encryption.

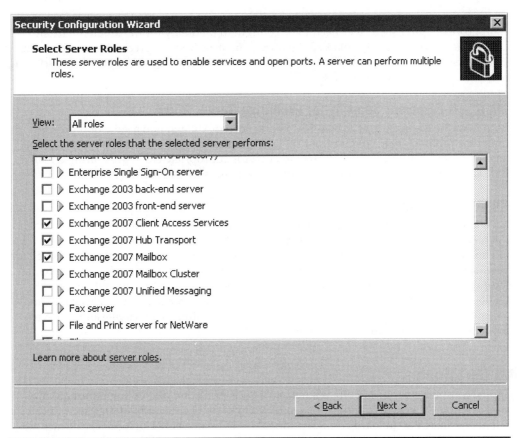

FIGURE 16-5   Security Configuration Wizard server roles on an internal Exchange 2007 server

Relays or smarthosts should not be storing messages beyond their queue and transport. Backup storage should use secured methods or secured media. For Outlook clients, there should be a personal archive policy. If users are allowed to save individual messages as .msg files or use personal folders (.pst files) in Outlook, then where are they stored and is their content secured?

Related Microsoft Products

Microsoft tries to be a comprehensive software solution for companies from start to finish. They have several products that, if deployed with Exchange 2007, make a more secure environment for messaging.

Internet Security and Acceleration (ISA) Server 2006

ISA 2006 is ideal for enhancing secure remote client access to Exchange 2007. ISA can securely publish the virtual directories used by the CAS server role, including Outlook Anywhere, ActiveSync, and Outlook Web Access, as well as preauthenticate users prior to reaching the internal network. ISA 2000 and 2004 can also be used to help secure Exchange 2007; however, published rules need to be configured manually for the different virtual directories without ISA 2006 or ISA 2004 with SP3. Because Microsoft recommends upgrading ISA to version 2006 for use with Exchange 2007, we will only consider ISA 2006 when discussing remote client access to Exchange 2007.

Microsoft Forefront Security for Exchange Server 2007

Born from the acquisition of Sybari, Microsoft evolved Antigen into a suite of products under the umbrella name of Forefront Security. For Exchange, Forefront provides multiple engines that scan for viruses, malware, and other inappropriate content. Securing e-mail in 2008 still requires a quality antivirus solution, and one is available from Microsoft.

Rights Management Server

Several years ago, Microsoft entered the realm of Digital Rights Management. Their focus is not media files that people like to share, but rather documents and messages that are intended for the eyes of the sender and recipient only. Rights Management Server (RMS) for Windows 2003 integrates with Microsoft Office and SharePoint to help protect confidential information. RMS activates the Information Rights Management functionality within Outlook, thus empowering the sender to prevent unauthorized access to a message. This can include prohibiting accidental (or intentional) forwarding of a message and can even prevent the printing of an e-mail by the recipient.

Digital Certificates

Digital certificates are used both as a means of encrypting and decrypting information, as well as signing messages digitally for sender validation. The majority of digital certificates fall under the X.509 standard certificate format outlined in RFC 2459. X.509 certificates are made up of the following fields:

- Version number
- Serial number
- Signature algorithm ID
- Issuer name
- Validity period (start and end dates)
- Subject name
- Subject public-key information
- Issuer unique identifier (versions 2 and 3 only)
- Subject unique identifier (versions 2 and 3 only)
- Extensions (version 3 only)
- Signature hash on the fields listed here

Exchange uses X.509 certificates to secure communication between servers and between clients and the Exchange server. There are several mechanisms for issuing and managing certificates for the purposes of securing e-mail systems and providing secure authentication. When Exchange 2007 is installed, it generates a self-signed certificate to secure point-to-point communication paths. When clients connect to a Client Access Server (CAS), they can use the self-signed certificate or another SSL certificate can be issued for use in its place. An alternative certificate would have to come either from a third-party authority or from a Windows Public Key Infrastructure (PKI).

X.509 certificates are supported in many areas, including TLS, SSL, S/MIME, HTTPS, SmartCard, and LDAPS.

Self-Signed Certificates

Typically used in a closed environment, applications can produce their own certificates, acting almost as a local Certificate Authority. These are not trusted by a public authority and therefore, are not good replacements for securing communication and authentication over networks not in administrator control.

Self-signed certificates find use in testing and development where a fully trusted certificate is not required. Microsoft even has a utility called MakeCert.exe for that purpose. Because self-signed certificates were not issued by a trusted authority, access will result in a warning that the certificate does not meet one or more of the three validation parameters for X.509 certificates:

- Was the certificate issued by a trusted authority?
- Is the date covered by the certificate still valid?
- Is the name on the certificate a valid name?

Users who access OWA with Internet Explorer 6 using the OWA server IP address might see the warning in Figure 16-6. IE 7 uses a custom web page to disclose the certificate error to the user. Users have the option to continue, even with the errors, or cancel the communication. In the enterprise, it is not sound practice to have users get into the habit of ignoring certificate error warnings.

Third-party Trusted Certificates

Many companies offer TLS/SSL certificate services, which work well for messaging solutions such as Exchange Server. Microsoft maintains a list of Certificate Authorities that it trusts through Windows by default in what the company calls their Root Certificate Trust program. Entrust, GoDaddy, and VeriSign are among those who have passed the audit process to qualify for this program. The use of X.509 certificates for cryptography is called *asymmetric encryption*. A pair of keys is generated—one public and one private—with one key, the public one, accessible through a trusted authority. The public key binds the identity of the private key holder to the certificate.

NOTE *Entrust has specific requirements for requesting a certificate for use in Exchange 2007, as outlined on their support page for Exchange (http://www.entrust.net/ssl-technical/msx2007/csr.cfm).*

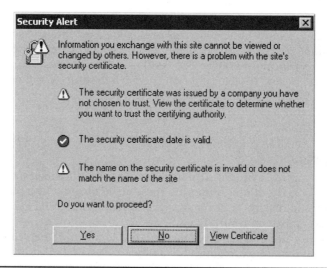

FIGURE 16-6   OWA over HTTPS certificate error warning in Internet Explorer 6

Engaging one of these companies for an SSL certificate for use within an Exchange environment requires the generation of a certificate request. This request is generated through the EMS as follows:

```
>New-ExchangeCertificate -GenerateRequest -subjectname "dc=com,dc=virtuec
orp,o=VirtueCorp,cn=mail.virtuecorp.com" -domainname e2k7-mb-02,e2k7-mb-
02.virtuecorp.com,mail.virtuecorp.com,autodiscover.virtuecorp.com -Pri-
vateKeyExportable $true -path c:\certificates\certrequest.req
```

In this example, the certificate has several domain names to use, and the SubjectName value reflects the X.500 format for the subject name. The Path parameter identifies where to save the text file that is the certificate request. The path needs to exist because the cmdlet will not create it. Executing this command will return a thumbprint, shown in Figure 16-7, which becomes a value we will need to reference for other EMS cmdlets affecting this certificate. The file certrequest.req is shown in Figure 16-8. This file is submitted to a trusted third-party vendor, often through a web interface. The vendor will return a certificate file that is to be imported from a saved file location using EMS again, as follows:

```
>Import-ExchangeCertificate -path c:\certificates\certificate.cer
```

The Import-ExchangeCertificate cmdlet installs the certificate on the Exchange server running the CAS role. This certificate will now be available for securing the various client access methods through the IIS Manager.

After the certificate is imported, it must be enabled. The Enable-ExchangeCertificate cmdlet has two required values consisting of the thumbprint and the services that the

FIGURE 16-7 Thumbprint output from the New-ExchangeCertificate cmdlet

certificate is being enabled to secure. The services options are SMTP, IIS, UM, POP, IMAP, and none. Here's an example of the syntax:

```
>Enable-ExchangeCertificate -ThumbPrint 85F96CFBB098D2A1ED4C939AFA77EC320217BDE0 -
Services "POP, IIS, SMTP"
```

FIGURE 16-8 Digital certificate request file

To delete an installed certificate, you also use the thumbprint value, as follows:

```
>Remove-ExchangeCertificate -thumbprint 85F96CFBB098D2A1ED4C939AFA77EC320217BDE0
```

Retrieving the thumbprint value is easily accomplished using the Get-ExchangeCertificate cmdlet, which will return a list of the certificates installed, including their thumbprints.

Public Key Infrastructure (PKI) Certificates

Public Key Infrastructure (PKI) is a trust hierarchy made up of protocols and systems for managing public keys. Typically, PKI is based on the X.509 certificate standard. The overall functionality it delivers includes:

- Generating digital certificates for signatures and encryption
- Enabling Secure Sockets Layer (SSL)
- Enabling digital signatures
- Facilitating authorization and access control

A basic PKI consists of several components. First, there needs to be a Certificate Authority (CA) responsible for generating digital certificates and Certificate Revocation Lists (CRLs). A Registration Authority (RA) validates user identity, which is bound to a public key. Certificates need to be stored in a directory, such as Active Directory. This is an extension of the trusted third-party CA to the enterprise.

A PKI is not a function of Exchange Server; however, Windows Server 2003 can host a solid PKI implementation. Certificate Services is a Windows component installed through the Add/Remove Windows Components option in Add/Remove Programs, accessed through the Control Panel. A Windows 2003 PKI is an expansion of the basic Windows CA to an enterprise solution. Deploying a PKI is not trivial and should be well planned. There are administrative roles to manage the PKI, much like the roles for Exchange 2007. Microsoft includes an Operations Guide for Windows 2003 PKI in TechNet online:

http://technet2.microsoft.com/windowsserver/en/library/e1d5a892-10e1-417c-be13-99d7147989a91033.mspx

Requesting a new certificate through a local Windows PKI is much the same process as with a third-party CA. Installing Certificate Services creates a website on the certificate server where certificate requests can be made through uploading the request .txt file to the local site, https://<Enterprise_PKI_CA_Servername>/certsvr, as shown in Figure 16-9.

NOTE *Known compatibility issues with the Windows 2003 PKI CA request web page and Windows Vista are outlined in Microsoft KB Article 922706.*

Interestingly, a Windows 2003 PKI with self-signed certificates does not work across forest boundaries, so it would not be effective for an Exchange 2007 resource forest topology. Users would not be able to send signed or encrypted messages across forest boundaries.

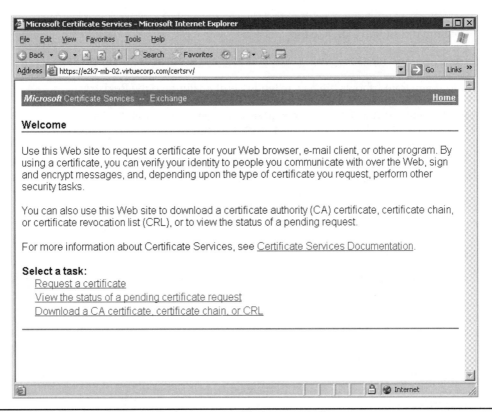

FIGURE 16-9   Windows 2003 certificate server certificate request site

Subject Alternative Name

Exchange 2007 complicates things a little relative to its predecessors. For a server with the CAS role installed, there may be numerous hostnames and Fully Qualified Domain Names (FQDNs) that reference the server and, more significantly, there are likely different URLs for external use versus internal use. In our New-ExchangeCertificate cmdlet example earlier in the chapter, we included several domain names for the server: e2k7-mb-02, e2k7-mb-02.virtuecorp.com, mail.virtuecorp.com, and autodiscover.virtuecorp.com. How do we apply multiple domain names? X.509 version 3 added an Extensions field, as listed earlier in this chapter. This field allows the certificate to carry multiple names to secure. This can be used by the CAs to allow for multiple names for a certificate.

Not all trusted Certificate Authorities are set up to allow for subject alternative names for their certificates. You may need to do some research before you "entrust" someone with this task.

Subject Alternative Name in Windows 2003 PKI CA

By default, a Windows 2003 CA will ignore multiple names for a Subject Alternative Name certificate request. Thankfully, a very useful tool called CertUtil.exe can add the field so the

CA can accommodate the request. CertUtil is installed with Certificate Services. The syntax for the command should look like this:

```
>certutil -setreg policy\EditFlags +EDITF_ATTRIBUTESUBJECTALTNAME2
```

The output generated shows the new extended edit attribute in the Registry:

```
SYSTEM\CurrentControlSet\Services\CertSvc\Configuration\Exchange\
PolicyModules\CertificateAuthority_MicrosoftDefault.Policy\EditFlags:

Old Value:

  EditFlags REG_DWORD = 11014e (1114446)

    EDITF_REQUESTEXTENSIONLIST -- 2

    EDITF_DISABLEEXTENSIONLIST -- 4

    EDITF_ADDOLDKEYUSAGE -- 8

    EDITF_BASICCONSTRAINTSCRITICAL -- 40 (64)

    EDITF_ENABLEAKIKEYID -- 100 (256)

    EDITF_ENABLEDEFAULTSMIME -- 10000 (65536)

    EDITF_ENABLECHASECLIENTDC -- 100000 (1048576)

New Value:

  EditFlags REG_DWORD = 15014e (1376590)

    EDITF_REQUESTEXTENSIONLIST -- 2

    EDITF_DISABLEEXTENSIONLIST -- 4

    EDITF_ADDOLDKEYUSAGE -- 8

    EDITF_BASICCONSTRAINTSCRITICAL -- 40 (64)

    EDITF_ENABLEAKIKEYID -- 100 (256)

    EDITF_ENABLEDEFAULTSMIME -- 10000 (65536)

    EDITF_ATTRIBUTESUBJECTALTNAME2 -- 40000 (262144)

    EDITF_ENABLECHASECLIENTDC -- 100000 (1048576)

CertUtil: -setreg command completed successfully.

The CertSvc service may need to be restarted for changes to take effect.
```

After the Certificate Service (certsvc) is restarted, the CA should accept Subject Alternative Name certificate requests using the New-ExchangeCertificate cmdlet, as shown earlier in the chapter.

Encrypted Transaction

So what happens in a typical secure message communication transaction? If a user trusts a particular Certificate Authority (CA), they can use its certificates to secure communications. Certificates bind an identity to a public key. The user creates a key pair (private and public). They then request a certificate from a Registering Authority (RA). The RA checks the user's ID and forwards the request to the CA. The public key gets posted to the directory. If the user signs or encrypts a message with their private key, the receiving party needs to decrypt or validate the sender. The recipient queries the trusted CA's directory. The recipient also checks the Certificate Revocation List (CRL) to ensure the certificate wasn't revoked. The recipient can now decrypt the message or validate the digital signature. Alternatively, a sender can encrypt a message with the recipient's public key, requiring the private key, which is in sole possession of the owner, to decrypt the message.

PKI eliminates the need for two entities to share passwords or exchange information prior to the secured message transaction. The public key component helps ensure a high success rate for completing the transaction because of accessibility.

Authentication

Quite simply, *authentication* is the mechanism for providing verified identity to a system. *Authorization* is the granting of access to resources, typically to an authenticated user. In Windows Server, users are most often authenticated based on their input of a username/password combination; however, other mechanisms can be used, including biometrics, smartcards, certificates on a chip, or a USB dongle.

Client Access Servers support several types of authentication, as detailed in Table 16-1. Forms-Based Authentication provides the best security for Outlook Web Access, especially with the use of ISA Server 2006.

Outlook Authentication

Outlook 2003 and 2007 both will attempt to use the current user's Windows logon credentials to access the Outlook profile and log onto the Exchange mailbox. To encrypt user credentials between the client and Active Directory, Outlook first tries to use Kerberos. Should that not work, it will fall back to NT LAN Manager (NTLM). This is controlled using the same tab as shown earlier in Figure 16-1. Navigate to Tools | Account Settings. Select the account, click Change, and then click the More Settings button. In the Security tab, the default Logon

CAS Authentication Type	Description
Standard authentication	Includes Basic, Windows Integrated, and Digest Authentication.
Forms-Based Authentication	Uses SSL-encrypted cookies to store passwords.
ISA Forms-Based Authentication	Proxies Forms-Based Authentication.
Smartcard/certificate/biometrics	Certificate on a smartcard or USB allows mutual authentication.

TABLE 16-1   Client Access Server Supported Authentication Types

FIGURE 16-10
Outlook 2007
Network Logon
Security setting

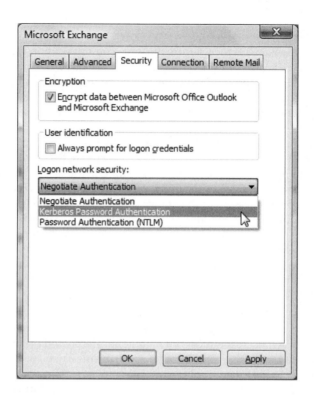

Network Security setting is Negotiate Authentication. The drop-down options there also
include Kerberos and NTLM, as reflected in Figure 16-10.

In the same tab, we can force Outlook to prompt for user credentials every time. Should
a user leave their desk unattended or someone otherwise gains access to the desktop, that
person will have to have the user's credentials to gain access to Outlook and Exchange
content. You can set this feature by checking the Always prompt for logon credentials box,
shown in Figure 16-10.

Client to Server

Security concerns with client communication are specific to the type of client and method of
connectivity to the server. There is a greater diversity of clients not seen in previous versions
of Exchange with several different protocols and services in use. Securing e-mail is slightly
different for each client type and (sometimes) version. Table 16-2 identifies the security used
for authentication and encryption for different client access methods.

Outlook 2007 Trust Center

As described in Chapter 11, the most recent version of Microsoft Office Outlook maintains a
Trust Center. This is a centralized interface for configuring security-related settings for
Outlook 2007. The E-Mail Security page is shown in Figure 16-11. Several aspects of e-mail

Client-to-Server Connection	Authentication	Encryption
MAPI	NTLM/Kerberos	RPC Encryption
OWA	Basic/forms-based	HTTPS
ActiveSync	Basic/certificate/token	HTTPS
POP3/IMAP4	Basic/NTLM/Kerberos	TLS/SSL
Outlook Anywhere	Basic/NTLM	HTTPS
CAS to UM	IP address	SIP over TLS
CAS to Mailbox	NTLM/Kerberos	RPC Encryption
CAS to CAS	Kerberos/certificate	HTTPS

TABLE 16-2   Client Access Security Methods for Exchange 2007

client security can be controlled in the Trust Center that need to be mentioned in a discussion on securing e-mail in the enterprise.

Some basic message hygiene controls are available in the Trust Center, including Attachment Blocking and Automatic Download of remote HTML content.

In the Trust Center, we can use digital certificates for S/MIME, encryption, or digitally signing e-mail messages. This functionality from the client perspective assumes the client has a Digital ID. Outlook 2007 has specific requirements for Digital IDs, and not all vendors have adopted that level of support yet.

MAPI Connections with Outlook

By default, messages sent with Outlook 2007 accessing Exchange 2007 mailboxes are sent with encrypted MAPI submission. This was not the case in previous versions. The Hub Transport can be globally set to check for encrypted MAPI submission through the following cmdlet:

```
>Set-TransportConfig -VerifySecureSubmitEnabled < $true | $false >
```

This value is set to $false by default. If it is set to $true, it will mark messages as "secure" for Outlook 2007 clients and "anonymous" for earlier versions or third-party MAPI providers.

TLS/SSL in Exchange 2007

When Exchange 2007 is installed, it includes a self-signed digital certificate to secure communication between Exchange servers and between clients and the CAS role. The biggest problem with depending on these default certificates is that they have not been issued by a trusted Certificate Authority. As a result, using them will prompt clients with a warning that the certificate does not meet the three validation requirements shown earlier in the chapter.

It is actually possible to trust the default self-signed certificate that installs with Exchange 2007. The default certificate can be exported to the local computer to be saved either in a trusted Certificate Authority or into the personal certificate store of each user on their

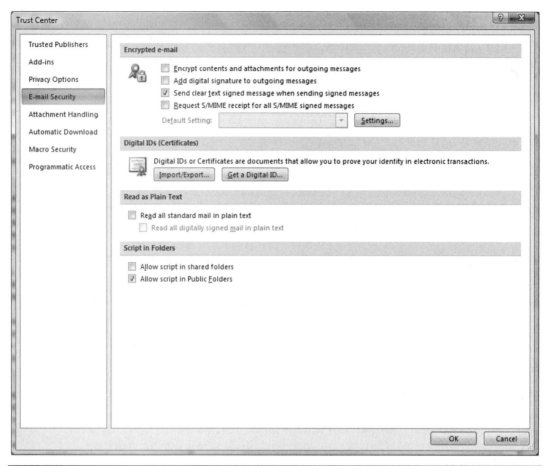

FIGURE 16-11   Outlook 2007 Trust Center's E-mail Security page

local machine. To export the certificate, we first have to obtain its thumbprint. The following command pipes that value to a .txt file, which will appear as shown in Figure 16-12.

```
>Get-ExchangeCertificate -DomainName e2k7-mb-02.virtuecorp.com >>excert.txt
```

FIGURE 16-12   Get-ExchangeCertificate output to obtain a thumbprint

The first thumbprint value is what is needed for the subsequent Export-ExchangeCertificate cmdlet syntax shown next. The Personal Information Interchange (.pfx) file can then be imported to a trusted store. Alternatively, when the clients receive the certificate warning, they can view the certificate and install it manually. Note the Install Certificate button at the bottom of Figure 16-13.

```
>Export-ExchangeCertificate -Thumbprint DE498B71B297BDFC51FB342A1DCCA783E19680CD
-BinaryEncoded:$true -Path c:\certificates\export.pfx -Password:(Get-Credential)
.password
```

Importing the default self-signed certificate into a trusted store for the client allows the use of SSL without acquiring a third-party certificate and eliminates the certificate error they may receive, especially when using a browser accessing OWA over HTTPS. This is not optimal because users may need secure access from multiple workstations, thus creating the need to address the certificate error at each unique workstation or logon prompt.

Securing Outlook Web Access (OWA)

As mentioned, OWA is secured with an optional self-signed certificate by default. This may not be optimal for users on the road accessing OWA on different computers or kiosks. For this reason, a trusted third-party-issued certificate or a PKI is a better solution.

FIGURE 16-13
Viewing certificate details

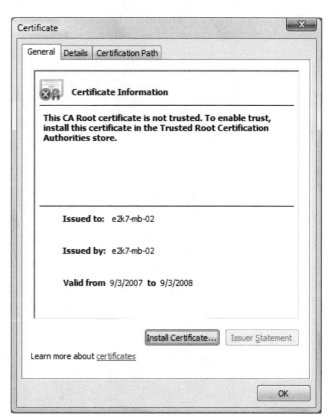

Outlook Web Access can use different authentication types. By default, OWA uses Forms-Based Authentication (FBA) and SSL. FBA provides the most security. It stores the username/password combination in an encrypted cookie. This allows Exchange to monitor timeout values for OWA and end the session after a set time is reached.

Windows Integrated Authentication requires a Windows operating system and Internet Explorer. Basic Authentication is supported across all browsers and will likely serve the OWA Light users on Safari on Mac OS X and Firefox on Linux.

OWA is configured to use SSL by default. This is reflected in Internet Information Service (IIS) Manager. Navigate to Default Web Site in the IIS Manager and right-click the Default Web Site where the Exchange virtual directories are hosted and select Properties from the context menu. Under the Directory Security tab, select the Edit button in the Secure Communications area. Figure 16-14 identifies the check box to require SSL for OWA client access.

Using a valid certificate from a trusted authority will eliminate the certificate error warnings when OWA is accessed.

Using the properties from the Default Web Site forces the use of SSL for the entire website of virtual directories. Alternatively, the same security option is available for each of the virtual directories beneath, should the administrator want to secure them individually.

Securing POP3 and IMAP4 with TSL or SSL

If your clients need Post Office Protocol v3 (POP3) or Internet Messaging Access Protocol v4 Rev1 (IMAP4) services through Microsoft Exchange, it is recommended that you secure this communication and authentication. SSL is easily implemented to secure client access with

FIGURE 16-14
IIS Manager's
Secure
Communications
dialog box

Client Access Protocol	Standard Port	Port with SSL
POP3	110	995
IMAP4	143	993

TABLE 16-3   Default Client Access Ports Used for POP3 and IMAP4 with and without SSL

these classic protocols, either with the EMC or through the EMS. Transport Layer Security (TLS) for POP and IMAP is new to Exchange 2007.

By default, accessing POP or IMAP from the client with SSL connects to a different port. These ports are outlined in Table 16-3. It is also possible to restrict access to port 110 and 143 and thus force SSL only.

Assuming you are at least a member of the Local Administrators group and a member of the Exchange Server Administrators group, you can use the EMC and navigate to the Client Access object under Server Configuration. From here, select the POP3 and IMAP4 tab. Highlight the protocol to secure with SSL and select Properties in the Actions pane. The process is the same for POP3 as it is for IMAP4. In the Authentication tab, enter the X.509 certificate name, as shown in Figure 16-15, and click Apply. In the same tab,

FIGURE 16-15
Configuring an
X.509 certificate in
the Authentication
tab

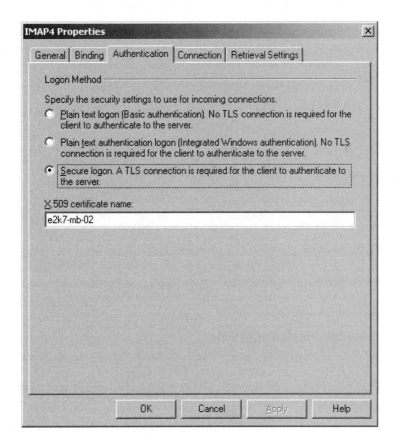

PART V

you can control the authentication method. You can force the need for TLS by selecting Secure Logon as the Logon Method setting. The Plain Text option does not provide any security. Plain Text Authentication Logon uses secure ports for authentication, but does not secure traffic.

In the EMS, POP3 and IMAP4 are managed with the Set-PopSettings and Set-ImapSettings cmdlets. To apply an SSL certificate to POP3 access on the Client Access Server, enter the following in EMS:

```
>Set-PopSettings -server <servername> -X509CertificateName <certificatename>
```

The logon method can also be configured using EMS, as follows:

```
>Set-ImapSettings -server <servername> -LoginType <PlainTextLogin |
PlainTextAuthentication | SecureLogin>
```

This command is for IMAP4, but again, the same syntax would apply for POP3, only the cmdlet would be Set-PopSettings.

SP1 *Service Pack 1 adds administration of POP3 and IMAP4 settings through the Exchange Management Console. This includes configuring SSL for those protocols.*

In both cases, the client protocol service on Exchange must be restarted before the SSL certificate can be used. This can be done directly in the Services console accessed through the Administrative Tools menu, or just as easily done through the command line, as follows:

```
>net stop MSExchangePOP3

>net start MSExchangePOP3
```

Both POP3 and IMAP4 can be configured to use nonstandard ports for authentication. This is configured only through the EMS, as follows:

```
>Set-ImapSettings -UnencryptedOrTLSBindings <IPaddress>:<Port>
```

Again, the service must be restarted to take effect:

```
>net stop MSExchangeIMAP4

>net start MSExchangeIMAP4
```

Microsoft recommends securing all client access, which includes POP3 and IMAP4 with SSL.

Securing Microsoft ActiveSync

ActiveSync supports three different authentication types, each with its own benefit and level of security. Basic Authentication is the simplest, with passwords being sent in plain text. Basic Authentication is enabled by default, but administrators should disable it unless they need it and have SSL in place.

Certificate-based authentication follows the same requirements as we outlined for the PKI implementation. There is a public and private key pair with an X.509 certificate issued by a trusted source properly named with a valid date. Not all mobile devices can use certificate-based authentication with Exchange, so it might be a good idea to verify mobile clients can still authenticate with this protocol.

Token-based authentication is called *two-factor authentication*. It requires a "key" on the connecting device. This key token may be software- or hardware-based. The token is an additional layer of authentication in the form of a physical device. Also a software application is typically required to administer this third-party authentication solution.

ActiveSync is really a different protocol from HTTP. Yet, as a web application, ActiveSync access is secured in a manner similar to Outlook Web Access. ActiveSync is its own virtual directory under the Default Web Site in IIS called Microsoft-Server-ActiveSync. Just like OWA, the requirement for SSL can be applied just to the ActiveSync virtual directory or to the Default Web Site above it.

If Basic Authentication is in use in particular, SSL should be enforced because passwords are being transmitted in plain text.

Securing Outlook Anywhere

Outlook Anywhere, formerly known as *RPC over HTTP(S)* is controlled using the RPC virtual directory in IIS. This directory was created when the RPC over HTTP Proxy Windows component was installed. As mentioned in chapter 7, Installing Exchange Server 2007, the RPC over HTTP Proxy component is a prerequisite for Outlook Anywhere (OA). It typically represents client access external to the network and is dependent on DNS. Outlook 2007 clients will try to connect to one of the following two URLs for the Autodiscover service:

https://www.virtuecorp.com/Autodiscover/Autodiscover.xml

https://Autodiscover.virtuecorp.com/Autodiscover/Autodiscover.xml

Outlook Anywhere cannot use the default self-signed SSL certificate; it must use a certificate issued by a trusted authority. An SSL certificate is installed in the CAS server through the certificate request and import process outlined earlier in the chapter. From there, SSL is enforced though the IIS Manager using the Properties page of the /rpc virtual directory.

Authentication options are Basic and NTLM. The latter is favored, but should be tested because not all firewalls will be able to pass that authentication through. ISA 2006 will handle it exceptionally, of course. Enforcing SSL is the same as we witnessed in OWA and ActiveSync through the /rpc virtual directory properties, as shown in Figure 16-16.

Outlook Anywhere is disabled by default and requires creation by those intending to use it. Outlook Anywhere can be enabled in the EMC by selecting the Server Configuration container and the Client Access node. The command to enable Outlook Anywhere is on the right in the Actions pane shown in Figure 16-17. You can also right-click the server where you want Outlook Anywhere enabled, and that option will appear in the context menu. Confirmation that OA is enabled will take us to the Application Event log, where the MSExchange RPC over HTTP Authconfig will report Event ID 3003 confirming that Outlook Anywhere has been updated.

FIGURE 16-16
Configuring SSL for
Outlook Anywhere
in IIS Manager

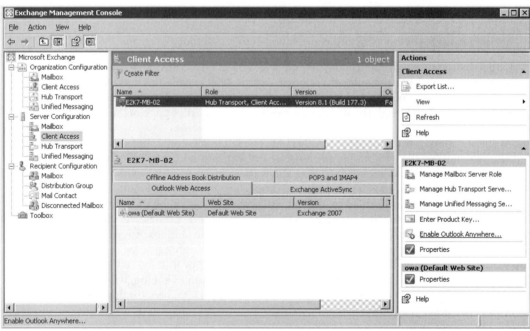

FIGURE 16-17   Enabling Outlook Anywhere in the EMC

Server-to-Server Connection	Authentication	Encryption
Hub to Hub	Kerberos	TLS
Edge to Hub	Direct Trust	TLS
Edge to Edge	Certificate (Anon)	TLS
Mailbox to Hub	NTLM/Kerberos	RPC encryption
Hub to AD	Kerberos	Kerberos
EdgeSync	Basic	LDAPS

TABLE 16-4   Server-to-Server Data Path Security Types for Exchange 2007

Server to Server

All server-to-server communication in Exchange 2007 is encrypted by default. Again, the self-signed certificate implemented at installation is used to secure SMTP traffic between Hub Transport servers using the Internet standard TLS. Communication occurs between other roles in Exchange also, especially when they exist on separate server systems and each seems to have its own specific authentication and encryption mechanism. Table 16-4 identifies the methods of securing server-to-server communication specific to which server components are participating.

Mutual and Opportunistic TLS

When Exchange 2007 connects with another SMTP server over port 25, it checks for the published SMTP command STARTTLS. At this point, Exchange will automatically initiate a secure session with that server. STARTTLS is an SMTP extension that Exchange uses as well, so mutual TLS is possible with other servers. This also increases the security of messaging because communication is secured whenever possible.

Summary

Both client access and server-to-server e-mail traffic are secured by default in Exchange 2007. Transport Layer Security (TLS) and Secure Sockets Layer (SSL) using X.509 certificates, form the basis for most of the secure communication in the Exchange organization. Exchange can make use of its self-signed certificate or use a PKI or trusted Certificate Authority for its certificates. In addition, Microsoft provides complementary applications that further expand and protect Exchange services.

CHAPTER

Anti-Spam

Spam has emerged as a major threat to messaging security over the past few years. To a large extent, this is facilitated by the fact that e-mail applications and standards, including Simple Mail Transfer Protocol (SMTP), were not written with spam or security in mind. In the early days of e-mail, getting messages delivered reliably was more of a concern than spam.

The earliest reported Internet e-mail that can be called spam is attributed to a message sent by Gary Thuerk at Digital Equipment Corporation (DEC) in 1978 to all ARPANet addresses on the West Coast, to announce a new DEC-20 computer. The sharp reaction it drew back then is no different from how most recipients react to spam today (refer to "Reaction to the DEC spam of 1978" at http://www.templetons.com/brad/spamreact .html), except for the fact that most spammers have mastered the art of remaining anonymous and untraceable, and are therefore beyond censure or punishment for most part. Nevertheless, it would not be incorrect to say that spam was practically nonexistent back then.

What Is Spam?

Spam, or junk mail, is also known by its quasi-legal name of *Unsolicited Commercial Email (UCE)*. It is e-mail that you get unsolicited. Typically, you do not have any relationship—as that of a customer, a vendor, or a subscriber of a mailing list or newsletter—with the sender. Spam is usually commercial in nature—offers for pills that can do wonders for your, ahem… health, as well as offers to sell insurance, to make a lot of money working part-time, to get the women of your dreams, or to claim millions of dollars left by some corrupt and now deceased Nigerian government official you would have never otherwise had the opportunity to know or hear from. They might even offer software products that will rid your computer of spyware—or even eliminate spam!

What about e-mail that is not commercial in nature—messages from religious or political groups and charities? Or ones detailing personal tragedies and asking for donations? According to the Controlling the Assault of Non-Solicited Pornography and Marketing Act of 2003, popularly known as the CAN-SPAM Act, such messages are not considered spam. Users and administrators of messaging systems may not agree with that legal definition of what constitutes spam, promulgated by U.S. senators Conrad Burns and Ron Wyden, the co-authors of the CAN-SPAM Act.

Unlike spam received in your mailbox, which requires a postage stamp for delivery, spam delivered by e-mail offers the added benefit of a disproportionately low cost, and certainly does not impose the incremental costs of spam sent by snail mail. An e-mail can be sent to a thousand recipients just as easily as it sent to a single recipient, with very little additional effort or cost involved. Additionally, the costs do not differ whether the spam is sent from a computer next door or from the other side of the planet, from a different continent.

The Problem

The problem is, the volume of spam received by mail servers has surpassed, by far, the volumes of legitimate e-mail. High volume of spam delivered to users' Inboxes impacts their productivity, as they spend valuable time sorting it from legitimate e-mail—or what an esteemed ex-colleague of mine likes to call "ham."

For mail system administrators, spam aggravates the problem of resource consumption—it takes more resources in terms of bandwidth, computing, and storage to receive more e-mail, to inspect messages, filter them, and to store what doesn't get filtered.

False Alarms

In addition to resource consumption and lost productivity of users, spam-fighting techniques bring additional problems with them—those of false positives and false negatives. Users want to receive as little spam as possible and cannot be blamed for not wanting to receive any, but they do not want a single valid message to be filtered out by spam-fighting techniques and filters. A valid e-mail being classified as spam—known as a false *positive* in anti-spam jargon—upsets many users disproportionately. For most users, and certainly so for business users, each piece of e-mail is valuable communication. False positives can potentially result in loss of business or damage customer relationships.

The challenge then is to stop as much spam from reaching a user's mailbox, without the risk of blocking legitimate messages.

The other challenge posed by spammers is their continuing innovation! Spammers come up with new methods and techniques for spamming almost as quickly as the anti-spam industry—I use this term to refer to vendors making anti-spam products as well as messaging system administrators dealing with the problem—comes up with new ways to filter or reduce spam. No single method, technique, or technology remains consistently effective in fighting spam for a long time.

Intelligent Message Filter

After the release of Exchange Server 2003, Microsoft felt the need to include some form of content-filtering mechanism in Exchange. Their answer was to release a free add-on for Exchange called Intelligent Message Filter (IMF). Never meant to be a complete anti-spam solution in itself, nor intended to provide any kind of competition to third-party anti-spam products, IMF became synonymous with Exchange Server's response to spam. Though many Exchange administrators were quick to point out its shortcomings (of which there were many), it became popular in smaller Exchange shops by the sheer virtue of its price tag ($0.00).

While discussing the anti-spam features in Exchange Server 2003, it is important to note that IMF is one of the many anti-spam filtering mechanisms in that version, which together provided a multilayered capability to combat spam.

An updated version of IMF became a part of Exchange Server 2003 Service Pack 2, with some minor user interface changes and the consequent addition of some new functionality via later hotfixes and Registry changes. Conspicuous by its absence was a whitelisting feature common to most anti-spam products, which allows adding a list of SMTP addresses or domains from which e-mail should not be filtered. Although a few third-party utilities stepped in to fill the void by providing such additional functionality, the anti-spam features in Exchange Server 2003 were little more than a reasonably good version-1 product and came up woefully short in comparison to most third-party anti-spam solutions.

Anti-Spam in Exchange Server 2007

Exchange Server 2007 brings a bonanza of anti-spam features that make it much more feature-rich and comparable to many third-party offerings. Many folks equate anti-spam with Intelligent Message Filter, and consider the anti-spam features in Exchange Server 2007 as nothing more than another version of IMF. It is important to consider the breadth and depth of these new anti-spam features—and if you do, I am fairly certain you will come to a different conclusion.

Before we get into the specifics of different anti-spam agents, a brief note about two features that make a lot of difference in how administrators and users work with anti-spam agents. Both of these features are related to reporting and determining the status of a message—how can an administrator or a user tell why a message showing up in the Inbox or the Junk Mail folder ended up there? And why were the ones that did not make it to the mailbox blocked?

The answer to the former question is provided by inserting anti-spam X-headers in a message. Message headers can be viewed easily in Microsoft Outlook and in Outlook Web Access (the Exchange Server 2007 version). Many administrators who have dealt with the convoluted procedures for making MAPI properties such as Spam Confidence Level (SCL) visible in Outlook will call this feature life-changing! By looking at the message header, a user or an administrator can determine which filters acted on a message, and why it was delivered to the Inbox or Junk Mail folder.

The anti-spam headers include a Spam Confidence Level (X-MS-Exchange-Organization-SCL:), Phishing Confidence Level (X-MS-Exchange-Organization-PCL:), SenderID (X-MS-Exchange-Organization-SenderIDResult) headers, and a comprehensive anti-spam report header (X-MS-Exchange-Organization-Antispam-Report:), which provides detailed information such as the versions of anti-spam signature (DAT) files used (see Figure 17-1). More details about anti-spam stamps can be found at http://technet.microsoft.com/en-us/library/aa996878.aspx.

The other important feature is the agent log, which is where actions taken by Exchange Server 2007's anti-spam agents are logged. Administrators can search and filter the agent log based on senders, recipients, IP addresses, and a number of other parameters (and combinations thereof) to determine the status of a message. This is particularly useful when troubleshooting mail flow to figure out if a message was ever received by Exchange or if it was indeed received but got devoured by anti-spam filters.

With the knowledge that both these features provide the required visibility into Exchange Server 2007's anti-spam functionality, let's move on to the anti-spam agents.

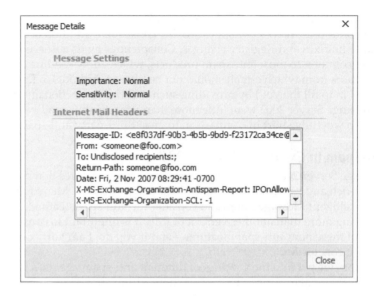

FIGURE 17-1
An anti-spam
stamp in a
message header

Exchange Server 2007 anti-spam agents are implemented as transport agents that act on SMTP connections and messages at different points in the lifecycle of an SMTP session. We'll take a look at these agents to understand their behavior.

Anti-Spam Features in Exchange Server 2007

Exchange Server 2007 expands on the multilayered approach to fighting spam that was first seen in Exchange Server 2003. The components of this multilayered system include the Connection Filtering agent, Content Filter agent, Sender ID agent, Sender Filter agent, Recipient Filter agent, and Protocol Analysis agent. Additionally, attachment blocking functionality is provided by the Attachment Filtering agent exclusive to Edge Transport servers.

The anti-spam agents are installed on Exchange Server 2007 servers running the Edge Transport server role. These can be installed on Hub Transport servers using the install-antispamagents.ps1 script, found in the Scripts folder in the Exchange Server 2007 install path (by default, this is C:\Program Files\Microsoft\Exchange Server\).

NOTE *Installing anti-spam agents on Hub Transport servers is only recommended in topologies where the Edge Transport server role is not deployed. In topologies with the Edge Transport server role, these typically serve as the gateway or entry point for inbound Internet e-mail. Performing messaging hygiene functions at the gateway is more efficient and provides the most benefit because a large proportion of messages are dropped there, thus shielding upstream mail servers from having to process them.*

After the anti-spam agents are installed successfully on a Hub Transport server, you can see the Anti-spam tab in the Organization Configuration | Hub Transport node in the Exchange Management Console (EMC). You can also verify the installation by using the

Get-TransportAgent command from the shell. It lists all the transport agents installed on a Hub Transport server, including anti-spam agents.

TIP *The Get-TransportAgent command works against a particular transport server and displays the agents installed and their priority on that transport server. When you view the anti-spam agents in the EMC's Anti-spam tab, the organization-wide configuration of those agents is displayed. Agents enabled or disabled from the Anti-spam tab are enabled or disabled throughout the organization. In the shell, this is the equivalent of using the corresponding Set command for a particular agent (such as Set-ContentFilterConfig) and setting it to $disabled. When an agent is disabled organization-wide and is active on a particular transport server, it continues to fire but does not take any action on messages. For more information, read the post titled, "Why Get-TransportAgent doesn't agree with the Exchange console," at http://exchangepedia.com/blog/2007/07/why-get-transportagent-doesnt-agree.html).*

Though at first it is easy to get confused by these multitude of agents and how they interact with the SMTP transport, if you visualize a typical SMTP session, you can see these different agents getting plugged into the transport and acting on the messages in a logical order. Before we get into the agents' interaction during message flow, it is important to understand what each agent does. Pointers have been provided to help you understand where in the message flow each agent acts within the explanation of each agent's functioning.

Connection Filtering Agent

An SMTP session is initiated by a sending SMTP host, called an SMTP *client*—even though the sending host may actually be a computer running a server operating system and SMTP *server* software, it is acting as an SMTP client when sending a message to another SMTP host (known as an SMTP *server*). An SMTP client creates a TCP connection to an SMTP server on the well-known TCP port (port 25).

If we can determine the authenticity of a connection, or how desirable it is to let a particular SMTP client connect, we can quickly decide whether the client should be allowed to connect or if it should be disconnected immediately, thereby avoiding any resource utilization by continuing the conversation. This is the job of the Connection Filtering agent.

One cannot underscore the importance of connection filtering enough. Given that a single SMTP client can deliver tens or hundreds of messages during a connection, this becomes the first line of defense—and perhaps one of the most important ones—against spam. Stopping that connection, if we are certain about the connecting client's intent of spamming or otherwise indulging in "inappropriate behavior," helps us avoid the tens or hundreds of messages that the client may end up sending us if it were to successfully establish that connection and proceed with message delivery.

The Connection Filtering agent makes these decisions based on IP Allow and Block Lists, IP Block List Providers, and IP Allow List Providers.

IP Block List

The IP Block List is an administrator-configured list of IP addresses that are known to be sources of spam, malicious code/viruses, or connections from which may not be desirable for other reasons.

NOTE In addition to the manually entered IP addresses or ranges, IP Block Lists also get populated dynamically by the Sender Reputation filter, discussed later in this chapter.

One can compare it with the Global Deny List used by the Connection Filter in Exchange Server 2003, but the IP Block List has three major differences:

- The Global Deny List is *global*—it applies to all SMTP virtual servers in the Exchange organization that have connection filtering enabled. Exchange Server 2007's IP Block List is *local* in scope—each transport server has its own list, which only impacts that particular server. Entries on the IP Block List are not propagated to or otherwise applied to all transport servers.

- Connections from IP addresses listed on the IP Block List are not disconnected immediately, which is a major change in behavior from that of the Global Deny List. (More about this change in the following paragraphs.)

- The other major difference is that entries on the IP Block List have a *life*—they can be expired, allowing you to block connections for a particular period of time. This is helpful when you're working with IP addresses that may need to be blocked temporarily, as the Sender Reputation agent does.

To add an IP address to the IP Block List using the console, follow these steps:

1. Expand Server Configuration.
2. Select Hub Transport to display Hub Transport servers.
3. From the center pane, select the Hub Transport server to which you wish to add the IP address or range to be blocked.
4. Click the Anti-spam tab.
5. Select IP Block List.
6. From the Actions pane, click the Properties shortcut to display the properties pages (alternatively, right-click IP Block List to select Properties from the context-sensitive menu).
7. On the Blocked Addresses tab, shown in Figure 17-2, click the Add button.
8. You can add a single IP address (for example, 1.2.3.4) or a block of IP addresses. For example, to add an entire range of IP addresses, from 192.168.1.1 through 192.168.1.255, type **192.168.1.0/24**. The /24 notation states the number of bits used by the subnet mask, which in this case is 255.255.255.0.
9. Optionally, you can set an expiration time for the entry. Connections from the IP address or range will be allowed after the expiration time. The dialog box displays the expiration time, if one is entered, and its current state—whether active or not.
10. Click OK twice to close the IP Block List properties.

SP1 In Exchange Server 2007 RTM, IP Block List and IP Accept List can be configured from the Anti-spam tab in the Organization container, thus contributing to the perception about the scope of these lists being global or organization-wide. In SP1, this has been moved to the Servers container, thus making it clear these are configured per server.

FIGURE **17-2**
Adding an IP
address to the
IP Block List

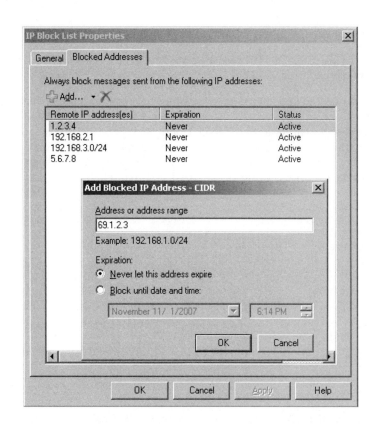

By default, IP addresses entered manually in the IP Block List configuration are set to never expire. However, under the hood, the expiration time for such entries is set to 12/31/9999 3:59:59 PM (as is evident from the ExpirationTime field in the output provided by the Get-IPBlockListEntry command).

To add an IP Block List entry from the shell, use the following command:

```
add-IPBlockListEntry -IPAddress 192.68.3.1
```

Here's how to add a range of IP addresses:

```
add-IPBlockListEntry -IPRange 192.168.3.0/24
```

And here's how to get the list of IP addresses or IP ranges on the IP Block List:

```
get-IPBlockListEntry
```

To restrict the list of IP addresses or ranges on the block list to those manually entered by an administrator, use this command:

```
get-IPBlockListEntry | where {$_.IsMachineGenerates -eq $false}
```

This can be further filtered to those entries that have not expired:

```
get-IPBlockListEntry | where {$_.IsMachineGenerated -eq $false -and
$_.HasExpired -eq $false}
```

It's critical to understand how Exchange Server, or more specifically a Receive Connector, behaves when a connection is made from an IP address that is listed on the IP Block List. As pointed out earlier in the chapter, Connection Filtering in Exchange Server 2003 immediately terminates sessions originating from IP addresses on the Global Deny List. Exchange Server 2007 not only allows the connection to be made and a HELO/EHLO handshake to occur, it waits for the MAIL command before responding with the following error:

```
550 5.7.1 External client does not have permissions to submit to this server
```

One often-heard complaint from many Exchange administrators about Connection Filtering in Exchange Server 2003 is the fact that there is no record of a connection dropped because it was listed on the Global Deny List. Not terminating a session upon connection allows such attempts to be logged, providing the much needed visibility to administrators.

However, the SMTP session is in fact kept alive, resulting in a condition where further attempts to send messages over that session can be made—although each one is greeted with a similar 5.7.1 response.

The preceding 550 response text can be configured by using the following command:

```
set-IPBlockListConfig -StaticEntryRejectionResponse "Your custom rejection
message"
```

Removing an IP Block List entry   An entry on the IP Block List can be easily removed using the EMC or the Exchange shell. When you remove an entry using the shell, the Remove-IPBlockListEntry command does not use the IP address or range to identify the entry. Each entry gets a unique numerical ID, which can be listed using the Get-IPBlockListEntry command and used in the Remove-IPBlockListEntry command, as seen in the following command:

```
 [PS] C:\>Get-IPBlockListEntry | select identity,iprangeIdentity     IPRange
 --------                                -------
1                                        216.22.18.153
181                                      192.168.2.10
```

The following removes the IP Block List entry:

```
Remove-IPBlockListEntry -identity 181
```

Or simply:

```
Remove-IPBlockListEntry 181
```

Tracking Messages Blocked by IP Block List   Exchange Server 2007 maintains an agent log that keeps track of actions taken by anti-spam agents. More details about the agent log can be found later in this chapter. For now, let's take a look at how to determine which senders were blocked by entries on the IP Block List. This is done using the Get-AgentLog command, which parses the agent log:

```
Get-agentog -StartDate "11/2/2007 6:00 am" | where {$_.agent -eq
"Connection Filtering Agent" -and $_.Reason -eq "LocalBlockList"}
```

This command provides a list of all messages blocked by the Connection Filtering agent because the sender's IP address was listed on the IP Block List. The agent log can be filtered using a number of different parameters, covered later in this chapter.

Disabling the IP Block List   The IP Block List functionality is part of the Connection Filtering agent and is enabled by default. The agent can be disabled on a particular transport server, but doing so also prevents other functionality provided by it—namely IP Allow List, IP Block List Providers, and IP Allow List Providers.

You can disable IP Block List functionality for the entire organization. This is done from the Anti-spam tab in the EMC or by using the following command from the shell:

```
Set-IPBlockListConfig -Enabled $false
```

IP Allow List

The IP Allow List feature works like the IP Block List, except it allows connections from IP addresses in the list. The behavior is similar to the Global Accept List in Exchange Server 2003—IP addresses listed here bypass anti-spam filters, including Connection Filtering's IP Block Lists, IP Block List Providers (a.k.a. "RBLs," which we'll discuss shortly), SenderID Filter, Content Filter, and Sender Reputation.

The IP Allow List should only be populated with trusted IP addresses belonging to senders such as customers, partners, vendors, and so on, that are trusted. It provides protection from IP addresses of senders being listed on RBLs, and otherwise having any of Exchange's anti-spam filters categorize e-mail originating from them as spam.

NOTE   *If an IP address appears on both the IP Allow List and the IP Block List, the IP Allow List gets preference. Messages from a listed host will be accepted even if the IP address is listed in the IP Block List or inadvertently gets listed on an RBL.*

To add an IP address or IP range to the IP Allow List using the EMC, follow these steps:

1. Expand the Server Configuration node and select Hub Transport.
2. From the details pane, select the Hub Transport server.
3. Select the Anti-spam tab.
4. Select IP Allow List.
5. In the Actions pane, select the Properties link to open the properties pages for the IP Allow List (or alternatively, right-click IP Allow List and select Properties from the context-sensitive menu).
6. Select the Allowed Addresses tab and click Add.
7. Add the IP address or range.

NOTE   *Unlike IP addresses added to the IP Block List, entries on the IP Allow List cannot be configured to expire.*

8. Click OK to add the IP address.

9. Click OK to close the IP Allow List Properties dialog box.

Here's how to add an IP address to the IP Allow List using the Exchange shell:

```
Add-IPAllowListEntry -IPAddress 192.168.3.10
```

To remove an IP address or IP range from the IP Allow List, we use the numerical identity of an entry that we used to remove entries from the IP Block List, instead of the IP address or range:

```
Remove-IPAllowListEntry -identity 185
```

The IP Allow List can be disabled for the entire organization using the EMC—the procedure is similar to the one described earlier for disabling the IP Block List. To disable IP Allow List using the shell, use the following command:

```
Set-IPAllowListConfig -enabled $false
```

The IP Block List and IP Allow List are administrator-defined lists. The IP Block List is also populated by the Sender Reputation filter, discussed later in this chapter. As any manually populated lists go, these lists come with the burden of having to manually manage them.

Next, let's take a look at what can be thought of as dynamic versions of these lists, which provide the benefit of offloading this function to third-party providers—the IP Block List Providers and IP Allow List Providers.

IP Block List Providers

IP Block List Providers, also known as Realtime Block Lists (RBLs) or DNS-based Block Lists (DNSBLs), provide a valuable service to messaging system administrators by maintaining DNS zones that list IP addresses that are known sources of spam, open proxies or open relays, compromised hosts, or hosts with dynamic IP addresses. Many RBLs are free to use, and configuring them involves little more than configuring Exchange to query the provider's DNS zone(s).

NOTE   *Exchange Server 2007 Management Tools—the console and the shell—use the term* IP Block List Providers *for RBLs/DNSBLs. In this chapter, these terms are used interchangeably—all three terms refer to providers of DNS-based Block Lists, where a mail server or MTA looks up a DNS zone maintained by the provider using a mechanism similar to the command-line utility* nslookup.

IP Block List Providers work differently from IP Block Lists. IP Block Lists are explicitly populated with IP addresses that are determined to be sending spam or otherwise belong to sources that you would rather not receive SMTP connections from (the process is initiated by an administrator). In case of IP Block List Providers, this is at the discretion of the provider. There are times legitimate senders may get listed in RBLs for a number of reasons. Also note that connections from IP Block Lists are disconnected after a few attempts and do not proceed beyond the MAIL command, whereas connections from IP addresses listed by IP Block List Providers are not. In fact, the behavior of Connection Filtering when IP addresses are listed by Block List Providers is to keep the connection alive and reject a message after the RCPT command is received.

The Exception List   Inspecting the recipient of a message in the RCPT command allows Exchange to look up a list of SMTP addresses that can still receive messages, even if the sender is listed by an IP Block List Provider. Take the postmaster address, for instance. You want to be able to provide sending domains a way to notify you that they have been listed (perhaps wrongly so in some cases) by an IP Block List Provider. This is facilitated by adding the postmaster's SMTP address—for example, postmaster@yourdomain.com—in the Exception List. Not only is this recommended for the postmaster address, it is in fact required by SMTP, according to RFC 2821.

There may be other addresses you want to receive messages for, even if the sender is listed by a IP Block List Provider—for instance, sales@yourdomain.com, info, and so on. If you do decide to do this, make sure you understand the implications—these addresses will be susceptible to receiving a higher amount of spam.

It is highly recommended that you add the postmaster and other such addresses to the Exception List before you configure a single IP Block List Provider.

To add SMTP addresses to the Exception List from the Exchange Management Console on an Edge Transport server, follow these steps:

1. Expand the Organization Configuration node and select Hub Transport.
2. In the details pane, go to the Anti-spam tab.
3. Right-click IP Block List Providers, select Properties, and click the Exceptions tab.
4. Click the Add button.
5. Click OK to close the properties dialog box.

In environments where no Edge Transport server exists and you are running anti-spam agents on the Hub Transport server(s), you can get to the Anti-spam tab by clicking the Hub Transport node.

To add an SMTP address to the Exception list using the Exchange Management Shell, use the following command:

```
Set-IPBlockListProviderConfig -BypassedRecipients postmaster@yourdomain.com
```

Multiple SMTP addresses can be added by using a comma as a separator:

```
Set-IPBlockListProviderConfig -BypassedRecipients postmaster@yourdomain.com,
sales@yourdomain.com
```

To get a list of SMTP addresses that are on the Exception list for IP Block List Providers, use the following command:

```
Get-IPBlockListProviderConfig | select BypassedRecipients
```

With our critical SMTP addresses safeguarded from IP Block List Providers, we can proceed with configuring the IP Block List Providers we will use. Before we do this, a word about IP Block List Providers.

Evaluating IP Block List Providers   Plenty of these providers offer their services for free, or a minimal charge. Before you decide to use one, investigate the reputation of those you are considering. Determine how they function and the reasons why they list an IP address. Is the listing merely based on the fact that someone complained, perhaps by entering an IP address on their web page, stating that it was a source of spam? Or does the provider follow any processes or have formal guidelines for listing IP addresses? Put yourself in the shoes of the victim—a sender with an IP address that is listed by one of these providers. What are the procedures to determine why your IP address is listed? How can you remove your IP address(es) from their list? Is it as simple as filling out a form on their website, asking them to remove your IP address(es)?

Expert opinion ranges from strong support for the concept of RBLs to a strong dislike and contempt for them. The downside of using RBLs, according to many experts, is the fact that you are denying messages based on someone else's judgment (the RBL provider's) about which IP addresses you should accept messages from—and more importantly, which ones you shouldn't. This makes the selection and testing of RBLs a very important part of planning, the importance of which cannot be understated.

The flip side of the argument is, you can in fact drop large amounts of spam by using RBLs. Some experts report dropping as much as 85% of spam based on RBLs. If you fear you may drop some legitimate mail because a valid IP address—perhaps belonging to an important customer or vendor—may be listed, mechanisms are in place to address that concern as well.

My personal experience strongly favors using RBLs. Have I used RBLs that may have listed a legit address, inadvertently or for a reason? Yes, but such instances have been infrequent and do not outweigh the high percentage of spam that is in fact blocked by using RBLs.

Once you are reasonably certain that the provider is reputable and follows reasonable practices for the listing and delisting of IP addresses, and you understand the response codes the provider returns for the different reasons an IP address is listed, you can proceed in configuring Exchange to use the provider.

Configuring Exchange Server 2007 to Use Real/External IP Block List Providers   In production, rather than setting up your own RBL or exclusively relying on an internal one, you are more likely to rely on third-party organizations that provide this service, many of which do a great job of listing sources of spam. What's more, many of these RBL services are provided for free!

You will need to select the IP Block List Providers you want to use and then configure them. Some of the popular providers are UK-based Spamhaus.org (www.spamhaus.org), Spam and Open Relay Blocking System (SORBS), NJABL (short for "Not Just Another Bogus List"; www.njabl.org). You can use the search engine of your choice to look for more providers. A directory of such providers can be found at http://www.dmoz.org/Computers/Internet/E-mail/Spam/Blacklists/.

Visiting the provider's website should get you the required information—the DNS lookup zone (or zones) of providers, the response codes, and the reasons these codes map to. Here's a list of some of the zones Spamhaus maintains:

- **sbl.spamhaus.org**   Lists "direct UBE sources, verified spam services, and ROKSO spammers," and uses the response code 127.0.0.2. ROKSO is Spamhaus's Register of Known Spam Operations. According to Spamhaus, these are known spam operations based on their information and evidence. This register includes spammers that have had their Internet services terminated by at least three ISPs for spam offenses. Spamhaus claims these senders are responsible for sending 80% of the spam to users in North America and Europe.

- **xbl.spamhaus.org**   This zone lists hosts that have been detected with "illegal third-party exploits, including proxies, worms, and trojan exploits." It also includes hosts on abuseat.org's Composite Block List (cbl.abuseat.org) and NJABL's list of open proxies. It uses the codes 127.0.0.4–127.0.0.6, where the response code 127.0.0.4 is returned for hosts listed on abuseat.org's CBL and 127.0.0.5 is returned for hosts listed on NJABL's list of open proxies.

- **sbl-xbl.spamhaus.org**   This zone combines hosts listed on the SBL and XBL. Using fewer IP Block List Providers reduces the number of queries your server sends to look up such providers. Using combined zones such as SBL-XBL ensures you can look up hosts listed in both the SBL and XBL zones by sending a single DNS query.

Configuring IP Block List Providers   Next, we configure Exchange to look up an IP Block List Provider. Here are the steps to follow:

1. In the Anti-spam tab on your Exchange server, right-click IP Block List Providers and select Properties.
2. Go to the Providers tab and click the Add button.
3. Enter a name for the IP Block List provider (for example, MyRBL or E12Labs MyRBL).
4. In the Lookup domain field, type the DNS zone name (for example, myrbl.e12labs.com).
5. In the Return status code section, you need to decide whether you will drop messages listed in the RBL for any reason, or just particular response codes such as 127.0.0.2 that map to a particular reason why a given IP address is listed. For this example, we will use a particular response code—127.0.0.2.
6. Select the option Match specific mask and responses.
7. In the field Match to any of the following responses, type **127.0.0.2** and click the Add button.
8. You can customize the error message a host listed in your RBL will get when trying to send a message to a recipient on your server. This is done by clicking the Error messages… button and selecting Custom Error Message in the IP Block List Provider Error Message dialog box.

FIGURE 17-3
A custom IP Block
List Provider error
message

Custom error messages can list the particular IP Block List Provider on which the sender's IP address is listed, as shown in Figure 17-3. You can additionally provide instructions to contact the postmaster address in your domain if the IP address is wrongly listed by the IP Block List Provider (this is the address we entered in the Exception List).

This provides the postmaster or mail administrator from the sending domain away to contact you on the postmaster address to inform you of the fact. The logic is, if you believe the sender is legitimate, you can add the sending IP address to the IP Allow List, bypassing the listing on a third-party IP Block List Provider.

For the purpose of this test, enter the following as the custom error message:

Your IP address %0 is listed on %2. If you need to send legitimate e-mail to this domain, please contact postmaster@e12labs.com

Click OK to close the Error Message dialog box.

9. Click OK to exit the Add IP Block List Provider dialog box (see Figure 17-4).

From Exchange Management Shell, this can be achieved by using the following command:

```
Add-IPBlockListProvider "E12Labs MyRBL" -LookupDomain myrbl.e12labs.com -
AnyMatch:$false -IPAddressMatch 127.0.0.2 -RejectionResponse "You are
listed on MyRBL.e12labs.com"
```

As you have seen, you can add IP Block List Providers easily from the console or the shell. The information you need to have from a provider includes their DNS lookup zone, their response codes (you need to determine the ones you want to block), and optionally any custom error message text you may want to use.

Testing IP Block List Provider Configuration   To test whether your IP Block List Provider configuration is working, and whether a given IP address is listed in a particular provider's zone, use the following shell command:

```
Test-IPBlockListProvider "E12Labs MyRBL" -IPAddress 192.168.1.10
```

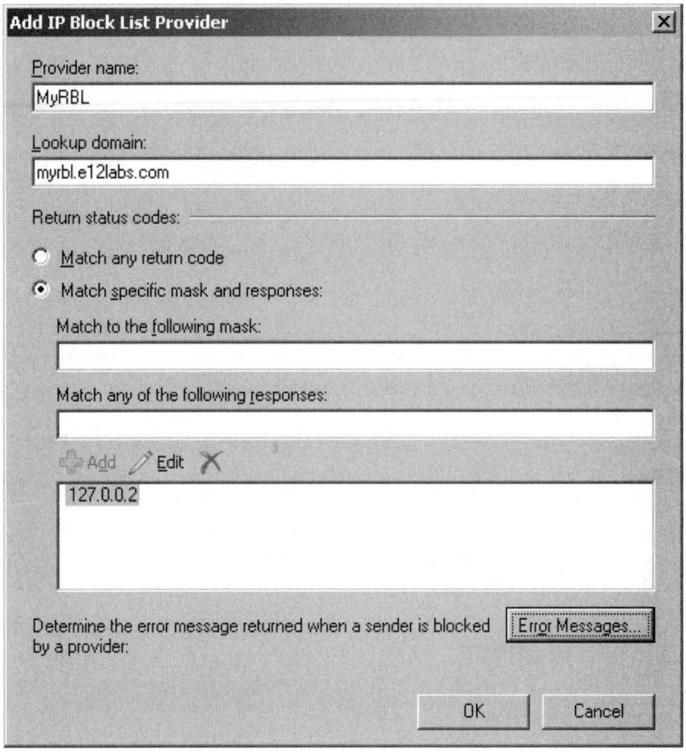

FIGURE 17-4
Add IP Block List
Provider dialog box

FIGURE 17-4
Add IP Block List
Provider dialog box

In this command, E12Labs MyRBL is the name of your IP Block List Provider, and the IP address 192.168.1.10 is the one you want to check. The command returns the name of the provider, a Matched value (which is True if an IP address is found to be listed, and False if it is not), and the ProviderResult, which provides the response code that the IP Block List Provider returns (in this case, it is 127.0.0.2).

Statistics, Reporting, and Monitoring   Once you start using IP Block List Providers, you should periodically check how they are performing. From time to time, you may need to determine why a particular message was blocked or which IP Block List Provider listed a particular IP address. This section lists some shell commands and scripts that will help you accomplish this.

To determine the number of messages blocked by each RBL provider, Microsoft has provided the Get-AntispamTopRBLProviders.ps1 script. This script resides in the *Exchange Server*\\Scripts folder, where *Exchange Server* is the directory in which Exchange Server 2007 was installed. To use this, fire up the Exchange shell, go to the \\Scripts directory, and issue the following command:

```
get-antispamtoprblproviders.ps1
```

The script outputs a list of the top 10 RBL providers with the messages blocked by each.

To determine why a particular message may have been blocked, use the following command:

```
get-agentlog | where {$_.IPAddress -eq "192.168.2.10"}
```

Here, 192.168.2.10 is the IP address of the sending host. The command outputs a list of all messages sent from IP address 192.168.2.10 that the anti-spam agents may have scanned and acted on.
Next, here's how to get a list of all messages blocked by RBL providers:

```
get-agentlog | where {$_.Reason -eq "BlockListProvider"}
```

To get a list of all messages blocked by a particular RBL provider (for example, E12Labs MyRBL), use the following command:

```
get-agentlog | where {$_.ReasonData -eq "E12Labs MyRBL"}
```

As with many shell commands, you can constrain the search from a particular start date to a particular end date. Further, you can limit your search by using fields in the agent log, such as Recipients, P1FromAddress, P2FromAddress, Agent, Event, Action, SmtpResponse, Reason, ReasonData, and so on.

Performance Counters
Performance of the Connection Filter can be monitored using the object MSExchange Connection Filtering agent.

IP Allow List Providers
IP Allow List Providers work similar to IP Block List Providers, except they *allow* connections from IP addresses listed by the DNS zones of the Allow List Provider.
Unlike IP Allow Lists, which will let the sending host bypass Connection Filtering and Content Filtering, IP Allow List Providers are looked up after IP Block Lists are applied. If an IP address exists on the IP Block List, it will be blocked regardless of whether it appears on a provider's IP Allow List. However, an IP Allow List Provider does have preference over the IP Block List Provider. The Connection Filtering Agent follows the following order: 1) IP Allow List 2) IP Block List 3) IP Allow List Provider 4) IP Block List Provider. Action is taken based on the first list in which the IP address match is found.
The configuration of IP Allow List Providers is not much different from that of IP Block List Providers, with one minor difference. When configuring IP Block List Providers, you can add a rejection response. Because IP Allow List Providers do not block messages, no response is required.

Internal SMTP Servers and Connection Filtering
Although it's easy to assume all messaging environments where Exchange is or will be deployed consist of Exchange servers only, the most common topologies in enterprise and most mid-size environments are the ones where Exchange servers sit behind one or more

layers of non-Exchange SMTP hosts that may act as SMTP gateways (a.k.a. *relay hosts* or *smarthosts*) and perform messaging hygiene (anti-spam/antivirus) or take policy-based actions such as archiving messages.

Another trend has been that of deploying security appliances that provide robust antivirus and anti-spam functionality. Appliances such as Ironport and Barracuda come to mind when talking about such plug-and-play functionality. Smaller organizations with network device or service limitations, or availability of IT resources, commonly rely on their Internet service providers (ISPs) to route inbound mail.

In any of these cases, Exchange does not directly accept inbound Internet mail from Internet senders. MX records in the organization's external DNS zones do not point to an Exchange server.

Each SMTP host that a mail message passes through adds a Received header that consists of the host's Fully Qualified Domain Name and IP address.

When inbound Internet mail is received by one or more trusted gateway hosts, you need to tell Exchange about these gateways.

SP1 *In SP1, Transport Settings can be configured using the EMC. If you are using the RTM version of Exchange Server 2007, you will need to use the shell to perform this task.*

To add internal SMTP servers to Exchange's Transport Settings using the EMC, follow these steps:

1. Expand the Organization Configuration node and select Hub Transport.
2. Select the Global Settings tab and select Transport Settings.
3. In the Actions pane, click the Properties link (or right-click Transport Settings and select Properties from the context-sensitive menu).
4. Select the Message Delivery tab.
5. Click the Add button under Enter the IP Addresses of internal SMTP servers....
6. Enter an IP address or a range of IP addresses for the internal SMTP servers, as shown in Figure 17-5.
7. Click OK to add the IP address(es).
8. Click OK to close the Transport Settings Properties dialog box.

To add internal SMTP servers using the Exchange shell, use the following command:

```
Set-TransportConfig -internalSMTPServers 1.2.3.4, 1.2.3.5, 1.2.3.6
```

This allows Exchange to apply Connection Filtering and SenderID filters by parsing SMTP message headers and being able to ignore the internal SMTP hosts. The external hosts that deliver a message can thus be identified.

NOTE *The term internal SMTP hosts is used loosely here to describe SMTP hosts that may actually be on the internal network, reside on a perimeter network, or belong to a third-party service provider.*

PART V

FIGURE 17-5
Adding internal
SMTP servers to
Transport Settings

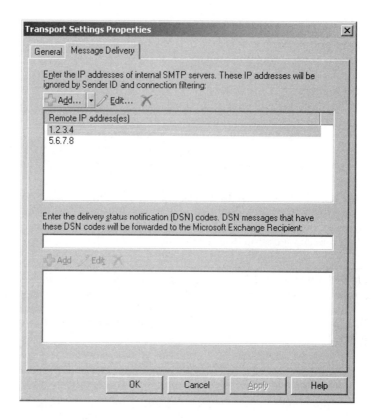

Sender Filtering

Having navigated through Connection Filtering's IP Allow List, IP Block List, IP Allow List Providers, and IP Block List Providers, the message now passes the Sender Filter. In an SMTP session, this occurs after the MAIL command. If the sender's SMTP address or domain is found on the Sender Filtering list, the message is rejected by default. The sending host gets the following error:

```
554 5.1.0 Sender Denied
```

To add an SMTP address to Sender Filtering's list of blocked senders from the EMC, follow these steps:

1. On the Anti-spam tab, right-click Sender Filtering.

2. On the Blocked Senders tab, click the Add button.

3. In the Add Blocked Senders dialog box, shown in Figure 17-6, the default selection is Individual e-mail address. Leave this selected.

4. Type the sender's SMTP address in the edit box (for example, foo@somedomain.com).

FIGURE 17-6
Adding blocked
senders (by
domain)

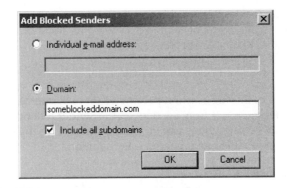

NOTE *To add a domain, first select Domain and then add the domain (for example, somedomain. com). To block the domain and all its subdomains, check Include all subdomains.*

5. Click OK to exit the Add Blocked Senders dialog box.

6. Click OK to exit Sender Filtering properties.

To add an SMTP address to the Sender Filter list from the shell, use the following command:

```
set-SenderFilterConfig –BlockedSenders foo@somedomain.com
```

NOTE *When you add a domain to Sender Filter, all subdomains of that domain are included. Not only will messages from *@somedomain.com be blocked, but messages from any subdomain (such as *@subdomainA.somedomain.com) will be blocked as well. If you do not intend to do that and want Sender Filtering to apply only to the particular domain, uncheck the box labeled "Include all subdomains."*

To use the shell to add a domain to the Sender Filtering configuration, use the following command:

```
Set-SenderFilterConfig –BlockedDomains somedomain.com
```

To reject messages from a domain and all its subdomains, use this command:

```
Set-SenderFilterConfig –BlockedDomainsAndSubdomains somedomain.com
```

Here's how to get a list of all blocked senders and domains:

```
Get-SenderFilterConfig | Select blocked* | fl
```

By default, Receive Connectors do not block messages from blank senders. This can be enabled by selecting the check box Block messages from blank senders.
To enable rejection of messages from blank senders, use the following command from the shell:

```
Set-SenderFilterConfig –BlankSenderBlockingEnabled:$true
```

The default Sender Filtering action of rejecting messages can be changed so that the messages are accepted but are stamped as being received from a blocked sender. This is done from the Action tab of the Sender Filtering properties or by using the shell, as follows:

```
Set-SenderFilterConfig -Action StampStatus
```

With Sender Filtering's Action parameter set to StampStatus, when the Content Filter agent examines messages from senders on the Sender Filtering list, it takes that fact into consideration when assigning a spam confidence level to the messages. You can read more about the Content Filter agent later in this chapter.

Disabling the Sender Filter

Like most filters, Sender Filtering can be disabled for the entire organization from the EMC. Here are the steps to follow:

1. Expand the Organization Configuration node, select Hub Transport, and then click the Anti-spam tab.

2. Select Sender Filtering.

3. In the Actions pane, click Disable (alternatively, right-click Sender Filtering and select Disable from the context-sensitive menu).

Here's how to disable Sender Filtering using the Exchange shell:

```
Set-SenderFilterConfig -Enable $false
```

Recipient Filtering

As we logically move through the SMTP session, we get to the RCPT command. This is where the sending host specifies a message recipient. Recipient Filtering can be configured to reject messages for recipients for which you do not want to receive external e-mail, including restricted distribution lists that should receive messages only from internal or authenticated senders.

This is done by adding those recipients to Recipient Filtering's Blocked Recipients list. To add a recipient to Recipient Filtering's Blocked Recipients list from the EMC, follow these steps:

1. Expand the Organization Configuration node and select Hub Transport.

2. From the details pane, select the Anti-spam tab.

3. From the Actions pane, select Properties (or alternatively, right-click Recipient Filtering and select Properties from the context-sensitive menu).

4. On the Blocked Recipients tab, check the box labeled "Block the following recipients," as shown in Figure 17-7.

5. Type the recipient's address in the edit box.

6. Click the Add button.

7. Click the OK button to exit the Recipient Filtering Properties dialog box.

FIGURE 17-7
Adding blocked
recipients and
blocking messages
for recipients not
listed in the GAL
using Recipient
Filtering

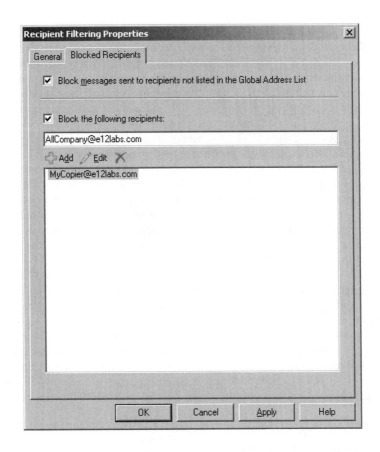

FIGURE 17-7
Adding blocked recipients and blocking messages for recipients not listed in the GAL using Recipient Filtering

To add a recipient to the Blocked Recipients list from the shell, use the following command:

```
Set-RecipientFilterConfig -BlockedRecipients someone@yourdomain.com
```

Here's how to add multiple recipients to the Blocked Recipients list, separated by commas:

```
Set-RecipientFilterConfig -BlockedRecipients
someone@yourdomain.com,someoneelse@yourdomain.com
```

NOTE *You can also prevent a recipient from receiving mail from unauthenticated sources by configuring the recipient's delivery restrictions to require that all senders be authenticated. This setting is available from the EMC in Recipient Properties | Mail Flow Settings | Message Delivery Restrictions, or from the shell by setting the recipient's RequireSenderAuthenticationEnabled property to $true.*

Recipient Validation

The ability to drop messages for nonexistent recipients existed in Exchange Server 2003's Recipient Filter. However, if Exchange does not directly receive inbound e-mail, this functionality cannot be extended to a non-Exchange host that received inbound mail. Exchange can still perform recipient validation and drop messages from nonexistent recipients, but rejecting or dropping most spam at the gateway is more efficient.

Many third-party anti-spam solutions can look up LDAP directories, including Active Directory, for recipients. Exchange Server 2007's EdgeSync feature brings synchronization of recipient info to an otherwise unmanaged mail gateway (in this case an Exchange Server 2007 server with the Edge Transport server role). This allows the Edge server to validate whether recipients exist in an Exchange organization before accepting messages and enables a Receive connector to drop messages for nonexistent recipients. A large proportion of spam received by most messaging systems consists of messages to nonexistent recipients. Rejecting such messages significantly decreases the load on other anti-spam components and on the messaging system in general.

Additionally, SMTP requires that a nondelivery report (NDR) be generated for each message accepted by a messaging system that cannot be delivered successfully. Validating recipients and rejecting messages for non-existent recipients during the SMTP session frees the system from the responsibility of generating NDRs for all such messages, which would have otherwise been accepted and necessitated the generation of NDRs.

To reject messages for nonexistent recipients, select the "Drop messages for recipients not listed in the Global Address List" check box on the Blocked Recipients tab in Recipient Filtering properties. This is the equivalent of the "Drop messages that do not exist in the directory" check box in Recipient Filtering properties in Exchange Server 2003.

To enable recipient validation from the shell, use the following command:

```
Set-RecipientFilterConfig -RecipientValidationEnabled $true
```

Disabling Recipient Filtering

Recipient Filtering can be disabled for the entire organization by following these steps in the EMC:

1. Expand the Organization Configuration node and select Hub Transport.
2. In the details pane, select the Anti-spam tab.
3. Select Recipient Filtering.
4. In the Actions pane, click Disable (or alternatively, right-click Recipient Filtering in the details pane and select Disable from the context-sensitive menu).

To disable Recipient Filtering from the shell, use the following command:

```
Set-RecipientFilterConfig -Enabled $false
```

Here's how to disable blocking of recipients in the Blocked Recipients list:

```
Set-RecipientFilterConfig -BlockListEnabled $false
```

This command disables lookups of the Blocked Recipients list to block messages, while allowing you to continue using recipient validation.

Address Harvesting and SMTP Tarpitting

Spammers use another clever trick to get a list of valid recipients on a messaging system. They send messages to different recipients in a domain, quite frequently using generic recipient names appended with the domain name (for example, john@somedomain.com). There may just as well be other means of receiving such lists of recipients. The messaging system either accepts the message (and nonreceipt of an NDR in such cases may imply that the address is "live") or the sending host may receive an error for a nonexistent recipient, such as the one discussed earlier generated by Recipient Filtering.

Yes, Recipient Filtering does make such attacks, known as address harvesting, easier. The server is freed from the responsibility of generating an NDR for nonexistent recipients, but in the process it provides an immediate response to the sending host about the validity of a given address.

Exchange Server 2007 uses a technique called *SMTP tarpitting* to defend against such attacks. It is quite simple in concept, yet it is one of the more effective ways to deter spammers. The goal is to make it more expensive for spammers to indulge in inappropriate SMTP behavior, including actions such as attempting to send messages to nonexistent recipients. So, let's discuss how this is accomplished.

When an SMTP host attempts to send a message to a nonexistent recipient, Exchange delays the 550 5.1.1 response by a few seconds. This increases the spammers' costs if they persist with such behavior—the time their systems may spend waiting for such responses would result in fewer messages sent. In other words, spammers require more resources to send the same amount of spam.

Fortunately, most spambots (which are scripts or software used by spammers to send mass e-mails) disconnect the session when they encounter such a delay. This results in an effective defense mechanism against address harvesting attacks, and it also reduces the amount of spam received by a messaging system.

However, SMTP tarpitting does come with some costs. On servers with a high volume of traffic, this may result in a higher number of open connections, which consumes more resources on your server. The risk of this happening, however, is quite low. I have not come across a lot of deployments where severe or noticeable performance degradation could be directly attributed to SMTP tarpitting.

The trick is to make this delay just long enough to discourage spammers, but not so long that it affects performance.

SMTP tarpitting was introduced in Windows Server 2003 Service Pack 1. (Note: Exchange Server 2003 uses the SMTP stack provided by IIS.) This requires the creation of a new Registry value to configure the SMTP tarpit delay interval. Exchange Server 2007 Receive connectors are configured for SMTP tarpitting by default. The default TarpitInterval on Receive connectors is five seconds, which is easily modified using the following shell command:

```
Set-ReceiveConnector "Connector Name" -TarpitInterval 00:00:10
```

> **TIP** *In a test environment when you're testing SMTP features, the tarpitting delay can become annoying (except, of course, when you're testing tarpitting itself). Tarpitting can be turned off by setting TarpitInterval to 0 seconds (00:00:00).*

The TarpitInterval value is in hours:minutes:seconds. Although the maximum TarpitInterval is 10 minutes, setting it to anything higher than a few seconds could result in performance issues, as discussed previously. After raising the TarpitInterval, it is generally advisable to observe the server's performance for some time to determine whether the change resulted in noticeable performance degradation. To disable SMTP tarpitting on a Receive connector, set this value to 00:00:00.

Curious to see SMTP tarpitting in action? It's easy to figure out what the sender may experience—simply telnet to the server's SMTP port and send a message to a nonexistent sender.

SenderID Filtering

As discussed earlier in this chapter, when the original standards that define SMTP behavior were written, spam was not foreseen as a major concern. As such, the protocol makes it quite easy to indulge in fraudulent behavior such as impersonating another sender or domain by providing a wrong address in message headers. Because Internet e-mail is exchanged with unknown or anonymous sending hosts that are not authenticated, spammers use the ability to provide nonexistent or incorrect addresses to avoid detection.

The technique—if it can be called that—is known as *spoofing*. Besides spam—which may otherwise be harmless—spoofing is also used by *phishing* messages.

Given that receiving Internet mail involves providing anonymous Internet hosts the ability to send mail without authentication, how can we make it easy to recognize practices such as spoofing? By using the same protocol that is used to direct inbound mail to your mail servers—namely DNS. Just as MX records are used to direct inbound e-mail for a domain to designated mail servers in an organization, we can use a DNS record to state which mail servers are designated mail senders for the domain.

The idea is largely credited to Paul Vixie, the brain behind Berkeley Internet Name Domain (BIND). Meng Wong wrote the specs for Sender Policy Framework (or SPF), now frequently referred to as SPF *classic*. Because no well-known resource record types existed in DNS to specify such information, it was and continues to be published in a text (TXT) record, commonly referred to as an SPF *record*.

SenderID is a combination of Wong's SPF classic and Microsoft's CallerID technology. SPF classic looks at a single field in SMTP message headers—the return-path field.

What Is Phishing?

Phishing is a term used to describe the act of masquerading as well-known or trustworthy organizations, such as banks, other financial institutions, government agencies, and the like, to collect sensitive information such as social security numbers, credit card and bank account numbers, usernames, and passwords. Needless to say, such information is used for identity theft, fraudulent use of credit cards, and other such activities.

E-mail messages are designed to appear as if they originated from the well-known organization, quite possibly one the recipient may recognize or have a customer relationship with, complete with logos, trademark information, and disclaimers in fine print. The recipient is asked to click a link that may appear to be an Internet address (URL) belonging to the well-known organization, and this link redirects the recipient to a web page that's nearly identical to the organization being impersonated. Given that such messages are very cleverly spoofed, and use very official-sounding language and layouts—including logos and other visual elements of known organizations—many recipients inadvertently end up providing valuable personal information.

Microsoft's SenderID uses an algorithm to extract what it calls Purported Responsible Address (PRA) from message headers. This is done by examining the From, Sender, and Resent-From headers in a message. Note that not all of these headers exist in all messages.

Once the original or purported responsible sender is determined, it is fairly easy to perform a DNS lookup query on the sending domain—or rather what is claimed to be the sending domain—and determine the hosts designated by it to send mail on its behalf. If the sending host is not designated by the domain, the message can either be rejected or forwarded to the Content Filter agent, which can then inspect such messages with a higher degree of suspicion.

- **Specifying internal SMTP servers**   As discussed previously in the Connection Filtering section, Exchange servers that are targets of MX records and receive Internet e-mail directly can determine the sending host's IP address easily—it is the same host that connects to your Exchange server and establishes an SMTP session. Exchange servers that are not Internet-facing (or otherwise receive inbound e-mail from a non-Exchange SMTP gateway or relay host) can determine who the external sending host is by examining the Received headers in a message. The list of internal SMTP servers needs to be populated with all the SMTP servers, including non-Exchange gateways and anti-spam appliances that handle inbound Internet mail.

- **Enabling SenderID Filtering**   SenderID Filtering is enabled by default on Edge Transport servers and on Hub Transport servers with anti-spam agents installed. The default action is set to stamp the SenderID status on the message and continue processing the message. No messages are rejected if SenderID lookups fail. The other options are to delete messages silently, without returning an NDR, and to reject messages during the SMTP session.

Understanding SenderID Lookups

When Exchange receives a message from a sender claiming to be from somedomain.com, the SenderID Filter determines the Purported Responsible Address by examining the From, Sender, and Resent From fields in message headers. Once the responsible sender is determined, Exchange performs a DNS lookup for the SPF record of somedomain.com. If an SPF record is published for the domain in that domain's (external or Internet-facing) DNS zone, it can be determined whether the sending SMTP host is authorized to send messages for that domain.

The following table shows the results of an SPF record lookup of a domain:

Status	What It Means
Pass	The sending IP address is permitted to send messages for the domain.
Neutral	The SPF record published in the sender's domain is explicitly inconclusive.
Soft Fail	The IP address may not be in the hosts authorized to send mail for the domain.
Fail	The IP address is not in the hosts authorized to send mail for the domain.
None	No data published in DNS.
Temp Error	Transient error (for example, DNS server unreachable).
Perm Error	Unrecoverable error (for example, error in SPF record format).

When configuring the SenderID Filter to reject or delete messages where the domain is spoofed, messages are rejected or deleted when the SPF record lookup returns a Fail status. In most cases, this means the sender is spoofing the domain/e-mail address.

To configure the SenderID Filter to delete or reject messages using the EMC, follow these steps:

1. Expand the Organization Configuration node and select Hub Transport.

2. Select the Anti-spam tab.

3. Select Sender ID.

4. From the Actions pane, select Properties (or alternatively, right-click Sender ID and select Properties from the context-sensitive menu).

5. From the Action tab, shown in Figure 17-8, select the appropriate action.

6. Click OK to close the Sender ID Properties dialog box.

To configure the SenderID to delete or reject messages using the shell, use the following command:

```
Set-SenderIDConfig -SpoofedDomainAction Action
```

FIGURE 17-8
Setting the spoofed domain action in Sender ID Properties dialog box

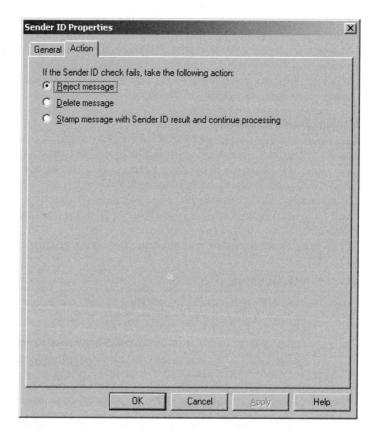

Replace the Action parameter in this command with either Delete or Reject.

Note that when you configure the SenderID Filter to drop or reject messages for spoofed domains, no action is taken if the SPF record lookup fails due to a transient error such as failure of the DNS lookup query. Messages are only dropped when the SPF record explicitly returns a Fail status—in other words, when the sending domain has an SPF record published that does not authorize the sending IP address to send e-mail for that domain.

The SenderID Filter can also be configured to delete or reject messages due to transient or temporary errors, such as the DNS server of the purported sending domain being unreachable. This can only be done from the shell:

```
Set-SenderIDConfig -TempErrorAction Action
```

By default, this is set to stamp the error status on messages and continue processing the messages. It can be set to Delete or Reject.

Bypassing Sender Domains and Recipients

The SenderID Filter can be configured with a list of bypassed domains; no filtering will be performed for such domains. To configure a list of domains to bypass the SenderID Filter, use the following command:

```
Set-SenderIDConfig -BypassedSenderDomains domain1.com,domain2.com
```

Similarly, the agent can be configured to not filter messages for certain Exchange recipients:

```
Set-SenderIDConfig -BypassedRecipients user1@mydomain.com,user2@mydomain.com
```

Disabling SenderID Filter

To disable the SenderID Filter for the entire organization from the EMC, follow these steps:

1. Expand the Organization Configuration node and select Hub Transport.
2. Select the Anti-spam tab.
3. Select Sender ID.
4. From the Actions pane, select Disable.

Here's how to disable SenderID using the shell:

```
Set-SenderIDConfig -Enabled $false
```

Monitoring SenderID

To get a list of messages rejected or deleted by the SenderID Filtering agent, use the get-agentlog command to parse the agent log:

```
Get-AgentLog -StartDate "11/2/2007" | where {$_.Agent -eq "Sender Id Agent"}
```

The resultant output is a list of messages that looks similar to the following example:

```
Timestamp           : 11/2/2007 2:34:28 PM
SessionId           : 08C9E9603BE090F0IPAddress        : 77.233.32.134
MessageId           :
P1FromAddress       : f-foo?mydomain.com-cmtopidhagamtfqxbmclpldldo@bounce.moiler.info
P2FromAddresses     : {sales@quotatank.com}
Recipients          : {me@mydomain.com}
Agent               : Sender Id Agent
Event               : OnEndOfHeaders
Action              : RejectMessage
SmtpResponse        : 550 5.7.1 Sender ID (PRA) Not Permitted
Reason              : Fail_NotPermitted
ReasonData          : sales@quotatank.com
Diagnostics         :
```

Note that the MessageID field in the preceding output is absent. The transport event on which the action is taken is OnEndOfHeaders. The message is rejected as soon as the headers are received, without letting the session proceed to the DATA command. The sender is not allowed to transfer the message payload or content. This means the Content Filter does not need to examine message content.

TIP *SenderID responses for an IP address can be checked via the Test-SenderID command using the PurportedResponsibleDomain. If the HELO/EHLO domain is different, it can be added as an additional parameter (–HelloDomain), as shown in the following example:*

```
Test-SenderID –IPAddress 131.107.115.215 –PurportedResponsibleDomain
Microsoft.com
```

Evaluating SenderID

As great as the concept of SenderID Filtering sounds, expert opinion is divided on its usage, just as it is on the use of RBLs. One of the many objections against SenderID is the fact that it treats SPF v1 records as SPF v2 records—something they were not intended for. Another objection stems from how certain mailing list software or remailers treat messages. Until recently, the way Exchange server itself handled distribution lists when the recipient is external made such messages forwarded by Exchange fail the SenderID check. (Refer to Microsoft KB Article 915863 for more information. The hotfix for Exchange Server 2003 referred to in the article can be requested online or obtained from Microsoft Customer Support Services.)

When evaluating techniques such as SenderID Filtering and its competitors, such as DKIM ("DomainKeys"), it is important to understand that SenderID is not meant to be a technique to fight spam. It is meant to counter spoofing of domains and e-mail addresses. It is quite easy for spammers to publish SPF records for their own domains. However, one of the consequences of preventing spoofing of domains in message headers is reduced spam. Additionally, preventing spoofing does provide protection from phishing, as well as possible identity theft to an extent. For these reasons alone, SenderID deserves serious consideration.

Regardless of whether you decide to use SenderID Filtering to reject or delete messages, publishing SPF records for domains you are responsible for is an easy decision. It helps messaging systems receiving mail from you or a spammer spoofing your domain to make that distinction.

SPF records are TXT (text) records in DNS. Many websites offer free web-based wizards that can help you format SPF records for your domain(s). Use your favorite search engine to look for them. Microsoft's own SPF Record Wizard can be found at the following location: http://www.microsoft.com/mscorp/safety/content/technologies/senderid/wizard/.

The Content Filter

After encountering all the different filtering agents in the course of an SMTP session, a message finally gets submitted to Exchange. This means the DATA portion of the message has been transferred, and Exchange now has access to message content. A large number of messages have possibly not made it to this stage, depending on the other filters you have enabled and what you have asked them to do with messages. This is good news for the Content Filter, because it probably has the hardest part of the job—inspecting the content and making a determination if it is spam or ham.

At its core, the Content Filter agent functions similarly to the Intelligent Message Filter in Exchange Server 2003. It stamps messages with a Spam Confidence Level (SCL) value— the higher the confidence, the higher the probability that a given message is spam. It uses the same SmartScreen technology developed by Microsoft Research to rate messages.

Nevertheless, the Content Filter can be thought of as IMF on steroids. Many user concerns related to usability and functionality have been addressed. Recipients can be bypassed from the filter, and sending domains or SMTP addresses can be added to a whitelist. The filter can be configured with keywords as good or bad words, allowing the CF agent to accept or reject messages based on presence of these good or bad words.

Whereas IMF had only one *gateway* threshold, and one corresponding action to either delete, reject or accept a message, the CF agent comes with three thresholds and gateway actions, allowing it to treat messages with different Spam Confidence Level values with different actions at the gateway—either delete them, reject them, or deliver them to a quarantine mailbox.

IMF's Store threshold is now called the JunkMail threshold. Messages with an SCL value below the JunkMail threshold are delivered to the Junk Mail folder in a user's mailbox.

Configuring Content Filter SCL Thresholds

The Content Filter agent is enabled by default. To configure the gateway thresholds and actions using the EMC, follow these steps:

1. Expand the Organization Configuration node and select Hub Transport.

2. Select the Anti-spam tab.

3. Select Content Filtering.

4. In the Actions pane, click Properties (or alternatively, right-click Content Filtering and select Properties from the context-sensitive menu) to open the property pages.

PART V

FIGURE **17-9**
Configuring SCL
thresholds and
actions

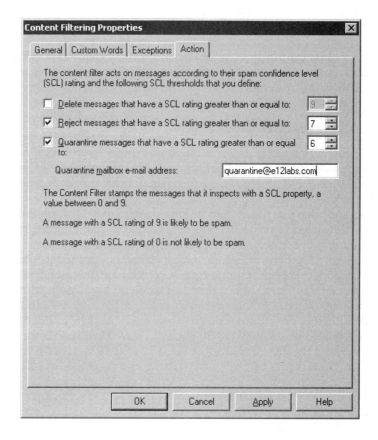

5. On the Action tab, shown in Figure 17-9, select the appropriate gateway actions:

- **Delete messages that have a SCL value rating greater than or equal to** Select this to delete messages higher than a particular SCL value. Enter an SCL value in the corresponding field. Messages equal to or greater than the SCL value entered will be deleted. The sender will not receive any notification of the message being deleted or not delivered.

- **Reject messages that have a SCL value rating greater than or equal to** Select this to reject messages higher than or equal to the corresponding SCL value. Enter an SCL value in the corresponding field. Messages equal to or greater than the SCL value entered will be rejected during the SMTP session. Because the message is never accepted, Exchange is not responsible for sending an NDR for the message. It is the sending server's responsibility to deliver an NDR to the sender.

NOTE *If the Delete action is selected, ensure the Reject threshold is lower than the Delete threshold. If a Quarantine threshold is selected, ensure the Reject threshold is higher than the Quarantine threshold. If the Quarantine threshold is not selected, but a Junk Mail threshold is selected, ensure the Reject threshold is higher than the Junk Mail threshold.*

- **Quarantine messages that have a SCL value rating greater than or equal to**
  Select this to quarantine messages equal to or higher than the corresponding value. Messages will be delivered to the quarantine message (configured in the next step). An administrator with access to the quarantine mailbox can examine messages and deliver them to the original recipient, if required.

NOTE *If the Reject action is selected, ensure the Quarantine threshold is lower than the Reject threshold. If the Reject action is not selected, but the Delete action is selected, ensure the Quarantine threshold is lower than the Delete threshold. Ensure the value is higher than the Junk Mail threshold.*

6. If you selected the Quarantine action and set the corresponding quarantine threshold, enter the SMTP address of the quarantine mailbox.

7. Click OK to close the properties pages.

NOTE *The quarantine mailbox can be an external SMTP address. Quarantined messages will be delivered to the external e-mail address. However, external e-mail addresses will not offer the functionality to inspect messages and deliver them to the original sender, as provided by Microsoft Outlook 2007.*

The Rule of Thumb for the Content Filter   Before you get too confused with the three different thresholds and actions, note that not all three need to be selected. You can select any of the three, or you can select none at all. The ability to have three different actions and thresholds simply provides you more control and the ability to treat messages with different SCL values differently.

The rule of thumb (depending on which actions and SCL thresholds you have selected) is that the Delete threshold should be higher than the Reject threshold, the Reject threshold should be higher than the Quarantine threshold, and the Quarantine threshold should be higher than the Junk Mail threshold.

Junk Mail Threshold   The Junk Mail threshold is configured in organization settings. Messages with SCL values higher than the Junk Mail threshold are delivered to the Junk Mail folder in a user's mailbox. The Junk Mail threshold can be configured using the shell, as follows:

```
Set-OrganizationConfig -SCLJunkThreshold 5
```

NOTE *Unlike the Delete, Reject, and Quarantine actions (the values of which should be equal to or higher than their corresponding threshold), for the Junk Mail action, the SCL value stamped on a message needs to be higher. This is similar to how IMF uses the Store threshold in Exchange Server 2003—the SCL value should be higher than the threshold to make its way to the Junk Mail folder. A tad confusing, for sure—and I cannot help myself from wondering, is this confusingly consistent, or consistently confusing?*

The Quarantine Mailbox   The quarantine mailbox improves on the archiving functionality of IMF, which simply delivered archived messages as files in the UceArchive folder, with no interface to manage them. Messages with an SCL rating higher than the quarantine threshold are delivered to the quarantine mailbox. Quarantined messages are wrapped in an NDR and appear to be from the postmaster address. The NDR wrapper or envelope displays the original message header, but the original sender and recipient(s) are not exposed.

NOTE   *A post detailing how to expose the original sender and recipient of a message can be found at http://exchangepedia.com/blog/2007/05/how-to-expose-original-senders-and_11.html.*

Microsoft Outlook and Outlook Web Access allow you to open the message envelope and click the Send Again button to *release* the message to its original recipient.

TIP   *An administrator or a user can be assigned full mailbox access to the quarantine mailbox, and the mailbox can be opened as an additional mailbox in the administrator's or user's MAPI profile (along with their own mailbox). However, when a message is released from the quarantine mailbox, the message delivered to the original recipient will appear to be sent from the user or administrator who released the message. To ensure the original sender is preserved, do not add the quarantine mailbox as an additional mailbox. Instead, log into the mailbox using a different Outlook profile or Outlook Web Access to release messages.*

Although an existing mailbox (perhaps belonging to an administrator) can be used as a quarantine mailbox when configuring the Content Filter, it is recommended that you create a separate mailbox for this purpose. Additionally, depending on the e-mail traffic in your organization and the quarantine threshold configured, you may see a large number of messages accumulate in the quarantine mailbox. Remember, the quarantine is for the entire organization, not specific to a certain set of users, an Exchange server, or an AD site.

It is important to ensure quarantine messages are not dropped because of issues such as mailbox quotas—messages thus dropped are lost forever.

Monitoring the quarantine mailbox is another management task added to the administrator's list. Unless a user complains about a missing message, it is possible for the mailbox to go unmonitored. To prevent the mailbox from growing to a very large size, collecting messages indefinitely, you can apply a Managed Folder Mailbox Policy to it to automatically archive messages older than a certain number of days.

TIP   *When you receive a user complaint, or when you want to monitor the number of messages delivered to the quarantine mailbox without logging onto the mailbox, use the get-agentlog command to search the agent log, as follows:*

```
Get-AgentLog -StartDate "11/2/2007" | where {$_.Action -eq "QuarantineMessage"} |
ft timestamp,P1FromAddress,Recipients
```

The Exception List   You can configure the Content Filter agent not to filter messages addressed to certain Exchange recipients by adding them to an exceptions list. Recipients' e-mail addresses can be entered on the Exceptions tab in the Content Filter properties.

Here's how to add an address to the exception list using the shell:

```
Set-ContentFilterConfig -BypassedRecipients postmaster@e12labs.com
```

Per-Recipient Content Filter Settings

In addition to exempting a recipient from Content Filtering altogether, individual SCL thresholds can be set on a recipient using the shell. This allows more granular control of how Content Filter settings are applied to messages for a particular recipient. Each Content Filter action—Delete, Reject, Quarantine, and Junk Mail—can be enabled or disabled, and the SCL threshold customized for each. Here's how to configure individual SCL settings on a mailbox using the shell:

```
Set-Mailbox "bsuneja@e12labs.com" -SCLDeleteEnabled $false
-SCLRejectThreshold 7 -SCLQuarantineEnabled $false -SCLJunkThreshold 6
```

TIP *To exempt a recipient from all anti-spam filters, set the recipient's –AntispamBypassEnabled parameter to $true.*

Finally, a Whitelisting Feature

One of the most frequently requested features in IMF—and certainly the most conspicuous by its absence—is the ability to whitelist sender domains and e-mail addresses to avoid false positives. Whitelisting is one of the more basic features offered by most anti-spam solutions. Although many experts prefer not to use whitelists because of the management overhead of manually maintained lists, as well as the potential for misuse given the ease with which SMTP headers can be spoofed, there is an equally large number of messaging systems administrators who would rather avoid blocking a single message from an important customer, partner, or vendor.

Additionally, consider the scenario where a message from a particular sender is blocked by a filter, and after more than a few minutes of troubleshooting, one simply needs to ensure that message flow from a particular sender or domain resumes quickly or continues uninterrupted. Whitelisting becomes a necessity under such circumstances, as a temporary measure to respond to business needs.

Finally, whitelisting has arrived in Exchange's Content Filter, and not a day too soon!

Senders and sender domains can be added to the BypassedSenders and BypassedSenderDomains parameters of the Content Filter configuration. This cannot be done from the EMC. To add bypassed senders and sender domains using the shell, use the following command:

```
Set-ContentFilterConfig -BypassedSenders foo@somedomain.com
Set-ContentFilterConfig -BypassedSenderDomains Microsoft.com,zenprise.com
```

Whitelisted senders get an SCL rating of -1. Yes, 0 is not the lowest SCL rating. Additionally, the anti-spam headers stamped in the messages reveal that Content Filter has been bypassed. Here's the anti-spam header from a message sent by a bypassed sender:

```
X-MS-Exchange-Organization-Antispam-Report:ContentFilterConfigBypassedSender
X-MS-Exchange-Organization-SCL: -1
```

To get the list of whitelisted senders and sender domains, use the following command:

```
Get-ContentFilterConfig | select BypassedSenders,BypassedSenderDomains
```

To get a list of messages where Content Filtering was bypassed, use the following command:

```
Get-Agentlog -StartDate "1/10/2008" | where {$_.Reason -eq "SCL" -and
$_.ReasonData -like "not available*" }
```

Using Custom Words to Control SCL Ratings

IMF v2 for Exchange Server 2003 included the Custom Weighting feature, which allowed an administrator to control the SCL ratings of a message based on keywords found in the subject or body of the message. This is a rudimentary feature found in most third-party anti-spam solutions, but its implementation in IMF v2 left a lot to be desired.

The Content Filter agent allows control of SCL ratings based on keywords. Keywords are added as good and bad words, and the lowest (0) or highest (9) SCL rating is applied to a message based on whether it contains good or bad words. Although it lacks the granular control of IMF v2's Custom Weighting feature, which allowed raising and lowering the SCL rating of a message by a specific value, there is no doubt it scores points for usability—configuring via the EMC or the shell certainly seems a lot more intuitive than creating the XML file–based configuration of IMF v2.

Here's how to add a custom word as a good word or bad word using the shell:

```
Add-ContentFilterPhrase "Project Ex2007TCR" -Influence goodword
Add-ContentFilterPhrase "Work from home" -Influence badword
```

Sender Reputation Filter

If one could track senders based on their SMTP behavior, their pattern of sending good or bad e-mail, and by conducting a number of tests such as a reverse DNS lookup, an open proxy test, and so on, over a period of time, one would start to accumulate enough information about different senders to determine whether they are valid senders or bad guys. This is what Sender Reputation does.

Senders are assigned a Sender Reputation Level (SRL) score from 0 to 9, as shown in Figure 17-10. Think of this as an SCL for an IP address (instead of messages), assigned based on a number of factors, including open proxy tests, examining domains and IP addresses used in HELO/EHLO commands, reverse DNS lookups, and the senders' track record based on SCL ratings assigned to the messages they send. With anti-spam updates enabled, Exchange also gets updates from Microsoft's own Block List and IP Reputation service. Senders with a poor reputation are automatically blocked—Exchange adds them to the IP Block List for a default period of 24 hours.

Yes, this is somewhat like automatically building your own RBL, except instead of adding IP addresses to a DNS zone, Exchange adds them to the IP Block List, for a configurable period of time.

Specific features of the Sender Reputation filter, such as performing open proxy tests, can be disabled. Sender Reputation comes with many configurable parameters. Details about these parameters can be found at http://technet.microsoft.com/en-us/library/bb124975.aspx.

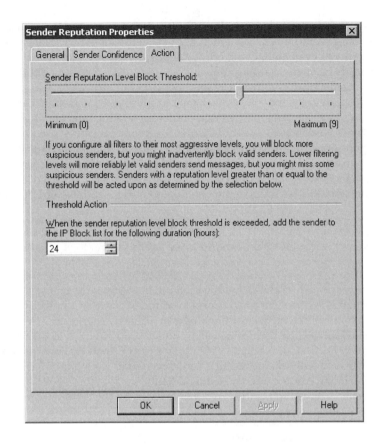

Figure **17-10**
Configuring the
Sender Reputation
Level (SRL)
threshold

To prevent Sender Reputation from blocking senders, use the following command:

```
Set-SenderReputationConfig -SenderBlockingEnabled $false
```

Here's how to get a list of IP addresses blocked by Sender Reputation (by adding them to the IP Block List):

```
Get-IPBlockListEntry | where {$_.IsMachineGenereated}
```

Safelist Aggregation: Reducing False Positives

As discussed earlier in this chapter, users have a very low tolerance for legitimate messages being blocked by a spam filter, also known as *false positives*. Important as it is to reduce the levels of spam users receive in their Inboxes, reducing the number of false positives often becomes the highest priority in most anti-spam efforts. The Safelist Aggregation feature aids significantly in this quest to reduce false positives.

Microsoft Outlook has allowed users to mark senders as safe (or blocked, in addition to safe recipients) since Outlook 2003. The safe and blocked senders lists reside in the user's mailbox, so the mailbox server has access to this information. However, this information has

PART V

been living in isolation from anti-spam filtering performed at the mail gateway or on Transport servers. Only when a message gets to the mailbox server can the safe or blocked senders list be evaluated. Quite often, the decision to block a particular message or sender has already been made at the gateway or on a Transport server, and the message is dropped before the mailbox server has a chance to see it.

Safelist Aggregation allows Exchange to collect the safe sender information from user mailboxes and populate them in Active Directory (AD), thus making this information available for use by the Content Filter. The information can be used by both the Edge Transport server, in topologies where it is deployed, and by the Hub Transport server with anti-spam agents installed. In topologies with the Edge Transport server role deployed, the Safe Senders list is replicated to the Edge Transport server as part of EdgeSync synchronization. This reduces the potential for false positives significantly.

TIP Even though safe senders are replicated to Edge Transport servers as part of EdgeSync, an Edge Transport server role is not required to use Safelist Aggregation. It can also be used by Hub Transport servers with anti-spam agents installed.

One reason why Safelist Aggregation can help you reduce false positives without any user action is the fact that the contacts residing in a user's Contacts folder in their mailbox are automatically trusted. Additionally, every time a user sends an e-mail to an external recipient, that recipient's address can be added automatically to the Safe Senders list when this option is selected in Microsoft Outlook's Junk E-mail Options, as shown in Figure 17-11. Exchange recipients, including all external recipients for whom a MailContact object has been created in AD, are also trusted by default.

Safelist Aggregation is triggered manually using the Update-Safelist command. By default, it pulls users' Safe Senders lists:

```
Update-Safelist-Type (SafeSenders | SafeRecipients | Both) -InludeDomains
```

A few considerations before you open the shell and type Update-Safelist:

- Using the Update-Safelist command for the first time may generate significant network and AD replication traffic. Without any additional parameters or filtering, it processes all users in the Exchange organization. However, it can be run against a particular user or number of users. It's a good idea to perform this in batches of a few users at a time, during off-peak hours. For instance, we can get mailboxes on one Exchange server or mailbox database, or all members of a distribution group, and run Update-Safelist only for those users, as shown in the following examples:

```
Get-Mailbox -Server E12Postcard | Update-Safelist
Get-MailboxDatabase "E12Postcard\SG4\E12Postcard-SG4-Mbx" |
Get-Mailbox | Update-Safelist
Get-DistributionGroupMember "USWest-Sales" | where {$_.RecipientType
-eq "UserMailbox"} | Update-Safelist
```

- For subsequent use, the Update-Safelist command can be set to run automatically on a schedule. If the command is not run, users' SafeSenders lists will not be automatically updated.

FIGURE **17-11**
Contacts are
automatically
trusted as "safe
senders" by
Microsoft Outlook

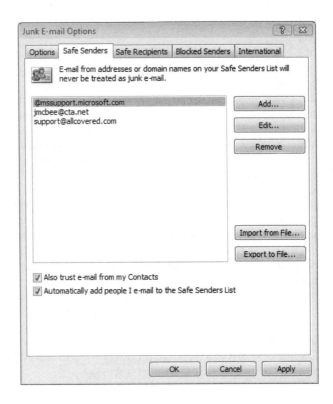

NOTE *More details about scheduling the Update-Safelist command to run automatically can be found at http://technet.microsoft.com/en-us/library/aa998280.aspx.*

- Update-Safelist does not include SafeRecipients by default. SafeRecipients can be included by using the –type switch with the value set to either SafeRecipients or Both. However, it makes little sense to do so, because the Content Filter agent ignores the SafeRecipients.

- In Exchange Server 2007 RTM, Safelist Aggregation also adds *safe domains*—these are domains users mark as safe in Microsoft Outlook. However, given that users can inadvertently mark entire domains as safe, including those of large service providers, this leaves them vulnerable to receiving large amounts of spam from such domains. In SP1, safe domains are not included unless explicitly specified via the –IncludeDomains switch.

After the initial processing of the Safe Senders list is complete and then updated on a regular basis, you should see a significant reduction in false positives. Over a period of time, you should survey users to determine their perception, particularly if false positives plagued your anti-spam implementation before implementing Exchange Server 2007 and Safelist Aggregation.

PART V

> **Greylisting**
>
> Greylisting is a technique similar to SMTP tarpitting. However, instead of a delay being
> introduced only when an SMTP client indulges in inappropriate behavior, all
> connections are subjected to the greylisting treatment—by dropping the connection
> when a new combination of an SMTP client IP address, sender, and recipient are
> encountered. The logic is that most spammers will not try sending the message again.
> Valid SMTP hosts will retry sending their message.
>
> After the message is dropped, a greylisting agent adds the triplet (sending IP
> address + sender + recipient) into a database. The next time an SMTP host retries
> sending the message with the same sender and recipient, the triplet will already exist in
> the database, resulting in acceptance of the message.
>
> Most messaging system administrators who use greylisting report a dramatic drop
> in the levels of spam—some reporting a drop as high as 80% to 90% attributed to this
> technique. Like tarpitting, greylisting increases the cost to spammers because each
> message with a new combination of sending host IP address/sender/recipient needs to
> be retried. If they have not done so already, spammers may find workarounds and
> adjust to this technique over a period of time.
>
> Exchange Server 2007 does not ship with native support for greylisting out of the
> box. The Exchange Server 2007 Software Development Kit (SDK) does include the code
> for a greylisting agent. The code needs to be compiled and the compiled agent installed
> on Exchange Server 2007 Transport servers. If you plan to use the agent code provided
> in the SDK, make sure it is tested in a production environment before you install the
> compiled agent on production Transport servers.

Managing the Agent Log

As mentioned earlier in the chapter, Exchange Server 2007 anti-spam agents log actions
taken in the agent log, which by default resides in the Exchange Server install path
(C:\Program Files\Microsoft\Exchange Server, by default) in \TransportRoles\Logs\
AgentLog. Logs are purged after 30 days, or when the size of the AgentLog directory
reaches 250MB.

In Exchange Server 2003 RTM, there are not many configuration options for the agent
log itself, except the ability to disable it. This is done by modifying the EdgeTransport.exe
.config file located in the \Bin directory in the path where Exchange is installed. Exchange
Server 2007 SP1 adds the ability to control maximum file and directory size, as well as the
maximum age of agent log files.

The agent log can be parsed using the get-agentlog command. It parses the agent logs
residing in the default location. If agent logs are archived to an alternate location, these can
be parsed by adding the –location parameter with the path where the archived agent logs
reside, as shown in the following command:

```
Get-AgentLog -Location "Z:\Antispam Agent Logs"
```

Get-AgentLog searches all the agent logs residing in the default path (or the path
provided using the –location parameter). Parsing a large number of agent logs accumulated

in the path can take a long time. The Get-AgentLog command can be constrained to a particular start date and time, and optionally an end date and time:

```
Get-AgentLog -StartDate "1/2/2008"
Get-AgentLog -StartDate "1/2/2008 7:00 am" -EndDate "1/2/2008 2:00 pm"
```

Here's a sample entry returned by the agent log:

```
Timestamp : 1/2/2008 12:39:49 AM
SessionId : 08C948C83FB951AC
IPAddress : 72.46.133.113
MessageId :
P1FromAddress : ret@noncornelan.com
P2FromAddresses : {}
Recipients : {foo@yourdomain.com}
Agent : Connection Filtering Agent
Event : OnRcptCommand
Action : RejectCommand
SmtpResponse : 550 5.7.1 Recipient not authorized, your IP has been found
on a block list
Reason : BlockListProvider
ReasonData : Spamhaus SBL-XBL
Diagnostics :
```

The agent log can be searched using these fields. Let's take a look at a few examples. To search by sending IP address, use the following command:

```
Get-AgentLog -StartDate "1/2/2008" -EndDate "1/3/2008" | where
{$_.IPAddress -eq "72.46.133.113"
```

To search by sender:

```
Get-AgentLog -StartDate "1/2/2008" -EndDate "1/3/2008" | where
{$_.P1FromAddress -like "ret@noncornelan.com" -or $_.P2FromAddress
-like "ret@noncornelan.com"}
```

To search messages for a particular recipient:

```
Get-AgentLog -StartDate "1/2/2008" -EndDate "1/3/2008" | where
[$_.Recipients -like "foo@mydomain.com"}
```

To search messages acted upon by a particular agent:

```
Get-AgentLog -StartDate "1/2/2008" -EndDate "1/3/2008" | where
{$_.Agent -eq "Content Filter Agent"}
```

To search messages with a particular SCL:

```
Get-AgentLog -StartDate "1/2/2008" -EndDate "1/3/2008" | where
{$_.Agent -eq "Content Filter Agent" -and $_.ReasonData -eq "8"}
```

PART V

To search by a particular SMTP response code:

```
Get-AgentLog -StartDate "1/2/2008" -EndDate "1/3/2008" | where
{$_.SmtpResponse -like "550 5.7.1*"}
```

These should give you a fair idea of how the agent log can be searched using different parameters. Explore the different fields and values logged in the agent log by different agents to understand the search parameters and values to use.

The agent log, in addition to the anti-spam headers stamped in messages, provides much needed visibility into the actions taken by the anti-spam agents. The Exchange shell provides the necessary flexibility in searching and parsing the logs in different ways to meet different needs—whether you're troubleshooting and looking for a single message for a particular recipient or reporting on actions taken by particular anti-spam agents.

In addition to the agent log, the Scripts folder in the Exchange Server install path has many useful scripts for reporting on anti-spam activity, such as Get-AntispamSCLHistogram .ps1, Get-AntiSpamTopBlockedSenderDomains.ps1, and so on. Explore these scripts and the reports they provide.

Summary

Exchange Server 2007 provides vastly improved messaging hygiene features that work together to provide a multilayered defense against spam. Although individually many of the features may not be as mature or provide all the functionality provided by third-party anti-spam solutions, together they provide a very attractive option to third-party solutions without any additional cost.

VI
PART

E-mail Continuity

Backup, Restore, and Disaster Recovery

In a survey commissioned by Postini, a leader in anti-spam and antivirus e-mail protection (now owned by Google), 98% of the CEOs and IT professionals surveyed said that e-mail was just as mission-critical to them as the telephone. When you consider that 15 years ago interoffice memos were still being typed on typewriters and distributed to physical inboxes on peoples' desks, e-mail has replaced both the means of transporting critical information and the storage of that data in almost every public and private sector. Few business and agencies would argue that data in their e-mail system is not critical. Especially now that the line between the telephone and e-mail communications is becoming narrower and narrower. The tolerance for system outages and data loss related to messaging system problems is steadily disappearing, if not altogether gone. It is not surprising to see a small business, with limited mail usage, identify the need to make their messaging system highly available. Larger organizations start with the premise that their messaging systems will be highly available and strive to design their systems to meet their requirements. Microsoft has provided the means to back up and restore Exchange since version 4.0. In the 1990s, Exchange backup and restore procedures constituted the majority of a disaster recovery plan. Today, these procedures have evolved and are faster and more dependable, but are only a part of the overall process of maintaining an Exchange organization. The events of 9/11 and Hurricane Katrina—and the data losses that ensued— elevated the awareness of our dependencies on electronic data. Many businesses simply closed their doors for business permanently after these events because they were unable to recover from their losses.

Numerous improvements have been made that make preemptively maintaining and rapidly recovering Exchange easier in each subsequent release. Exchange 2007 comes with an unprecedented amount of features and tools specifically for operational continuity and high availability. Part VI of this book provides you with the information you need to implement Exchange to meet your organization's e-mail continuity requirements. Chapter 18 details backup and restore procedures. Chapter 19 details the latest high-availability features: Local Continuous Replication, Cluster Continuous Replication, and Standby Continuous Replication. Chapter 20 details the maintenance, monitoring, and optimizations procedures that will allow you to proactively protect your servers from failures and minimize outages when they do occur. Chapter 21 details the tools, methods, and resources that allow you to successfully troubleshoot an Exchange organization.

Backups

The least common denominator in a disaster recovery plan is the backup. Backups provide the first level of operational continuity. The technology that is employed by an organization to back up and restore Exchange data has a far-reaching effect on the overall design of Exchange 2007. Therefore, the decision you make on how you back up Exchange should be made before you deploy Exchange 2007. All other data storage and disaster recovery procedures will follow. The Exchange administrator must ensure that decision makers (management) understand that the critical data and the associated backup of that data go beyond the mail stores. It is the responsibility of an organization to not just safeguard the mailbox data, but all Exchange related data and the various servers they reside on.

Critical Exchange Data

Exchange 2007 is composed of five distinct roles. Each role has unique configuration data that is critical to its function. The Mailbox role and Transport role servers also store critical e-mail data. Additionally, Exchange 2007 has a dependency on Exchange data stored in Active Directory. In order to recover Exchange 2007, you must be able back up all critical data. In Figure 18-1 you can see the various data types that are critical to the Exchange organization.

The following sections provide the data types for each server role and the location where the data is stored. All the data listed is critical to Exchange servers. The data locations should be monitored for performance and security. Microsoft installed all the server-side

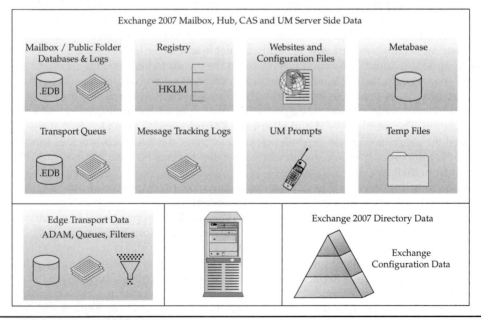

FIGURE 18-1 Exchange 2007 critical data

data into the C:\Program Files\Microsoft\Exchange Server\ directory by default. Any changes to the paths will need to be documented for disaster recovery planning.

Client Access Servers

The Client Access Server role has a default configuration that facilitates Outlook Web Access and Mobile clients' connectivity to mailboxes. But the Client Access Server (CAS) performs other critical functions. Features such as Autodiscover, ActiveSync, IMAP4, and POP3 are also part of the Client Access Server's configuration.

Mailbox Servers

Although the configuration data for a mailbox server stored in Active Directory is critical to the Mailbox server role, it is not the most important data on that server. Unlike the other server roles, the most important information on a server with the Mailbox role is the users' mailbox and, if they are used, public folder data. When a mailbox server is being designed, care is taken to design the disk storage so that databases and transaction logs are stored on separate disk volumes for performance and availability. For more information on Exchange 2007 storage and the Mailbox server role, see Chapter 6. The same care should be taken to design the Exchange backups to project the users' data. The physical location of the mailbox data affects the backup solutions available for you to choose from. Make sure you are aware of not only the critical data paths, but also the storage technology. For example, if you are storing the databases and transaction logs on a storage area network (SAN), you will need specific knowledge in order to configure the SAN. Even the RAID controllers for direct-attached storage (DAS) have complex features that must be understood in order to properly configure them.

Hub Transport Servers

The default configuration of a Hub Transport server role will allow Exchange 2000, 2003, and 2007 servers to process and transport messages within an organization. Although there is a Queue database on the Hub transport, the data is deleted from the database as soon as the transport has completed relaying the message to the appropriate destination. Administrators who are carefully monitoring Hub Transports may additionally have Message Tracking logs and Protocol logs stored on the Hub Transports.

Edge Transport Servers

The Edge Transport default configuration allows SMTP hosts to relay messages securely to the Internet. The Edge Transport is typically configured to receive all mail from the Internet on behalf of one or more SMTP domains. It can obtain its configuration from Hub Transport servers and maintain a synchronized LDAP directory with Active Directory (AD). However, the Edge Transport server role is the only role that does not store its configuration in Active Directory. Because it is designed to exist as a standalone e-mail security solution, it is not technically part of the Exchange organization. This isolation is intentional and allows the server to exist in less-secure environments such as a network's demilitarized zone (DMZ). Understanding where and how the data is stored on an Edge Transport can help you keep it secure.

The Edge Transport shares the same transport stack with the Hub Transport, so you can see the same file system structure for the Queue database and transaction logs. Message tracking and protocol logs can also be enabled and monitored by administrators. The Edge Transport differs from the Hub Transport in a few ways when it comes to data storage.

For example, content filtering is enabled by default (optional on the Hub Transport). The most significant difference in data storage is the ADAM (Active Directory Administrative Mode) directory database.

Unified Messaging Servers

The Unified Messaging server role's default configuration will not allow voicemail to flow to mailboxes in Exchange 2007. A significant amount of customization is required for the Unified Messaging server role. This translates into a greater need to document and ultimately back up the custom configurations. The custom voice prompts created for your organization reside on the Unified Messaging server as well as the actual voicemail items as they are being processed. They are kept in a temp directory until they can be delivered to the intended recipient.

Active Directory Domain Controllers

Although Active Directory domain controllers are not technically Exchange 2007 servers, they are the Exchange 2007 directory servers. With the exception of the Edge Transport server role, every Exchange 2007 server stores and retrieves its configuration information on domain controllers. The schema defines what you can and can't create in the directory. Exchange 2007 Setup extends the schema with the objects and attributes used by Exchange 2007. The Domain partition stores users, contacts, distribution groups, and other recipient objects. The Configuration partition stores all other Exchange 2007 configuration data.

For more information on protecting Exchange 2007 data and specific details on the data paths, see http://technet.microsoft.com/en-us/library/bb124780.aspx.

Backup Solutions

When you hear the word *backup*, what comes to mind? Is it different from the way you thought of backups 5 years ago? 10 years ago? How about 20+ years ago? Some big advances have been made in storage technology that have changed the face of backup solutions (see Figure 18-2).

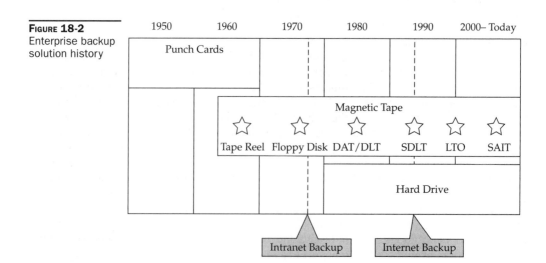

Figure 18-2 Enterprise backup solution history

Admittedly, the history in this figure is abridged. Certain technologies are not listed, such as optical disc storage (CD, DVD, Blue-ray, HD) as well as RAM and flash memory enhancements that can be used for backup purposes. However, in the context of backing up Exchange data as opposed to personal data, the scope of backup solutions is narrower. If you are interested in a more holistic history of backups, see http://www.backuphistory.com.

Two paradigm-shifting technologies are illustrated in Figure 18-2. The first technology that was used to define and shape the backup strategies of today was magnetic tape. Even today, magnetic tape continues to advance. It has evolved from a technology that could hold 12,000 punch cards' worth of data on a single magnetic reel to the Sony SAIT Helical-scan technology, which can store approximately 2TB of data per tape. The technology today that has posed the greatest challenge to magnetic tape backup is disk-to-disk backups. The hard disk drive was first invented by IBM in the 1950s, but it was not mainstream until the 1980s when hard drives became a standard feature in personal computers (PCs) and servers. Today, the cost of hard drive space has gone down so dramatically that it is often less expensive and more reliable than magnetic tape as a backup technology. According to Zsolt Kerekes, the editor for StorageSearch.com, in 4 to 10 years we can expect solid state drives (SSDs; also know as *Flash drives*) to challenge hard disk drive solutions. For more information on SSDs, see http://www.storagesearch.com/soliddata-art2-comparisons.pdf.

Backup software has also evolved over time (see Figure 18-3). The choice of what backup software you will use is as important a choice as the storage technology you will be backing up to. In the early days of backing up Exchange, we were completely dependent on the backup software vendor to provide us with both agents for Exchange and drivers for the storage devices. Microsoft has made it easier to support a variety of new storage technologies with the inclusion of the Removable Storage Service (RSS) with the operating system. In Windows Server 2003, the Volume Shadow copy Service (VSS) was added and offers an alternative to traditional streaming backup methods used by legacy backup agents for Exchange. We will cover the VSS in more detail later. The latest advances in backup software technology utilize VSS to provide faster backup and recovery times.

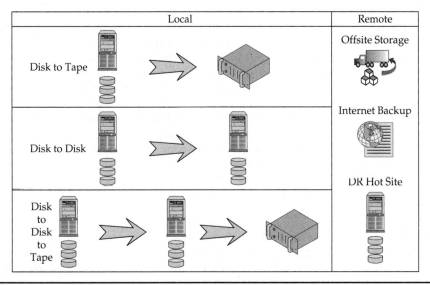

FIGURE 18-3 Backup solution choices

Exchange Retention Strategies

A retention strategy is an organization's policy on the limits for the number of days backups are kept before they are overridden or disposed of. This used to be an administratively defined period of time dictated by a backup rotation cycle. Today, more often than not, it is largely defined by legal counsel and governmental regulations. In the context of Exchange backups, a retention strategy must also include the Exchange storage settings for Deleted Item Retention and Deleted Mailbox Retention. Not included in the backup strategy, but part of the overall organizational retention strategies, are the settings for managed folders. Managed folders are outside the scope of this discussion, but you can find more detail on them in Chapter 15.

Deleted Item Retention

Deleted Item Retention is a mailbox database setting that maintains deleted items in a dumpster for an administratively defined period of time. Microsoft has doubled the default retention period from 7 days (Exchange 2000/2003) to 14 days in Exchange 2007. Items stored in the dumpster do not count against the users' mailbox storage limits. However, additional space considerations must be made in order to compensate for the amount of deleted items you will be storing. Although the numbers will vary in each environment, at 14 days you should plan for Deleted Item Retention to be approximately 20% of the total users' mailbox sizes on each mailbox database. Deleted Item Retention is also enabled by default on Public Folder databases. You will disable Deleted Item Retention if you set the retention length to 0 days. The Deleted Item Retention period begins only after an item is deleted from its original location and then deleted from the Deleted Items folder. The exception is public folders, where the retention period will begin as soon as the item is deleted.

You can configure Deleted Item Retention at two levels. An Exchange organization administrator can configure the Mailbox databases with default Deleted Item Retention. Exchange recipient administrators can set exceptions for individual users' mailboxes. The details of these procedures are covered in Chapter 6 and Chapter 10.

Deleted Mailbox Retention

Deleted Mailbox Retention is similar to Deleted Item Retention in that Exchange will keep deleted data in the Mailbox database for a set period of time. It is different in that it is the collection of all data in the deleted users' mailboxes. The Deleted Item Retention settings do not apply to the data in a deleted mailbox. It is difficult to determine the amount of space required for Deleted Mailbox Retention. It has a great deal to do with the turnover rate and the deletion policies of an organization. The default setting is to maintain deleted mailboxes for 30 days. The retention period does not begin until after the user object is deleted or the mailbox is removed from the user object in Active Directory.

Deleted Mailbox Retention settings can only be configured on the Mailbox databases by an Exchange organization administrator. The details of this procedure are covered in Chapter 6.

Media Retention

The two most common choices for backup media are magnetic tape and hard drives. Just like magnetic tape technology, the hard drive backup solutions vary. Hard drive failure can be mitigated by Redundant Array of Independent Disk (RAID) configurations. The three options for backing up to disk are direct attached storage (DAS), network attached storage (NAS), and storage area network (SAN). If hot-swappable drives are used for your storage array, you only need to replace the media when a drive fails—and you will not have to worry about outages.

Regardless of the magnetic tape technology you are using to back up Exchange, you can use the following formula to determine the amount of media required on an annual basis. Because tape costs are a large expense for any size organization, you might want to run the numbers against the following formula for each technology you are considering (or are already using) and compare that with the cost of disk-to-disk backups.

Number of backup drives × Number of tapes in backup set × Number of sets in rotation × Number of rotations annually = Number of tables required

Tape rotations are necessary to help prevent media failures from getting in the way of restoring data.

Retention Enforcement

The retention settings you configure for Deleted Item Retention and Deleted Mailbox Retention are enforced during the online maintenance process. It is possible to configure online maintenance to skip retention enforcement if a successful backup has not been performed since the last maintenance period. If you would like more detail on online maintenance, see Chapter 20. In Exchange 2003 it was possible to use Exchange Policies to apply retention settings to information stores. Although the Exchange Policy objects no longer exist, it is possible to configure the settings on all mailbox databases in Exchange 2007 at the same time by using the Exchange Management Shell. The following one-liner can enumerate all Mailbox databases and apply the default retention settings uniformly:

```
[PS] C:\>Get-MailboxDatabase | Set-MailboxDatabase -DeletedItemRetention
7.00:00:00 -MailboxRetention 45.00:00:00
```

To customize this one-liner, modify the duration with the days.hours:minutes:seconds you want to apply.

Exchange Backup Strategies

Exchange 2007 backup strategies can be as varied as the backup technologies available. In general, two strategies can be used for backing up Exchange: streaming backups and Volume Shadow copy Services (VSS) backups. Keep in mind that the critical data that needs to be backed up is not just the data on the Exchange server but also the configuration information stored in AD. Of course, the primary focus of any Exchange-related backup is the databases and transaction logs stored on mailbox servers and the local server information for each server role.

Streaming Backups (Legacy)

For many years now, Exchange backup software applications have utilized the Exchange Extensible Storage Engine (ESE) backup API. Vendors provide backup agents to install on the Exchange servers that utilize the legacy ESE API. The agents are then used to stream backup data from the live production database to a flat backup file, hence the name *streaming backups*. Streaming backups can back up mailbox and public folder databases while they are still online. This allows for backups to occur without incurring downtime.

However, streaming backups cannot fully take advantage of the new Exchange Server 2007 backup and restore features. Microsoft even recommends against using streaming backup for Exchange 2007.

SP1   *In Exchange 2007 SP1 and higher, the ability to perform remote streaming backups has been disabled by default. If you run third-party backup software that still uses the legacy ESE API, you will need to follow the instructions in the Exchange 2007 SP1 Release Notes to enable remote streaming backups.*

A streaming backup strategy involves a full backup (a.k.a. normal backup) at the beginning of the backup cycle. The remaining backups in the cycle can either be incremental, differential, or full backups (see Figure 18-4):

- **Full (normal)**   With a normal backup, Exchange databases and transaction logs for the storage groups you select are backed up regardless of how their archive bit is set. After the backup, the archive bit is set to "off"; this indicates that the Exchange files were backed up. The backup software then purges the transaction logs from the Exchange server.

- **Incremental**   With an incremental backup, Exchange transaction logs for the storage groups you select are backed up if their archive bit is set to "on". After the backup, the archive bit is set to "off"; this indicates that the Exchange files were backed up. The backup software then purges the log files from the Exchange server.

- **Differential**   With a differential backup, Exchange transaction logs with the archive bit set to "off" (for the storage groups you select) are backed up. After the backup, the archive bit is not changed. No transaction logs are purged after a differential backup.

Only an online normal (full) backup of the Exchange Server 2003 storage groups will back up the information stores and transaction logs, perform error checking on the database, and then purge the archived transaction logs. The downside to a normal backup is

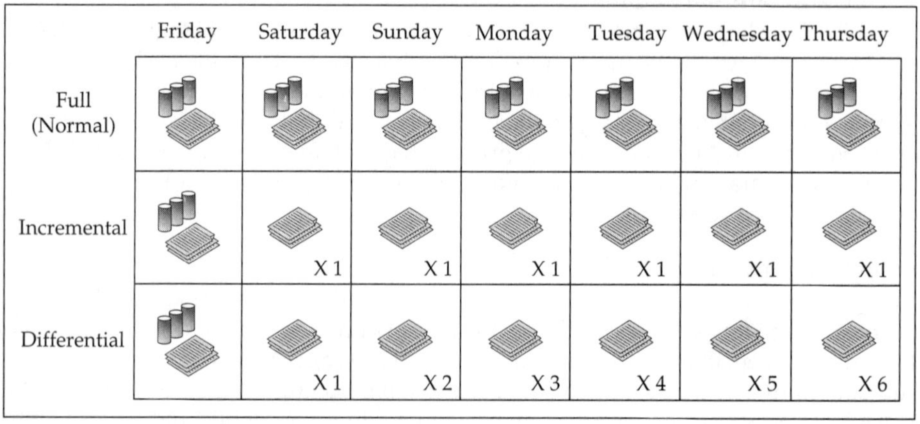

FIGURE 18-4   Streaming backup strategies

the amount of space it takes up on your tape backups. If space is at a premium in your tape backup solution, you can look at implementing incremental or differential backups.

With an incremental backup, you still need a normal backup at the beginning of a rotation. The incremental backup only backs up the changes made since the last full or previous incremental backup. Incremental backups will purge the transaction logs. When you restore from an incremental backup, you need the normal backup plus all incremental backups up to the point of failure. If even one of the incremental backups failed, you will not be able to restore up to the point of failure. You will, however, be able to restore up to the failed incremental backup.

With a differential backup, you make one normal backup at the beginning of a rotation. Then each day you back up only the changes made since the last normal backup. Differential backups do not purge the transaction logs. When you restore, you will need two backups: the normal backup and the last differential backup.

An additional backup type exists for the streaming backup strategy: the offline (copy) backup. With a copy backup, the Exchange databases must be dismounted first. As the database is dismounted, the transaction logs are committed to the database. The copy will back up the selected database and transaction logs regardless of how their archive bit is set. After the backup, the archive bit is not changed in any file. Offline copies can provide additional insurance for your streaming backup strategy.

VSS Backups

The Volume Shadow copy Service (VSS) was introduced in Windows Server 2003. The generic functionality allows snapshot copies of files to be made. Unfortunately, the generic functionality is not designed for Exchange. What's more, the backup tool that comes with Windows Server 2003 cannot perform Exchange VSS backups. Only some independent software vendors (ISVs) and Microsoft's new System Center Data Protection Manager (DPM), Version 2, support the Exchange 2007 enhanced version of VSS. DPM is a proprietary backup solution from Microsoft that provides continuous data protection for Microsoft application and file servers. We will take a look at how DPM is used to back up Exchange 2007 later in this chapter.

So what is so special about the Exchange 2007 VSS? It has the ability to coordinate the requests from the backup applications (requestors), the communications to and from the Exchange 2003 information store and Exchange 2007 store (writers), and the calls to the hardware/software (providers) that create the snapshots. Without the Exchange 2007 enhancements to the VSS, this would not be possible. Exchange 2007 improves upon the Exchange 2003 VSS by adding a new writer. The new writer is called the Replication Writer. The Replication Writer allows the requestors to back up the offline copy of the Cluster Continuous Replication (CCR) database or the Local Continuous Replication (LCR) "copy" of the production database. This changes the dynamics of backups even further by allowing backups to occur during normal daily operations without impacting end users' performance at all. Even though the Exchange 2007 Store Writer is on all servers with the Exchange 2007 mailbox servers and the Replication Writer is on all servers with CCR or LCR enabled, without an Exchange 2007-aware requestor and provider, VSS backups will not be possible, as Figure 18-5 illustrates.

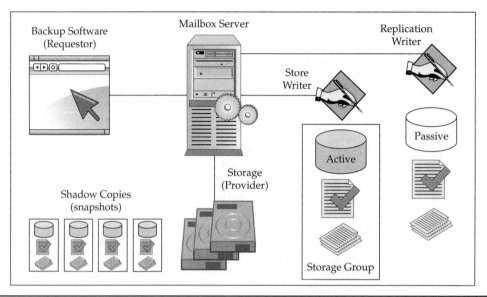

FIGURE 18-5 Exchange 2007 VSS architecture

The components that make up the VSS architecture work together to perform backups and restores of Exchange 2007. As mentioned, the VSS coordinates the components. Here is an overview of the shadow copy process:

1. The VSS requestor (backup software) sends a command to make a shadow copy of a storage group (or storage groups).

2. The VSS communicates with the appropriate Exchange writer to lock down the storage group for a snapshot:

   - Prohibit administrative actions

   - Check disk volume dependencies

   - Suspend all write operations to the database and transaction logs

3. The VSS communicates with the storage provider and creates a shadow copy of the storage volume that contains the storage group.

4. The VSS releases the Exchange 2007 storage group to resume normal operations.

5. The VSS requestor (backup software) performs a consistency check.

6. Exchange 2007, not the requestor, truncates the transaction logs for the active storage group upon a successful backup, even if the Replication Writer was used to perform the backup.

Because the VSS is an advanced form of backup, the backup strategies are different. The backup schedule for VSS is different from a streaming backup schedule. Rather than being driven just by the size of the databases you are backing up or the time of day in which a backup can occur, the VSS backups are based on the recovery goals you specify. Here are some factors you might consider:

- **Data loss tolerance**   The maximum amount of Exchange data loss, measured in time, that is acceptable
- **Retention range**   How long you need the backed-up Exchange data available (both short term and long term)
- **Recovery point schedule**   Establishes how many incremental snapshots should be created
- **Full backup schedule**   Establishes the beginning of each VSS backup cycle

The way your organization defines these variable becomes your VSS backup strategy. Your backup strategy also reflects your organization's recovery goals. In Figure 18-6, you can see a VSS backup strategy based on some tolerance for Exchange data loss.

For the example in Figure 18-6, the maximum amount of time between snapshots is three hours, which means at no time will there be more than three hours worth of unprotected data. For an organization with very low tolerance for data loss, the Exchange 2007 VSS will allow you to set a snapshot schedule as frequently as every 15 minutes. The tradeoff is the additional disk storage requirements for the additional snapshots.

NTBackup and Exchange 2007

When Microsoft released Windows NT 3.51, the first backup software vendor that supported it was Arcadia Software, with a product called Backup Exec. Backup Exec actually has a long and interesting history that predates Windows. By the time Exchange 4.0 was in the market, Microsoft was including a lightweight version of Backup Exec with the Windows NT 4.0 operating system, which Microsoft called NTBackup. Arcadia was acquired by

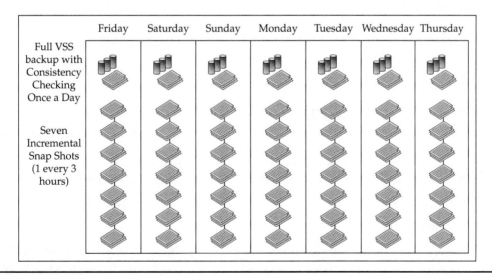

FIGURE 18-6   VSS backup strategy example

Seagate in 1996 after the release of Exchange 4.0. In 1999, the Seagate Software management division was acquired by Veritas. In June 2005, Veritas merged with Symantec, who is now the current owner of Backup Exec. Microsoft has continued to include NTBackup with Windows Server 2003. The Windows 2003 version of NTBackup will support backing up Exchange 5.5, 2000, 2003, and even Exchange 2007 once the Exchange management tools are installed. The bad news for NTBackup fans is that it is no longer available in Windows Server 2008.

NTBackup uses the legacy streaming backup APIs and not the Exchange 2007 VSS writers. It is limited in that it can only back up the local machine's data. It cannot back up another Exchange server over the network. It can, however, save its backups to a network drive—and network backup software can be used to back up the NTBackups.

Backing Up Exchange 2007 to Disk with NTBackup

Use the following steps to create a backup job for Exchange Server 2007 with NTBackup:

1. Click Start | Run, type **ntbackup.exe**, and click OK.

2. Select the Advanced Mode link on the Welcome page.

3. Click the Backup tab.

4. Expand Microsoft Exchange Server, expand an *exchange_servername,* and select the check box next to the storage group you want to back up.

5. Verify that path is in the in the Backup destination list.

6. In the Backup media or file name box, type the path and filename for this backup (for example, C:\E2K7Backups\1stBackup).

7. On the Tools menu, click Options. Verify that the Default Backup Type is Normal and then click OK.

8. Click Start Backup, review the backup job information, and verify that the settings are appropriate.

9. Click Advanced, enable Verify data after backup, and click OK.

10. Click Start Backup.

It is possible to use the Schedule Jobs option to automate the Exchange backups and enforce your backup strategy.

VSS Backup for Exchange 2007

The Data Protection Manager, Version 2, from Microsoft fully supports VSS backups of Exchange Server 2007. Some, but not all third-party vendors do. Be careful when looking at Exchange 2007 backup software that you choose a vendor that supports Exchange 2007's VSS. Here is a list of some of vendors that provide VSS backup solutions for Exchange 2007:

- Symantec Backup Exec
- CommVault Simpana

For a current list of Microsoft backup/archive ISV partners for Exchange Server 2007, see http://www.microsoft.com/exchange/partners/2007/backup.mspx. If you currently have a backup ISV, check with them to confirm their support for Exchange 2007 VSS. ISV solutions that are compliant with the Exchange 2007 VSS will be able to do the following:

- Back up the Exchange 2007 database, transaction log, and checkpoint files with the Exchange 2007 VSS writers
- Validate the integrity of the shadow copy backup set
- Restore the Exchange 2007 database, transaction log, and checkpoint files with the Exchange 2007 VSS writers

The planning, installation, configuration of Data Protection Manager (DPM), Version 2, is outside the scope of this book. However, because DPM is the Microsoft Exchange 2007 VSS backup solution, we will detail the backup and restore process using DPM. You can find out more about DPM at https://www.microsoft.com/systemcenter/dpm/default.mspx. You can download the 32-bit version of DPM at the following site:

https://connect.microsoft.com/Downloads/DownloadDetails.aspx?SiteID=205&DownloadID=6741

The 64-bit version can be downloaded here:

https://connect.microsoft.com/Downloads/DownloadDetails.aspx?SiteID=205&DownloadID=6740

Backing Up Exchange 2007 to Disk with DPM

The following steps illustrate how to create a new protection group and configure DPM to back up an Exchange 2007 mailbox server:

1. On the server running DPM, Version 2, open the DPM v2 Administrator Console.

2. Click the Management button and then the Agent tab. Verify that the Exchange server you want to protect has an agent installed on it. If not, use the console to install the agent, as shown next. (Note: This will require a restart on the Exchange 2007 mailbox server.)

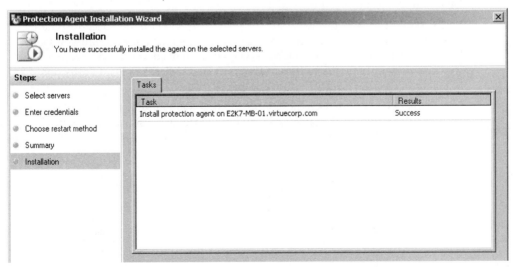

3. Click the Disks tab. Verify that there is at least one DPM storage pool disk configured, and that there is enough unallocated space for your backups. If not, you will need to add a disk to the DPM server with enough free space to back up your Exchange 2007 server.

4. Click the Protection button and then select Create Protection Group from the Actions pane.

5. Click Next when the Welcome page appears.

6. Expand the Exchange server you want to protect and check the box for each storage group you want to protect, as shown here. Click Next.

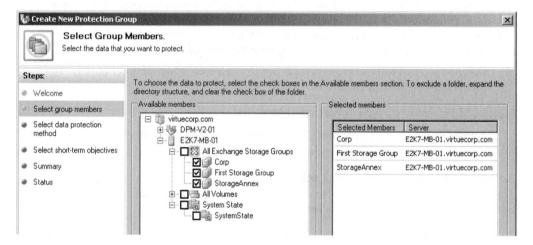

7. Type a name in the Protection group name field that reflects the scope of the protection group.

8. Verify that the check box "I want short-term protection using:" is selected and that Disk is the protection method. Click Next.

9. Verify that Run Eseutil to check data integrity is selected on the Specify Exchange Protection Options page and click Next. (Note: If the Exchange administrative tools have not been installed on the DPM server, you will need to manually copy the ese.dll and eseutil.exe files to the C:\Program Files\Microsoft Data Protection Manager\DPM\bin directory from another machine.)

10. Specify the retention range, synchronization frequency, and frequency of the express full backup on the Specify Short-Term Goals page, shown here. Click Next.

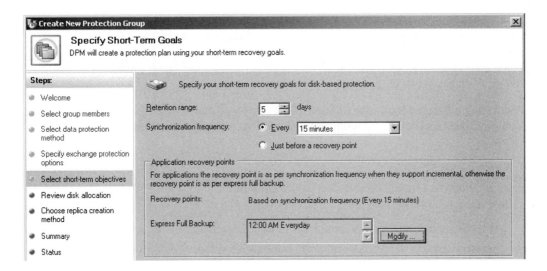

11. Verify the Disk Allocation settings and confirm that there are not any free space errors. Click Next.

12. Leave the default Replica Creation Method set to Automatically and click Next. (Note: If the database is very large, you can choose to create the replica at a different time. Or you can choose to manually transfer the data with removable media in low-bandwidth situations.)

13. Review the protection group members and the protection group settings and then click Create Group.

14. Verify that all task results on the Status page are successful. Click Close.

15. Click the Monitoring button and select the Jobs tab. Review the status of the jobs that you scheduled.

Basic Recovery

The purpose of a backup strategy is to facilitate an organization's recovery requirements. In this section we are going to look at how the data retention strategies and basic backup strategies can be used as the first line of recovery available to Exchange users and administrators. This includes recovering individual e-mail items, reconnecting deleted mailboxes, and restoring databases from streaming backups. We will additionally look at the basic uses for the recovery storage group.

Recovering Deleted Items

When a user deletes a message, it goes to the Deleted Items folder. Once removed from the Deleted Items folder, the message is finally considered deleted by Exchange. A keyboard action that will hard-delete an item from a mailbox, from any folder, is SHIFT-DELETE. When the SHIFT key and DELETE are used to delete an item, that item bypasses the Deleted Items folder and is fully deleted. The prior case is the most common, so most item recovery will take place from the Deleted Items folder. Users will not need an administrator to recover deleted items as long as Deleted Item Retention is enabled. If the default setting is still in place, an end user can perform the following procedure up to 14 days after the Deleted Items folder has been emptied.

Recovering a Deleted Item with Outlook 2007

Each user can recover deleted items using the following simple steps from their Outlook client.

1. Open Outlook.
2. Select the Deleted Items folder in the mailbox.
3. From the Tools menu, select Recover Deleted Items.
4. Select the item(s) you want to recover and then click Recover Selected Items.
5. Move the item to a folder other than the Deleted Items folder.

Outlook 2007 clients will also be able to perform this procedure from any folder in their Outlook mailbox to recover deleted items that were hard-deleted. This is because the DumpsterAlwaysOn parameter is enabled by default. Outlook 2003 clients will not be able to do this by default. The Registry can be modified on an Outlook 2003 client to allow deleted item recovery from any folder.

Enabling DumpsterAlwaysOn for Outlook 2003

To configure Outlook 2003 clients to behave like Outlook 2007 clients, you can enable the DumpteralwaysOn setting as follows:

1. Click Start, click Run, type **regedit**, and then click OK.
2. Navigate to HKLM\SOFTWARE\Microsoft\Exchange\Client\Options.
3. Click the Edit | New and select DWORD Value.
4. Type **DumpsterAlwaysOn** and then press ENTER.
5. Double-click DumpsterAlwaysOn.
6. Type **1** in the Value data area and then click OK. The following illustration shows the result.

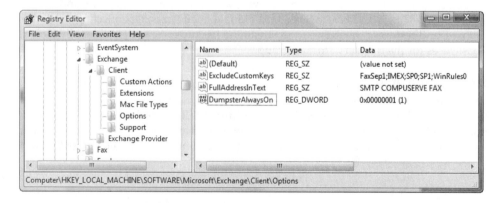

7. Close the Registry Editor.

8. Restart Outlook for the change to take effect.

Recovering Deleted Items with Outlook Web Access 2007

It is also possible to restore deleted items from Outlook Web Access. Here are the steps to follow:

1. Connect to the CAS server (https://*cas_servername*/owa).

2. Log on using your domain\username and password.

3. Click the Options link in the upper right of the OWA window.

4. Select Deleted Items from the option list on the left side of the OWA window.

5. Locate and select the item(s) you want to recover and then click the Recover to Deleted Items folder link.

Recovering Deleted Mailboxes

Every organization has a policy regarding mailboxes when it comes to employees who resign or are terminated. In both of these situations, organizations seek to minimize the intentional or unintentional damages caused by an employee leaving the company. Although the policies vary from informal manual procedures to strict automated procedures, they do exist. Let's say that your organization has a policy that requires your Windows administrators to disable a user's account as soon as they have left the company. In addition to that, they are required to maintain that account for 60 days after which they delete the user account, which in turn deletes the mailbox from Active Directory as well. However, the content of that user's mailbox will not be removed from the Exchange 2007 Mailbox database until the Deleted Mailbox Retention settings have expired and online maintenance completes. In Exchange 2007 that is an additional 30 days.

Now let's say that the user's manager requests access to the user's mailbox 61 days after they have left the company. The content is still on the mailbox server, but you will need to find a way to give the manager access. The process of recovering a deleted mailbox is called a *connect*. Connecting the mailbox with a user object will make the content available to whichever user account the mailbox is connected to. However, you cannot connect a mailbox to a user account that already has a mailbox.

Connecting a Deleted Mailbox with the EMC

Once a deleted mailbox has been identified you can connect the mailbox to a non-mailbox enabled user with the following steps.

1. Open the Exchange Management Console (EMC).

2. Expand the Recipient Configuration work center.

3. Select Disconnected Mailbox.

4. In the Actions pane, click Connect to Server, click Browse, select the server that contains the deleted mailbox's contents, click OK, and then click Connect.

5. Select the mailbox you want to reconnect to a user object and click Connect from the Actions pane.

6. Select the mailbox type and click Next.

7. Select Matching User if the original user still exists or Existing User if you want to specify an alternative user object. Click Browse and select the user object. Click OK and then click Next.

8. Click Connect.

9. Click Finish.

Reconnecting a Deleted Mailbox with the EMS

The first step to using the Exchange Management Shell to reconnect a deleted mailbox is to enumerate the disconnected mailboxes, like so:

```
[PS]C:\> Get-MailboxStatistics -Server E2K7-MB-01 | where
{ $_.DisconnectDate -ne $null } | select DisplayName,DisconnectDate
```

The next step is to reconnect a disconnected mailbox to a user object that is already in Active Directory:

```
[PS]C:\> Connect-Mailbox -Database "Mailbox Database" -Identity "Rich Luckett"
```

Of course, you will need to replace the variables with your specific server names, database names, and mailbox names.

Recovering Databases

Many factors determine how long it will take to recover a database, such as the size of the database, the type of backup that was performed, and the type of Exchange server (standard mailbox server, LCR, CCR, or SCR). As a rule of thumb, it generally takes about twice as long to restore a database as it take to back it up. In your initial design of the mailbox server, the smaller you designed the databases to be, the faster your restores will be. In your backup design, the choice of VSS over streaming backups will make the recover process faster. Your choice to deploy highly available servers such as the LCR, CCR, or SCR will give you the fastest database recovery times.

Yet another fact that has a great impact on the recovery process is the reason for the restore. If the database is corrupted, what cause the corruption? What is a hardware failure? What is an operator's error? In other words, what needs to be done before you can restore the database? In all database recovery scenarios, the problem that forced you to restore the database must be resolved first and then the database restore can be done. In extreme cases, as we will discuss later, the database can be restored to an alternate location when the problem cannot easily be resolved on the original server.

Recovering a Database with NTBackup (Streaming)

Use the following steps to recover a database from an NTBackup streaming backup:

1. Open the Exchange Management Console.

2. Expand the Server Configuration work center and select Mailbox.

3. Select the mailbox server from the results pane that contains the database you want to restore.

4. Expand the storage group in which the mailbox database resides, right-click the database, and select Properties.

5. Verify that you have the General tab selected and check the box "This database can be overwritten by a restore." Click OK.

6. Select Dismount Database in the Actions pane and click Yes to confirm.

NOTE *Alternatively you can replace steps 1–6 by using the following cmdlets in the EMS:*

```
[PS]C:\>Set-MailboxDatabase "Mailbox Database" -AllowFileRestore $true
[PS]C:\>Dismount-Database "Mailbox Database"
```

7. Click Start | Run, type **ntbackup.exe**, click OK, and choose Advanced Mode.

8. Click the Restore and Manage Media tab and then select the Exchange storage group or database you want to restore.

9. In the Restore files, Original location should be grayed out.

10. Click Start Restore.

11. Leave the default, Restore to server. Type a path for the temporary location for log and path files.

12. Check the boxes for Last Restore Set and Mount database after Restore and then click OK.

13. Click OK to verify the backup file location.

14. You can click the Report button when the restore is finished to verify the status of the restore. When you are done, close the NTBackup tool.

What you do not want to do is mix backup types. Trying to restore an old streaming backup to a system that is currently being backed up by VSS is not supported.

Recovery Storage Groups

Although recovery storage groups (RSGs) may not share the spotlight with other Exchange features, it is one of the most significant additions to the Exchange administrator's arsenal of tools. It was first introduced with Exchange 2003 Server and has expanded the recovery options available to organizations of all sizes. How you add and configure recovery storage groups has changed significantly in Exchange 2007. In Exchange 2003, it was possible to use the Exmerge tool to extract data from the RSG to a Personal Storage Table (PST). With Service Pack 1 for Exchange 2003, the merge and copy operations were integrated with the Exchange Task Wizard. In Exchange 2007, both have been replaced by the Restore-Mailbox cmdlet in the Exchange Management Shell and the Exchange Disaster Recovery Analyzer (ExDRA). Before we go into detail on the procedures, there are some technical aspects of the recovery storage group that you should understand.

The recovery storage group was originally designed to replace the need to set up a separate forest and recovery server for single-item restorations, which were mandatory for Exchange 2000 and earlier versions. The special characteristics of the recovery storage group make this possible. Once a recovery storage group has been added to a server, the Exchange information store automatically redirects all restore operations to the recovery storage group.

An administrator then creates an empty placeholder database in the recovery storage group to be overwritten by a restore. When the restore is performed on the RSG server, the information store service will attempt to redirect it to the recovery storage group. If a placeholder database has not been created by an administrator, the restore operation fails. If it does exist, the restore succeeds. The best part of this process is that it is transparent to the backup application. It does not know that the restore is being redirected and, therefore, doesn't require any special configurations to work with the recovery storage group.

As a safety precaution, the following limitations have been imposed on recovery storage groups to preclude them from production use:

- Exchange clients cannot connect to an RSG database.
- All restored mailboxes will be disconnected from Active Directory and cannot be connected to user objects.
- Retention settings and Folder Management Policies do not apply to RSGs.
- All RSG databases are dismounted by default and have to be manually mounted.
- The restore path for the RSG cannot be changed after it is created.
- Public folder databases cannot be restored in an RSG.
- You can only create one RSG per server, but you can restore a database from any server in the organization to the RSG server.
- RSGs do not support CCR or LCR replication.
- You cannot back up an RSG database.

It is also possible to recover e-mail items from a restored database in the recovery storage group to a mailbox on a production database in the organization. Two operations are supported in the RTM (Release to Manufacture) version of Exchange 2007:

- Merge with a mailbox
- Copy to a subfolder

It is possible to merge the recovered data into a mailbox even if the user is logged onto their mailbox. Any item that is not already present will be merged with the expectation of mailbox rules and custom search folders. It is possible to limit the merge by configuring filters for specific data. An alternative is to copy the recovered data to another folder in the user's mailbox and allow the user to extract the item(s) they need.

SP1 *SP1 includes a new cmdlet called Export-Mailbox to allow exporting mailbox data to a PST. However, this is not supported with the recovery storage group (http://technet.microsoft.com/ en-us/library/bb266964.aspx).*

Because of differences between Exchange 2000/2003 and Exchange 2007 storage, it will not be possible to restore databases from Exchange 2000/2003 to Exchange 2007. To create a new recovery storage group, you will need to have the Exchange Server Administrator role and be a member of the local Administrators group on the Exchange 2007 server. To restore recovered data to a mailbox, you will need to have the Recipients Administrators role.

Individual Mailbox Restore with the Recovery Storage Group

It is faster in most cases to use the Exchange Management Shell to create recovery storage groups and recover mailbox data. However, the Exchange Disaster Recovery Analyzer (ExDRA) tool provides workflow process that may be easier for an administrator with limited experience with the EMS. The first of the following examples shows how to use the ExDRA, and the second shows how to use the EMS.

ExDRA-RSG   Follow these steps to use the ExDRA to create a recovery storage group and recover mailbox data:

1. Open the Exchange Management Console.

2. Select the Tools work center and double-click Disaster Recovery Management.

3. Click Go to Welcome Screen.

4. Type **E2K7 Recovery Storage Group** for the identifying label.

5. Verify that the server name and domain controller name are correct and click Next.

6. Select Create a recovery storage group.

7. Select First Storage Group (or whatever storage group you would like to link to) and click Next.

8. Verify that the default path has enough free space to perform the restore. If not, change the path and then click Create the recovery storage group.

9. Verify that the database(s) were also added into the recovery storage group when it was created in the result pages.

10. Repeat the "Recovering a Database with NTBackup (Streaming)" exercise from earlier in this chapter.

11. Switch back to the Microsoft Exchange Troubleshooting Assistant window and click Go back to task center.

12. Select Mount or Dismount databases in the recovery storage group.

13. Check the box next to Mailbox Database (or the database you recovered).

14. Click Mount selected database.

15. Click Go back to task center.

16. Select Merge or copy mailbox contents.

17. Click Gather merge information.

18. Click Show Advanced Options. Change the setting for Bad item limit to 3, as shown next.

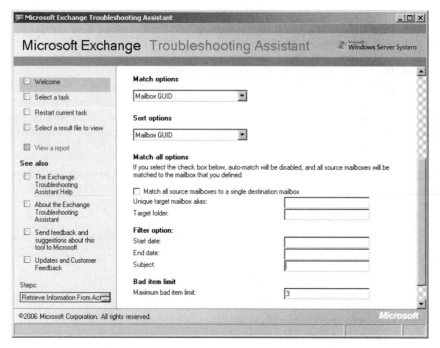

19. Click Perform pre-merge tasks.

20. Select the mailbox(es) you want to merge or copy data for and click Perform merge actions, shown next.

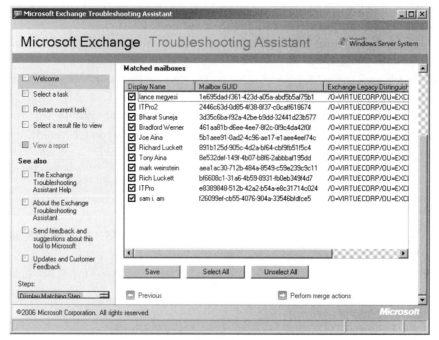

21. Confirm that the mailboxes were restored on the Merge Results page.

22. Click Go back to task center.

23. Use the ExDRA to dismount the databases in the RSG and then remove the RSG.

24. Close the tool.

It will be necessary to clean up the files in the RSG recovery path because they are not deleted when the RSG is removed—especially if you want to regain the free space so you can create an RSG as a later point in time to the same path.

EMS-RSG   Behind the curtain of the ExDRA is the underlying EMS cmdlets. By learning the cmdlets, you can increase the speed at which recoveries take place. The following exercise illustrates how the same procedure just performed from the ExDRA can be done from the Exchange Management Shell (EMS). Here are the steps to follow:

1. Create a recovery storage group:

```
[PS]C:\>New-Storagegroup -Server "E2K7-MB-01" -LogFolderPath
"C:\RSG01\" -Name "RSG01" -SystemFolderPath "C:\RSG01\" -Recovery
```

2. Add a recovery database and set the recovery database to allow overwrites:

```
[PS]C:\>New-Mailboxdatabase -MailboxDatabaseToRecover "Mailbox
Database" -StorageGroup "E2K7-MB-01\RSG01"
```

3. Repeat the "Recovering a Database with NTBackup (Streaming)" exercise from earlier in this chapter.

4. Mount the recovery database by running the following Exchange Management Shell command:

```
[PS]C:\>Mount-Database "E2K7-MB-01\RSG01\Mailbox Database"
```

5. Recover the mailbox of an existing user to an existing mailbox by running the following Exchange Management Shell command:

```
[PS]C:\>Restore-Mailbox "Rich Luckett" -RSGDatabase "E2K7-MB-01\
RSG01\Mailbox Database"
```

It is possible to use the Restore-Mailbox cmdlets to merge or to copy. In the previous example, Merge mode was used. In Copy-to-folder mode, you can specify a folder to restore the recovered data to. It can even be the folder of a different user's mailbox.

Advanced Recovery

What makes a recovery process an advanced restore procedure (versus a basic restore procedure) is not necessarily that it is a more complex procedure or will take more time to complete. The term *advanced* simply implies that the restore procedure is taking advantage of the latest tools and features to make the more difficult service loss scenarios easier to recover from. We explored the new features and new technology supported by Exchange 2007 for backing up Exchange 2007. Now, we will take a look at how the same advanced features can be used to rapidly recover critical Exchange server data.

Database Portability

Exchange 2007 introduces, for the first time ever in the Exchange product's history, the native capability to restore any mailbox database in an organization to another production mailbox server in the same organization. Previous releases of Exchange imposed restrictions that prevented databases from being mounted on different servers. Exchange 2007's database portability removes the restrictions and makes it possible. However, there are two limitations: You cannot mount databases from outside of the organization, and public folders are not supported.

Although much emphasis has been put on the latest clustering technologies, database portability deserves much attention in the context of disaster recovery. The option to recover a database (or databases) of a failed server onto a functioning server can mean a minimal outage, whereas a lengthy outage would be expected. Database portability can also come in quite handy during forklift hardware upgrades as well.

Recovering Databases to Different Servers

Imagine that you have a SCSI RAID controller failure for one of your storage groups. You have been making backups with software that uses the legacy backup API and the only good copy you have of the database is on tape. You do not have any additional space on the server with the failed controller. However, you do have another Windows 2003 server with the Exchange Server 2007 mailbox role installed that does have enough free space. You can take advantage of database portability and use the backup file to restore the database to the other server. The process is illustrated in the following steps:

1. Create a target storage group with same name as the source storage group:

   ```
   [PS]C:\>New-StorageGroup CORP -Server E2K7-MB-02
   ```

2. Create a target database in the target storage group with the same name as the source database:

   ```
   [PS]C:\>New-MailboxDatabase -StorageGroup E2K7-MB-02\CORP -Name
   "Sales"
   ```

3. Set the target database so that it can be overwritten:

   ```
   [PS]C:\>Set-MailboxDatabase "Sales" -AllowFileRestore $true
   ```

4. Click Start | Run, type **ntbackup.exe**, click OK, and choose Advanced Mode.

5. Click the Restore and Manage Media tab and then select the Exchange storage group or database you want to restore.

6. The *Restore files Original location* option should be grayed out.

7. Click Start Restore.

8. Change the Restore To setting to the target server. Type a path for the temporary location for log and path files, as shown here.

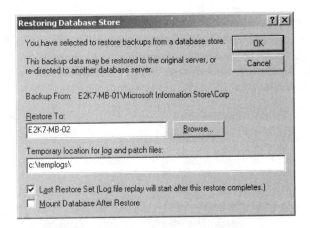

9. Check the box for Last Restore Set and click OK.

10. Click OK to verify the backup file location.

11. You can click the Report button when the restore is finished to verify the status of the restore. When you are done, close the NTBackup tool.

12. Mount the database on the target server:

```
[PS]C:\>mount-database "Sales"
```

Relocating Databases

In the previous example, you saw how a streaming backup could be used to restore access to users' mailbox data on another server in the organization. Another example of how database portability works is to move a production mailbox database from one mailbox server to another mailbox server within the organization. Here are a few scenarios where this could be beneficial:

- The final steps in the dial-tone recovery process
- Decommissioning hardware
- Optimizing performance and managing database growth

The relocation process is similar to recovering from a streaming backup to a new server:

1. Dismount the source database:

```
[PS]C:\>Dismount-Database "E2K7-MB-01\StorageAnnex\SuperSizedMBX"
```

2. Create a target storage group with same name as the source storage group:

```
[PS]C:\>New-StorageGroup StorageAnnex -Server E2K7-MB-02
```

3. Create a target database in the target storage group with the same name as the source database:

```
[PS]C:\>New-MailboxDatabase -StorageGroup E2K7-MB-02\StorageAnnex
-Name "SuperSizedMBX"
```

PART VI

4. Set the target database so that it can be overwritten:

```
[PS]C:\>Set-MailboxDatabase "SuperSizedMBX" -AllowFileRestore $true
```

5. Move the database files (.edb files, log files, and Exchange Search catalog) to the appropriate location, as shown next. (Note: You can find the path to the database to view its properties with the EMC or via a cmdlet in the EMS.)

```
[PS]C:\>Get-MailboxDatabase "SuperSizedMBX" | FL Name,EdbFilePath
```

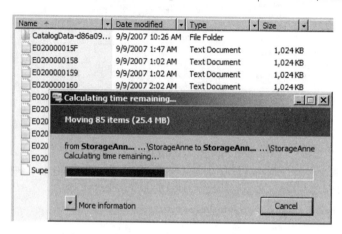

6. Mount the target database using the following command:

```
[PS]C:\>Mount-Database "SuperSizedMBX"
```

7. Update the source database's mailbox-enabled user objects in Active Directory with the new database location:

```
[PS]C:\>Get-Mailbox -Database "E2K7-MB-01\StorageAnnex\SuperSizedMBX" |
where {$_.ObjectClass -NotMatch "(SystemAttendantMailbox|
ExOleDbSystemMailbox)"}| Move-Mailbox -ConfigurationOnly
-TargetDatabase "E2K7-MB-02\StorrageAnnex\SuperSizedMBX"
```

There may be some additional work depending on the type of Exchange clients that connect to the database. Table 18-1 summarizes the way in which different clients will be able to connect to the relocated database.

Exchange Client	Redirection Method
Outlook 2007	Redirected automatically with the Autodiscover service
Outlook Web Access	Automatically redirected
Outlook 2003 and earlier	Manually configured to point to the new server or to use an outlook.prf file

TABLE 18-1   Client Redirection

Dial-tone Restores

Dial-tone restores have been used by Exchange administrators as long as there have been Exchange servers. Because the mailbox is a Directory object stored in a directory database, and the mailbox content is stored separately in an Exchange database, it is possible to quickly restore basic e-mail functionality even if an Exchange database takes hours to repair. The only way this could be done in Exchange 2003 and earlier versions of Exchange was to replace the failed database with an empty database. Then, after the data was restored on a recovery server, it could replace the "dial-tone" database. It was a difficult procedure to retain the data in the dial-tone database and merge it back with the restored database.

By adding portability to the dial-tone recovery process in Exchange Server 2007, Microsoft has significantly simplified the overall process. Dial-tone portability allows a user's mailbox to be moved to a different database, even on a different server, without the original database needing to be replaced with an empty database. Outlook 2007 and Outlook Web Access clients will automatically be redirected to the new server, or new database on the same server, when they connect. As they log on, they will not have access to all messages, rules, forms, views, and other mailbox information associated with the original database. However, at a later point in time when the original database is recovered, it is possible to merge the data in the dial-tone database back into the original database—and it is a much easier process than it was in previous versions. If you want to use the original procedure, you can mount an empty database in place of a single failed database, and the new Disaster Recovery Analyzer (DRA) tool will simplify swapping dial-tone databases with recovered databases.

We have reviewed the key components of database portability, such as the Move-Mailbox –ConfigurationOnly cmdlet and the DRA, and how they are used to recover an entire database. In the following section, you will see how the dial-tone database is created and how it can be merged back with the original database. In an earlier example, I asked you to imagine that your SCSI RAID controller had failed, but you had a good backup that you could restore to another server. Now I would like you to imagine that you do not have a recent good backup, but you are able to replace the failed controller card. Unfortunately, you have identified that the database was corrupted when the controller failed. You have to call for offsite storage to deliver an archived tape backup or perhaps even try some more drastic recovery techniques with Eseutil (Extensible Storage Engine Utility). In either case, you will have to leave the production database down for a lengthy period of time. Your manager has informed you that if you cannot restore e-mail functionality, the company will lose millions of dollars every hour it is down. With that in mind, you decide to perform a dial-tone recovery so that your company can continue to receive and send e-mail and buy some time to repair the corrupted database.

Performing the Dial-tone Recovery

Use the following step to provide users with continued messaging services during a disaster recovery situation.

1. Move any files from the failed database to another location. You may still be able to use them when recovering the corrupted database.

2. After the failed database files have been removed from the EdbFilePath, use the EMC or EMS to mount the database. Because there are no files in the path, you will

receive the following warning. Click Yes to create an empty database. You do not need to use the Move-Mailbox–ConfigurationOnly cmdlet in this case; the server and storage group are the same.

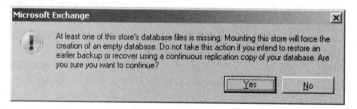

3. Open the EMC and select the Toolbox work center. Double-click the Database Recovery Management tool.

4. Configure a recovery storage group on the server for the failed database. See "Individual Mailbox Restore with the Recovery Storage Group," earlier in the chapter, if you need to review the steps.

5. Restore the backup of the failed database to your recovery storage group, copy any log files from the failed database that were saved off to another folder earlier, and mount the database in the recovery storage group.

6. Choose the option Swap database for "dial-tone" scenario.

7. Verify the mounted database in the RSG is the correct database and click Gather swap information.

8. Click the Perform swap option.

9. Confirm that the swap was successful, as shown here.

Display Database Swap Result

Server name: e2k7-mb-01
Recovery storage group name: RSG01
Linked storage group name: First Storage Group
Selected database name: Mailbox Database
Linked database name: Mailbox Database

Database swap result:

The configurations for original and recovery database have been swapped successfully, and the databases have been remounted.

10. Choose the option Merge or copy mailbox contents. See "Individual Mailbox Restore with the Recovery Storage Group," earlier in the chapter, if you need to review the steps.

11. Remove the recovery storage group. Note that the swap procedure changed the directory path, so you will want to move the recovered database to an appropriate storage volume.

Even though you have swapped the database back into place, some users' profiles may experience issues from being in dial-tone mode. This is especially true if the users have customized any settings while using the dial-tone database. If you experience problems with user profiles, you can refer to the Microsoft KB article, "Considerations and best practices when resetting an Exchange mailbox database," at http://support.microsoft.com/kb/282496/en-us.

This procedure worked because the data in Active Directory was intact. But what happens when the data that is lost is in Active Directory? Microsoft has developed a script and a procedure that allows you to recover missing user accounts in Active Directory from a copy of an Exchange database. For more information on the script, see the TechNet article, "How to Generate Active Directory Accounts By Using the Mailbox Information in the Mailbox Database," at http://technet.microsoft.com/en-us/library/bb430758.aspx.

VSS Restores for Exchange 2007

The Volume Shadow copy Service is the preferred method of backing up Exchange 2007, and the Disaster Protection Manager (DPM) is the only Microsoft backup software that supports Exchange 2007 enhanced VSS backups and restores. If you followed the VSS backup example earlier in the chapter, you will be able to perform the following steps for restoring Exchange data using DPM.

Recovering an Exchange 2007 Database with DPM

Use the following steps to recover an Exchange database from a VSS backup with DPM.

1. Open the EMS on the Exchange 2007 server on which you want to recover the database.

2. Configure the database to be overwritten by a restore:

   ```
   [PS]C:\>Set-MailboxDatabase "Sales" -AllowFileRestore $true
   ```

3. Open the DPM Administrator Console on the DPM server.

4. Click the Recovery button, shown at the top of the following illustration.

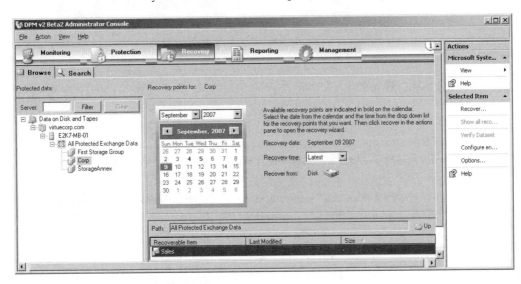

5. Expand the Domain object | Exchange 2007 Server | All Protected Exchange Data. Select the storage group that contains the database that needs to be restored.

6. Select the day in the calendar with the recovery point you would like to use.

7. Verify that Latest is selected in the Recovery time drop-down list. (Note: If you want to restore the data to an alternate location, such as the recovery storage group, you can choose a recovery time prior to the latest recovery point.)

8. Click Recovery in the Actions pane.

9. Click Next when the Review Recovery Selection page in the Recovery Wizard appears.

10. Verify that Recover to original Exchange Server location is selected and correct, as shown next. Click Next.

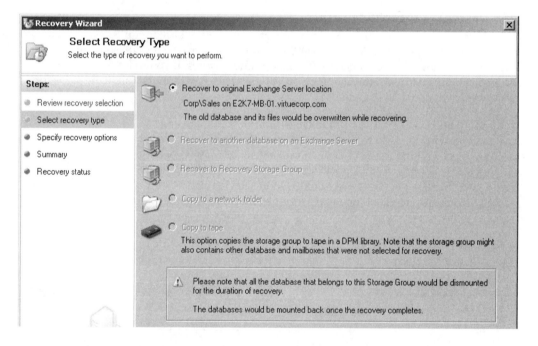

11. Verify that the check box Mount the databases after they are recovered is selected. Click Next.

12. Verify the information on the Summary page and click Recover.

13. Click Close.

14. Click the Monitoring button and expand the In Progress jobs. When the job is complete, confirm that is was successful.

15. Switch to the Exchange 2007 server and verify that the database was mounted successfully and that users can access their mailboxes.

Failed Server Recovery

This topic has one disclaimer: It does not apply to a single node failure in a cluster. This is because a new node can be added to replace the failed node without impacting service levels. So when we talk about failed server recovery, we are talking about an Exchange server with one or more Exchange roles installed that must be restored in order to recover the appropriate service levels in an organization. There are many reasons a server could become unavailable. Here are the three most common:

- Server hardware failure
- Facility/site failure
- Software/data corruption

In general, you can recover a specific server by restoring the system state with a full Exchange backup set or by using the Setup /m:RecoverServer procedures. Although a system state backup has the potential to be the fastest recovery plan, it lacks flexibility. The system state restore requires the exact same hardware configuration so that when the Registry is restored there are no invalid configurations. At an installation for a client, I restored a system state backup of a machine that was made before a hardware upgrade. Immediately following the restore the system hard drive became unavailable because the RAID controller drivers and parameters in the Registry were invalid. If you do not keep your system state backups up to date after each hardware change, they become a liability as opposed to an asset.

The Exchange Setup utility, on the other hand, can be used to recover a server regardless of the hardware changes. This is because the configuration information for the Mailbox server, Hub Transport server, Client Access Server, and Unified Messaging server roles is stored in Active Directory. The setup utility pulls the configuration from Active Directory when the /M:RecoverServer option is invoked. If you have to purchase a new server or utilize an existing server to restore your Exchange 2007 server, you will want to use the Exchange Setup /m:RecoverServer option. Before you use this option, you must make sure you have no plans of bringing the server you are replacing back online.

Using Setup /m:RecoverServer

Before a new computer can take the place of the failed Exchange 2007 server, you must reset the computer account in Active Directory. Resetting the computer account will allow the new server to join the domain without losing all the permissions and configurations associated with the failed server. You never want to delete the existing computer object for the failed server because this will purge Active Directory of the critical Exchange Server data.

Follow these steps to reset the computer account:

1. Open Active Directory Users and Computers.
2. Navigate to the computer object for the lost server. By default, it will be in the Computers container.
3. Right-click the server name and select Reset Account.

The server that you use to replace the failed server doesn't have to have exact matching hardware. However, it is a good idea to use equivalent or better hardware. Also, you need to configure the server with the same number of disk drives (LUNs) as the original server and assign the disks with the same drive letters so that the recovered configuration data matches the available paths. This includes connecting it to the same SAN if one exists. Connecting back to the SAN can be tricky with new hardware. The new host bus adapter (HBA) will have a different world wide number (WWN) from the failed server. Check with your SAN vendor on how to register the new HBA and configure it to have access to the same LUNs as the failed server. If you would like more detail on what a WWN is, see http://searchstorage.techtarget.com/expert/KnowledgebaseAnswer/0,289625,sid5_gci1159703,00.html.

Here are the steps to follow to build the replacement server:

1. Install Windows 2003 on the new server.
2. Install all service packs and hotfixes that the failed server had applied. Do not install patches that have not yet been applied to the failed server.
3. Change the name on the server to be the failed server name.
4. Join the Active directory domain of the failed server.
5. Open Computer Management and navigate to Disk Management.
6. Change the drive letters of each disk present in Disk Management to match the drives of the failed server.
7. Insert the Exchange 2007 media. Click Start | Run, type **<SourceDrive>:\setup .com /m:recoverserver** (as shown next), and click OK.

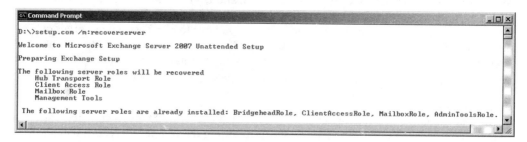

Based on the configuration information available in Active Directory for the failed server, setup will perform a custom installation. Specifically, the roles that were running on the failed server will be reinstalled. Any customizations made locally on the failed server will be lost, however. Once the recovery is complete you will need to manually reapply the custom settings to the server.

Recovering Transport Servers

Microsoft created the two transport roles (Hub Transport and Edge Transport) in the Exchange 2007 architecture to work together to process the e-mail messages both inside and outside the Exchange organization. They are both based on the same SMTP transport stack, so they share the same basic components. A failure on a transport server can prevent mail flow. Depending on the design you implement, you may or may not be able to continue to send and receive e-mail when a single transport server goes down. Because the majority of the Hub Transport configuration information is stored in AD, a failed Hub Transport can simply be replaced. In fact, just adding a new Hub Transport server in the same Active Directory site as the failed server will provide an alternative route for mail to flow through. Edge Transport servers are not as easy to replace. The configuration of an Edge Transport server role resides on the server, not in Active Directory. Typically, there are numerous customizations to the Edge Transport server for anti-spam and antivirus protection. Therefore, it is important to back up this configuration information. To do this, you can use ExportEdgeConfig.ps1, which is provided by Microsoft.

Backing Up an Edge Transport Server with ExportEdgeConfig.ps1

Use the following steps to backup the configuration of an Edge Transport server.

1. Log onto the Edge Transport server.

2. Open the Exchange Management Shell.

3. Type **./ExportEdgeConfig.ps1 -cloneConfigData: "<Drive>:\EdgeBackupFile.xml"** and press ENTER. (Note: <drive> is the location where you want to save the file, and EdgeBackupFile.xml is whatever name you want to call the file.)

4. Verify that the confirmation message shows a successful export, as shown next.

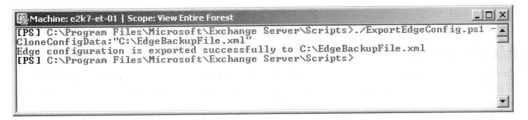

5. Move or copy the .xml file to a server on your internal network where it can be backed up.

Unfortunately, local configuration information is not the only casualty when a transport server fails. It is possible that undelivered messages are still in the queues. If you can still access the queue database, you might be able to recover and resubmit those messages. Another issue that faces the transport server is limited disk space. If a queue database becomes too large to fit on the drive, it could become corrupted. If the database becomes corrupted, it may be necessary to repair the queue database in order to recover and replay messages stuck in the queue. These procedures are outlined in the Microsoft TechNet article, "Working with the Queue Database on Transport Servers," at http://technet.microsoft.com/en-us/library/bb124343.aspx.

Restoring an Edge Transport Server with ImportEdgeConfig.ps1

Use the following steps to backup the configuration of an Edge Transport server.

1. Install Windows 2003 on the new server.

2. Install all service packs and hotfixes that the failed server had applied. Do not install patches that have not yet been applied to the failed server.

3. Change the name on the server to be the failed server name and add the DNS suffix for the Exchange organization.

4. Leave the server as a member of a workgroup.

5. Install the Edge Transport role.

6. Open the Exchange Management Shell.

7. Create an answer file that will work with your configuration file by using the following cmdlet:

```
[PS]C:\> ./importedgeconfig.ps1 -cloneConfigData
"<Drive>:\EdgeBackupFileName.xml" -isImport $false -CloneConfigAnswer
"<Drive>:\EdgeAnswerFile.xml"
```

NOTE *It is not necessary to edit the answer file, but you should review it to confirm that there are no undesirable settings.*

8. Type **./ImportEdgeConfig -cloneConfigData:"<Drive>:\EdgeBackupFileName .xml" isImport $true -CloneConfigAnswer "<Drive>:\EdgeAnswerFile.xml"** and press ENTER.

9. Verify the confirmation message shows a successful export.

10. Configure EdgeSync between the new server and AD.

Disaster Recovery

So far in this chapter we have reviewed the backup and restore procedures supported by Exchange Server 2007. These procedures are the building blocks that allow you to create a disaster recovery plan. Disaster recovery plans run the gamut—from minimal backups with high tolerance for failures and outages, to full backups with little or no tolerance for outages. It is not likely that you will find an environment that can tolerate any data loss. That is why backups are essential to any disaster recovery plan. Here is a list of outages you should be aware of so that you can plan appropriately:

- Deleted mail items
- Deleted mailboxes
- Failed database or storage groups
- Failed mailbox server (data still intact)
- Failed mailbox server (data lost)
- Failed Client Access Server
- Failed node in an Exchange 2007 cluster
- Failed storage subsystem
- Failed cluster (all nodes)
- Network failures and network service failures (DC, GC, DNS, LDAP, and so on)
- *Force majeure* (acts of nature or mankind that causes the loss of an entire site)

The comprehensiveness of your plan will depend on your ability to be prepared for some or all of these events. In the event that your backup strategy fails to provide you with the ability to restore your data, you should become familiar with the additional tools available to assist you in restoring service and repairing databases.

Exchange 2007 Recovery Tools

Earlier in the chapter, we reviewed procedures for recovering databases and mailboxes. The tool that makes that process easier to accomplish is the Database Recovery Management (DRM) tool. DRM is collection of tools you can use when you have to recover data. DRM is a subset of a larger collection of tools called the Microsoft Exchange Server Performance Troubleshooting Assistant (ExTRA) tool as shown in Figure 18-7.

Database Recovery Management Tool (DRM)

The DRM tool is fairly complex to navigate. Table 18-2 defines the various DRM tasks that you can perform.

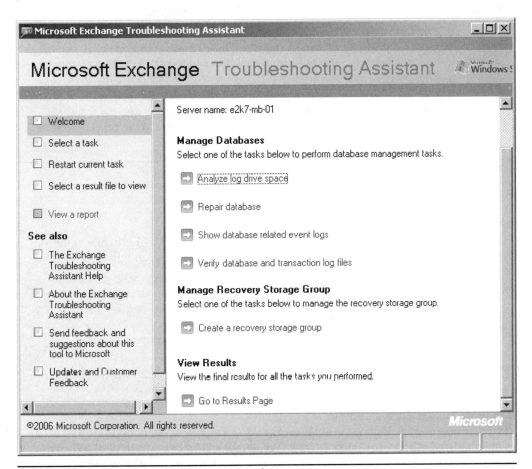

FIGURE 18-7   Database Recovery Management tasks

DRM Task	Description
Analyze log drive space	Determines drive space issues for databases and log files.
Repair database	Repairs corrupted databases.
Show database related event logs	Generates a report on database errors in the Application Event log.
Verify database and transaction log files	Determines the reason why databases fail. Also used to verify file availability for restore procedures.
Create a recovery storage group	Creates a recovery storage group for restoring mailbox data.
Merge or copy mailbox contents	The RSG task that restores mailbox content.
Mount or dismount the databases in the recovery storage group	This RSG task is necessary as the the RSG databases are not visible in the EMC. You can use this tool to mount and dismount the recovered databases as well.
Remove the recovery storage group	This RSG task removes the existing recovery storage group after restores are complete.
Set up "Database can be overwritten by restore" flag	This is a mandatory step for production databases prior to a restore. Empty databases added to the RSG will automatically have this value set.
Swap databases for "dial-tone" scenario	Used to swap the temporary database with the recovered database. The paths are changed, and the configuration information in AD is updated.

TABLE 18-2   DRM Task Descriptions

Database Troubleshooting Tool

The Database Troubleshooting Tool will analyze events generated by Exchange in the Application log related to the Mailbox and Public Folders databases. It will attempt to do the following:

- Troubleshoot why the database will not mount
- Troubleshoot why the log files are inconsistent
- Troubleshoot why the log file generation has run out of numbers to name the log files
- Identify events that indicate low disk space on volumes containing Exchange databases and transaction logs

Extensible Storage Engine Utility

The Extensible Storage Engine Utility (Eseutil.exe) is a low-level command-line tool used to maintain and in some cases repair Exchange database files (see Figure 18-8). When a database cannot be repaired by a restore from backup, it may be possible to repair it

```
C:\WINDOWS\system32\cmd.exe - eseutil /?

C:\Program Files\Microsoft\Exchange Server\Bin>eseutil /?

Extensible Storage Engine Utilities for Microsoft(R) Exchange Server
Version 08.01
Copyright (C) Microsoft Corporation. All Rights Reserved.

DESCRIPTION:  Database utilities for the Extensible Storage Engine for Microsoft
(R) Exchange Server.

MODES OF OPERATION:
     Defragmentation:   ESEUTIL /d <database name> [options]
            Recovery:   ESEUTIL /r <logfile base name> [options]
           Integrity:   ESEUTIL /g <database name> [options]
            Checksum:   ESEUTIL /k <file name> [options]
              Repair:   ESEUTIL /p <database name> [options]
           File Dump:   ESEUTIL /m[mode-modifier] <filename>
           Copy File:   ESEUTIL /y <source file> [options]
             Restore:   ESEUTIL /c[mode-modifier] <path name> [options]

<<<<<  Press a key for more help  >>>>>
D=Defragmentation, R=Recovery, G=inteGrity, K=checKsum,
P=rePair, M=file duMp, Y=copY file, C=restore
=>
```

FIGURE 18-8   Eseutil

using Eseutil. Eseutil is located in the Microsoft Exchange BIN directory (C:\ProgramFiles\
Microsoft\Exchange Server\BIN). Although this tool has traditionally been used to
administer Mailbox and Public Folders databases, its scope of administration now includes
the Hub Transport and Edge Transport server roles. If multiple versions of Exchange coexist
in your organization, you need to be cautious about which version of Eseutil you are using.
The Exchange 2007 version is not compatible with previous versions of Exchange. Use the
Exchange 2003 Eseutil to manage and repair 2000/2003 Exchange database files.

Offline defragmentation (Eseutil /D) is a common task that administrator use to
optimize Exchange database performance. Offline defragmentation and other optimization
tasks are covered further in Chapter 20. Eseutil /D is also used as part of the database repair
procedure to create a stable database after the repair procedure is complete. A repaired
database will be considered consistent. However, due to the nature of the repair process, it
could be unreliable.

Eseutil scans the logical structure of the database tables and records. If the logical
structure is inconsistent with the physical data on the disk, Eseutil will attempt to repair the
data. If the repair fails, the logical reference to the data is removed from the database tree
structure. In other words, it makes the database consistent by removing the reference to the
missing data. A defragmentation will move all the consistent data to a new database and
delete the original database, leaving a single consistent and reliable database. Table 18-3 lists
the various modes that Eseutil can run in and gives a brief description of each mode.

Information Store Integrity Tool

After Eseutil is used to perform a low-level repair (Eseutil /P) of a Mailbox or Public Folders
database, it is often necessary to fix the reference made to the database from the Exchange
application itself. Otherwise, users' mailbox items or public folder posts will inaccurately
represent the data that is in the database. The Information Store Integrity tool (Isinteg.exe)
will fix the inconsistence between the application and the database (see Figure 18-9). In some
cases, Isinteg can restore relationships between mailboxes, folders, items, and attachments

Eseutil Mode (Switch)	Description
Defragmentation (Eseutil /D)	Defragments the database offline and can be configured to leave the previous database intact or to purge it.
Repair (Eseutil /P)	Repairs a corrupted database by removing pages that point to data that cannot be repaired.
Restore (Eseutil /C)	Displays restore log file (Restore.env file). Can be used to force a hard-recovery after restoration from streaming backups.
Recovery (Eseutil /R)	Replays transaction log files that have not yet been committed to the database.
Integrity (Eseutil /G)	Scans the database and reports on integrity issues. It does not repair the database.
File Dump (Eseutil /M)	Displays headers of database files, transaction log files, and checkpoint files. Also displays database page header information as well as database space allocation and metadata.
Checksum (Eseutil /K)	Verifies checksums on all pages in the database, log files, and checkpoint files.
Copy File (Eseutil /Y)	Performs a fast-copy of very large files.

TABLE 18-3   Eseutil Mode Descriptions

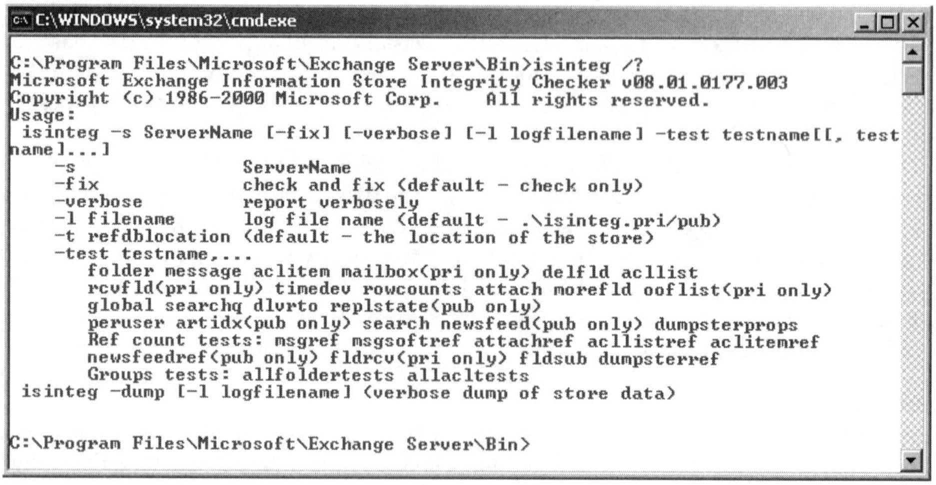

```
C:\WINDOWS\system32\cmd.exe                                              _ □ ×

C:\Program Files\Microsoft\Exchange Server\Bin>isinteg /?
Microsoft Exchange Information Store Integrity Checker v08.01.0177.003
Copyright (c) 1986-2000 Microsoft Corp.    All rights reserved.
Usage:
 isinteg -s ServerName [-fix] [-verbose] [-l logfilename] -test testname[[, test
name]...]
    -s               ServerName
    -fix             check and fix (default - check only)
    -verbose         report verbosely
    -l filename      log file name (default - .\isinteg.pri/pub)
    -t refdblocation (default - the location of the store)
    -test testname,...
        folder message aclitem mailbox(pri only) delfld acllist
        rcvfld(pri only) timedev rowcounts attach morefld ooflist(pri only)
        global searchq dlvrto replstate(pub only)
        peruser artidx(pub only) search newsfeed(pub only) dumpsterprops
        Ref count tests: msgref msgsoftref attachref acllistref aclitemref
        newsfeedref(pub only) fldrcv(pri only) fldsub dumpsterref
        Groups tests: allfoldertests allacltests
 isinteg -dump [-l logfilename] (verbose dump of store data)


C:\Program Files\Microsoft\Exchange Server\Bin>
```

FIGURE 18-9   Isinteg

that cannot be restored by Eseutil. Isinteg should only be used as a disaster recovery tool—never as a maintenance utility. It patches the information store after a restore from an offline backup.

Summary

The least common denominator in a disaster recovery plan is the backup. Backups provide the first level of operational continuity. The technology that is employed by an organization to back up and restore Exchange data has a far-reaching effect on the overall design of Exchange 2007. Exchange administrators must ensure that decision makers (management) understand that the critical data and associated backup of that data goes beyond the mail stores. A number of changes in Exchange 2007 are designed to make Exchange more reliable and highly available. However, it is critical to create a disaster recovery plan for Exchange 2007.

In Exchange 2007 SP1 and higher, the ability to perform remote streaming backups has been disabled by default. If you run third-party backup software that still uses the legacy ESE API, you will need to follow the instructions in the Exchange 2007 SP1 Release Notes to enable remote streaming backups. Microsoft's new System Center Data Protection Manager (DPM), Version 2, supports the Exchange 2007-enhanced version of VSS. DPM is a proprietary backup solution from Microsoft that provides continuous data protection for Microsoft application and files servers.

How you add and configure recovery storage groups has changed significantly in Exchange 2007. In Exchange 2003, it was possible to use the Exmerge tool to extract data from the RSG to a PST. With Service Pack 1 for Exchange 2003, the merge and copy operations were integrated with the Exchange Task Wizard. In Exchange 2007, both have been replaced by the Restore-Mailbox cmdlet in the Exchange Management Shell and the Exchange Disaster Recovery Analyzer (ExDRA).

Exchange 2007 introduces, for the first time ever in the application's history, the native capability to restore any mailbox database in an organization to another production mailbox server in the same organization. Previous releases of Exchange imposed restrictions that prevented databases from being mounted on different servers. Exchange 2007's database portability removes the restrictions and makes it possible. The configuration of an Edge Transport server role resides on the server, not in Active Directory. Typically, there are numerous customizations to the Edge Transport server for anti-spam and antivirus protection. Therefore, it is important to back up this configuration information. To do this, you can use ExportEdgeConfig.ps1, which is provided by Microsoft. A complete set of tools are provided by Microsoft with Exchange 2007 for administering, troubleshooting, and recovering Exchange servers and data including: DRM, the Database Troubleshooting Tool, the Extensible Storage Engine Utility (Eseutil), and the Information Store Integrity tool (Isinteg).

High Availability

Perhaps one of the most important tasks confronting Exchange administrators or the messaging team, as well as IT departments in general, is ensuring the availability of messaging as a service. Exchange Server 2007—RTM and SP1—has plenty of new features and functionality to meet the high availability needs of many deployments. Exchange Server 2007 documentation covers high availability in a lot of detail. Frankly, the amount of information available is mind-boggling, to say the least. At the time of this writing, SP1 is headed through its final iterations toward an eventual release. New documentation and changes to existing docs continue to surface. This chapter is an attempt to cover high availability in general and the features available in Exchange Server 2007 SP1 to an extent that you have a good understanding of them.

More importantly, a note about what this chapter is not: It is not an exhaustive, in-depth coverage of the high availability features and how to deploy and manage them. Such coverage may require a separate book on Exchange Server 2007 high availability, and the Exchange UE team is doing a great job of documenting the how-to's and all the nuances of using these features.

Another note before proceeding: Make yourself comfortable with the acronyms used in this chapter. There are plenty of TLAs (three-letter acronyms) related to high availability, starting with SLAs (or Service Level Agreements).

Understanding High Availability

High availability is generally driven by Service Level Agreements (SLAs) between IT departments and business units. Business units want a messaging service that is always available, with reliable performance. It is IT's job to deliver on those expectations.

Availability means different things to different segments of IT professionals and the user community. A delay in e-mail delivery by more than a few minutes, the inability to schedule a meeting or to access scheduling information (Free/Busy) for recipients, the inability to send or receive e-mail on a mobile device, and so on, may be perceived by users as e-mail being unavailable. Messaging systems may be up, but network connectivity could be sluggish or unavailable. Exchange is dependent on a number of components, including Active Directory, DNS, and network infrastructure such as routers, switches, and firewalls. It is important to consider these different aspects and define them clearly in SLAs.

Going a step further, Exchange high availability can be further segmented into the availability of each of its services—Outlook/MAPI availability, Outlook Web Access availability, Exchange ActiveSync availability, message delivery or transport server availability, and new to Exchange Server 2007-Unified Messaging availability. In the Exchange Server 2007 context, availability of Mailbox and Hub Transport (and optionally Edge Transport) servers can provide Outlook/MAPI connectivity and message delivery. An outage of the Client Access Server or Unified Messaging server(s) does not impact these.

For many organizations, availability and reliability go hand in hand. SLAs in such organizations can be quite granular, down to defining and measuring the time it takes for a message to be delivered within a particular office or geographical area, between two locations, and between a location and Internet recipients. Yet another layer of granularity may be measuring all of these areas for different message sizes. All of these are measures of reliability—e-mail may be *available*, or even *highly available*, but how reliable is it?

Measuring High Availability

Availability is measured by the percentage of uptime. If you are expected to provide service availability for 365 days a year, 7 days a week, 24 hours a day, it adds up to 525,600 minutes or 8760 hours a year. One-hundred percent uptime would translate into a service always being available—an ideal that has since long been considered close to unachievable by many IT organizations.

NOTE *It is possible to provide 100% availability for a shorter duration, such as a day or a week. However, Service Level Agreements are more concerned with availability over a period of time, and results of service delivery are reviewed at different levels on a monthly, quarterly, or yearly basis. Although it's not quite uncommon to see some top-tier infrastructure providers such as ISPs, hosting companies, and power companies guaranteeing 100% availability, I have not worked in an IT department that guarantees 100% availability of messaging services without any caveats.*

If 100% availability remains all but unachievable for most IT departments, what is achievable and respectable? For instance, although 99% availability Sounds reasonable, it actually translates into 5256 minutes, or 87 hours, or 3.65 days of lost productivity! For most businesses this would be unacceptable.

Between 99% and 100% uptime lie the proverbial "nines" of availability, as illustrated in the following table:

	Downtime	
Availability %	**Minutes**	**Hours**
99.999%	5.26	0.09
99.99%	52.56	0.88
99.9%	525.60	8.76
99.7%	1576.80	26.28 (a little over 1 day)
99%	5256	87.60

As is evident from this table, the holy grail of 99.999% availability, also known as *five nines*, affords you a little over five minutes of downtime every year. Planning to apply that emergency hotfix that requires restarting the server? Then consider yourself in violation of the SLA, depending on whether such maintenance is done within a planned outage window, and if such planned maintenance windows are defined in SLAs.

What High Availability Costs

The other side of this high availability and SLA coin is cost. It should come as no surprise that high availability comes with high costs attached to it—costs for building adequate redundancy or fault tolerance into systems, networks, and the IT infrastructure, as well as costs for redundant power supplies in servers and network equipment, redundant CPUs, network interfaces, switches, routers, Internet connectivity from multiple providers, and so on. Costs are directly proportional to availability, up to a certain point. Beyond that, they rise exponentially (for instance, the costs of multiple redundant datacenters if site redundancy is required, electricity from different power grids to eliminate the utility company as a single point of failure, and the like).

The cost of high availability becomes an important factor in deciding how far one can move the goalpost in terms of percentage of uptime.

The Cost of Not Having High Availability

Entire books have been written on high availability, redundancy, fault-tolerant computing, and Service Level Agreements, with a common theme—the cost of downtime. Vendors of high-availability hardware, software, and solutions often cite the cost of downtime in their marketing collateral. For messaging, the cost of downtime due to a large number of users affected by an e-mail outage can be staggering. The cost of a datacenter outage, or an entire organization without access to e-mail for an extended period of time, is even more so. An outage may last for a few minutes, but its impact is felt by users for much longer and has a cascading effect on dependent business processes.

It is this cost of downtime that is used by most vendors to justify the cost of high availability.

Not too long ago, Zenprise commissioned the independent analyst firm Osterman Research to determine the cost of downtime for e-mail and that of troubleshooting the root causes of e-mail outages and fixing them. Though focused on quantifying the cost of troubleshooting e-mail-related problems, which can be quite complex in larger organizations and involve multiple departments in addition to the Exchange/messaging team, the report provides an insight into the costs of e-mail outages as well. According to the report, the downtime costs an organization of 5000 employees an average of $520,000 per year in lost productivity. For larger organizations, the curve is much higher. The complete report is available on the Zenprise website at http://www.zenprise.com/resources/pdfs/Zenprise-RP_Osterman.pdf.

This cost of downtime is not the same across different types of organizations. For instance, in environments where e-mail is not very critical to operations—and I am sure such businesses exist—downtime may not be nearly as damaging. Many small businesses may not be as concerned about downtime, and certainly do not incur the same type of costs should downtime inevitably occur. Yet many other organizations may fully understand the implications and costs of downtime, but may have budgetary constraints that do not allow for elaborate high-availability implementations, or even any type of high availability at all.

The good news is, Exchange Server 2007 has plenty of new features to aid your high-availability efforts. For the rest of this chapter, we will look at high-availability features in Exchange Server 2007, how they work, and how to set these up.

High Availability Features in Exchange Server 2007

Out of all the server roles in Exchange, the Mailbox server role is perhaps the one that needs the most high availability "love and care." Mailbox servers host mailboxes, and they provide access to MAPI clients such as Microsoft Office Outlook. An outage of a Mailbox server most immediately and most severely impacts all Exchange users, regardless of the client used. Outlook clients using MAPI or Outlook Anywhere, or those using IMAP, POP, Outlook Web Access (OWA), or Exchange ActiveSync (EAS) are equally impacted by it.

Previous versions of Exchange have relied on server clusters and Microsoft Cluster Service (MSCS). MSCS traces its roots back to Windows NT 4.0 and "Wolfpack," the first version of MSCS, released as a part of Windows NT 4.0 Service Pack 3. (As some of the examples and screenshots in this chapter will reveal, that codename and the metaphor are used through the rest of this chapter—that of individual cluster nodes as wolves, and together the cluster nodes as a pack of wolves, or a "wolfpack.")

With each version of Windows and Exchange since then (Windows 2000 + Exchange 2000, and Windows Server 2003 + Exchange Server 2003), Exchange clusters have grown increasingly sophisticated in ease of deployment, stability, scalability, and ease of management. From the two-node model of the original Wolfpack release, MSCS clusters can now scale up to as many as eight nodes in Windows Server 2003, and as many as 16 nodes in Windows Server 2008. However, the underlying "shared nothing" model hasn't changed much, nor has the reliance on a bunch of shared disk volumes used to maintain the cluster quorum data and Exchange's Information Store. Needless to say, the shared storage has been the proverbial Achilles' heel for Exchange clusters utilizing MSCS (in addition to the network used for public communication, the outage of which can result in cluster failure).

NOTE *Windows Server 2003 allows the use of Majority Node Set (MNS) quorum, thus freeing MSCS clusters from the conundrum of a single copy of the quorum residing on a shared volume. A post-SP1 hotfix (KB 921181) adds support for a File Share Witness to MNS quorum. Windows Server 2003 SP2 includes this hotfix.*

Many third parties have stepped in to provide an interesting framework of solutions, including replication of shared storage or data, the ability to use geographically dispersed clusters (or *geo-clusters*), and replacements for MSCS altogether. Needless to say, each layer added on top of Exchange or MSCS is another layer of complexity in deployment, operations, and support.

Exchange administrators and messaging architects have long demanded a better clustering and high-availability model—one that doesn't require specially tested and cluster-certified hardware, that doesn't suffer from the single point of failure inherent in shared storage and a single copy of the Information Store, and one that is simple to set up and operate.

How MSCS Clusters Work

The simplest of MSCS clusters can be implemented using two servers running the Enterprise edition of the Windows Server operating system and shared storage. The shared storage can be an external *parallel* SCSI box, shared by the two nodes, or more expensive storage area networks (SAN) or network attached storage (NAS). (As mentioned later in this chapter, Windows Server 2008 failover clusters do not support parallel SCSI.)

No matter what storage you use, it should appear as a local volume to the cluster. SANs typically use Fiber Channel transport. Storage adapters known as Fiber Channel Host Bus Adapters (HBAs) are installed in the servers, which can talk to SAN storage directly or through a Fiber Channel switch. NAS uses plain-vanilla network interfaces (the familiar Ethernet variety found in most servers) and proprietary protocols. Software utilities and drivers are installed on the servers to make the NAS disk volumes appear as locally attached volumes. In recent years, a new protocol called iSCSI has become increasingly popular.

Other components of a cluster include:

- **Network interfaces, networks, and IP addresses**   Each server participating in a cluster is known as a *cluster node*. Each node has two network interfaces (NICs). One NIC is connected to the *public* network, to allow client computers and other servers to connect to the cluster. The second NIC is connected to a *private* network on a different IP subnet, for internal cluster communication. This communication consists of small User Datagram Protocol packets, called *heartbeats*, allowing each cluster node to communicate its state. Another IP address from the public network is assigned to the cluster itself, allowing management applications to connect to it and manage it.

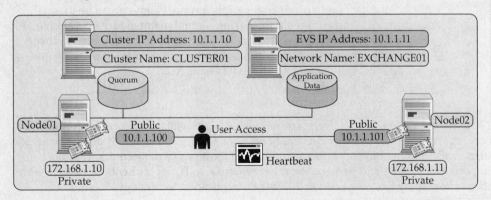

- **Cluster resources**   Server and application resources are exposed by the operating system and cluster-aware applications such as Exchange Server to the cluster service using resource DLLs. These resource DLLs allow the cluster service to abstract the actual resources, allowing cluster resources to be moved from one node to another in a way that is mostly transparent to users of the application or

(Continued)

PART VI

other servers interacting with it. Resources can be owned by only one cluster node at any time. Cluster resources can be hardware resources (such as physical disk), logical resources (such as Network Name or IP address), or application resources (resources made available by cluster-aware applications. For Exchange Server, these include resources such as System Attendant, the Information Store, and so on, exposed by Exchange Server's resource DLL - EXRES.DLL).

- **Cluster resource groups**   Cluster resources are grouped together in cluster resource groups, which work as a *failover unit*. In other words, an entire group can fail over from one node to another—resources in a group may be brought online or offline individually, but cannot be selectively failed over to another node. All clusters have at least one resource group—the one that owns the *quorum*. Each resource group has an IP address and a Network Name resource. Additionally, it may have other resources, including physical disk resources and application resources.

- **Cluster quorum**   The cluster quorum is a database of cluster configurations. It tells the cluster which nodes are participating, the cluster groups created and resources available, the state of each resource (whether online or offline), and which node owns a resource at any given point. It also provides arbitration in deciding which node is active or has ownership of a cluster group and its resources in split-brain scenarios when cluster nodes cannot communicate with each other. The term also refers to the disk volume used to store the quorum database, which traditionally only resided on a shared volume until Windows Server 2003.

- **Failover**   Failover is the process when one cluster group is moved from a node that has ownership of the group to another node that participates in the cluster and can assume ownership of the group. Failovers can be manual (performed by an administrator during normal maintenance operations). However, the term *failover* is generally associated with automated failovers triggered by the failure of a particular resource in a group or by the failure of the node that has ownership of cluster resources.

Exchange Server 2007 delivers a multilayered high-availability solution for mailbox servers, with a combination of clustered and standalone (nonclustered) deployments for high availability within and across geographical locations or datacenters. The most important features—and perhaps the most beneficial to IT departments of all sizes—are those afforded by Exchange Server 2007's new replication technology.

Continuous Replication

The replication is asynchronous, accomplished by initially copying a baseline database (EDB) from the active copy to the passive replica—a process known as *seeding*—followed by continuous replication of closed transaction logs from the active copy of a Storage Group to the replica. After transaction logs are copied to the replica, they are inspected for integrity by running a checksum on the files and inspecting their logical properties such as the signature. Once log files pass the inspection process, they are committed to the replica database in batches. The entire replication process is handled by the Microsoft Exchange Replication Service. The Replication service manages the truncation of log files on the active and passive copies of a storage group. Files that have not been replayed to the replica are not truncated on the active copy after a successful backup, with the exception of SCR, where truncation behaves a little differently because there can be one source replicated to many targets.

More technical details about replication architecture can be found in an excellent blog post by Scott Schnoll at http://snipurl.com/20j12.

Replication is used by three new high-availability features: Local Continuous Replication (LCR), Cluster Continuous Replication (CCR), and Standby Continuous Replication (SCR).

These high-availability features are enabled per storage group, and they have the same basic requirement: Replication can be enabled for only those storage groups that have a single database. Additionally, there are some restrictions on replicating storage groups that contain Public Folder database(s), which are discussed with each feature in the remainder of this chapter. Let's take a look at each of these.

LCR: Database and Storage Redundancy

Local Continuous Replication (LCR) is the poor man's cluster—or perhaps more appropriately, the poor man's non-cluster. It replicates (production) storage groups to another volume on the same server, providing protection from failure of the volume where the primary storage group resides, as well as protection from database corruption.

LCR is set up on a per–storage group basis. It makes sense to use a separate physical volume to store the LCR replica, as opposed to separate logical partitions on the same physical volume. For the price of a few disks, one can have the redundancy that many Exchange administrators—particularly those in smaller IT shops with limited resources—have desired for a long time.

Yes, you may religiously back up your Exchange server every night or perhaps several times during the day. Yes, you may religiously verify your backups every other day. However, the benefit of LCR becomes immediately apparent when you can have users with mailboxes on a corrupt database or one residing on a failed disk volume back in business in less time than it takes to find a backup tape.

Is there a price to pay besides the storage? Yes, albeit a minor one. Because replication only happens on a single server, the integrity of replicated logs is checked, and logs are replayed to the replica database on the same server, the server ends up spending about 20% of CPU cycles. Given the strides in processing capacity, as predicted by Moore's Law, it's not something you should spend any more cycles thinking about.

Additionally, Microsoft recommends servers with LCR enabled be provisioned with an additional 1GB of RAM.

NOTE *Exchange Server 2007 RTM requires the volume with the LCR replica to have two to three times the disk IOPS (I/Os per second) as the volume where the active copy of the database is located. This has been optimized in Exchange Server 2007 SP1 to require the same I/O performance as the volume with the active copy.*

With LCR enabled, and the replica database functioning as the first line of defense in case of failure, the recovery times are significantly reduced.

New Exchange administrators often question how large mailbox databases should be allowed to grow. The common response to such questions has been, as large as they can be to allow your backup product/technology to restore within a reasonable amount of time, which is within the SLAs. LCR enables an organization to maintain larger databases and to quickly switch to the replica. However, should the first line of defense fail for some reason, you will need to restore from a backup. When defining SLAs for Exchange Server 2007, make sure you consider both these factors. For LCR-enabled databases, Microsoft recommends the maximum database size of 200GB, double the recommend 100GB size of databases that do not utilize replication.

If you don't have the budget to go the clustering route, LCR can be the first step on the road to high availability on a limited budget.

Setting Up Local Continuous Replication for an Existing Storage Group

LCR can be set up quite easily using the EMC or the Exchange shell. Here are the steps to follow to set up LCR for a storage group using the EMC:

1. Expand the Server Configuration container and select Mailbox.

2. From the Details pane, select the Mailbox server.

3. From the Database Management tab, select the storage group to be replicated.

4. Click the Enable local continuous replication link on the Action pane to start the Enable Storage Group Local Continuous Replication Wizard, shown in Figure 19-1.

5. On the Introduction page, verify that the correct storage group is selected and that it has a single database. Click Next.

FIGURE 19-1
Enabling LCR on an existing storage group using the EMC

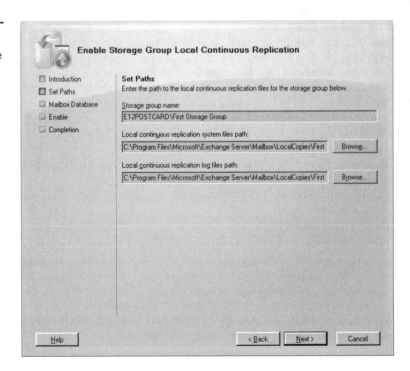

6. On the Set Paths page, select the paths for system files and transaction logs. Click Next.

7. On the Mailbox Database page, select the path where the database should be replicated to and click Next.

8. On the Enable page, review the paths selected in the previous steps. Click Enable to enable LCR replication.

9. On the Completion page, review the output to ensure LCR was enabled successfully. Then click Finish to close the wizard.

To enable LCR using the Exchange shell, use the following commands:

```
Enable-DatabaseCopy "E12Postcard\SG3\SG3-MBX2" –CopyEDBFilePath
"E:\SG3-MBX2\SG3-MBX2.EDB"
```

In these commands, E12Postcard is the server name, SG3 the storage group, and SG3-MBX2 the mailbox database. Note that the path includes the EDB filename. Next, enable LCR on the storage group:

```
Enable-StorageGroupCopy "E12Postcard\SG3" –CopyLogFolderPath "C:\SG3-Logs"
–CopySystemFolderPath "C:\SG3-Logs"
```

Once an LCR replica is created on a server, the server cannot be a *target* of a Standby Continuous Replication (SCR is discussed later in this chapter) replica from another Exchange server. However, you can replicate a storage group from this server to any other server using SCR, including any storage groups that are already being replicated locally using LCR.

Enabling LCR for New Storage Groups

When you're creating new storage groups using the EMC, the New Storage Group Wizard provides the ability to enable LCR for the storage groups and to select replica log and system file paths during creation. To create a new storage group and enable LCR for it, use the following command:

```
New-StorageGroup –Server "E12Postcard" –Name "E12Postcard-SG4"
-SystemFolderPath C:\SG4-Logs" -LogFolderPath "C:\SG4-Logs" -HasLocalCopy
$true –CopyLogFolderpath "E:\SG4-Logs" –CopySystemFolderPath "E:\SG4-Logs"
```

A storage group without a database is of no particular use. In fact, if you leave a storage group in this state with LCR enabled, the Microsoft Exchange Replication Service will take the opportunity to chastise you for it, by logging Event ID 2062 in the Application event log. The event reminds you that there are no databases to replicate—you should either create one or delete the storage group. Being the good Exchange geeks that we are, we will not provide any Exchange service to complain or be dissatisfied with our attitude to it. In the next step, we create a new mailbox database and enable replication for it.

The New Mailbox Database Wizard behaves like the New Storage Group Wizard—it allows you to specify the path for the LCR replica database. Here's how to create a new mailbox database and enable it for LCR using the Exchange shell:

```
New-MailboxDatabase –StorageGroup "E12Postcard-SG4" –Name "E12Postcard-SG4-MBX1"
-EDBFolderPath "C:\SG4-MBX1" -CopyEDBFolderPath "E:\SG4-MBX1"
```

Keeping an Eye on Replication: Monitoring Replication Health

With LCR enabled, one should keep a close eye on replication health. We want to ensure the replica is marching in lockstep with the active copy of the storage group, that copy and replay queues are not building up, and that there is not a huge gap between the time when logs are closed by the active storage group and when they are copied, inspected, and replayed to the replica.

This can be done using the EMC by viewing the properties of a storage group, as shown in Figure 19-2, or you can do it from the shell.

As you may already have noticed when working with the EMC and the shell, the latter generally provides more information. Here's the command to use:

```
Get-StorageGroupCopyStatus "E12Postcard\E12Postcard-SG4"
```

TIP *If storage group names are unique, you can omit the name of the server from the command. If the identity of an object that is the target of a particular shell command is the first parameter you use after the command, you can also get by without having to type "–identity" every time.*

The preceding command outputs replication status in brief, by displaying four important parameters—SummaryCopyStatus, CopyQueueLength, ReplayQueueLength, and LastInspectedLogTime. The SummaryCopyStatus parameter can be Healthy, Seeding, Copying, Stopped, Disabled, or Failed. The CopyQueueLength parameter, as the name

FIGURE 19-2
The Local Continuous Replication tab displays replication health and related statistics

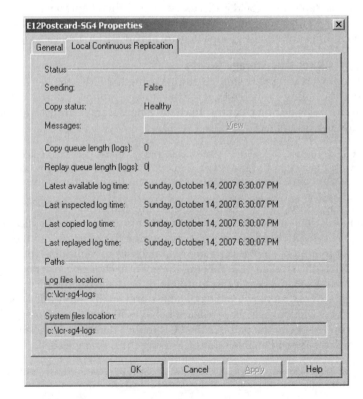

suggests, indicates the number of log files yet to be copied from the active copy. The ReplayQueueLength parameter indicates the number of copied logs to be replayed to the replica database. To get a complete list of all the parameters, pipe the output of the preceding command to a list using the following command:

```
Get-StorageGroupCopyStatus "E12Postcard\E12Postcard-SG4" | fl
```

NOTE *The same command is also used to get replication status for CCR and SCR. LCR cannot be enabled for storage groups hosted on a CCR cluster. On servers that do not serve as SCR targets, storage groups can be enabled for LCR to replicate to another volume locally, and also to use SCR to replicate to another server. To get the replication status for the SCR replica, use the optional –StandbyMachine parameter to specify the name of the SCR target server.*

To get a list of all storage groups enabled for LCR, use the following command:

```
Get-StorageGroup | where {$_.HasLocalCopy} | select name,*path | fl
```

To get the replication status for the preceding LCR-enabled storage groups, we can pipe the list to the Get-StorageGroupCopyStatus command, as follows:

```
Get-StorageGroup | where {$_.HasLocalCopy} | Get-StorageGroupCopyStatus
```

To get a list of storage groups where replication is not healthy (this can include states such as Initializing, Failed, and so on), use the following command:

```
Get-StorageGroup | where {$_.HasLocalCopy} | Get-StorageGroupCopyStatus |
where {$_.SummaryCopyStatus -ne "Healthy"}
```

The Test-ReplicationHealth command runs a bunch of replication-related tests and reports the results:

```
Test-ReplicationHealth
```

LCR provides a good starting point to get comfortable with replication and replication-related commands. As noted earlier, these commands will also help you to keep tabs on the replication health of CCR and SCR. Use them, get comfortable with them, and understand the output.

The Replication service also logs a number of events to the Application event log. Replication errors and warnings logged by the Replication service (MSExchangeRepl) should be monitored (see Figure 19-3).

Getting into the Replication Frame of Mind: Managing Replication

Needless to say, replicated storage groups and databases should be treated a little differently than the ones that are not replicated. Besides monitoring replication health, one needs to get used to the procedures of suspending and resuming replication when required. This is equally true for CCR and SCR, as it is for LCR. If you need to move the paths of the LCR source storage group or database, or those of the LCR replica, replication will need to be suspended. Need to indulge in any disk maintenance goodness? Replication will need to be suspended.

Figure **19-3**
Errors and
warnings logged by
the Replication
service should be
monitored

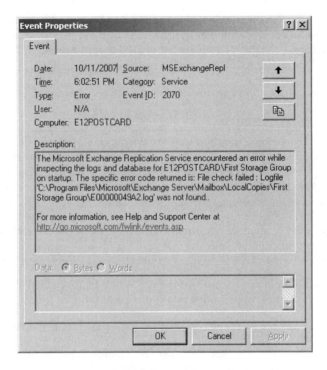

With an LCR-enabled storage group selected, you can suspend and resume LCR by clicking the shortcuts in the Action pane. For shell jockeys, use the following command to suspend LCR:

```
Suspend-StorageGroupCopy "E12Postcard\E12Postcard-SG4"
```

Here's how to resume replication of an LCR-enabled storage group:

```
Resume-StorageGroupCopy "E12Postcard\E12Postcard-SG4"
```

Seeding and Reseeding Replicas

When enabling LCR on a storage group, the Replication service copies the database to the path specified in the –EDBFilePath parameter. This initial copying of the database is called *seeding*. At times, the database may need to be reseeded. This may be required when replication cannot continue due to corrupt log files, or when the original/active and the replica databases diverge from each other—such as when the database is defragmented offline.

Reseeding could be one of those pain-inflicting moments for Exchange administrators, depending on the size of the database, the server, and storage. Large databases will take a while to be copied, thus taxing the server and the storage in the process. This is another one of those tasks that are best performed during periods of low user activity.

To reseed the database using the EMC, select the Storage Group and click Update Storage Group Copy in the Action Pane.

When using EMC to reseed, Exchange suspends replication, reseeds the storage group, and resumes replication. When using the Exchange shell, you need to suspend replication first using the following command:

```
Suspend-StorageGroupCopy "E12Postcard\E12Postcard-SG4" -SuspendComment
"Need to reseed"
```

After suspending replication, you need to delete all files in the LCR target path. Next, the storage group can be reseeded using the following command:

```
Update-StorageGroupCopy "E12Postcard\E12Postcard-SG4"
```

After the storage group is reseeded, the preceding command resumes replication automatically. Optionally, you can bypass the automatic resumption by adding the –ManualResume parameter to the command and using the Resume-StorageGroupCopy command when replication needs to be resumed.

Besides using Exchange's built-in reseeding feature via the EMC or the shell, you can also perform reseeding by manually copying the EDB file to the LCR replica's EDBFolderPath.

CAUTION *To manually reseed using this option, replication needs to be suspended first and the database taken offline.*

Yet another option to reseed is to disable LCR and enable it again.

Disabling LCR
LCR can be disabled on a storage group using the EMC. Select the storage group and click the Disable Local Continuous Replication link in the Action pane. To disable LCR using the shell, use the following command:

```
Disable-StorageGroupCopy "E12Postcard\E12Postcard-SG4"
```

When Disaster Strikes: Activating the LCR Replica
All the technical jargon, detailed descriptions, and procedures outlined so far are of little use unless you need to switch to the replica copy at some point. This may be necessary if the active copy of the storage group is corrupt, or if the volumes on which these reside decide to prove the Mean Time Between Failure (MTBF) statistics cited by storage vendors is nothing but wishful thinking.

At such times, the first step should be assessing the cause of the damage and the health of the replica. The latter can be done using the Get-StorageGroupCopyStatus command or the EMC, as described earlier in this section.

You can activate the replica in a number of ways:

- **Similar paths used by the active storage group and LCR replica**   The paths used by the active copy of the storage group/database are the same, except the drive letter, as in the following example:

Copy	Storage Group System and Log Files	Database
Active	D:\SERVER1-SG1	E:\SERVER1-SG1-MBX1\SG1-MBX1.EDB
LCR replica	F:\SERVER1-SG1	G:\SERVER1-SG1-MBX1\SG1-MBX1.EDB

In this case, you can simply use the Disk Management console to change the drive letter assignments. A similar change can also be done if volume mount points are used—the mount point assignments can be easily reconfigured.

- **Move files**   This involves copying files from the LCR replica location to the location of the active copy. Copying large databases can take much longer, with every minute counting against your SLA performance—not something management likes to see.

- **Change paths**   The preceding methods make activation of the replica possible without changing the storage group configuration in AD—it still points to the same path of the active copy. Another quick alternative is to simply change paths and point Exchange to the replica. Although Microsoft doesn't recommend it, there is no particular reason for not choosing this method. The downside: Another administrator may be surprised to come back to work and find the storage group files now reside in F:\Local Copies\SG1 and the database in G:\Local Copies\SG1-MBX1.EDB. However, with adequate change control procedures, communication, and documentation, this should not be a major issue. Plus, it has the advantage of providing the quickest and "most automated" recovery.

The actual method used will differ in each case, depending on what's easier and quicker to accomplish in your configuration. The mission: Minimize downtime.

Use the following procedure to activate the replica:

1. If the Database is still mounted, dismount it using the EMC or the Dismount-Database command from the shell.

2. Prepare the replica to be mounted. If changing drive letter assignments, reconfiguring volume mount points, or copying files from the replica to the original location, use the following command:

   ```
   Restore-StorageGroupCopy "E12Postcard-SG4"
   ```

NOTE   *After the preceding command is used, perform the appropriate disk management procedure to ensure the storage group and database files from the replica magically appear in the original location, unless the –ReplaceLocations switch will be used to change paths.*

If you're changing the storage group and database paths, use the following command (see Figure 19-4):

```
Restore-StorageGroupCopy "E12Postcard-SG4" –ReplaceLocations $true
```

```
[PS] C:\>Restore-StorageGroupCopy e12postcard-sg4 -ReplaceLocations
     Base name: e03
     Log file: e:\sg4-logs\E030000005A.log
     Csv file: c:\lcr-sg4-logs\IgnoredLogs\ymiojkca.pp2

     Base name: e03
     Log file: c:\lcr-sg4-logs\E030000005A.log
     Csv file: c:\lcr-sg4-logs\IgnoredLogs\yq40jf0w.efy

Integrity check passed for log file: c:\lcr-sg4-logs\inspector\E03.log
WARNING: The Restore-StorageGroupCopy operation for storage group copy E12Postcard-SG4 was
successful, and production paths were updated. All logs were successfully copied.
[PS] C:\>Mount-Database e12postcard-sg4
```

FIGURE 19-4   Using Restore-StorageGroupCopy with –ReplaceLocations switch

3. The database is now ready to be mounted using your tool of choice—the EMC or the Mount-Database command from the shell.

4. If the original or additional volumes are available, enable LCR again to create a new replica. To set up LCR again for the storage group, use the Enable-DatabaseCopy command to enable LCR for the database, and use Enable-StorageGroupCopy for the storage group. If the volumes containing the logs and database from the formerly active copy are available, you can use the same paths used earlier (in effect, reversing the direction of LCR replication this time, from the now-active copy to the paths used by the previously active copy). This will avoid reseeding.

   If the database was dismounted because of corruption, reseeding will be required. The logs and database on that volume will need to be deleted.

   If new disk volumes are being used, the database will be seeded.

5. (Optional at this point.) If the MTBF figures cited by the storage vendor proved to be hot air, send them an e-mail. Brag to your manager as well as their manager about the less-than-X-seconds/minutes of downtime your well-planned and well-implemented Exchange deployment suffered. Ask for a day off, as you prepare to receive the most valuable employee of the year award from the CEO! (Recommended: Send a thank you e-mail to the Exchange marketing gods for not requiring an Enterprise edition license to use LCR.)

It's not hard to see why LCR (and other replication features) has many Exchange administrators and messaging teams excited.

Single Copy Cluster: Server Redundancy

Single Copy Clusters (SCCs) can be thought of as Exchange clusters as we know them from previous versions of Exchange Server. They use shared storage, which becomes a single point of failure "out of the box," unless augmented by third-party solutions that provide redundancy to the storage. As such, SCC provides the benefit of server redundancy, but does not provide any storage or database redundancy.

Failure of shared storage—particularly the SAN and NAS variety that comes with plenty of redundancy built in, depending on the implementation—is not very common. However, it is a risk nevertheless that needs to be understood and mitigation steps taken.

PART VI

Another important factor to keep in mind is the comparatively more stringent hardware requirements for SCC—hardware used for nodes of a cluster should be similar, and the entire solution should be listed in the Cluster Solution category on the Windows Server Catalog of Tested Products.

Together, these requirements drive up the cost of high availability and may affect your choice of the type of clusters to deploy.

With that out of the way, Single Copy Clusters do have some notable features lacking in the CCR model, including the ability to scale up beyond the two-node limitation of CCR, to as many as eight nodes on both Windows Server 2003 and Windows Server 2008. Organizations with significant investments in expensive, redundant storage, and perhaps third-party solutions in use to provide replication and geographically dispersed clustering solutions, may find it beneficial to stick with this known model. If you decide to take this route, make sure the existing solutions are compatible with Exchange Server 2007, and determine whether any upgrades are required for compatibility.

SCC benefits from Exchange Server 2007's reduced number of cluster resources— remember, there is no support for any other server role except the Clustered Mailbox Server. There are no equivalents of protocol virtual server resources such as HTTP, SMTP, POP3, and IMAP. The only resources exposed by Exchange Server 2007 are System Attendant, Information Store, and Exchange Database instances, in addition to the Network Name and IP Address resources that must exist in a CMS. This adds to the simplification of the cluster resource dependency model, resulting in faster failovers in most deployments.

NOTE *Exchange Server 2007 SCC clusters should have one or more Physical Disk resources. These are shared volumes on which Exchange Server 2007 databases and transaction logs reside. Additionally, the Cluster group may use the traditional shared quorum resource, or the quorum may reside locally on each node if the Majority Node Set quorum is used, or optionally the MNS quorum with a File Share Witness may also be used for SCC.*

Cluster Continuous Replication: Server and Storage Redundancy

Cluster Continuous Replication (CCR) is the brave, new child of Exchange Server 2007's high availability bandwagon. It uses Windows Server's Cluster Service and provides the same automated failover capabilities that have characterized Exchange clusters since we have known them. However, in addition to providing server redundancy, it also provides storage redundancy.

Gone is the requirement of using shared storage, which forced one to use the kludgy parallel/shared SCSI that many administrators shied away from in the past, or more expensive NAS/SAN storage that became the *de facto* clustering requirement and made Exchange clusters quite attractive to the bottom line of storage companies.

Following are some of the notable benefits of CCR:

- **CCR does not require shared storage; local/direct attached storage can be used**   CCR uses Exchange Server 2007's continuous replication technology to replicate transaction logs from an active node to the passive node. In addition to server redundancy, CCR provides storage and database redundancy out of the box. If one server becomes unavailable, or its storage fails completely, a Clustered Mailbox Server using CCR will fail over, survive, and continue to provide service. Besides its replication features, it capitalizes on Windows Server's Majority Node

Set quorum with a File Share Witness, which eliminate shared quorums as the single point of failure in MSCS clusters. That's a major leap over the shared storage model of clustering in previous versions of Exchange.

- **CCR provides storage *and* database redundancy**   CCR drives down the cost of clustering. In addition to not requiring expensive shared storage implementations, it allows the use of hardware that's neither similar nor cluster-certified—or even listed on the Clustering Solutions list. Hardware listed on the Windows Server list can be used instead. Although not a best practice, two cluster nodes do not need to have matching specs, thus allowing one to redeploy and reuse one-off servers.

- **CCR is cheaper to implement**

Here are a couple other advantages of CCR:

- **Backups from passive node**   CCR provides the ability to perform VSS backups from the replica on a passive node, without taxing the performance of the active node.

- **Reduced backup requirements**   With previous versions of Exchange, it is not uncommon to see frequent backups of the Exchange Information Stores being performed to ensure very little data is lost in case of a disaster—and what's on the backup media is as up-to-date as possible. In fact, in a large number of deployments, backups are performed multiple times a day. Performing such backups requires more storage, either online or on *near-line* disks (a term used for slower, cheaper disk-based storage offered by most storage vendors) or on tape. Having a replica of Exchange storage groups readily available reduces backup requirements. The replica serves as the first line of defense in case of a disaster.

How Cluster Continuous Replication Works

CCR uses Exchange Server 2007's continuous replication technology, which is also used by Local Continuous Replication (LCR) and Standby Continuous Replication (SCR, discussed later in this chapter). Simply put, replication copies a baseline database from an active node to the passive node, and uses *log shipping* to copy transaction logs from the active node to the replica on the passive node.

Replication is asynchronous. Transaction logs are copied by the passive node after they are closed by the active node. The Microsoft Exchange Replication Service provides this replication functionality. No additional CPU load is placed on the active node, because the logs are copied by the passive node.

NOTE *One concern expressed by many IT departments with the active/passive clustering topology in previous versions of Exchange Server and SCC in Exchange Server 2007 is the fact that the passive node is completely idle. It does nothing besides waiting for a failover to happen. Many consider this a waste of resources, and some use this to profess an active/active topology, where both the nodes in a cluster host an EVS/CMS (an instance of Exchange server). An active/active topology is no longer offered in Exchange Server 2007. Passive nodes in CCR clusters are not really passive—they are actively involved in the replication process, copying log files from the active node, inspecting them for integrity, and replaying them to their own replica of the database. Additionally, backups can be performed on the passive CCR node, which happily bears that load.*

In previous versions of Exchange Server, the size of transaction logs is 5MB. In Exchange Server 2007, it has been reduced to 1MB. This ensures that less data is locked by the active node, and transaction logs are copied faster because of their smaller size.

However, at any given point of time, the active node in a CCR cluster will have data that has not been replicated to the passive node. A natural question to ask at this point is, what happens after a failover? Will you see messages missing on the replica residing on the passive node, which becomes active after a failover? This is where a new feature called the Transport Dumpster comes in.

The Transport Dumpster is a *cache* of recent messages held on Hub Transport servers. Remember, every message delivered to an Exchange Server 2007 mailbox must pass through a Hub Transport server, including those sent by senders to recipients on the same server. In the event of a failover, Hub Transport servers deliver messages from the Transport Dumpster to the new active node. Messages already existing in a mailbox are filtered out, and missing messages are delivered to the mailbox shortly after a failover occurs.

Does the transport dumpster guarantee that there will be no data loss at all? One wishes this were the case, but imagine the few scenarios where messages have not made it to the Hub Transport servers. These include messages a user may have stored in the Drafts folder when Outlook is in online mode (another reason to use the Microsoft Outlook client in Cached Mode), messages still in transit to the Hub Transport server, appointments and tasks.

Cluster Continuous Replication Requirements

In addition to the prerequisites for the standalone Mailbox server role, installing Exchange Server 2007 SP1 on clusters involves the following requirements:

- **Windows Server Enterprise or Datacenter edition**   All cluster nodes need to be running Windows Server 2003 Enterprise or Datacenter edition or Windows Server 2008 Enterprise edition. Nodes running different operating system versions are not supported in the same cluster.

- **Windows Server 2003 SP2**   If Windows Server 2003 is being run, Service Pack 2 is required on both nodes before you install Exchange Server 2007 SP1.

NOTE *In addition to SP2, at the time of this writing, the hotfixes in Microsoft KB Article 931836, "August 2007 Cumulative TimeZone Update," and KB Article 926776, "Hotfix for .Net Framework 2.0," are also required. If these are not installed, Exchange setup will prompt you to install them. KB 931836 has been superseded by KB, December 2007 cumulative time zone update for Microsoft Windows operating system.*

- **Domain membership**   All cluster nodes must be members of the same Active Directory domain. Nodes running Exchange Server 2007 must not be domain controllers or members of different domains.

- **Cluster Service account**   Windows Server 2003 clusters use a Cluster Service account. This account must be a domain user account and a member of the local Administrators group on each cluster node. Windows Server 2008 Failover Clusters do not require a service account—Cluster Service runs as the LocalSystem account.

NOTE *The MSDTC component, a requirement for Exchange clusters in previous versions, is not required on cluster nodes running Exchange Server 2007. No MSDTC resource needs to be created to setup SCC or CCR.*

- **File Share Witness** Microsoft recommends locating the file share used for file share witness (FSW) on a Hub Transport server. However, any server running a Windows Server operating system that's a member of the domain can host the FSW.

- **Number of cluster nodes** CCR supports only two nodes. Sure, you can create a failover cluster using the Majority Node Set (MNS) quorum and a File Share Witness with more than two nodes. However, the additional nodes are not utilized by CCR. The FSW acts as a *voting node* to avoid split- brain scenarios, where the two nodes are disjointed and both claim ownership of resources. It is important to understand that the FSW is merely a computer with a shared folder and voting rights to form a majority. It is not a cluster node *per se* and cannot own any cluster resources.

- **Network interfaces** Each cluster node requires at least two network interfaces. One is connected to a *public* network for all communications with clients and other servers. The second network interface is connected to a *private* network using a different subnet dedicated to the cluster.

NOTE *The term* public *network does not imply the use of public or external IP addresses reachable on the Internet. Although you can use external IP addresses accessible from the Internet on the public network, the term* public *is used here in the context of client computers and other servers such as AD domain controllers, DNS, Hub Transport servers, and Client Access Servers.*

If the servers are in close proximity in the same datacenter, the private interfaces on both nodes can be connected to each other directly using a crossover cable. In fact, many a clustering document with illustrations show two nodes as being connected directly to each other, implying the use of crossover cables. However, consider this: When a crossover cable is used, if one of the nodes becomes unavailable, the Windows OS treats the network interface as being down, even on the node that is up. Therefore, it is recommended that you use a network device such as a hub to connect the two.

- **IP Addresses** A two-node cluster requires at least six IP addresses
  - Two for the public network
  - Two for the private network
  - One for the cluster
  - One for the Clustered Mailbox Server (CMS)

- **Hardware** Windows Server 2003 or Windows Server 2008 cluster nodes in a CCR environment do not need hardware that is certified for clustering. It is no longer required to have identical hardware—cluster nodes can use dissimilar hardware. It is recommended that cluster nodes have similar specs, however, to maintain the same level of performance after a failover.

PART VI

Network Configuration for Failover Clustering

Failover Clustering, whether SCC or CCR, requires at least two network interfaces (NICs) on each cluster node. One interface is connected to a public hub or switch, to make the nodes accessible to clients and other servers connecting to a Clustered Mailbox Server. The other interface is used for private communication between cluster nodes, often referred to as *heartbeats*.

It is a good idea to rename the network interfaces Public, Private, or Heartbeat, or any other appropriate name that make it easier to identify which networks they are connected to or what their intended purpose is—whether for public connectivity with other servers and clients, or for private communication with other cluster nodes.

Configuring the Network Connection Order

1. On the Network Connections control panel, select the Advanced menu and then select Advanced Settings.

2. On the Adapters and Bindings tab, under Connections, ensure the connections appear in the following order: Public, Private/Heartbeat, Remote Access Connections.

Additionally, on the NIC used for private communication, follow these steps:

1. In Network interface's properties, uncheck File and Print Sharing for Microsoft Networks and Client for Microsoft Networks.

2. No default gateway or DNS server addresses need to be entered.

3. On the DNS tab, uncheck Register this connection's addresses in DNS.

4. On the WINS tab, select Disable NetBIOS over TCP/IP.

Setting Up Cluster Continuous Replication

Setting up CCR involves similar steps on Windows Server 2003 and Windows Server 2008, with some differences. This assumes all prerequisites have been met.

1. Configure the two network interfaces on each node with appropriate public and private IP addresses. Make the necessary changes to the network configuration for the NIC used for private cluster communication (see the earlier section on network configuration).

2. Form a cluster using the cluster.exe command-line utility or using the Cluster Administrator tool on Windows Server 2003. On Windows Server 2008, the tool is called Failover Cluster Management (console).

3. Add the second node to the cluster.

NOTE   *On Windows Server 2008, both nodes can be added to the cluster during cluster formation. On Windows Server 2003, adding the second node is an additional step.*

4. Change the quorum type to Majority Node Set with File Share Witness on Windows Server 2003, or to Node and File Share Majority Quorum on Windows Server 2008.

5. Install Exchange Server 2007 as an Active Clustered Mailbox Server on the first node, and as a Passive Clustered Mailbox Server on the second node.

Setting Up Exchange CCR on Windows Server 2003

To set up CCR on Windows Server 2003, start with the first step of cluster formation. To create the cluster using the Cluster Administrator tool, use the following procedure:

1. Start the Cluster Administrator console from Administration Tools. When this console is started for the first time, it brings up the Open Connection to Cluster dialog box, with the default action set to Create a new cluster. Click OK to create a new cluster.

2. On the Welcome page, click Next.

3. On the Cluster Name and Domain page, (Figure 19-5), make sure the correct domain name is selected in the Domain drop-down.

4. In the Cluster name field, enter a name for the cluster. This name is used as the Network Name resource for the cluster group. Click Next.

5. On the Select Computer page, make sure the name of the first node you are installing the cluster on is selected. Click Next.

6. On the Analyzing Configuration page, validation checks are run to check cluster feasibility. The wizard displays a warning that no sharable quorum resources could be found and a local quorum will be created. The quorum type will be changed later and a File Sharing Witness configured. Click Next.

7. On the IP Address page, specify the cluster IP address.

8. On the Cluster Service Account page, enter the Cluster Service account name and password. Make sure the correct domain name is selected in the Domain drop-down. Click Next.

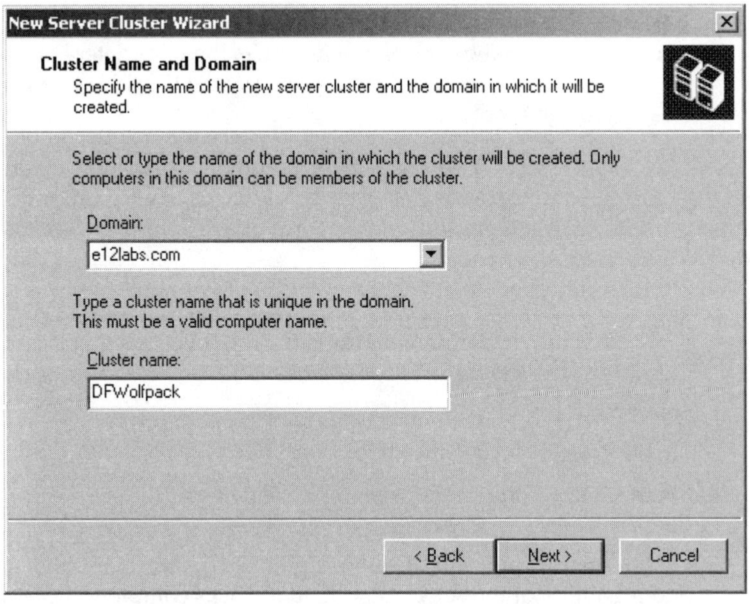

FIGURE 19-5
Specifying the cluster name on the Cluster Name and Domain page. This name is used as the Network Name resource for the cluster group.

9. On the Proposed Cluster Configuration page, click Quorum. Change the quorum to Majority Node Set from the drop-down and then click OK.

10. Verify the configuration parameters, including the cluster name, IP addresses, the service account, and the quorum type. Click Next.

11. On the Creating the Cluster page, the wizard creates the cluster and configures the Cluster Service. The cluster group is created during this process. Network Name, IP Address, and quorum resources are created in the group. Review any errors or warnings that may appear during cluster formation. If all tasks complete successfully, click Next.

12. Click Finish to close the New Server Cluster Wizard.

The new cluster is created at this point. Now is a good time to review the cluster group and all the resources created in it—namely, the Cluster IP Address, Cluster Name, and the Majority Node Set (quorum) resources. Inspect the properties of the resources.

- The General tab of each resource lists the node(s) that are the possible owners for a resource.

- The Dependencies tab lists which cluster resource this resource is dependent on. This helps you understand the cluster dependency model. The Network Name resource has no dependencies. This is the first resource that is brought online. The IP Address resource is dependent on the Network Name resource. The Majority Node Set resource also has no dependencies. On a cluster where a shared quorum is used, the quorum is dependent on the shared disk where the quorum resides.

- The Advanced tab lists the heartbeat polling settings, how a resource should be treated when it fails, and whether the failure of a resource affects the entire resource group.

- The Parameters tab is available if there are any associated values for a selected resource. For the Network Name resource, the parameter is the name you selected for the cluster. For the IP Address resource, the IP address you entered during cluster setup is displayed.

Next, we add the second server as an additional node to the cluster. This can be done from the Cluster Administrator tool or using the cluster.exe command-line utility from the first node itself. Alternatively, you can perform this task from the second server that is to be added to the cluster as a node.

To add the second node using Cluster Administrator, follow these steps:

1. Right-click the cluster name. This is the top-level container displayed in Cluster Administrator, shown in Figure 19-6.

2. Select New | Node.

3. On the Welcome page, click Next.

4. On the Select Computers page, type the name of the second server, click Add, and then click Next.

5. On the Analyzing Configuration page, the wizard checks the cluster configuration and feasibility of the selected node. If all tasks complete successfully, click Next.

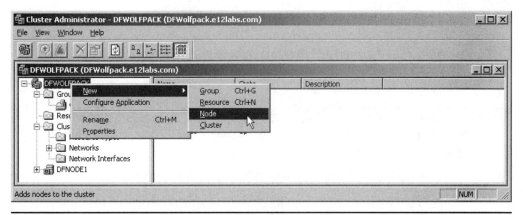

FIGURE 19-6   Adding a new node to the cluster

6. On the Cluster Service Account page, the Cluster Service account you used to create the cluster is already populated. Enter the password for the service account. Click Next.

7. On the Proposed Cluster Configuration page, verify the configuration parameters. Click Next.

8. On the Adding Nodes to the Cluster page, the wizard performs the final validation checks, adds the server as a new node to the cluster, and modifies the cluster configuration and resources to include the new node. If all tasks complete successfully, click Next.

9. Click Finish to close the Add Nodes Wizard.

Review the cluster group and resource configuration in Cluster Administrator again. Note the new node has been added as a possible owner on the General tab of each resource in the group. Under Networks, the network interfaces of the new node have been added to the appropriate Public and Heartbeat networks.

Optionally, you can test failover of the cluster group by right-clicking the cluster group and selecting Move Group. To do this from the command line via the cluster.exe utility, use the following command:

```
Cluster Group "Cluster Group" /Move:DFNODE2
```

All resources in the group are taken offline and then brought online on the second node. After failover, the second node is listed as the owner of all resources.

You can move the cluster group back to the first node using this procedure by replacing the name of the node with the (now) passive node DFNode1.

Verifying Heartbeat Network Communication

It is important to ensure the Heartbeat network is used for internal cluster communication only. In Cluster Administrator, expand Cluster Configuration | Heartbeat | Properties. On the General tab, select Internal cluster communication only (private network).

PART VI

Configuring a File Share Witness

With the cluster formed, we need to perform one more step before we move on to installing Exchange Server 2007 SP1. The quorum needs to be changed from Majority Node Set to Majority Node Set with File Share Witness. A shared folder needs to be created on the server that will act as a File Share Witness.

NOTE *If a node in a clustered environment using Majority Node Set quorum with File Share Witness fails, the computer hosting the File Share Witness shared folder should be available for the cluster to fail over successfully.*

Follow these steps to create the shared folder for the File Share Witness:

1. Log onto the server that will host the File Share Witness, using an account that has local Administrator privileges. The server can be any server running the Windows Server operating system, located in the same AD site as the cluster nodes. Microsoft recommends using a Hub Transport server for this purpose.

2. Create a new folder on any disk volume on the server using Windows Explorer or the command prompt. For this example, we create a new folder called FSW-DFWolfpack on the C:\ drive. If you're doing this from the command prompt, use the following command:

   ```
   Mkdir C:\FSW-DFWolfpack
   ```

3. Share the folder and assign Full Control share permission to the Cluster Service account. This can be done using Windows Explorer from the Share tab of the folder's properties, or using the command line. To do this from the command line, use the following command:

   ```
   net share FSW-DFWolfpack=C:\FSW-DFWolfpack /GRANT:e12labs\clustersvc,FULL
   ```

4. Assign Full Control NTFS permission for the folder to the Administrators group and the Cluster Service account. This can be done using Windows Explorer from the Security tab of the folder's properties, or using the Change Access Control Lists utility from the command line. To do this from the command line, use the following command:

   ```
   cacls C:\FSW-DFWolfpack /G BUILTIN\Administrators:F e12labs\clustersvc:F
   ```

5. Log onto either cluster node using the Cluster Service account. Using Windows Explorer or the command line, verify that the account can access the share using the Universal Naming Convention path—for example, \\Servername\FSW-DFWolfpack.

NOTE *Microsoft recommends creating an alias (a CNAME record in DNS; for example, witness .mydomain.com) for the server holding the shared folder and then using the fully qualified alias in the UNC path for this procedure. This is particularly helpful when nodes reside in different datacenters. In case of a datacenter outage, if the active node and File Share Witness in that datacenter are not available, the CNAME record can be quickly changed to point to a server in the second datacenter where the passive node resides.*

With the folder created and the share and NTFS permissions configured and verified from either node, the quorum on the cluster can be changed to use Majority Node Set with File Share Witness.

***

CAUTION *When using a CNAME to access a file share on a Windows Server 2003 server, you need to disable strict name checking on the server hosting the file share. This is done by adding a Registry value, as discussed in Microsoft KB 281308.*

To change the quorum type for the cluster, log onto a cluster node using an account that has local Administrator privileges and follow these steps:

1. To change the quorum to use a File Share Witness, we need to set a property of the Majority Node Set quorum. This is done from the command line using the cluster.exe utility:

   ```
   Cluster DFWolfpack res "Majority Node Set" /priv MNSFileShare=\\
   e12postcard\FSW-DFWolfpack
   ```

   In this example, DFWolfpack is the name of the cluster. E12Postcard is the Hub Transport server hosting the shared folder that will be used for the File Share Witness. FSW-DFWolfpack is the share name of the folder.

2. If the property change completes successfully, cluster.exe will state that the property has been changed, but will not take effect until the next time the resource is brought online.

3. Move the cluster to the second node and then move it back to the first node.

4. Verify the MNSFileShare property of the Majority Node Set resource using the following command:

   ```
   cluster DFWolfpack res "Majority Node Set" /priv
   ```

You now have a cluster up and running, with a Majority Node Set quorum that uses the File Share Witness. Now we can install Exchange Server 2007 SP1 on both nodes, one at a time.

Installing Exchange Server 2007 SP1 on the First Node

To install the Active Clustered Mailbox Server role using the Exchange Setup Wizard, follow these steps:

1. From the Installation Type page, select Custom and click Next.

   (Optional) You can change the path where Exchange Server is installed by clicking the Browse button. The default path is C:\Program Files\Microsoft\Exchange Server. If you change the path, remember to use the same path when installing Exchange on the passive node.

2. On the Server Role Selection page, shown in Figure 19-7, select Active Clustered Mailbox Role and click Next.

3. Take the following actions on the Cluster Settings page:

   a. Under Cluster type, select Cluster Continuous Replication.

   b. In the Clustered Mailbox Server Name field, enter a name for the Clustered Mailbox Server (CMS). This is used as the Network Name resource for the CMS, and it appears as an Exchange server in Exchange management tools.

   c. (Optional) You can change the path where Exchange databases will be created by clicking the Browse button and selecting the correct path.

FIGURE 19-7
Installing Exchange
Server 2007 SP1
on the first node

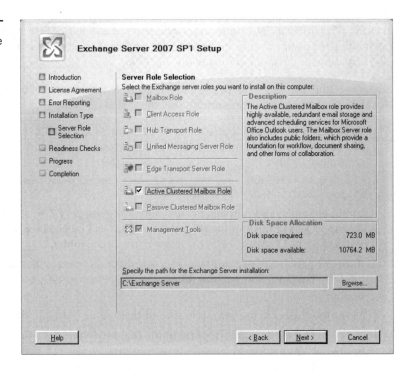

FIGURE 19-7
Installing Exchange
Server 2007 SP1
on the first node

4. On the Cluster IP Address Configuration page, shown in Figure 19-8, enter an IPv4 address for the CMS and click Next.

NOTE *The options to use a dynamically assigned (by a DHCP server) IPv4 address, to use an IPv6 address, and to add an IP address for the CMS are grayed out. Support for these is only available when setting up Exchange Server on a Windows Server 2008 Failover Cluster.*

5. On the Readiness Checks page, ensure there are no errors or warnings under Mailbox Role Prerequisites or Clustered Mailbox Server Prerequisites. Click Install.

6. This brings you to the Progress page, which shows the different steps setup takes to install Exchange and create the CMS. It will take a while to complete, so now's a good time to take a break, get a cup of coffee, or simply get some fresh air. If all goes well, you will return to a completed installation and can click Finish.

As part of the installation, Exchange Server 2007 creates a group for the new Clustered Mailbox Server. The group name is the same as the CMS name. Before we move ahead with installing Exchange Server on the passive node, let's take a look at Cluster Administrator and inspect the new resource group created by Exchange setup, as well as the cluster resources in it. Just like in the cluster group, you will find a IP Address resource and a Network Name resource. Additionally, you'll find the following Exchange server resources: System Attendant, Information Store, and Storage Group (see Figure 19-9).

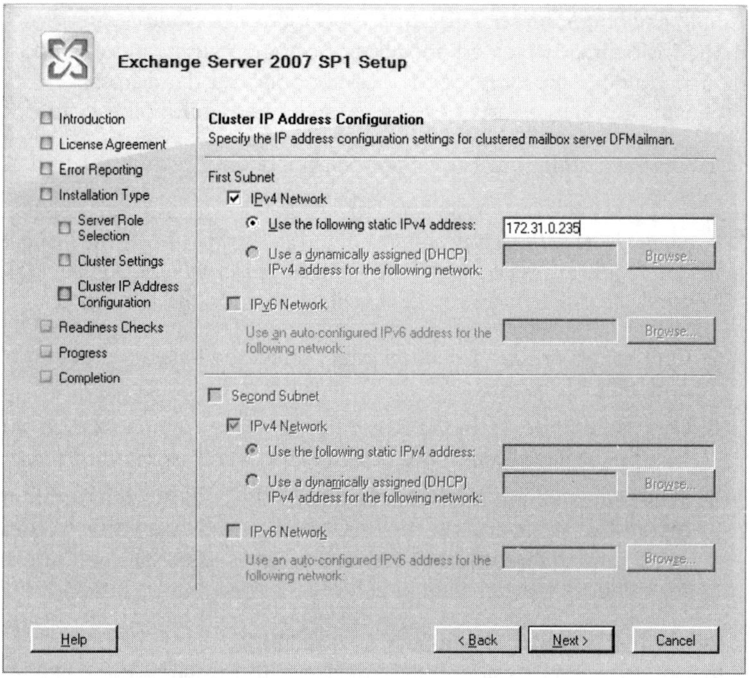

FIGURE 19-8
Adding an IP
address for the
CMS

If you look at the General tab in the properties of each resource in the new resource group, you will find the active node is the only possible owner of those resources. The properties of the Cluster Group resources show both nodes as possible owners. Once we install Exchange Server on the passive node, the node will be added as a possible owner of the newgroup.

FIGURE 19-9   Exchange setup creates a resource group for the CMS, with Network Name, IP Address, System Attendant, Information Store, and Storage Group resources

Installing Exchange Server 2007 SP1 on the Passive Node

With the CMS already created, installing Exchange on the passive node involves fewer steps. You do not get prompted for a CMS name and IP address.

To install Exchange Server on the passive node, follow these steps:

1. On the Installation Type page, select Custom Installation and click Next.

NOTE *If you changed the setup path to a non-default path during the installation of the Active Clustered Mailbox Server, make sure you change the path during installation of the Passive Clustered Mailbox Server as well, to match the one on the active node.*

2. On the Server Role Selection page, select the Passive Clustered Mailbox Server role and click Next.

3. On the Readiness Checks page, ensure there are no errors or warnings under Mailbox Role Prerequisites or Clustered Mailbox Server Prerequisites. Click Install.

4. This brings you to the Progress page, which shows the different steps setup takes to install Exchange and create the CMS. It will take a while to complete, so now's a good time to take another break. If all goes well, you will return to a completed installation and can click Finish.

New Clustering Features in Windows Server 2008

Windows Server 2008 brings some remarkable improvements to MSCS. The feature is now called Failover Clustering, but the name of the Cluster Service remains unchanged. Some of the new features include:

- **New Failover Cluster Manager console**   The Cluster Administrator tool has been replaced with a new console based on Microsoft Management Console 3.0. This brings it on par with the Exchange Management Console (EMC) in Exchange Server 2007, with a similar three-pane window and plenty of configuration wizards and shortcuts in the Action pane on the right.

- **New quorum model**   Failover Clustering supports a new hybrid quorum model. The quorum type can be selected either during cluster setup or after setup is complete to change from one quorum model to another (see Figure 19-10). The four quorum models include:

  - **Node Majority**   Node Majority is recommended for clusters with an odd number of nodes. Each node is given a vote, and the cluster can continue to run as long as a majority of the nodes is available. As such, it only makes sense to use it in clusters with three or more nodes. Failure of half the nodes minus one node ((Nodes/2) – 1) can be sustained. In a three-node cluster, failure of one node can be sustained. In a five-node cluster, failure of two nodes can be sustained. Node Majority can be used for SCC clusters with three or more nodes. However, CCR replication is only supported between two nodes. As such, although adding a third node to a CCR cluster to be able to use Node Majority is possible, you are essentially wasting a node by doing so.

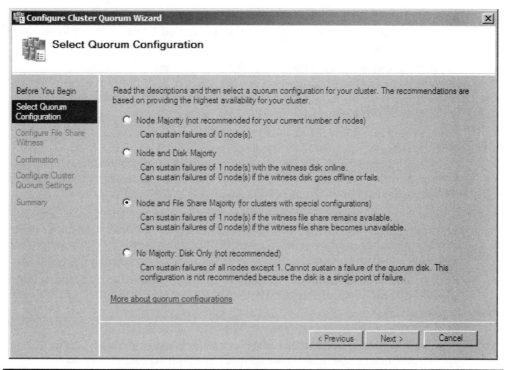

FIGURE 19-10   The Configure Cluster Quorum Wizard in Windows Server 2008 Failover Cluster Manager console displays the quorum choices and makes recommendations based on cluster configuration, nodes, and storage

- **Node and Disk Majority**   Node and Disk Majority is recommended for clusters with an even number of nodes. Each node gets a vote, and so does the quorum (a.k.a., the "witness disk") residing on shared storage like *traditional* quorums in previous versions of Windows Server. A failure of half the total number of nodes can be sustained if the witness disk remains online. The cluster can also remain up if the witness disk is lost but a majority of the nodes are online.

- **Node and File Share Majority (for clusters with special configurations)**   This is the equivalent of Majority Node Set with File Share Witness in Windows Server 2003, and is recommended for two-node clusters. It is also similar to Node and Disk Majority, except the witness disk is replaced by a File Share Witness (FSW). The FSW has a vote in forming the majority in case of a node outage, but it is hosted on a shared folder on a server that does not participate in the cluster.

- **No Majority: Disk Only**   This is the equivalent of a *traditional* shared quorum, residing on a shared storage volume. Outage of the quorum results in outage of the cluster.

- **IPv6 support**   Windows Server 2008 supports Internet Protocol version 6 (IPv6). This support is extended to Failover Clustering as well. Cluster nodes can now use IPv6 addressing.

- **Support for dynamic IP addresses**   Failover Clustering supports the use of dynamically assigned IP addresses. Exchange Server 2007 allows the use of dynamic IP addresses if it's running on Windows Server 2008, but I am yet to see the light on why this is a good idea.

- **Stretch clusters**   Failover Clustering supports two cluster nodes residing on different subnets. As a result, Exchange Server 2007 SP1 supports stretch clusters, or cluster nodes residing in different datacenters on different IP subnets, without the need to stretch the same IP subnet to another datacenter. However, Exchange Server 2007 requires that both IP subnets be associated with the same AD site.

- **Cluster Service runs as LocalSystem**   On Windows Server 2003, the Cluster Service requires a service account that is a domain user account and member of the local Administrators group on each node. On Windows Server 2008, the service runs as the LocalSystem account.

- **Built-in cluster validation tool**   A built-in cluster validation tool is included in the Failover Cluster Manager console. The tool can be used before setting up a Failover Cluster to validate the node configuration, and after cluster setup to validate the cluster configuration.

- **Set up multiple nodes simultaneously**   Failover Clustering allows you to add both or all cluster nodes to a cluster during cluster formation. This saves time because the nodes do not need to be added to the cluster one at a time.

- **No support for parallel SCSI**   Storage that does not support Persistent Reservations, as specified in the SCSI Primary Commands-3 (SPC-3) standard, is not supported by Windows Server 2008 Failover Clusters. Fiber Channel, iSCSI, and Serial Attached SCSI (SAS) all support Persistent Reservations; parallel SCSI does not. This means no support for parallel SCSI. In the earlier days of clustering, it wasn't quite uncommon to see clusters implemented with two nodes and an external SCSI storage enclosure with a bunch of RAIDed disk volumes serving as shared storage. Parallel SCSI is a pain to manage, even when it's not shared between cluster nodes. Adding the *shared* element of clusters to these is a sure ticket to clustering Waa-Waa-land! Ms. Parallel Scsi will not be missed.

- **Support for GUID partition tables**   Failover Clustering supports GPT disk volumes, thus allowing the use of volumes larger than 2TB (terabytes). Exchange Server 2007 has a maximum database size limit of 16TB. You are now free from allowing databases hosted by Exchange clusters to grow to a size that can take a few days to back up, but perhaps with volumes that size you may never need to back up. *(Disclaimer: The author of this chapter owns no stock in any storage company at the time of this writing, but that may change if you take this suggestion to heart.)*

- **No NetBIOS dependencies**   Finally, Windows Server Failover Clusters are free from any dependency on NetBIOS.

- **Extensive use of Windows event logs**   Another welcome move is the more extensive use of Windows event logs for logging clustering-related events, compared to previous versions. Parsing the cluster log is something we can all do without. Windows event logs allow management and monitoring apps to detect clustering-related events easily, given the structure and accessibility event logs provide over parsing a text file. They also make it much easier for administrators to detect, troubleshoot, and report such events, compared to the often-cryptic cluster log. Events in Windows event logs have event IDs, making Internet searches for documents, forum posts, and blogs a lot easier compared to looking for strings from the cluster log. The revamped Event Viewer console in Windows Server 2008 also makes it a lot more *fun* to deal with event logs.

Setting Up Cluster Continuous Replication on Windows Server 2008

The following prerequisites need to be installed on Windows Server 2008 servers to be able to install Exchange Server 2007 SP1:

- **Active Directory management tools**   To install AD management tools on Windows Server 2008, use the following command:

```
ServerManagerCmd -i RSAT-ADDS
```

NOTE *Installation of Active Directory management tools may require a reboot post-installation. The remaining commands in this list can be copied to a batch file and run together. However, if the installation of AD management tools is clubbed with them and then a post-installation reboot is required, the remaining commands will fail.*

- **Windows PowerShell**   Windows PowerShell is included in Windows Server 2008, but is not installed by default. To install it, use the following command:

```
ServerManagerCmd -i PowerShell
```

- **Internet Information Server (IIS) components**   The IIS components required on mailbox servers are a subset of those required for the Client Access Server role. To install the necessary IIS components, use the following commands:

```
ServerManagerCmd -i Web-Server
ServerManagerCmd -i Web-Metabase
ServerManagerCmd -i Web-Lgcy-Mgmt-Console
```

- **Failover Clustering**   Install Failover Clustering using the following command:

```
ServerManagerCmd -i Failover-Clustering
```

Creating a Failover Cluster on Windows Server 2008

With the prerequisites installed, and the public and private network interfaces configured, a Failover Cluster can be formed. To create a two-node Failover Cluster, use the following procedure:

1. Start the Failover Cluster Manager console from Administration Tools.
2. Click the Create a cluster option to create a new Failover Cluster.

3. Enter the names of both the cluster nodes and click Next.

4. On the Validation Warning page, click Yes to run cluster validation tests if you haven't run these before. Click Next.

5. On the Access Point for Administering the Cluster page, enter a name for the cluster in the Cluster Name field, as shown in Figure 19-11. This is the Network Name resource for the cluster group.

6. The networks suitable for the cluster group are displayed. Check the appropriate network and enter the IP address from that subnet in the Address field next to it. If you're using iSCSI storage, make sure the IP address is not used for communication with iSCSI storage. Click Next.

7. On the Confirmation page, ensure the correct cluster name, cluster nodes, and cluster IP address are displayed.

8. Click Finish to complete cluster formation.

The cluster has been created at this point. Windows Server 2008 has a built-in cluster validation tool that includes a number of tests to validate the cluster configuration. However, the cluster does not pass the validation checks at this point because it is set to use a Majority Node quorum, and you only have two nodes in the cluster. The quorum type

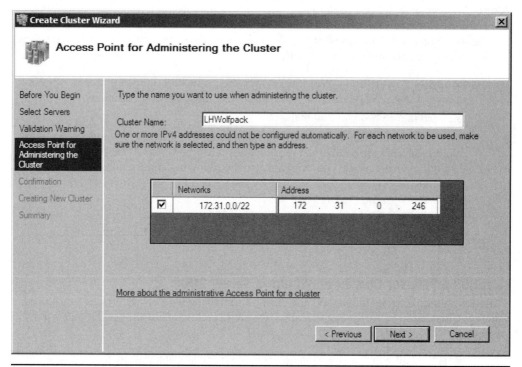

FIGURE 19-11   Providing a network name and IP address for the cluster

needs to be changed to Node and File Share Majority. Before configuring the quorum type, you need to create a shared folder on another domain-joined computer.

Creating a Shared Folder for File Share Witness

Microsoft recommends locating the File Share Witness on a Hub Transport server, but it can be located on any server running Windows Server OS that's a member of the domain.

Follow these steps to create a shared folder for use as a File Share Witness:

1. Log onto the server with a domain user account that is a member of the local Administrators group on the server.

2. Create a new folder. It is recommended that you use a uniform and descriptive naming convention for the File Share Witness folder. In this example, we call it FSW-LHWolfpack.

3. Share the folder. Assign the account or group that will be used to change the quorum type Full Control permission on the share. This can be done from the Share tab of the folder's properties in Windows Explorer, or from the command line using the following command:

```
net share FSW-LHWolfpack=C:\FSW-LHWolfpack /GRANT:E12labs\
SetupAccount,FULL
```

In this command, FSW-LHWolfpack is the name of the shared folder. C:\FSW-LHWolfpack is the folder that is shared. SetupAccount is the admin account used when changing the quorum type.

With the File Share Witness folder created and shared, and adequate permissions assigned, we can now change the quorum type on the cluster to use Node and File Share Majority.

Changing the Quorum Type to Node and File Share Majority

To configure the cluster quorum to use Node and File Share Majority quorum, use the following procedure:

1. Start the Failover Cluster Management console on any cluster node.

2. In the Actions pane, click Configure Cluster Quorum Settings.

3. Review the information on the Before You Begin page and click Next.

4. On the Select Quorum Configuration page, select Node and File Share Majority (for clusters with special configurations). Click Next.

5. In the Configure File Share Witness page, enter the UNC path to the shared folder created earlier for the File Share Witness.

6. If appropriate permissions to the file share cannot be verified, an error message is displayed. If permissions are verified, the Confirmation page appears. Review the UNC path entered and the quorum type selected. Click Next.

7. On the Summary page, ensure the quorum settings were configured successfully. Click Finish to close the wizard.

With the quorum configured to use Node and File Share Majority, we are now ready to set up Exchange Server on both the nodes. You can do this using the command line in a two-step process. The first step installs Exchange Server 2007 SP1 on the node(s) using the following command:

```
setup.exe   /roles:mailbox
```

The second step actually creates the Clustered Mailbox Server (CMS). To create the CMS, use the following command:

```
setup /createcms /cmsname:"CMS Name" /cmsipaddress:x.x.x.x
```

If you're using the Exchange Setup Wizard, follow these steps:

1. From the Installation Type page, select Custom and click Next.

   (Optional) You can change the path where Exchange Server is installed by clicking the Browse button. The default path is C:\Program Files\Microsoft\Exchange Server.

NOTE *If you change the installation path, remember to use the same path when installing Exchange on the passive node.*

---

2. On the Server Role Selection page, select Active Clustered Mailbox Role and click Next.

3. Perform the following actions on the Cluster Settings page:

   a. Under Cluster type, select Cluster Continuous Replication.

   b. In the Clustered Mailbox Server Name field, enter a name for the Clustered Mailbox Server (CMS). This is used as the Network Name resource for the CMS, and it appears as an Exchange server in Exchange management tools.

   c. (Optional) You can change the path where Exchange databases will be created by clicking the Browse button and selecting the correct path.

4. On the Cluster IP Configuration page, we provide an IP address for the CMS. Note the following differences between Exchange setup on Windows Server 2003 and on Windows Server 2008 (see Figure 19-12):

   • Under First Subnet, select the appropriate IP address type (IPv4 or IPv6).

   • If you're using a static IP address (recommended), select Use the following static IPv4 address. Then enter the IP address in the text field next to it.

   • If you're using a dynamic IP address, select Use a dynamically assigned (DHCP) IPv4 address for the following network. Then enter the network address in the corresponding text field.

   • If you're using IPv6, in the corresponding field for Use an auto-configured IPv6 address for the following network, enter the IPv6 network address.

FIGURE 19-12
Windows Server
2008 supports
cluster nodes
residing on
different IP
subnets and the
use of IPv6.
Exchange Server
2007 SP1 setup
allows you to
specify IP
addresses from
two subnets.

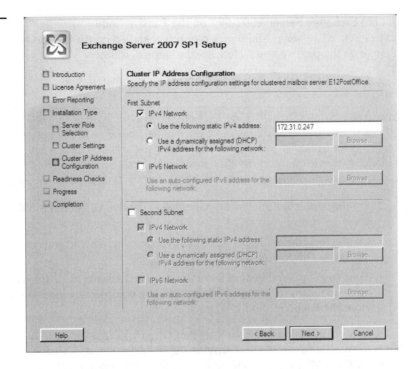

NOTE *Windows Server 2008 allows two cluster nodes to reside on different subnets. This makes it easier to locate the nodes in different datacenters or geographical locations. The Exchange setup GUI allows you to add the second IP address from the remote subnet to be associated with a CMS. Windows Server 2008 makes changes to the logic used for the IP address resource—from AND (both or all IP address resources associated with a cluster resource group should be online) to OR, resulting in a cluster resource group's ability to be brought and remain online if any of the IP address resources in the group is online. Although this allows CCR nodes to be on different subnets, it is important to note that Exchange Server 2007 requires both subnets be associated with the same AD site. Additionally, it is recommended to lower the TTL of the A record created in DNS by the CMS. With a lower TTL, the DNS resolver cache on client computers expire the record in less time, queries DNS again for the record, and discovers the new IP address from the second subnet with which the CMS is associated post-failover.*

5. On the Readiness Checks page, ensure there are no errors or warnings under Mailbox Role Prerequisites or Clustered Mailbox Server Prerequisites. Click Install.

6. This brings you to the Progress page, which shows the different steps setup takes to install Exchange and create the CMS. It will take a while to complete, so now's a good time to take a break. If all goes well, you will return to a completed installation and can click Finish.

Installing Exchange Server 2007 SP1 on the Passive Node

With the Active Clustered Mailbox Server role installed on the first node, it's time to install Exchange on the passive node. Here are the steps to follow:

1. On the Installation Type page, select Custom Installation.

NOTE *If you changed the path where Exchange is installed when setting up the active node, ensure the same path is selected during installation of the passive node. For example, if you created a folder called **Exchange Server** on the C:\ drive, so the path is C:\Exchange Server, click the Browse button when setting up the passive node to create a new folder on the C:\ drive and give it the same name (Exchange Server). Select this folder as the installation path.*

2. On the Server Role Selection page, select Passive Clustered Mailbox Role and click Next.

3. On the Readiness Checks page, ensure there are no warnings or errors when the readiness checks complete. Click Install.

4. Time to get up and get another cup of coffee or some more fresh air. If all goes well, you can return in about 20–30 minutes to a complete installation. Click Finish to close the Exchange Setup Wizard.

The new cluster is now set up. Note that when you're setting up the passive node, the options to create a new CMS and provide the IP address and name for the CMS are not displayed. The CMS is already created when the active node is set up.

Managing Exchange CCR

Managing Clustered Mailbox Servers is not very different from managing standalone Exchange Server 2007 servers. There are some things one needs to know and be careful about, however. For instance, unlike standalone servers, Exchange-related services should not be started and stopped using the Services console. You can use the Cluster Management console (or the Failover Cluster Management console in Windows Server 2008) or cluster.exe to move a CMS from one cluster node to another, but failover typically takes much longer and comes with the inherent risks of the databases not mounting or the cluster group going offline. Exchange Server 2007 management tools—the EMC and EMS—provide the necessary cluster integration and management hooks to move a CMS from one node to another. Additionally, replication health needs to be monitored. When you're undertaking maintenance tasks, replication may need to be suspended and then resumed when maintenance is complete. If replication issues occur, or a cluster node is recovered from a disaster, rebuilt, or a new cluster node added to replace a lost node, the replica needs to be reseeded.

The Exchange Server 2007 SP1 documentation details many procedures related to these tasks. The following sections detail some of the important concepts and tasks one should know about before setting up CCR.

Moving CMS to a Passive Node and Rolling Upgrades

Every once in a while, maintenance needs to be performed on cluster nodes. Firmware may need to be upgraded, or an operating system or Exchange update rollup or service pack may need to be applied. One of the big benefits clustering provides is the ability to perform such operations at any time, without much noticeable impact to operations or uptime. With Exchange cluster nodes running Exchange Server 2000/2003 and Exchange Server 2007's Single Copy Cluster (SCC), it is common to see such operations being performed in the middle of a busy working day, perhaps because of the luxury of having more number of passive nodes available in a cluster. The process, commonly referred to as *rolling upgrades*, allows passive nodes to be updated and restarted, if required, and the Exchange virtual server (or the Clustered Mailbox Server in Exchange Server 2007) moved to the updated passive node. After the move, the formerly active node becomes passive so the same updates can be applied to it. Users using Outlook 2003/2007 in cached mode do not generally notice such failovers, or get a chance to complain. Failover times range from as little as a few seconds to a few minutes.

NOTE *This is by no means an endorsement for performing such rolling upgrades during peak hours. It is mentioned here to illustrate considerations for such maintenance for Exchange Server 2007 cluster nodes running CCR.*

Although this may be acceptable in a cluster with additional nodes to fail over to, CCR has the limitation of being a two-node implementation. The passive node isn't really passive, as in previous versions and SCC clusters. It is actually busy replicating logs from the active node, inspecting them, and committing or replaying them to the replica database. An extended outage of the passive node leaves the CMS without the ability to fail over to another node. Additionally, an extended outage of a passive node results in accumulation of transaction logs on the active node, which cannot be truncated until they are replicated and replayed by the passive node. Further, if a node is lost during maintenance and needs to be rebuilt and added again to the cluster, the seeding of database(s) will be required. Seeding large databases may tax the storage subsystem and degrade performance on the active node.

Therefore, it is advisable to plan any maintenance to be performed on CCR nodes, test any updates or patches in a lab before applying them to production nodes, and strive to schedule such changes to occur during planned maintenance windows.

CAUTION *In earlier versions of Exchange, the Cluster Administrator console or cluster.exe utility is used to move an EVS to a passive node. In Exchange Server 2007, you can move a CMS using either the cluster tools (Cluster Administrator or cluster.exe utility) or the Exchange management tools (the Exchange shell and post-SP1 EMC). It is recommended that you use the Exchange management tools in a CCR environment, because these perform the necessary checks related to replication health and status that the cluster tools do not, and they block the move if they find that one or more databases may not mount due to replication issues. Once these checks are done, the Exchange tools use Cluster API to move the CMS.*

A CMS can be moved from an active node to a passive node using the Exchange shell in Exchange Server 2007 RTM. SP1 brings this functionality to the console as well.

NOTE *Using the Exchange tools to move a CMS does not move the cluster group. Before performing maintenance on a node, make sure both the CMS and the cluster group have been moved to another node.*

To move a CMS to a passive node using the Exchange shell, use the following command:

```
Move-ClusteredMailboxServer CMSName -TargetMachine NODE2 -MoveComment
"Testing Failover to NODE2"
```

NOTE *Neither the Exchange shell nor the console allow you to move a CMS without adding a comment. This allows an organization to maintain a record of why a CMS was moved to another node.*

To move a CMS to a passive node using the Exchange console, use the following procedure:

1. Expand the Server Configuration node and select Mailbox.
2. In the Action pane on the right, click Manage Clustered Mailbox Server. This starts the Manage Clustered Mailbox Server Wizard.
3. On the Introduction page, select Move the Clustered Mailbox Server to another node. Click Next.
4. On the Move Clustered Mailbox Server page, enter the following settings:
   - **Select target node**   Click Browse to select the target passive node to which the CMS should be moved.
   - **Move comment**   Enter a brief comment indicating the reason for the move.
5. On the Progress page, make sure the correct passive node is selected. Click Move.
6. On the Completion page, ensure the move was successful. Click Finish to close the wizard.

NOTE *When a CMS is moved from the active node to the passive node, CCR is automatically reconfigured to reverse the direction of replication of storage group(s) on the cluster. A node functioning as a replication target when it is passive starts functioning as the replication source when it becomes active after a move. No admin intervention is necessary to make this change. Figure 19-13 provides more details about such a move.*

Configuring the Transport Dumpster

As mentioned earlier in this chapter, the Transport Dumpster is a cache of recent messages that are routed by a Hub Transport server. These are delivered to a CMS after a failover, which delivers any missing messages to mailboxes. The Transport Dumpster is enabled by default. It retains messages for seven days, or until it reaches the default maximum size per storage group of 18MB.

In SP1, both these properties can be configured from the EMC by selecting Organization Configuration | Hub Transport | Global Settings tab | Transport Settings | Properties.

Here's how to configure these properties using the Exchange shell:

```
Set-TransportConfig -MaxDumpsterSizePerStorageGroup 20Mb -MaxDumpsterTime
8.00:00:00.
```

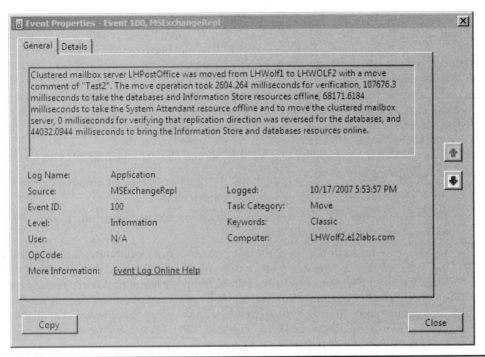

FIGURE 19-13   Event ID 100 is logged by the Replication service after a CMS move. This provides more details about the move, including the time taken and the fact that the direction of replication was reversed.

This command sets the maximum size per storage group to 20MB and the maximum age of messages in the dumpster to eight days.

Transport Dumpster Recommendations   Microsoft recommends the Transport Dumpster be set to at least 1.5 times the maximum message size allowed in an organization (or 15MB in organizations without a maximum message size) and that the maximum age of dumpster items be set to seven days. A logical question at this point would be: Wouldn't setting large dumpster values provide more protection? Consider this: The Transport Dumpster is used by CCR and LCR (the latter in SP1). SCR cannot use it. The size of transaction logs is 1MB. If your replica located in the same datacenter is behind by more than a few logs, or more than seven days' worth of logs have not been replicated to a CCR or LCR replica, you probably have other issues to worry about. For CCR across the WAN, if an entire datacenter is lost, the Hub Transport servers in that datacenter cannot reach the remote CCR node to deliver items from the Transport Dumpster.

Transport Dumpster Statistics   The Get-StorageGroupCopyStatus command can be used with the optional –DumpsterStatistics switch to display the number of items and size of the Transport Dumpster.

PART VI

Configuring Failover Behavior: AutoDatabaseMountDial

By default, after a failover the database(s) on a CMS will mount if there are up to six transaction log files in the replication queue. These are logs that have not been copied by the passive node. (Yes, the Lazy Passive Node Syndrome, or LPNS, if you really want another acronym at this point. We can make them up as we go!) Given that the transaction log file has been changed to 1MB in Exchange Server 2007, this does not represent a lot of data. The Transport Dumpster is likely to have all messages that are in the log files not copied by the lazy passive node. Hub Transport servers will graciously deliver these messages again after a CMS fails over.

This tolerance for potential data loss can be configured using the AutoDataBaseMountDial parameter of a Mailbox server. Here are the possible values:

- **BestAvailability** The default. It allows the database to mount automatically if there are a maximum of six logs in the replication queue.

- **GoodAvailability** This allows the database to mount automatically if there are up to three logs in the replication queue.

- **Lossless** If this setting is used, the database does not mount automatically until all logs are copied to the passive node. It prevents lossy failovers, but you should consider the implications carefully. If the active node is lost or not in a responsive mood, it virtually guarantees a database will not mount after a failover. If Lossless is your choice, you will have to learn to live with the potential of reduced availability. In other words, the Recovery Point Objective (RPO) takes precedence over the Recovery Time Objective (RTO).

SP1 *In Exchange Server 2007 SP1, the AutoDatabaseMountDial parameter can be configured from the Cluster Continuous Replication tab in a CMS's properties in EMC.*

To configure the AutoDatabaseMountDial parameter using the shell, use the following command:

```
Set-MailboxServer "Server Name" -AutoDatabaseMountDial GoodAvailability
```

NOTE *If the databases do not mount automatically after a failover due to the AutoDataBaseMountDial setting, an administrator can still mount them manually.*

Managing and Monitoring Replication

CCR relies on a good replica of a storage group on the passive node to be able to fail over. This makes the health of replication an important aspect of the high availability that CCR clusters provide. A bad replica can result in a CMS going offline after an attempted failover, or not failing over at all.

The Exchange shell provides the necessary tools to monitor and control replication. To monitor replication health for a particular storage group, use the following command:

```
Get-StorageGroupCopyStatus "Server\Storage Group"
```

This command provides a brief summary of replication health, by displaying SummaryCopyStatus (healthy or not healthy), CopyQueueLength (the number of logs that need to be copied by the passive node), ReplayQueueLength (the number of logs the passive node needs to replay to its copy of the database), and LastLogInspectTime (the last time when copied logs were inspected by the passive node).

To get more details about the replication health of the storage group, use the following command:

```
Get-StorageGroupCopyStatus "Server\Storage Group" | fl
```

SP1   *In Exchange Server 2007 SP1, a subset of the preceding replication health and status details is available from the Cluster Continuous Replication tab of a storage group's properties in the Exchange console. The tab is only available if the storage group is hosted by a CMS.*

The Test-ReplicationHealth command runs a number of tests to determine whether replication is in a healthy state. It can be used with the optional –MonitoringContext $true switch to include replication-related events logged to the Application event log and performance counter data:

```
Test-ReplicationHealth-MonitoringContext $true
```

The Get-ClusteredMailboxServerStatus command displays CMS status—whether or not it's online, the nodes in the cluster, which node is active, and which node owns the quorum or the cluster group.

Moving Storage Group or Database Paths

Databases hosted on a CMS can be mounted and dismounted from the Exchange console or the shell, just as you would on a standalone/nonclustered Exchange server. However, moving a storage group or a database to an alternate path requires that replication be suspended and the database be dismounted. Once the storage group or database paths are changed, the database can be mounted and replication of the storage group resumed.

Suspending Replication

Replication needs to be stopped to perform maintenance procedures on the active or the passive node. Moving the storage group or database paths, or performing maintenance operations on cluster nodes, requires replication to be temporarily halted or suspended.

SP1   *In Exchange Server 2007 SP1, the functionality to suspend, resume, and update a storage group copy is available from the Actions pane when a storage group is selected in EMC.*

Here's how to suspend replication for a storage group from the Exchange shell:

```
Suspend-StorageGroupCopy "Server\Storage Group Name"
```

This command suspends replication for a particular storage group on a CMS. If the maintenance procedure only impacts one storage group (for example, changing the storage group or database path), only that storage group needs to be taken offline. If the maintenance procedure impacts all storage groups on a CMS (one that requires a node to be taken offline), you can suspend replication of all storage groups hosted by the CMS using the following command:

```
Get-StorageGroup -server "Server Name" | Suspend-StorageGroupCopy
```

CAUTION *Suspending replication for extended periods of time is not recommended. For storage groups that have replication enabled, transaction logs are not truncated after successful backups until the logs are replicated to the target. Suspending replication for extended periods results in accumulation of transaction logs, which may eventually result in the disk volume running out of space.*

Resuming Replication

Once maintenance is complete, replication can be resumed using the following command:

```
Resume-StorageGroupCopy "Server\Storage Group Name"
```

Seeding and "Reseeding" a Storage Group Replica

Seeding is the process of creating a replica of a database on the passive node. When a new CCR cluster is set up, seeding occurs automatically after the installation of Exchange Server on the passive node. Similarly, when a new storage group is created on an active CCR node, seeding happens automatically and a replica is created on the passive node. In both these cases, the first transaction log file generated for the storage group is still available. The database can be created on the passive node if all log files, starting with the first one, are available. No admin intervention is required for the initial creation of the replica in both cases.

However, at different times a replica may need to be "reseeded."

NOTE *The term* reseeded *is used because the database was already seeded once when the second node was added and replication enabled during the process, or when a new storage group was created.*

This may happen in the following situations:

- When the replica has a missing or corrupt transaction log file that cannot be replayed to the replica database.
- The checkpoint file is corrupt.
- Offline defragmentation is performed on the production database.
- The log file generation sequence for the storage group is reset to log1.
- When a node is recovered after a disaster.
- When a new node is added to the cluster after a node is lost.

To reseed the storage group copy using the Exchange console, follow these steps:

1. Select the storage group. From the Action pane, click the Update Storage Group Copy link to start the Update Storage Group Copy Wizard.
2. On the Introduction page, make sure the correct storage group is selected. Click Next.
3. On the Update Storage Group Copy page, click the Update button.

NOTE *The wizard suspends replication of the storage group before reseeding it, and resumes replication after reseeding is completed successfully.*

4. On the Completion page, review the summary of tasks completed and whether reseeding was successful. Click Finish to exit the wizard.

To reseed a storage group replica using the Exchange shell, use the following commands:

```
Suspend-StorageGroupCopy "Server\Storage Group Name"
Update-StorageGroupCopy "Server\Storage Group Name"
```

> **NOTE** *Seeding/reseeding traffic travels over the public NIC. SP1 allows specifying which networks should be used for such traffic using the optional –DataHostNames parameter. For more details on how to configure this, refer to http://technet.microsoft.com/en-us/library/bb629629.aspx.*

After the Update-StorageGroupCopy command is used to reseed, replication resumes automatically. Alternatively, you can use the Update-StorageGroupCopy command with the optional –ManualResume parameter and then resume replication of the storage group using the following command:

```
Resume-StorageGroupCopy "Server\Storage Group Name"
```

Another method for reseeding a replica storage group involves suspending replication, dismounting the production database, copying the database EDB file manually to the target node, and mounting the database again. This method results in service unavailability for users on the dismounted database.

Standby Continuous Replication: Site Redundancy

As far as high availability features go, it seems Microsoft saved the best for the last. Standby Continuous Replication (SCR) was the missing piece in Exchange Server 2007's high availability story. It is available in Service Pack 1. Just as CCR replicates storage groups from an active cluster node to a passive node, SCR replicates to a standby Exchange server. Although intended to provide site redundancy by replicating to an Exchange server in a remote datacenter, it can also be implemented to replicate to a server in the same datacenter.

The beauty of the SCR solution is the fact that it can be implemented in clustered or nonclustered environments, or a combination of the two. The production Exchange server, called the SCR source, can be a CMS that uses either CCR or SCC, or a standalone/nonclustered Exchange server. The target Exchange server can also be either a cluster (with no CMS) or a standalone/nonclustered Exchange server. A combination of SCC or CCR and SCR can also be used to provide high availability with automated failovers between active and passive cluster nodes in a local datacenter, and to a standalone Exchange server or a SCC/CCR cluster in a remote datacenter that can be *activated* manually.

What SCR does not provide is the capability to automatically fail over to an SCR target. One needs to consider whether such automated failover to a server in a remote datacenter is actually required or desirable. Do you want a system to decide by itself that an entire datacenter or site is unavailable, and fail over automatically to a server in a remote site? If that is a requirement, SCR is clearly not the solution you are looking for. If manual intervention is desirable to switch to a remote site, SCR provides a low-cost solution out of the box, without the complexity of considering, understanding, buying, and implementing any third-party replication or geo-clustering add-ons. This is not to say that SCR does not come with some of its own complexity, given the wide number of combinations in which it can be deployed—for instance, a CMS (SCC or CCR) as the source and a standalone Exchange server as the SCR target, a standalone source and a clustered (SCC or CCR, without a CMS created) as the target, and all the combinations in between.

Site Redundancy: CCR vs. SCR

One question that has been frequently asked ever since the early details of SCR were made public is: Should I use CCR over a WAN link to a remote datacenter, or is SCR a better option?

The answer is: It depends on whether you require failovers across datacenters—something only CCR provides out of the box. SCR, on the other hand, requires manual activation of the SCR target. It lets you create multiple layers of protection with different replay and log file truncation lags for different targets of the same source storage group.

Additionally, consider the Windows Server clustering requirements. Windows Server 2003 requires cluster nodes to be on the same IP subnet. The result: a subnet stretched over WAN Links using VLANS, which adds complexity at the network layer using VLANs. Windows Server 2008 allows cluster nodes to be on different subnets. (Note: Exchange Server 2007 requires that both subnets be associated with the same AD site.) Finally, consider the requirement of placing the File Share Witness. If it's placed in the same datacenter as the active node hosting the CMS, in the case of a datacenter failure the passive node located in a remote datacenter does not have access to the FSW. As a result, no automated failovers are possible. Microsoft recommends placing the FSW in a third datacenter. For more details, read the Exchange team blog post titled "Placement of the File Share Witness (FSW) on a Geographically Dispersed CCR Cluster" at http://msexchangeteam.com/archive/2007/04/25/438185.aspx. It is important to carefully plan such topologies, and consider having multiple redundant links between the data centers hosting, each node, and the third data centers where the FSW resides.

Although CCR can be used to achieve site redundancy across datacenters, be aware of the caveats.

SCR, on the other hand, is designed to provide site redundancy. There is no requirement for a File Share Witness, or even clustering. SCR also allows for a delay in replaying and truncation of truncation of transaction logs on SCR targets. However, activation of an SCR replica or target is manual and can be time consuming, depending on the method used for activation.

A combination of CCR and SCR may provide better availability. CCR can be used to provide high availability within the same datacenter. SCR can be used to provide site redundancy. An SCR replica in the remote datacenter can also be a CCR/SCC cluster, albeit without a CMS created. This allows for quicker recovery by using the /RecoverCMS option, as discussed later in this chapter.

SCR Requirements

Here are some requirements to keep in mind when planning to implement SCR:

- **Exchange Server 2007 SP1**   SCR is available in Exchange Server 2007 SP1. Exchange Server 2007 SP1 is required on both the SCR source and the SCR target servers.

- **Same Windows Server versions on SCR source and target**   SCR requires both the source and the target servers to have the same version of the Windows Server operating system. An Exchange Server 2007 SP1 server running Windows Server 2008 cannot be a SCR source or target for an Exchange Server 2007 SP1 server running Windows Server 2003, and vice versa.

- **One Mailbox database per storage group** As with LCR and CCR, SCR requires that each replicated storage group contain only one database. SCR cannot be enabled for a storage group that has more than one database, nor can additional databases be created in a storage group that is being replicated using SCR.

- **Exchange Server editions** SCR is available on both Standard and Enterprise editions of Exchange Server 2007 SP1. If the SCR source is clustered or needs to host more than five databases, Exchange Server 2007 Enterprise edition is required. Similarly, if the SCR target is to be clustered or needs to host more than five databases, the Enterprise edition of Exchange Server 2007 is required.

- **Matching storage group paths on SCR target and source** SCR target servers replicate a storage group to the same path(s) on the target where they reside on the source servers. For instance, if the Exchange database resides on E:\Database and transaction logs on F:\Logs on the source server, the same paths should be available on the SCR target, and not contain any other files. With careful planning, this can be done at the deployment stage. Alternatively, transaction logs and databases on the source can be moved to match the available drivesletters/paths on the SCR target before SCR is enabled.

***

TIP *Although SCR requires that the SCR source and target servers use the same paths to store the database and transaction logs, the same storage group names can be used from multiple source servers to replicate to one (or more) SCR target server. For instance, the first/default storage group created on all servers is called "First Storage Group," and the first (Mailbox) database is called "Mailbox Database." You can enable SCR for the First Storage Group from ServerA and the First Storage Group from ServerB to an SCR target ServerC, as long as both the source servers use different paths. However, this can be confusing in real-world implementations. It is a best practice to ensure a consistent and descriptive naming convention is used for naming storage groups and databases, one that makes these easily identifiable—for example, on ServerA, SRVA-SG1 for the storage group, and SRVA-SG1-MBX1 for the Mailbox database. This should be done regardless of whether any replication—LCR, CCR or SCR—is being used, and it becomes even more important in an environment where storage groups are being replicated.*

- **No LCR on SCR targets** A server that is an SCR target cannot use LCR to replicate any storage groups, including the ones it hosts itself (that is, the ones that are not replicated from an SCR source).

- **SCR and public folders** Just like CCR, SCR cannot be used to replicate storage groups containing a Public Folder database if more than one server hosts public folders in the organization. Public folders have their in-built replication mechanism, which should be used for the high availability of public folders.

SCC does not use the continuous replication technology of Exchange Server 2007. Storage groups containing Public Folder databases hosted on an SCC can be replicated to an SCR target, as can those on standalone servers that are not being replicated locally on that server using LCR. Yes, that does sound a tad complicated. Simply put, SCR is not supported for any storage group with a Public Folder database that is being touched by any other type of replication—LCR, CCR, or the built-in Public Folder replication mechanism.

With those basic questions and considerations out of the way, let's take a look at implementing SCR.

Setting Up SCR

Setting up SCR is a relatively simple task. The New-StorageGroup and Enable-StorageGroupCopy commands used for LCR and CCR are enhanced in Exchange Server 2007 SP1 to handle SCR, with the –StandbyMachine, –ReplayLagTime, and –TruncationLagTime parameters added.

ReplayLagTime

The default ReplayLagTime, which is the time an SCR target waits before *replaying* or committing transaction logs to the replica database, is 24 hours. It can be set to as high as 7 days, or as low as 0 seconds. However, setting it to a very low interval takes away from the capability to provide protection against database corruption of the SCR source. It is recommended to set this to a few hours, to ensure enough time has lapsed to allow for the detection of database corruption on the SCR source and avoid having the SCR target in the same state.

Once this is enabled, you may not see much activity on SCR replicas if the source storage group has less than 50 transaction logs. By default, SCR has a copy lag of 50 log files.

TruncationLagTime

In addition to be able to delay replaying transaction logs to a replica, SCR also allows you to delay truncation of transaction logs after they have been replayed to the target database. The maximum truncation lag can be seven days. Note that this value cannot be changed after it has been set—that is, without disabling and reenabling SCR for a storage group.

This begs the question: When do files get truncated on the SCR source and replica? When using LCR and CCR, it makes sense to truncate log files after they have been replicated and replayed to the passive copy. SCR introduces the ability to delay replay and truncation. Further, a source storage group can have one or more SCR targets, perhaps with different replay and truncation lags. When would it be safe to flush these logs at the source and at the target?

It is logical to expect that the source should not wait for all SCR targets to replay the logs. It can truncate them as soon as they are replicated and inspected (but perhaps not replayed because of the replay lag) by all SCR targets, and a backup of the source completes successfully. Additionally, if the source has LCR enabled or is hosted on a CCR cluster, it should wait until the LCR or CCR replica has replayed the logs. In most deployments, one can expect the latter to happen rather quickly.

On the SCR target, log files are truncated if the log file generation sequence (log files in a storage group are numbered sequentially) is below the log file that the storage group's checkpoint file points to, *and* the file is older than the replay and truncation lag times combined.

NOTE *For more details about how Exchange Server 2007's transaction logging works, as well as how the checkpoints are maintained and used, refer to "Understanding Transaction Logging," in the Exchange Server 2007 documentation. This is available online at https://technet.microsoft .com/en-us/library/bb331951(EXCHG.80).aspx.*

SCR can be enabled for a new storage group when it is created, using the following command:

```
New-StorageGroup -Server "DFMailman" -Name "DFMailman-SG2" -LogFolderPath
"E:\Logs" -SystemFolderPath "F:\Database" -StandbyMachine MIRROR
```

This command creates a new storage group called DFMailman-SG2 on server DFMailman, sets the log folder path and system folder (database) path, and enables SCR replication to the target server named MIRROR. If required, the –ReplayLagTime and –TruncationLagTime parameters can be added to this command.

NOTE *If you're using the Exchange Management Console to create a new storage group, no options exist to enable SCR. All SCR-related configuration is done using the Exchange shell.*

To enable SCR for an existing storage group, use the following command:

```
Enable-StorageGroupCopy "Server\Storage Group Name" -StandbyMachine
"Standby Server Name"
```

NOTE *The storage group path on the SCR target must match the one on the SCR source. If the store (EDB) is located at D:\First Storage Group\Database, and the transaction logs at E:\First Storage Group\Logs, SCR will replicate these to the exact same paths on the SCR target. If those paths are not available on the target, the preceding command will fail. Additionally, the folders must not contain any Exchange databases or transaction logs on the target server.*

After SCR is enabled, you would want to find out the replication status. If you try to do this right after enabling SCR, you may not see much activity if the source storage group has fewer than 50 transaction logs. Once the log replication starts, you will see the replay queue build up. Remember, the default replay log time of 24 hours means no logs will be replayed to the target database until that time has elapsed.

To verify the status of SCR replication, use the same Get-StorageGroupCopyStatus command used for LCR and CCR, with the –StandbyMachine parameter (see Figure 19-14):

```
Get-StorageGroupCopyStatus "Server\Storage Group" -StandbyMachine "Standby
Server Name"
```

The result displayed is similar to the output for the LCR and CCR replication status, when the command is used without the –StandbyMachine switch. Note that the copy queue length and the replay queue length are shown separately. Using the preceding command and formatting the output as a list displays more detailed replication statistics.

```
[PS] C:\>Get-StorageGroupCopyStatus "DFMailman\First STorage Group" -StandbyMach
ine MIRROR

Name                  SummaryCopySt CopyQueueLeng ReplayQueueL LastInspecte
                      atus          th            ength        dLogTime
----                  ------------- ------------- ------------ ------------
First Storage Group   Healthy       0             100          10/10/200...
```

FIGURE 19-14   Get-StorageGroupCopyStatus command with the –StandbyMachine switch displays SCR replication status

Disabling SCR

To disable SCR for a storage group, use the following command:

```
Disable-StorageGroupCopy "Server\Storage Group" -StandbyMachine "SCR Target
Server Name"
```

Listing All Storage Groups with SCR Replicas

The following command lists all storage groups replicated by the SCR, source server, target server, log file path, and database path:

```
Get-StorageGroup | where {$_.StandbyMachines -ne $null} | select
name,server,logfolderpath,systemfolderpath,standbymachines
```

Recovering from Failure Using SCR

Switching from an SCR source to an SCR target server is called activation. It is important to note that SCR is not designed for temporary server outages. The right approach to protect from such temporary server outages is by using failover clustering—either CCR or SCC. SCR should be a second line of defense, to be used when there is significant failure, and other recovery mechanisms, such as restoring from backup, will take too long. In an SCC scenario, if the shared storage on which Exchange storage groups reside fails, or a database is corrupt, SCR activation can be the next line of defense. In a CCR scenario, if both the cluster nodes fail or the databases on both nodes becomes corrupt, SCR can be the next line of defense.

In a site failure scenario, SCR provides the important capability of getting users up and running in the shortest amount of time, compared to recovering from a backup.

There are two paths you can take to activate an SCR target.

The first one involves recovering a server or a CMS—depending on whether the source is a CMS or a standalone server. The second one involves using Database Portability to mount the replica database to the SCR target server, followed by moving users to the SCR target using the –with the Move-Mailbox command ConfigurationOnly switch.

The starting point for both methods is to disable SCR and make the SCR replica on the target server ready for mounting. This is done using the following command:

```
Restore-StorageGroupCopy "SourceServer\Storage Group Name" -StandbyMachine
"SCR Target Server Name"
```

This command ensures all transaction logs from the source storage group have been copied to the replica on the target server. Attempts are made to copy any missing files to the replica. However, if the source server is unavailable, the command should be used with the –Force switch appended.

The Path to Recovery

When planning to use SCR, you need to consider recovery scenarios and choose a recovery path from the two choices outlined earlier.

TIP *Although SCR allows using a CMS (SCC or CCR) as the source and a standalone server as a target, as well as the other way around, such combinations eliminate one path of recovery, or at least make it considerably more time consuming. For instance, a source that is clustered cannot be recovered using /RecoverServer if the target is a standalone server. It makes sense to use a clustered target for a clustered source to be able to use /RecoverCMS instead. You do not need additional servers in a typical two-node configuration to use a clustered target—a single node suffices. The only difference in cost is the Enterprise edition of Windows Server that failover clustering requires.*

(Alternatively, if the target for a clustered source is a standalone server, you can uninstall Exchange, install and configure the Cluster Service, and then use /RecoverCMS. However, as stated earlier, this makes recovery more time consuming).

Similarly, if the source is a standalone Exchange server, it is logical to expect the target be a standalone server as well, although SCR allows the use of a clustered target in this scenario.

In the case of a failure of a source server or CMS with multiple storage groups being replicated to an SCR target, recovering a CMS provides the fastest path. If the source and target servers are clustered, Exchange is already installed on the SCR target cluster, but no CMS has been created. Using Setup /RecoverCMS creates the CMS on the target.

TIP *It may be desirable to locate the SCR target on a cluster, even if it consists of a single node. This provides the ability to use Setup /RecoverCMS on an already existing Exchange installation for a speedy activation of the standby cluster.*

When /RecoverServer is used, Exchange is installed on the server, which gets the identity of the server being recovered. In other words, the server gets the same server name and is associated with the same msExchExchangeServer object in the Configuration container. Obviously, this is not possible on the SCR target server without uninstalling Exchange Server from it—it already has an identity (unlike a cluster with no CMS created). In this case, Exchange Server needs to be uninstalled and reinstalled with the /RecoverServer option.

If the failure is limited to a storage group or two (for instance, due to database corruption or the loss of a disk volume), it is easier to use Database Portability and point the affected users to the SCR target using the move-mailbox command.

Recovering a CMS to a SCR Target Cluster Node
If the SCR source and target are clustered, the following command is used to activate the SCR target:

```
Setup /RecoverCMS /CMSName:"CMS Name of SCR Source" /CMSIPAddress:x.x.x.x
```

Once setup completes, the CMS is created on the standby cluster. Databases can be mounted at this point using the EMC or the Mount-Database command from the shell.

Note that if the SCR target is in a different subnet (typically in a remote datacenter), the IP address used in the preceding command is likely to be a different IP address than the original CMS IP address, and may belong to a different subnet than the source server. If the SCR source and target clusters are running on a Windows Server 2008 server, the HostTTLRecord property can be set on the Network Name resource of the CMS to change the TTL from its default of 20 minutes. Microsoft recommends setting this to 5 minutes (300 seconds). A lower TTL allows quicker client connectivity to the CMS post-recovery. The TTL should be changed after the CMS is set up on the source cluster, and after SCR activation on the standby cluster. To set the TTL, use the cluster.exe command line on Windows Server 2008:

```
cluster.exe res "CMSName" /priv HostRecordTTL=300
```

Activating a Storage Group on the SCR Target

The second recovery option uses Database Portability to mount the database on the SCR target. AD accounts for users with mailboxes on the affected database are changed to point to the SCR target server using the Move-Mailbox command with the –ConfigurationOnly option. If the original server is still online and responding to requests, it redirects Outlook 2003 and later clients to the SCR target, where their mailboxes now reside. If the original server is unavailable, Outlook profiles for the affected users may need to be modified to point them to the correct server.

Outlook 2007 clients rely on the Autodiscover service to locate their maiboxes automatically. As soon as AD replication updates the change to the domain controllers used by Client Access Servers, these users can start Outlook and have access to their mailboxes.

NOTE *Detailed steps for activating the SCR target using database portability can be found at http://technet.microsoft.com/en-us/library/bb738132.aspx.*

Summary

The high availability functionality in Exchange Server 2007 provides a number of new features (as well as enhancement to old ones) that allow organizations to ensure higher availability and to reduce downtime. The built-in replication features can be used in different combinations to meet the high availability goals in organizations of all sizes, as detailed in the following table.

Features and Requirements	LCR	CCR	SCC	SCR
Storage and database redundancy.	Yes	Yes	No	Yes
Server redundancy.	No	Yes	Yes	Yes
Datacenter redundancy (site resilience).	No	Yes[1]	No[2]	Yes
Uses Cluster Service.	No	Yes	Yes	No[3]
Requires "cluster-certified" hardware. (The entire solution should be on the Cluster solution category of Windows Server Catalog of Tested Products.)	No	No	Yes	No
Requires shared storage.	No	No	Yes	No[4]
Requires Windows Server (2003/2008) Enterprise or Datacenter edition.	No	Yes	Yes	No[5]

Features and Requirements	LCR	CCR	SCC	SCR
Requires Exchange Server 2007 Enterprise edition.	No	Yes	Yes	No[5]
Maximum number of nodes.	N/A	2[6]	8	N/A
Maximum number of databases per storage group.	1	1	5[7]	1
Supported on dissimilar hardware.	N/A	Yes	No	N/A
Automated failovers.	No	Yes	Yes	No
Uses Exchange Database Continuous Replication.	Yes	Yes	No[8]	Yes
Supports multiple replication targets.	No	No	N/A	Yes
Supports configuration of lag times for log file replay and truncation.	No	No	N/A	Yes
Supports VSS backups from replica.	Yes	Yes	N/A	No
Uses Transport Dumpster.	Yes[9]	Yes	No	No
Supports public folder replication.	No[10]	No	Yes[11]	No
Coexistence with other Exchange Server 2007 server roles.	Yes	No	No	Yes[12]

1. CCR can provide datacenter redundancy. If the operating system is Windows Server 2003, both nodes need to be on the same subnet, thus requiring the subnet to be stretched using VLANs. If you're using Windows Server 2008, both nodes can be on different subnets. The placement of the File Share Witness should be considered carefully in such topologies, as mentioned earlier in this chapter.

2. SCC does not provide datacenter redundancy out of the box—Exchange databases, and generally the quorum, reside on shared storage. Third-party solutions can be used to implement datacenter redundancy.

3. SCR works with standalone or clustered source and target servers. If the source or target servers are clustered, the Cluster Service is used. SCR by itself does not require the Cluster Service.

4. If the SCR source or targets are Clustered Mailbox Servers using SCC, they require shared storage.

5. SCR source and target servers can be in a clustered environment using SCC or CCR. All Exchange servers participating in a cluster require Windows Server 2003/2008 Enterprise or Datacenter edition, and Exchange Server 2007 Enterprise edition.

6. Clustered Mailbox Servers can be set up in a cluster environment where more than two nodes exist in the cluster. However, only two nodes can participate in CCR replication and become possible owners of a CMS. As such, only two-node clusters are recommended with a Majority Node Set (MNS) quorum with File Share Witness.

7. If a Clustered Mailbox Server using SCC is required to participate in SCR replication, SCR supports only one database per storage group.

8. SCC cluster nodes do not replicate Exchange databases/storage groups to each other. However, they can participate in SCR replication as SCR sources, and replicate to one or more SCR targets. SCC clusters without a CMS can also act as SCR targets.

9. In Exchange Server 2007 SP1, LCR uses the Transport Dumpster feature to request messages from Hub Transport servers in the site after recovery to an LCR replica.

10. Public folder replication is not supported if any of the storage groups containing a Public Folder database is being replicated using LCR, CCR, or SCR.

11. A Clustered Mailbox Server using SCC supports replication of Public Folder databases. However, storage groups containing Public Folder databases that use Public Folder replication are not supported as an SCR source.

12. If SCR source or target servers are clustered, only the Clustered Mailbox Server role is supported. If either the SCR source or target servers are not clustered, the standalone/nonclustered servers can coexist with other Exchange Server 2007 server roles, except the Edge Transport Server role.

Although the log shipping and replication techniques have been around in different products and high-availability solutions for a long time, they are quite new to Exchange Server. Investments will need to be made in testing and piloting such deployments before they are put in production, and in training Exchange administrators and IT staff to get a fair understanding of the different features available, the different combinations they can be used in, and overall to be comfortable with them.

If you're using CCR or SCR to replicate storage groups over WAN links, the issue of bandwidth utilization and availability needs to be considered as well. However, bandwidth considerations are no different from those with similar third-party replication products offering synchronous or asynchronous replication.

NOTE *According to Microsoft, less data is moved by continuous replication than most third-party solutions. Comparative test results and information is not available yet (from Microsoft, ISVs, and third parties) that quantifies the actual data moved and the bandwidth consumed by Exchange's continuous replication and replication solutions provided by ISVs.*

At this time of writing, not much time has elapsed since the release of Exchange Server 2007 RTM, and the release of SP1 is just around the corner. Best practices emerge over a period of time—there isn't an abundance of such advice at this time.

When considering which high-availability feature or product to use, you should consider solutions provided by third-party vendors and compare them with those offered natively in Exchange Server 2007. If keeping the costs of high availability low, using "out-of-the-box" or *native* features, and keeping deployments simple and support restricted to as few vendors as possible are important, Exchange Server 2007 SP1 offers all these features today.

CHAPTER

Maintenance and Optimization

I n order to ensure that the infrastructure of servers you deploy for Exchange Server 2007 today continues to function properly in the future, you will need to properly maintain the environment. As your organization's needs and usage patterns change, you will need to monitor the environment and identify trends. Once you identify trends, you can make changes to optimize the organization's infrastructure and, when necessary, proactively scale to meet future needs.

Operations Overview

Microsoft provides Exchange administrators with tools to maintain their organizations. Not all the tools are well known. Some are rudimentary tools associated with a specific operational task. It is important to understand the operational tasks that Microsoft recommends and to incorporate the associated tools into your administrative routine. Some of the operational tasks require Windows Server tools, whereas other tasks need tools unique to Exchange Server 2007. The process of maintaining, monitoring, and optimizing Exchange Server is a tedious one that is more complex in larger organizations. The process is critical to the health and well being of any size organization. Microsoft and a number of third-party vendors provide applications and tools, above and beyond what comes with Exchange, to assist administrators in their efforts to increase the availability and performance of their Exchange servers.

Lifecycle Management

Although this book includes information that pertains to the entire lifecycle of Exchange 2007, the majority of time spent administering Exchange 2007 will be spent in the day-to-day maintenance of the servers. Collectively, the process of deploying and maintaining a server is referred to as *lifecycle management*. Microsoft uses a methodology called the Microsoft Operations Framework (MOF) to define their best practices for deploying and maintaining Microsoft servers. This framework can be applied to any of their products. Here is a high-level overview of the lifecycle:

- Changing
  - Change Management
  - Configuration Management
  - Release Management

669

- Operating
  - System Administration
  - Security Administration
  - Directory Services Administration
  - Network Administration
  - Service Monitoring and Control
  - Storage Management
  - Job Scheduling
- Supporting
  - Service Desk
  - Incident Management
  - Problem Management
- Optimizing
  - Service-Level Management
  - Financial Management
  - Capacity Management
  - Availability Management
  - Workforce Management
  - Security Management
  - Infrastructure Management

Because it is a lifecycle, MOF implies that the process is circular in nature—from Changing, to Operating, to Supporting, to Optimizing, over and over again.

Online Maintenance

To help keep the system in good operating condition, the Microsoft Exchange team built a maintenance utility into the application. It performs the following tasks in the following order:

1. **Purge database indexes**   The index aging table is examined. If the index is older than 40 days, the index is removed.

2. **Maintain tombstones**   Removes deleted public folder items from Public Folder databases that were not properly replicated after the item was originally deleted.

3. **Clean up the Transport Dumpster**   Better know as *Deleted Item Retention,* the Transport Dumpster contains messages deleted by clients. Deleted messages that have exceeded the administratively set retention period (14 days by default) are permanently removed from Transport Dumpster when this process runs. Mailbox folders that have retention periods set are processed as well.

4. **Remove public folders that have exceeded the expiry time**   Removes public folders that have expiration polices. If you have two or more instances of a folder, it is possible to have different expiration policies per replica.

5. **Remove deleted public folders that have exceeded the tombstone lifetime**   Removes public folders that were deleted over 180 days ago.

6. **Clean up conflicting public folder messages**   The owners of public folders have 180 days to manually resolve conflicts, after which the message that was last saved is kept and all other conflicting versions are deleted.

7. **Update server versions**   Updates the version information on Public Folder databases that contain replicas of a system folder(s).

8. **Check Schedule+ Free Busy and Offline Address Book folders (OAB)**   The Public Folder database verifies that the Schedule+ Free Busy and Offline Address Book folders exist. When OABs are deleted from Active Directory, the associated OAB public folder is deleted approximately one week later. The Schedule+ Free Busy folders that are associated with administrative groups are never deleted.

9. **Clean up deleted mailboxes**   Deletes mailbox content from the Mailbox database that has not had an associated user object for the administratively defined retention period. The default period is 30 days.

10. **Check message table for orphaned messages**   The message table in each mailbox database is examined for messages without any references. All orphaned messages are deleted.

11. **Clean up reliable event tables**   The reliable event table is cleaned so it does not contain events older than one week. This table is used by the Edge Transport server during EdgeSync.

These 11 tasks must be performed during the maintenance window defined by the Exchange administrator. The maintenance schedule can be defined individually, for each Mailbox database and Public Folder database, using the Exchange Management Console or the Exchange Management Shell. If the maintenance window ends or a backup routine interrupts the tasks, they will resume where they left off during the next scheduled maintenance window. See Chapter 6 for more information on configuring database settings. Chapter 18 details setting retention policies for your organization.

Once any of these maintenance tasks completes on a database, an attempt to perform an online defragmentation of the database begins. Once all the 11 tasks have completed as well as online defragmentation, the database is scanned and all the unused pages are set to zero. Then the page checksums for every page in the database are updated with the new format. The new checksums are used by backup applications and tools such as the Eseutil to identify database errors and facilitate repair procedures.

Operation Tasks

Microsoft recommends a set of operational tasks and provides checklists for the Exchange 2007 administrator to perform. If these operational tasks are performed, the chances of having a serious service outage are largely reduced. The following tasks are broken down into daily, weekly, and monthly.

Daily Tasks

There are a number of tasks that, if repeated daily, will help you proactively identify problems before they cause service outages. Daily tasks can also help you identify security breaches and environmental conditions that can adversely affect Exchange. Here are the daily tasks recommended by Microsoft:

- Perform physical environmental checks:
  - Review physical security (doors, locks, security cameras, biometrics, and so on) for functionality.
  - Verify room temperature, humidity levels, power/UPS availability, and other environmental factors for normal operating conditions.
  - Inspect network infrastructure components, including cables, switches, routers, and network access points to verify functionality.
- Perform and monitor backups:
  - Perform an online streaming (legacy) or VSS backup of all Exchange databases.
  - Perform a backup of the System State of all Exchange servers and domain controllers.
  - Monitor the Application log on all Exchange servers and domain controllers for Event ID 8000 (backup started) and Event ID 8001 (backup complete).
  - Analyze and respond to errors and warnings during the backup operation.
  - Rotate the backup media if you are using a tape solution.
  - Verify that the transaction logs were truncated (full and incremental backups only).
  - Erase or dispose of tapes that contain data older then the allowed data-retention period (could be done weekly or monthly, depending on your policy).
- Check disk usage:
  - Check for free disk space on Exchange Database volumes.
  - Check for free disk space on Transaction Log volumes.
  - Check for free disk space on the Operating System and Pagefile volumes.
  - Check for free disk space on the SMTP Queues volumes.
  - Use Performance Monitor to check performance on disks.
- Check the Event Viewer:
  - Review the Application log for Exchange-related events.
  - Review the Security log to identity unauthorized access attempts.
  - Review the System log for events logged by hardware drivers and systems services.
  - Filter for information events created by Online Maintenance and backups that you know should be occurring daily.
  - Filter for errors and cautions, and look for repetitive entries.
- Monitor server performance:
  - Use Performance Monitor's System Monitor to view performance counters for critical Exchange resources on each Exchange server and document the readings:
    - Processor: %Processor Time

- Memory: Available MBs
- Memory: % Committed Bytes in Use
- Use Performance Monitor's System Monitor to view performance counters for IIS and Web services (particularly the CAS role):
  - Active Server Pages counters (OWA and other ASP applications)
  - FTP Service counters (FTP and BITS)
  - Web Service counters (WWW service)
  - Web Service Cache counters (WWW service cache)
- Create counter logs with Performance Monitor to use in trend reporting.
- Create alerts that will notify you when performance thresholds are crossed.
- Check the Exchange Mailbox Server roles:
  - Document the number of transaction logs generated each day. Try to identify upward trends that could impact performance.
  - Verify that production databases are mounted.
  - Check public folder replication status.
  - With test mailboxes, verify the logon of each database and the send/receive capabilities.
  - Verify that database indexes are up to date and searchable.
- Monitor Outlook client performance:
  - Examine Outlook counters in System Monitor on the Outlook Client machine.
  - Examine Event Viewer logs on the client machine.
  - Verify that a test account can log onto the Exchange server and has send/receive capabilities from the Outlook test account.
  - Compare the current counters against a baseline counter log (RPC average latency/RPC and requests/RPC operations).
- Monitor network performance:
  - Run NetDiag.exe to validate TCP/IP configuration and network connectivity.
  - Examine network activity on the Exchange servers using Network Monitor.
  - Run scripts and/or WMI applications to identify network problems.
  - Monitor SNMP traps on network adapters and network devices that are used by Exchange.

Verify the Database Indexes

The following cmdlet can be used to verify the database indexes are up to date:

```
[PS]C:\>Get-Mailboxdatabase -Identity | Get-mailbox | Test-ExchangeSearch -
indextimeout 20 | Format-table
```

- Check mailflow:
    - Check queues for each server in each administrative group using the Queue Viewer tool in the Exchange Management Console.
    - Record the queue size.
    - Send messages between internal servers using test accounts.
    - Check and verify that messages deliver successfully.
    - Send outgoing messages to non-local accounts.
    - Check and verify that outgoing messages deliver successfully. With the test account on the external host, verify that mail comes in.
    - Send messages across any connectors to Exchange organizations, Lotus Notes, and Novell GroupWise recipients.
    - Verify successful message transfer across connectors and routes.
- Check security features:
    - View the Security Event log on Event Viewer and match security changes to known, authorized configuration changes.
    - Investigate unauthorized security changes discovered in the Security Event log.
    - Check security news for the latest viruses, worms, and vulnerabilities.
    - Update and fix discovered security problems and vulnerabilities.
    - Verify that SMTP does not relay anonymously, or lock down to specific servers that require functionality.
    - Verify that the Message Tracking log does not have the Everyone group listed in the ACL permission. You can also do this task weekly.
    - Verify that SSL is functioning for configured secure channels.
    - Update virus signatures hourly.

Weekly Tasks

Not all tasks need to be performed daily. In smaller organization, some of the daily tasks can be performed weekly due to limited mailflow and usage. However, it will not hurt to perform all the daily tasks daily, even if this is a bit of overkill, because you will develop good habits you can use regardless of the size of the environment you administer. The following tasks should be performed weekly, at a minimum:

- Archive event logs, especially the Security event log.
- Archive mailbox content you no longer want to store on the Exchange servers. For example, the mailboxes of users who have left the company can be exported to a .pst file and saved off of the Mailbox server.
- Create performance reports:
    - Use daily data from the event log and System Monitor to create reports.
    - Report on disk usage.
    - Create reports on memory and CPU usage.

- Generate uptime and availability reports.
- Generate database and mailbox sizes.
- Create capacity reports from messages sent and client logons.
- Create reports on queue use, size, and growth.
- Create incident reports:
  - List the top generated, resolved, and pending incidents.
  - Create solutions for unresolved incidents.
  - Update reports to include new trouble tickets.
  - Create a document depository for troubleshooting guides and postmortems about outages.
- Review e-mail security:
  - Perform a virus scan on each computer, but exclude drives that are specifically for Exchange (SMTP/Exchange databases/logs, and so on).
  - Verify that the Message Tracking log does not have the Everyone group listed in the ACL permission.
- Status meeting:
  - Get server and network status for the overall organization and segments.
  - Monitor organizational performance and availability.
  - Collect overview reports and incidents.
  - Perform risk analysis and evaluation, including upcoming changes.
  - Perform capacity, availability, and performance reviews.
  - Verify Service Level Agreement (SLA) performance and review items that have not met target objectives.
- Perform a restore from backup to the recovery storage group and verify the restored data's integrity.
- Verify the Exchange routing topology:
  - Run WinRoute to ensure connectivity (Exchange 2000/2003 only).
  - Run the Routing Log Viewer (Exchange 2007 SP1 and higher only)

Monthly Tasks

The daily and weekly tasks, when aggregated together, will show trends in usage, performance, and security. Monthly tasks are the action items that result from the analysis of these trends.

- Capacity Planning
  - Check capacity and performance against Service Level Agreement requirements.
  - Review SLA requirements and capacity figures from the previous month.
  - Produce and implement an upgrade path based on projected growth from the previous growth data.

- Updates
  - Maintain a list of applied hotfixes, service packs, update rollups, and security updates.
  - See if there are new hotfixes for Microsoft Windows Server.
  - See if there are service packs for Windows Server.
  - See if there are updates to complementary services, such as Internet Information Services (IIS), AD directory service, and DNS service.
  - Apply updates uniformly across servers and workstations in the organization.
  - Perform critical security updates as soon as possible, based on company policy.
- Fire drills
  - Perform a simulated outage of one or more of the Exchange 2007 critical services or dependencies to test the procedures for restoring service.
  - Analyze and correct any issues discovered during the fire drill.

Monitoring Objectives

The maintenance operations procedures are often considered the first step of troubleshooting. When you are performing the day-to-day maintenance of your messaging system, it is then that you are most likely to identify the problems as they occur. Identification of a problem is the first step in troubleshooting. Monitoring, in a way, is the automation of routine maintenance tasks. Even in a small business, monitoring every aspect of Active Directory and Exchange 2007 would be a full-time job. Monitoring tools make it easier to maintain complex systems. Some of the monitoring tools available today are so sophisticated that they not only monitor an Exchange organization and alert administrators to problems as they occur, they also troubleshoot problems and prescribe a course of action for an administrator to correct them. When administrators implement a monitoring system, they are persuing the following objectives:

- Centralizing the monitoring console or portal
- Reducing administration
- Receiving notification of service failures and performance bottlenecks
- Getting real-time status and health information on Exchange Server's hardware, software, and services
- Performing trend analysis and reporting

Problem Identification and Remediation

As mentioned earlier, sophisticated monitoring tools do much more than tell you what is up and what is down. Ideally, the tool(s) can be integrated into all aspects of your operating procedures. Many administrators are faced with the growing challenge of maintaining server farms that keep growing as new IT projects are rolled out. In many cases, administrators are expected to do so without any additional help. It is this predicament that has led to a boom in the managed services industry. It is no longer a matter of whether or not an organization can afford to implement monitoring software internally or use a managed service from a third party; it is how can they afford *not* to do so when the complex systems they depend on go down. To make sure the mission-critical systems, such as Exchange, stay up and running, the monitoring tools have to do more than just alerting. They have become smarter—to the point where they know, in detail, the software applications they are monitoring. The more the monitoring tools are aware of the specific applications they are monitoring, the sooner they can identify problems as well as issues that could lead to problems if they are not addressed.

Ultimately, administrators need a tool or tool set that can help them identify problems or potential problems and then assist with their remediation. The assistance can come in many forms. It can be reference information that describes a known issue with a product. It can be prescriptive to the point of providing the step-by-step instructions on how to correct a problem. Or it can just fix the problem and generate a report letting administrators know what corrective actions were taken. Managed service solutions fill the gap between what tools can do and what a reduced support staff and/or one with a limited skill set cannot. A managed service provider can offer 24/7 support and remote into your servers to perform remediation steps on demand.

Optimization

It is easy to see monitoring and maintenance as a necessary administrative effort to thwart outages. What is not so easy to see is how the data collected by those mandatory efforts can be used to optimize the performance of the infrastructure that is already in place. For example, every day you document the size of each database. Over time you may even notice a trend that all the database sizes are growing. From a maintenance standpoint, you may just be looking at the capacity of each server independently. If you look at it from an optimization standpoint, you will look for databases that are growing faster than others. In your weekly meetings, you can begin to report on this. Then monthly you can look at moving mailboxes based on user usage patterns and mailbox database sizes in the attempt to optimize the performance of the system and in turn improve the client experience.

If the monitoring tools come with built-in reporting, the reports will often identify the trends that are leading to degradation in performance. These reports are not only valuable for their ability to illustrate trends and to help administrators optimize their environments, they are also indispensible when it comes time to justify the budget for upgrades when they are necessary.

Monitoring Tools

As stated in the beginning of the chapter, Microsoft provides administrators with the tools they need to maintain Exchange Server 2007. This section introduces you to the monitoring tools you can use with Exchange 2007. At the end of this section, you'll find a list some third-party tools that support Exchange 2007. Here's a list of the tools provided by Microsoft:

- Exchange Server User Monitor
- Performance Console
- Queue Viewer
- Exchange Best Practices Analyzer
- Server Performance Advisor
- Microsoft Exchange Server Profile Analyzer
- Microsoft Operation Manager and Exchange Server 2007 Management Pack for MOM

Exchange Server User Monitor

No matter how powerful and reliable the Exchange servers are, it is ultimately the users' experience with their e-mail client that matters most. To be able to evaluate user experience, Microsoft developed the Exchange Server User Monitor (ExMon) to collect the performance data from an Exchange server about MAPI (Outlook) clients. Figure 20-1 shows the server-side information displayed by ExMon.

Server Latency

The Exchange Mailbox servers communicate directly with MAPI clients. Any latency generated by poor server performance will affect the client experience. The Avg. Server Latency and Max. Server Latency columns show how much time it takes for user requests to be processed. The higher the number, the slower the user's response time will be (in other words, the worse their experience will be). The Performance Monitor tool will display the average Remote Procedure Call (RPC) latency for each database, but only ExMon can show you how that breaks down at the user level.

Client Latency

By monitoring network latency, as well as the number of RPC communications a client has to make for a request to be processed, the ExMon tool can calculate the client-side latency as well. This information is displayed on the By Clientmon tab, as shown in Figure 20-2.

Online mode (non-cache mode) MAPI clients are most affected by latency because all their requests must be made to the Exchange Mailbox server. A high average client latency (100ms or higher) could cause the client to complain about poor performance. To correct the problem, the client could be switched to cache mode, where latencies up to 500ms are unperceivable to the user.

Performance Console

Probably the best-know monitoring tool in a Windows environment is Performance Monitor (PerfMon). Even third-party tools and other Microsoft tools derive much of their information from the performance objects and counters that were written by programmers for Performance Monitor. Just about everything that you need to monitor the health

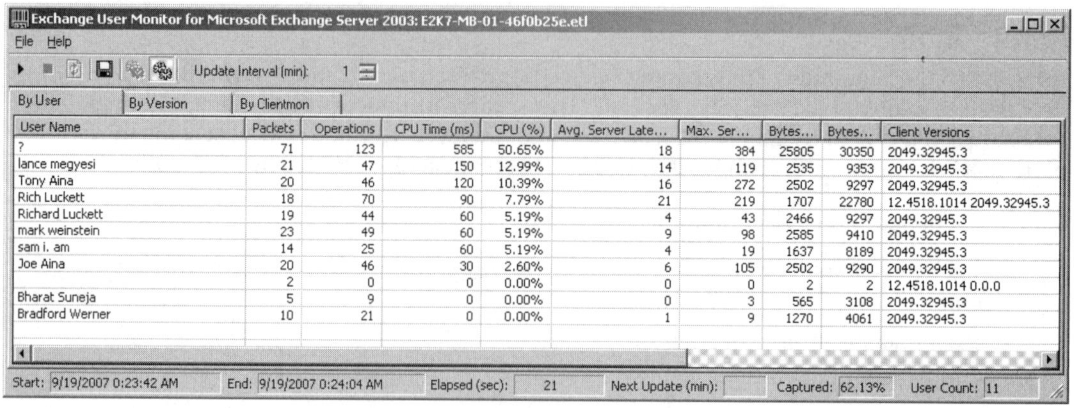
Exchange User Monitor for Microsoft Exchange Server 2003: E2K7-MB-01-46f0b25e.etl
File Help
Update Interval (min): 1
By User
By Version
By Clientmon
User Name | Packets | Operations | CPU Time (ms) | CPU (%) | Avg. Server Late... | Max. Ser... | Bytes... | Bytes... | Client Versions
? | 71 | 123 | 585 | 50.65% | 18 | 384 | 25805 | 30350 | 2049.32945.3
lance megyesi | 21 | 47 | 150 | 12.99% | 14 | 119 | 2535 | 9353 | 2049.32945.3
Tony Aina | 20 | 46 | 120 | 10.39% | 16 | 272 | 2502 | 9297 | 2049.32945.3
Rich Luckett | 18 | 70 | 90 | 7.79% | 21 | 219 | 1707 | 22780 | 12.4518.1014 2049.32945.3
Richard Luckett | 19 | 44 | 60 | 5.19% | 4 | 43 | 2466 | 9297 | 2049.32945.3
mark weinstein | 23 | 49 | 60 | 5.19% | 9 | 98 | 2585 | 9410 | 2049.32945.3
sam i. am | 14 | 25 | 60 | 5.19% | 4 | 19 | 1637 | 8189 | 2049.32945.3
Joe Aina | 20 | 46 | 30 | 2.60% | 6 | 105 | 2502 | 9290 | 2049.32945.3
 | 2 | 0 | 0 | 0.00% | 0 | 0 | 2 | 2 | 12.4518.1014 0.0.0
Bharat Suneja | 5 | 9 | 0 | 0.00% | 0 | 3 | 565 | 3108 | 2049.32945.3
Bradford Werner | 10 | 21 | 0 | 0.00% | 1 | 9 | 1270 | 4061 | 2049.32945.3
Start: 9/19/2007 0:23:42 AM
End: 9/19/2007 0:24:04 AM
Elapsed (sec): 21
Next Update (min):
Captured: 62.13%
User Count: 11

FIGURE 20-1 The ExMon tool showing server latency data

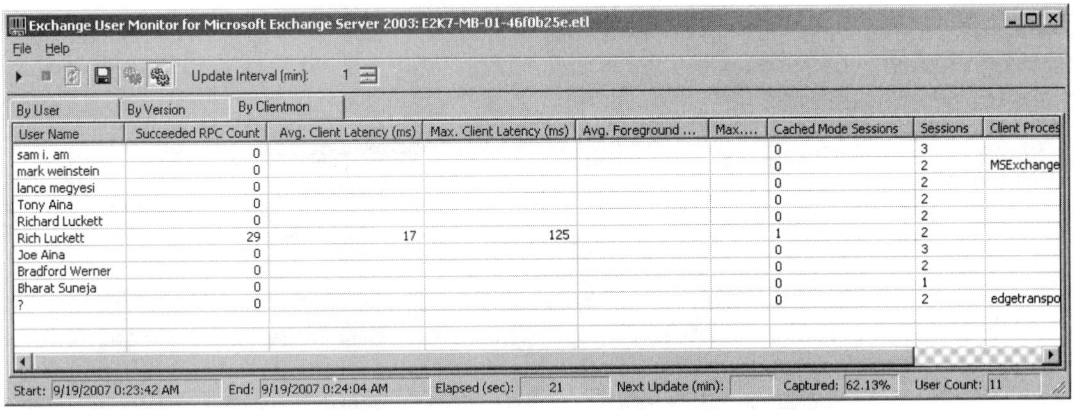

User Name	Succeeded RPC Count	Avg. Client Latency (ms)	Max. Client Latency (ms)	Avg. Foreground ...	Max....	Cached Mode Sessions	Sessions	Client Proces
sam i. am	0					0	3	
mark weinstein	0					0	2	MSExchange
lance megyesi	0					0	2	
Tony Aina	0					0	2	
Richard Luckett	0					0	2	
Rich Luckett	29	17	125			1	2	
Joe Aina	0					0	3	
Bradford Werner	0					0	2	
Bharat Suneja	0					0	1	
?	0					0	2	edgetranspo

Start: 9/19/2007 0:23:42 AM   End: 9/19/2007 0:24:04 AM   Elapsed (sec): 21   Next Update (min):   Captured: 62.13%   User Count: 11

FIGURE 20-2   The ExMon tool showing client latency data

and performance of an Exchange server is included with the Performance Monitor. The downside is that it is not terribly intuitive. For an administrator new to Windows and Exchange, the performance objects and counters are cryptic at best. To understand the results of counters, even the ones that seem to make sense, requires a depth of knowledge of the interdependencies of the resources being monitored so that you can distinguish between a symptom and the source of a problem.

Fortunately, Microsoft provides built-in descriptions of almost all the performance object counters. And the application groups such as the Microsoft Exchange team publish helpful documentation on monitoring the performance of their applications using the Performance Monitor. The Exchange team at Microsoft also created a number of Exchange-specific performance objects that can also be used to monitor numerous aspects of your Exchange organization. Although the standard Performance Monitor tool can be opened by typing **perfmon.msc**, a version of PerfMon is included with Exchange 2007 in the BIN directory called ExchPrf.msc. In Figure 20-3, you can see how the System Monitor in Performance Monitor was customized for Exchange 2007.

Although the Performance Console is best known for its ability to show real-time performance information, the most important monitoring function it performs is benchmarking. Performance benchmarking is the process of gathering performance data that can be used for analyzing performance at a later point in time.

Queue Viewer

Simple Mail Transfer Protocol (SMTP) utilizes a folder at the file system level called the Queue directory for processing mail items. Exchange 2007 optimizes the SMTP protocol by using Microsoft's Extensible Storage Engine (ESE) database in place of flat files for the mail queue. It is not possible to view the content of the mail Queue directory with a simple text editor. Because administrators need the ability to be able to monitor queues and at times clean out messages in a queue, Microsoft has developed tools that expose the contents of the queues in all their releases of Exchange. Exchange 2003 had a very refined version of the Queue Viewer. Due to the changes in the SMTP transport stack and administrative tools in Exchange 2007, the Queue Viewer had to be changed. The new Queue Viewer is show in Figure 20-4.

PART VI

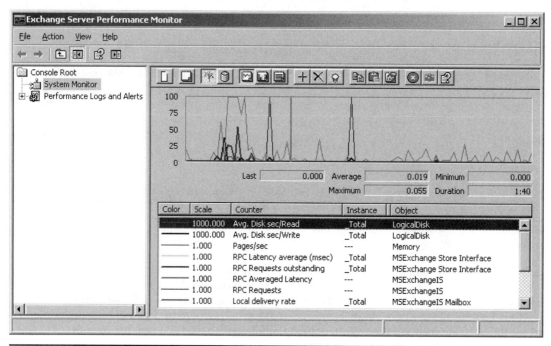

FIGURE 20-3   ExchPrf custom console

Exchange 2007 Queue Viewer uses MMC 3.0 and like the Exchange Management Console (EMC) its information is derived from the execution of cmdlets in the Exchange Management Shell (EMS). Information about each item in the queues can also be viewed in the Queue Viewer, as shown in Figure 20-5.

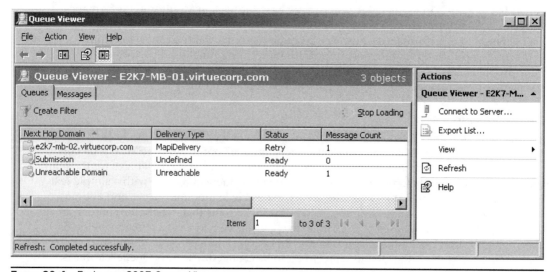

FIGURE 20-4   Exchange 2007 Queue Viewer

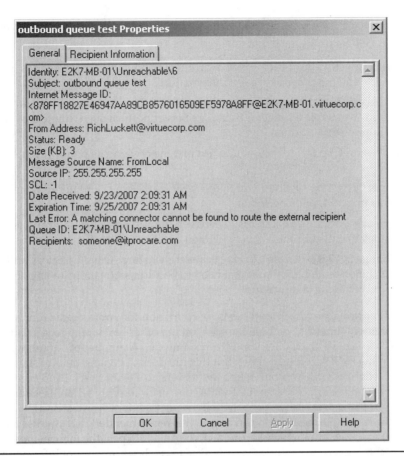

FIGURE 20-5   Item properties in the Queue Viewer

By default, you can use the Queue Viewer to sort and filter queues based on the following information:

Identity, Subject, Message ID, From Address, Status, Size, Message Source Name, Source IP, SCL Rating, Date Received, Expiration Time, Last Error, Queue ID, Recipients

It is also possible to manage the queues by suspending a queue or a message in the queue. When necessary, it is possible to delete items in a queue.

Exchange Best Practices Analyzer

The Exchange Best Practices Analyzer (ExBPA) is a multifaceted tool. Because of its versatility, we have covered its benefits in previous chapters in this book. In the context of this chapter, the ExBPA is being used as a monitoring tool. The ExBPA allows you to run the following scans:

- **Health Check**   Checks for errors, warnings, nondefault configurations, recent changes, and other configuration information.
- **The Health/Performance Check**   Performs the Health Check scan and then proceeds to sample a range of Exchange Server performance counters over a two-hour period of time.
- **Permission Check**   Allows you to test just the credentials you will be using to run the scan.
- **Connectivity Test**   Allows you to test your connections and permissions before performing a Health Check scan.
- **Baseline**   Performs a comparison between the current values for various Exchange parameters with administratively defined baseline values. Reports on the differences.
- **Exchange 2007 Readiness Check**   Scans the existing Active Directory and Exchange organization to identify issues that need to be addressed before joining an Exchange 2007 server to the organization.

The Health/Performance Check scan can be used to monitor your organization with limited configuration requirements. The Baseline scan, on the other hand, may require additional work in order to specify the values you want to compare. A number of default values are configured in the ExBPA.config.xml file. But this file doesn't contain default source values for all the baseline options. You can define the servers you want to scan and edit the source values for the baseline options with the ExBPA tool, prior to running the Baseline scan, as shown in Figure 20-6.

Due to the resources required to run a scan, it is recommended that you use a dedicated management machine from which to run the ExBPA tool. Expect the management machine to use 50–75% of its processor during a scan. Due to the large amount of information being requested from a domain controller, you may see the processor usage on the domain controller used by ExBPA go up to 50% utilization during the scan. The good news is that even if you run a scan during the middle of the day, it will have nominal effects on the actual Exchange servers you are scanning as long as you do not install and run the ExBPA on an Exchange server.

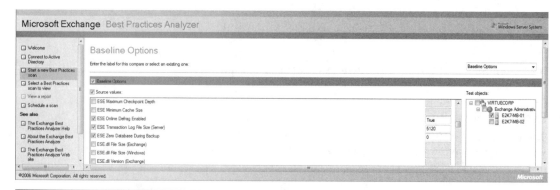

FIGURE 20-6   Baseline scan options

Windows Server 2003 Performance Advisor

The Windows Server 2003 Performance Advisor (SPA) is a hybrid monitoring and reporting tool. It allows you to monitor configuration settings, performance counters, and tracing information. Because Exchange 2007 runs on 64-bit hardware only, you will need to make sure you use SPA Version 2, which offers additional benefits over Version 1 besides 64-bit support. You can control the way in which collected data is stored by setting size restrictions and enabling circular logging. You can generate trend reports based on the performance counters you monitor. Additional information about IIS has been included in new XML templates. A new DNS data collector group has been added. You can download the Windows 2003 Performance Advisor at http://www.microsoft.com/downloads/details .aspx?familyid=61a41d78-e4aa-47b9-901b-cf85da075a73&displaylang=en. Here's a list of the data collector groups you can use:

- System Overview
- Active Directory
- ADAM
- IIS
- Print Spooler
- Performance Counters
- File
- Context Switch
- DNS

These role-based collector groups are defined by the Template_Server_Roles.xml file. You can configure the SPA to use one or more of these collection groups by using the Add/Repair Data Collector Groups option in the Edit menu. SPA Version 2 is shown in Figure 20-7.

Additional templates are available for creating custom data collator groups, including the following:

- Additional IIS Roles (Template_Enhanced_IIS.xml)
- Kernel Tracing (Template_Kernel_Special.xml)
- IT Study Roles (Template_IT_Study.xml)
- Multiple Providers Sample (Template_Multiple_Provides_Sample.xml)
- Custom Provider Sample (Template_Custom_Sample.xml)

Microsoft Exchange Server Profile Analyzer

One of the more difficult monitoring tasks to accomplish is mailbox profiling. Yet the ability to profile individual mailboxes is the most essential element for capacity planning. In the day-to-day maintenance and monitoring of Exchange 2007 Mailbox servers, you will want to capture information about the mailboxes servers, storage groups, databases, and the mailboxes themselves. You could spend money on one of the third-party tools available, and it would likely be worth the investment. At a minimum, you will want to use the Microsoft Exchange Server Profile Analyzer (EPA). The statistics you can derive from running the EPA

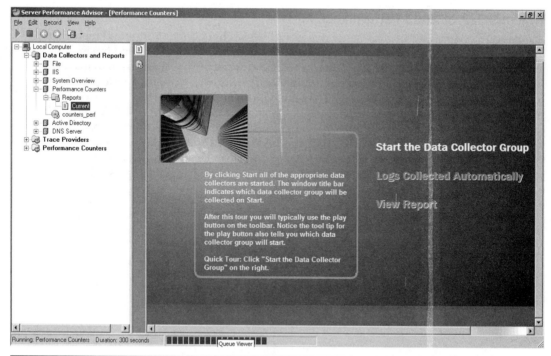

FIGURE 20-7   Windows Server 2003 Performance Advisor

will help you make critical capacity planning and maintenance decisions. Figure 20-8 shows the epawin.exe (GUI) interface. It is also possible to run the EPA tools from the command line as well.

Because this tool retrieves mailbox statistics at the server, store, and mailbox levels, there are explicit permissions that the monitoring account will need for the tool to run successfully. The minimum permissions required are as follows:

- Exchange View-Only Administrator
- Full Mailbox access to all mailboxes

You can use the EMC or the EMS to add the EPA monitoring account to the View-Only Administrator role. But you will need to use the Add-ADPermissions cmdlet from the EMS in order to grant Full Mailbox access to mailboxes on an Exchange 2007 server. It is possible to grant permissions to an entire Exchange server, as shown in Figure 20-9.

For more details on the EPA, see the TechNet article, "Microsoft Exchange Server Profile Analyzer," at http://technet.microsoft.com/en-us/library/bb508856.aspx.

Microsoft Operation Manager

The monitoring tools we have reviewed so far either come with Windows or Exchange or they are free to download and use. However, they tend to have specific uses, and some are a little more intuitive than others. You could easily spend the majority of each day performing

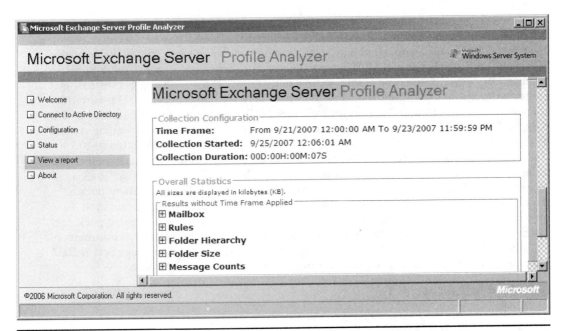

FIGURE 20-8   Exchange Server Profile Analyzer Tool

all the operation tasks necessary to keep Exchange running smoothly. In many environments this in unrealistic due to limited personnel. When this is the case, additional tools that take the burden of monitoring the organization off of the administrator are necessary. This is where a tool such as Microsoft Operations Manager (MOM) comes into play.

```
Machine: E2K7-MB-01 | Scope: virtuecorp.com

[PS] C:\Documents and Settings\Administrator>Get-ExchangeServer e2k7-mb-01 | Add
-ADPermission -user epa -AccessRights extendedright -ExtendedRights "send-as"

Identity             User              Deny  Inherited  Rights
--------             ----              ----  ---------  ------
E2K7-MB-01           VIRTUECORP\epa    False False      Send-As

[PS] C:\Documents and Settings\Administrator>Get-ExchangeServer e2k7-mb-01 | Add
-ADPermission -user epa -AccessRights extendedright -ExtendedRights "receive-as"

Identity             User              Deny  Inherited  Rights
--------             ----              ----  ---------  ------
E2K7-MB-01           VIRTUECORP\epa    False False      Receive-As

[PS] C:\Documents and Settings\Administrator>_
```

FIGURE 20-9   Granting EPA account permissions

Microsoft Operation Manager is not free—and it has additional requirements that make its deployment much more complex than the other tools we have looked at so far. However, once you have MOM installed, you'll find it to be the most powerful monitoring tool available from Microsoft. The latest version of MOM is available as part of the new System Center from Microsoft. However, at the time of this writing, native support for Exchange Server 2007 is limited to Microsoft Operations Manager 2005. Ironically, Exchange Server 2003 is currently supported in System Center. Support for Exchange 2007 comes in the form of a management pack. MOM by itself is limited in its monitoring "know-how" to the Windows operating system. Its knowledge can be extended by importing management packs, as shown in Figure 20-10.

Although MOM is not free, the Exchange Server 2007 management pack is free. It can be found at http://www.microsoft.com/downloads/details.aspx?FamilyID=30eebc7c-a35a-41ae-9cd1-2047847fde85&DisplayLang=en. Once the Exchange 2007 management pack is imported into MOM, it can begin to provide administrators with valuable information. To provide administrators with information quickly, the Exchange 2007 management pack takes advantage of cmdlets in the Exchange Management Shell (EMS) to gather information about the health of Exchange 2007. Just through the installation of the Exchange Server 2007 management pack, MOM will be preconfigured to run the following cmdlets:

- Test-MAPIConnectivity
- Test-Mailflow
- Test-ExchangeSearch
- Test-ServiceHealth
- Test-SystemHealth
- Test-UMConnectivity
- Test-EdgeSynchronization

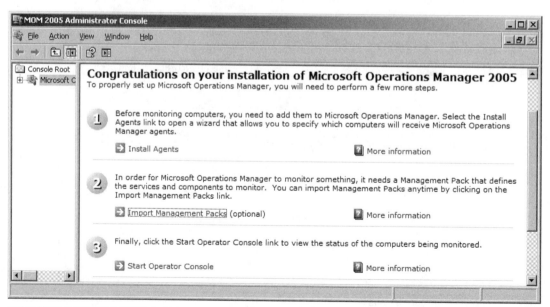

FIGURE 20-10   Importing a management pack

Although additional Exchange 2007 cmdlets can provide information to MOM, they have to be manually configured to do so. Some are specific to the server roles they test. The Exchange 2007 management pack takes less time to configure than previous versions of Exchange management packs because it is already preconfigured to monitor each of the different Exchange 2007 roles independently. For status information you can view the state of the entire organization collectively, see each role grouped together, or see each server independently. Perhaps the most attractive feature of MOM is its reporting services. The Exchange 2007 management pack will import Exchange 2007-specific reports that can assist with change management and capacity planning.

Third-party Monitoring Tools

There are a number of third-party vendors that provide monitoring tools. However, there is only a handful specializing in monitoring Exchange Server 2007. Table 20-1 shows some of the more prominent monitoring tools.

Vendor/Product	Description and Link
Zenprise for Exchange	Zenprise provides real-time, automated diagnosis and resolution of operational problems across the Microsoft Exchange and BlackBerry environments. Zenprise automatically provides resolutions to complex e-mail problems, which enables enterprises to spend less time and money manually troubleshooting issues while simultaneously improving overall service levels. For example, user complaints about sending, receiving, or viewing e-mails, will require an administrator to analyze multiple infrastructure components such as Active Directory, DNS, and network devices to pinpoint the root cause of the problem—a process that can be unduly tedious and time consuming. A customer's monitoring systems will detect numerous errors across the infrastructure. Zenprise complements these systems by automatically correlating errors across the infrastructure components to not only quickly detect the underlying cause of these errors, but also to provide detailed resolution steps to the administrator. The automated diagnosis and resolution of the problem allows the issue to be resolved in minutes, rather than the hours, days, or weeks traditionally spent troubleshooting. (Go to http://www.zenprise.com/products/exchange.aspx.)
Quest Software's Spotlight on Exchange and MessageStats	Helps administrators protect mission-critical messaging environments with Exchange troubleshooting that quickly diagnoses exactly where and what the problems are and resolves the problems from a single, easy-to-use interface. (Go to http://www.quest.com/intelligent-messaging/end-user-experience.aspx.)
Promodag Reports	Retrieves vital information easily as well as measures the use of your electronic messaging system, analyzes traffic patterns and mailbox and public folder content, and establishes the cost of using the system. (Go to http://www.bi101.com/products/solutions/promodag/index.php.)
ENow's Mailscape	Mailscape is a unique and innovative systems management tool that combines all the key elements for Exchange monitoring, administration, and maintenance in a single solution. Mailscape's sleek dashboard provides vital information about each server's current state and growth rate to facilitate proactive Exchange management. Mailscape manages Exchange proactively to optimize system performance and minimize downtime. It also increases helpdesk efficiency to improve the level of end-user service. (Go to http://www.enowinc.com/mailscape/overview.asp.)

TABLE 20-1   Third-party Monitoring Tools

Monitoring Exchange 2007

Although Microsoft Operations Manager with the Exchange 2007 management pack is the most comprehensive tool from Microsoft for monitoring Exchange Server 2007, it will benefit you to know how other tools can be used. In this part of the chapter we will look at how these various tools can be used—in some cases in conjunction with one another—to monitor clients, individual server roles, system resources, and services. We will also take a look at how you can configure tools to send alerts so that you can be notified in the event that an issue arises or a failure occurs.

Monitoring Clients

To make sure users have the best experience possible with the infrastructure you have, you should monitor the clients, the servers, and the network on which they communicate with each other. Clients tend to be the canaries in the coalmine when it comes to monitoring Exchange Server or network connectivity problem in many organizations. With proper monitoring, it may be possible to identify problems before the end users get a chance to call the helpdesk.

Outlook (MAPI)

The client that is most dependent on the network for its performance is the MAPI client. Outlook 2007, Outlook 2003, and Outlook 2002 are supported MAPI clients. Outlook 2000 and earlier clients were not tested with, and are not supported by, Exchange Server 2007. There are MAPI connections made to Exchange that are not Outlook connections. Monitor the version number of the MAPI connections being made to your Exchange 2007 mailbox servers. If you see a connection with a version older than 10.0.2627.2625, that connection is unsupported and could be a problem waiting to happen. For example, if a line of business application uses MAPI to interface with Exchange 2007, make sure it supports a version of MAPI higher than Outlook 2002 (10.0.2627.2625). Monitoring the version numbers of the MAPI connections could help identify problems.

You can use the Exchange Server User Monitor (ExMon) to identify the client versions and IP addresses used by the clients. In Figures 20-1 and 20-2, earlier in the chapter, we looked at how ExMon displays RPC connection latency data for MAPI clients. On the client machine you can capture performance information with Performance Monitor (PerfMon). In Figure 20-11, you can see the Outlook Performance object and the available performance counts associated with the object for a Outlook 2007 client on a Vista machine.

You can use the Exchange Management Shell to test MAPI connectivity to the Mailbox databases. The cmdlet is Test-MAPIConnectivity. It will display the results of the test, as shown in Figure 20-12.

If you are running MOM with the Exchange 2007 management pack, this test will be performed automatically and will appear in the Operator Console under Performance Views.

Internet Clients

Outlook Web Access, Internet Mail Access Protocol (IMAP), Post Office Protocol (POP), and Exchange Active Sync (EAS) clients do not connect directly to the Mailbox Server role. To monitor these clients, you will need to monitor the Client Access Server connections. For clients that are external to your network, you may need to simulate connections with test accounts and client devices/machines so that you can monitor and validate their experience.

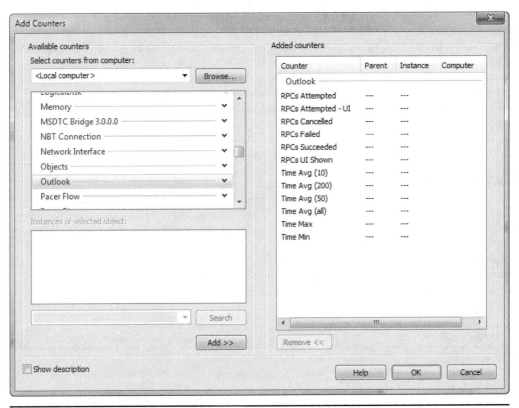

Figure 20-11   Outlook performance object

Monitoring Servers

The Exchange Server 2007 architecture is broken into five distinct roles. From a maintenance perspective, this means that five separate roles must be monitored. This is especially important to understand when a single server may have multiple roles installed. A typical

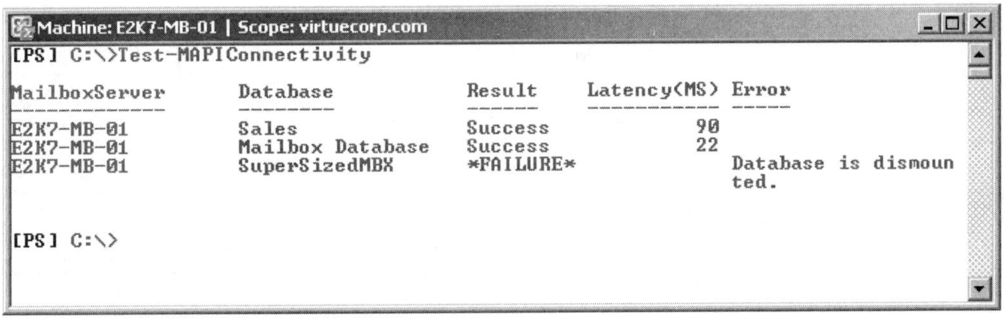

```
Machine: E2K7-MB-01 | Scope: virtuecorp.com                                  _ □ ×
[PS] C:\>Test-MAPIConnectivity

MailboxServer         Database            Result      Latency(MS) Error
------------          --------            ------      ----------- -----
E2K7-MB-01            Sales               Success              90
E2K7-MB-01            Mailbox Database    Success              22
E2K7-MB-01            SuperSizedMBX       *FAILURE*                 Database is dismoun
                                                                    ted.


[PS] C:\>
```

Figure 20-12   Test-MAPIConnectivity results

installation of Exchange Server 2007 will have three roles installed (Client Access Server, Hub Transport server, and Mailbox server). Monitoring tools will have three views associated with that single server. In some cases, the same data will be visible from all three perspectives (for example, the event logs for the server). On the other hand, there is data that can only be collected from a specific role. For example, only the Mailbox role will have information about the number of mailboxes on the server. So what should be monitored based on role? The information in Table 20-2 is collected by the Exchange 2007 management pack for MOM 2005.

Although MOM has these settings preconfigured, it is possible to use other tools such as the Event Viewer and Performance Monitor to gather the same information. However, it will take longer to analyze the information that you gather without the help of the logic built into the Exchange 2007 management pack.

Another tool that can be helpful in monitoring the Exchange 2007 roles is the Microsoft Exchange Server Best Practices Analyzer Tool (ExBPA). It collects configuration information from Active Directory, the Windows Server Registry, the IIS metabase, and server/application performance objects to learn about all the Exchange Server roles you have deployed. By comparing the information that it retrieves with the Microsoft Best Practices database, you can monitor for inappropriate settings throughout the organization.

Server Role	Role-Specific Items to Monitor
Client Access	• ActiveSync Connections • OWA Connections • Web Services Connectivity
Edge Transport	• Transport Delivery Status Notification (DSN) • Transport Queues • Agents
Hub Transport	• Transport Delivery Status Notification (DSN) • Transport Queues • Agents

Mailbox	• Information Store
	  • Public Receive Queue Size
	  • Client RPC
	  • Database
	  • RPC
	• Mailbox Count
	• Mailflow
	• MAPIConnectivity

Unified Messaging	• UM Connectivity

TABLE 20-2 Monitoring Server Roles

Alerts and Notifications

Monitoring tools such as MOM allow you to centralize all your monitoring and then store and analyze the results from a central location. This is ideal for the maintenance cycle. But one of the requirements that administrators have for any monitoring solution is for it to be able to identify problems and then notify an administrator so that the problems can be resolved. If you do not have MOM, it doesn't mean you can't have notifications. The Performance Monitor has an alert feature built in. One bit negative to PerfMon alerts is that they do not have an integrated e-mail message notification option. Here are the actions you can take when an alert is triggered:

- Log an entry in the application event log (default)
- Send a network message to
- Start performance data log
- Run this program

Configuring a PerfMon Alert

1. Open the Performance Monitor on your management machine.
2. Expand Performance Logs and Alerts and select Alerts.
3. Right-click Alerts and select New Alert Settings.
4. Type **Low Disk Space** and click OK.
5. Type **Free Disk Space Alert** in the Comment field.
6. Click the Add button.
7. Select the Exchange server you want to monitor from the Select counters from computer drop-down box.
8. Select Logical Disk from the Performance object drop-down box, and select Free Megabytes from the Select counters from list box.
9. Verify that the drive instance you want to monitor is selected. Click Add once and then click Close.
10. Select Under from the Alert when the value is drop-down box and type a number in MB that represents 20% of the total disk space (for example, 4000 is 20% of a 20GB drive).
11. Change the Sample data every settings to once per day.
12. Click the Actions tab and select the method for which you would like to be alerted, as shown next.
13. Click the Schedule tab and configure the time that the alert should run. You can set it to manually start as well.
14. Click OK.

PART VI

15. Either manually start the alert or verify that the alert starts at the time you scheduled it to.

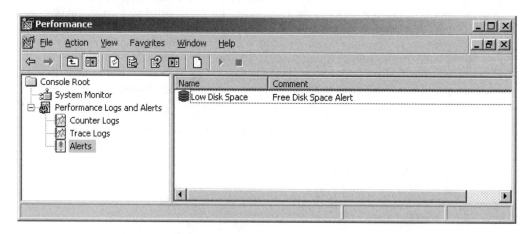

You can add other alert counters for resources that are critical to Exchange Server 2007, or you can create additional alerts for separate counters. The key is not to set the update interval to run too often so that it will not adversely affect the system you are monitoring.

Optimizing Performance

Once you begin monitoring your organization in a structured way, patterns will begin to emerge. You will start to see inequity in resource utilization from server to server. Optimization is the next step beyond remediation of a problem. Optimizing performance is the natural conclusion to the operations' lifecycle.

Establishing a Baseline

Over time, as the patterns and trends emerge, it is possible to overlook the fact that resources are slowing being depleted on the Exchange servers. In order to truly quantify the changes taking place, you will need a reference point. You can create a reference point by establishing a baseline. Without a baseline, the information you are currently seeing when you monitor Exchange can easily be taken out of context and lead you to make unjustified decisions. The easiest way to create a baseline for Exchange 2007 is to use the Baseline scan that is built into the latest version of the Exchange Best Practices Analyzer, as shown in Figure 20-6, earlier in this chapter. After the baseline is established, you can run a tool such as the Windows Server 2003 Performance Advisor (refer to Figure 20-7) to provide you with real-time performance monitoring that you can use to compare with the baseline data.

Mailbox Server Optimization

In Chapter 6, we covered administering mailbox servers. The optimization settings are covered in depth in this chapter as design best practices. But even the best design may need performance tweaking over time. Continue to profile your users' Input/Output per Second (IOPS) on a per-mailbox bases. Profiling your users on mailbox servers will provide you with the most accurate way to plan for resource capacity changes. ExMon provides quick and accurate profiles for your users. It may not be as full featured as some of the third-party tools, but it is far better than having to manually calculate the information from PerfMon. For more details on profiling users and optimizing disk IOPS, see Chapter 6.

Transport Server Optimization

In Chapter 7, we covered administering Hub and Edge Transport servers. Optimization settings are also covered in Chapter 7, which goes into the deployment and administration of Transport Server roles. The Hub Transport servers depend greatly on the Active Directory sites and site links to build a routing topology. Active Directory sites and services are managed on domain controllers.

If your Exchange servers are in Active Directory domains where the domain controllers have not yet been upgraded to the 64-bit version of Windows, you may be able to double the performance of your Exchange servers by upgrading your domain controllers. If you would like to read more about how upgrading your domain controllers can have a positive effect on Exchange 2007, see "Guidance on Active Directory design for Exchange Server 2007" at http://msexchangeteam.com/archive/2007/03/28/437313.aspx.

Optimizing the Client Experience

Outlook 2003 and higher can be optimized with literally a click of a button. In fact, the default configuration for each profile on Outlook 2003 and higher is set to optimize performance. What are we talking about? Why cache mode, of course. A number of organizations have either disabled cache mode or have not upgraded to a version of Outlook that supports cache mode. The legacy connection mode is called *online mode*. The impact of cache mode goes beyond conserving network bandwidth. The benefits of cache mode were discussed in detail in Chapter 11. In addition to the benefits listed in Chapter 11, hardware vendors such as NetApp have released performance documents that show how cache mode clients use less processor, memory, and disk I/O on the mailbox servers they connect to. If you would like to see the results of NetApp's performance testing/comparison of cache mode vs. online mode, see "Exchange Server 2007 Performance Characteristics Using NetApp iSCSI Storage Systems," at http://www.netapp.com/library/tr/3565.pdf.

Analysis and Reporting

Microsoft Operations Manager gathers performance and availability information from Exchange and stores the information in a central database. The database is used by the Operations Console to display information about monitored servers, as you have seen earlier. Sometimes it is difficult to be able to decipher the information you see. In most cases, it is difficult to connect the dots and see how the information you are looking at affects the other components of the Exchange 2007 architecture. If you are running the SP1 version of Microsoft Operations Manager 2005 or later, an additional database, referred to as the *Data Warehouse*, is created to store information for the SQL Reporting Services to access. The SQL Reporting Services make it possible for administrators to easily aggregate the gathered data and run the Exchange 2007 management pack reports. By default, data is transferred from the operational database to the data warehouse database at 1:00 A.M. daily. This can be changed by modifying the scheduled task on the SQL server with the data warehouse.

Exchange Reports

When the Exchange 2007 management pack is imported to MOM 2005 SP1, the Exchange 2007 reports can be imported at the same time or separately. A variety of reports are available to administrators. As shown in Figure 20-13, they are grouped into categories: Exchange 2007 Anti-Spam, Exchange 2007 Metrics, and Exchange 2007 Service Availability. It is easy to share the information in the reports because the Exchange 2007 management pack reports will render graphs, charts, and tables that are easy to read and understand (see Figure 20-13).

Anti-Spam

- **Attached File Filter**   effectiveness of the Attachment Filter agent
- **Connection Filter Report**   effectiveness of the Connection Filter agent
- **Content Filter**   effectiveness of the Content Filter agent
- **Protocol Analysis**   effectiveness of the Protocol Analysis/Sender Reputation agent
- **Recipient Filter**   effectiveness of the Recipient Filter agent
- **Sender Filter**   effectiveness of the Sender Filter agent
- **Sender Id**   effectiveness of the Sender Id agent

Metrics

- **Client Performance**   Indicates clients' experience by gathering the percentage of successful RPC client/server operations between Outlook clients and Exchange 2007.
- **Mailbox Count**   Shows the distribution of mailboxes across storage groups and databases.
- **RPC and Database Performance**   Shows the relationship between RPC and database I/O performance.

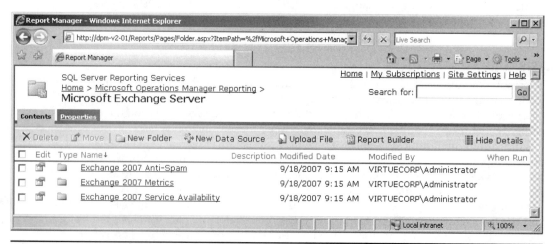

FIGURE 20-13   Exchange 2007 report categories

- **Unified Messaging Call Summary**   Shows a summary of telephone calls received and placed by Exchange 2007 Unified Messaging servers.

- **Unified Messaging Message Summary**   Shows a summary of voice and fax messages processed by Unified Messaging servers.

Service Availability

Figure 20-14 shows the list of the service availability reports provided by MOM.

- **Service Availability Summary**   Summarizes the availability of Exchange 2007 services such as Mailbox, Mailflow, Microsoft Outlook Web Access, Microsoft Exchange ActiveSync, and Unified Messaging. Service Availability Summary can also be used to discover a timeframe of a bottleneck that can be used to filter events in the logs.

- **ActiveSync Internal Service Availability**   Shows the internal service availability of Exchange ActiveSync as measured by the Test-ActiveSyncConnectivity cmdlet.

- **Mailbox Service Availability**   Shows the MAPI connectivity availability for the mailbox server. Utilizes the Test-MAPIConnectivity cmdlet.*

- **Mailflow Local Service Availability**   Shows the availability of Mailflow Local service. Utilizes the Test-Mailflow cmdlet.

- **Mailflow Remote Service Availability**   Shows the availability of the Mailflow Remote service. Utilizes the Test-Mailflow cmdlet.

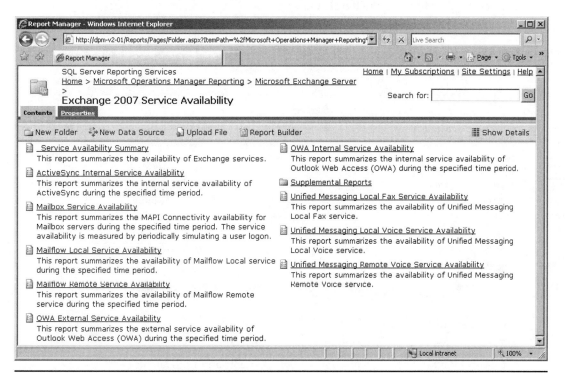

FIGURE 20-14   Exchange 2007 Service Availability reports

- **Outlook Web Access External Service Availability** Shows the external service availability of Outlook Web Access. Utilizes the Test-OWAConnectivity cmdlet.*

- **Outlook Web Access Internal Service Availability** Shows the internal service availability of Outlook Web Access. Utilizes the Test-OWAConnectivity cmdlets.*

- **Unified Messaging Local Fax Service Availability** Shows the availability of the Local Fax service. Utilizes the Test-UMConnectivity cmdlet.

- **Unified Messaging Local Voice Service Availability** Shows the availability of the Local Voice service. Utilizes the Test-UMConnectivity cmdlet.

- **Unified Messaging Remote Voice Service Availability** Shows the availability of the Remote Voice service. Utilizes the Test-UMConnectivity cmdlet.

  * These reports require a test mailbox account or other additional manual configurations. See http://technet.microsoft.com/en-us/library/bb691294.aspx for additional details.

Establishing a Service Level Agreement (SLA)

The Service Availability reports can additionally be configured to monitor SLA thresholds that you manually define. If the threshold is exceeded, the display will show the results in red as opposed to the default color (black). Use the following steps to set a permanent SLA percentage number for a Service Availability report:

1. Start the Reporting Console.

2. Open a report to configure the SLA for.

3. Select the Properties tab, shown next.

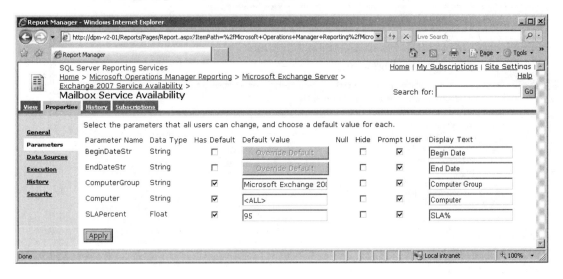

4. Click Parameters on the left.

5. Type a number from 1 to 99.9 in the SLAPercent field.

6. Deselect the HasDefault check box for BeginDateStr and EndDateStr.

7. Click Apply.

Export a Report

After running a report, you may want to share the report with others. MOM 2005 supports exporting reports to a number of file formats. Use the Select a format drop-down box to select one of the following file formats:

- XML file with report data
- CSV (comma delimited)
- TIFF file
- Acrobat (PDF) file
- Excel

Depending on the version of SQL you are using, you may have additional export options, including the following:

- HTML with Office Web Components
- Web archive

Summary

Microsoft provides Exchange administrators with tools to maintain their organizations. The process of maintaining, monitoring, and optimizing Exchange Server is a tedious one that is more complex in larger organizations. However, the process is inescapable because it is critical to the health and well being of any size organization. It is important to consider using a lifecycle management model like MOF in order to cover all your bases.

Microsoft has built in a number of maintenance tasks performed by Exchange 2007 during online maintenance. However, a number of daily, weekly, and monthly maintenance tasks are recommended. Monitoring tools should be utilized to keep a close eye on the health of your organization. The goals of monitoring include:

- Centralized monitoring console or portal
- Reduced administration
- Notification of service failures and performance bottlenecks
- Real-time status and health information on Exchange Servers' hardware, software, and services
- Trend analysis and reporting

The benefits you derive from monitoring your organization closely are numerous. Preemptively identifying problems before they become disasters is good for obvious reasons. Identifying potential bottlenecks so you can balance out server resources and optimize the users' experience takes monitoring to the next level.

When monitoring Exchange 2007 becomes too time consuming for the personnel that you have administering Exchange, you can incorporate third-party monitoring tools and/or Microsoft Operations Manager. Microsoft provides an Exchange Server 2007 management pack that can be imported into Microsoft Operations Manager 2005. A variety of reports are included in the Exchange 2007 management pack and are preconfigured for administrators to use right out of the box. They are grouped into three categories: Exchange 2007 Anti-Spam, Exchange 2007 Metrics, and Exchange 2007 Service Availability. It is easy to share the information in the reports because the Exchange 2007 management pack reports render graphs, charts, and tables that are easy to read and understand.

Troubleshooting Exchange 2007

Exchange Server 2007 is a complex application being placed in very different scenarios at enterprises around the globe. Some companies push their servers to their limits; others hardly use them at all. Inevitably, there will be some failure of hardware, software, or infrastructure that impacts the Exchange environment. A big part of troubleshooting various issues with Exchange Server involves knowing where to look for issues, what tools are available for troubleshooting, and how to use those tools to identify and resolve problems.

Exchange Server Troubleshooting Tools

Microsoft provides several tools to work with Exchange Server 2007. Many perform preventative maintenance and can be used to determine a baseline or benchmarks for Exchange performance. Others are a little more forensic in that they are designed to identify problem areas in an existing environment. There are also other steps that administrators can perform that assist in troubleshooting down the road.

The Importance of a Baseline

Knowing a baseline for the performance of a system can help expose deviations from normal operations. Identifying these trends can help resolve issues before they are noticed by users or have a negative impact on a Service Level Agreement (SLA). Performance Monitor and ExBPA are examples of tools that can determine baseline settings against which you can compare day-to-day statistics. Baseline measurements of systems during off-peak times and peak times should be regularly compared to current operational levels to identify negative trends. Although this is a function of monitoring, it also can help in troubleshooting.

Administrator Documentation

If you are troubleshooting a system that has always been under your control, you may be intimately aware of various nuances of the configuration and even user behavior patterns, but if you are called in to troubleshoot an existing system that has problems, you are often handicapped. It seems the more relevant information you can gather, the better off you are from the start.

Although not many administrators seem to enjoy the task of system documentation, Microsoft provides an Exchange 2007 Visio template with icons for the Exchange roles and other expected messaging-related network components. Administrators can easily maintain a network diagram with this template. The download consists of two Visio files to add to the My Shapes folder under the My Documents or Documents folder and is found at http://www .microsoft.com/downloads/details.aspx?familyid=45f7ea49-ceb2-4b04-8d46-2b0ae5e10694.

Event Viewer

Exchange Server is a Windows application, and as such reports certain events to the Application event log. Checking the Application event Log, whether manually or by some reporting software, should be part of a regular maintenance routine. Outside of such a routine, the Application event log is one of the first places to check for information in the presence of e-mail difficulties. As we know, problems with Exchange systems are not limited to Exchange Server itself, so the System event log should also be monitored for Windows errors or warnings.

Exchange also posts informational events to the Application event log that serve as confirmation of completion. One of the most relevant of these posts involves the online maintenance process, which includes an online defrag of the information stores. Event ID 1221 confirms successful passes of online defragmentation through the information stores, public or private, by reporting available whitespace. Figure 21-1 shows a sampling of Application event log entries for Exchange 2007, including errors, warnings, and informative entries.

Exchange Server 2007 Management Console Tools

Within the Exchange Management Console is a portal to a set of Exchange tools that can help with troubleshooting a variety of issues. Figure 21-2 shows the Toolbox menu in the EMC.

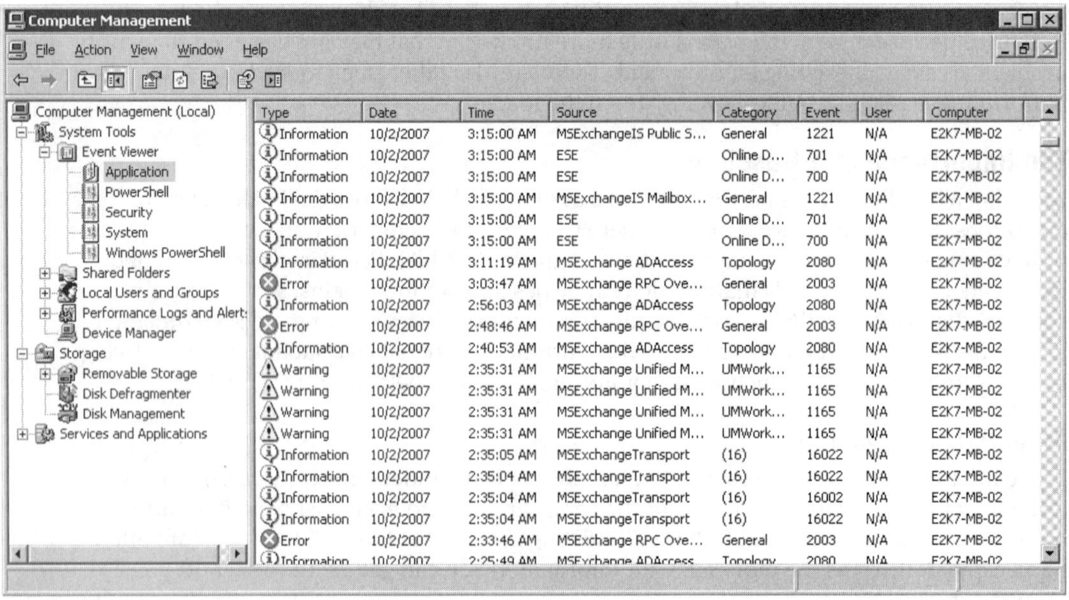

Figure 21-1 Exchange Server 2007 Application event log sample

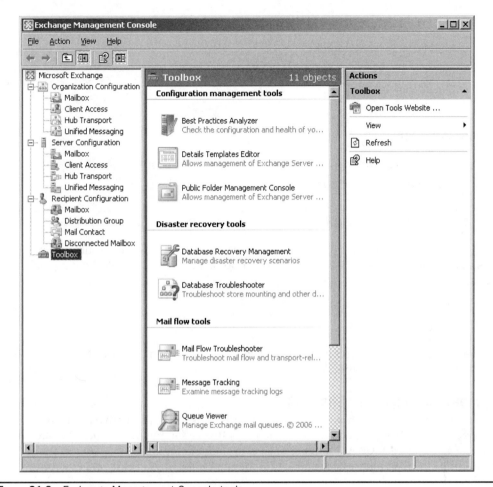

FIGURE 21-2   Exchange Management Console tools

Not all the tools here are specifically for troubleshooting, and they are separated into four different sections:

Configuration Management Tools

- Best Practices Analyzer
- Details Templates Editor
- Public Folder Management Console

Disaster Recovery Tools

- Database Recovery Management
- Database Troubleshooter

PART VI

Mail Flow Tools

- Mail Flow Troubleshooter
- Message Tracking
- Queue Viewer
- Routing Log Viewer

Performance Tools

- Performance Monitor
- Performance Troubleshooter

SP1 *Service Pack 1 adds the Public Folder Management Console to the EMC Tools section.*

The three "Troubleshooter" tools listed launch the Exchange Server Troubleshooting Assistant, shown in Figure 21-3. This is another portal just for the troubleshooting tools and adds a couple of other tools:

- Process Failure Analysis
- Trace Control

We will discuss these tools and their role in resolving certain problems that may arise in an Exchange 2007 organization.

Exchange Management Shell (EMS)

We have used the EMS as much as possible in this book as an alternative to the user interface. During troubleshooting, there are many things that the EMS can do that are not (yet) available in the GUI. At the same time, everything in the GUI is available in the EMS. In addition, the EMS allows access to all the command-line functionality experienced with cmd.exe, such as the basic networking tools, ping and telnet.

In addition, a set of cmdlets is available that performs tests. Entering **Get-ExCommand** lists all the Exchange-specific cmdlets in alphabetical order. These "Test-" cmdlets are listed next:

- Test-ActiveSyncConnectivity
- Test-EdgeSynchronization
- Test-ExchangeSearch
- Test-ImapConnectivity
- Test-IPAllowListProvider
- Test-IPBlockListProvider
- Test-Mailflow
- Test-MAPIConnectivity
- Test-OutlookWebServices
- Test-OwaConnectivity
- Test-PopConnectivity
- Test-ReplicationHealth
- Test-SenderId
- Test-ServiceHealth
- Test-SystemHealth
- Test-UMConnectivity
- Test-WebServicesConnectivity

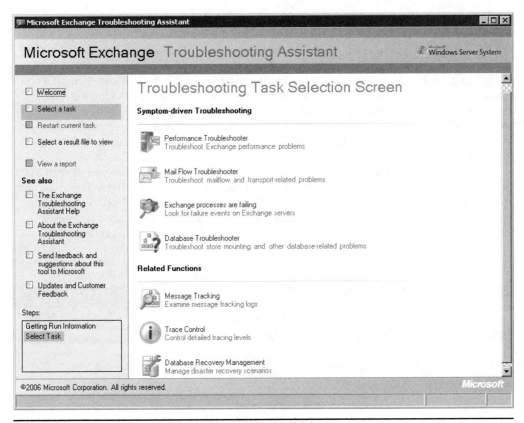

FIGURE 21-3   Microsoft Exchange Server Troubleshooting Assistant

As an example, Test-SystemHealth is like a mini ExBPA for the EMS. It performs checks based on the results of the installed roles and reports.

Microsoft Exchange Server Best Practices Analyzer

When the ExBPA was first released as a free tool in 2004 for Exchange, it was one of the most relevant applications for Exchange configuration, maintenance, and troubleshooting we have seen. It is the Swiss Army knife of Exchange utilities and something that every Exchange administrator should at least be familiar with. It can be run proactively to identify potential problem spots as well as reactively when something is preventing optimized Exchange performance.

ExBPA depends on a configuration file called ExBPA.config.xml for its actions and calls on various components to collect data about the Exchange implementation, including the IIS metabase, Active Directory, WMI, and the local Exchange server. The English version of this config file is stored in %programfiles%\microsoft\exchange server\bin\en\. ExBPA configuration files are available in 11 languages as of Exchange 2007 Service Pack 1. It represents the knowledge base of tests and checks that ExBPA runs during a scan. Both ExBPA and its configuration files may be updated through Microsoft update, with Roll Up updates, or with Exchange Service Pack application.

Starting the ExBPA returns the welcome screen shown in Figure 21-4 and then offers an opportunity to enter an account with access to Active Directory after checking for updates. The minimum permissions required for the account executing ExBPA are threefold: domain administrator for AD queries, local administrator on each Exchange server, and Exchange View-Only Permissions on the Exchange organization. If the account running ExBPA has these permissions, the account option to access AD is not necessary.

After connecting to Active Directory, ExBPA presents options for the type of scan to execute, which are listed as Health Check, Permissions Check, Connectivity Test, Baseline, and Exchange 2007 Readiness Check. These are shown in Figure 21-5. ExBPA runs these scans and returns a report of its findings relative to Exchange best practices. From a troubleshooting perspective, ExBPA does highlight problems and brings them to the

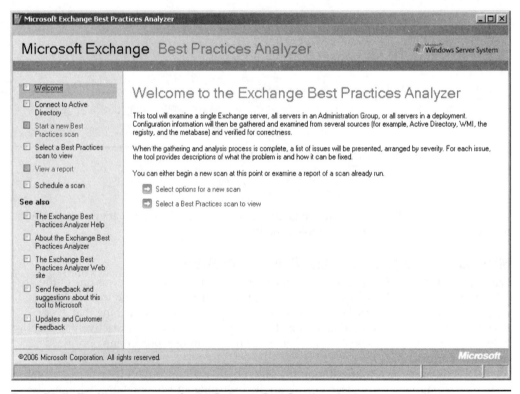

FIGURE 21-4 The Welcome screen for the Exchange Best Practices Analyzer

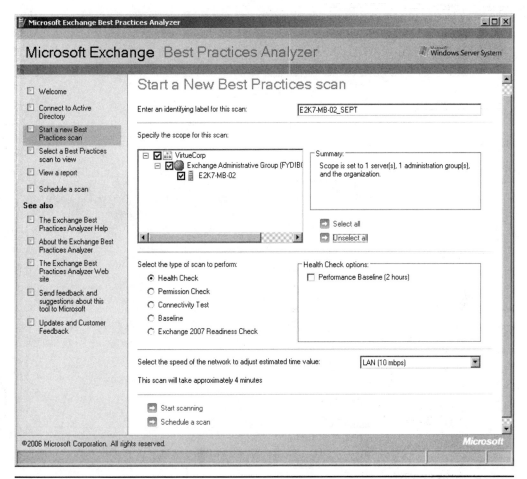

FIGURE 21-5 Starting a New Best Practices scan in the ExBPA

attention of the administrators in the reports. Figure 21-6 shows a detailed scan report as an example.

Also, scans can be saved and compared against a baseline scan for differences. Figure 21-7 shows several scan reports saved for future viewing. These can be referenced any time you might need to see what has changed since the scan was last executed. ExBPA is an invaluable tool for both proactive assessment and troubleshooting.

ExBPA also has a command-line version called ExBPACmd.exe. This is useful for scheduling scans and running them silently. ExBPACmd.exe has the same configurable components as the GUI version, including the scope of the scan, the scan type, and the configuration file to use.

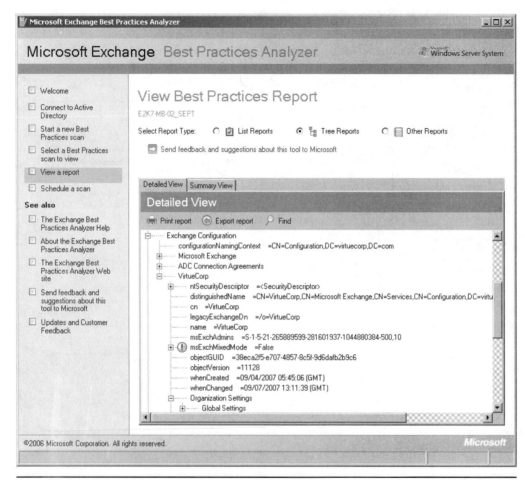

FIGURE 21-6 A Detailed View scan report

Queue Viewer

The Queue Viewer is accessed through the EMC and lists SMTP messages, inbound or outbound, that have not completed their journey. These may be delayed deliveries because the destination server is offline, DNS resolution is failing, or disruptions have occurred between Hub Transport servers, as well as many other issues. The Queue Viewer will identify all messages specific to a domain and can show the status of each message in the queue. Queue contents are filterable where specific message types can be presented in the window based on dates, message IDs, addresses, and SCL values. Figure 21-8 shows a simple example where messages are not making it to the smarthost.

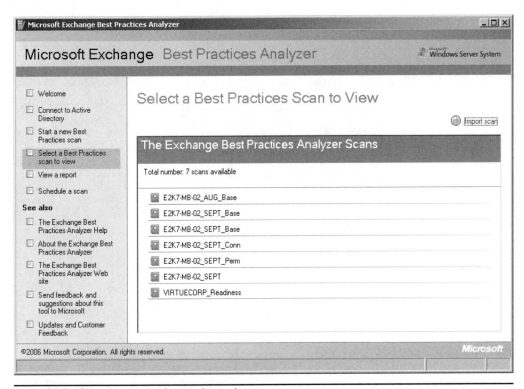

FIGURE 21-7 Stored scans to view on demand

The Queue Viewer does enjoy a new architecture in Exchange 2007, maintaining its own Extensible Storage Engine (ESE) database under %programfiles%\Microsoft\Exchange Server\TransportRoles\Data\Queue\. As you can see in Figure 21-9, the database and transaction logs coexist in the same folder and therefore on the same physical drive. While troubleshooting message flow, it is conceivable that on busy servers the STMP queue itself can be a bottleneck. If there is insufficient drive space, a minimum of 4GB of free space, or the server is exceptionally busy, then the SMTP queues can slow e-mail traffic. This back pressure algorithm changes in Service Pack 1, allowing the minimum free drive space to go down to 500MB. The location of the Queue database and its transaction logs are controlled through a configuration file. Oddly, the file is called EdgeTransport.exe.config and is located in %programfiles%\Microsoft\Exchange Server\bin\. This is the configuration file for the Edge Transport role or the Hub Transport role queues, depending on which is installed on the Exchange Server.

SP1 *Exchange 2007 SP1 improves the back pressure algorithm. This allows for a reduction in the minimum free drive space on an Exchange 2007 Hub Transport server from 4GB to 500MB.*

PART VI

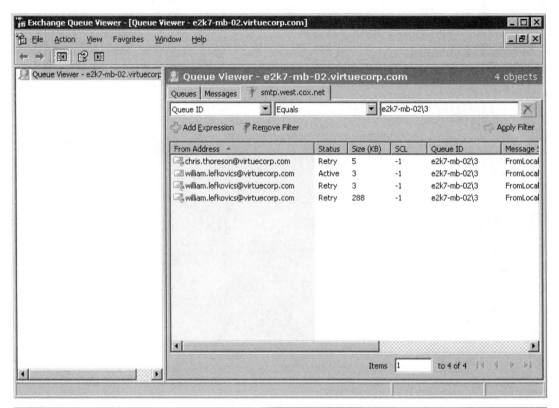

FIGURE 21-8   The Queue Viewer

After the following tags have been edited in the configuration file, the MSExchangeTransport service needs to be restarted for the change to take effect:

```
<add key="QueueDatabasePath" value = "<full path>" />
<add key="QueueDatabaseLoggingPath" value = "<full path>" />
```

On a busy Hub Transport server, especially one that shares drives with the Mailbox role, it may be beneficial to isolate the SMTP Queue database on a separate spindle.

As we expect, the SMTP queues in Exchange 2007 can also be managed using the EMS. The cmdlet Get-Queue returns the equivalent output, shown in Figure 21-10, as the Queue Viewer does in Figure 21-8. Other cmdlets that can manipulate the SMTP queues include Suspend-Queue, Resume-Queue, and Retry-Queue. Should your system be suspected of sending lots of messages as a result of some virus or bot infection, running Suspend-Queue to stop message flow will help with troubleshooting.

Exchange Troubleshooting Assistant

In the Tools section of the EMC are several tools with "Troubleshooter" as part of their name. Launching any of these will start the Exchange Troubleshooting Assistant (ExTRA).

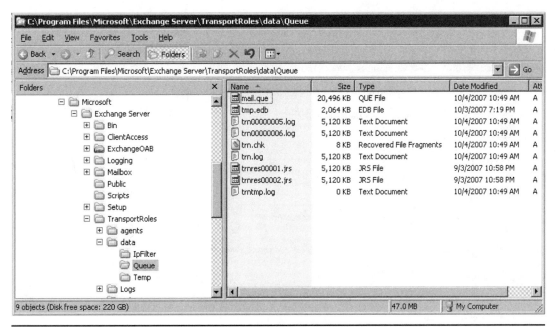

FIGURE 21-9   Windows Explorer showing the SMTP Queue database and logging path

Figure 21-3, earlier in the chapter, showed the Welcome page for ExTRA. The ExTRA essentially becomes another portal to the Troubleshooter tools. It is intended to host the tools used in reaction to issues rather than maintenance tools. The ExTRA tools can be run locally on the server in question, or remotely from another Exchange server or a server with the Management Tools installed. In addition, version 1.1 of the Exchange Troubleshooting Assistant can be downloaded and installed on Windows 2003 or Windows XP with the .NET Framework Version 1.1 installed. The Exchange Troubleshooting Assistant, shown in Figure 21-11, divides the list of tools into two sections, as follows:

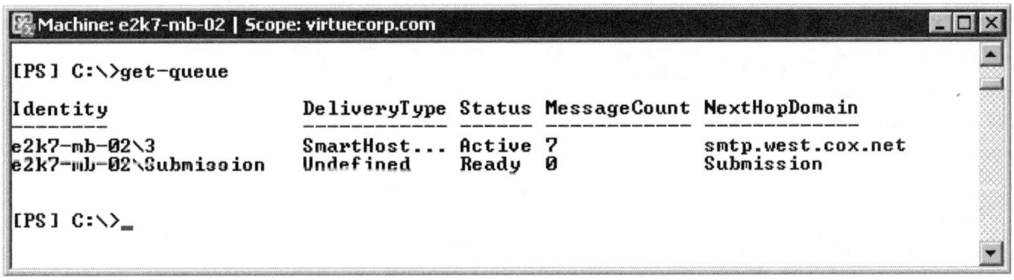

```
Machine: e2k7-mb-02 | Scope: virtuecorp.com                        _ □ X

[PS] C:\>get-queue

Identity            DeliveryType Status  MessageCount NextHopDomain
--------            ------------ ------  ------------ -------------
e2k7-mb-02\3        SmartHost... Active  7            smtp.west.cox.net
e2k7-mb-02\Submission Undefined  Ready   0            Submission

[PS] C:\>_
```

FIGURE 21-10   Get-Queue output in the EMS

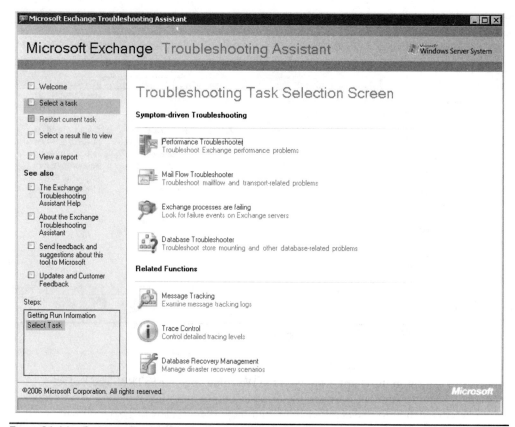

FIGURE 21-11   Exchange Troubleshooting Assistant Task Selection

Symptom-Driven Troubleshooting

- Performance Troubleshooter
- Mail Flow Troubleshooter
- Exchange processes are failing
- Database Troubleshooter

Related Functions

- Message Tracking
- Trace Control
- Database Recovery Management

Performance Troubleshooter

If you are experiencing performance issues on a single Exchange server, this tool will use a combination of logs, Exchange configuration, and a capture of active data to determine the problem and possibly a remedy. Because of the data capture component, it is best to run this tool while the issue is occurring to get the best results.

Performance Troubleshooter can focus on three specific Remote Procedure Call (RPC) connectivity symptoms, and it provides a drop-down box for the administrator to choose from:

- Multiple users are complaining of delays when they are using Outlook, or are frequently seeing the Outlook cancelable RPC dialog box.
- The number of RPC operations per second is higher than expected.
- The number of outstanding RPC requests is high.

Figure 21-12 shows the output for a Performance Troubleshooter analysis. Most of the visible output is from the Exchange configuration information in Active Directory.

Mail Flow Troubleshooter

The Mail Flow Troubleshooter also offers the administrator a set of symptoms to troubleshoot against. The logical steps toward resolution vary with the symptom selected.

- Users are receiving unexpected nondelivery reports when sending messages
- Expected messages from senders are delayed or are not received by some recipients

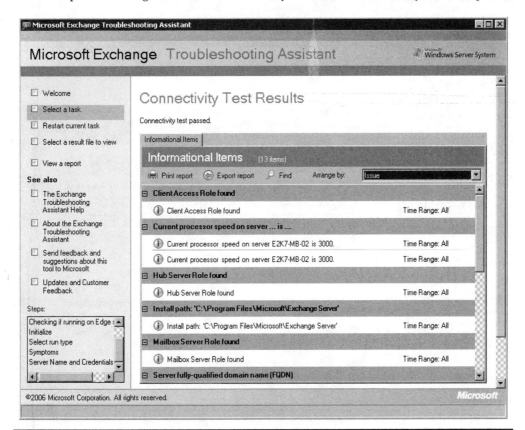

FIGURE 21-12   Exchange 2007 Performance Troubleshooter output

- Messages destined to recipients are delayed or are not received by some recipients
- Messages are backing up in one or more queues on a server
- Messages sent by users are pending submission on their mailbox server (Exchange 2007)
- Problems with Edge Server synchronization with Active Directory (Exchange 2007)

Mail Flow Troubleshooter gathers information from the Exchange server with WMI and from Active Directory and reports on the selected symptom with a link to the related page in technet.microsoft.com. Earlier we intentionally misconfigured a smarthost for our server to put some messages in the queue. Running the Exchange Message Flow Analyzer tool verified the state of the queue and reported it as shown in Figure 21-13.

Exchange Processes Are Failing

The name sounds more like an issue than a tool. As part of the Exchange Troubleshooting Assistant, this utility checks all Exchange servers or a specific Exchange server for failure events. It is a simple health check for Exchange Service failures logged on each server.

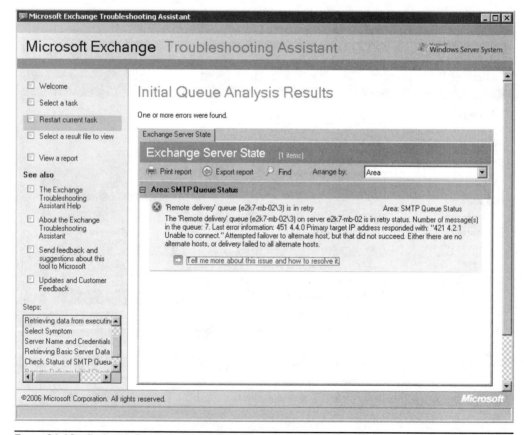

FIGURE 21-13   Exchange Troubleshooting Assistant—Mail Flow Troubleshooter output for SMTP queue delays

Database Troubleshooter

The Database Troubleshooter first logs onto Active Directory and gathers Exchange information, either using the credentials of the administrator running the tool or an account the administrator provides when the tool is launched. It then parses the event log for entries pertaining to Exchange database issues and reports on basic, but critical issues such as the following:

- Databases failing to mount
- Inconsistencies in transaction logs
- Lack of free drive space for databases and logs

Message Tracking

Message Tracking has been a part of Exchange for a long time, with an evolving interface. In Exchange 2007, Message Tracking is configured using the EMS, but the interface is accessed through the EMC Tools section. Message Tracking can follow the path of a message through the Exchange organization from Edge to Mailbox, or vice versa, by querying a log file for attributes of the message in question. Figure 21-14 shows the input screen for a Message Tracking query. Like many places in the GUI, the Message Tracking parameter window also shows the equivalent EMS cmdlet updated as options are entered in the GUI. By default, the

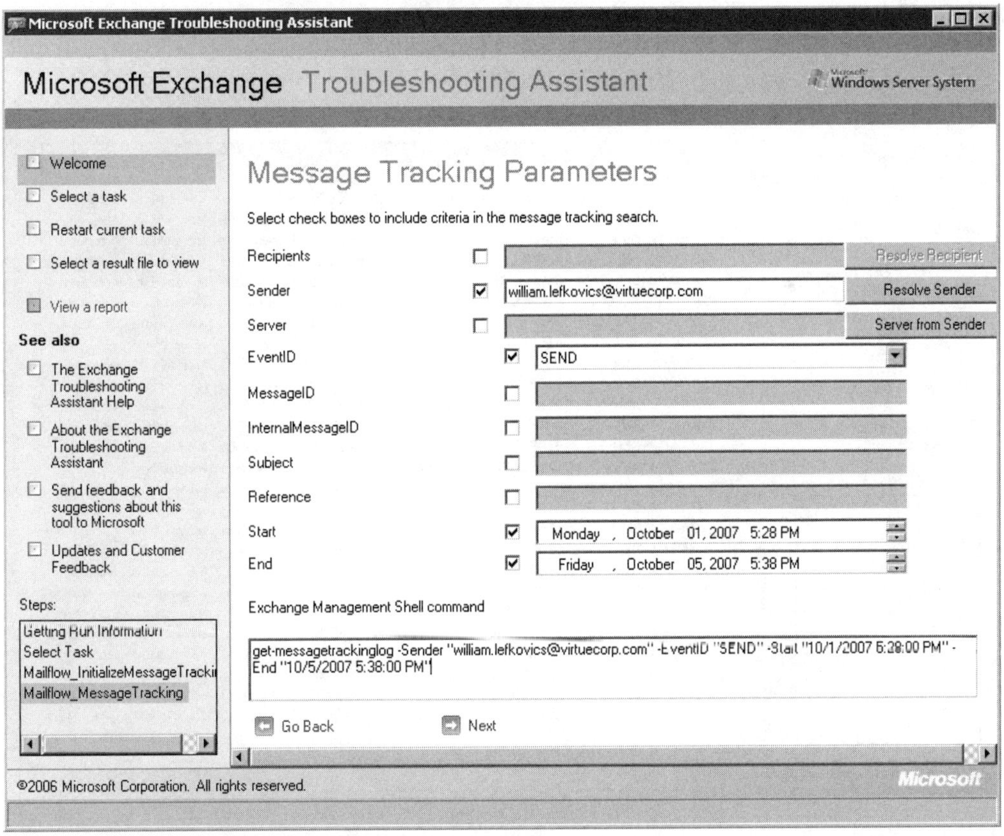

FIGURE 21-14   Exchange 2007 Message Tracking parameters

Message Tracking interface provides a 10-minute window for the start and end times for the query. If you are looking for a message from earlier, then those dates and times need to be changed accordingly. You can select the date or time value and use the up and down arrow keys to change that value.

SP1 *Service Pack 1 provides a better mechanism for incrementing the date values in the Start and End parameters in the Message Tracking interface (for those who prefer the mouse) by clicking the up/down arrows at the end of the date/time fields.*

The Message Tracking tool applies the criteria to its search and returns the matching content summary. You can select individual messages from those messages returned by the filtered query by selecting them and clicking Next at the bottom. Before showing the single message, the tool will first show the parameters screen with unique identifiers in place to extract the single message from the Message Tracking logs. Figure 21-15 shows the initial results page from our query. The columns headings are clickable to sort the output page by that value.

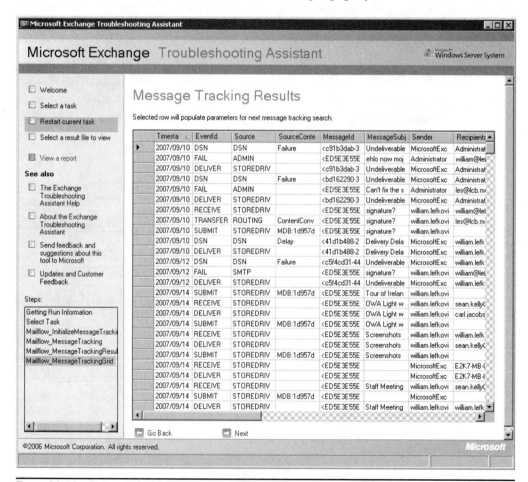

FIGURE 21-15 Exchange 2007 Message Tracking output

Message Tracking is enabled by default, which is different from its predecessors. The log file location has also been updated for Exchange 2007. The Message Tracking log is now found in %programfiles%\Microsoft\Exchange Server\TransportRoles\Logs\MessageTracking\. As mentioned, Message Tracking is configured using the EMS. The location of the Message Tracking log is easily moved with the following cmdlet:

```
>Set-TransportServer <servername> -MessageTrackingLogPath <Full_path>
```

For example, to move our Message Tracking log to D:\Exchange\Tracking Log\, we would employ the following command:

```
>Set-TransportServer E2K7-MB-02 -MessageTrackingLogPath "d:\Exchange\Tracking Log"
```

The server name here is required, and the path must be the complete path local to the server. If the path does not exist, it will be created when the command is executed. The folder, by default, has a maximum size of 250MB. Older tracking logs are deleted as new ones are created to fit within that limit. The maximum folder size is easily configured, again using the EMS. The log files compress well also, and a script can be used to compress and archive older tracking logs on a regular basis if company policy dictates that they need to be saved. To set the maximum tracking log folder size, issue the following cmdlet:

```
>Set-TransportServer <servername> -MessageTrackingLogMaxDirectorySize 750MB
```

The tracking log file size and age are also controlled by similar parameters. We use Set-TransportServer to enable or disable Message Tracking as follows:

```
>Set-TransportServer <servername> –MessageTrackingLogEnabled <$true | $false>
```

The cmdlet that initiates queries as you have seen using the GUI is Get-MessageTrackingLog. Entering **Get-MessageTrackingLog** without any parameters will return the entire log file. A sample filtered query using the EMS might look like this:

```
>Get-MessageTrackingLog -Sender "sean.kelly@virtuecorp.com" -EventID "FAIL" -
MessageSubject "Monthly Report" -Start "9/9/2007 8:00:00 AM" -End "9/9/2007
10:30:00 AM"
```

Trace Control

When you first launch Trace Control from the ExTRA, a pop-up advises you that no reader is available on the server for Exchange trace logs, as shown in Figure 21-16, and that you should enlist the assistance of Customer Service and Support (CSS). Trace Control writes very granular debug tracing information to a file called ExchangeDebugTraces.etl, located by default at %programfiles%\Microsoft\Exchange Server\. This tool is really for use when troubleshooting symptoms not revealed through standard administrator troubleshooting and the assistance of Microsoft CSS is required.

Database Recovery Management

This tool is partly an administrative tool for restoring content and partly a troubleshooting tool. It goes deeper than the Database Troubleshooter, but still can parse the event logs for

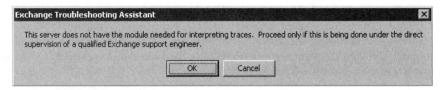

FIGURE 21-16 Exchange Troubleshooting Assistant trace control warning

database-related entries and perform other simple analysis tasks. Figure 21-17 shows the task options for the ExDRA in sections, as follows:

Manage Databases

- Analyze log drive space
- Repair database
- Show database related event logs
- Verify database and transaction logs

FIGURE 21-17 Exchange Troubleshooting Assistant database recovery management

Manage Recovery Storage Group

- Create a recovery storage group

View Results

- Go to Results Page

From a troubleshooting perspective, the ExDRA returns relevant content from the analysis of log drive space, the summary of database-related event log entries, and the verification of the Exchange database and transaction logs. Figure 21-18 shows the results of the log drive space analysis.

NOTE *Microsoft uses a consistent abbreviation system for the family of Exchange Analyzers:*

ExBPA   *Exchange Best Practices Analyzer*

ExTRA   *Exchange Troubleshooting Assistant*

ExMFA   *Exchange Mail Flow Analyzer*

ExDRA   *Exchange Database Recovery Analyzer*

ExPTA   *Exchange Performance Troubleshooting Analyzer*

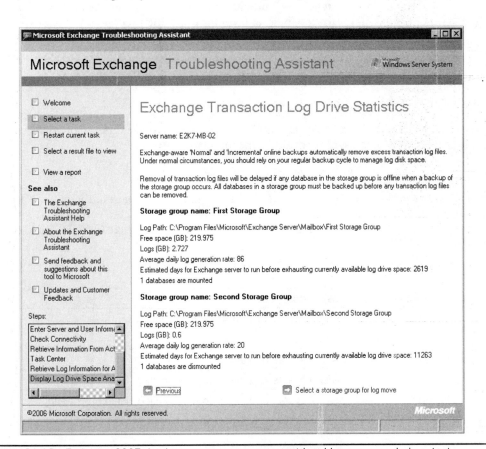

FIGURE 21-18   Exchange 2007 database recovery management log drive space analysis output

Diagnostic Logging

Exchange processes use the Application event log to record events, including information, warning, and error events. The types of events that are logged are controlled by logging levels applied to each individual process. The levels for diagnostic logging are Lowest, Low, Medium, High, and Expert, as shown in Table 21-1. By default, all but two processes are configured at the Lowest logging level, with MSExchange ADAccess\Topology and MSExchange ADAccess\Validation set to Low by default.

What gets written to the event log by a process at each level of diagnostic logging is determined in source code. Raising the logging level of a process does not automatically mean that a marked increase in what is logged will occur, but that is the concept. Increasing diagnostic logging on a process should be a temporary means of gathering more information on what is happening with that process through the Application event log. The size of the Application event log should also be monitored as well during elevated diagnostic logging because the size can grow quickly. Performance may be slightly compromised as well. In other words, always return logging to its original value after troubleshooting is complete.

The diagnostic logging level is configured using the EMS or manually through the Registry. The EMS provides a few cmdlets for controlling diagnostic logging. The Get-EventLogLevel will return the logging level for a specific process or processes:

```
>Get-EventLogLevel <Exchange_process>
```

To adjust the diagnostic level, we use the Set-EventLogLevel cmdlet, as follows:

```
>Set-EventLogLevel <Exchange_process> -Level <number>
```

If we wanted to set the diagnostic logging level of the MSExchange OWA\Core process to Medium, the EMS cmdlet syntax would be the following:

```
>Set-EventLogLevel "MSExchange OWA\Core" -Level 3
```

The Exchange process is in quotation marks because there is a space in the name. Also, the level number or the corresponding name, as shown in Table 21-1, can be used for the -Level parameter in the cmdlet. Figure 21-19 shows the MSExchange OWA\Core logging level at 3 (Medium).

Level	Level Name	Description
0	Lowest	Critical events, error events, and level 0 events
1	Low	Level 1 events and lower
3	Medium	Level 3 events and lower
5	High	Level 5 events and lower (formerly called "Maximum")
7	Expert	Level 7 events and lower (formerly called "Field Engineering" level)

TABLE 21-1   Exchange 2007 Diagnostic Logging Levels

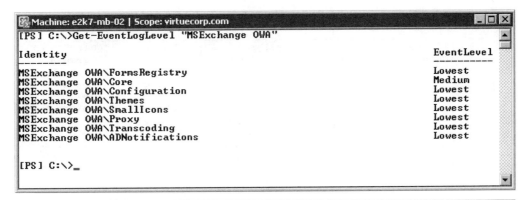

```
Machine: e2k7-mb-02 | Scope: virtuecorp.com                    _ □ ✕
[PS] C:\>Get-EventLogLevel "MSExchange OWA"

Identity                                                EventLevel
_____                                                _____
MSExchange OWA\FormsRegistry                            Lowest
MSExchange OWA\Core                                     Medium
MSExchange OWA\Configuration                            Lowest
MSExchange OWA\Themes                                   Lowest
MSExchange OWA\SmallIcons                               Lowest
MSExchange OWA\Proxy                                    Lowest
MSExchange OWA\Transcoding                              Lowest
MSExchange OWA\ADNotifications                          Lowest


[PS] C:\>_
```

FIGURE 21-19   Exchange 2007 diagnostic logging level shown with EMS for MSExchange OWA

The Exchange processes that can be configured each have a Registry object with a key called Diagnostics with one or more DWORD values against which logging levels can be adjusted. Here's the typical path in the Registry Editor (regedit.exe):

>HKLM\SYSTEM\CurrentControlSet\Services\<MSExchange_ProcessName>\Diagnostics\

Under that key are numbered processes that can have their logging values configured with the numbers shown in Table 21-1. Figure 21-20 shows the process of MSExchange OWA\ Core set to logging level 3 (Medium).

There is an extensive list of Exchange processes for which diagnostic logging can be adjusted for troubleshooting. Running the EMS cmdlet Get-EventLogLevel without any parameters will return the entire list.

Message Transport Logging

As part of message flow troubleshooting, several aspects of message transport in Exchange 2007 have logging capabilities. These include connectivity logging, agent logging, routing table logging, and protocol logging.

Connectivity Logging

As the name might suggest, connectivity logging tracks connections (in this case, ones made through outbound SMTP connectors on either Edge Transport servers or Hub Transport servers). Connectivity logging does not provide for individual messages, but only confirms outbound connections to destination SMTP servers or smarthosts. The most important information that is provided through connectivity logging is detailed information when an SMTP connection fails, including name resolution issues.

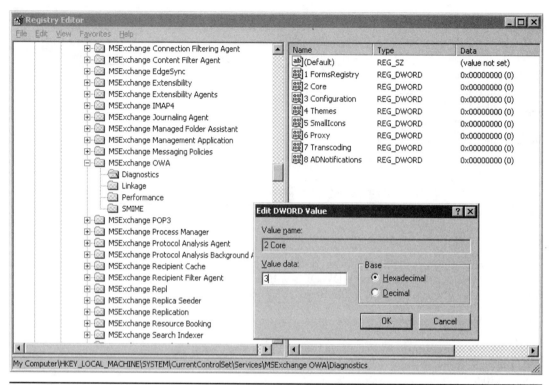

FIGURE 21-20 Exchange 2007 Registry Editor showing a DWORD value to change the logging level for the MSExchange OWA\Core process

Connectivity logging is disabled by default. It can be enabled through the EMC or using the EMS. Figure 21-21 shows the check box selected for connectivity logging. The default path of %programfiles%\Microsoft\Exchange Server\TransportRoles\Logs\Connectivity\ can also be changed in this interface.

A few settings for connectivity logging can be configured from the EMS:

```
>Set-TransportServer <servername> -ConnectivityLogEnabled <$True | $False>
```

Log file age and size can be configured in the EMS. The EMS-configured settings for connectivity logging are shown with the following cmdlet and in Figure 21-22:

```
>Get-TransportServer <servername> |fl *connectivity*
```

SP1 *Connectivity logging configuration was added to the EMC for Exchange 2007 Service Pack 1.*

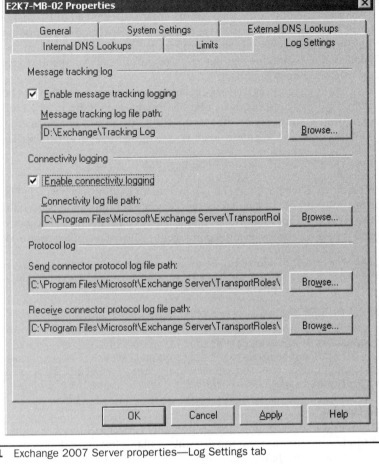

FIGURE 21-21   Exchange 2007 Server properties—Log Settings tab

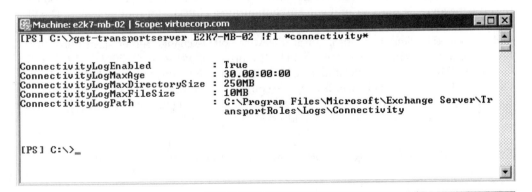

FIGURE 21-22   Exchange 2007 EMS Get-TransportServer cmdlet showing connectivity logging settings

Agent Logging

On an Edge server or when the anti-spam agents are installed on a Hub Transport server, how do we know how well the agents are performing? Agent logging reports on the activities of the anti-spam agents. Agent logging is enabled by default, when the anti-spam agents are installed, and maintains log files at %programfiles%\Microsoft\Exchange Server\TransportRoles\Logs\AgentLog\.

Unlike connectivity logging, agent logging has only one parameter that can be configured, and it is found in the EdgeTransport.exe.config file. Again, even if this is for a Hub Transport server, the configuration file contains the word *Edge*. To disable or enable agent logging, amend the following entry in the EdgeTransport.exe.config file with either TRUE or FALSE:

```
<add key="AgentLogEnabled" value="<TRUE | FALSE>" />
```

The other parameters we have seen for other types of logging, such as Log File Age and Log File Size, are not exposed for agent logging. The only configuration is to enable or disable the feature. The log file output for agent logging is fairly comprehensive because it follows SMTP messages through the various anti-spam agents. The list of values captured are:

```
Timestamp, SessionId, LocalEndpoint, RemoteEndpoint, EnteredOrgFromIP, MessageId,
P1FromAddress, P2FromAddresses, Recipient, NumRecipients, Agent, Event, Action,
SmtpResponse, Reason, ReasonData
```

A sample log file entry for Agent logging might read as follows:

```
2007-10-07T00:24:49.302Z,08C9D4976DAB9639,74.93.100.161:25,24.161.13.143:
2868,24.161.13.143,<0f9901c80878$75e181f0$8f0da118@Salvador>,jramirez@bppr
.com,Salvador@bppr.com;,ca82f8a7@virtuecorp.com,1,Content Filter Agent,
OnEndOfData,DeleteMessage,,SclAtOrAboveDeleteThreshold,8
```

Routing Table Logging

Exchange 2007 does not use a routing table as previous versions did. It does, however, take a snapshot of routing configuration and topology at regular intervals and records the values in an .xml file. Each time the Exchange Transport Service is restarted or a change occurs in the configuration of routing components, such as the Send connector properties, a new snapshot of the routing table is logged. This is valuable if you are troubleshooting mail flow, if you need to verify the lowest cost route, or if you are configuring a Hub site for routing e-mail. The files are named in the unique format of RoutingConfig#<number>@<creationdate-time_UTC>.xml and are located by default at %programfiles%\Microsoft\Exchange Server\TransportRoles\ Logs\Routing\. A sample file name would be RoutingConfig#18@10_01_2007 07_10_29.xml.

In the EMC Toolbox is a Routing Log Viewer that renders the .xml snapshots in a GUI. One of the features of this viewer is a log file comparison showing what changed in the routing. Figure 21-23 shows that the Send connector was changed from the Fully Qualified Domain Name of a smarthost to its IP address.

SP1 *Service Pack 1 for Exchange 2007 adds a Routing Log Viewer to the EMC Toolbox.*

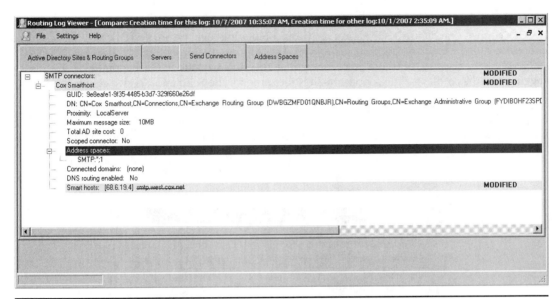

FIGURE 21-23   Exchange 2007 EMC Routing Log Viewer showing a log file comparison

The frequency of the snapshots is controlled through a tag in the EdgeTransport.exe.config file, again as follows:

```
<add key="RoutingConfigReloadInterval" value="12:00:00" />
```

Additional parameters can be configured using the EMS. Their default values are shown in Figure 21-24.

SMTP Protocol Logs

In Exchange 2000/2003, the SMTP Service in Internet Information Services (IIS) was extended to provide SMTP for Exchange. In Exchange 2007, SMTP is brought back into the application. In addition to diagnostics logging for processes, we can also maintain logging for the different protocols. SMTP protocol logging can save entire SMTP conversations between servers, either intra-org or external servers. This information can be used to troubleshoot a number of mail-flow issues.

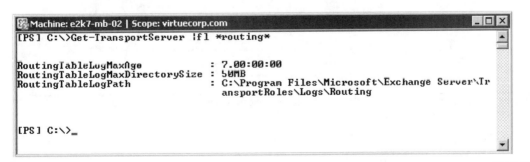

FIGURE 21-24   Exchange 2007 EMS Get-TransportServer values for a routing table log

Protocol logging is disabled by default, but is enabled on individual SMTP Send and Receive connectors. Figure 21-25 shows the protocol logging level on an SMTP Send connector called Cox Smarthost, set to Verbose. The options are Verbose and None.

EMS can be used to configure protocol logging as well. To enable or disable protocol logging, use the cmdlet for the connectors. It is the same for the Send and Receive connectors.

```
>Set-SendConnector <connectorname> -ProtocolLoggingLevel <None | Verbose>
```

Even though logging is enabled with this cmdlet, the settings for that logging are controlled using the Set-TransportServer cmdlet, with the current settings shown in Figure 21-26.

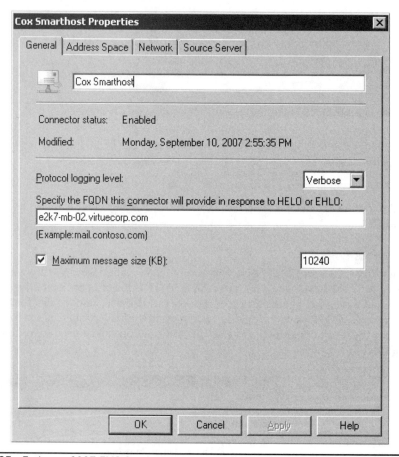

FIGURE 21-25   Exchange 2007 EMC Send connector properties showing protocol logging level of Verbose

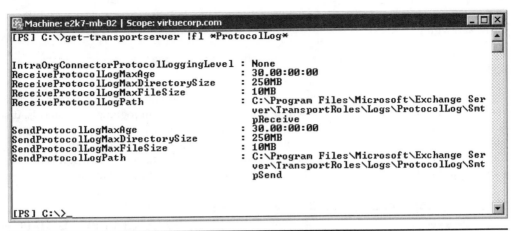

Machine: e2k7-mb-02 | Scope: virtuecorp.com

[PS] C:\>get-transportserver |fl *ProtocolLog*

IntraOrgConnectorProtocolLoggingLevel : None
ReceiveProtocolLogMaxAge   : 30.00:00:00
ReceiveProtocolLogMaxDirectorySize   : 250MB
ReceiveProtocolLogMaxFileSize   : 10MB
ReceiveProtocolLogPath   : C:\Program Files\Microsoft\Exchange Ser
                                        ver\TransportRoles\Logs\ProtocolLog\Smt
                                        pReceive

SendProtocolLogMaxAge   : 30.00:00:00
SendProtocolLogMaxDirectorySize   : 250MB
SendProtocolLogMaxFileSize   : 10MB
SendProtocolLogPath   : C:\Program Files\Microsoft\Exchange Ser
                                        ver\TransportRoles\Logs\ProtocolLog\Smt
                                        pSend

[PS] C:\>_

FIGURE 21-26   Exchange 2007 EMS cmdlet showing the protocol logging settings under the EMS

The logs for the Receive connectors and Send connectors are kept separate under %programfiles%\Microsoft\Exchange Server\TransportRoles\Logs\ProtocolLog\. From here, each is kept in either the SMTPSend or SMTPReceive folder. The parameter controlling the log file path, like the others shown in Figure 21-26, is configurable through the EMS as follows:

```
>Set-TransportServer <servername> -ReceiveProtocolLogPath <LocalFilePath>
```

SP1 The log file location for SMTP protocol logging is configurable in the EMC on Exchange 2007 servers running Service Pack 1.

POP3 and IMAP4 Protocol Logging

On Exchange 2007 servers with the CAS role installed, we can enable client Internet protocol logging. POP3 and IMAP4 logging will help identify client access issues for the Internet protocols. Sometimes the client themselves also have protocol logging that could be enabled simultaneously. Both POP3 and IMAP4 logging are enabled through their own configuration files. The files Microsoft.Exchange.Pop3.exe.config and Microsoft.Exchange .Imap4.exe.config are located by default in %programfiles%\Microsoft\Exchange Server\ ClientAccess\PopImap\. For both POP3 and IMAP4, the process to enable logging is the same. This line in the configuration file must be amended to read **value="true"**. This line is found near the end of the file in the <application settings> area.

```
<add key="ProtocolLog" value="false" />
```

The default log path is also in the configuration file. The logs will be written to %programfiles%\Microsoft\Exchange Server\Logging\<protocol>\, where <protocol> is either POP3 or IMAP4. Also by default, a new file will be created daily. The values logged fit these headings (except for context, which is listed in the log file, but not used for POP3 or IMAP logging):

```
date-time,connector-id,session-id,sequence-number,local-endpoint,remote-
endpoint,event,data,context
```

Some e-mail clients, including Outlook, can perform their own protocol logging from the client. In Outlook 2003 and 2007, this setting is a single check box for logging all protocols. It is found in Tools | Options | Other. In the General section, select the Advanced Options button. Select the check box beside Enable logging (troubleshooting). Like diagnostics logging, this settings has an effect on performance and should be turned off when it is no longer required. Outlook needs to be restarted for the logging change to take effect.

Messaging Application Programming Interface (MAPI) Editor

In previous versions of Exchange, the equivalent of this tool was called MDBVue32. MAPI Editor itself is the evolution of MFCMAPI. This tool allows us to look into a MAPI message store and even manipulate data in the tables. The Microsoft Exchange Server MAPI Client and Collaboration Data Objects 1.2.1 represent a prerequisite for installing MAPI Editor on Exchange 2007. Figure 21-27 shows a screenshot of the MAPI Editor connected to an Exchange mailbox.

Networking Tools

Of course, the effectiveness of your Exchange deployment is dependent on the underlying network. Many networking tools can assist you in troubleshooting networking issues.

Ping

Packet Internet Groper (ping) is a simple command-line Internet Control Message Protocol echo utility for verifying connectivity of a TCP/IP host on the network. If a user cannot connect to a resource, a common question arises: "Can the user ping it?" This utility also can assist as a quick test for name resolution as well when you need to issue a ping to the server name and not its address.

Telnet

Telnet is used to connect to the ports that Exchange is expected to be using. The banner that is returned in a telnet session validates that Exchange services are available. It is simple to verify SMTP services by opening a telnet session to SMTP port 25 and sending a message manually:

```
>telnet <servername> 25
```

If an SMTP server is listening on port 25, such as the Microsoft Exchange ESMTP Service, a 220 reply returns a configured name for the listening server service:

```
220 e2k7-mb-02.virtuecorp.com Microsoft ESMTP Service Ready at <date and time>
```

You can also validate other messaging-related ports in this manner, including POP3 and IMAP4. A telnet to port 110 would return the MSExchange POP3 service banner if it was configured to allow POP3 without SSL.

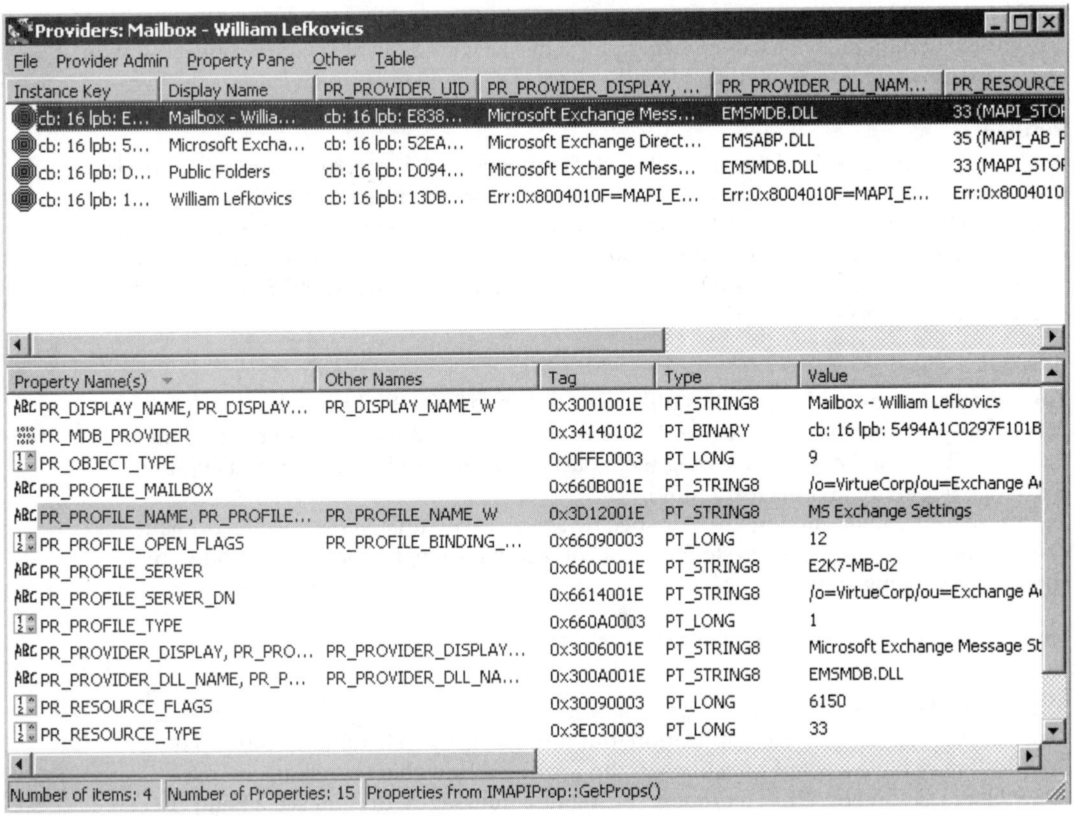

FIGURE 21-27   MAPI Editor on an Exchange 2007 mailbox server

IPConfig

IPConfig is another command-line utility that can verify TCP/IP settings on a workstation or server. Running ipconfig /all from the command prompt should return the IP configuration for all adapters. Microsoft KB 314850 covers the various parameters that are defined for use with this tool.

NSLookup

NSLookup validates hostname resolution on the network through general or specific queries against a certain Domain Name Services (DNS) server or for a certain query type, such as MX records. Exchange and Outlook require a functioning DNS infrastructure to operate effectively.

RPCPing

Exchange and Outlook use Remote Procedure Calls (RPC) to communicate. Microsoft provides the RPCPing utility in the Windows Server 2003 Resource Kit to verify connectivity between the Exchange server and the MAPI client. Running RPCPing on the Exchange server verifies that it is able to accept Remote Procedure Calls. The real intent is to run RPCPing from the workstation that may be experiencing problems. RPCPing can also verify connectivity for Outlook Anywhere, formerly RPC/HTTPS.

NetDiag

As the name suggests, NetDiag is a network diagnostic tool. It can run a series of network tests to confirm the health of the network, reporting per-interface results and global results of diagnostic tests. Along with DCDiag, it is a valuable tool to ensure your system is ready to install Exchange 2007. By the same measure, it can also be helpful to identify network issues in an existing system. NetDiag is installed with the Windows 2003 Support Tools found on the Windows 2003 CD.

DCDiag

The Domain Controller Diagnostics utility is a command-line tool from the Windows 2003 Server Support Tools that runs several tests analyzing the state of domain controllers. In Exchange 2003, NetDiag and DCDiag were part of the prerequisite tests run using the Exchange deployment tools (exdeploy).

These tests can be run together, or specific tests can be run against specific domain controllers. For example, the systemlog test run against a single domain controller might show the following syntax:

```
>dcdiag /s:<DC_Hostname> /test:systemlog
```

Logic and Tools Summary

Okay, logic is not a software application, but it does apply to troubleshooting. The helpdesk may have a set of questions in the form of a flowchart to ask users in a controlled assessment: "If you are not getting new messages, do you see a Send/Receive error in Outlook? If no, then Question A. If yes, then Question B." The administrator needs to combine the input from those experiencing problems with what the computers are showing in error dialogs and warnings to determine the scope of the issue (single user? single server? whole enterprise?) and what tool(s) to use to identify or confirm the problem and resolve it. Clearly the SMTP logs are not going to help you with MAPI connectivity concerns. In addition, there are a lot of different sources of information to assist with troubleshooting. Sometimes the biggest challenge is actually determining which tool to use when faced with something to troubleshoot. Table 21-2 is a simplified categorization of most of the tools we have considered so far.

Category	List of Possible Tools to Use for Diagnosis
Clients	Connectivity and protocol logging
Network	Ping, Telnet, RPCPing, IPConfig, NetDiag
DNS/AD	NSLookup, DCDiag, event logs
Exchange Server	Diagnostic logging (on Exchange processes), Troubleshooting Assistant (and its tools), EMS Test cmdlets

TABLE 21-2   List of Troubleshooting Areas and Tools to Use in Each Area

Microsoft Product Support Services

Sometimes called Customer Service and Support (CSS), this Microsoft helpline can be used to find successful resolutions to problems where troubleshooting has failed or time constraints do not allow the luxury of researching a problem. This costs a little bit of money, but for some the time saved pays for itself multiple times over. For others, this helpline is to be used only when all else fails. Product Support Services can be reached through localized numbers from the Microsoft main site at http://support.microsoft.com/.

Client Connectivity

Troubleshooting client connectivity can point to many different possibilities from the Exchange server hosting the CAS role, to the actual client in use, to the path between the client and the server. Outlook 2007 is the recommended client for Exchange 2007, and its versatility means it could be using one of several protocols to communicate with Exchange. Other components of Exchange broaden the points of client access to a large number of potential problem areas.

MAPI Clients

The first step in troubleshooting client access to a server resource is to identify the scope of the issue. Troubleshooting takes a completely different direction if only one user is experiencing the issue relative to an entire department or location. MAPI uses RPC to communicate with Exchange. If a client is not able to retrieve e-mail using Outlook and MAPI, we can engage our toolset to identify the cause. If the scope of the issue is restricted to one workstation, that becomes the focus of troubleshooting. The following is a typical troubleshooting path for an Outlook MAPI client.

1. Is TCP/IP configured correctly on the client workstation?
We can use IPConfig to ensure TCP/IP on the client workstation is configured to participate in the network.

2. Can the client workstation communicate with the Exchange server (and domain controller)?
A simple ping using the command line or the EMS will return a set of ICMP echoes to verify TCP/IP connectivity between the client and the Exchange server.

3. Is DNS resolution working effectively from the workstation?
An NSLookUp from the workstation will confirm whether the appropriate DNS and _srv records are being returned for the client to access the appropriate resources.

4. Can the workstation reach the Exchange server with RPC?
RPCPing will confirm whether the client can communicate with Exchange using MAPI.

Should the workstation pass these tests, the answer most likely lies elsewhere—namely the Exchange server hosting the Mailbox role. Our tests on the client so far simultaneously eliminated the CAS role to client connectivity as a likely source of the problem. It still may be a problem, but it allows client connections.

5. Is the mailbox properly configured on the server?

Mailbox configuration is readily accessed in the Exchange Management Console. We can see the mailbox properties showing the appropriate protocols enabled. The EMS also can return whether the mailbox has MAPI enabled with the following command:

```
>Get-CASMailbox <MailboxName> | fl mapienabled
```

6. Are the mailbox permissions configured correctly on the mailbox?

The EMS provides easy access to permission information on a mailbox. The cmdlet Get-MailboxPermission returns who has what level of permission on the mailbox.

For Outlook 2007, a CTRL-click on the Outlook icon in the taskbar adds a couple options to the context menu: Connection Status and Test E-Mail AutoConfiguration. Figure 21-28 shows the connection status between Outlook and Exchange, as well as the connection status of an Outlook 2007 client to the Exchange 2007 CAS server role.

Outlook performance is tied to several factors including mailbox size, indexing activity, and add-ons. Mailbox size is fairly liberal, but it is the number of items in the critical folders that can impact performance even more. If a user complains of Outlook performance, ensure that they are using a secondary folder or a subfolder to store large numbers of items. Microsoft recommends a critical folder limit of 5000 items. The size of those items is secondary to their number.

Outlook Web Access

Within the options in OWA 2007 is a button labeled About at the bottom of the list. Selecting this option presents configuration and versioning information describing the working

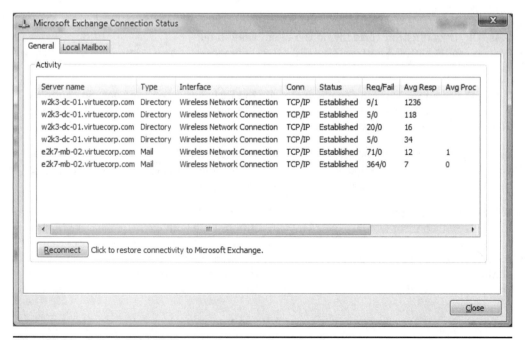

FIGURE 21-28   Outlook 2007 MAPI connection status from the client

OWA environment, as shown in Figure 21-29. This information could be vital for a helpdesk trying to resolve OWA problems.

As with MAPI troubleshooting, we need to identify the scope of the troubleshooting issue. Multiple individuals experiencing the same symptom redirects initial troubleshooting to the server first. If there are multiple users with the same issue, is there a connection between the users? Perhaps they are on the same server, either CAS or mailbox. Confirmation that the client's environment meets or exceeds policy is the next step. The user should probably be accessing Exchange with the current version of the browser—that is, Internet Explorer 7 for the Premium OWA 2007 experience. Can they open the OWA logon page? Is the SSL certificate giving an error? Does OWA Light work? Once the user's settings are confirmed, we need to focus on the server side.

The EMS provides many test cmdlets. A relevant one here is Test-OWAConnectivity. This is run from the server or an administration workstation with the appropriate Exchange tools installed. If OWA on the CAS is working according to tests, consider whether the mailbox is OWA-enabled and the user has the right permissions to use it.

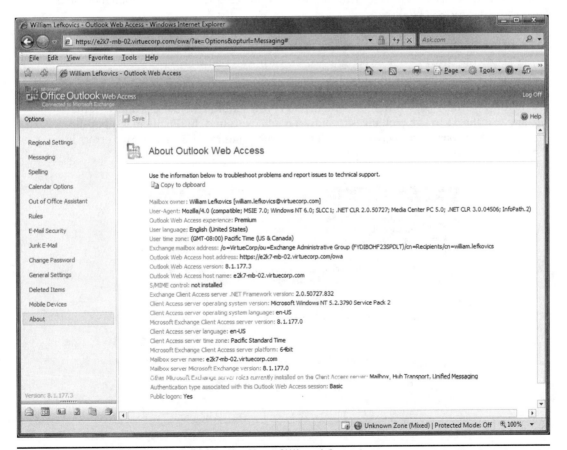

FIGURE 21-29   Outlook Web Access 2007—the About OWA environment

A workflow for OWA troubleshooting might read as follows:

- **Verify user environment**   Correct client software version? Configuration correct?
- **Verify connectivity and name resolution**   Can the client resolve and connect to the remote server?
- **Verify the SSL certificate**   Is secure access causing issues?
- **Verify the server configuration**   Is the server working properly? Are others connecting?
- **Verify the client settings on server**   Is the user configured for this access type?

OWA is a web application, of course. The IIS WWW Service logs are also a great resource of information.

SSL Certificate Issues

When you're connecting to the OWA site with HTTPS and the correct URL (which should match the certificate), a certificate error may occur. If the certificate does not match in three key areas, an error will be shown.

- Was the certificate issued by a trusted authority?
- Does the URL match that assigned to the certificate?
- Is the date on the certificate valid (or is it expired)?

In IE7 a warning page is first presented, and if you should take the risk and visit the site anyway, the address bar changes to show a red background. In IE6, there is a pop-up identifying what part of the certificate violates the rules. Figure 21-30 shows two errors in the certificate used to secure a web page.

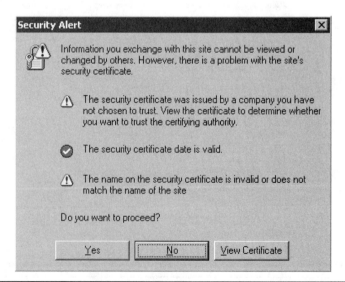

FIGURE 21-30   Certificate errors in Internet Explorer 6

Certificate errors are easiest to see in a web browser, but will cause problems with ActiveSync, Outlook Anywhere, and Outlook Web Access.

Internet Clients

Internet clients represent all the clients that access Exchange 2007 with the classic Internet protocols POP3 and IMAP4. Troubleshooting these clients requires some of the same basic steps as MAPI clients. First, identify the scope of the problem. Is there only one client that is reporting an issue? The next step is to verify connectivity from the client with networking tools such as ping. The client can also issue a telnet to the standard protocol port to verify they can reach the service.

From the server, we can enable client protocol logging and check how far the client is getting in the protocol conversation. For many e-mail clients, it is also possible to log connections, including Outlook 2007. If there is nothing pertinent to the issue at hand recorded in those logs, we can check the Application event log and even increase diagnostic logging on the client protocol processes, such as "MSExchange POP3\General."

To initiate logging in Outlook 2007, navigate to Tools | Options | Other within Outlook. Then select the Advanced Options button. Select the check box beside Enable Logging (Troubleshooting). By default, logging is disabled in Outlook, and for good reason. Performance can be significantly hampered with logging enabled. The Main Outlook window even tells the user it is enabled with the text across the top reading "Microsoft Office Outlook (Logging Enabled)." Unfortunately in Outlook, logging is not granular. If you have multiple accounts, it is not possible to engage logging just for the IMAP account, for example.

Mobile Clients

Windows Mobile clients that use ActiveSync have their own set of issues. There is an EMS test cmdlet for ActiveSync as well. Test-ActiveSyncConnectivity will simulate an ActiveSync session and report on the results.

Windows Mobile emulator software can be used to virtually represent a Windows Mobile client to troubleshoot connectivity, including ActiveSync issues. The emulator assists more with identifying server-side connectivity issues with mobile clients. Microsoft provides downloads of localized versions of Windows Mobile 5 and 6 images for use in development and troubleshooting.

Unified Messaging

A couple of tools are available to help us troubleshoot Unified Messaging (UM) issues. MSExchangeUM writes information, errors, and warnings to the Application event log, and diagnostics logging can be increased on UM objects, as listed in Table 21-2, to record more information to the Application event log. If we need to test phone connectivity, Microsoft includes an IP phone simulation application on the Exchange 2007 DVD. ExchangeUMTestPhone.exe is located in \setup\serverroles\common.

The Test-UMConnectivity cmdlet is run on a local Exchange 2007 server with the UM role installed. A SIP call is initiated, and the cmdlet returns perceived health of the connection. Figure 21-31 shows the output of this cmdlet without any optional parameters. This is important because connectivity to the IP/VoIP gateway can sometimes be a troubleshooting opportunity.

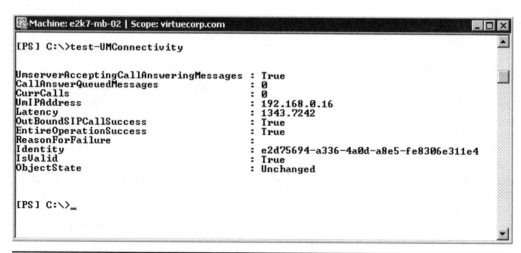

FIGURE 21-31   Test-UMConnectivity cmdlet output in the EMS

Transport Pipeline

Mail routing requires monitoring, especially in larger Exchange organizations. Quality monitoring with a product such as Microsoft Operations Manager (MOM), now called Systems Center Operations Manager (SCOM), will reduce the time spent troubleshooting as questionable conditions create alerts within SCOM for administrators to address prior to them becoming issues. Still, we may have to spend time answering questions from users wondering why they didn't receive an e-mail that was sent from a colleague.

Whenever the Application event log is mentioned as a consideration for troubleshooting, it could also include a possible increase in diagnostic logging to try to draw more information out of the process(es) that might be failing.

Internal Mail Flow

Exchange 2007 no longer maintains its own routing engine. The old Resource Kit tool called WinRoute does not help us find the routes Exchange is using. That is why we now have the Routing Log Viewer. If mail just isn't making it to its destination, there are a few places to look. The messages don't just disappear, so a likely place for them would be in the queue. The Queue Viewer or EMS Get-Queue cmdlet will reveal if that is the case. Message Tracking should show the logical steps the messages took in the Exchange organization. Finally, the Routing Log Viewer may show that there isn't a valid route configured for the messages to get to their destination.

The ExTRA will help identify issues related to internal mail flow within the organization. Of course, the Application event log can help as well.

External Mail Flow

All mail must travel through a Hub Transport server. External mail either arrives through a Receive connector or leaves through a Send connector, although the connectors may be on the Edge Transport server. When you subscribe an Edge Transport server to the Exchange organization, a Send connector is created by default. If you are not using an Edge Transport server, then a Send connector must be configured. In the EMC, this is done in the Organization Configuration container in the Hub Transport settings. There is a configuration value on these connectors that can cause mail flow interruptions. In the Send connector properties, you'll find a value for Address Space. This value represents domains that the Send connector can actually send to. I have seen people enter their own domain where the asterisk resides in Figure 21-32. The asterisk is a wildcard which, when alone, means *all* domains.

Likewise, the Receive connector can be restricted by permissions. Figure 21-33 shows that only Exchange users can connect to this Receive connector. Permissions form a basis for securing Receive connectors.

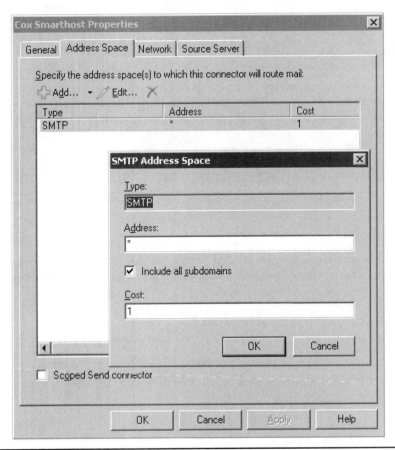

FIGURE 21-32   The Address Space tab of the Send Connector Properties dialog box

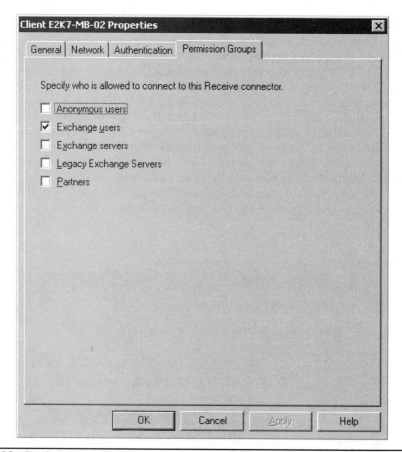

FIGURE 21-33   The Permission Groups tab of the Receive Connector Properties dialog box

The Receive connector will give an SMTP error code for connections it does not accept, including connections where the client does not hold the necessary permissions.

- **535 5.7.3**   Authentication unsuccessful.
- **530 5.7.1**   Client was not authenticated.
- **550 5.7.1**   Client does not have permission to submit to this server.
- **550 5.7.1**   Client does not have permission to send as this sender.
- **550 5.7.1**   Client does not have permission to send on behalf of the from address.
- **550 5.7.1**   Unable to relay.

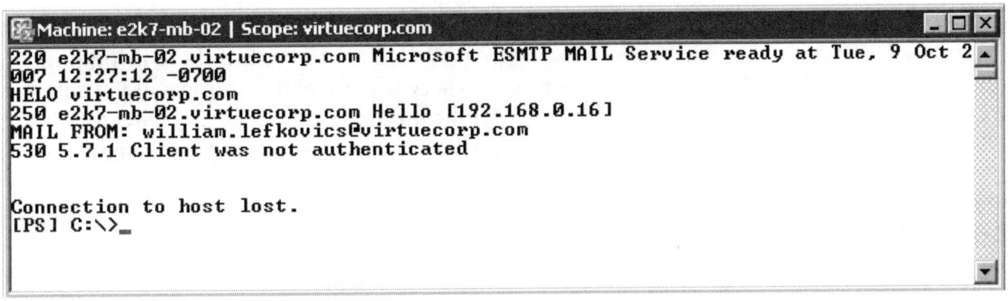

```
Machine: e2k7-mb-02 | Scope: virtuecorp.com                    _ □ X
220 e2k7-mb-02.virtuecorp.com Microsoft ESMTP MAIL Service ready at Tue, 9 Oct 2
007 12:27:12 -0700
HELO virtuecorp.com
250 e2k7-mb-02.virtuecorp.com Hello [192.168.0.16]
MAIL FROM: william.lefkovics@virtuecorp.com
530 5.7.1 Client was not authenticated


Connection to host lost.
[PS] C:\>_
```

FIGURE **21-34**   Exchange 2007 telnet to port 25 without client authentication

Figure 21-34 show a telnet session where the client was not authenticated and got served with a 530 5.7.1 error code. The telnet session works just as well from the Exchange Management Shell.

Unreachable Queue

When outbound e-mail is addressed to a domain for which a server was not available, the messages are moved to a queue called "unreachable." This may be the result of a network outage, a DNS change, or even a misconfiguration somewhere. These messages will time out and bounce back to the sender. During the standard SMTP timeout, administrators can go into the queue and resubmit messages to the categorizer. It is one place to look when a user says their message did not make it to its destination. The message can be resubmitted using the EMC or the Retry-Queue cmdlet in the EMS.

Edge Transport Server

The Edge Transport role provides message hygiene and gateway functionality for your messaging infrastructure. It is critical to message flow and also requires a special subscription to get basic AD information for message hygiene filtering. The EMS has one of its great test cmdlets just for this setup. Test-EdgeSynchronization has only one required parameter: -VerifyRecipient. This cmdlet can check for a specific user to see if synchronization has copied that user's information to AD Application Mode.

SP1   The Test-EdgeSynchronization cmdlet was added in Exchange 2007 service Pack 1.

Smarthost

When configuring a Send connector for a smarthost, you have the option to enter the smarthost as an IP address or an FQDN. For servers out of your control, you really should use the FQDN because that is less likely to change addresses. Should the IP address of the smarthost change, you won't be troubleshooting why e-mail stopped going out.

Logs

Exchange 2007 can log the progress of its logging. Well, maybe not, but there is logging for troubleshooting at almost every point. From a server perspective, almost always in troubleshooting the event logs are checked—Application, System, Security, Directory, DNS, and even PowerShell. Event logs are a constant in troubleshooting Exchange.

Mailbox Servers

Mailbox servers basically hold the data. They maintain storage groups with the Exchange databases and transaction logs.

Databases

Data stored in the Information Store databases represents the information that each user considers critical to their job, and therefore to the Exchange administrator's job. Monitoring storage should all but eliminate the need to troubleshoot the back end. Probably your greatest friend here is the Application event log. Online maintenance runs nightly by default. It will report the success of that maintenance in the Application event log. It will report issues that may need to be addressed. If online maintenance is not completing each night, either the window for online maintenance is too short or perhaps a backup or other process is interfering with online maintenance. Those entries should be monitored.

Transaction logs are written for everything going into the database. Regular online backups will commit and purge those transaction logs. If these logs are not being removed with regular backups, there is some troubleshooting to do. Are the backups completing successfully? Failure to ensure transaction logs are being purged can result in Exchange running out of drive space for the logs.

The Exchange Best Practices Analyzer will report on the configuration of the databases and note less-than-optimum setups.

Mailboxes

Mailboxes represent virtual segmentations of databases. Their integrity goes along with that of the database as a whole. A common issue for users is quota enforcement. When users get a message indicating their mailbox is full, they have a hard time reconciling that to what their client shows. Sent and deleted items are, of course, included. In Outlook, have the user right-click their mailbox atop the folder tree and select Properties. The Folder Size button will expose where that volume is hiding.

Mailboxes sometimes must be moved to different servers. Some administrators do not register that mailbox moves generate transaction logs. It is not out of the question to run out of drive space for transaction logs just from moving mailboxes to a new storage group. The Application event log will describe the issue simply. After large mailbox moves, it would not hurt to run the ExBPA again to identify any unnoticed issues and even to create a new baseline to reference.

Public Folders

Public folders are not installed by default in a pure Exchange 2007 organization. They are available as an optional installation to support clients of Outlook 2003 or earlier. The ExBPA can summarize suspected issues with public folders. Troubleshooting public folders involves replication, storage, and client access. The Application event log, with help from Diagnostics Logging settings, will advise you on issues from public folder replication.

SP1 *Exchange 2007 Service Pack 1 adds a User Interface for public folder administration to the EMC.*

Client Access Servers

Client Access Servers manage all forms of clients and protocols. They require IIS and have special requirements with security certificates for securing client communication.

Autodiscover and Availability Service

Calendaring information for Free/Busy is provided to clients using the Exchange web service called the Availability service. Problems getting calendar information from other mailboxes may be a problem with the Availability service. Errors in the Availability service are posted to the Application event log, typically. The Availability service is dependent on the Autodiscover service, so sometimes troubleshooting it requires consideration of both services.

Similarly, if AutoConfiguration is used for creating an Outlook profile, a call is made to the Autodiscover service. If AutoConfiguration cannot complete, there is a chance that the Autodiscover service is not available. Maybe the service is not available or something in between the client and the server is not cooperating. The Autodiscover service's Web service name has to resolve for the user. If it fails to do so, maybe a record for it was not created in the DNS server. Alternatively, in certain circumstances, an equivalent entry in the user's HOSTS file will suffice, although this is not the preferred solution.

Exchange 2007 makes a significant move to Web services, such as the Autodiscover and Availability services. Among the many Test cmdlets in EMS, an important test for Outlook access is available in the Test-OutlookWebServices cmdlet, which checks these vital services. The output for this test is shown in Figure 21-35.

AutoConfiguration

AutoConfiguration uses the Autodiscover service to automatically create a profile for Outlook 2007. If Autodiscover is not available, through missing DNS entries or otherwise, then the Autodiscover service will not be available, and subsequently the AutoConfiguration functionality will not work.

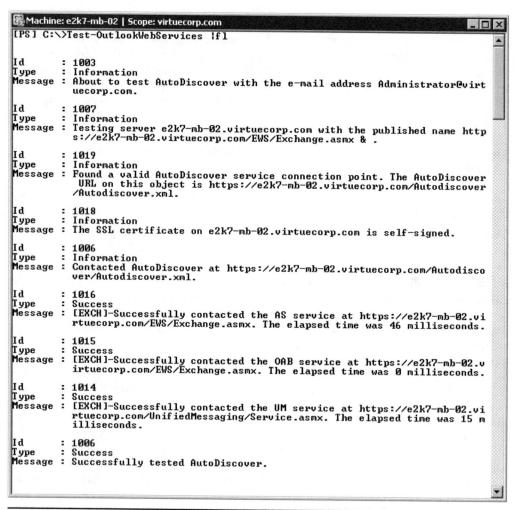

```
Machine: e2k7-mb-02 | Scope: virtuecorp.com                    _ □ ✕
[PS] C:\>Test-OutlookWebServices !fl


Id       : 1003
Type     : Information
Message  : About to test AutoDiscover with the e-mail address Administrator@virt
           uecorp.com.

Id       : 1007
Type     : Information
Message  : Testing server e2k7-mb-02.virtuecorp.com with the published name http
           s://e2k7-mb-02.virtuecorp.com/EWS/Exchange.asmx & .

Id       : 1019
Type     : Information
Message  : Found a valid AutoDiscover service connection point. The AutoDiscover
           URL on this object is https://e2k7-mb-02.virtuecorp.com/Autodiscover
           /Autodiscover.xml.

Id       : 1018
Type     : Information
Message  : The SSL certificate on e2k7-mb-02.virtuecorp.com is self-signed.

Id       : 1006
Type     : Information
Message  : Contacted AutoDiscover at https://e2k7-mb-02.virtuecorp.com/Autodisco
           ver/Autodiscover.xml.

Id       : 1016
Type     : Success
Message  : [EXCH]-Successfully contacted the AS service at https://e2k7-mb-02.vi
           rtuecorp.com/EWS/Exchange.asmx. The elapsed time was 46 milliseconds.

Id       : 1015
Type     : Success
Message  : [EXCH]-Successfully contacted the OAB service at https://e2k7-mb-02.v
           irtuecorp.com/EWS/Exchange.asmx. The elapsed time was 0 milliseconds.

Id       : 1014
Type     : Success
Message  : [EXCH]-Successfully contacted the UM service at https://e2k7-mb-02.vi
           rtuecorp.com/UnifiedMessaging/Service.asmx. The elapsed time was 15 m
           illiseconds.

Id       : 1006
Type     : Success
Message  : Successfully tested AutoDiscover.
```

FIGURE 21-35   Output from the Test-OutlookWebServices cmdlet

AutoConfiguration can be tested in Outlook 2007. CTRL-right-clicking the icon in the taskbar adds the Test E-Mail AutoConfiguration option to the context menu. To see if AutoConfiguration is working, enter a valid e-mail address and password. Then deselect the "GuessSmart" feature options. Figure 21-36 shows a successful run of the AutoConfiguration test.

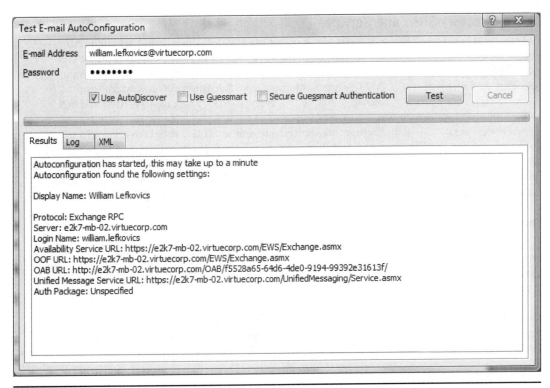

FIGURE 21-36   Testing e-mail AutoConfiguration

Network Services

Sometimes issues that arise are not specific to Exchange, but rather the underlying network infrastructure. In a perfect world, all networking issues would be resolved prior to Exchange 2007 being introduced.

Domain Controllers and Global Catalogs

Obviously, domain controllers maintain Active Directory. AD allows for user authentication and also stores Exchange configuration information. Directory lookups are performed through AD, and the Offline Address Book is created from AD.

If Exchange is not allowing users to access their mailboxes, there may not be a domain controller available to service authentication requests. If there is only one Global Catalog or domain controller server and it is rebooted, Exchange will record its displeasure in the Application event log. DcDiag.exe is a domain controller diagnostics tool that, if run from the Exchange server, verifies whether specific domain controllers pass a battery of tests to ensure it can service the requests of the Exchange server.

Active Directory Sites and Services

AD Sites and Services manages the AD topology for the Windows network. Exchange 2007 no longer uses routing groups to control message delivery paths, but rather depends on the AD site topology. Exchange 2007 is "site-aware." This means that both changes to the Exchange topology and changes to the AD site topology must take the other into consideration. Exchange uses the Microsoft Exchange Active Directory Topology service to verify Exchange server membership in each site.

AD sites can be associated with more than one IP subnet. If IP subnets overlap in a site, Exchange will not be able to use its topology service to identify where the other Exchange servers are. This will make troubleshooting routing a challenge. Thankfully, Exchange will tell the Application event log that it is having trouble with Exchange server site membership collection. DCDiag tests can verify intersite connectivity, topology, and replication success.

Domain Naming System (DNS)

DNS is critical to Exchange and Outlook working well together. This reality is further emphasized in the combination of Exchange 2007 and Outlook 2007. As you have seen, the Autodiscover service depends on the clients being able to find specific URLs for the Autodiscover Web service.

DNS entries also support SenderID and other anti-spoofing technologies. A properly formed Mail eXchanger (MX) record is considered a prerequisite for a messaging infrastructure. NetDiag and DCDiag both have DNS tests that can identify problems with DNS, whereas NSLookup can verify the resolution of hostnames.

TCP/IP Configurations

It seems almost trivial at this point, but TCP/IP addressing is also critical to Exchange Server. Issuing the command IPConfig /all from a command prompt or an EMS prompt returns all TCP/IP setting information for all adapters on a server or workstation. That information can provide TCP/IP troubleshooting input. Message routing in the network is dependent on a solid TCP/IP communication infrastructure. SMTP messages cannot travel where TCP/IP cannot. Ping and Tracert can confirm TCP/IP paths.

Finally, several Exchange components have IPv6 configurations already prepared for Windows 2008 Server which was recently released to manufacturing (RTM).

SP1   *Service Pack 1 adds IPv6 support, but it will require Windows 2008 Server. There are some places in Exchange 2007 where IPv6 values can be entered, but Exchange 2007 is not supported with IPv6 on any Windows 2003 Server version.*

Summary

Troubleshooting complex applications in various environments—some possibly not anticipated by the supplier—is not always a perfect process. For Exchange 2007, Microsoft provides plenty of tools and resources to help resolve issues that may arise. If you know what tool can provide the information needed to solve a troubleshooting riddle, you are well on your way to solving it.

Index